CLASSIFIED: THE INSIDE[R GUIDE] TO 500 SPY SITES IN L[ONDON]

Plus 250 Associated London Intelligence Sites

Incorporating Highlights and Significant Moments of over 100 Years of British Secret Service

By Mark Birdsall and Deborah Plisko
Eye Spy Intelligence Magazine

Additional research Peter Thompson. Photography unless stated © Snapperjack of London, Eye Spy Intelligence Magazine and Hala Al-Ayoubi

FIRST EDITION 2015

In memory of Donald - an NSA Arlington Hall analyst

Published by Eye Spy Publishing Ltd (ESPL)
P.O. Box 10, Skipton, Leeds City Region, North Yorkshire, BD23 5US, UK
Empire State Building, 350 5th Avenue, 59th Floor, New York, NY 10118, USA

First published in Great Britain 2015
Copyright © 2015 Mark Birdsall, Deborah Plisko, Eye Spy Intelligence Magazine
ISBN. 978-0-9564530-1-3
Typeset and design by ESPL
Printed and bound in Great Britain by Cambrian Printers

Additional copies are available from ESPL via its UK or USA offices
Telephone: 01756 770199 UK or Toll Free 877 309 9243 USA

Similarly, you can order via Eye Spy Intelligence Magazine's website: www.eyespymag.com

Eye Spy Intelligence Magazine

CONTENTS

Introduction: — III

Chapter 01: Seeds of Secret Service - *The Long Arm of British Covert Influence* — 1
Chapter 02: Emergence of the Spy Services - *Strange Origins of British Intelligence* — 13
Chapter 03: The Dark Spies - *Propaganda, Front Companies and Spy Rings* — 55
Chapter 04: First London Spy Wars - *MI5 Battles Spies, Communists and Nazis* — 89
Chapter 05: The Fourth Spy Agency - *Emergence of Spy Tradecraft* — 105
Chapter 06: An Early MI5 Success - *Maxwell's Dark Agents Strike* — 127
Chapter 07: Propaganda & Codebreakers - *Deception, Disinformation and Ultra* — 135
Chapter 08: A Very Dirty Business - *The Irregulars - Throwing Away the Rule Book* — 153
Chapter 09: Exiles and Guests - *London Homes for Friends in Need* — 177
Chapter 10: A Most Secret War - *OSS, MI9 and Hidden Tunnels* — 189
Chapter 11: The Illusionists - *Ministries for Disinformation and Mischief* — 207
Chapter 12: British Security Coordination - *MI6 and a Man Called Intrepid* — 223
Chapter 13: Interrogation and Interpretation - *Deceit, Danger and Aerial Spies* — 249
Chapter 14: Games of Deception - *Operation Mincemeat and Jermyn Street* — 267
Chapter 15: The D-Day Spies - *Double Cross, XX Committee and Victory* — 285
Chapter 16: Street of Strange Secrets - *Rutland Gate and People of the Serpentine* — 313
Chapter 17: KGB Spies, Treason & Venona - *Communist Spies in London* — 321
Chapter 18: Room at the Top - *MI5, Internal Suspicion and KGB Spy Games* — 355
Chapter 19: Too Hot to Handle - *Spy Case that Shook the Establishment* — 381
Chapter 20: Spy Tradecraft - *Dead Letter Drops and Brush Passes* — 397
Chapter 21: Menaces and Moves - *More Spies and Relocation of Service Sites* — 409
Chapter 22: The New Professionals - *Cold War Ends as New Millennium Beckons* — 445
Chapter 23: British Intelligence Shaken - *Terrorists Strike in London - 7/7* — 471
Chapter 24: Intelligence Services Evolve - *Spies, Assassins, Honeytraps and Plots* — 479

Postscript — 528
Index, Guide and Maps: — 532

London - the Spy Capital of the World!

Mark Birdsall - Editor
Eye Spy Intelligence Magazine

Deborah Plisko
Eye Spy Intelligence Magazine

Introduction

1909 was the inception date of Britain's Secret Service Bureau (SSB). It consisted of a handful of military intelligence officers and public figures drawn together more by chance than design. Five years later the Great War erupted, but fortuitously by then, the SSB had already evolved into what could be described as an intelligence service; albeit naive in stature and still searching for an identity. It struggled to find its place in a country where the military still ruled supreme in respect of intelligence collection.

A little over a decade later the Bureau expanded and fragmented; born were several new agencies, most famously MI5 and MI6 - the domestic and foreign arms of British Intelligence. The Government Code and Cipher School (GC&CS) also emerged, later renamed GCHQ (Government Communications Headquarters). Retracing their journey and the many famous characters linked to the agencies has been absorbing and fascinating.

Though these are the organisations that people are familiar with today, others have played their part in creating what is still one of the world's most powerful intelligence forces, including the Special Operations Executive (SOE), Naval Intelligence Division (NID), which pre-dates every service, Room 40 codebreakers, British Security Coordination, Special Forces and the Intelligence Corp.

This guide allows you to walk back in time to various eras when the 'cloak and dagger' game of espionage was crucial to the well being of the nation's security.

And London is central to the telling of the story of British Intelligence. A city unlike no other in respect of its long association with the world of espionage. Spies, assets, double agents, traitors, heroes and villains from every continent have played out their shadowy games of cunning, deceit and treachery on the streets of Britain's capital. However, there are hundreds of famous people - 'surprise spies' - from every walk of life who are also linked to the spying game.

The skill and skulduggery of the most famous spies and spycatchers were honed in a plethora of London buildings, apartments, inconspicuous

Eye Spy Intelligence Magazine

houses, alleyways, streets, parks, churches, tea rooms, train stations and yes... even pubs.

Some locations associated with the city's spylore are known, others are only familiar to spy aficionados and those who have worked in this secret industry. But, using this guide, you too can follow the paths of many legendary and infamous spies who have made London an international espionage institution. And it's a path one should take with due haste - as every year buildings associated with the UK's intelligence and espionage history disappear.

The commentary in this guide, which is threaded to a candid overview of 100 years of British Intelligence, is just sufficient to give readers a tantalising glimpse of the people and 'ghosts' who once plied their trade on London's streets, though naturally we would urge further research.

It's still possible to stand on London's streets and view the buildings where some of the greatest spy operations were planned and actioned; where the spies lived, worked, played and ultimately where they were caught, jailed, executed and sometimes even assassinated.

Inside this book, readers will find over 700 places to visit, many of these have never been previously associated with the spying game in London. Along the way, we have included other sites: covert hiding places, agent meeting points, front companies, spy training schools, dead letter drops, mail opening centres, secret underground sites, safe houses and recruitment clubs linked to the greatest spy operations of all time. Fascinating spy stories born in hotels, restaurants, theatres, cinemas, clubs, dance halls, cafes etc. also have a place in this book. Ordinary locations concealing extraordinary facts.

Classified: The Insider's Guide to 500 Spy Sites in London reveals the city's enduring liaison with the world of spying from the beginning of the last century to the present. An illuminated history of the secret wars hosted by one of the greatest cities in the world... indeed, the spy capital of the world!

ESPL DISCLAIMER: Every effort has been made to make this book as accurate as possible. However, the information should be used only as a general guide and not as the ultimate source for the information you seek. We therefore accept no liability for any inaccuracies or any loss, damage or injury arising from the use or reliance on the information contained in this book. ESPL cannot be held responsible for any injury, damage, loss, accident or inconvenience to persons engaged in following the information contained herein. Please familiarise yourself with privacy and counter-terrorism laws before using this guide.

All rights reserved. No part of this publication may be reproduced, stored in a retrieval system, or transmitted, in any form, or by any means, electronic, mechanical, photocopying, recording or otherwise, without the prior permission of the publishers. This book is sold subject to the condition that it shall not be, by way of trade or otherwise be lent, resold, hired out or circulated without the publisher's prior consent in any form or binding or cover other than that in which it is published and without a similar condition including this condition being imposed on the subsequent purchaser.

SPY SITES OF LONDON

Seeds of Secret Service
The Long Arm of British Covert Influence

Intelligence gathering and covert operations by Britain (in a form recognisable today), can be traced back to Queen Elizabeth I's secretary of state Sir Francis Walsingham. Born into a very wealthy and well connected family, he grew up in large manor house in **SCADBURY, BROMLEY [001•99]**. The ruins of the building can still be found in Scadbury Park. In the 16th century, Walsingham despatched dozens of undercover agents to seek out Catholics plotting against the throne. He oversaw many intelligence operations in Europe, and conspired in the plot which resulted in the execution of Mary, Queen of Scots. A close intelligence associate was Thomas Phelippes - a cryptographer who deciphered many coded communications created by Elizabeth's enemies. One in particular sealed the fate of Mary. Phelippes forged a short postscript to a letter sent by Mary in reply to a request for support from Anthony Babington, a young Catholic nobleman. He wanted approval to assassinate Queen Elizabeth. In 1586, Phelippes intercepted Mary's coded response, and added the gallows sign as well as asking for the names of Babington's associates. A few days later he and several colleagues were arrested and executed in St Giles Fields near Holborn. Mary had been in captivity for nearly for 20 years, but on 1 February 1587, Queen Elizabeth signed her death warrant. A week later she was beheaded in the Great Hall at Fotheringhay Castle, Northamptonshire.

001•99 Scadbury Park

Ruins of Walsingham's manor house at Scadbury

A seventeenth century engraving of Queen Elizabeth. On the right - Francis Walsingham - the first recognised spymaster of Britain

As a reward for his spying activities, Walsingham was given a large manor house - **BARN ELMS, RICHMOND UPON THAMES [002•36]**. Sadly this incredibly important location no longer exists.

Also convenient was the fact that his brother, Edmund, held the post of

Eye Spy Intelligence Magazine

1

Queen Elizabeth I, Sir Francis Walsingham, Charles II and Mary, Queen of Scots

FORGERIES AND CIPHERS

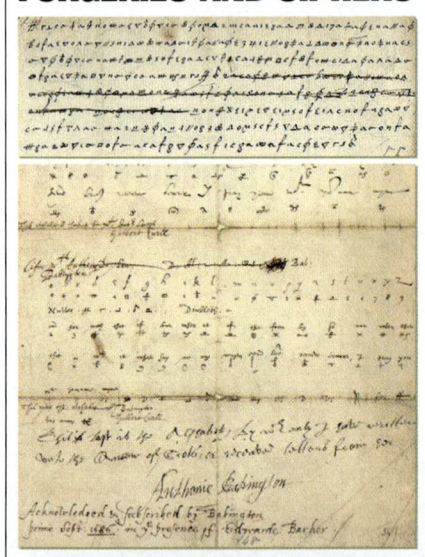

Mary, Queen of Scots letter to Babington and Phelippes forged cipher postscript

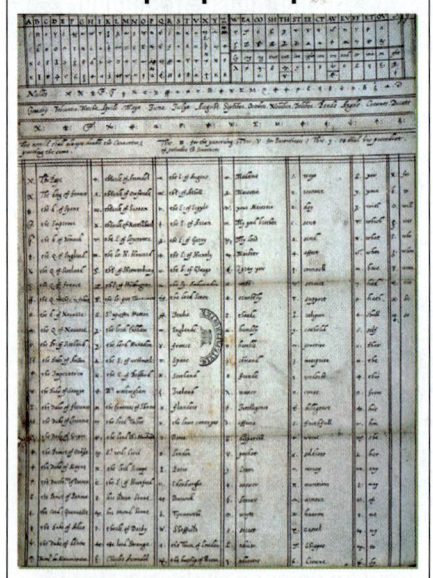

Mary, Queen of Scots cipher code

Execution of Queen Mary at Fotheringhay Castle in 1587

lieutenant in the notorious Tower of London. For the next 400 years this location would be used to house hundreds of suspected spies.

PLOT TO ASSASSINATE A KING AND BLOW UP PARLIAMENT

Less than 20 years later another group of assassins gathered in London. And just like Anthony Babington, they too were disgruntled about the treatment of Catholics in England. The 1604 Gunpowder Plot as it is known today, involved several men, the most famous being Guy Fawkes, a Yorkshireman. However, the operation was actually led by Robert Catesby who wanted to assassinate Protestant King James. The group met at an inn called the Duck and Drake on the Strand to discuss the plot. A room (cellar) was hired under the House of Lords which would be used

Barn Elms fields, Richmond upon Thames
The first spy headquarters

002·36

Site of Barn Elms an old medieval Manor House. Queen Elizabeth bought the lease on the building in 1579 as a reward for Sir Francis Walsingham's services to the crown. The Queen visited Britain's first recognised spycatcher on three occasions. The original building was demolished in 1694 and replaced with a new manor house. In 1954, the house was destroyed in a fire

Eye Spy Intelligence Magazine

003·42

SPY SITES OF LONDON

Government officials discover the cellar and arrest Guy Fawkes

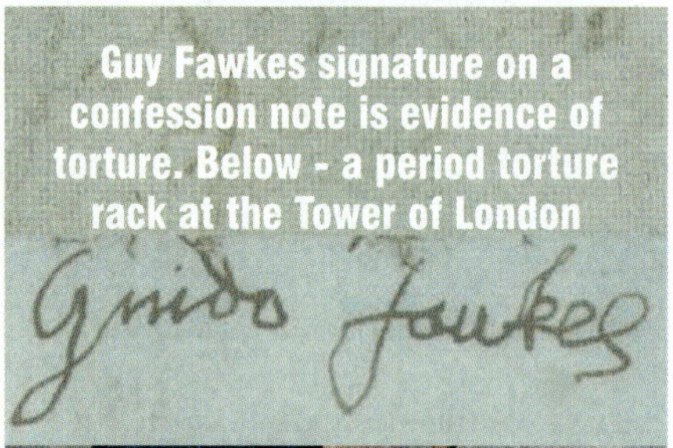

Guy Fawkes signature on a confession note is evidence of torture. Below - a period torture rack at the Tower of London

Houses of Parliament

to store barrels of gunpowder. To avoid detection, the barrels were moved in gradually and a date set for the attack - November.

Less than two weeks before the attack, Lord Monteagle received an anonymous letter warning him to stay away from Parliament. This was passed on to the government and soon a major search began in, around and under the buildings of Westminster. In the early hours of 5 November, Fawkes was seen leaving the cellar and duly arrested. The plot had been rumbled and one by one all the conspirators arrested, tried and executed.

In 1605, Londoners were encouraged to celebrate the King's close call on the anniversary of the bomb plot. And since then, the public still commemorate what many people call Guy Fawkes Night, marking the occasion with firework displays, bonfires and conviviality. However, the event was one of terrorism, and had Fawkes, who had already placed the gunpowder

Contemporary engraving of the conspirators - Guy Fawkes is third from right

Eye Spy Intelligence Magazine

244-278 Crondall Street

John Thurloe

barrels on piles of wood, lit the fuse, experts today conclude the attack would have been catastrophic resulting in many casualties and the destruction of most of the **PARLIAMENT BUILDINGS [003•42]**. This would not be the last terrorist attempt to cause mayhem on the city's streets...

Of further interest, a plaque has been erected near the exact location where Lord Monteagle lived and received his warning not to venture near Parliament. This can be found at **244-278 CRONDALL STREET [004•09]**.

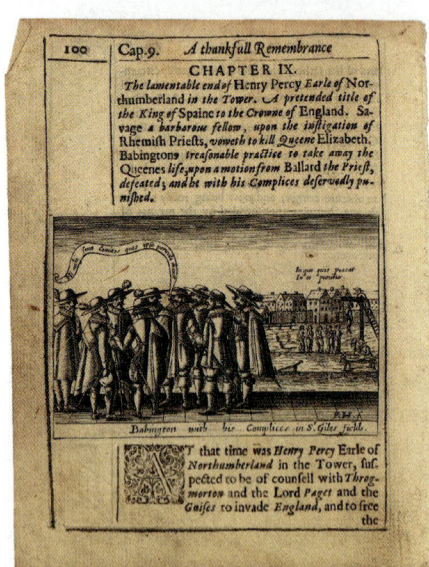

CROMWELL'S INTEL CHIEF

Another early spymaster was John Thurloe. After Oliver Cromwell's rise to power in the mid-1600s, Thurloe became his head of intelligence collection and developed a nationwide network of spies and informants to supply information on plots and anti-Cromwell sentiment. His reach was not restricted to Britain and he also ran operatives in Europe, including Dutch diplomat Lieuwe van Aitzema and mathematician John Wallis. Wallis in fact established a codebreaking unit. Thurloe's secret team helped thwart a 1657 plot created by Miles Sindercombe to assassinate Cromwell. However, one of his own team, Samuel Morland would then betray Thurloe by supporting the Royalists. Nevertheless, the advantages of having a secret service were slowly being recognised by leading figures in government. Thurloe lived at **24 OLD BUILDINGS, CHANCERY LANE [005•62]**.

Interestingly, Thurloe documented much of his secret work which was discovered at 13 Old Buildings hidden in the ceiling of the attic. Thankfully these papers were removed during the reign of William III because the building was later destroyed. These important files can now be viewed at the Bodleian Library in Oxford.

About 50 years later, in the reign of Charles II, regular monies were put aside for a Secret Service Fund, evolving into an annual Secret Service Vote in Parliament. The monies were

An engraving showing Babington meeting his co-conspirators in St Giles Fields. Ironically, they would all be executed here

John Wallis

SPY SITES OF LONDON

005·62

CHANCERY LANE WC2

Samuel Morland

24 Old Buildings, Chancery Lane

Queen Victoria

Sir Charles Dickens

Bodleian Library, Oxford

supposed to have been used as payment to British informants who spied on the country's enemies both at home and abroad. It later transpired that about half of it actually fell into the hands of dubious politicians who used it for bribes and other underhand tactics. Despite this, Britain was receiving extremely useful intelligence from its overseas spies, many of whom had begun infiltrating political groups, foreign armies, European governments, royal families etc. One official later described the operation as "the long arm of British covert influence."

Many great things emerged under the rule of Queen Victoria, the Industrial Revolution being one, and you could be forgiven for believing the secret services would have blossomed, but the exact opposite happened. During Victoria's reign, the use of agents and skulduggery to obtain information inside the UK was unusual, primarily because Britain was secure with almost a third of the world map coloured a bright shade of pink. The position was virtually the same abroad and intelligence collection rare. Reflecting on this situation and the burgeoning power of Britain and its people, the great Charles Dickens wrote: *'This most rabid demagogue can say in this free country what he chooses... he speaks not under the terror of an organised spy system'*.

Dickens was of course correct, but by the end of the nineteenth century Britain's navy and army services began to note the rumblings of possible conflict all over the globe. In an effort to bolster tactical and strategic intelligence gathering, the services established intelligence divisions, though they were not secret.

Much of the intelligence gleaned by forces' directorates came via open sources, newspapers, publications, meetings and from the notes of their respective officers when travelling or operating abroad. Other information came from representatives at Britain's

Eye Spy Intelligence Magazine

The original nineteenth century headquarters of the Metropolitan Police Force can be found behind 4 Whitehall. Also of interest, the building to the right is still used by the police for its mounted officers

3-5 and 7-13 Great Scotland Yard, Whitehall

3-5 Great Scotland Yard, Whitehall

was thrown from his horse as he rode in Constitution Hill near Buckingham Palace. He died three days later from his injuries. A statue of him can be found in Parliament Square.

EARLY TERRORIST ATTACKS IN THE HEART OF LONDON

In 1883, Scotland Yard established the Special Irish Branch in response to several Irish Fenian bomb attacks. This soon became known simply as Special Branch. At this time there were two rebellious countries in the British Empire where Special Branch operated its shadowy network of spies and informants - Ireland and India.

In 1867, the police had to deal with a major terrorist incident which happened in Corporation Row, Coldbath Square - just outside Coldbath Prison walls. Fenian operative Michael Barrett detonated a bomb on 13

vast network of foreign embassies and trading companies dotted across the globe.

SPECIAL IRISH BRANCH AND GENESIS OF SCOTLAND YARD

In 1829, Home Secretary Robert Peel established the Metropolitan Police Force at 4 Whitehall Place. Many adjoining buildings were requisitioned as the Service grew, including **3-5 GREAT SCOTLAND YARD [006•42]**. This soon became the public entrance and somehow the name Scotland Yard became synonymous with London police. Interestingly, the building used as stables by the police - **7-13 GREAT SCOTLAND YARD [007•42]** is still occupied by New Scotland Yard and serves its mounted division. After departing the premises in 1890 - moving close to Parliament on **VICTORIA EMBANKMENT [008•42]** - the Force retained its metonym - Scotland Yard. However, 'New' was added as a prefix.

Robert Peel, who would eventually become prime minister, lived for many years with his father at **16 UPPER GROSVENOR STREET [009•55]**. His demise was rather unexpected and a little poignant; in late June 1850, he

Sir Robert Peel founded New Scotland Yard in 1829

6

Eye Spy Intelligence Magazine

SPY SITES OF LONDON

December which killed several civilians. He was arrested and became the last person ever hanged in public in England. The sentence was carried out at a gallows constructed outside Newgate Prison in front of a watching crowd of several thousand people. Newgate Prison, which can trace its roots back to 1188 was demolished in 1904. The Central Criminal Court, better known as the Old Bailey, was built in its place and named as such after the street. In later years it would host several high profile spy trials as we shall soon discover. Famous Newgate prisoners include assassin John Bellingham.

In early 1812, Bellingham visited a tailor who he asked to manufacture a suit with a secret pocket designed to conceal a firearm. His target was in fact Prime Minister Spencer Percival. On 12 April that year Bellingham waited in the lobby of Parliament, and when Percival arrived he calmly shot him dead through the heart. It is the only occasion a British prime minister has ever been assassinated. Like Barrett, he was hanged at Newgate.

As for Coldbath Prison, it was closed in 1885 and the land given to the General Post Office. Gradually the buildings were demolished and by 1929, little remained of the original site. Today it is occupied by Britain's biggest postal sorting office - Mount Pleasant, though a street called **COLDBATH SQUARE [010•08]** - that was identified as the site of the bombing, remains.

3-5 Great Scotland Yard, Whitehall

New Scotland Yard, Victoria Embankment

THE CATO STREET CONSPIRACY

Eight years after Bellingham shot Percival, an even more audacious conspiracy was unfolding in London. A group of men calling themselves the Spencean Philanthropists (taking their name from the radical speaker

Scotland Yard's second headquarters near Parliament is now called the Norman Shaw Buildings

Eye Spy Intelligence Magazine

SPY SITES OF LONDON

Sir Robert Peel fell from his horse in Constitution Hill

Bellingham shoots dead Spencer Percival

Thomas Spence), plotted to kill Prime Minister Lord Liverpool and his entire Cabinet. The assassins learned Lord Liverpool and his Cabinet were to meet at 39 Grosvenor Square (now number 44). On the night of 23 February 1820, the group met at a public house on **CATO STREET, MARYLEBONE [011•55]** to finalise their plot. Unbeknown to them, two undercover government agents from the famous Bow Street Runners,

Arthur Thistlewood - one of the Cato Street conspirators

regarded as Britain's first police force, had infiltrated the group. Outside the pub around a dozen more agents were waiting to pounce. At 7.30pm that evening, the government men were joined by soldiers from the Coldstream Guards. In the ensuing fight a policeman was killed. Some of the conspirators escaped, but were arrested days later. On 1 May 1820, the group were executed - some were hanged - others beheaded. Interestingly, at the trial of the men, some information presented by the prosecution was not accepted because it had been provided by a spy!

The Bow Street Runners were formed in 1749 by author Henry Fielding. The name was given to them by the public because they worked out of his office at 4 Bow Street. The building has long gone but a splendid plaque noting the history of famous residents who lived on Bow Street can be found at nearby Broad Court. The officials did not patrol but issued various court documents such as writs and arrested offenders on behalf of the authorities. Fielding lived at **MILBOURNE HOUSE, BARNES GREEN [012•36]**.

Prime Minister Lord Liverpool

Sir Robert Peel's statue in Parliament Square

8

Eye Spy Intelligence Magazine

Newgate Prison

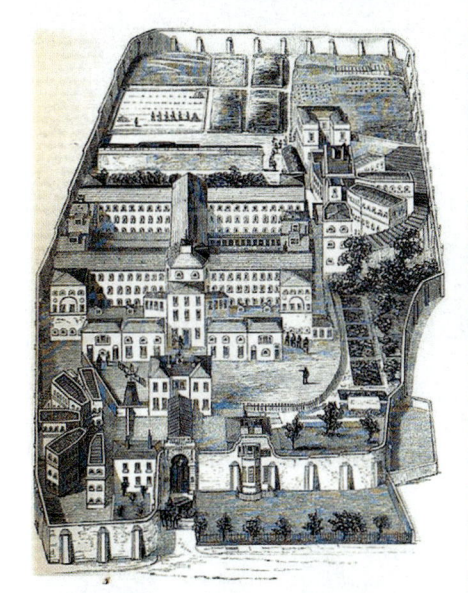

Coldbath Prison. The site of the former sprawling prison is now dominated by Mount Pleasant sorting office - the biggest in Britain

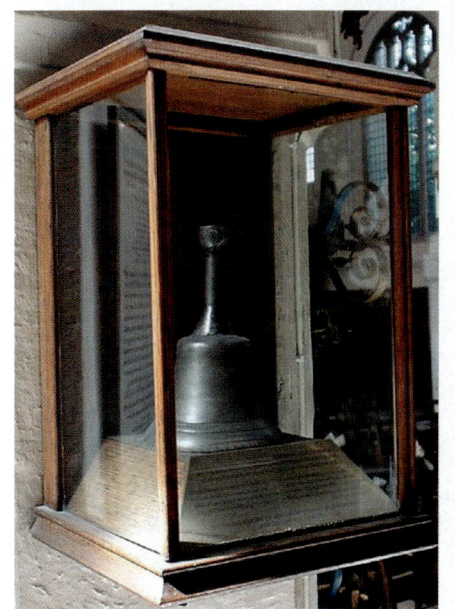

Newgate Prison execution bell

16 Upper Grosvenor Street

Mount Pleasant Sorting Office

Eye Spy Intelligence Magazine

Coldbath Square

OLD BAILEY EC4
CITY OF LONDON

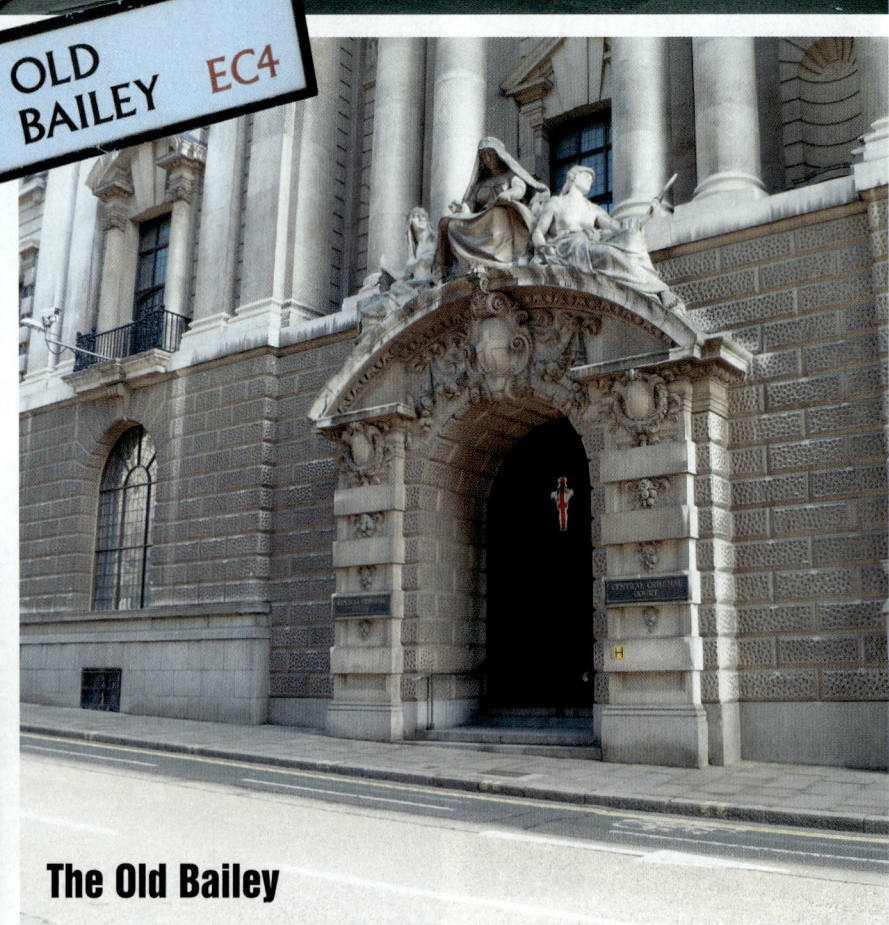

The Old Bailey

Eye Spy Intelligence Magazine

Arrest of the Cato Street conspirators by the Bow Street Runners

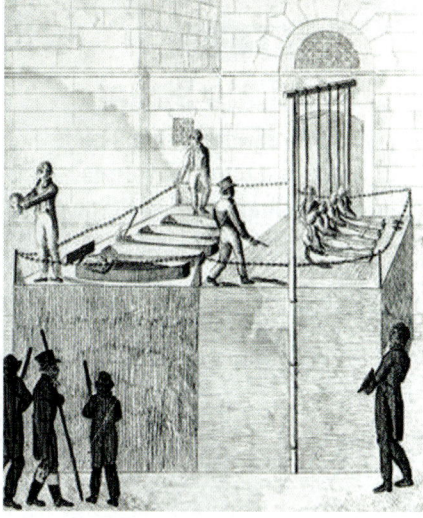

SPY SITES OF LONDON

Execution of the Cato Street gang

The original Tudor building no longer exists though parts of the structure, including the Elizabethan fireplace are contained in a new building overlooking the town's pond. This is perhaps poignant as Robert Beale, Sir Francis Walsingham's secretary (Elizabeth I's spymaster) also lived here.

Members of the British Establishment dance around the heads of the Cato Street conspirators

BOW STREET WAS FORMED ABOUT 1637. IT HAS BEEN THE RESIDENCE OF MANY NOTABLE MEN — AMONG WHOM WERE — HENRY FIELDING (NOVELIST), SIR JOHN FIELDING (MAGISTRATE), GRINLING GIBBONS (WOODCARVER), CHARLES MACKLIN (ACTOR), JOHN RADCLIFFE (PHYSICIAN), CHARLES SACKVILLE EARL OF DORSET (POET), — WILLIAM WYCHERLEY (DRAMATIST). LCC

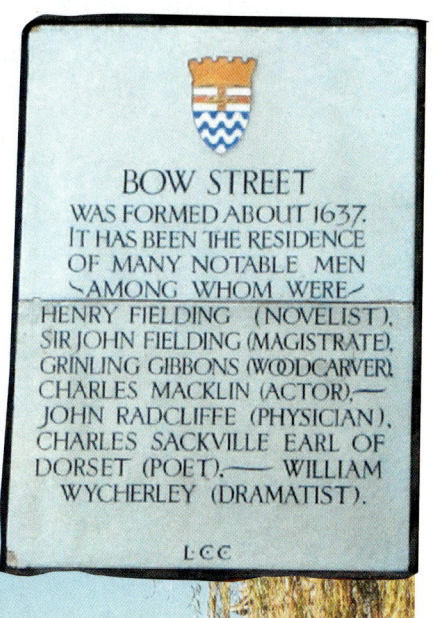

Milbourne House, Barnes Green
Henry Fielding, founder of the Bow Street Runners lived here

Henry Fielding

Eye Spy Intelligence Magazine   11

SPY SITES OF LONDON

011 • 55

1A Cato Street

Site of a former public house where a gang plotted to assassinate British Prime Minister Lord Liverpool

SPY SITES OF LONDON

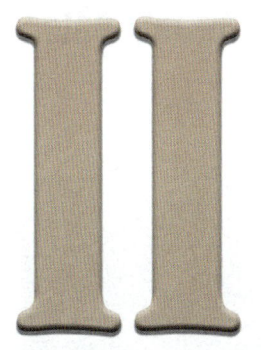

Emergence of the Spy Services
Strange Origins of British Intelligence

When the Boer War of 1889-1902 erupted, and reports started to emerge of Germany's expanding military and industrial might, those in charge of analysing and combating such issues were left grasping for information. The massive shortcomings of Britain's inadequate intelligence collection capability were revealed. This led to the creation of the Committee of Imperial Defence in 1905, and the country's intelligence activities were soon on the agenda. The armed forces held joint conferences in 1906 and 1907 and acknowledged the situation was at best poor, at worst dire. However, the Foreign Office disliked the notion of spying,

Old War Office, Whitehall

describing it as "ungentlemanly and underhand." As for the notion that a home-based secret service be formed to identify subversives and foreign spies, this was seen as being against Britain's "liberal traditions."

Yet there were those in Whitehall who recognised the need to construct and put in place (at the very least), a competent and secure mechanism to gather information. One man tasked with lobbying for change was Lieutenant Colonel James Edmonds. He had participated in the Boer War, which from an intelligence perspective, had been a dreadful affair. Edmonds, however, had run a successful unit called Section H - which examined (and censored) cables and mail flowing in and out of South Africa. Unbeknown to Edmonds at the time, he was actually laying the foundations of Britain's Security Service - MI5.

Another well known British military figure in the war was Horatio Herbert Kitchener. Controversy surrounded Kitchener who became best known as

Eye Spy Intelligence Magazine

13

SPY SITES OF LONDON

016 • 42

16 Queen Anne's Gate

Boer fighters

the face in the World War One poster proclaiming *'Your Country Needs You'*. However, like Edmonds, he recognised the importance of intelligence and in later years forged associations with several key intelligence men. He would also succumb to the devious methods of an undercover German spy in Europe.

MILITARY OPERATIONS 5 (MO5)

In 1907, because of his experience, Edmonds was selected to join MO5 - a specialist, but tiny element within the

George MacDonogh

Directorate of Military Operations, **WAR OFFICE, WHITEHALL [013 • 42]**. George MacDonogh headed the section, which besides its counter-espionage activities, was also responsible for protecting ciphers and the censorship of post and telegrams. Also involved was Sir Walter Kirke, who worked under MacDonogh and has been credited with helping to establish the Intelligence Corp prior to WWI. An archive document written by Kirke, notes that MO5's CE (counter-espionage) unit was headed by Major Vernon Kell. Kell was effectively head of MI5 from its inception in 1909 until 1940. MacDonogh, incidentally, controlled the activities of a certain Captain Mansfield Cumming (Royal Navy), who would later emerge as the Chief or 'C' of MI6 (C standing for Cumming - not Chief).

DECEPTIONS AND IMAGINARY GERMAN SPIES

The British Army Military Intelligence Division occupied **16-18 QUEEN ANNE'S GATE [014 • 42]** from 1884 until 1901. After the army moved out, Admiral of the Fleet Lord John Fisher moved in until 1910. Fisher

14

Eye Spy Intelligence Magazine

SPY SITES OF LONDON

[015•42]

Winchester House, 21 St James's Square

Ernest Rutherford

recognised the importance of submarines and urged their rapid development. He also served shortly as chairman of the Admiralty's Board of Invention and Research until 1918. One of Fisher's colleagues was New Zealand-born chemist and physicist Ernest Rutherford, regarded widely as the 'father of nuclear physics'.

Whilst attached to the navy, Rutherford worked on acoustic methods of detecting submarines. All of this important research quickly found its way to the Naval Intelligence Division (NID).

By 1900, Senior Army Military Intelligence Division officials were also based at **WINCHESTER HOUSE, 21 ST JAMES'S SQUARE [015•42]**. Here they analysed numerous military reports submitted from around the Empire. The building was far bigger than Queen Anne's Gate which could explain the 1901 move.

MacDonogh was also close to Lord Curzon who would chair the War Cabinet Committee. (MI5 would later site its headquarters on Curzon Street in London).

One of Edmond's first tasks was to put in place several operations aimed at assessing the spy threat posed by Germany. His conclusions stunned Whitehall and moves were afoot to strengthen domestic security - especially against German spies who were seemingly everywhere. The liberal values of Queen Victoria's Britain were slowly being replaced by nationalism and xenophobia. This was reflected in the media which warned about large numbers of German spies in Britain; the Kaiser's growing and impressive navy, and a secret army that had been put in place to rise against the UK at a moment's notice. Lord Northcliffe's *Daily Mail* led the charge of alarmist reports and even published Germany's 'invasion plans'. The newspaper was not alone; a letter written in April 1907, by an army colonel in *The Globe* read: *'The Streets of London swarm with Germans... where do they go? They are comfortably dressed and well nourished... they are undoubtedly soldiers'*.

There was even a report that reached Whitehall suggesting German soldiers were operating as waiters in restaurants, a notion dispelled by Edmonds.

Yet as we shall see, Edmonds was to fall for the paper talk. The grumblings of his peers that spies were walking London's streets and alleys, and being

Eye Spy Intelligence Magazine

SPY SITES OF LONDON

Lord George Curzon

The first heads of MI6 and MI5. Sir Mansfield Cumming 'C' (left) and Sir Vernon Kell. Below - caricature of Richard Haldane - Secretary of War who did not believe German spy stories

Another view of the Old War Office - a busy intelligence hub

sent to the country's docks and ports to spy on its ships, convinced Edmonds there was some substance to the reports.

SPY RINGS IN LONDON

All of this was hysteria of course, but the outcome was a serious and fresh look at how Britain should position itself when dealing with global and domestic security matters. And this at a time when its Empire was being threatened by an ever-growing, dominant and powerful Germany. Bizarrely out of character for a man like Edmonds, he ultimately concluded in a report to the War Office, that a vast underground network of German spies was indeed roaming the countryside and being operated centrally from England's capital.

His report ended up on the desk of Major General Spencer Ewart, the Director of Military Operations, essentially Edmond's superior. Ewart was angry, not because he disagreed with its content, but because he wanted to establish his own network of spies in Germany. If emphasis was placed on counter-espionage, his plans for a foreign intelligence collection service could be set back. Ewart then played a masterstroke. He announced that the only way to compensate and support both objectives, was by creating an organised

Richard Haldane

L-R: Planning for war - General von Hindenburg, Kaiser Wilhelm II and General Erich Ludendorf

Secret Service Bureau and strengthening the Official Secrets Act. At this very moment lay the origins of Britain's modern intelligence services.

Not everyone agreed with Ewart, including the Secretary of State for War, R. B. Haldane. But shortly thereafter in 1909, came the timely writings of a certain William Tufnell Le Queux. The *Weekly News* ran a series of features that swelled public opinion that spies were everywhere. Le Queux's stories - *The Spies of the Kaiser* - featured fictional heroes and story-lines not unlike those that Ian Fleming would scribe decades later on the activities of a certain James Bond. Staggeringly, this prompted the government to act, primarily because of the public's support for Le Queux, who was starting to mix a little fact with a lot of fiction.

The *Weekly News* was a much sought-after publication, and with a tantalising reader offer of £10 to any person who could identify a German spy, the reports of spy activity increased. Men with wigs, Germans with maps (tour-

William Le Queux - the fantasy spy writer who caused mayhem in the country - but whose features inadvertently helped create British Intelligence

ists), people dressed in German-made suits and foreign registered cars, all came under suspicion. And woe to those with a foreign accent or were seen in the vicinity of a pigeon!

STRANGE ORIGINS OF THE SECRET SERVICE BUREAU (SSB)

The Committee of Imperial Defence discussed the 'rampant spying' but was not totally convinced by Edmond's report. It did, however, conclude the Germans were conducting espionage and that the Kaiser had authorised a plan to invade Britain to be drawn up.

In July 1909, a sub-committee recommended that police be given more powers to question aliens and prevent sabotage. Yet its most important decision was to agree with Ewart - a move post haste towards establishing the Secret Service Bureau - SSB.

Spencer Ewart

A French postcard depicting the Kaiser as a war monger

Eye Spy Intelligence Magazine

The original Secret Service Bureau headquarters. The building was knocked down and replaced by this huge tower block (below)

Ashley Mansions, Vauxhall Bridge Road

64 Victoria Street

The plan was for the SSB to be a single entity engaged in both domestic and overseas intelligence activities. But by 1910, it seems the Bureau had already begun to separate. Officials opted to form a military and naval section. The military section would have domestic and overseas arms - basically a security service engaged in counter-espionage, while the naval section would help create Britain's network of foreign agents and run collaborators. Its first headquarters were at **64 VICTORIA STREET [016•42]** - long since gone. Cumming lost no time in searching out a second location to plan his Service's development - and one he could live in. **ASHLEY MANSIONS, VAUXHALL BRIDGE ROAD, WESTMINSTER [017•42]**, was purchased and soon became the location of many meetings between military and government officials. This in-house arrangement suited Cumming, and some intelligence watchers believe the term 'MI6 headquarters' could easily have been attributed to this building.

Sir Vernon Kell, who resigned his army position because of the new model, designated MO(t) as the actual name of his counter-espionage organisation. The operation was run from a single room in the War Office with an incredibly low budget of just £7,000. One of his first tasks was to create an Alien Registry by gathering

SPY SITES OF LONDON

Drawing of the original building shortly after it was completed in 1831

8-9 Carlton House Terrace [018•42]

PALACE ROAD [019•42], would go on to arrest several spies who found themselves interrogated in the dark and less than glamorous belly of **THE TOWER OF LONDON [020•08]**.

In early 1911, and in a bid to save money, Kell's fledgling agency moved its headquarters to the **PAPER BUILDINGS** in **TEMPLE [021•08]**. The building had no proper electricity or water supply - a situation which probably explains why Kell preferred the Rubens Hotel. Also in 1911, MO(t) had become aware of a German journalist, Max Schulz, who lived on a houseboat in Exeter. He was sending reports on the Royal Navy to a Gustav Steinhauer, a former detective of the Pinkerton Agency and one-time bodyguard to the Kaiser himself. The correspondence was sent to addresses in London where it was forwarded by German agents to a bogus address in Potsdam c/o Steinhauer. Kell became suspicious and probed deeper.

Schultz's mail was opened and copied by General Post Office (GPO) specialists. And though they discovered everything Schultz was writing appeared open source, the addresses of the middlemen and contacts soon put Kell's officers onto the Kaiser's agents. Heinrich Grosse was arrested working as a stoker aboard the Royal Navy destroyer HMS Foxhound and Dr. Armgaard Graves near the dock yards in Glasgow. Kell was careful not to let details slip out into the media and thus alert the rest of the Steinhauer spy ring. The end game to this operation, which was effectively MI5's first successful counter-espionage activity, came about with the arrest of Royal Navy gunner George Parrot in

and researching the names of some 30,000 UK-based Germans. He also started investigating Le Queux's theory that the Germans had established a major spy network in southern England.

Kell obtained the cooperation of police forces and by 1914, the year when war would explode across Europe, MO(t) had details of 11,000 Germans. The operation was of course doomed before it began, because in reality, there was no German spy network and the Kaiser did not have a viable and concrete invasion plan.

The German Embassy at **8-9 CARLTON HOUSE TERRACE [018•42]** was naturally kept under surveillance. And following the departure of the Kaiser's officials, German interests were initially overseen by the United States, until it sided with Britain in the war.

Kell, who for a time held office in the **RUBENS HOTEL, BUCKINGHAM**

Eye Spy Intelligence Magazine

SPY SITES OF LONDON
019•42
Rubens Hotel, Buckingham Palace Road

MI5 head Sir Vernon Kell disliked his stuffy office and for a time directed operations from a plush suite at the Rubens Hotel, Buckingham Palace Road. On the outside wall of the hotel a plaque notes that it was used during WWII as the headquarters of the exiled Polish government

November 1912. It transpired that the man who had recruited Parrot, a certain Karl Hentschel, tried to blackmail German intelligence officials by threatening to reveal Parrot's role to the British. Kell was alerted and gave Hentschel £30.00 to tell everything he knew about the spy ring - which he promptly did.

Kell's agency was gaining credibility and a reputation in Whitehall and beyond. And despite the incorrect assessment on the huge network of spies, it was of some importance that when war broke out, Kell's intelligence, due to the earlier surveillance operation, was central to the detention of about 200 'undesirable' Germans and 22 suspected agents. As it later transpired, only one of the 22 people was charged with espionage. He was a hairdresser working at 402A Caledonian Road. Acting as an agent,

The Kaiser's spymaster Gustav Steinhauer

SPY SITES OF LONDON

021•08
Vernon Kell's fledgling Service relocated here for a brief period in February 1911. For reasons still unknown, it was regarded as unsuitable

3 Paper Buildings in Temple

the man had been forwarding mail to Steinhauer for a fee of just £1.00 per week. Sadly, this historically important location no longer exists, replaced by modern housing.

Nevertheless, premier Herbert Asquith was delighted at the outcome and visited Kell. On the wall of his office, Kell had prepared a somewhat dubious map highlighting where the German spies were based in the UK. This too impressed Asquith who said it was a "major victory."

Prime Minister Herbert Asquith "delighted with spy arrests"

RAID ON THE BANK OF ENGLAND

Gustav Steinhauer's opposite number in MI5 was former Special Branch chief William Melville - later known simply as 'M'. The breaking of the Kaiser's spy ring led officers to further information that exposed a most daring operation in the city. German spies had plotted to destroy the gold reserves at the **BANK OF ENGLAND, THREADNEEDLE STREET [022•08]**, effectively crippling the British economy. Steinhauer considered robbing the gold, but believed this was impossible. Regardless of his ambitious scheme, the plot was exposed and stopped well before planning even began.

Eye Spy Intelligence Magazine

SPY SITES OF LONDON

020•08

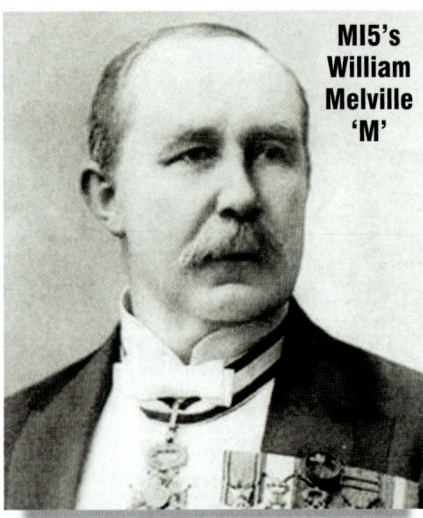

MI5's William Melville 'M'

The Tower of London

Several German spies were held here, interrogated and if found guilty - executed by firing squad. The original wooden 'death chair' containing dozens of bullet holes still exists. Another famous 'resident' in later years was Rudolf Hess - Hitler's wartime deputy (right)

wife Amelia and four children. It was from this address that he joined MI5. Similarly, he may well have retired to **24 ORLANDO ROAD [025•45]** as his police pension was sent here. Melville, who was born in 1850, is regarded as the first true spymaster of Britain's modern intelligence services. It is also believed he was instrumental in the recruitment of master spy Sidney Reilly who would become an important MI6 operative in Russia. His exploits are examined shortly.

THE RECRUITMENT OF MANSFIELD CUMMING - 'C'

Meanwhile, the foreign intelligence collection arm of the Secret Service Bureau, now designated MI-1(c), sought to appoint its first proper head, and 50-year-old Commander Mansfield Cumming was its preferred choice. Cumming had been retired from the Royal Navy for 20 years. A constant sufferer from sea sickness meant his career in the navy was affected, but he had proven himself useful in intelligence matters.

The Hon A. E. Bethell, the Director of Naval Intelligence (DNI), and a member of the CID was responsible for finding a suitable naval candidate

Details of this incredible story emerged in 2009, following extensive research by intelligence historian Andrew Cook. He is convinced that the incident was the stimulus for Ian Fleming, himself an MI6-NID man, to write the 007 book - *Goldfinger*. Another extraordinary fact uncovered by Cook, was that legendary escape artist Harry Houdini was employed by Melville to help train British agents! During his time in England, the Austrian-Hungarian born American lived at **84 BEDFORD COURT MANSIONS [023•62]**. Britain's Security Service was up and running.

As for Melville, the 1911 census shows the Irishman living at **16 LYDON ROAD [024•45]**, together with his

SPY SITES OF LONDON
The Bank of England, Threadneedle Street

022•08

The Bank of England - the location of a dramatic 1914 German spy plot to destroy the UK's gold reserves. The operation was thwarted by MI5

to head the Foreign Section. On 10 August 1909, Bethell wrote to Commander Mansfield Cumming:

'My dear Mansfield Cumming, Boom defence must be getting a bit stale

024•45

16 Lydon Road

025•45

24 Orlando Road

Eye Spy Intelligence Magazine

23

SPY SITES OF LONDON
HARRY HOUDINI AN UNLIKELY AND SURPRISING SPY TRAINER

American boxers Jack Dempsey (left) and Benny Leonard in a playful mood with Harry Houdini (centre)

An unlikely MI5 spy trainer - Harry Houdini pictured in 1918

MI5's William Melville befriended stage magician Harry Houdini before the war when he visited Scotland Yard. He reportedly showed the police and other watching officials just how easy it was to remove handcuffs. Melville recognised some of his feats could be useful for his own agents, no doubt in connection to tradecraft. In later years Houdini spent time training MI5 officers in various arts, including escapology

with you and the recent experiments with Ferret rather discounts yours at Southampton. You may therefore perhaps like a new billet. If so I have something good I can offer you and if you would like to come and see me on *Thursday* about noon I will tell you what it is'.

ESPIONAGE - A 'CAPITAL SPORT'

He spoke of his new position to colleagues as "exciting" and described

84 Bedford Court Mansions
Harry Houdini's London residence

One of the most famous documents in the MI6 archives - the Bethell Letter. This brief note invited Cumming to take charge of the fledgling Foreign Section of the Secret Service Bureau

Sir Mansfield Cumming

Pentland House, Old Road

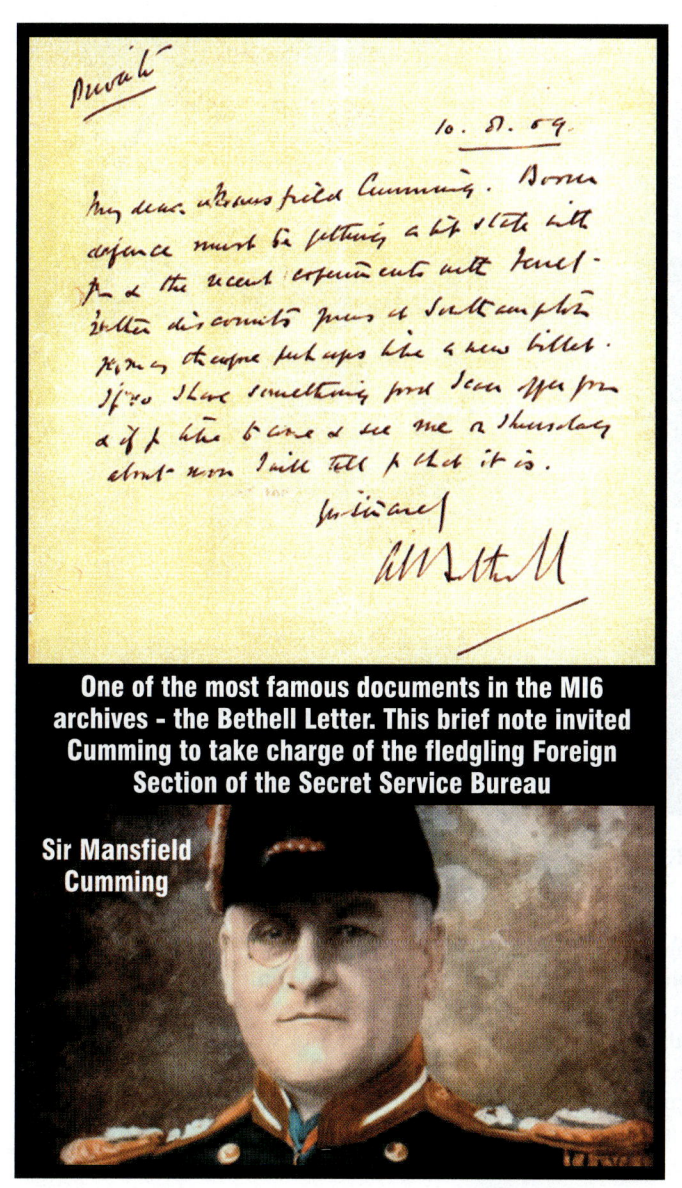

Below: A rare photo showing the interior of Pentland House - 1885. Cumming would have been 16-years-old

espionage as "a capital sport." And as for the man himself, he was actually born Mansfield George Smith - the date being 1 April 1859, which some commentators jokingly believe may explain his oft eccentric behaviour!

The location of his birth was a splendid residence called Foellt House (built in 1685 and named as such by his father - Colonel John Thomas Smith) in the South London district of Lee (Lewisham). In later years the building served as a hall of residence for Goldsmiths College, though today is called **PENTLAND HOUSE, OLD ROAD [026•26]** and is divided into private flats. It is the oldest surviving domestic building in the borough and retains much of its original interior.

Eye Spy Intelligence Magazine

25

Pentland House, Old Road

LIKE FATHER, LIKE SON

Spy writers have long noted Cumming's eccentricity, and the man who often wore a monocle and only wrote in green ink, would add another chapter to his legacy after a car crash near Paris in 1914.

At that time the Cumming's family, including Alastair, his son, resided at 22 FITZJAMES AVENUE, KENSINGTON [027•54].

Cumming was being driven by Alastair when their car crashed into a tree at high speed. His son was flung from the vehicle and fatally injured. Unable to reach Alastair because his own leg was trapped and crushed, he allegedly (and calmly) took out his penknife and started to chop away at his leg until he was free. He then reached over and put a coat over his dying son. The report of his penknife bravery has been rejected by many researchers. Just what Cumming was doing in France with Alastair has long remained a mystery, but we discovered he did have connections to the Farman [Air] School, Etampes, where he obtained his flying certificate. Also of interest, Eye Spy discovered a document

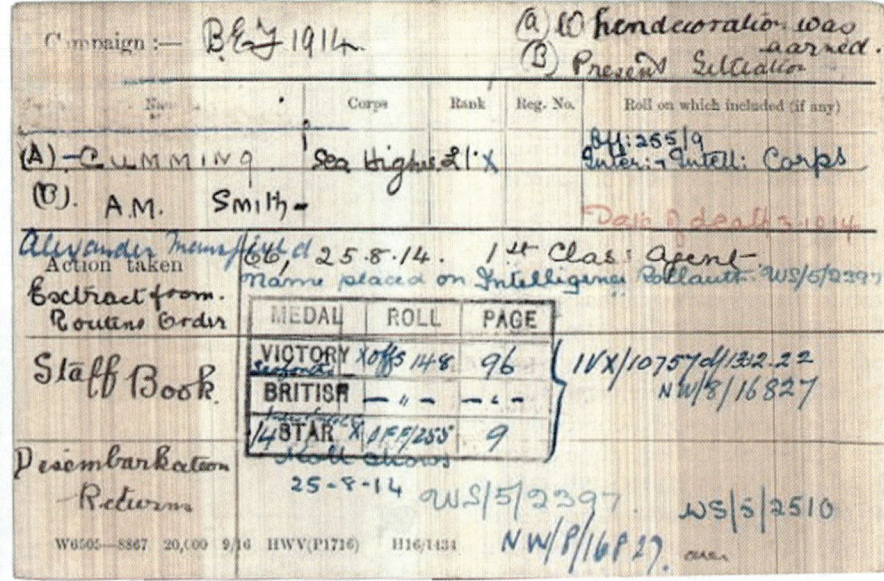

Document identifying Alastair Cumming as a '1st Class agent' in the Intelligence Corp. It also reveals the date of his death - 3 October 1914

26

Eye Spy Intelligence Magazine

27 Westminster Mansions, Great Smith Street

029•42

showing Alastair was part of the British Expeditionary Force (BEF) and an officer in the Intelligence Corp. A note described him as a *'1st Class Agent',* thus it seems just like his father, he had decided to embark upon a career in the intelligence world. As for the crash, there is much speculation Alastair was driving far too fast according to reports. Alastair was born on 5 February 1890 to Cumming's second wife Leslie Marian May.

There has been a persistent rumour amongst intelligence historians that Alastair was involved in a plot to assassinate Grigori Rasputin - advisor to the powerful House of Romanov and Tsar Nicholas II. The operation is said to have gone terribly wrong and the young agent killed. None of this can be verified at the moment, but interestingly, Andrew Cook did uncover some extraordinary information on Oswald Rayner, a member of MI6, who was working at the Russian court in St Petersburg at the time of Rasputin's assassination on 16-17 December 1916. It seems likely the

```
            Also French Cert. No. 1568.            727
CUMMING, Mansfield Smith.
       2, Whitehall Court, London, S.W.
                                      ─────────

Born  1st April, 1859,   at  London
Nationality  British
Rank or Profession   Commander, Royal Navy
Certificate taken on   Maurice Farman Biplane
At    The Farman School, Etampes, France
Date     10th November, 1913
```

Mansfield Cumming described as a Commander in the Royal Navy was issued with his flying certificate following training at the Farman School, Etampes, France. The address shown is MI6 headquarters

Grigori Rasputin

Eye Spy Intelligence Magazine

27

22 Fitzjames Avenue, Kensington

This photograph is from Cumming's pilot licence

great romancer was removed to stop a deal between Russia and Germany that would have freed thousands of German troops allowing them to move to the Western Front. Britain was fearful of his influence on Tsar Nicholas II and Tsarina Alexandra.

The Cummings relocated to **9 HOLLAND PARK TERRACE, PORTLAND ROAD [028•52]**. However, Cumming's main residence was **27 WESTMINSTER MANSIONS, GREAT SMITH STREET [029•42]**. His neighbour there, at number 28, just happened to be Edgar Rees Jones, Britain's WWI Minister of Munitions.

After returning to London, Cumming's new wooden leg was definitely something of a talking point in Whitehall itself. He had a tendency to tap his new appendage with a knife, much to the puzzlement of others. Outside his office his behaviour was equally as baffling, and apparently it was not unusual for him to be seen dashing about the corridors on a child's scooter.

Beyond Whitehall Court, Cumming was notorious for donning disguises and terrifying the public as he drove quickly and dangerously through the streets of London in his Rolls Royce. How this was interpreted and received by fellow members, intelligence colleagues and officials at the **ROYAL AUTOMOBILE CLUB (RAC), 89 PALL MALL [030•42]** is anyone's guess.

Cumming and his inner circle were regular visitors to the club, despite many members casting doubt on his ability to drive safely. Indeed, in this

Oswald Rayner - MI6

area of London several gentlemen's clubs exist - all of which can boast hundreds of famous members - including many from the intelligence community. Besides the RAC, three other significant establishments can be found neatly aligned on Pall Mall. Throughout the last century and beyond, they have been recognised as prime intelligence recruiting ground. **THE ATHENAEUM CLUB, 107 PALL MALL [031•42], TRAVELLERS CLUB, 106 PALL MALL [032•42]** and the

Eye Spy Intelligence Magazine

028•52

Holland Park Terrace, Portland Road

Reform Club, 104 Pall Mall **(See Chapter 9)**.

Established in 1837, another 'gentleman only' venue which also attracted senior military and intelligence people was **THE RAG ARMY AND NAVY CLUB, 36-39 PALL MALL [033•42]**. MI6 Chief Hugh Sinclair was a notable member in the 1920s. The original building was demolished in the late 1950s to make way for the modern construction.

As for its unusual name, this followed an incident shortly after it opened. A returning British Army officer was appalled at the lack of fare on offer comparing it to a "rag and famish affair" which was a known squalid gaming house. Members were amused and decided to form a 'Rag and Famish' dining club. In time the second part of the name was dropped. The club should not be confused with the Navy and Military Club **(See Site 356•42)**.

Cumming's appalling driving terrified Londoners

In May 1916, MI6 moved its headquarters to **2 WHITEHALL COURT [034•42]**. Unbeknown to many in the intelligence world, Cumming's office could only be accessed by a series of bizarre entrances. He built a mechanism of levers and peddles which he himself controlled. Once pressed, a false wall would open revealing a hidden staircase to his office! This address also featured on his pilot's accreditation.

Eye Spy Intelligence Magazine

29

2 Whitehall Court

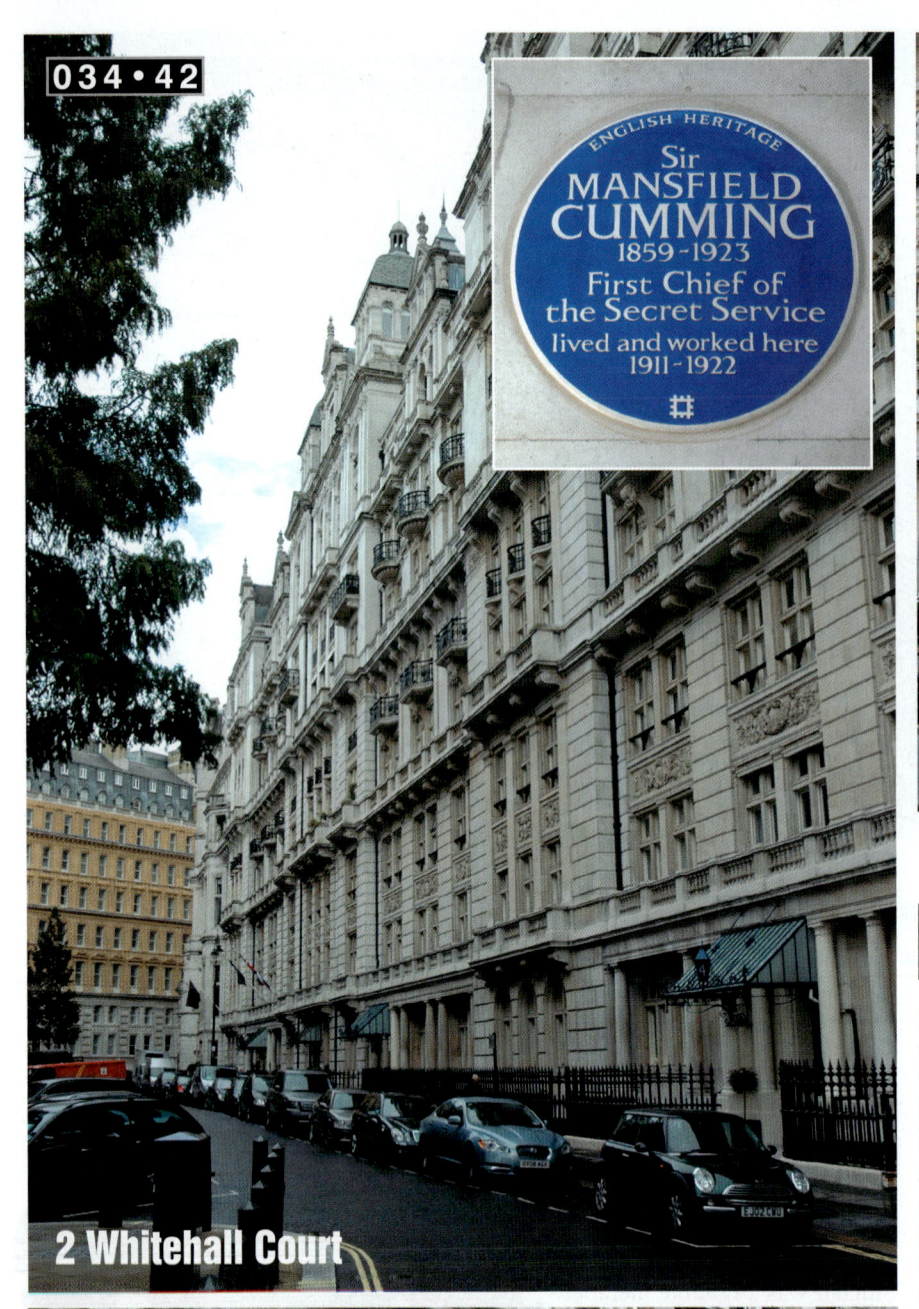

The entrance to 2 Whitehall Court - MI6's new home by 1916

NAVAL INTELLIGENCE AND THE ADMIRALTY

MI-1(c), unlike MO(t) was placed under control of **THE ADMIRALTY, WHITEHALL [035•42]** which traditionally had been the dominant organisation in intelligence collection. A year after MI-1(c)'s formation, navy officers Captain Trench and marine, Lieutenant Brandon, were arrested by German police and charged with espionage. And though they were operating under the auspices of the Admiralty, not Cumming's MI-1(c), it was a wake-up call for London that the great game was one not to be taken too light-heartedly.

As early as 1910, Cumming had started to enlist the occasional support of travelling British businessmen, industrialists, arms dealers and others to help gather information. This was particularly successful in Europe, especially Rotterdam and Brussels. Both these locations would play a significant role in the development of Britain's Passport Control Office (PCO) spy network. But the fledgling Service still had a lot to learn. For example, in Brussels, Cumming's men were offered a secret German code book. They requested permission to buy the book for £600.00 - a sum duly paid by MI-1(c). To Cumming's shock, the book turned out to be a forgery. Nevertheless, with war looming, at least Cumming had some agents in place at the edge of what would be a huge battlefield on the Western Front.

By this time, Kell's MO(t) had a name change to MO(g) and one year into the war (1915), it was officially renamed MI5 (Military Intelligence 5). Kell's staffing levels had also increased from just 14 operatives and a tight budget of a few thousand pounds, to 850 employees and a war purse of £100,000. Besides operating in the UK against possible German spies and collaborators, MI5 operated the Military Port Control Service - checking on all the comings and goings of foreigners (see the Alien Registry). Agents were also sent to Europe and a new section created called the Detection Branch. Already the signs were there that MI5 had arrived and was now starting to expand rapidly.

In neutral Holland, MI5 had been providing useful intelligence on the war, until its under cover agent - a man called James Dunn of the *Daily Mail* - was arrested by the neutral Dutch authorities in 1915. Cumming's Rotterdam bureau then took over the operation to send back intelligence.

Counter-espionage activities were ongoing, but the Kaiser's spies, at least those who were identified, were no match for Kell and his team. One hapless operative - Karl Hans Lody - was infiltrated into Britain using a stolen American passport. His mail was opened by an MI5 censor which showed him corresponding with a

German WWI warships in formation. Cumming sensed intelligence from abroad would be vital to defeat a formidable enemy

Athenaeum, Travellers and Reform clubs

Eye Spy Intelligence Magazine

31

Athenaeum Club 107 Pall Mall

THE HISTORIC GENTLEMEN'S CLUBS OF PALL MALL, LONDON

Royal Automobile Club, 89 Pall Mall

SPY SITES OF LONDON

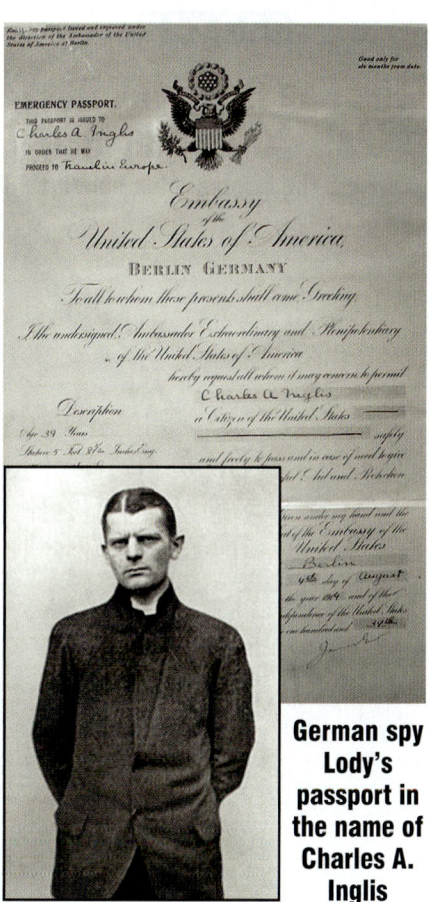

Travellers Club, 108 Pall Mall

German spy Lody's passport in the name of Charles A. Inglis

June 1915, but not before he shook the hand of each member of the firing squad. Hahn was given a prison sentence.

known German agent in Sweden. He was executed by firing squad in the Tower of London on 6 November 1914. He would be joined by 11 of his fellow spies as MI5 sought out German agents at British ports, airfields and weapons factories.

Also arrested was British national Peter Hahn who was caught helping a German spy by the name of Karl Muller distribute information. This came about after Hahn's attempts to conceal his location using invisible ink were discovered. The Londoner had fallen into severe debt in 1913 which probably explains why he was targeted.

Police detained Hahn at his address at **201 DEPTFORD HIGH STREET [036•33]** and found a complete invisible ink kit issued to him by Muller - including a lemon. Muller's arrest soon followed and his effort to explain why he too had a lemon on his person didn't impress MI5. The juice of the fruit was of course used as invisible ink. The German spy was shot in the Tower of London on 23

Karl Muller executed in 1915

Eye Spy Intelligence Magazine

SPY SITES OF LONDON
033 • 42

The Rag Army and Navy Club, 36-39 Pall Mall
Inset: The original club building

Frederick Duquesne pictured in Boar uniform. In later years he would create a formidable German spy network in the United States

Lord Kitchener

THE STRANGE DEMISE OF LORD KITCHENER

Recruiting young (and older men) for the British armed forces was a task championed by Lord Kitchener. He had many friends in British Intelligence, but also plenty of enemies, including some with very long memories about his behaviour in the Boer War. Thus the rumour mill was sent spinning when Kitchener perished along with over 600 men of HMS Hampshire west of the Orkney Isles on 5 June 1916. The ship was on a diplomatic mission to Russia when it reportedly hit a sea mine deposited by a marauding German U-boat.

Some years later a man by the name of Frederick Duquesne, who fought against Kitchener in the Boar War and disliked him very much, claimed involvement in the sinking of the Hampshire. Duquesne, in the employ of the British allegedly signalled the U-boat and then made good his escape on the submarine. Of course today, Duquesne is more famous for his role as a German spymaster who later ran a successful spy ring in America before his luck ran out and he was arrested

SPY SITES OF LONDON

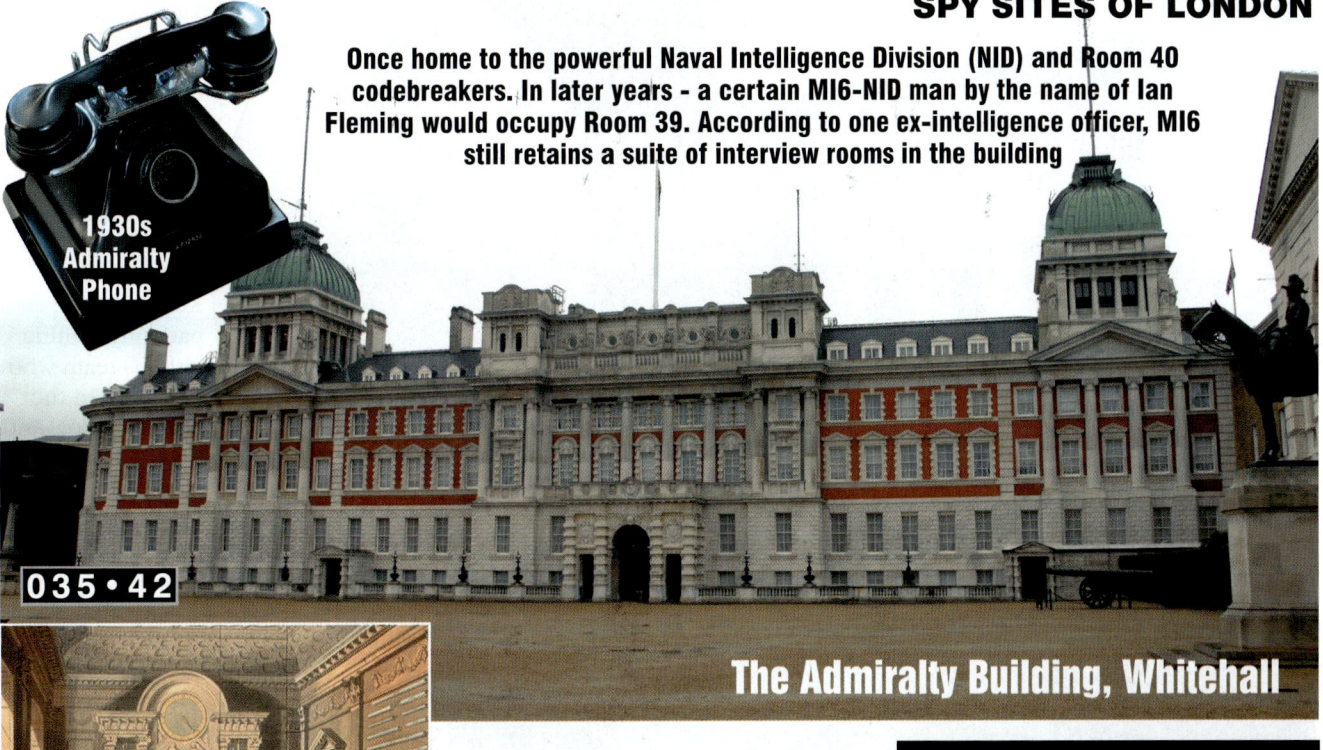

Once home to the powerful Naval Intelligence Division (NID) and Room 40 codebreakers. In later years - a certain MI6-NID man by the name of Ian Fleming would occupy Room 39. According to one ex-intelligence officer, MI6 still retains a suite of interview rooms in the building

1930s Admiralty Phone

035•42

The Admiralty Building, Whitehall

An 1808 engraving of the Admiralty board room. The room is still used today to host important meetings

by the FBI in the early stages of WWII. Thirty three members of his network were tried and convicted. As for Kitchener, who lived at **2 CARLTON GARDENS, [037•42]** his body was never found. And by now, the Kaiser had all but given up on the notion German spies could operate freely in Britain and produce valuable intelligence.

BRITISH INTELLIGENCE BEGINS TO FORM AND DIVIDE

MI5's Vernon Kell had a little more success against those who were funded by German spy financiers. Take for example the case of Robert

036•33

201 Deptford High Street

Eye Spy Intelligence Magazine

35

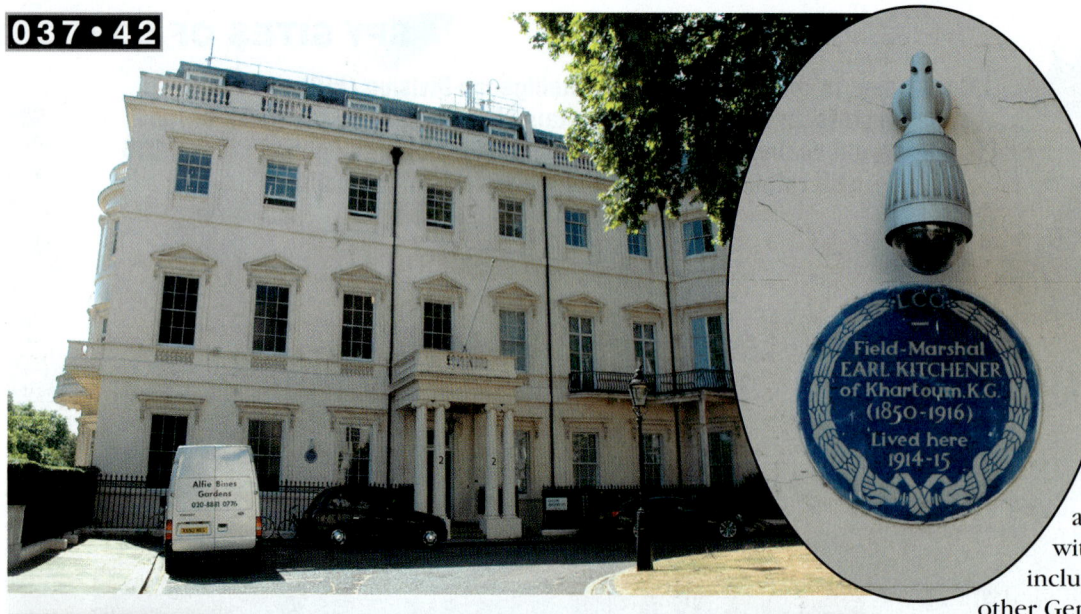

2 Carlton Gardens

opened it. A few weeks later, Rosenthal took a boat from Holland and arrived at the docks in Newcastle-upon-Tyne. Kell had been patiently waiting with his team who duly arrested the unknowing spy. And though Rosenthal agreed to provide MI5 with every assistance, including the names of other German agents, Kell was guarded because his prize catch was a brilliant ex-forger and cocaine addict.

By 1918, MI5 had nearly 140,000 files of individuals and 'persons of interest' in its Alien Registry.

Rosenthal. He had written a letter to his Berlin handler from his home in Copenhagen giving details of a forthcoming secret spy mission to Britain. The letter had somehow found its way into a post bag marked 'London'. Days later it was discovered by an inquisitive MI5 censor who duly

Hundreds of men gather at the former headquarters of Scotland Yard - used as a recruitment centre following Kitchener's request

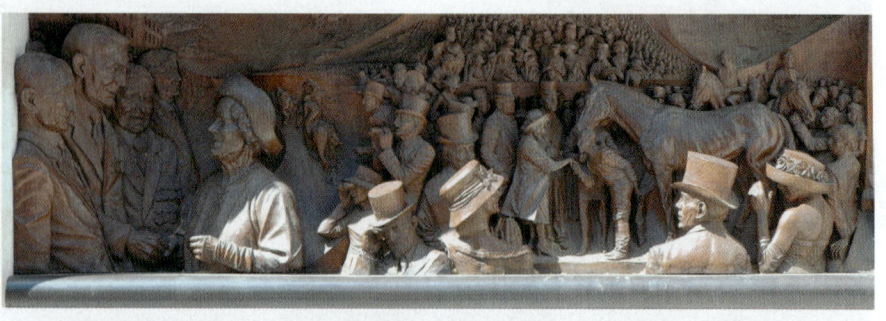

2 Carlton Gardens sits behind the splendid Queen Mother Memorial

Eye Spy Intelligence Magazine

CORK STREET W1
CITY OF WESTMINSTER

The Cryptanalytic Bureau operated from this address from 1916-1919. Interestingly, the same building was used as overflow offices for MI5 in the 1950s and early 1960s - this as the Security Service battled spies across London from the KGB

Captured members of Frederick Duquesne's German spy network

5 Cork Street, Mayfair

THE RELUCTANT NAVAL INTELLIGENCE DIVISION (NID)

Cumming's foreign intelligence section meanwhile, was still playing second fiddle to two powerful agencies operating in the intelligence arena. Firstly, there was the Naval Intelligence Division (NID) which was reluctant to simply allow MI-1(c), a clear run in overseas intelligence collection. Its role had become crucial following the outbreak of war. And then there was the British Army's Intelligence Corp, already playing a pivotal role in the battlefields of Europe. By 1916, MI-1(c) had moved from its offices in the Admiralty to the War Office. It was now but one of four sections employed in the field of intelligence gathering and analysis. The War Office also ran the fledgling Cryptanalytic Bureau MI1(b) from **5 CORK STREET, MAYFAIR [038•55]** but the Admiralty would soon acquire this codebreaking 'gem'.

HMS Hampshire hit a sea mine and sank with the loss of 600 men - including Lord Kitchener

Eye Spy Intelligence Magazine

SPY SITES OF LONDON

039·42
Admiralty Arch

Admiralty Arch built two years before the outbreak of WWI adjoins the Old Admiralty Building on the Mall. This splendid architectural 'gem' has many naval intelligence links, and as late as 2000 hosted Cabinet Meetings. It was also the headquarters of Downing Street's Strategy Unit. In 2011, this Grade I listed building was put up for sale

Director of Naval Intelligence - the legendary Captain William Reginald 'Blinker' Hall

NAVAL CODEBREAKERS OF ROOM 40

The NID was perhaps the defining agency at that moment, primarily because it was best placed to control SIGINT (Signals Intelligence). This was further augmented by the delivery of a German code book from the Russians, who had discovered the 'jewel' in the pocket of a dead German naval officer from the battleship Magdeburg. The Director of Naval Intelligence was a legendary figure known as Captain William Reginald 'Blinker' Hall. Hall, recognising the clear advantage which breaking codes and secure communications offered, set about forming a section which was central to the understanding of German radio traffic. Room 40 of the Admiralty operated in great secrecy and played an underhand role in getting the Americans 'on board' with the British in their fight against the Germans. In January 1917, a German telegram sent by the Kaiser's Foreign Minister Arthur Zimmermann, to the German Ambassador in America, was intercepted. After Room 40 decoded the signal, British Intelligence knew they had the document that would force America's hand. The telegram said that Mexico should be encouraged to join Germany in its fight, and in return, it would help guarantee a huge section of the southern United States. There was also a reference to

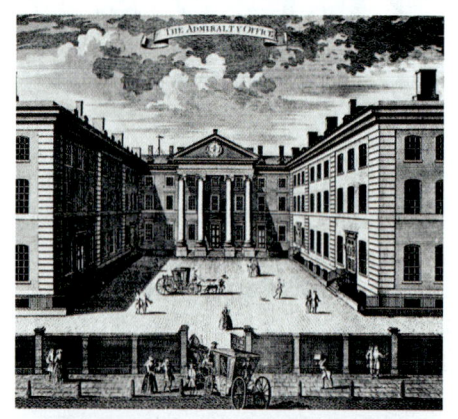

Engraving of the Ripley Building, Whitehall built in 1726 and still in use. The famous Room 40 codebreakers occupied part of the first floor

unrestricted warfare which essentially meant Germany was prepared to target neutral shipping, including US vessels sailing the Atlantic. British foreign officials, intelligence in hand, showed the document to President Woodrow Wilson who was naturally furious. America soon decided it would no longer remain neutral and Parliament cheered.

British naval intelligence officials used many Whitehall residences to host

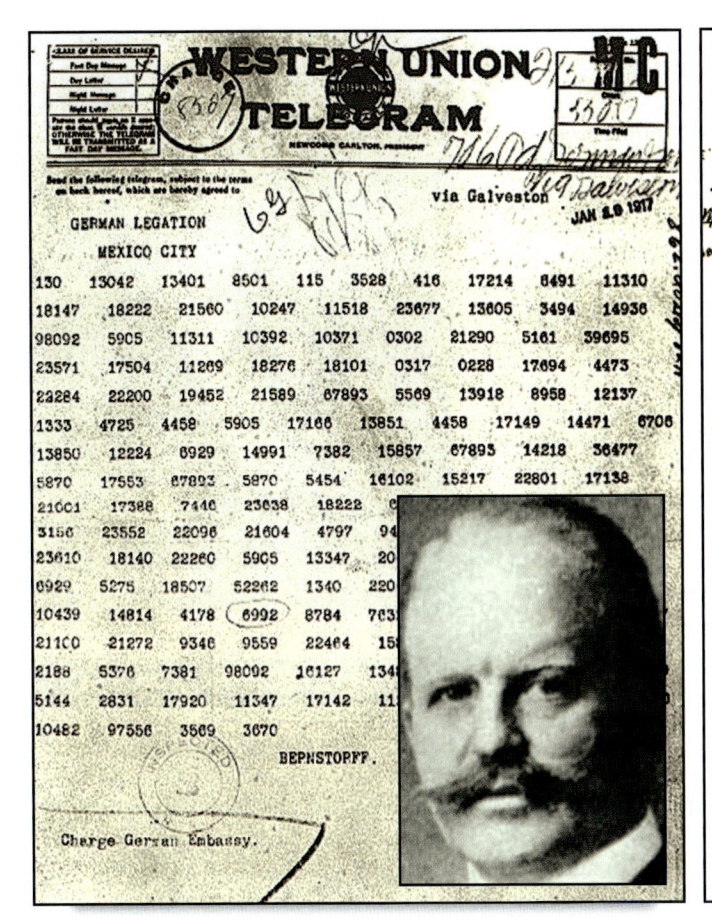

The coded German telegram (left) which was intercepted by British Intelligence and deciphered (right). A copy was delivered to Washington which effectively resulted in the United States entering WWI. Inset: Arthur Zimmermann

important meetings, and one such venue was the impressive **ADMIRALTY ARCH [039•42]** - a southern gateway to the Mall near Buckingham Palace.

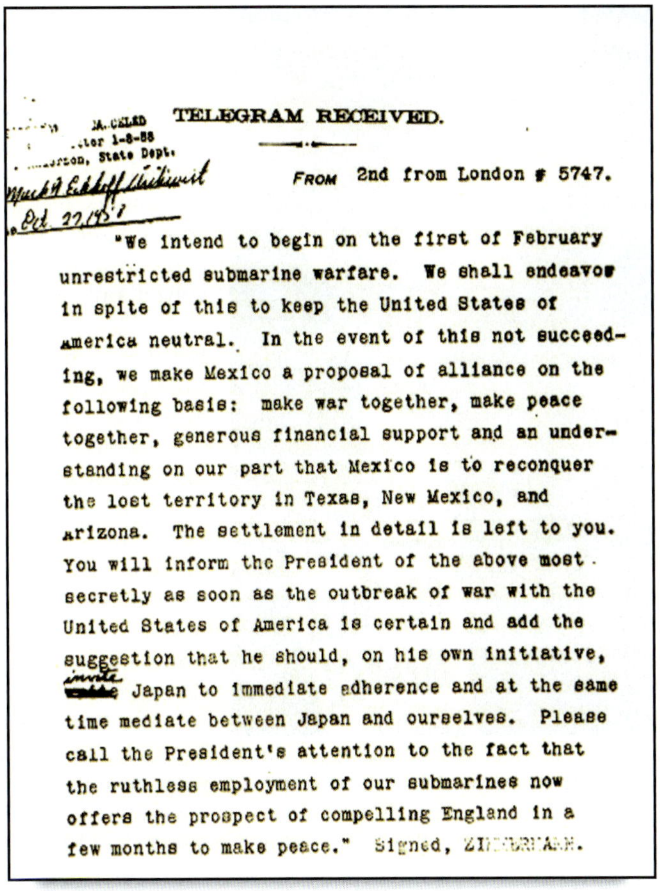

BUILDING SPY NETWORKS

MI-1(c) and the Intelligence Corp had, by late 1916, developed their own spy networks in Europe. As part of the General Staff, the Intelligence Corp was charged with gathering tactical intelligence, while Cumming and his team focused on strategic intelligence. There was conflict, and relations were not good.

The German light cruiser SMS Magdeburg lies helpless after running aground near the island of Odensholm. Russian sailors seized three intact code books and passed them to the British - allowing London to decode communications - including the now famous Zimmermann Telegram

US President Woodrow Wilson

Undeterred, Cumming continued to develop his operation and there were already several elements and networks operating under MI-1(c). One section, codenamed Frankignoul after one of its senior agents, had a dedicated team

Eye Spy Intelligence Magazine

SPY SITES OF LONDON

of about 30 agents who monitored train movements. But disaster was to strike and following the interception of reports from a steamer in the North Sea, the network was compromised and ten MI-1(c) agents were executed in 1917. Cumming persisted and built new networks and developed existing ones, including the largest of them all - the Dame Blanche - originally devised by military intelligence. This train-watching group numbered a staggering 1,000, and passed a variety of intelligence about troop and armaments' movement, and high-profile figures seen in different towns and cities. Of the 1,000 people involved, only 35 were ever arrested.

Besides the European theatre, Cumming began deploying his forces further and further afield - this laying the genesis for today's global MI6 intelligence operation. This worldwide ambition had actually started quietly in September 1914. Indeed, the first office which could be described as an MI6 Field Station opened in Petrograd, Russia. Here, Cumming appointed Major Archibald Campbell with a task to augment and support Russian signal's intelligence. Typically, Cumming inserted a somewhat devious caveat... Campbell was instructed to create an underground network of his own MI-1(c) agents. However, because of Foreign Office rivalries, Campbell was soon back in the UK. Despite this, on 7 November 1917, Britain was in a position to understand and observe the collapse of her former Imperial ally to Communism and the take-over by revolutionary Bolsheviks.

MI6 officer Somerset Maugham

THE BOLSHEVIK MENACE

Five months earlier, Cumming despatched the revered novelist and MI6 officer William Somerset Maugham to Petrograd in a last gasp effort to help White Russia. On 31 October he returned to London carrying an urgent message - a desperate appeal for arms. Helpless, a Downing Street official replied "can't help." Maugham, who would participate in other intelligence operations, lived at **6 CHESTERFIELD STREET [040•55]** in the heart of Mayfair.

A Russian White Army poster warning of the dangers and menace of Trotsky and the Bolsheviks

6 Chesterfield Street
Former home of MI6 officer Somerset Maugham

Eye Spy Intelligence Magazine

Vladimir Lenin

044•08 Marxist Memorial Library, 37A Clerkenwell Green

Britain maintained an unofficial mission in Russia, and because the country was still an ally, Cumming used his skills to bolster MI6's intelligence gathering ability. The mission was headed by Bruce Lockhart and he would soon liaise with one of MI6's most legendary spies - Sidney Reilly (real name Schlomo Rosenblum) - a brilliant disguise expert and described by Cumming as a "sinister man who I could never trust." Their objective was to overthrow the new government of Vladimir Ilyich Lenin. Reilly lived with his wife Margaret at **63 EARLS COURT SQUARE [041•46]**.

Lenin actually visited London on six occasions, spending much time studying at the British Library, where it's said he was first introduced to the works of Karl Marx. He fled Germany in 1902 because of persecution and transferred production of *Iskra*, the journal of the Russian Social Democracy Labour Party to London. He had various residences in the city, but one location is marked by a blue plaque - this on the site of **16 PERCY CIRCUS [042•62]**. And interestingly, some researchers believe he met another soon-to-be famous socialist at the **CROWN TAVERN, CLERKENWELL [043•08]** in 1905 - Joseph Stalin. A short distance from the pub one can also find the **MARXIST MEMORIAL LIBRARY, 37A CLERKENWELL GREEN [044•08]**. A bust of Lenin is on display at the Islington Museum, 245 St John Street. Lenin also met with another famous Marxist revolutionary in London - Leon Trotsky. The two men had much in common and discussed the future of Russia at 30 Holford Square, King's Cross. The building no longer exists, but a memorial board near the square is a reminder of its historical importance.

MI6 disguise artist Sidney Reilly was known as the 'Ace of Spies'

Two years later in 1907, the Bolshevik congress was held in a meeting room on **FULBOURNE STREET, WHITECHAPEL [045•01]**. As for Marx, in the 1850s he was a regular visitor to a debating club which held meetings above the **RED LION PUBLIC HOUSE, GREAT WINDMILL STREET AND ARCHER [046•55]**. Here he plotted with others to assassinate Queen Victoria. Today the pub is called B@1. Marx died in London in 1883 and was buried in **HIGHGATE CEMETERY [047•14]**. Here an impressive tomb can be found commemorating his philosophy.

In World War One, and amidst this once popular district for all things

047•14

Highgate Cemetery
The tomb of socialist Karl Marx who plotted to kill Queen Victoria

Eye Spy Intelligence Magazine 41

SPY SITES OF LONDON
042•62
16 Percy Circus

'foreign and Communist', British Intelligence chose the nearby Post Office **MOUNT PLEASANT SORTING OFFICE, FARRINGDON ROAD [048•08]**, to host its secret Letter Interception Unit or LIU. Here dozens of staffers would sift through incoming and outgoing mail to and from the continent. Anything that looked suspicious or contained information which was deemed helpful to the enemy was seized and acted upon.

Together with Imperial Censorship, the LIU would go on to help identify a number of important German spies, including Carl Hans Lody.

And it was against this backdrop of deep suspicion Reilly and Lockhart were despatched to conspire with anti-Bolsheviks. The Latvian Plot, as it was known, was aborted in 1918, and perhaps this was best for Cumming. The British intelligence officers had made contact with two Latvians of the Kremlin Guard who claimed troops were ready to take on the Bolsheviks. However, it would later transpire the men were actually agents of the Cheka - the Bolsheviks secret police and ultimate forerunner to the KGB. There were other plots to assassinate Lenin, and one in particular forced Reilly into hiding. He eventually escaped on a Dutch freighter, while Lockhart and another officer were arrested. Both were eventually returned to the UK in a very early spy exchange involving a Bolshevik official who had been detained in London by Kell's MI5. Lockhart was no doubt glad to return to his home at **48 WALTON STREET [049•44]**.

By 1918 and the end of World War One, Britain's fledgling MI5 and MI-1(c) had proven themselves worthy additions to the intelligence community. Both services had played important parts in helping the Allies defeat the Kaiser. Indeed, Kell and Cumming were awarded knighthoods. With victory against Germany assured, MI5 was run down again, and given a

L-R: Karl Marx 1875, Leon Trotsky 1897 and Lenin in disguise 1917

SPY SITES OF LONDON

046•55

MI6 officer Bruce Lockhart

paltry operating budget of just £25,000 a year. MI-1(c) fared even worse - and most of its experienced staff were lost to other departments. In 1920, MI-1(c) was officially re-named Military Intelligence 6 (MI6) to align itself with MI5's designation. The UK now operated dedicated foreign and domestic intelligence agencies. In later years, MI5 would become known as The Security Service, while in 1921, MI6 took on the official title of Secret Intelligence Service or SIS.

Winston Churchill wanted to create a unified intelligence service

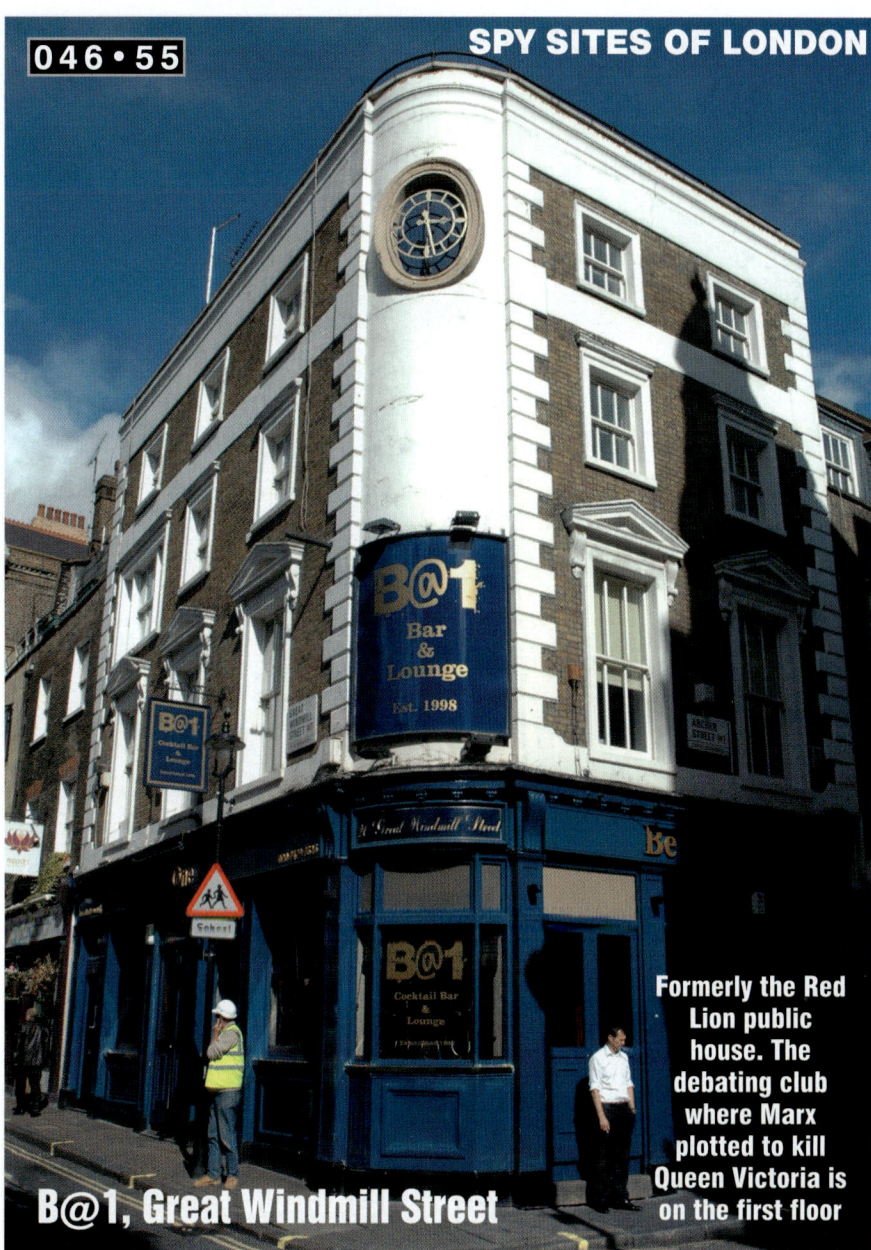

B@1, Great Windmill Street

Formerly the Red Lion public house. The debating club where Marx plotted to kill Queen Victoria is on the first floor

MI5's G-Branch. Note the military uniforms. CIRCA. 1918

Eye Spy Intelligence Magazine

43

SPY SITES OF LONDON

043•08

Crown Tavern, Clerkenwell

048•08

Mount Pleasant Sorting Office, Farringdon Road

With respect to the decline of MI5 and MI6, things could have turned out even worse. In 1921, Winston Churchill returned to the notion that Britain should have a unified Secret Service Bureau. Kell and Cumming resisted, though a new service, the Directorate of Intelligence (DOI), which had been formed a year earlier, took over the responsibilities of tackling subversion in Britain. Kell eventually succeeded in convincing ministers that this was a job MI5 could do itself - without the creation of yet another agency. The DOI imploded shortly thereafter, and ten years later, another intelligence arm, the Special Branch, was also absorbed by MI5.

CUMMING'S 'LAST HURRAHS'

In 1923, MI6 under Cumming, snatched Room 40 away from the Admiralty's NID. With a plethora of skilled cryptographers, Cumming helped shape what is today known as GCHQ - Government Communications Headquarters. However, before that in 1919, Room 40 was renamed the Government Code and Cypher School (GC&CS). Interestingly, some staffers used the initials to spell out a very different organisation - the 'Golf, Cheese and Chess Society'!

MI6 officer T. E. Lawrence - 'Lawrence of Arabia' 1919

44

Eye Spy Intelligence Magazine

045•01
Fulbourne Street, Whitechapel

SPY SITES OF LONDON
Stalin, Trotsky and Lenin all spoke at conferences in this building. In 1907 the Bolshevik congress was held here

© LOUIS BERK

049•44
48 Walton Street

Cumming relocated GC&CS to one of his favourite MI6 operational sites - **WATERGATE HOUSE, 13-15 YORK BUILDINGS [050•62]**. This suited him to a tee as just a short distance away, his favourite disguise provider ran a shop!

Throughout his early endeavours to turn MI6 into a formidable organisation, Cumming was fortunate to have around him a number of brilliant intelligence officers, one of whom was his friend - Russian-born Harry Carr. The super-secretive Carr would go on to play a significant role in future operations across Europe, the Baltic and Russia. Vehemently opposed to the Bolsheviks he was eventually appointed Helsinki Field Station Chief. Carr lived at **11 FORDHAM COURT, DE VERE GARDENS, KENSINGTON [051•60]**. Sadly, Harry Carr was murdered in 1981.

Another interesting Cumming recruit - Lt. Colonel Thomas Edward Lawrence - better known by his nickname

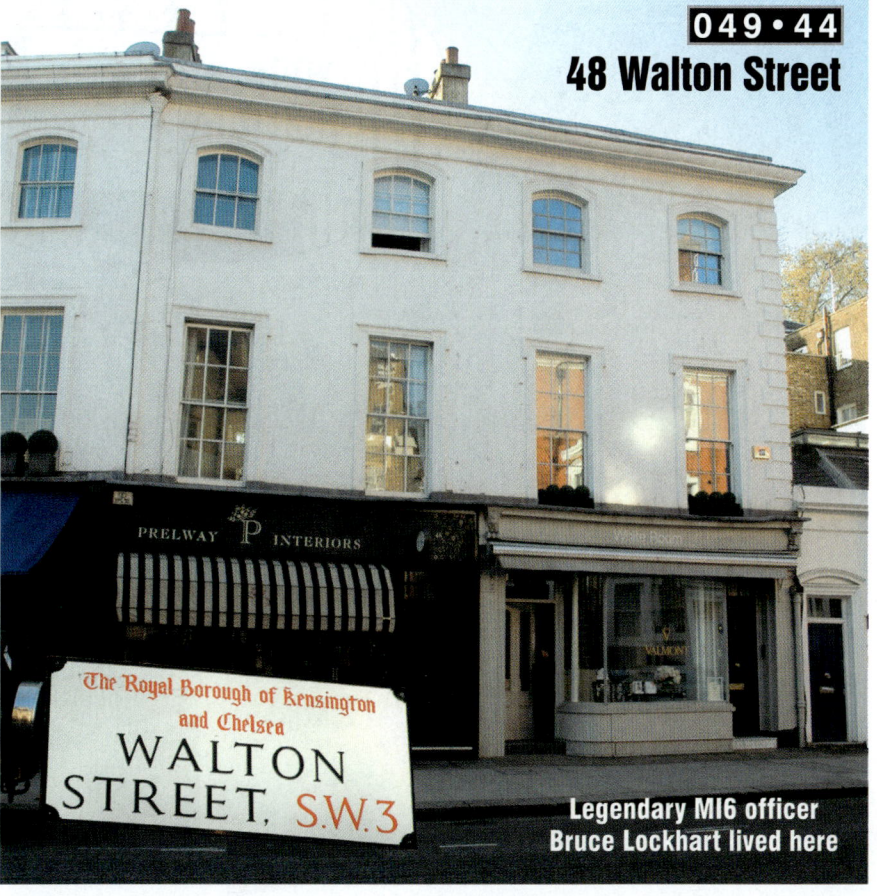

Legendary MI6 officer Bruce Lockhart lived here

Eye Spy Intelligence Magazine

45

051•60

The super-secret MI6 officer Harry Carr lived here

11 Fordham Court, De Vere Gardens, Kensington

The Royal Borough of Kensington and Chelsea
DE VERE GARDENS, W.8.

050•62

YORK BUILDINGS WC2
CITY OF WESTMINSTER

Watergate House, 13-15 York Buildings
GC&CS HQ in 1919

WATERGATE HOUSE
13-15 YORK BUILDINGS

14 Barton Street

052•42

46   Eye Spy Intelligence Magazine

'Lawrence of Arabia', helped attract (some in the intelligence world prefer to use the word recruit) many interesting and important figures to MI6. Lawrence himself played a pivotal role as a liaison during the Arab revolt against Ottoman Turkish rule between the years 1916-1918. Lawrence's experiences of his wartime work were published in the historically important book - *Seven Pillars of Wisdom*. This was written whilst Lawrence lived at **14 BARTON STREET [052•42]**. Many interesting visitors to this address would, in years to come, find themselves in the service of MI6 and MI5, including playwright, composer, actor and director Sir Noel Coward. The flamboyant Londoner was born at **131 WALDEGRAVE ROAD, TEDDINGTON [053•50]** in 1899, though during his important years working for British Intelligence and the War Ministry, lived at **17 GERALD ROAD, BELGRAVIA [054•42]**. In WWII, Coward would play a crucial role in the British propaganda directorate as we shall soon discover. In 2006, following much refurbishment, the Albery Theatre in St Martin's Lane was renamed the **NOEL COWARD THEATRE [055•62]** in his honour, though this was entirely due to his work in theatre and not his undercover dealings with MI6! As for Lawrence, even Winston Churchill frequently discussed intelligence happenings with him at his home.

An early MI6 disaster which deeply affected Cumming should be recorded. In Ireland, an IRA attack in 1920, left 14 of his London-trained agents dead. This resulted in the Service pulling most of its personnel out of the country.

Cumming also recognised the importance of using celebrities who could travel with near impunity across borders and for propaganda purposes.

MI6 contact man - Noel Coward

© ALLAN WARREN

131 Waldegrave Road, Teddington

053•50

Lillie Langtry's 'liaisons' were of concern to British Intelligence

Eye Spy Intelligence Magazine 47

17 Gerald Road, Belgravia
054•42

Noel Coward Theatre, 131 St Martin's Lane
055•62

Though the plaque on the wall identifies 17 Gerald Road, the actual house cannot be seen as it is tucked between two rows of houses - perhaps just as Coward would have wished in respect of his privacy. However, the house which can be seen and is often mistaken for 'number 17' did play host to another war hero - whose brother was a most important KGB spy (See Chapter 17)

This early tradecraft would be developed by MI6 in future years and would become crucial in WWII. Of course with celebrity comes risk, and this was evident with one famous stage performer and actress - Lillie Langtry. Amongst her inner circle of friends and associates were the likes of Robert Peel, Oscar Wilde and film producer Alexander Korda. Korda would eventually work for MI6, and like Coward and some other surprising stage and film figures, his work will be discussed later.

Amidst the liaisons, there were even rumours that senior MI6 man Claude Dansey may have been seduced by Wilde's first lover - Robbie Ross. As for Langtry, some of her productions were regarded as British propaganda, but she moved in very secretive circles and had access to all manner of information, some of it undoubtedly useful to

Oscar Wilde

Eye Spy Intelligence Magazine

Edward VII - 1901 painting

Prince Louis of Battenberg and a wartime propaganda drawing of him sweeping away his German ties

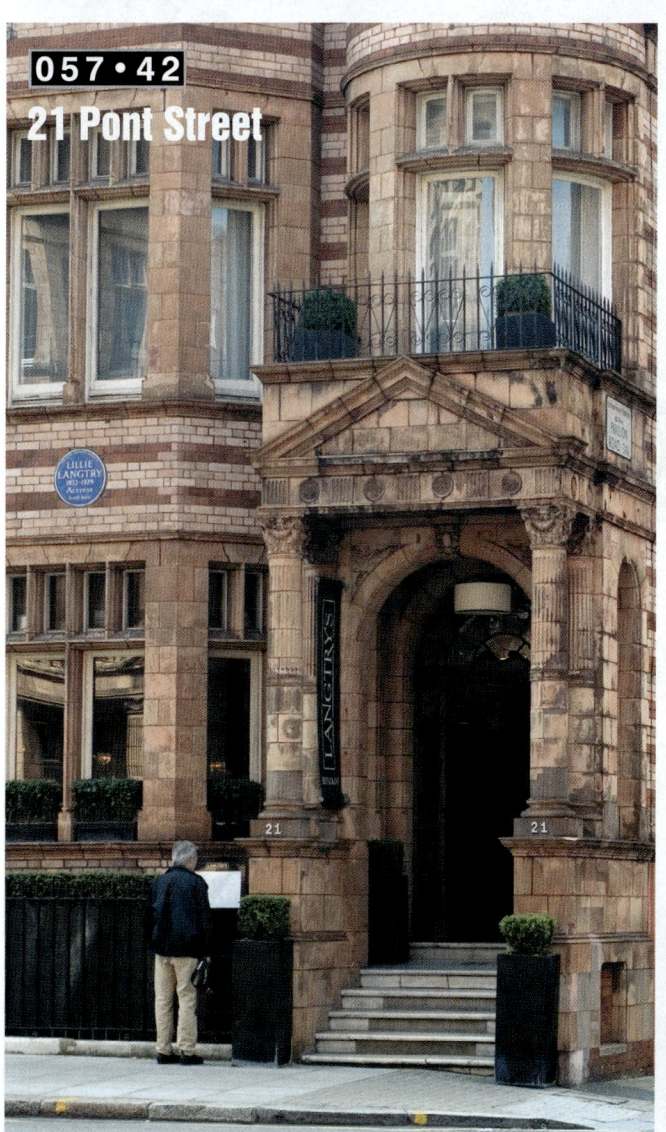

21 Pont Street   057•42

5 Wilton Place   056•42

Eye Spy Intelligence Magazine   49

SPY SITES OF LONDON

Adelphi Building, 1-11 John Adam Street

The architecture of the Adelphi is truly splendid. Unbeknown to most of its residents, the building once hosted an important MI5 office

058•62

MI6 and MI5. However, it was her liaisons with a number of very high profile figures that concerned senior officials. There were stories of affairs with King Edward VII and Prince Louis of Battenberg, a German prince related to the Royal Family. In 1912, he was appointed First Sea Lord, but as war loomed with Germany he was forced to step down. In 1917, at the height of the war, a propaganda drawing was published in the British press showing the prince 'sweeping away his German ties'. Nevertheless, he would later marry a granddaughter of Queen Victoria and was the father of a certain Admiral of the Fleet - Louis Mountbatten. Two addresses associated with Langtry can be found

Trafalgar Square and Nelson's Column

© DAVID CASTOR

50

Eye Spy Intelligence Magazine

061•47

73-75 Queen's Gate
Early post WWI offices of MI5

in London - **5 WILTON PLACE** [056•42] and **21 PONT STREET** [057•42] - if walls could talk!

However, most historians recognise Cumming had overseen the birth of a truly global institution, but sadly, he passed away in 1923. He was found dead in his office at 1 Melbury Road, the Service's headquarters.

MI5 WARTIME EXPANSION - AND A POOR REWARD FOR HELPING DEFEAT GERMANY

Watergate House had supported MI5 staffers up until around 1916 along

041•46

63 Earl's Court Square
MI6's 'Ace of Spies' lived here at the time of his recruitment into British Intelligence

Eye Spy Intelligence Magazine　　51

SPY SITES OF LONDON
062•42

Girl Guides pictured in 1918

with the neighbouring **ADELPHI BUILDING, 1-11 JOHN ADAMS STREET [058•62]**.

However, wartime expansion meant that the organisation needed additional space for personnel. It moved its centre of operations to **WATERLOO HOUSE, 16 CHARLES STREET, HAYMARKET [059•55]**. Staff were apparently pleased because it had a large canteen and provided excellent views of Trafalgar Square and Nelson's Column! Additional premises were also taken at **GREENER HOUSE, 66-68 HAYMARKET [060•42]**. These buildings would be used by MI5 staffers for many years and all have retained their original architecture.

MI5's reward for helping to defeat Germany? - a huge cut in its budget - down from £100,000 a year to just over £35,000. The Service was also on the move again and relocated from Charles Street to cheaper premises at **73-75 QUEEN'S GATE [061•47]**.

17-19 Buckingham Palace Road

Sidney Reilly

Eye Spy Intelligence Magazine

SPY SITES OF LONDON

35 Albemarle Street, Mayfair

063·55

060·42

Greener House, 66-68 Haymarket

Here it would remain for almost a decade. Today the location is known as Queens Court and the numbering has also changed. However, the building retains its original facade.

By 1919, Kell had lost around 80 per cent of his wartime staff - from 844 to just 151 and he was in a desperate fight to keep the Service alive.

THE SECRET RUNNERS

One wartime secret MI5 did manage to conceal from the media concerned its recruitment of Girl Guides and Boy Scouts to act as local couriers and observers.

Girl Guides were seen as less suspicious than boys who were more difficult to manage. They were aged between 14 and 18-years-old and paid a weekly sum of 10 shillings (50p) plus they received a food allowance. Interestingly, like all members of the Service the youngsters had to take a

Pepita Bobadilla

Greener House was occupied by MI5 counter-espionage officers for part of the Great War

Eye Spy Intelligence Magazine

53

SPY SITES OF LONDON

Waterloo House, 16 Charles Street, Haymarket

pledge of secrecy and swear allegiance to the Crown. The Girl Guides were headquartered at **17-19 BUCKINGHAM PALACE ROAD [062•42]**. Like many of the full time staffers after the war had ended, they too were shown the door!

There was also a blow for MI6 in 1925 when Russian OGPU spies lured Sidney Reilly to his death in woods outside Moscow. The order to assassinate the MI6 officer had been made by Stalin himself.

Two years earlier he had married Pepita Bobadilla - his third wife - at the Registrar Office, Henrietta Street, Covent Garden. They lived together in an apartment at **35 ALBEMARLE STREET, MAYFAIR [063•55]**.

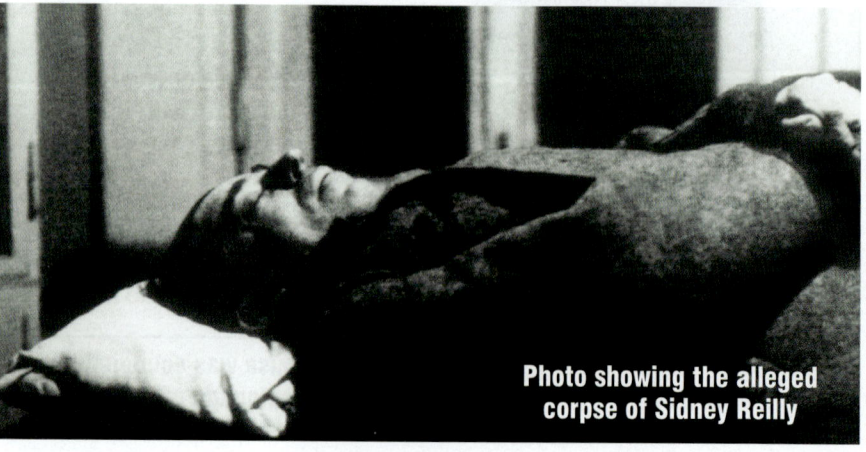

Photo showing the alleged corpse of Sidney Reilly

COURTESY: ANDREW COOK

SPY SITES OF LONDON

III

The Dark Spies
Propaganda, Front Companies and Spy Rings

Lord Northcliffe's (Alfred Harmsworth) *Daily Mail* had championed the threat of invasion by Germany - even though few government officials supported such a scenario. Along with that 'artful dodger' William Tufnell Le Queux, the powerful publisher had been a little underhand in fermenting talk of German spies wandering about the countryside and spying on British ports etc. Nevertheless, even though such stories were little more than tales, they were convincingly written. Thus when war did break out, Northcliffe was summoned to Whitehall and chosen to oversee and direct one of the most secretive organisations ever created by the government - the British War Propaganda Bureau (WPB).

Unbeknown to most members of Parliament, Northcliffe, together with a number of senior military, intelligence and political figures, managed to secure the services of some of the world's best known media people, authors and historians. This monumental effort was to convince the international community Germany

064•08

Fleet Street

Eye Spy Intelligence Magazine 55

SPY SITES OF LONDON

065•08

Lord Northcliffe

Ye Old Cheshire Cheese, 145 Fleet Street

was a global menace, and that they should back Britain. At one time the WPB had threads to virtually every newspaper owner and editor on **FLEET STREET [064•08]** - the home of Britain's newspaper industry. Here stories of German atrocities and less than truthful reporting were 'fed' to editors and duly published. Reports of British heroism and battlefield successes were also delivered, though some were undoubtedly false. It made good copy for the newspapers, and at the same time was a definite morale boosting venture. Several senior overseas correspondents also chose to gather information on events in Europe and pass it to British Intelligence. Disinformation was 'king' and deception the name of the game. In later years when news of the Fleet Street liaison emerged, some commentators criticised the decision to use such tactics, but these were desperate times indeed.

YE OLD CHESHIRE CHEESE, 145 FLEET STREET [065•08] is one of the oldest public houses in the city - . The pub was frequented by literary authors, newspaper editors and intelligence people working for the propaganda houses. No doubt too those from the War Propaganda Bureau.

Northcliffe secured many intelligence connections and, despite what some historians say, he helped ferment an atmosphere of suspicion in London. This was especially true of those officials who did not believe the country really needed a powerful intelligence community. During the war, Northcliffe was a senior orchestrator of propaganda at the behest of War Office and MI6 officials.

By chance or design, the media magnate fell victim to a German assassin whilst on operational duty for the British armed forces in Holland.

His death in August 1922 came as a shock to the country. As a former owner of *The London Times, Daily Mirror* and of course *Daily Mail*, he was a well known public figure. However, it is the circumstances surrounding how the 57-year-old died and where that is something of an intelligence mystery. This is examined shortly.

THE PROPAGANDA HOUSES OF WELLINGTON AND CREW

At the beginning of World War One, much of the propaganda work was conducted by the War Office Directorate of Military Operations Department MI7, the Admiralty and a number of other organisations, including the Foreign Office News Department. Also created was an intelligence 'corridor' to the major British newspapers (Fleet Street) via the humorously named Neutral Press Committee.

Many operations were performed by an organisation known as Wellington

Wellington House, Buckingham Gate

House, which operated from 2 September 1914 until 1918. Its name derives from the building used as headquarters for the British War Propaganda Bureau. Situated at **70 BUCKINGHAM GATE [066•42]** a new build still retains the name - Wellington House. A century ago it was occupied by the National Insurance Department - making it an ideal front organisation for the super-secret activities of the WPB.

Journalist-come-politician Charles F. G. Masterman was selected as Wellington House Director. Masterman lived and worked from **46 GILLINGHAM STREET, ECCLESTON SQUARE [067•42]**. Part of the original building has been replaced. Masterman invited many leading British authors, including Arthur Conan Doyle, Rudyard Kipling, H. G. Wells and historian G. M. Trevelyan to a conference which outlined the nature of his work at Wellington House. He also explained what the organisation sought to achieve. Doyle lived at **12 TENNISON ROAD [068•29]**, but he wrote and worked from **2 UPPER WIMPOLE**

Rudyard Kipling | **Sir Arthur Conan Doyle** | **John Buchan** | **Herbert George Wells**

Eye Spy Intelligence Magazine

SPY SITES OF LONDON

Charles Masterman

STREET [069•55]. Wells lived and died at 13 HANOVER TERRACE [070•15]. Kipling lived at 43 VILLIERS STREET now renamed KIPLING HOUSE [071•62].

Masterman's team published a decidedly biased monthly *History of the War* and recruited the brilliant author John Buchan to head its production. In 1915, Buchan of course, wrote the iconic *Thirty Nine Steps* - a novel involving German spies which remains a hugely popular book, film and play. Indeed, it still retains its allure. In 2012 the play was hosted by the **CRITERION THEATRE, 2 JERMYN STREET [072•55]**. This building has its own spylore in that during WWII its basement was used as a covert BBC broadcasting studio, and as we shall discover, a KGB agent meeting point.

In 1918, Buchan was made Director of Intelligence for Wellington House. He lived at **76 PORTLAND PLACE [073•55]**, sadly this is now a new build and the site occupied by the Institute of Physics. However, inside the foyer a plaque notes his residence. Besides paper media, the organisation

Criterion Theatre, 2 Jermyn Street 072•55

Spymaster and author John Buchan's iconic *39 Steps* remains as popular as ever - here being hosted at the Criterion Theatre. In WWII its basement was used as a covert BBC broadcasting studio

A frame from the propaganda motion picture produced by Wellington House - *The Battle of the Somme*

068•29
12 Tennison Road

58   Eye Spy Intelligence Magazine

SPY SITES OF LONDON
070·15
H. G. Wells lived and died here

43 Villiers Street (Kipling House)

13 Hanover Terrace

formed a cinema section, which went on to produce the famous 1916 propaganda film-documentary - *Battle of the Somme.*

At the same time, Sir Max Aitken, better known of course as Lord Beaverbrook, owner of the powerful *Daily Express,* was made Minister of Information. Masterman then relinquished overall control, but was made Director of Publications.

Twenty years later, Beaverbrook would be called upon again as a minister for

Lord Beaverbrook

Eye Spy Intelligence Magazine — 59

073•55

William Fisher, Lord Downing - Minister of Information

JOHN BUCHAN
AUTHOR & STATESMAN
Lived in a house on this site from 1912 until 1919

76 Portland Place

Committee which was headquartered at **CREWE HOUSE, 28 CHARLES STREET [076•55]**. Also relocated to this impressive building were the Political Intelligence Bureau and the Enemy Propaganda Bureau. Today the building serves as the Embassy of Saudi Arabia. One key member was

075•60

Thorney Court

disinformation and play a pivotal role in one of the greatest deception operations of all time - to help draw America into WWII.

William Fisher, Lord Downham, took over from Beaverbrook in 1917. He lived and had offices at **13 BUCKINGHAM PALACE ROAD [074•42]**.

Another well known media man, Robert Donald, editor of the *Daily Chronicle* was made Director of Propaganda. He was charged with targeting neutral countries. Donald resided at **12 THORNEY COURT, KENSINGTON [075•60]**. The original building has long since been replaced, but at least planners retained the original stone gates to the site. Many of these organisations merged in 1917, forming the short-lived Department of Information. A year later it was renamed Ministry of Information.

In 1918, Lord Northcliffe was made chief of the section which aimed propaganda at enemy nations. The Ministry of Information was also dissolved in this year. Northcliffe was placed in charge of a new propaganda endeavour called the Crewe House

Eye Spy Intelligence Magazine

067•42

Gillingham Street, Eccleston Square

074•42

13 Buckingham Palace Road

Eye Spy Intelligence Magazine

Crewe House
This photograph actually shows the rear of Crewe House

historian Arnold Joseph Toynbee, who in 1943, was made director of the important Research Directorate at the Foreign Office, this after serving four years as head of the Royal Institute of International Affairs (RUSI). The Toynbee family lived at **49 WIMBLEDON PARK SIDE [077•41]**.

Another surprising man who worked with the propaganda bureaus and intelligence world was only discovered in 2013, thanks to the release of intelligence files by the National Archives. He was Alan Alexander Milne, author of the famous *Winnie the Pooh* books. Milne resided at **13 MALLORD STREET [078•44]**.

An assistant editor of *Punch* magazine and a critic of war, despite the fact he joined the army, Milne decided to speak out in support of the British war effort. This was for MI7B - military intelligence and his writings and

Crewe House, 28 Charles Street

A. A. Milne with his son Christopher Robin

49 Wimbledon Park Side

The former Toynbee residence is now a hospital

reflections distributed through Crewe House. However, in 1934 he wrote a book denouncing the war again titled *Peace with Honour*. When WWII broke out he changed the title again to *War with Honour* - perhaps a sign he had rejoined the propaganda elements of British Intelligence.

Arnold Joseph Toynbee featured on the cover of *Time* magazine

THE STRANGE DEATH OF LORD NORTHCLIFFE

In the months following the end of World War One in November 1918, Lord Northcliffe complained of stomach pains and had great difficulty in sleeping. He was also said to suffer from acute paranoia - this evidenced by one strange event when he aimed a gun at his own dressing gown believing it contained a body. Thereafter he kept the firearm loaded next to his bed whilst sleeping.

His close confidantes later revealed that he was "incarcerated for his own safety," in a specially built wooden shed on the roof top of 2 Carlton Gardens. This splendid residence, just off The Mall, was of course a government building frequently used by British Intelligence and military officials.

A source from Northcliffe's inner circle also explained that the media and MI6 contact man believed his health problems could be traced back

G. M. Trevelyan - Wellington House propaganda advisor

to a wartime encounter with a shadowy group of Germans on the Dutch border. He said the men may have been deliberately tipped-off about his location after a German spy had recognised him.

At some point he ate an ice cream which the spy had somehow managed to lace with poison. After digesting the treat, Northcliffe suddenly felt poorly, and from that moment on he never regained his health. Officially, his

Eye Spy Intelligence Magazine

SPY SITES OF LONDON

069•55

2 Upper Wimpole Street
Work place of Sir Arthur Conan Doyle

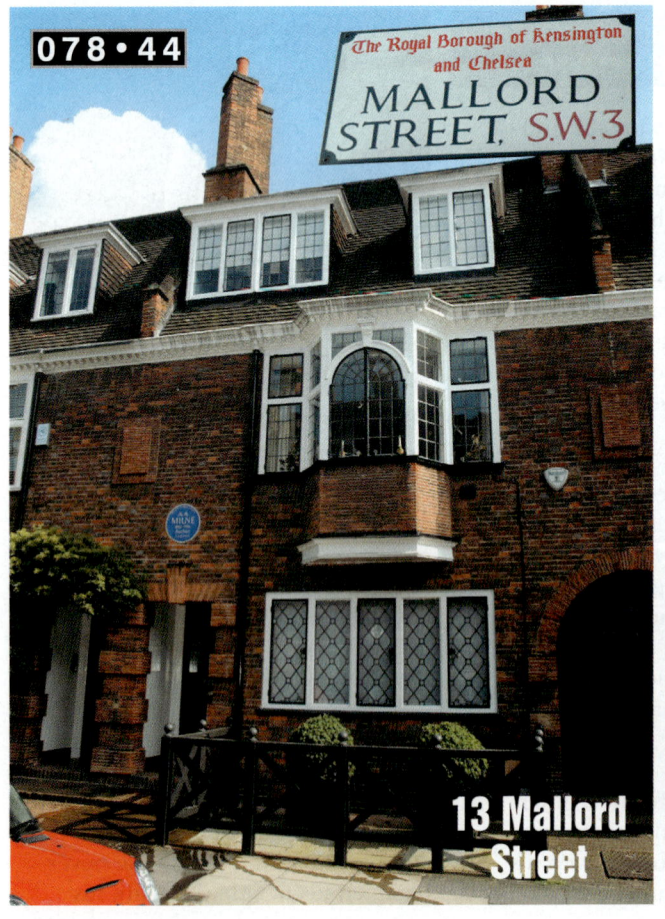

078•44

13 Mallord Street

2 Carlton Gardens

The sun sets over this once important intelligence location - scene of a most mysterious death

079•21

31 Pandora Road

A photo said to show Lord Northcliffe with three unidentified men presumably in London - date unknown

Another view of 31 Pandora Road

cause of death was the result of streptococcus, an infection of the bloodstream which causes heart and kidney malfunction. Some described this as, "general paralysis of the insane."

There was one final twist to this sad affair. Northcliffe had been a fierce critic of British war hero Lord Kitchener and had repeatedly questioned his tactics. However, this didn't go down too well with the public and his newspaper circulation plummeted.

Nevertheless, the attacks continued until Kitchener's demise following the sinking of HMS Hampshire in June 1916. "The British Empire has just had the greatest stroke of luck in its history," Northcliffe proclaimed.

That Northcliffe, who founded the Pandora Publishing Company from his home at **31 PANDORA ROAD, HAMPSTEAD [079•21]** in 1890, should die on the rooftop of 2 Carlton Gardens is a mystery in itself. For ironically, this was once the home of Lord Kitchener...

A little over thirty years later this building would host a Top Secret meeting between senior MI6 and CIA officials. On the agenda was a Cold War operation to dig deep under East Berlin, intercept vital communications and penetrate the heart of Soviet Intelligence.

THE EMERGING COMMUNIST THREAT AND SEEDS OF THE COLD WAR

In 1920, the League of Nations was founded as a result of the Paris Peace Conference that ended the Great War. Its principal mission was to ensure and maintain world peace. The architect of the organisation was the 1st Viscount Robert Cecil of Chelwood, an intelligence contact man and Under Secretary of State for Foreign Affairs. He lived at **18 EATON PLACE [080•42]**.

British Intelligence likened the emerging Russia to a Hydra

Eye Spy Intelligence Magazine

65

Robert Cecil

080•42
18 Eaton Place

One of the countries who signed up to the League of Nations was Germany, but as history shows, they pulled out in 1938 along with Italy and Japan. This would prove a pivotal moment. But for now, with the war against the Kaiser now behind them, MI5 and MI6 sought to establish themselves alongside Britain's still predominantly military intelligence community. Successes during the conflict meant that their credibility had been assured and both the Services' respective heads, Vernon Kell (MI5) and Mansfield Cumming (MI6), were regarded as heroes in Whitehall.

However, the Naval Intelligence Division (NID) - sometimes called Room 39 - after its room number at Admiralty headquarters, was still far and away the most respected and powerful of intelligence organisations. Indeed, in late 1918 as the embers of WWI were beginning to fade, the NID's chief, Admiral Sir William Reginald 'Blinker' Hall, warned of a new emerging threat - that of Bolshevism in Russia: "Hard and bitter as the battle has been, we now have to face a far, far more ruthless foe. A foe that is hydra-headed and whose evil power will spread over the whole world... that foe is Soviet Russia," Hall said.

Hall, who lived at **59 ONSLOW GARDENS [081•47]**, with his wife Ethel, insisted British Intelligence focus much of its attention in an easterly direction. And this London duly did, using all its experience in the dark arts of espionage as we shall discover.

Hall and his NID officers were revered in London, unlike some emerging figures in British Intelligence. He surrounded himself with a variety of brilliant methodical thinkers, analysts and tacticians, many in the codebreaking field. Alastair Denniston - a Room 40 codebreaker for example. He of course had by now been appointed head of the Government Code and Cypher School (GC&CS). Another associate worthy of mention is Scottish physicist and engineer James Alfred Ewing. He was head of the NID codebreakers and had played a significant role in the interception and decoding of the Zimmermann Telegram which helped bring America into the war. It is of no surprise Ewing was also a member of the incredibly important Royal Society of London, a learned society for science. Founded in 1660, and during Ewing's membership, it was based at the impressive **BURLINGTON HOUSE, PICCADILLY [082•55]**.

SPY SITES OF LONDON

59 Onslow Gardens
Admiral Sir William Reginald 'Blinker' Hall - one of Britain's most famous intelligence officers lived here

Alastair Denniston

Early drawing of Burlington House - first home to The Royal Society

James Alfred Ewing

In 1967, the society relocated to **6-9 CARLTON HOUSE TERRACE [083•42]**, and today acts as a scientific advising body to the government.

MI6, THE PASSPORT CONTROL OFFICE (PCO) AND THE MYSTERY OF MELBURY ROAD

In 1919, some MI6 officers began working under 'diplomatic cover' at established British passport offices. The use of such official mechanisms had been under MI5(e) control, but because MI6 was the foreign arm of British Intelligence, Cumming wrestled the Passport Control Office (PCO) away from Vernon Kell's authority.

MI6 officers working under the guise of the PCO, sent intelligence back to officials in London. The operation was controlled by legendary intelligence figure Claude Dansey. Twenty years later, Dansey would also be responsible for creating another shadowy and powerful MI6 spy network called the Z Organisation.

In 1923, MI6 moved out of Whitehall Court to 1 Melbury Road in Holland Park. The building - described as a "red brick mansion" - was allegedly knocked down years ago and today visitors will find a number of expensive residences displaying this address. At least this is according to bits of official literature. However, when we first sought out the location, we noted the closest number to the address is **2 MELBURY ROAD (MELBURY COTTAGE) [084•54]**, the former residence of famous sculptor Sir Hamo Thornycroft. Similarly, the numbers of the buildings have also been changed, for example, 29 is now number 9. The entire street was once described as a "bohemian enclave of artists, musicians, actors and architects." Indeed, over half a century earlier, in 1859,

Eye Spy Intelligence Magazine   67

082•55

BURLINGTON HOUSE

In the 19th century, Burlington House was used as headquarters for a British Army regiment known as the Artists Rifles. A hundred years later this unique unit would evolve into the famous Special Air Service (SAS)

Burlington House, Piccadilly

© MIKE PEEL

083•42

6-9 Carlton House Terrace

Headquarters of the Royal Society

several of its esteemed residents volunteered to join the British Army in a regiment creatively named the Artists Rifles. Interestingly, and perhaps not a coincidence, in 1860, its headquarters were based at Burlington House. By 1900, the Artists Rifles strength had increased to twelve companies and continued to attract many recruits from Public Schools and universities. It was disbanded at the end of the Second World War, but reinvented in 1947 and transferred to the Army Air

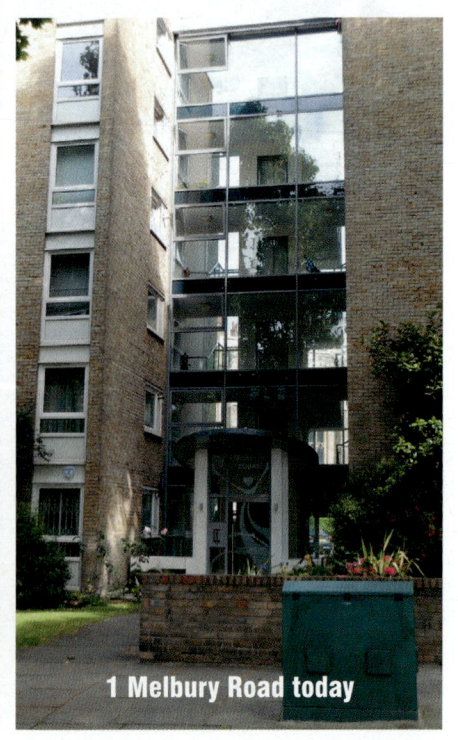

1 Melbury Road today

084•54

2a Melbury Road
A blue plaque was erected in 1957 honouring Sir Hamo Thornycroft

SPY SITES OF LONDON

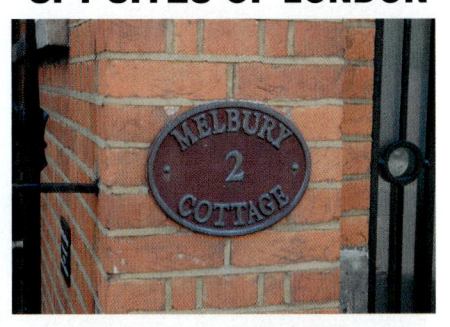

Caricature of William Hamo Thornycroft which appeared in a 1892 edition of *Vanity Fair*

Minshall called his autobiography *Guilt Edged*

Corp as the now famous 21st Special Air Service Regiment (Artists Rifles).

Yet further investigation into architectural addresses on Melbury Road and its many wonderful and fascinating residents, did reveal some unusual facts.

MERLIN MINSHALL AND THE DISCOVERY OF 1 MELBURY ROAD

Through other sources Eye Spy learned that one of Reginald Hall's Room 40 naval codebreakers had connections to this part of London - the aptly named Merlin Minshall. He was a close friend and colleague of NID-MI6 man - Ian Fleming. Some historians believe Fleming based his fictitious character James Bond on Minshall, but then many spies are said to have been the inspiration for the film agent. We will examine other intelligence figures and their connection to Fleming later.

Nevertheless, archive records suggested Minshall's mother worked for British Intelligence in World War One - and his father just happened to be Colonel Thomas Herbert Minshall, a well known newspaper proprietor who in 1941 wrote a book titled - *What to do with Germany?*.

Minshall and Fleming became friends in the 1930s and when war broke out,

Eye Spy Intelligence Magazine

69

SPY SITES OF LONDON
The Tower House, Melbury Road

085•54

Research of MI6 officer Merlin Minshall led Eye Spy to this iconic building on Melbury Road, London. Merlin's father (Colonel Thomas) was a newspaper publisher whose wife it transpired, was recruited by MI6 Chief Mansfield Cumming in World War One.

In the 1920s the building became the Minshalls family home - this was an important discovery, but it's what our researchers found at the end of the street that provided a shock...

1 Melbury Road
MI6's 1920s headquarters now assigned the numbers 9-11

086•54

Fleming actually requested that Merlin be assigned to him in naval intelligence.

Minshall was undoubtedly a chancer and had a desire for adventure, which on more than one occasion almost cost him his life. He and his first wife Elizabeth, once took their boat - Sperwer on a voyage to the Black Sea. Whilst enroute and sailing down the River Danube, the couple encountered a beautiful German woman who asked if she could accompany them a little of the way. Merlin agreed, but the liaison had not been one of chance, she was in fact a German agent. After seducing Merlin she then tried to poison him, but he survived. Berlin had apparently gleaned information that Minshall may have been engaged by MI6 to investigate points on the coast which could be used to store oil. His subsequent ordeal must have made for interesting reading in London. Of course his marriage to Elizabeth didn't last, but Merlin would go on to marry another three women.

Built in 1878, The Tower House has been home to various well-known people - but will be forever associated with the Minshall family

Minshall was also a lover of speed - and he competed in the Monte Carlo Rally twice. In 1937, he also won a race in Italy, and was presented with a trophy by none other than Italian dictator Benito Mussolini.

Eye Spy Intelligence Magazine

SPY SITES OF LONDON

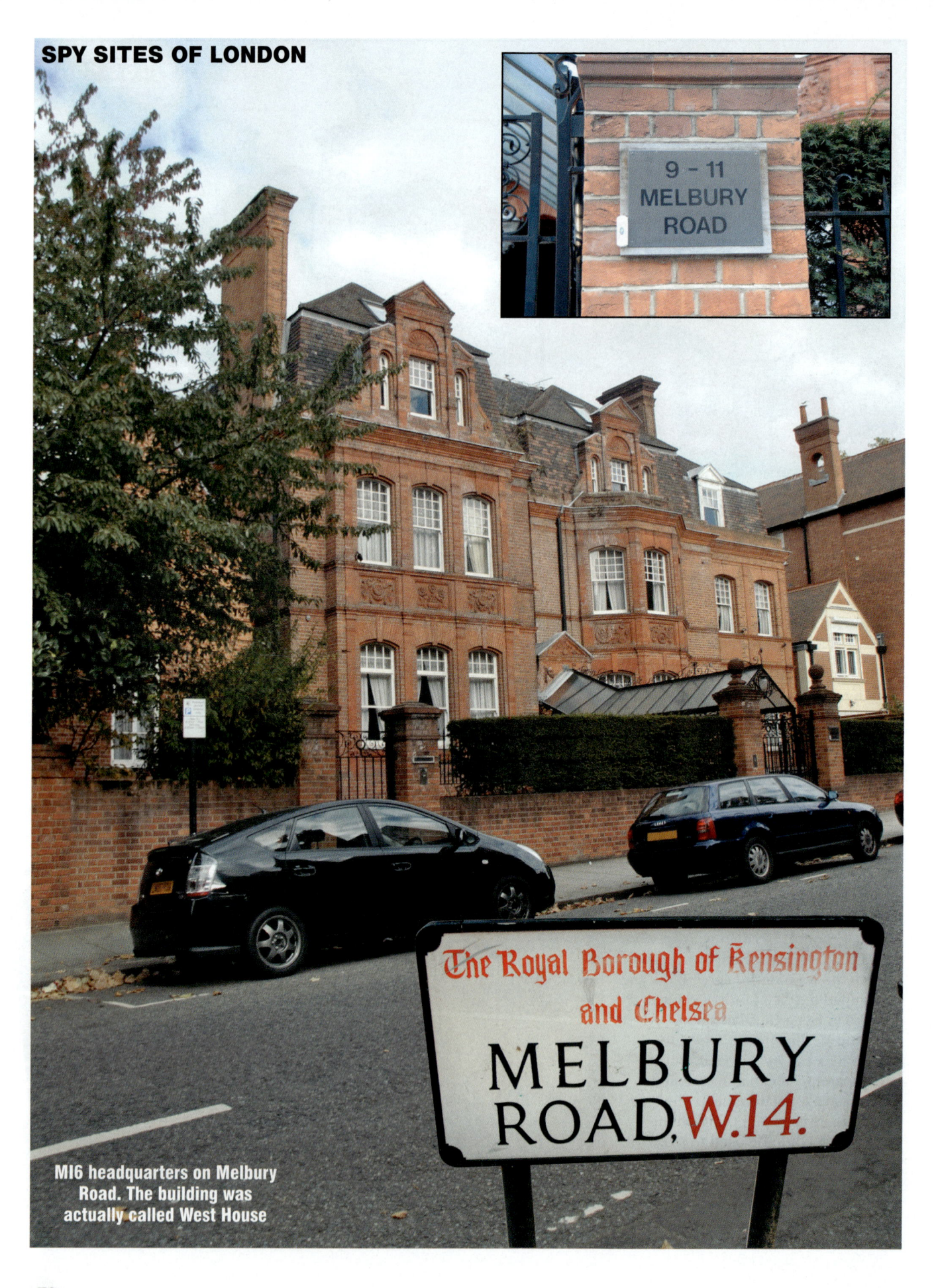

MI6 headquarters on Melbury Road. The building was actually called West House

SPY SITES OF LONDON

A unique view from inside Sir Mansfield Cumming's office at Melbury Road. Sir Hamo Thornycroft's residence can be seen opposite

Sir Mansfield Cumming's office. The MI6 Chief died in the building

In 2013 the building underwent a massive internal refurbishment. Its architecture and primary features were carefully retained and restored to their former glory. Interestingly, the front door to the building has always featured green paint - Cumming's favourite colour which he used to sign off all his correspondence

His adventures didn't stop there. He became the first person to cross the Sahara Desert on a motorcycle and in the Congo, reportedly came across a secret German Army unit. He also had a face-to-face encounter with Field Marshal Hermann Goring, head of Germany's Luftwaffe.

In 1940, he was duly summoned back to war work as a member of the Royal Naval Volunteer Reserve. A little later he joined Fleming in the Naval Intelligence Division and then moved to the Special Operations Executive. He would subsequently participate in many important operations and even helped New Zealand organise a special naval intelligence element.

Additional research soon revealed his mother had indeed been recruited by MI6's Mansfield Cumming. British author Len Deighton notes this in his foreword to Merlin's book - *Guilt-Edged* published in 1977. Deighton, of course, wrote the iconic spy novel *The IPCRESS File,* later made into a movie starring Michael Caine.

MERLIN MINSHALL AND THE TOWER HOUSE

At the end of Melbury Road sits a most impressive and unusual building - **THE TOWER HOUSE [085•54]** - quite appropriate for a man with a name like Merlin. Indeed, for it transpired this was the 1920s family

Eye Spy Intelligence Magazine

73

6 Melbury Road, Little Holland House

home of the Minshalls! Merlin would have been a young man at the time. Archive records, however, show the address as 9 Melbury Road, but today it is numbered 29. This immediately alerted our research team to another very interesting possibility - for Sir Mansfield Cumming, the original 'C' of MI6, died at the Service's first headquarters - 1 Melbury Road. We again began examining information on all the address numbers. After learning of further renumbering, and a search of additional names and addresses, we can reveal that the former MI6 headquarters' building remains intact and sits at **9-11 MELBURY ROAD [086•54]**. It was a significant discovery.

Was Merlin Minshall the inspiration for James Bond? It's an impossible question to answer, especially because Fleming gave so little away in his interviews. However, Eye Spy believes Fleming's character is not based on any single individual, more likely he is a composite of many people. Similarly, the adventures of the agent and other characters in his books are drawn from people Fleming met, whom he worked with and, the MI6 and NID reports which crossed his desk.

William Morris

A STREET OF HEROES, KINGS, SPIES, VILLAINS AND TRAITORS

Several significant people involved with government and intelligence also resided on this important street, including original troopers from the Artists Rifles. Luke Fildes and Marcus

Wilfred Owen

74

Eye Spy Intelligence Magazine

SPY SITES OF LONDON

Luke Fildes

087•54

8 Melbury Road

Valentine Cameron Prinsep at his home in Melbury Road

Sir Frederic Leighton - an early commanding officer of the Rifles

Over the Top - a 1918 painting by John Nash depicts an attack by the Artists Rifles in 1917. Sixty-eight soldiers in the regiment died in the battle near Cambrai

Stone, both artists and illustrators lived at **8 MELBURY ROAD [087•54]**. Other Artists Rifles soldiers living on the street included WWI poet Wilfred Owen; Frederic Leighton commanding officer of the Rifles in 1869; William Morris textile designer, poet and novelist and Valentine Cameron Prinsep - a founding member. The Rifles were headquartered at **OLD DRILL HALL, DUKES ROAD [088•62]**.

Of further interest, Cetshwayo - King of the Zulus 1872-1879 - lived at **6 MELBURY ROAD, LITTLE HOLLAND HOUSE [089•54]** and at number 3, a rather unsavoury character in the person of Ezra Pound. His activities in London and Europe would eventually make him an MI5 'person of interest' and one of America's most wanted.

Pound was a poet, writer and radical whose work is said to have inspired men like T. S. Eliot and Ernest Hemingway. However, he became disillusioned with life in Britain after WWI and in the 1930s he embraced Benito Mussolini and supported Adolf

088•62

Built in 1888 the building was used as the headquarters of the Artists Rifles

© CERIDWEN

Old Drill Hall, Duke's Road

090•55

Note proximity to Yorkshire Grey public house

48 Langham Street

Cetshwayo - King of the Zulus 1872-1879

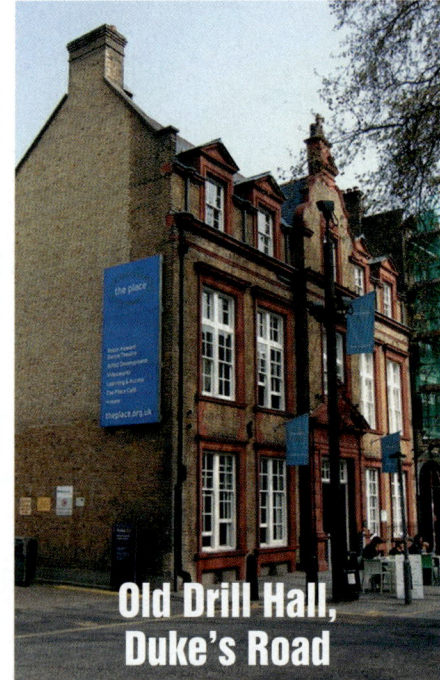

Hitler. Pound arrived in London from America in 1908 and found lodgings at **48 LANGHAM STREET [090•55]**, ironically just feet from the Yorkshire Grey public house, which would be used by British Intelligence to coerce US journalists in WWII **(See Site 312•55)**. A year later he moved to **10 KENSINGTON CHURCH WALK [091•60]** before eventually ending up in Melbury Road.

He also worked closely with the British fascist Oswald Mosley and during WWII was invited to Italy by Mussolini to produce numerous propaganda broadcasts. Pound was arrested in 1945 by US forces and charged with treason. He spent the next 12 years in prison.

Eye Spy Intelligence Magazine

092•54
Melbury House, 22 Melbury Road

SPY SITES OF LONDON

Outside the old MI6 headquarters looking towards The Tower House

Benjamin Britten

Ezra Pound

Benjamin Britten lived here

091•60

10 Kensington Church Walk

Thereafter upon his release, he returned to Italy and resumed his controversial writing career.

Another famous person who lived at **MELBURY HOUSE, 22 MELBURY ROAD [092•54]** was Benjamin Britten. He caused controversy at the beginning of WWII when he opted to go to America. A conscientious objector and pacifist, MI5 described him in a Registry file as *'a man of Communist appearance'*.

In 1935 he began working for the General Post Office film agency, which was controlled by the propaganda house Ministry of Information - more on this organisation later. Even MI6 had a file on Britten because the Service feared he was in contact with foreign concerns.

How much truth there is to the suspicions of British Intelligence about Britten remains unclear, however he did go to school with two notorious Russian spies - Guy Burgess and Donald Maclean. Indeed, in 1963, Britten - on a concert tour of the USSR - actually visited Burgess who had defected a decade earlier.

There are other aspects about his private life that also drew the attention of the authorities.

Old Star Public House, 66 Broadway

54 Broadway Buildings

The Old Star catered for many of Broadway's MI6 occupants. The former MI6 headquarters' building is to the right

Eye Spy Intelligence Magazine

SPY SITES OF LONDON

THE 'ILLUMINATE' OF QUEEN ANNE'S GATE AND THE BROADWAY BUILDINGS

It was also on Melbury Road that Cumming died on 14 June 1923. His replacement, Rear Admiral Hugh 'Quex' Sinclair, was instrumental in the 1926 relocation of the Service to one of its most famous homes - **54 BROADWAY BUILDINGS [093•42]** near to St James's Park Tube Station.

There are many wonderful stories associated with the move to Broadway, including one occasionally told by London's ever popular cabbies. To protect MI6's operations within the building, Sinclair approved a plaque that was mounted above the bell on the front door. It proclaimed the headquarters of the Minimax Fire Extinguisher company. London cabbies, who had themselves been puzzled by all the comings and goings were having none of it. They knew exactly what went on behind the front doors. One morning Sinclair woke to find a big chalked message on the pavement outside the HQ - *'This way to the British Secret Service Office'* it read. The Minimax plaque was quickly removed by order of 'C'!

There's also a rumour that for several years a blind matchstick seller often seen standing opposite Broadway, outside **ST JAMES'S PARK STATION [094•42]** was in fact a German spy - a story that has never been confirmed.

Unbeknown to most Londoners, 54 Broadway also had a secret entrance cleverly tucked away in an adjoining street at **21 QUEEN ANNE'S GATE [095•42]**. This building sits in a quiet area behind Broadway and Sinclair opted to use a fourth floor apartment as his own residence. In no time at all builders changed part of the structure and created a small corridor that led into the Broadway Buildings. Also convenient for MI6 staffers, the **OLD STAR [096•42]** public house sits just a few yards from the building's main entrance.

Hugh Sinclair

MI6 soon started to take over other parts of Queen Anne's Gate and in

St James's Park Station
The matchstick seller would stand here and watch all the comings and goings at MI6's headquarters

Former staff entrance to MI6's Broadway headquarters

Minimax Fire Extinguisher Company

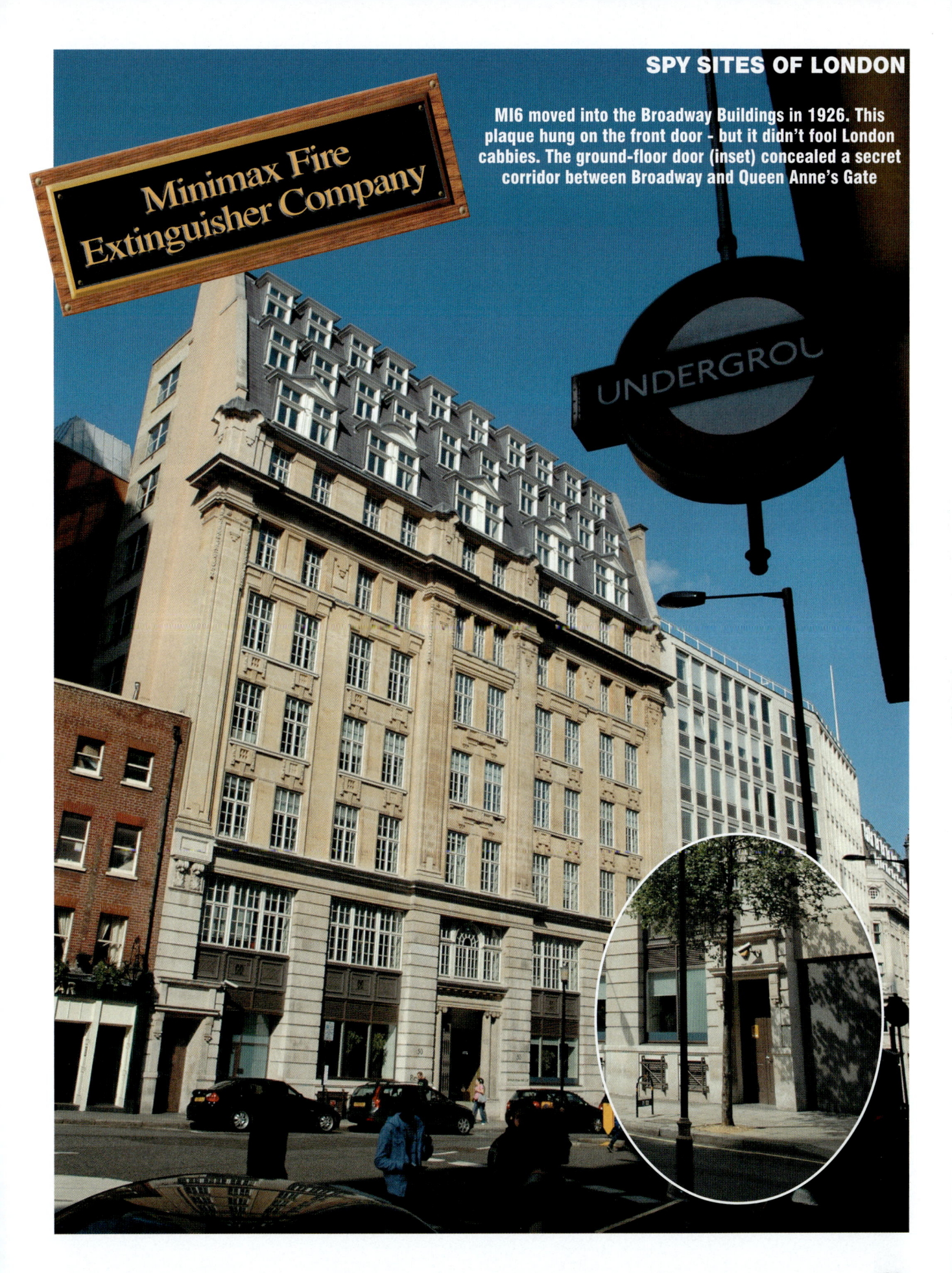

SPY SITES OF LONDON

MI6 moved into the Broadway Buildings in 1926. This plaque hung on the front door – but it didn't fool London cabbies. The ground-floor door (inset) concealed a secret corridor between Broadway and Queen Anne's Gate

Eye Spy Intelligence Magazine

INTELLIGENCE SQUARE OF QUEEN ANNE'S GATE

HM PCO
BRITISH GOVERNMENT
PASSPORT CONTROL OFFICE

21 Queen Anne's Gate
MI6 ran its secret front agency – the Passport Control Office from here

3 Queen Anne's Gate

SPY SITES OF LONDON

"The lamps are going out all over Europe... we shall not see them lit again in our time."

PCO coordinated a multitude of operations in Europe and beyond.

As for MI6's Broadway headquarters, in later years, the notorious KGB agent and MI6 officer Kim Philby described the building as "dingy - one that hid a warren of wooden partitions and was served by an ancient lift." Despite obvious concerns about its location, parking and interior design, MI6 would remain here until 1966.

Another famous resident of the 'Square' was Lord Haldane, former Secretary of State for War. He lived at

1922, GC&CS moved much of its operation here occupying the fifth floor. Another shadowy MI6 front was also relocated here in 1926 - Claude Dansey's Passport Control Office. From its first floor headquarters the

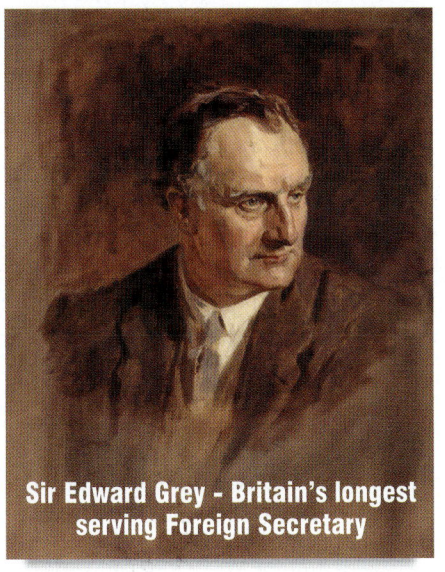

Sir Edward Grey - Britain's longest serving Foreign Secretary

21 Queen Anne's Gate was the secret rear entrance to MI6 headquarters at Broadway

28 Queen Anne's Gate Lord Haldane, former Secretary of State for War lived here

16 Queen Anne's Gate

Eye Spy Intelligence Magazine 83

An historic club is located at **34 QUEEN ANNE'S GATE [100•42]**. St Stephen's Club can trace its genesis back over 100 years and to numerous locations in the city. Founded by Benjamin Disraeli in 1870, it is widely associated with politicians of a Conservative affiliation. Notable members include Prime Ministers Harold Macmillan and Margaret Thatcher.

And of course, the British Army military intelligence branch occupied 16-18 Queen Anne's Gate **(See Site 014•42)** from 1884 until 1901. After the army moved out, Admiral of the Fleet Lord John Fisher moved in until 1910.

Fisher served shortly as chairman of the Admiralty's Board of Invention and Research until 1918. One of his colleagues on the committee was of

Admiral of the Fleet John Fisher lived and worked from 16 Queen Anne's Gate

Statue of Queen Anne in Queen Anne's Gate

28 QUEEN ANNE'S GATE [097•42]. Haldane had long opposed an intelligence gathering system but ironically found himself living side-by-side with many people who worked in the industry!

Sir Edward Grey, the longest serving British Foreign Secretary (1905-1916) lived at **3 QUEEN ANNE'S GATE [098•42]**. Grey is remembered today for his famous words spoken at the outbreak of World War One: "The lamps are going out all over Europe... we shall not see them lit again in our time." Few doubt he had liaisons with a host of British intelligence officials responsible for the creation of the country's secret services.

At **4 QUEEN ANNE'S GATE [099•42]** a medical practise operated on behalf of British Intelligence. Just a few doors away from the head of MI6 - 'C' and the staffers at Broadway, it was very convenient. This building would prove invaluable in WWII as the strain of war and operations began to take its toll on the health of officers and agents including some from outside MI6. As well as physical injuries, psychological problems were also treated here.

4 Queen Anne's Gate

84

Eye Spy Intelligence Magazine

100•42

18 Queen Anne's Gate

34 Queen Anne's Gate
St Stephen's Club can boast a plethora of famous members

Dining Room - St Stephen's Club

Prime Minister David Cameron at St Stephen's Club

course New Zealand-born chemist and physicist Ernest Rutherford **(See Chapter 2)**.

ADMIRALTY RESEARCH LABORATORY (ARL)

Many of Rutherford's team, including the likes of sonar scientist Albert Beaumont Wood, Charles Darwin and Hans Geiger, co-inventor of the Geiger counter joined the secret **ADMIRALTY**

German WWII contact mine

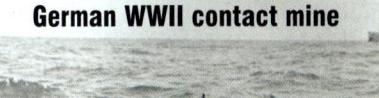

RESEARCH LABORATORY (ARL), QUEENS ROAD, TEDDINGTON [101•50] established in 1921 as the centre for naval research. Its remit was to investigate and expand the underlying science to technological advances made during WWI. ARL rapidly became capable of supporting urgent needs; early examples being the development of the Echo Depth Sounder, Navigational Plotting Tables and later, Underwater Television. During WWII, ARL developed degaussing techniques to reduce a ship's magnetic signature as a level of protection against sea-mines.

Eye Spy Intelligence Magazine   85

ADMIRALTY RESEARCH LABORATORY (ARL)

Admiralty Way, Queens Road
The brick pillars on Queens Road which once supported two giant wooden gates to the entrance of the ARL still exist. However, This was not the original entrance

Undoubtedly, the busiest and most productive time for ARL was during the Cold War. ARL research enabled major advances in submarine stealth, weapons and sonar, including streamlining, faster and quieter Pump-Jet propulsion and Towed Array long-range passive sonar. Further, ARL expertise in sonar signal processing, as well as overt and covert acquisition, analysis and assessment of noise radiated by NATO and Soviet ships and submarines, underpinned a key maritime acoustic intelligence unit.

Darwin would later become its director in World War Two, but he also played a pivotal role in America's top secret Manhattan Project - the building of the atomic bomb.

A former notable employee was Reginald Victor Jones, a scientific military intelligence expert who in WWII was instrumental in the success of many top secret projects. His work on air defence was key to British security, though he was heavily involved with covert endeavours enabled by MI6, including the Double Cross System which is examined later.

Hans Geiger

Charles G. Darwin - scientist and intelligence contact man who headed the important WWII National Physical Laboratory and worked on America's Manhattan Project

86   Eye Spy Intelligence Magazine

SPY SITES OF LONDON

Entrance to ARL in Bushy Park near gate known as Upper Lodge. Much secret work in the 1960s was conducted here, including work related to the stealth and detectability of nuclear submarines

Memorial at Upper Lodge shows an original gearwheel of the drive mechanism of the rotating beam ('whirling arm') and a plaque describing other work undertaken at the ARL

R. V. Jones pictured in 1993 with CIA Director James Woolsey and Jeannie Rousseau, an Allied WWII spy who passed Jones vital intelligence on the V1 cruise missile and V2 rocket

Whirling Arm building, Upper Lodge - the only remaining and recognisable building at this famous site

A rocket and radar expert, he was honoured by US Intelligence in 1993, when he became the first recipient of the R. V. Jones Intelligence Award created by the CIA in his honour. His book, *Most Secret War*, is regarded as one of the most fascinating ever written that reveals the incredibly important role science played during WWII.

© NIGEL R. D. GODSELL www.arl.g3w1.com

Eye Spy Intelligence Magazine

87

Admiralty Way, Queens Road
Site of the Admiralty Research Laboratory, Teddington

IV

First London Spy Wars
MI5 Battles Spies, Communists and Nazis

British Intelligence in all its guises was deeply concerned about the post-World War One Bolshevik threat and embarked upon operations to expose its supposed growing influence in the UK. However, sometimes mistakes were made. For example, Lieutenant Colonel Ronald Meiklejohn, MI6 Station Chief in Estonia, was given snippets of information from a number of telegrams originating from Russia's Foreign Office. Those in MI5 and MI6 who were deeply suspicious that a plot to infiltrate British society was forming were delighted, for it offered them an opportunity to react and seek additional resources. The documents apparently showed the Bolsheviks were bank-rolling a Sinn Fein operation in Ireland in the hope that revolution would ensue. It later transpired the papers were bogus.

And though this threat turned out to be false, in future months and years officials had legitimate concerns about one Moscow bank-rolled organisation, and another with a sympathetic ear for the emerging Nazi Party led by a certain Adolf Hitler in Germany.

128 New Bond Street

SPY SITES OF LONDON

Established in 1920, the Communist Party of Great Britain (CPGB) was a revolutionary movement that at best was a nuisance, at worst an entity which required monitoring. The party further attracted the interest of MI5 and MI6 when it was learned that Russia had started to communicate and pass monies to some of its leaders. Analysts believed this was an undercover attempt to create political unrest. MI5 discovered that thousands of pounds were being sent to London by the Profintern (Red International of Labour Unions) in Moscow to its British Bureau at **128 NEW BOND STREET [102•55]**. The Profintern was established in 1921 to coordinate Communist activities in trade unions, but it was clearly intent on creating trouble even during its fledgling years.

Entrance to 128 New Bond Street

103•42
Russian Embassy 1920s

Union chief Mikhail Tomski was instrumental in establishing good relations between the Profintern and British Communists

Early 1920s logo of the organisation

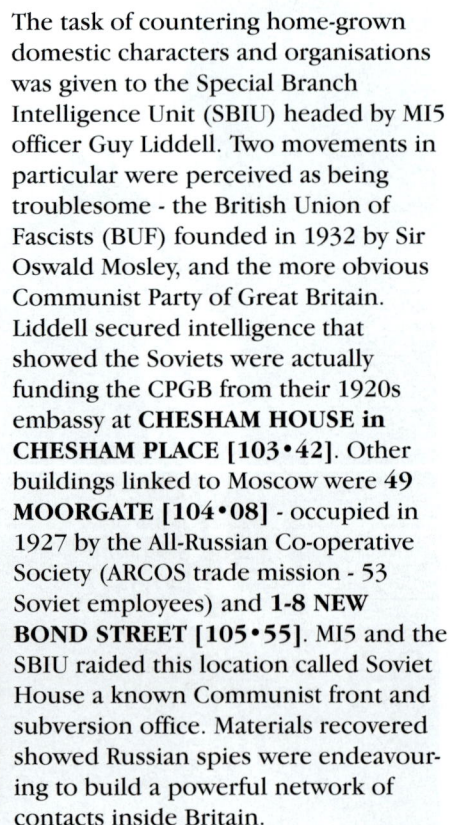

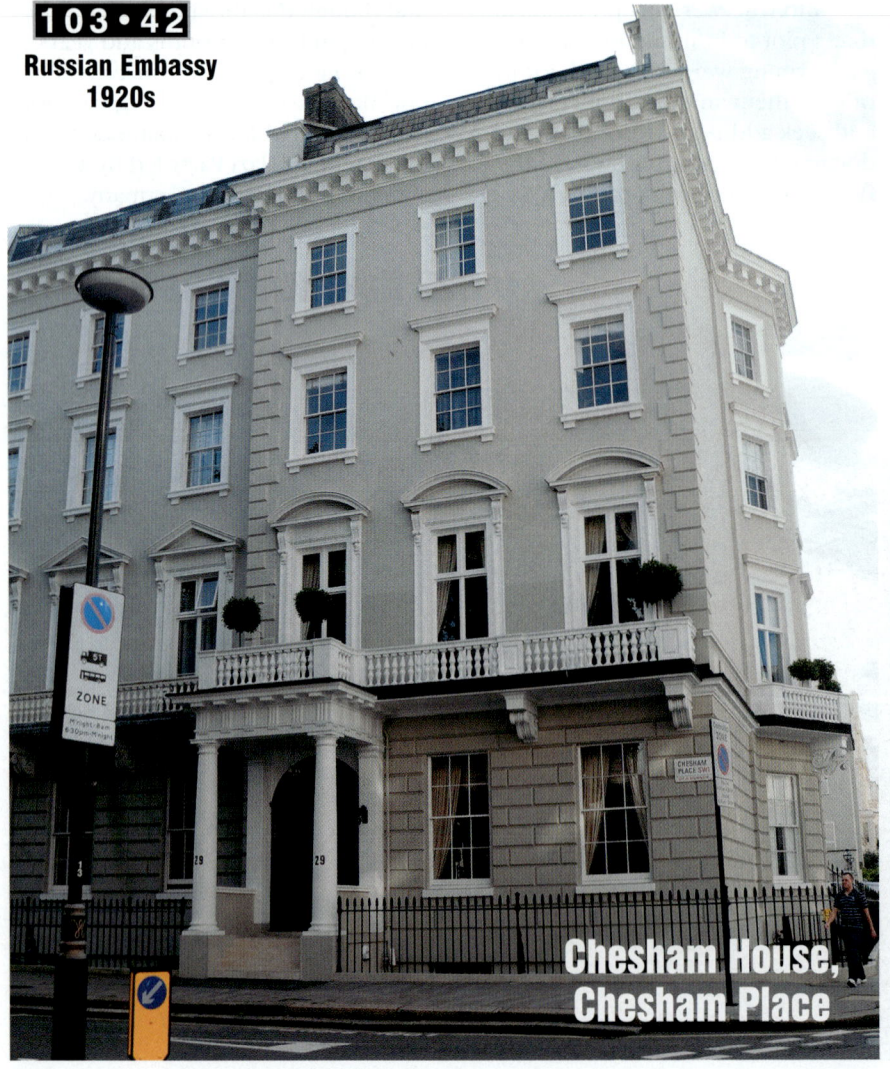

The task of countering home-grown domestic characters and organisations was given to the Special Branch Intelligence Unit (SBIU) headed by MI5 officer Guy Liddell. Two movements in particular were perceived as being troublesome - the British Union of Fascists (BUF) founded in 1932 by Sir Oswald Mosley, and the more obvious Communist Party of Great Britain. Liddell secured intelligence that showed the Soviets were actually funding the CPGB from their 1920s embassy at **CHESHAM HOUSE in CHESHAM PLACE [103•42]**. Other buildings linked to Moscow were **49 MOORGATE [104•08]** - occupied in 1927 by the All-Russian Co-operative Society (ARCOS trade mission - 53 Soviet employees) and **1-8 NEW BOND STREET [105•55]**. MI5 and the SBIU raided this location called Soviet House a known Communist front and subversion office. Materials recovered showed Russian spies were endeavouring to build a powerful network of contacts inside Britain.

Chesham House, Chesham Place

Eye Spy Intelligence Magazine

SPY SITES OF LONDON

Legendary MI5 officer Guy Liddell was born at 64 Victoria Gardens - which was used as an early Secret Service Bureau headquarters (See Site 016•42). Liddell was considered an authority on the 'Russian Menace'

105•55

1-8 New Bond Street

MI5 spycatcher Guy Liddell

Though the Russian Embassy (as a provider of support and cash for the CPGB) was upper most in the minds of MI5, there was another organisation, and a surprising one, which Liddell's team had their eyes on. This was the Federated Press of America.

The FPA London was an organisation that had been established in 1923 by foreign affairs writer William Ewer, with the connivance of American political activist and media man Carl Haessler. The agency was simply a front company providing Russia with a

109•62

Former headquarters of the Communist Party of Great Britain (CPGB). MI5 bugged the building

16 King Street

SPY SITES OF LONDON

104•08

49 Moorgate
New office building at 51 Moorgate has replaced 49 Moorgate

The detailed architecture of The Outer Temple building is remarkable

'legitimate' investigative media presence in London. Operational until the late 1920s, and based at **50 OUTER TEMPLE (222 STRAND) [106•62]** the organisation's supposed dealings with its American parent company were almost non-existent, a cause for concern to those MI5 officials who were convinced Ewer was a Russian spy. In 1950, Ewer claimed that only Haessler and not other members of the FPA London were involved in espionage-related activities, but this was not true.

By the mid-1920s, MI5 discovered that the FPA produced hardly any legitimate journalism, and existed only as an espionage and money channelling firm. Ewer had 'pricked' the imagination of MI5 in 1924 when the FPA posted a strange advertisement in the *Daily Herald* asking for *'information and details from anyone who has ever had any association with or been brought in touch with any Secret Service department or operation'*. Hardly discreet, and likely to attract the attention of MI5 news watchers.

A subsequent MI5 operation proved the FPA on the Strand was being funded by the Russian Embassy with an allocation of money set aside for the CPGB. Agent Ewer was therefore also a courier, but he was seemingly not the only 'person of interest'. He may also have been on the payroll of Russian spy Nikolai Klishko, indeed, some intelligence writers believe the entire ruse was the brainchild of Klishko.

Ewer had contact with Eva Collet Reckitt, founder of the once famous, yet controversial and radical Collet's bookshop. As a former member and financial backer of the CPGB, she had fallen under MI5's radar following her support of other Communist and left-wing concerns. MI5 intercepts released decades later show she was regarded as the party's 'milch [milk] cow' due to her significant contributions - monies she originally inherited from her family - part of the famous British mustard firm Reckitt and Colman. Dozens of intelligence files reveal her shadowy connections to Ewer and the CPGB.

The London office of FPA also acted as a clearing house for information that could be described as intelligence. This material - of a sensitive nature - was passed to Moscow probably via Klishko for analysis. Additional intelligence was routed through the FPA from France. MI5 raided the premises in 1929 and several staff were interrogated.

In 1934, Collet established the first of three bookstores at **66 CHARING CROSS ROAD [107•62]** calling it

Eye Spy Intelligence Magazine

106•62

SPY SITES OF LONDON

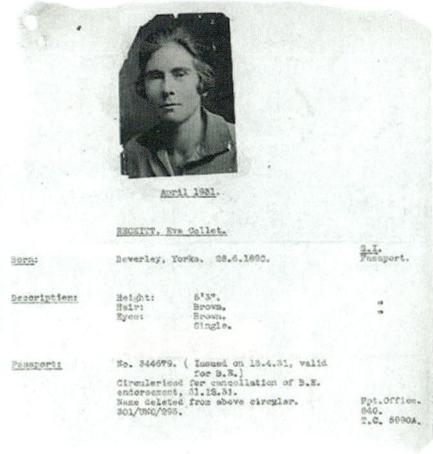

50 Outer Temple (222 Strand)
Former headquarters of the London Federated Press of America (FPA) - a known Russian Intelligence front company

MI5 Registry file on Eva Collet

ture Dealer. Lakey's effectiveness disappeared in the early 1930s following an intelligence breach - this as MI5 finally managed to uncover most of the spy network.

The BUF was based at **1 SANCTUARY BUILDINGS [108•42]** near Westminster Abbey, and the CPGB at **16 KING STREET [109•62]**. The latter retained its presence in King Street until 1980. Former MI5 officer Peter Wright acknowledged his service had bugged the location for years. As for Mosley, who had a plethora of ties to many leading Nazis, and whom the government considered a genuine threat to national security, his career effectively ended in 1940 when he was interned.

Besides tackling the Communists in London, MI5 also watched another organisation spread its wings in the capital - the National Fascist Party of Italy. Founded in Rome in 1921 by Benito Mussolini, this outfit soon claimed **25 NOEL STREET, SOHO [110•55]** as its headquarters.

The extremist party ruled Italy from 1922 to 1945 and its type of fascism would in less than a decade, be copied by Adolf Hitler's Nazi Party.

British Intelligence had every right to fear the NFP, for its agents had reported Oswald Mosley and Mussolini had corresponded and agreed to form a relationship. Indeed, just three years before WWII broke out, Mosley

Collet's - The Political Bookshop. For the record, Collet's (as it was renamed some years later), finally closed its doors in 1989. The location is now occupied by a Chinese medicine store. In the National Archives there exists a plethora of MI5 files on Collet and her liaisons with Russian-backed associates.

Moscow had planted its spies at the heart of the CPGB and FPA. Arthur Francis Lakey was one such agent, and as a former disgruntled police detective he held all the appropriate credentials. Operating under the pseudonym Albert Allen, he first joined the CPGB in 1920. Two years later he found himself working from an office at the FPA Strand address. Lakey performed counter-intelligence operations against MI5 and was involved with various surveillance outfits which monitored British military establishments. He was replaced as the main CPGB insider in 1924 by Jim Finney - another Moscow-financed spy - codenamed the Furni-

Eye Spy Intelligence Magazine   93

66 Charing Cross Road
Once occupied by Collet's - The Political Bookshop

Oswald Mosley on his wedding day

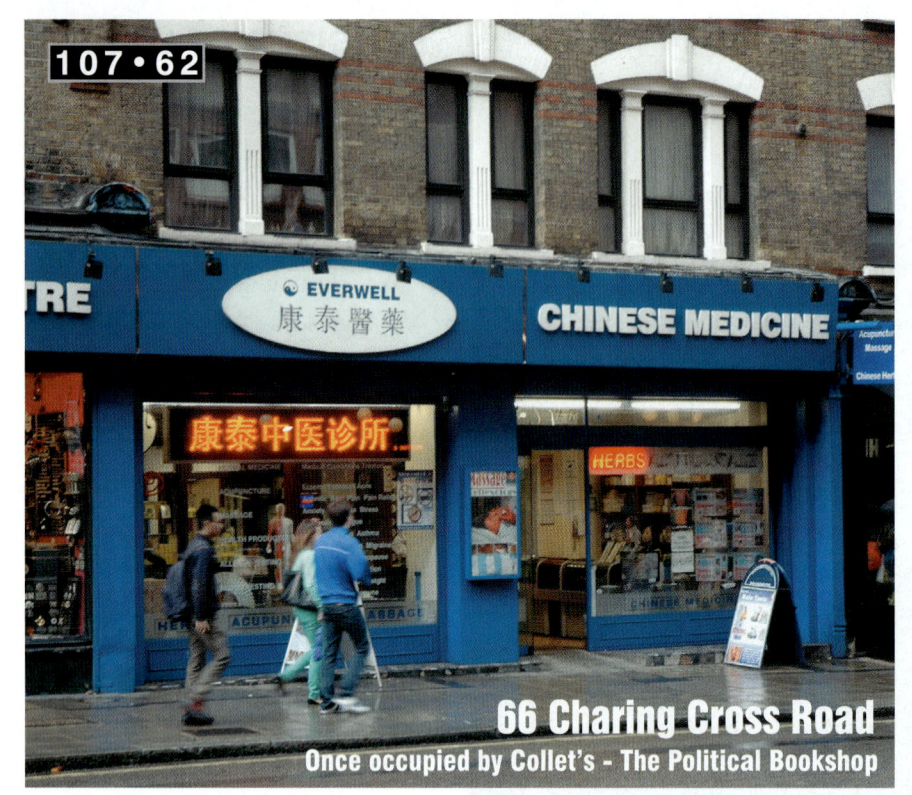

appeared alongside Mussolini at a rally.

In 1931, a most strange incident involving MI5 and Mussolini then occurred. A British agent had become aware of interesting liaisons taking place at a delicatessen at **37 OLD COMPTON STREET [111•55]**. The Service soon started surveillance on the owner of the establishment - an Italian anarchist and businessman by the name of Emidio Recchioni.

Besides other well known anarchists and fascists who visited the shop, such as Emma Goldman and Sylvia Pankhurst, Recchioni welcomed the likes of George Orwell. Orwell would be used by MI6 in later years. There is also evidence to suggest Recchioni

1 Sanctuary Buildings
Former headquarters of the British Union of Fascists

94

Eye Spy Intelligence Magazine

25 Noel Street

Location of former headquarters of the National Fascist Party of Italy

37 Old Compton Street

MI5 watched a number of strange happenings which could have led to scandal in Parliament

Benito Mussolini - founded the National Fascist Party of Italy

was a friend of Labour Party leader Ramsey MacDonald.

MI5 had been tipped-off by Italian Intelligence that Recchioni was allegedly funding a daring plot to assassinate Mussolini in Rome. He was followed by a British agent to Brussels where he met with suspected hitman Angelo Sbardellott.

The operation was somehow compromised and Sbardellott was arrested in Rome. Italy soon demanded that Recchioni be returned to stand trial, but the affair was swept under the carpet.

Details of the case and Recchioni's connection, were published by the *Daily Telegraph*. Recchioni denied the charges, sued and was duly awarded about £1,000 by a court. So sensitive was the case that relevant MI5 material

Mussolini and Oswald Mosley share a platform in Rome 1936. Such liaisons resulted in the Briton being detained when war broke out

was kept out of the public's gaze until the early 2000s.

That MI5 did not pursue the affair is most puzzling indeed. However, the timing of the incident seems to offer a clue... in 1931 Ramsey MacDonald won the election and became leader of the country! As for Recchioni he

Eye Spy Intelligence Magazine 95

SPY SITES OF LONDON

Another view of Old Compton Street

MI5 and Special Branch opted not to investigate alleged plot against Mussolini because of threads to premier Ramsey MacDonald

died a couple of years later, but his son, Vero, became a long-time friend of George Orwell and a noted publisher of anarchist materials. The 37 Old Compton Street address is today a popular Italian restaurant!

THE RECRUITMENT OF 'MR SCOTT'

Besides the increasing threat of anarchists, fascists and other organisations intent on causing trouble, MI5 also had its hands full trying to combat foreign spies and traitors. One such person who falls into both categories was cipher clerk Ernest Holloway Oldham. He worked at the **FOREIGN OFFICE, KING CHARLES STREET [112•42]** and had offered his

Russian-born anarchist Emma Goldman's trips to Recchioni's shop were monitored by MI5. Goldman had caused much concern to authorities in the United States which led to her deportation back to Russia. After arriving in London, she continued her political activism

This photograph shows the proximity of 1 Sanctuary Buildings (centre), former headquarters of the British Union of Fascists in relation to Parliament. Little wonder British Intelligence feared the movement and its growing connections to similar organisations abroad

SPY SITES OF LONDON

The impressive building today houses the department responsible for overseeing and supporting global MI6 operations - Foreign and Commonwealth Office

Foreign Office, King Charles Street

services to the Soviets in the late 1920s. The extent of his activities were eventually revealed by Walter G. Krivitsky, a Russian intelligence officer who defected to Britain shortly before WWII. Krivitsky told MI5 that Oldham had provided valuable intelligence on UK government policy (through examination of embassy signals) to his handler Dmitri Bystrolyotov. This is relevant because the date coincides with the closure of the Soviet front operation - Federated Press of America (FPA). His motive, however, was driven by financial considerations rather than anything ideological.

Oldham had initially presented himself to the Russians at their Embassy in Paris as Mr Scott. After dropping off a package of diplomatic codes, officials realised that he did have access to important material, and henceforth began searching for him in London. A short while later a Dutch artist calling himself Hans Galleni travelled to the city and visited a police station. He explained to the desk sergeant that he was seeking a man called Mr Scott because he had been witness to a car crash involving his sister in Paris. He also said that the, "Englishman told me he worked at the Foreign Office."

Galleni had cleverly selected the specific date which coincided with Oldham's visit to drop off the diplomatic codes in Paris. The impressed policeman duly telephoned the Foreign Office who provided the names of four diplomatic staff who had been in Paris on that date. Armed with this knowledge, Galleni duly visited each address before identifying Oldham as he walked near Pembroke Gardens. Galleni crossed

Ernest Holloway Oldham

Walter G. Krivitsky - Russian defector and MI5 agent

Eye Spy Intelligence Magazine

113•60   31 Pembroke Gardens

Residence of Russian spy Ernest Oldham who was probably assassinated by Russian agents in an effort to conceal other London-based operatives

Oldham, who lived at **31 PEMBROKE GARDENS [113•60]** was said to have been discovered in his Kensington flat with his head in a gas oven. Sadly, in 1950, his wife Lucy who some allege had an affair with Bystrolyotov, decided to take her own life by jumping into the River Thames.

SPY CODES - ONE-TIME PADS - REORGANISATION

In 1927, and with relations with Moscow deteriorating, British government officials bizarrely quoted from an intercepted Russian diplomatic message. The codebreakers of GC&CS were naturally horrified, but the action, of course, meant that Russia was now fully aware British Intelli-

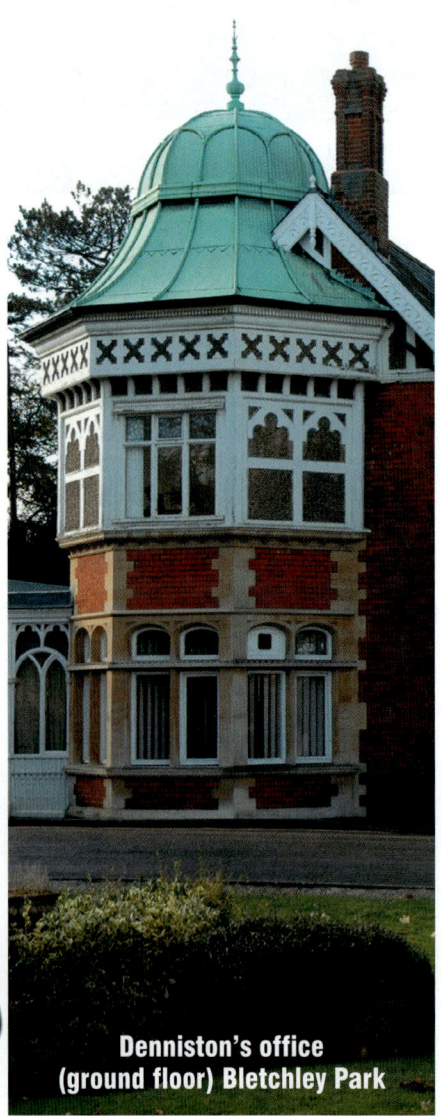

the road towards his target and duly pushed an envelope into his hand containing at least £2,000. Like it or not, Oldham was now a bona-fide Russian spy.

Much documentation is contained in an MI5 report known as the Arno File, named as such after Oldham's Russian codename. He was said to have fallen under intense suspicion following a bumbling attempt to duplicate keys to the Foreign Office's cipher room. British Government documents note his use of drink (indication of alcoholism), and domestic violence towards women. His death was said to be suicide. But there is much suspicion he was murdered.

THE ASSASSINATION OF 'MR SCOTT'

Officially, Oldham resigned his post with the Foreign Office in 1933, however, our sources say that assassins sent by Moscow entered his home and killed him, this in an effort to stop MI5 securing valuable intelligence on other Russian agents and contact people still operational in the city. Eye Spy Intelligence Magazine had been told Oldham was killed to protect the affairs of senior spy handler Bystrolyotov. And of course, it has now been revealed that Dutch artist Hans Galleni and Dmitri Bystrolyotov were one and the same man.

KGB Colonel and MI6 agent Oleg Gordievsky described Bystrolyotov, often referred to as 'Stalin's Romeo Spy', as "the nearest thing to James Bond." Other historians recognise that this particular spy supplied vast amounts of superior intelligence to Moscow. Any information therefore secured by MI5 from Oldham, may have exposed this top agent.

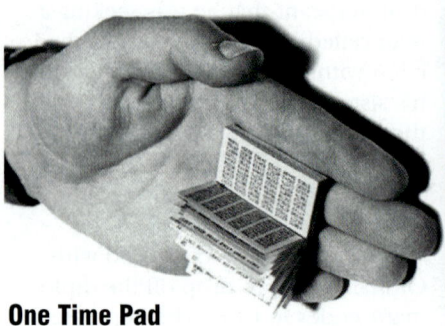

One Time Pad

Denniston's office (ground floor) Bletchley Park

98   Eye Spy Intelligence Magazine

gence had managed to capture and decode supposedly secure signals.

The Soviet response was to devise a communications system called one time pads for enciphering.* This put an end to GC&CS's ability to read secret messages and prompted an angry outburst from its head, Commander Alastair Denniston, who complained that his own government had "compromised the organisation's work beyond question." These were powerful words from Denniston - one of Britain's most important intelligence figures. He of course, would later be appointed the first head of the country's most secret codebreaking site - Bletchley Park. More on that later. During his time in London, Denniston lived at **48 TEDWORTH SQUARE, CHELSEA [114•44]**, just a short distance from the former residence of Mark Twain the famous American writer. He resided at number three. Sadly, Denniston's part of the square was controversially knocked down in 1974 and new apartments built.

MI5'S ECCENTRIC SPYCATCHER - 'M'

By 1931 the Special Branch Intelligence Unit (SBIU), had been absorbed into MI5, but they decided to keep Liddell as its Communist section head. Liddell himself worked under one of the Service's greatest officers - Maxwell Knight. It was also around

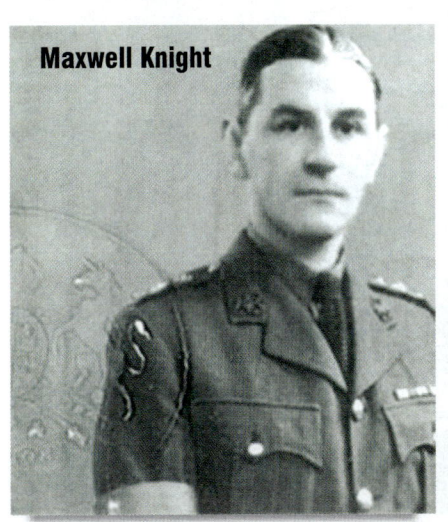

Maxwell Knight

115•47

In the early 1930s, MI5 moved its headquarters to this address

124-126 Cromwell Road

114•44

Former home to codebreaking genius Alastair Denniston

Tedworth Square, Chelsea

* One time pad - collection of random numbers for single use in enciphering messages - used properly the system is mathematically unbreakable

Eye Spy Intelligence Magazine

99

116•42

38 Sloane Street

this time that MI5 relocated to new headquarters at **124-126 CROMWELL ROAD [115•47]**.

Interestingly, Knight had been recruited by MI5 Director Vernon Kell around 1925, despite being advised of his rather controversial association with a right-wing outfit - the Rotha Lintorn-Orman's British Fascisti. The group had formed soon after Mussolini had established his own fascist organisation. Working from an apartment in London's Dolphin Square, the eccentric Knight, known as 'M' to his colleagues, ran agents in various left-wing outfits (Knight kept a variety of exotic pets in his flat, including a baboon, snakes and even a bear). He resided and worked from **38 SLOANE STREET [116•42]**, and members of the public in Chelsea would often see him taking his baby baboon for a walk.

Knight's counter-intelligence work against the Communists became legendary, so too the endeavours of

---

A flat at 82 Holland Road was surveilled by MI5 watchers from the opposite side of the street. Here agents of the Russian NKVD - the forerunner of the KGB would visit Glading and exchange information

118•54

82 Holland Road

Eye Spy Intelligence Magazine

The Beresford Gate of the former Royal Arsenal, Woolwich building built in 1829. It is now separated from other remaining buildings in the complex by a busy road. The site is definitely worth a visit and important blocks such as the Laboratory Square, Royal Cartridge Factory and Royal Brass Foundry still exist. Some buildings date back to 1696. Pictured is the Old Military Academy building (above)

117•28 The work location of the infamous Woolwich Spy Ring which included Percy Glading

Beresford Gate, Woolwich

Workers end their shift at Royal Woolwich Arsenal and exit via the Beresford Gate. This postcard dates from around the end of the nineteenth century

119•62

Charing Cross Station

CPGB member Percy Glading following his arrest in 1942

his agents. One of whom was Olga Gray, a young 19-year-old recruited by Knight in 1930. She was asked to join and infiltrate The Friends of the Soviet Union, a task which she conducted with vigour. Eventually she secured a secretarial post and the trust of a certain Percy Glading... a senior Communist sympathiser; member of the CPGB and an official of the League Against Imperialism. He had been under MI5 surveillance since 1922 and was also suspected of espionage. This rapport would be crucial in the breaking of the infamous Woolwich Arsenal Spy Ring.

In 1937, Glading, employed at the Royal Navy's **ROYAL ARSENAL, WOOLWICH [117•28]** in south-east London, discussed his spying in more detail with Gray. She pretended to be enthusiastic and rented a room at **82 HOLLAND ROAD [118•54]** where she and Glading took photographs of secret documents - many of which had been secured from Woolwich Arsenal and were designs of British weaponry. MI5 watchers noted all the comings and

SPY SITES OF LONDON

Knight's MI5 team was called Knight's Black Agents

120•42 Dolphin Square

The Dolphin Square sign. Note Collingwood and Hood - both buildings housed Maxwell Knight's MI5 apartments

goings and soon identified two persons who they believed were secreting the documents out of the armoury. Another surveillance operation resulted in the identification of Glading's Soviet handler who was being presented with an array of useful intelligence.

MI5 asked Special Branch to arrest key figures in the spy ring, but the Russian element had already left the country. Glading, however, was detained at **CHARING CROSS RAILWAY STATION [119•62]** - this as he received another package from a Woolwich Arsenal employee.

THE BIG HOUSE WITH A BIG SPY HISTORY

Knight's officers deployed against the Soviets were called Knight's Black Agents taken from the book *Macbeth*

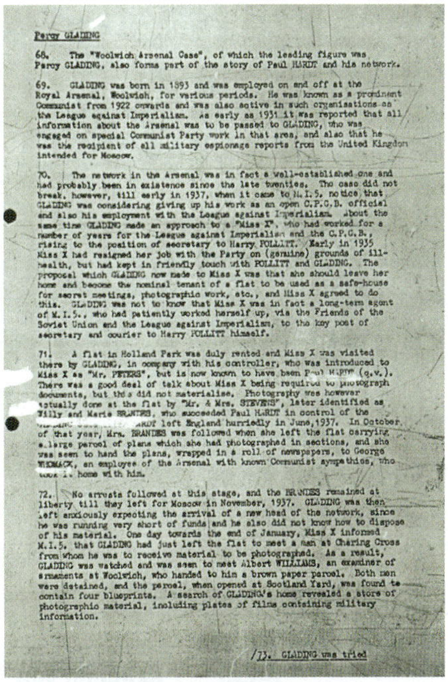

SPY SITES OF LONDON

Joseph Stalin greets Joachim von Ribbentrop at the signing of the non-aggression pact between Russia and Germany - 23 August 1939. A year earlier, Ribbentrop had been a resident of 8-9 Carlton House Terrace in his capacity as German Ambassador to Great Britain. German Intelligence - the Abwehr - undoubtedly had a presence within the building

COURTESY: NATIONAL ARCHIVES

Percy Glading's Woolwich Spy Ring features in this extensive MI5 overview of Russian spies - 1935-1955. It is just one of thousands of reports available on the subject of espionage and intelligence from the National Archives
www.nationalarchives.gov.uk

which referred to the *'Night's black agents'*. His flat in **DOLPHIN SQUARE, PIMLICO [120•42]** was assured anonymity, at least Knight believed this, because it was under his wife's name.

In later years it is believed German Intelligence became aware of just exactly who resided here. Knight had two addresses in the Dolphin Square complex - one at 308 Hood House which doubled as an office and MI5 safe house, and the other at 10 Collingwood House which he used as an operations and briefing centre.

Knight's demise came about in the early 1950s after internal wranglings and a change in MI5's leadership. However, some historians believe had he remained in the Service, his experience and contacts inside the CPGB might have exposed MI5 man and KGB agent, Anthony Blunt.

As a footnote to Maxwell Knight, who some historians believe is another

man Ian Fleming based his famous 007 agent on, he also played drums for a jazz band at the famous **HAMMERSMITH PALAIS DE DANSE, 242 SHEPHERDS BUSH ROAD [121•59]**, built in 1909. Besides being a popular entertainment venue, this building like many in the city held a secret. In its large basement was a work force building tanks! The original building was demolished but visitors to the site can still see its frontage and iconic signage that was retained.

Another famous incident that happened in Dolphin Square occurred in the 1960s and involved society girl Christine Keeler and John Profumo, Secretary of State for War. Keeler had

Hitler with associates in 1930

an apartment here and besides dating Profumo, she also had a liaison with a Soviet GRU intelligence officer by the name of Yevgeny Ivanov. There were deep concerns that the affair may have been orchestrated by the Russians

The German Embassy, Carlton Terrace as it appeared in the 1930s

Eye Spy Intelligence Magazine

103

SPY SITES OF LONDON

121•59
Hammersmith Palais de Danse

242 Shepherds Bush Road

with the ultimate goal of blackmail and then recruitment. However, any hopes of a honeytrap-type sting were dashed when Keeler went public.

Another person who resided in Dolphin Square was British civil servant John Vassall. In 1954, after serving just one year as a clerk in the Naval Attache's office of Britain's Moscow Embassy, Vassall agreed to pass intelligence to the Soviets. This followed a successful KGB honeytrap operation: undercover agents photographed him in a compromising situation with other men at a party.

To Moscow's delight, Vassall was soon reassigned to a position in Naval Intelligence at the Admiralty. This gave him access to a plethora of secrets and poor security allowed him to simply pop documents into his *London Times* newspaper and walk out of the front door. More on both these intriguing spy cases later.

Thus Dolphin House, in one way or another, has played host to several important figures in the history of British espionage, and much of it threaded to its long 20th century battle with the Soviet Union.

But just as MI5 and MI6 were winning the intelligence war with the Communists in the 1930s, another even more deadly threat was emerging inside Europe - Adolf Hitler and his dreaded Nazis. Some had already arrived in Britain, including Joachim von Ribbentrop in 1936. Ironically, as German Ambassador to Great Britain, he was making himself at home in his country's embassy at 8-9 Carlton House Terrace **(See Site 018•42)** along with a strong delegation of Abwehr agents and officials.

Joachim von Ribbentrop

Former entrance to the famous Hammersmith Palais de Danse

104

Eye Spy Intelligence Magazine

SPY SITES OF LONDON

The Fourth Spy Agency
Emergence of Spy Tradecraft

Conflicts tend to fast-track technologies and projects that otherwise may move ahead at a leisurely pace, or stagnate altogether. War also sees ingenuity come to the fore which often results in the creation of an entirely new generation of products - the objective being to give your side an advantage, or at the very least an opportunity to understand what an adversary or opponent may be intending or developing. It's no different in the world of intelligence collection. But in 1939, the truth is MI6 simply did not see WWII coming, and with the might of Germany poised to launch Operation Sea Lion and invade Britain, there were real fears that the country would be quickly overrun.

Claude Dansey - Colonel Z

One MI6 endeavour that should have provided more clues via its work in Europe was the spy network known as the Passport Control Office (PCO). This experienced front organisation had

14 Cromwell Place
1876 birthplace of the famous MI6 officer Claude Dansey. The building now houses the French Embassy's language section

Eye Spy Intelligence Magazine 105

SPY SITES OF LONDON

been operating for 20 years, but many intelligence watchers believe much more could have been done in the 1920s and 30s to expand its role.

In 1929, MI6 man Claude Dansey, who was born at **14 CROMWELL PLACE [122•47]**, was quietly invited by the Foreign Office to create a secondary intelligence network separate from the Passport Control Office and out of MI6's overall jurisdiction. The new network, called the Z Organisation stuttered at first, but it began to take shape after Hitler became Chancellor in 1933. Dansey started to recruit all manner of people who had a legitimate reason to travel: business persons, merchant seamen, industrialists, bankers, filmmakers etc. Instead of seeking just educated sorts and

Buckingham Palace [123•42]

[125•08] **Liverpool Street Railway Station - GER Memorial**

Sir Henry Wilson was assassinated shortly after opening this impressive memorial at Liverpool Street Station - dedicated to the men of the Great Eastern Railway who died fighting in World War One

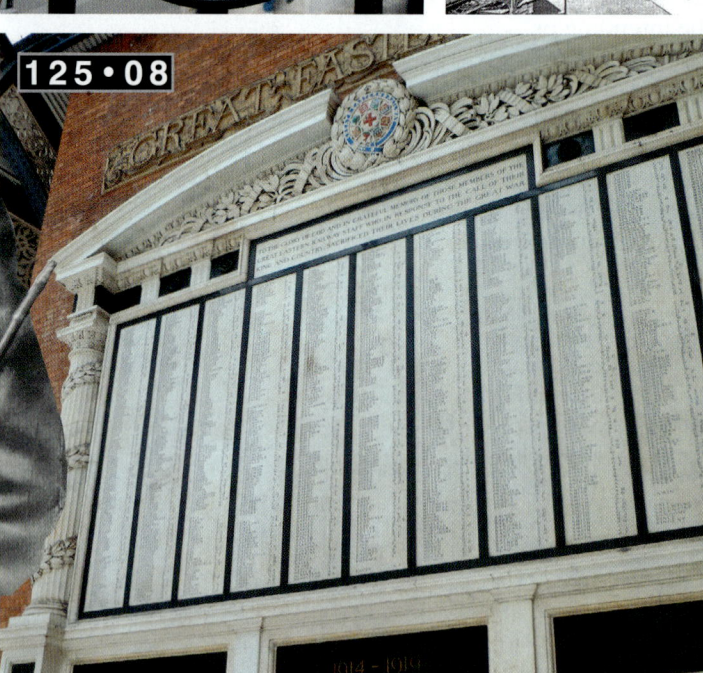

106

Eye Spy Intelligence Magazine

Sir Henry Wilson's memorial

The brave Charles Fryatt

Charles Fryatt memorial

Sir Henry Wilson's memorial sits next to that of Captain Charles Fryatt who attempted to ram a U-boat in 1915. Even though he was classed as a non-combatant the Germans executed him

recommendations from the Establishment,* Dansey - one of the Service's first authentic spy recruiters - started to think 'out of the box'.

Dansey had already garnished support from many of his peers after he successfully thwarted a proposed dynamite attack on **BUCKINGHAM PALACE [123•42]** by members of an Irish nationalist movement. In this case he received intelligence from associates in Ireland. Had such an attack occurred, one can only image the implications.

Some historians believe the proposed attack on the Royal Family had its roots in the case of Roger Casement, an Irish nationalist who was executed in 1916. Other intelligence analysts believe the reason is not so simplistic and point towards a 1938 IRA operation codenamed S-Plan. Either way, several bomb explosions attributed to this IRA endeavour occurred in London and in other cities in 1939. That Germany's Abwehr was involved still remains a point of debate.

THE IRA STRIKE AGAIN

On 22 June 1922, two IRA men shot and killed Field Marshal Sir Henry Hughes Wilson, a military and political advisor to Downing Street, and later senior advisor on Northern Ireland affairs, as he returned to his home at **36 EATON PLACE [124•42]**. Just hours earlier Wilson had unveiled a splendid war memorial at **LIVERPOOL STREET STATION [125•08]** for the workers of the Great Eastern Railway who had made the ultimate sacrifice in World War One.

IRA volunteers, Reginald Dunne and Joseph O'Sullivan were immediately captured. However, within 60 minutes of Sir Henry's death, the two pistols used by the assassins were taken to the Cabinet Room at 10 Downing Street and placed on a table before David Lloyd George and Winston

Roger Casement

36 Eaton Place 124•42
Sir Henry Wilson was assassinated close to his home

* Perceived dominant closed group, small or large - elite power controlling body in society

Eye Spy Intelligence Magazine

107

SPY SITES OF LONDON

126•42

22 Hans Place, Knightsbridge

IRA intelligence man Michael Collins

Churchill. Churchill said, "there was no Henry Wilson."

This incident followed the signing of an Anglo-Irish Treaty that was negotiated on 6 December 1921, to help prevent further violence in Ireland and on the mainland. The Irish delegation was headed by Michael Collins. A top-level diplomatic meeting had been held at **22 HANS PLACE, KNIGHTSBRIDGE [126•42]** between various officials and individuals and a cease fire agreed. However, just a few weeks after the murder of Sir Henry, Michael Collins was himself assassinated in Cork in July 1922. Many intelligence watchers believe the Collins attack was in retaliation for the murder of Sir Henry Wilson. Either way, 'The Troubles', as they became known, would continue for most of the century.

WATCHING THE GERMAN MILITARY BUILD-UP

With an eye on Germany's huge military build-up, MI6's PCO started to pass intelligence back to London. Dansey was still fully involved with the organisation, but kept details of his emerging Z network secret. Perhaps this was a good idea, for the PCO had been compromised as early as 1935 by the Abwehr which set up a radio listening post close to a barge in Holland that was doubling as an MI6 field station. When Dansey suspected the PCO had been exposed, he cleverly continued its operation: the intention being the Germans would believe the British had yet to learn of its demise.

SECTION D AND SECTION V

Despite these apparent failures, in March 1938, MI6 Chief Sinclair created a force that would later expand and be duplicated by others. It began as Section D (D standing for Destruction). Headed by Major Lawrence Grand, D operatives were to study sabotage techniques, subversion and be trained for operations behind enemy lines. Section D was burgeoning and its overall strength of 140 persons was as big as the rest of MI6 put together. Also at this time, greater emphasis was placed on MI6's counter-espionage wing - Section V - headed by Major Valentine Vivian. (Vivian would later recruit the infamous Kim Philby into the ranks of British Intelligence). Section V was reconstructed and strengthened

SPY SITES OF LONDON

Clive House, 70 Petty France

Senior MI6 officer Colonel Valentine Patrick Vivian - head of the Service's counter-espionage Section V

Meanwhile Section V performed extremely well and uncovered Nazi agents in Spain, Portugal and elsewhere. Some of these were recruited as spies by MI6 officers, whilst others led the Service to enemy agents.

THE HOUSE OF TRICKS AND DECEPTION

The Z Organisation found its home on the eighth floor of **BUSH HOUSE, WESTMINSTER [128•62]** which just happened to host the Soviet Union's Tass press agency, and the vast radio network controlled by the BBC's overseas concerns known as The Empire Service.

Built by American Irving Bush in the 1920s, Bush House would also be used for a plethora of other fascinating schemes. Operational MI6 front companies were also based here as we shall soon discover.

Despite this seemingly secure address, and in keeping with his reputation as a cautious spy, Dansey rented the premises under the name of C. E. Moore. The initials C. E. M.* were of course his own. Dansey himself chose to move into one of his favourite

immensely. The Radio Security Service (RSS) was to become an important MI5 element known at the time (in intelligence circles) as MI8c or Section 8, and had originally fallen under the auspices of the intelligence directorate of the War Office. During World War One it actually operated within Wormwood Scrubs Prison, but by the beginning of World War Two, and following a bitter dispute with MI5 chiefs, it was absorbed into MI6 in May 1941. The decision was met with hostility and dismay by a furious MI5.

MI6 built a listening post atop the Passport Office at **CLIVE HOUSE, 70 PETTY FRANCE [127•42]**. Together with personnel from the RSS, the Service began intercepting communications' traffic from the Abwehr. RSS information that should have been controlled and distributed by MI5, was now in the hands of Vivian and Section V. How much material was shared is a matter of some debate. However, for the record, it should be noted that a facility known as Hanslope Park, which became fully operational in the Autumn of 1942, played a significant role in British radio intelligence and was supportive of the RSS and other electronic collection organisations.

*C. E. M. - Claude Edward Majoribanks Dansey

Eye Spy Intelligence Magazine

SPY SITES OF LONDON

128•62

Bush House, Westminster
This imposing building played host to a variety of British Intelligence elements and fronts - including MI6's Z Organisation

General de Gaulle made a famous broadcast from Bush House to his countrymen on 18 June 1940

districts of London - close to a number of clubs and MI6 houses.

CLUBS, RECRUITMENT AND SPY GAMES

Dansey, who was known as Colonel Z (1) (other Z agents were given codenames Z-2, Z-3 etc.) selected **3 ALBEMARLE STREET [129•55]** just across from Piccadilly as his place of residence and work. It was a nondescript building that suited him because his operation was 'hidden' from other MI6 fronts. More importantly, it was just 100 yards from his club - **BOODLE'S - 28 ST JAMES'S STREET [130•42]**! Hugely popular with MI6 officers and a genuine recruitment centre, one of its most famous clients was naval intelligence officer and MI6 man Ian Fleming. He would later comment that the "food served there was the best in London."

"THIS IS LONDON..."

Eye Spy Intelligence Magazine

SPY SITES OF LONDON

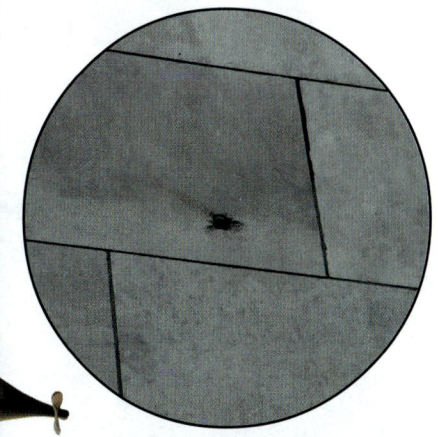

On 21 June 1944, a German V1 cruise missile narrowly missed Bush House, but damaged parts of its facade. Shrapnel marks (above) can still be seen on the building and road

American Irving T. Bush, built Bush House in the 1920s

could offer his organisation assistance and operate in difficult arenas.

Menzies's dreadful recruiting skills did not go unnoticed with MI6's hierarchy. Section IV MI6 Air Intelligence (head)

Lord Shelburne

Boodle's: A favourite haunt of Dansey and other MI6 officers. Besides staffers enjoying a drink or two, MI6 used the club as a recruiting venue. Back in the eighteenth century it was known as the Savoir Vivre, but changed its name to Boodle's in 1782. Its founder, Lord Shelburne, who would become Prime Minister, had an establishment known as Boodle's originally at Pall Mall. The club was named as such after its head waiter - Edward Boodle

In Fleming's books depicting the imaginary MI6 agent James Bond, he does in fact make reference to Boodle's on at least two occasions. The Blades Club mentioned in his novels is based upon Boodle's. Perhaps more interesting, in the 1979 motion picture *Moonraker*, the producer chose to use its real name!

Interestingly, rumour has it that Dansey also liked Boodle's, this because his boss - Chief of MI6 Colonel Stewart Menzies, never ventured there, preferring the equally classy **WHITE'S CLUB** at nearby **37-38 ST JAMES'S STREET! [131•42]**.

Menzies, who was born at **46 UPPER GROSVENOR STREET [132•55]**, saw White's as an important location for recruitment. However, those who knew him say he was an appalling judge of character. Menzies sought to 'tap' the shoulder of Establishment types, while Dansey liked those who

Eye Spy Intelligence Magazine   111

White's Club, 37-38 St James's Street
MI6 Chief Colonel Stewart Menzies' favourite club

Boodle's Club, 28 St James's Street

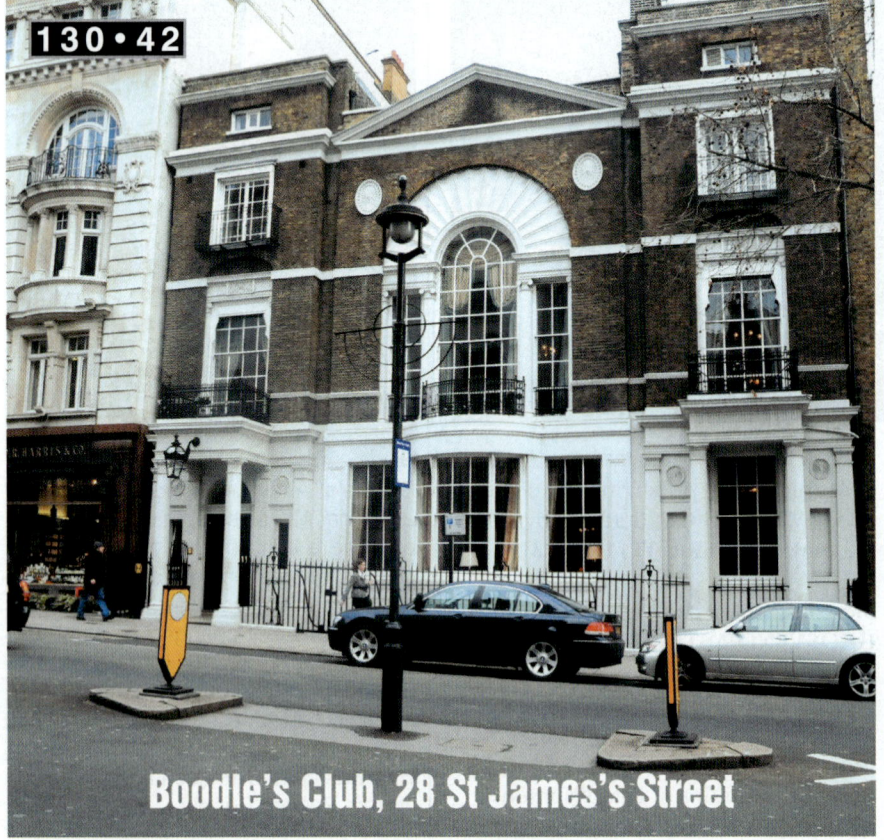

Group Captain Frederick Winterbotham, who during World War Two supervised ULTRA Intelligence, said he was a "terrible judge often finding employment for totally unsuitable characters." Indeed, after a weekend's recruiting, Menzies errors were usually rectified on a Monday morning by a bemused front office staff who had to politely tell those who turned up for work - "it's a mistake." Menzies lived at **4 DAVIES STREET, MAYFAIR [133•55]**. As for the clubs - they remain hugely popular in London with a loyal clientele.

One lesser known recruiting club that for decades was used to secure the services of preferred staff was the **DEVONSHIRE CLUB, 50 ST JAMES'S STREET [134•42]**. This was first mentioned by spy author William Le Queux long before MI5 and MI6 had been established! The club closed in 1976 and its membership merged with the **EAST INDIA CLUB, 16 ST JAMES'S SQUARE [135•42]**. Interest-

Eye Spy Intelligence Magazine

A slightly damaged but rare WWI photo of Colonel Stewart Menzies (right) and his brother Keith

3 Albemarle Street

ingly, Eye Spy learned that a secret tunnel linked the Devonshire Club with White's Club across the road. Also, in 2011, 50 St James's was purchased by a Russian billionaire for £75 million!

MI6 SPIES, AGENT WESTMINSTER AND A STRANGE TWIST OF FATE

Whilst the PCO carried on valiantly in neutral countries, when war broke out it was inevitable Z agents would sometimes find themselves working in the same area and occasionally, on the same projects.

The existence of the secret Z Organisation was made known to the PCO after MI6 sent a memo to Station Chief Major Stevens at the Hague Station on 4 September 1939 - just three days after Germany had invaded Poland:

'You are to place yourself in touch with Captain S. Payne Best and give him all facilities which he may require in regard to communications and otherwise and also money he may want. Best is a highly experienced man of great ability. Beyond giving your services you are not to interfere in his arrangements...'

Devonshire Club, 50 St James's Street

Eye Spy Intelligence Magazine

113

SPY SITES OF LONDON
East India Club, 16 St James's Square

135•42

The Backus Cafe, Blerik near Venlo. A German sting operation resulted in the capture of two senior MI6 men

Walter Schellenberg

MI6 Hague Station Chief, Major Stevens (left) and Z Organisation man Captain Sigismund Payne Best

convince British Intelligence he was trustworthy and opposed to Hitler.

Reinhard Heydrich, the ruthless Nazi chief of the SD, whose SS intelligence service often competed with the Abwehr, gave the go-ahead to shatter MI6's Hague Station. A series of bogus meetings with German plotters was arranged by Fischer and on 9 November 1939, Best and Stevens were lured to the Backus Cafe at Blerik near Venlo, about five miles from the

1905 photo showing the street (Nieuwe Uitleg) in the Hague where MI6 ran its Dutch operation

Though Stevens was head of MI6 in Holland, he had never heard of Best, nor was he aware of the Z Organisation - primarily because PCOs were not told, but also because Z agents and officers were not given radios. This meant there was no radio traffic to intercept - no clues to their existence. Z agents simply used meetings, the post or dead letter drops* (DLD) to forward and receive intelligence. But the Abwehr, headed by Wilhelm Canaris, knew of the PCO operation in Holland and was watching.

The information was gleaned by a Dr. Fischer, a double agent working for Germany's Sicherheitsdienst (SD - Security Service) who had managed to

Dead letter drops - innocuous locations for depositing and retrieving information and/or items etc.

SPY SITES OF LONDON

132•55
46 Upper Grosvenor Street

A rare intelligence find... WWII MI6 Chief Stewart Graham Menzies was born here in 1890. Menzies would replace Sinclair as 'C' in 1939

Walter Schellenberg flew to Portugal in an audacious attempt to secure the services and support of the Duke and Duchess of Windsor

German border. Heydrich's assistant, SS-Oberfuhrer Walter Schellenberg lay in wait with an armed German intelligence unit. Both MI6 men were abducted at gun point along with their chauffeur Jam Lemmens. Lieutenant Klop, a Dutch intelligence officer who travelled with the Britons, tried to intervene but was shot dead. According to German propaganda neither British officer put up much resistance when questioned, and gave a "remarkable comprehensive overview of the MI6 organisation." The officers photographs were splashed all over the newspapers, and the PCO operation was effectively dead. To add to one of the Service's lowest points in its history, Admiral Sinclair died just hours before the Venlo incident on 4 November, leaving MI6 leaderless. As for Schellenberg, he was awarded the Iron Cross and in 1944, following the abolition of the Abwehr, became head of the SS foreign intelligence section.

And as a final footnote to this incident, and relevant to the history of British Intelligence, there is strong evidence that Schellenberg was sent on a secret mission that could have affected the outcome of the war. Schellenberg had flown to Portugal in 1940 to try and meet with the Duke and Duchess of Windsor (Wallis Simpson). This, as part of an ambitious attempt to persuade them to join Germany, or at the very least to secure their support. Simpson lived at **16 CUMBERLAND TERRACE [136•15]**, an address almost certainly known to German Intelligence. In the end, the SD operation was a dismal failure. Nevertheless, Schellenberg was a highly regarded intelligence officer,

Eye Spy Intelligence Magazine

SPY SITES OF LONDON

133 • 55

4 Davies Street, Mayfair

Night falls on Davies Street. Chief of MI6 Colonel Stewart Menzies lived here in the 1930s

Reinhard Heydrich (holding document), whose organisation ran its own powerful intelligence service, pictured with Heinrich Himmler (far left) in 1939

MI6 underestimated the Abwehr and its spy chief Wilhelm Canaris. This would quickly change as the Nazis outwitted and overran a seemingly defenceless Europe. He also recruited a number of surprising spies including Coco Chanel - agent 7124 - codename Westminster

Wilhelm Canaris   **Coco Chanel**

116

Eye Spy Intelligence Magazine

Wallis Simpson lived and worked from an apartment here overlooking Regent's Park

16 Cumberland Terrace

and in later years he was prominent in the hunt for members of the very famous Russian Red Orchestra spy network. Some intelligence watchers believe he had forged personal liaisons with leading Irish nationalists who were still opposed to British rule.

Paris-based historian Hal Vaughan says Schellenberg also had a relationship with the famous Coco Chanel and that this iconic lady was herself an agent of the Abwehr using the codename Westminster. After the war Chanel was arrested, but strangely Winston Churchill is said to have intervened and she was released just hours later. As for Schellenberg, he was sent to jail for six years. The short sentence may reflect his willingness to provide key intelligence on his associates to MI6 and American intelligence officials. This enabled prosecutors to gather a vast amount of incriminating evidence against several leading Nazi suspects which was presented and used at the Nuremberg Trials.

MI6 AND BRITAIN'S 'OSKAR SCHINDLERS'

Another PCO officer whose work for MI6 against the Nazis has only recently been honoured is Frank Foley.

Born in 1894, Foley was an unassuming and quiet man. In the 1930s, before the outbreak of WWII, Foley was despatched by MI6 to take charge of the Berlin Station, whilst working in the passport section of Britain's Berlin embassy. The job was simply a front as he secured intelligence on the growing menace of Hitler's Germany. Despite this, and not because of his MI6 role, he soon found himself issuing visas, passports and travel documentation to more and more European Jews wanting to leave the

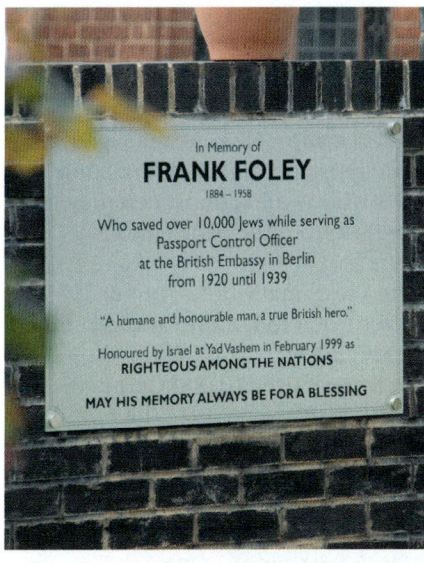

MI6 officer Frank Foley

In Memory of FRANK FOLEY 1884–1958

Who saved over 10,000 Jews while serving as Passport Control Officer at the British Embassy in Berlin from 1920 until 1939

"A humane and honourable man, a true British hero."

Honoured by Israel at Yad Vashem in February 1999 as **RIGHTEOUS AMONG THE NATIONS**

MAY HIS MEMORY ALWAYS BE FOR A BLESSING

Eye Spy Intelligence Magazine 117

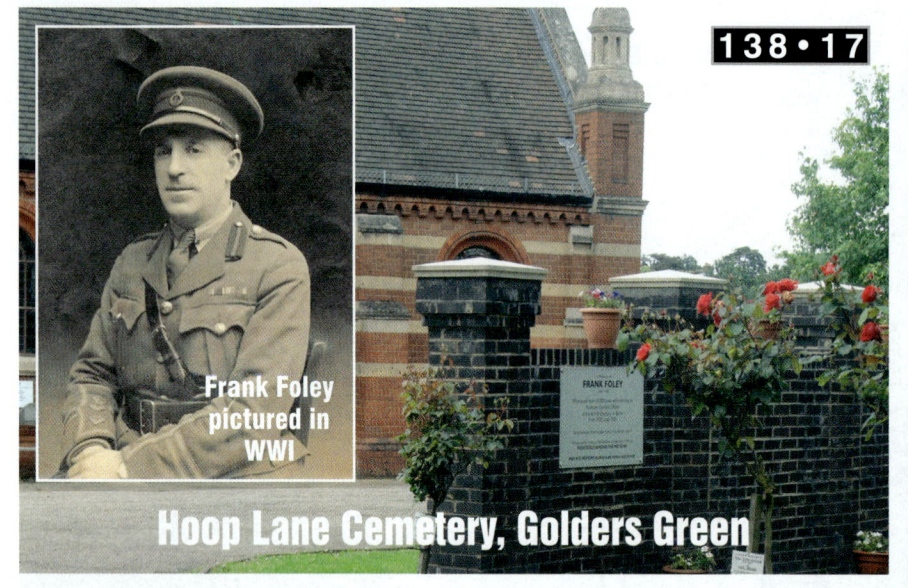

Frank Foley pictured in WWI

Hoop Lane Cemetery, Golders Green [138•17]

15 Sunnymead Road [137•38]

country. And of course, he had no genuine cover provided for by diplomatic immunity. If his unofficial escape operation was discovered, he would have been arrested.

Following the infamous Kristallnacht*, life for Foley, and more so for many European Jews, became even more dangerous. Yet every day he continued to stamp visas and on some occasions, even used his apartment to shelter those wanting to flee. Perhaps more noteworthy were his travels to concentration camps. Here he managed to issue more permits and save some Jews who would almost certainly not have survived the nearing war.

When war finally broke out in 1939, he returned to London and continued his intelligence work. Foley had saved the lives of over 10,000 German-Jewish civilians. In 1942, he found himself interrogating Hitler's deputy Rudolf Hess, and later still, he was part of the secret British Intelligence agent-running operation known as the Double Cross System. He was also an important member of the British Security Coordination (BSC). After the war, armed with his knowledge of Berlin, he returned to Germany in an effort to identify leading Nazis.

Prior to the war this great unassuming wartime spy lived at **15 SUNNYMEAD ROAD [137•38]**. However, following the end of hostilities he moved into a flat at Nell Gwynn House. Eye Spy understands MI6 used at least one apartment here for its officers and agents. Another famous occupant was SOE agent Vera Atkins **(See Site 193•44)**. In 1949, Foley retired to the town of Stourbridge and sadly died in obscurity in 1958.

A number of plaques and statues have since been unveiled of Frank Foley, the latest in July 2012, at **HOOP LANE CEMETERY, GOLDERS GREEN [138•17]**. It was London's Jewish community which organised the plaque - not just to thank the man for his life-saving work, but also in the hope that his story will be remembered in future days. Rabbi Baroness Neuberger said: "This is nowhere near enough recognition for someone who did what Frank Foley did."

The ceremony was attended by some of the people Foley got out, including Nachum Stechler. "He got me a Polish passport because I was in a camp on the border of Poland," said Stechler. "Because of that I was able to come to London."

In 1999, he was recognised as a Righteous Among the Nations by Israel's Yad Vashem Holocaust Museum. Belatedly, in 2010, Frank Foley was posthumously named a British Hero of the Holocaust by the UK government.

Another man who helped Europe's Jewish community and was knighted for his services in 1993, is Sir Nicholas Winton, aged 105. In 2014 he was awarded the Order of the White Lion at a ceremony in the city of Prague,

Sir Nicholas Winton

Sir Nicholas Winton receives the Order of the White Lion from Czech President Milos Zeman

*Kristallnacht - attacks on Jewish owned shops and synagogues 9-10 August 1938 in Germany. Authorities failed to intervene

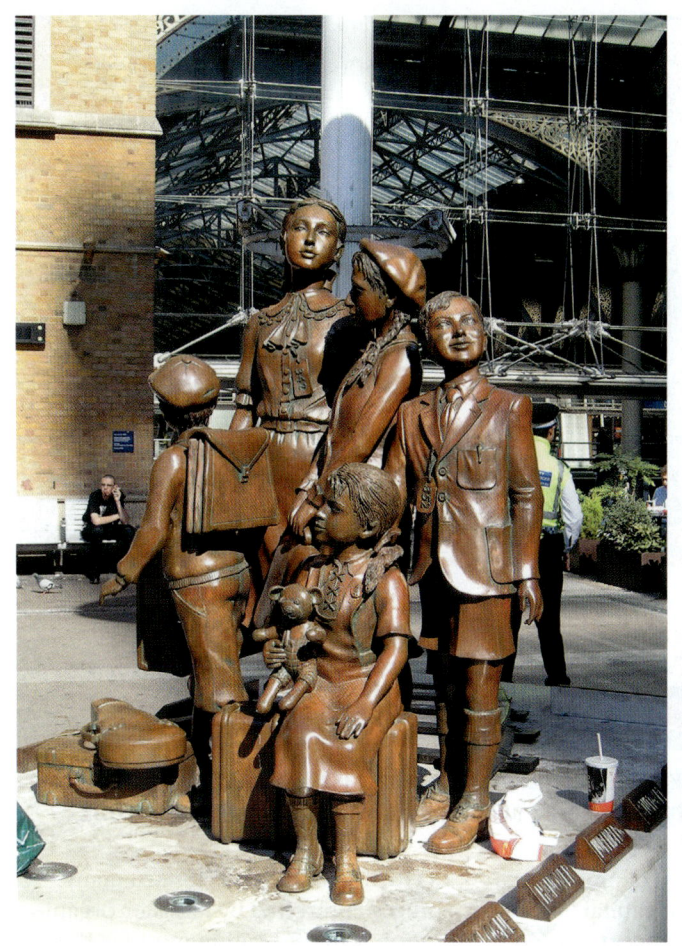

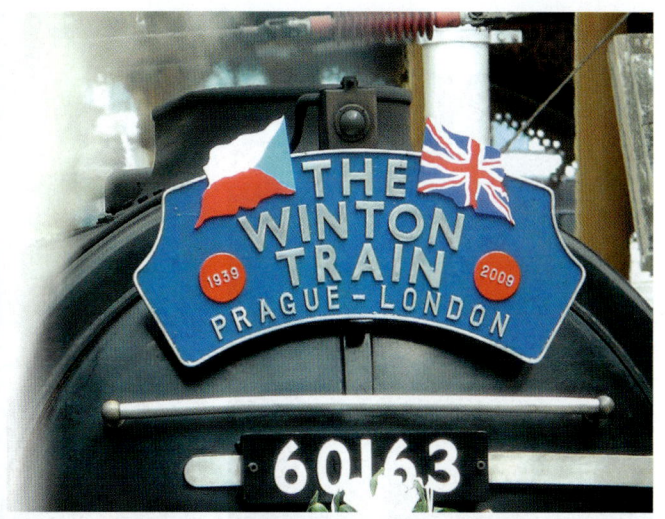

Sir Nicholas Winton Memorial at Liverpool Street Station

Two 'Winton children' at the ceremony

Czech Republic. The Czech Defence Ministry actually despatched a military aircraft to fly him to the event, this out of respect for his wartime endeavours which saved hundreds of young Czech Jews from Hitler's death camps.

In 1939, on the eve of Germany's invasion of Europe, Winton, recognising the threat to Jewish citizens, organised the rescue of over 600 youngsters to Britain where he found them foster homes. The operation became known as the Czech Kindertransport because he used some eight trains to transport them across Europe.

On 1 September 2009, to mark the 70th anniversary of the operation, a train renamed the Winton Train, comprising of the original locomotive and several carriages used in 1939, left Prague Station on its journey to London. Some of the people who made the original journey so many years ago were on the train.

The Czech Government said he had "given children the greatest possible gift: the chance to live and be free." Today, there are an estimated 6,000 people who are descendants of those he managed to help. Czech President Milos Zeman, who made the presentation, said he felt ashamed that Winton had to wait so long to be honoured, but that it was "better late than never."

What Winton did can perhaps be best assessed by examining the train journey which never was. After youngsters on the eight trains successfully reached Britain, Winton attempted to organise his biggest operation yet - a ninth train. This had been booked to carry over 250 children to freedom. Sadly war broke out and the Nazis occupied the Sudentenland area of Czechoslovakia; the train, scheduled to depart on 3 September was cancelled. All those who were intended to travel were killed in the months and years that followed. An estimated one million Czech Jews perished in Auschwitz alone.

Winton did not disclose details of his tremendous work until the 1990s, when his wife found his wartime

Memorial to Sir Winton at the main train station in Prague

Eye Spy Intelligence Magazine

119

SPY SITES OF LONDON

With war declared on Germany, MI6 soon found itself looking for additional London-based premises. Caxton Street and nearby St. Ermin's Hotel became a hub of activity after being occupied by MI6 and the emerging SOE

scrapbook. A splendid memorial to Sir Winton can be found at the entrance of Liverpool Street Station **(See Site 125•08).**

MI5 EXPANSION, NEW PREMISES AND REORGANISATION

Just as MI6 was finding it difficult to operate in a Europe fast succumbing to Hitler's army, MI5 was desperately trying to reorganise itself. By 1937 it had already occupied more offices at **HORSEFERRY ROAD [139•42]** (adjacent to its new headquarters at Thames House), and was recruiting officers apace. Sadly, some of those selected by MI5 (and MI6) would turn out to be nothing more than traitors. MI6, meanwhile, had begun to occupy premises at **2 CAXTON STREET** including part of the impressive **ST. ERMIN'S HOTEL [140•42].**

MI5's Registry of 'persons of interest' (and now menace) was expanding so a decision was made to fragment its offices to other parts of London and beyond. To accommodate its growing directorates (MI5 call these branches), in 1939 the Service moved to **WORMWOOD SCRUBS PRISON [141•53].**

Besides a number of training offices scattered around the capital, MI5 relocated its main London Central operation to **57-58 ST. JAMES'S STREET [142•42]** - close to many offices controlled by its sister organisation MI6. But within months, the important Registry (for the first time

Continued on page 122

In 1939, MI5 moved its headquarters to this unlikely setting. The Radio Security Service was also operating from this building

141•53

Wormwood Scrubs Prison

Eye Spy Intelligence Magazine

ST. ERMIN'S HOTEL - A FASCINATING INTELLIGENCE AND SPY LOCATION

Every year St. Ermin's Hotel hosts the important Intelligence Book of the Year Award

St. Ermin's Hotel, Caxton Street

St. Ermin's Hotel has a long and rich connection with a variety of UK and foreign secret organisations. First opened as a hotel in 1899, its close proximity to the Broadway Buildings, the headquarters of the British Secret Intelligence Service (MI6) throughout the 1930s and 40s, made it a convenient and discreet venue to meet agents.

In fact, the hotel became so familiar to the British intelligence community that in March 1936, MI6 took over an entire floor to accommodate a new organisation known as Section D (D for Destruction). Headed by Colonel Lawrence Grand, its task was to prepare plans for sabotaging strategic sites in Europe that might fall in the event of another world war.

In 1938, Arthur Owens, the double agent codenamed Snow by the British and Johny by the Abwehr, was interrogated by the Naval Intelligence Division as well as MI5 officers. Later, when Snow attempted to penetrate the British Union of Fascists, he claimed that the hotel was one of several fronts run for the benefit of what he described as "the British Secret Services."

In July 1940, Section D was absorbed into an entirely new organisation - the Special Operations Executive (SOE) based in Baker Street. SOE continued to use the hotel as a meeting place and operational headquarters. It also extended into an adjacent block where there was a suite of unmarked offices.

In his memoirs, *My Silent War,* KGB agent Kim Philby recounted how he had been interviewed at the hotel when he was first approached to join MI6 and had visited Guy Burgess at his office in the building.

Cambridge Spy Ring traitors Philby and Maclean frequented the Caxton Bar whilst the hotel's proximity to government and security offices ensured its use by intelligence officers both domestic and foreign.

Hugh Dalton - Minister for Economic Warfare played a pivotal role in helping establish the SOE

Horseferry Road
In 1937, an expanding MI5 moved some of its operations to Thames House and also occupied offices on Horseferry Road

In 1940, Churchill sacked long-time MI5 head Vernon Kell and started plotting the creation of a most formidable pro-active spy organisation - the Special Operations Executive (SOE)

MI6 ran the imaginary Albany Trust from Abbey House, now lost under this building. The front company operated solely to gather intelligence

Victoria Street

ever) was moved outside the city to the relative safety of Blenheim Palace in the Oxfordshire countryside, the birthplace and ancestral home of Prime Minister Winston Churchill. Here it would remain for much of the duration of the war.

Churchill then delivered a shock to the Service. In 1940 he fired long-time Director-General Sir Vernon Kell who had headed MI5 since its birth in 1909. Churchill eventually appointed David Petrie in 1941, replacing acting director Brigadier A. W. Harker. Petrie would lead MI5 throughout the remainder of the war until 1946.

MORE MI6 FRONT COMPANIES

Z officer Captain Sigismund Payne Best had communicated with the Z Organisation via an MI6 front company - Menoline Limited - based at **24 MAPLE STREET [143•55]** off London's Tottenham Court Road. Sadly, like a growing number of famous spy haunts in the capital, the building no longer exists - replaced by rows of apartments and offices. Menoline was but one of several fictitious businesses used and/or created by Dansey that allowed MI6 to conduct its intelli-

SPY SITES OF LONDON

Maple Street

This site was once occupied by the MI6 front company Menoline Ltd

143•55

142•42
57-58 St. James's Street
In 1939, MI5 moved its central London operation here

gence collection operations all over the world. The Albany Trust run from **ABBEY HOUSE, VICTORIA STREET [144•42]** was another used by Dansey to conduct interviews. Today the magnificent building which once stood on Victoria Street has gone - in its place a modern structure. The interviews at Abbey House were overseen by a Colonel Haywood, an MI5 officer specially chosen by Dansey. However, some historians believe Haywood was in fact Dansey himself.

If selected and approved, the agent would be given a Z number. Other Z Organisation front companies included the export arm of international fine art dealers Geoffrey Duveen & Company; H. Sichel & Sons, the wine shipper and holiday firm - Lammin Tours. Of course, dozens of Z agents were already in place working overseas for genuine firms. By far the most important of these commercial covers, was London Films - a feature film company headed by Hungarian-born Alexander Korda. His work along with that of his brother Zolan would be of immense help in developing another crucial intelligence organisation as we shall discover.

Whilst MI6's operations were being shaped by additional finances and a great desire to thwart Hitler, Churchill provided support for other even more shadowy organisations - the Political Warfare Executive (PWE) and the far-reaching British Security Coordination (BSC) - of which Claude Dansey would provide support in the shape of spy tradecraft and recruitment. Together with the newly formed Special Operations Executive (SOE), which Hugh Dalton, Minister of Economic Warfare played a pivotal role in its establishment, this trio of organisations provided the UK with a powerful military and psychological intelligence arm. Dalton, who lived at **ASHLEY GARDENS, AMBROSDEN AVENUE [145•42]** next to Westminster Cathedral, advised Churchill that Colin Gubbins should be appointed as head of the SOE. Gubbins himself lived at **CAMPDEN HILL COURT, CAMPDEN HILL ROAD, KENSINGTON [146•60]**.

Of interest, one early recruit (1940) to the PWE was the wartime Foreign Secretary and future Prime Minister Anthony Eden. He lived in a flat at **4 CHESTERFIELD STREET [147•55]** -

Eye Spy Intelligence Magazine

SPY SITES OF LONDON

After a brief spell as head of MI5, Brigadier A. W. Harker (right) was replaced by David Petrie in 1941

interestingly right next door to the secretive MI6 officer Somerset Maugham.

By 1942, much of the deception work of these agencies would be controlled by an even more shadowy organisation - the London Controlling Section (LCS). More on the LCS later.

A SPY TO THE LAST

At the end of the war, deputy head of MI6 and now Sir Claude Dansey, moved out of the city with his wife to the countryside and into a fine residence known as Bathampton Manor near Bath. Seeking solace in the area, the man known as Colonel Z woke one morning to find someone had drawn a 'Z' on his front door. Despite his intelligence skills, he never managed to solve this particular puzzle!

A life in the spying game proved too much for Dansey and he died peacefully in 1947 in Lansdowne Grove Nursing Home, Bath, with his wife Frances holding his hand. But there was one more twist in the legend of Claude Dansey... when Frances was going through his papers, she discovered six of his passports all in different names. A consummate spy to the last...

Ashley Gardens sits next to the magnificent Westminster Cathedral

Sir Anthony Eden

Eye Spy Intelligence Magazine

SPY SITES OF LONDON

145•42

Acting on the advice of his minister for Economic Warfare, Hugh Dalton, Churchill asked that Colin Gubbins be seconded into the newly formed Special Operations Executive (SOE). Gubbins name would become synonymous with the SOE and many of its famous intelligence-led operations

Sir Colin Gubbins

Hugh Dalton

147•55

4 Chesterfield Street

Ashley Gardens, Ambrosden Avenue

146 • 60

46 Campden Hill Court, Campden Hill Road

GENESIS OF THE MI6 Z ORGANISATION - NAVIGATION SURROUNDING CLAUDE DANSEY

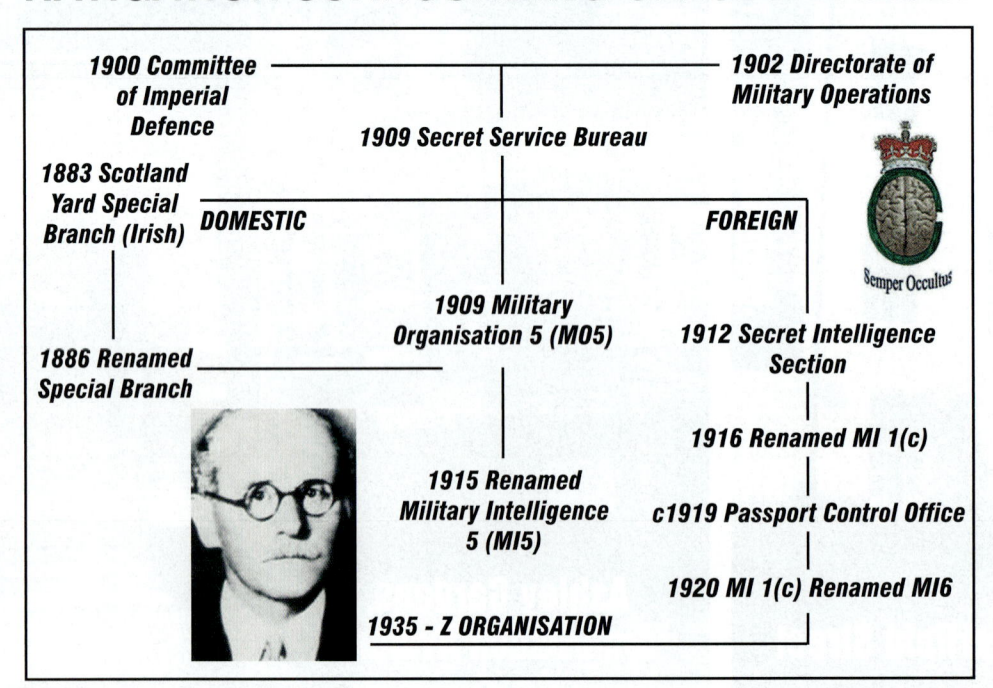

- 1900 Committee of Imperial Defence
- 1902 Directorate of Military Operations
- 1909 Secret Service Bureau
- 1883 Scotland Yard Special Branch (Irish)

DOMESTIC

FOREIGN

- 1909 Military Organisation 5 (MO5)
- 1912 Secret Intelligence Section
- 1886 Renamed Special Branch
- 1916 Renamed MI 1(c)
- 1915 Renamed Military Intelligence 5 (MI5)
- c1919 Passport Control Office
- 1920 MI 1(c) Renamed MI6
- 1935 - Z ORGANISATION

Semper Occultus

Eye Spy Intelligence Magazine

SPY SITES OF LONDON

VI
An Early MI5 Success
Maxwell's Dark Agents Strike

There were several innocuous-looking buildings spread across the capital that during the war became of great interest to MI5's counter-espionage and subversion branches. And the goings-on in one particular building could have had serious implications for America's entry into the war. At **24 ONSLOW SQUARE [148•47]** pro-Nazi British politician Captain Archibald Henry Maule Ramsay was surveilled by men from MI5 and detained by accompanying police officers. His arrest on 23 May 1940, followed the detention of other activists who were judged to be legitimate threats to security.

Ramsay's anti-Jewish rhetoric was bad enough, but MI5 had become deeply concerned about a group he formed to promote English-Nazi friendship. Other concerns came in the person of a certain Anna Volkov, who was an admirer of Ramsay and a lover of Tyler Kent, a cipher clerk who worked at the US Embassy of a still-neutral America. The building, at **1 GROSVENOR SQUARE [149•55]** is today partly used by the Government of Canada and its High Commission.

In the late 1930s, Kent had a liaison with a female agent of the NKVD (forerunner of the KGB) called Danischewsky and made monies from Moscow by passing on communications - this he later said was to

US cipher clerk Tyler Kent

24 Onslow Square

148•47

SPY SITES OF LONDON
149•55
1 Grosvenor Square

Former US Embassy at 1 Grosvenor Square was occupied by Canadian diplomats after the Americans requirements outgrew the building. The building is currently called MacDonald House

Franklin D. Roosevelt

"augment his government salary." MI5 Watchers* had Kent surveilled across London and their attention was heightened when he met with a suspected Nazi agent.

With access to the classified material Kent was stealing, there was a real possibility Ramsay could destabilise the UK-USA relationship, especially as Britain was still trying to get the United States to join them in the war. Kent and Volkov met frequently at her home at **18 ROLAND GARDENS** [150•47]. MI5 believe all manner of secrets were being taken to this address. Occasionally, Volkov, who actually met Hitler's deputy Rudolf Hess just before the war, travelled to Kent's apartment at **47 GLOUCESTER PLACE [151•42]**.

It was here on 20 May, several MI5 and Special Branch officers broke into his second floor residence and recovered over 1,000 official US government communications. Chillingly, some letters were private correspondence between Churchill and US leader Franklin D. Roosevelt. It was a huge security breach.

In some respect this was a relief to both Washington and London, for officials had privately suspected US Ambassador to Great Britain, Joseph P. Kennedy, of filtering such correspondence to his contacts back in Berlin. Kennedy believed Britain was actually involved in a covert programme to secure American war assistance, and even said Churchill would "blow up the US Embassy and blame Germany" in an effort to draw the United States into the war.

Kennedy's business interests in Germany and his passionate belief Britain could not win a war with Hitler's Wehrmacht, meant he became an obvious target for MI5. When the Service learned that secret Roosevelt-Churchill cables were being quoted in intercepted German communications by British codebreakers, this only confirmed its belief that security at the embassy had been breached.

It is highly likely this surveillance was sanctioned by Roosevelt who had been embarrassed by Kennedy's appeasement policy towards Hitler.

US AMBASSADOR BUGGED

We learned a most secret and unprecedented event then took place to establish who was leaking material. British spies bugged Kennedy's private

* Name given to operational surveillance officers from MI5. Today such officers operate within the Service's A4 Branch

18 Roland Gardens

14 Princes Gate, Kensington

The private residence of US ambassadors to Great Britain until the early 1960s. The building was bugged by MI5 in 1940 whilst occupied by Ambassador Joesph P. Kennedy. Officials believed he was passing on secret Churchill-Roosevelt cables to the Germans

residence at **14 PRINCES GATE, KENSINGTON [152•47]**, whilst GPO specialists attached to MI5 recorded all incoming and outgoing calls.

Kent, of course, worked under Kennedy, thus when he was identified as the prime culprit, Kennedy was forced to publicly denounce his spy actions - ironically from the steps of his bugged home at Princes Gate.

The incident signalled the end of this most anti-British ambassador, who held the post from 1938. He was quickly replaced and left the country in October 1940. As for Kent, he received a seven-year prison sentence.

Interestingly, and many years later, it emerged Kent's girlfriend and Soviet agent - Danischewsky - was in fact the aunt of the famous British actress Helen Mirran - Mrs Irine Danischewsky, whose maiden name

Joseph P. Kennedy and his wife Rose pictured in 1940 during his role as US Ambassador to Great Britain

Eye Spy Intelligence Magazine

151•42

47 Gloucester Place

was Mironoff - the original family name of the Mirrans. Danischewsky was also jailed for seven years.

Not long after, Anna Volkov was arrested at another well-known far-right haunt that had become a place of interest for Maxwell Knight's undercover MI5 agents. She was the daughter of Admiral Nikolai Volkov, the last naval attache of the Tsar's imperial forces before the Bolsheviks took control. He decided it was best to stay in England and opened the Russian Tea Rooms at **50 HARRINGTON ROAD [153•47]**.

Known for its good food, the address concealed a menacing secret, for above its dining room - a flat used by a group started by Ramsay - the far-right Clandestine Right Club. This outfit gave MI5 all manner of problems. However, Knight's agents infiltrated the organisation and following the detention of Kent, over 2,000 members (including 800 from the British Union of Fascists) were arrested. So too was Anna Volkov just as she was about to help serve tea to diners.

Ramsay's rants about a global Jewish conspiracy being behind capitalism, Communism, Masonry, Vatican spy rings and just about every other underworld subject, caused much unease with intelligence officials. He spent most of the war in detention and out of harms way.

Volkov eventually received a ten-year prison sentence, but she could easily have been hanged. As for Ramsay, he was never charged, but 24 Onslow Square represents one of the most keenly surveilled addresses in wartime London, and an early, but major success for MI5.

A STRANGE TWIST OF FATE

There were many other persons high on the list of MI5's WWII Registry, including former German intelligence officer Captain Franz Rintelen (von Kleist). His daring WWI exploits surely reflect the highs and lows of a spy. A

Captain Franz Rintelen

130

Eye Spy Intelligence Magazine

153 • 47

Anna Volkov

50 Harrington Road
Former Russian Tea Rooms

Spy and 'paymaster general' Heinrich Albert

Lt. Commander in the German Navy, Rintelen was given a bogus Swiss passport in the name of his brother-in-law - Emil Gasche, and sent to the United States in 1915.

His first mission was the dangerous task of interfering with armaments sailing from New York to England. Using his bogus name and various other identity and business ruses, the German established himself in America. With the help of trusted agents and massive finance from Berlin, Rintelen began smuggling incendiary bombs into the depths of cargo ships carrying ordnance.

His operation was run from New York with an associate - Heinrich Albert. Albert was a solicitor attached to the German Embassy diplomatic staff: in effect a spy and paymaster of the operation known as the Great Phenol Plot. However, because of his association with George Sylvester Viereck, editor of a pro-German magazine called *The Fatherland,* who was already under surveillance by US authorities, the scheme would eventually unfold.

As a director for a front company called Bridgeport Projectile, Rintelen decided to use the name Frederick Hansen. With a legitimate certificate in hand, it enabled the men to purchase all manner of weaponry and explosives. Under instructions from his spy handler in Berlin, Rintelen then attempted the daring purchase of the du Pont [gun] powder factory. This endeavour ended in failure, but it did not stop the spy.

AN ENLARGED OPERATION TO SQUEEZE AMERICA

Working with a small number of trusted contacts, Rintelen manufactured bombs which were assembled with timers. These were planted on ships carrying legitimate weapons traversing the Atlantic towards England. When they exploded (and several did with much success) the authorities simply believed the ship's deadly cargo had somehow detonated.

David Lamar

Eye Spy Intelligence Magazine

131

SPY SITES OF LONDON

SOUTH KENSINGTON - A STATION FOR ALL SEASONS AND REASONS

In 1927, part of this deep-level station, an unused westbound tunnel, was occupied by British military intelligence and used as a radio signalling school. In 1939, at the onset of WWII the facility closed or moved to another site. The site then housed vital equipment used to detect unexploded Luftwaffe bombs that had fallen into the River Thames. This was considered vital as any damage to the flood gates would have resulted in severe problems for the city. Its very deep location also meant it was an ideal bomb-proof storage area. During the First World War, treasures from Buckingham Palace and the Victoria and Albert Museum were secreted away in the darkest depths of the station.

During the height of the Cold War, MI5 had a permanent presence at the station to monitor Soviet agents. The station was close to numerous locations used by the KGB and British Intelligence

Buckingham Palace

Victoria and Albert Museum

Victoriano Huerta (centre)

Rintelen was then ordered to create unrest in US trade unions, and used the services of a shadowy American in the person of David Lamar who was only too pleased to act as an agent - this in return for huge sums of money.

Yet Rintelen's most daring mission involved trying to get Mexico involved in World War One - fighting against the US and the Allies. He even managed to contact Victoriano Huerta, a senior Mexican military figure and hated dictator in an effort to secure support for U-Boat operations. Rintelen hoped Huerta would also wage war in his country in an effort to become leader. Another vital aspect of the ruse was to obtain the support of political figures in Japan and Ireland. Substantial sums of monies were wired to the spy from the German Embassy in Washington.

Rintelen's stay in America was brief, and in any event, British Room 40 codebreakers were already intercepting communications destined for his front companies. One signal was contained in a complaint by future intelligence contact man Franz von Papen, who would become Chancellor of Germany. Von Papen was supposedly concerned about the huge sums of money Rintelen was spending. However, there is some evidence to suggest this communication was

Franz von Papen

Women peace protesters aboard the MS Noordan in April 1915 on their way to a peace convention in Holland. Rintelen used this event as cover to leave the USA believing the focus of attention would be on the women. MI5, tipped-off by US authorities, were waiting for him as the ship docked in the UK

generated by British Intelligence as a ruse to convince America to join Britain in its fight against Germany.

As Rintelen made his way back to Germany aboard the sailing ship MS Noordam in April 1915, a British marine contingent was waiting for him. The ship docked in Ramsgate [some reports suggest he was detained in Southampton] and he was arrested. Interestingly, he had chosen a vessel packed with women protesting against the war who were enroute to a peace protest in Holland. At around the same time, Berlin was the intended venue for a meeting of the International Woman Suffrage Alliance. Rintelen used these events as cover to slip out of America.

One of the first officers to interview him in Britain was MI5's Vernon Kell. He was reportedly unsure of the German's activities, but another key British intelligence officer was convinced of his guilt - Admiral 'Blinker' Hall of Room 40. Hall's section had intercepted many supposedly secret signals leaving the codebreaker utterly convinced Rintelen was a "dangerous spy and operator."

Rintelen's adventure ended there; he was jailed for nearly two years and served a further three years detention in America. However, he was released early in 1920. As an indication of his importance to Berlin, the Germans offered to exchange him for 20 Allied officers. We understand that by the mid-1920s, Rintelen had returned to Europe and moved to England. Five years later he renounced his allegiance to Germany. But his rhetoric did not impress the UK's Alien Tribunal Board and he failed to get British citizenship.

He was interned in 1940 when war broke out again. And for the next five years was held in an open camp on the Isle of Man. After his release he thought his luck might change, but with little money and absolutely no job prospects at all, he found solace in a tiny room in **EVELYN GARDENS, KENSINGTON [054•47]**.

South Kensington Station

155•47

Eye Spy Intelligence Magazine

Evelyn Gardens, Kensington

Eye Spy Intelligence Magazine has failed to find any explanation of how he ended up there, but did learn that his flat just happened to be right next door to that of his former MI5 intelligence adversary - Sir Vernon Kell who had been dropped by Churchill.

Similarly, he had befriended Admiral Hall. Both Hall and Kell had interviewed Rintelen years earlier after he was arrested. This is simply too much of a coincidence, though the truth remains elusive. What we can confirm is that on 30 May 1949, a train guard found the body of an elderly man in his early 70s in a tube train at **SOUTH KENSINGTON STATION [155•47]**. He was holding a government document that entitled him to find work... it was Rintelen - known to British Intelligence as the Dark Invader.*

* Captain Franz Rintelen wrote two books - The Dark Invader and The Return of the Dark Invader (1930s)

SPY SITES OF LONDON

VII
Propaganda & Codebreakers
Deception, Disinformation and ULTRA

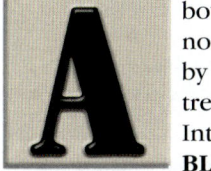

About one hour's drive north of London (less by train), is one of the treasures of British Intelligence - **BLETCHLEY PARK, MILTON KEYNES [156•99]** - the WWII codebreaking centre. This establishment played a pivotal role in the intelligence war with Germany. Similarly, it had threads to many locations in London and elsewhere.

This huge site was once occupied by over 10,000 people who worked to break Germany's secret communications. Churchill ordered its creation in 1939, and housed the Government Code and Cypher School under the auspices of MI6 here. Indeed, the site was also known as Station X because it was MI6's tenth facility, and the Service occupied the top floor of the mansion house. Here it established a tiny radio communications room that was tucked away in the tower. War meant Britain needed to expand its Y Service - a series of wireless stations that listened to Germany's Morse code traffic. MI6's main Y Station antenna at Bletchley Park was concealed within a giant tree in front of the mansion - this

Mansion House facade

The Mansion House, Bletchley Park
The tall tree on the right concealed an MI6 Y Station antenna

tree still grows today. GC&CS, plus other military elements, occupied all of the rooms on the ground floor. The secret military intelligence gathered in this way was codenamed ULTRA. And though MI6 moved out of Bletchley Park in 1941, the codebreaking centre continued to develop.

Bletchley Park would soon become central to a global network of stations

Continued on page 139

Eye Spy Intelligence Magazine

135

'THE GEESE THAT LAID THE GOLDEN EGGS BUT NEVER CACKLED'

156•99

The Colossus codebreaking machine and the museum's late Tony Sale

British Artist Steve Williams' haunting depiction of the tiny MI6 communication room which operated from within the tower of the mansion house. The codebreaking centre was also known as Station X because it was the tenth such operational MI6 facility

Bletchley Park's MI6 agent communications room was hidden away in this tower

Films were projected into the conference room via this orifice

MI6 analysts and war officials would meet in this room to discuss the latest happenings and watch secretly acquired film footage and reconnaissance images gathered by Allied agents

Inside the MI6 communications room

Dillwyn (Dilly) Knox
was the pioneer UK Enigma cryptanalysist
23 July 1884 - 27 February 1943

The first German message was broken here in January 1940

German Enigma machine

Alan Turing (inset) - one of the world's most famous codebreakers lived in this house on the Bletchley Park site

Eye Spy Intelligence Magazine

SPY SITES OF LONDON

2 Warrington Crescent

Birthplace of Alan Turing, perhaps the world's greatest-ever codebreaker

SPY SITES OF LONDON

Another view of 2 Warrington Crescent

Alan Turing statue at Bletchley Park

that captured German, Italian and Japanese messages, especially those produced by German Enigma machines. The messages were gathered and collated in London and sent by either an MI6 dispatch rider or teleprinter for decoding at Bletchley Park. Once decoded, they were returned posthaste in a similar fashion and because they were not sent by radio, the Germans could not intercept them. At the height of the war, couriers entered and left the grounds of Bletchley Park 24-hours-a-day.

It was actually MI6 Chief Admiral Hugh Sinclair who used his own personal wealth to buy Bletchley Park in 1938. Sinclair, who lived at **8 BEAUMONT STREET [157•55]** headed the Service from 1923 and remains the longest serving 'C' of MI6.

THE DULWICH BOYS

A little known fact connects Bletchley Park with the well known poet T. S. Eliot. He worked from a small flat at the School of Oriental Studies (SOAS) at the **FABER BUILDING, 24 RUSSELL SQUARE [158•62]**. The codebreaking centre, fearful it had a lack of Japanese linguists, turned to the War Office for help. With a prompt by Eliot, who had liaisons with the British propaganda ministries, SOAS opened a unit dedicated to supply the centre with experienced personnel who became known as the Dulwich Boys. Eliot himself produced radio broadcasts directed towards the people of Germany telling them they were being misled by Hitler.

TURING AND KNOX

Poignantly, a plaque inside one of the rooms at Bletchley Park hails Dillwyn

Beaumont Street

SPY SITES OF LONDON

Faber Building, 24 Russell Square

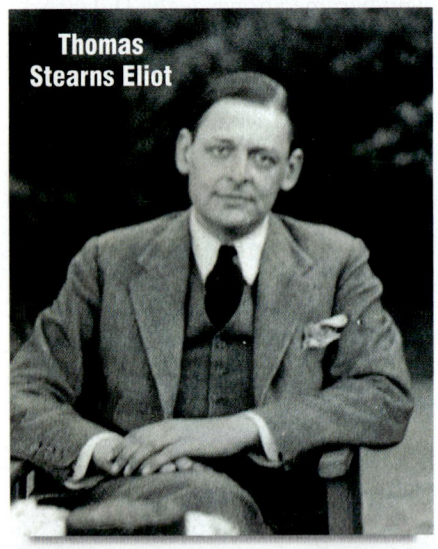

Thomas Stearns Eliot

Knox - *'the pioneer UK Enigma cryptanalyst'*, and notes the first German message was broken in January 1940. Other famous codebreakers who worked at Bletchley Park are honoured, including Alan Turing. He was born at **2 WARRINGTON CRESCENT, WESTMINSTER [159•61]**. The fact that it was a Polish team who first broke the Enigma communications in the late 1920s, is also noted by a monument in the grounds of the mansion.

An MI6 communications room actually overlooks an upper-floor bedroom reserved for Winston Churchill. It was fully restored in 2008 and contains some of the original 1940s radios and equipment. Churchill himself called those involved at Station X the "geese that laid the golden eggs but never cackled."

GC&CS occupied Bletchley Park throughout the war, but by 1946 the scale of the operation was already being run down. Codebreaking continued until 1952, but after the organisation was renamed Government Communications Headquarters (GCHQ) it was eventually relocated to a massive site in Cheltenham.

Besides Bletchley Park's involvement with codebreaking, GC&CS also had an on-going undercover operation in the heart of London at **7-9 BERKELEY STREET [160•55]**. This building, which housed many brilliant codebreakers in luxury apartments, handled diplomatic decrypts.

Another intelligence effort was ULTRA - the interception and decoding of German radio communications. Its success lay solely with GC&CS and the codebreakers of Bletchley Park. Wanting to play a part, MI6 tried to influence the way in which the organisation worked, but in reality it only distributed the decoded communications. MI6 Chief Menzies still wanted to take the credit for the work of the codebreakers, and every day he would send a box of the best material to Winston Churchill. Churchill, not realising that Menzies was standing on GC&CS's toes, was delighted.

Another MI6 side-swipe aimed at MI5 and relevant to communications had already happened. This of course resulted in MI5 losing its Radio Security Service (RSS). But how did this come about? The RSS monitored Abwehr signals in Britain, but after it had learned of an agent Snow, MI5 turned its listening devices on wider

Eye Spy Intelligence Magazine

Y Station Commemorative Badge

In 2009, the UK government honoured surviving Y Station workers with this long-overdue award

160•55

7-9 Berkeley Street

GC&CS LONDON SECTION
The organisation decrypted enemy, neutral and friendly communications including USA codes

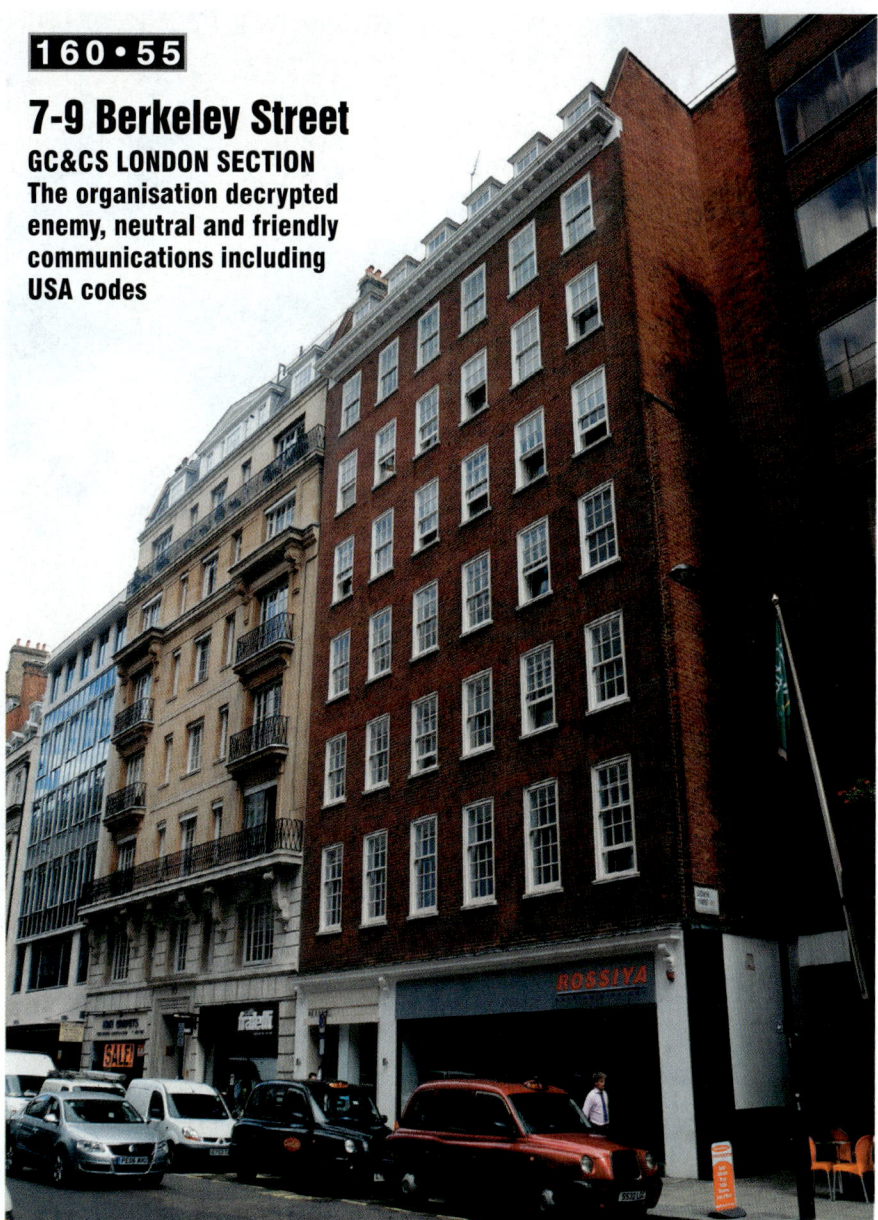

transmissions. Menzies was furious over what he considered "domestic MI5 interference," and schemed with others to secure Churchill's support. The result was the RSS simply fell into the grateful hands of MI6's counter-intelligence Section V. In effect, an MI6 ruse had been played against its sister organisation!

The Services were of course competitive, however, this rarely proved problematic in that both organisations were fighting a common foe. Indeed, they were often willing to share locations just as they were intelligence - at least that's the official line. And one such location was Imperial House **(See Site 373•55)**. Interestingly, the building had been used earlier by Russian spies and Communists, probably members of the CPGB in the 1920s and 1930s, but by the beginning of the war, they had departed. MI5 now operated a team of officers in some rooms, whilst MI6 decided to conceal several front companies and agent runners in others.

Perhaps a little humorous, one company based at the address which was eventually liquidated, was called Co-Optimists Entertainment Syndicate Ltd.

MI6 seemed intent on dictating intelligence policy. Indeed, with its Section D, established just prior to the war, enabling undercover operatives to perform subversion and sabotage operations, the Service seemed the dominant force. That was until Churchill ordered the formation of a military intelligence organisation known as the Special Operations Executive (SOE) [within the newly formed Ministry of Economic Warfare] in July 1940. For a very short period SOE was based at **BERKELEY SQUARE HOUSE [161•55]** headquarters of the ministry before moving to Caxton Street. On the side of the building at **17 BRUTON STREET [162•55]**, visitors will find a plaque dedicated to HM Queen Elizabeth II who was born in a town house on the site on 21 April 1925.

162•55

17 Bruton Street

Eye Spy Intelligence Magazine 141

Berkeley Square House

Once home to the powerful Ministry of Economic Warfare, the building also hosted RAF intelligence staffers and for a short time, was headquarters of the Special Operations Executive

161•55

Berkeley Square House as seen from London's famous Berkeley Square

UNDER-THE-COUNTER INTELLIGENCE ELECTRA HOUSE AND MOORGATE

Churchill's orders to SOE were simple - "set Europe ablaze." Soon it absorbed Section D and about 40 of its officers from MI6. From April 1939, until its closure, Section D had operated from Caxton Street. Also thrown into the SOE model, whose first head was Sir Frank Nelson, a shadowy British Intelligence outfit called Department EH. This ultra-secret Foreign Office front agency had ties to MI6 and was essentially a propaganda organisation headed by Canadian media magnate and *London Times* man, Sir Campbell Stuart. Interestingly, the EH designation came from the building it once occupied - Electra House.

Opened in 1902, **DEPARTMENT EH - ELECTRA HOUSE** - was originally sited at **84 MOORGATE [163•08]**. It was home to the Eastern and Associated Telegraph Companies. In 1933, the administration centre was transferred to a new building on Victoria Embankment. This building served as headquarters for Imperial and International Communications, which in the following year became Cable and Wireless Ltd. Also of significance, the building was used as an alternative terminal for Britain's main overseas communications' system.

It should be noted, after a V1 missile struck the Moorgate building, all work conducted here was transferred to Electra House, Embankment.

In 1939, Cable and Wireless operated nearly half of the 350,000 miles of

cable that spanned the globe and also ran around 130 of the permanent wireless circuits. As in accordance with the Official Secrets Act, the company, like other cable operators, had been compelled to supply copies of all the communications' traffic to the government for investigation by GC&CS.

Another covert operation performed by Electra House, Embankment, concerned secret conduits laid to the building from the **CENTRAL TELEGRAPH EXCHANGE, 72 FORE STREET, MOORGATE [164•11]**. These monitored the telephone lines of every foreign embassy in London. If the Moorgate site was damaged, Electra House, Embankment, had sensors to take over. A third entity, and much more important, made up SOE - a guerrilla research warfare unit established by the War Office in 1938 known as Military Intelligence Research (MI(R)), a small effort within a section known as General Staff (Research) (GS[R]). Section D, Department EH, which had its own first class intelligence section, and General Staff all had ties to each other before the formation of the SOE.

GPO/BT building - (telegraph) - once the MI5 cable entry point to capture telephone communications

164•11

72 Fore Street, Moorgate

EMERGENCE OF THE POLITICAL WARFARE EXECUTIVE - PWE

SOE's early propaganda wing, known by the designation SO1, was boosted by Department EH staffers and eventually turned over to a new and emerging body called the Political Warfare Executive (PWE) established in 1941.

This powerful organisation was heavily involved in radio propaganda and created several clandestine and bogus radio stations. This left SOE to focus on active subterfuge operations.

The PWE would eventually absorb SO1 and other elements associated with black propaganda, including the Joint Broadcasting Committee (JBC) which was formed shortly before the start of WWII. The JBC, which had an MI6 liaison, was based at **71 CHESTER SQUARE [165•42]**. Until SOE's formation it transmitted a variety of disinformation to Germany via a series of radio posts presumably set up by MI6 agents in Europe.

Electra House, 84 Moorgate
The intelligence section EH was but one of three elements that made up the SOE

163•08

PWE broadcaster Sefton Delmer

Eye Spy Intelligence Magazine

143

165•42

Home to the short-lived Joint Broadcasting Committee

169•62

9 KINGSWAY

71 Chester Square

Ingersoll House, 7-9 Kingsway

Like several MI6 fronts - the PWE's London headquarters was at Bush House. Broadcasts were sent out across Europe, many included factual information to mask that of a subversive nature. One leading figure recruited by the PWE from the BBC was German-born British journalist Sefton Delmer. He was fluent in German and before the war had actually interviewed Adolf Hitler. Delmer's broadcasts infuriated the Nazis and he was placed on a 'most wanted' list. Delmer lived at 12 Arlington Street which has been demolished. However, across from this address is the **BLUE POSTS PUBLIC HOUSE, 6 BENNETT STREET [166•42]** where PWE staffers met and discussed operations.

A leading official drafted into the PWE was Ivonne Kirkpatrick. An experienced diplomat formerly based in Berlin, he understood the German mindset. Kirkpatrick, who also worked for the BBC, lived at **160 CRANMER COURT [167•44]**.

Another important PWE man was Richard Crossman who headed the German Section. He produced anti-Nazi radio broadcasts for Radio of the European Revolution - an SOE front. Crossman lived at **9 VINCENT SQUARE [168•42]**.

Though the organisation occupied the entire three upper floors of Bush House, so big was the PWE that some of its directorates were housed in nearby buildings including **INGERSOLL HOUSE, 7-9 KINGSWAY [169•62]**. This location is but 100ft away. In our later researches we discovered it was connected to a most

PWE official Ivone Kirkpatrick

© IMPERIAL WAR MUSEUM

144

Eye Spy Intelligence Magazine

FITZMAURICE PLACE W1
CITY OF WESTMINSTER

170•55

2 Fitzmaurice Place

fascinating underground complex operated by MI6 **(See Site 248•62)**.

At **2 FITZMAURICE PLACE** near **BERKELEY SQUARE [170•55]**, the PWE based its important military section. Major elements of its controlling office were moved to the historic **WOBURN ABBEY**, **BEDFORDSHIRE [171•99]**, about one hour's drive from the capital. Here the focus was indeed on intelligence operations. MI6 officer Bruce Lockhart would later become its Director-General. When operational in London, Lockhart lived and worked from an apartment at **78 MARGARET STREET [172•55]**. The Admiralty played a central role in securing premises for the PWE. After Woburn Abbey the **BANKRUPTCY BUILDINGS, CAREY STREET [173•62]** were soon acquired - here more PWE officers were housed.

The original template for the PWE was Britain's WWI propaganda organisation Crewe House **(See Site 076•55)** and its primary aim was to damage enemy morale. Securing the services of a plethora of skilled intelligence officials, media experts, military and political thinkers, the PWE expanded its operations and added a Central Intelligence Directorate and a Central Planning Section. Working closely with the BBC and other ministries, the organisation used the airwaves to distribute information. Leaflet drops containing all manner of false stories and disinformation were carried out and intended to confuse the Germans.

PWE's cover name was the Political Intelligence Department, though its staffers - called 'Peewits' by those in

Woburn Abbey

171•99

In WWII Woburn Abbey was used as a central intelligence hub to deliver propaganda across Europe. It was a key site staffed by members of the PWE, Ministry of Information, MI6 and the SOE

© CHRIS NYBERG

Eye Spy Intelligence Magazine

172•55 **78 Margaret Street**

174•62

The Seven Stars,
53 Carey Street

© BASHER EYRE

An interesting, and perhaps revealing wartime drawing of Brendan Bracken released by the National Archives. Bracken was Minister of Information and an important organiser in Britain's propaganda war with Germany. George Orwell worked in his department

the intelligence world, would often used the phrase 'Pee Wee'. A popular meeting point for officials was the oldest public house in London - **SEVEN STARS, 53 CAREY STREET [174•62]**.

The work undertaken by the BBC's monitoring and listening section should not be underestimated. At **CAVERSHAM PARK, BERKSHIRE [175•99]**, the corporation listened to, recorded and transcribed one and a quarter million words everyday. This information was distributed accordingly to the intelligence, military and political offices of Britain.

Caversham was supplied much of its signals information from the corporation's important receiving station at **CROWSLEY PARK, OXFORDSHIRE [176•99]**, about three miles to the south.

At its headquarters in **PORTLAND PLACE [177•55]** similar liaisons were formed and developed. As for the PWE, Andrew Roberts who wrote the

146

Eye Spy Intelligence Magazine

167•44

160 Cranmer Court

166•42

The Blue Posts, 6 Bennett Street

168•42

9 Vincent Square

Bankruptcy Court, Carey Street

introduction to David Garnett's excellent *The Secret History of the PWE* said: "Sir Winston Churchill once said that in war the truth needed to be protected by a 'bodyguard of lies'. This is the story of the men and women who constituted that bodyguard."

MI6 also ran confusion operations in Europe, some performed by the Z Organisation. But it often found itself competing for resources with SOE. Relations between the organisations was fraught and bitterness occasionally ensued. MI6 was increasingly nervous about the high-grade intelligence acquired and returned to London from SOE operatives.

Another surprising location which helped British and American Intelligence confuse the Nazis, and also understand Hitler's own propaganda recordings, was the now famous

2008: Redevelopment of BBC headquarters, Portland Place, London begins. The BBC is the biggest provider of open source intelligence to British Intelligence. Its broadcasts are certainly utilised by foreign intelligence services

Portland Place

148   Eye Spy Intelligence Magazine

SPY SITES OF LONDON

178·22

Abbey Road Studios, 3 Abbey Road

Roundell Palmer replaced Hugh Dalton on the PWE committee. From 1942-1945 he served as Minister of Economic Warfare

"In war the truth needed to be protected by a bodyguard of lies..."
Winston Churchill

Eye Spy Intelligence Magazine

149

SPY SITES OF LONDON
Caversham Park

175•99

The BBC listened to, recorded and transcribed a million and a quarter words a day in thirty languages, all of which were translated into English...

recording studio - **ABBEY ROAD STUDIOS, 3 ABBEY ROAD [178•22]** in St John's Wood. Built in 1831, the building was purchased in 1929 by emerging recording house EMI.

Abbey Road is a must-visit location made famous by the Beatles, and few people have not seen the iconic photo of the Liverpool band as they walked across the zebra crossing. However, in World War Two highly skilled technicians and music specialists at the studio played their part in defeating Germany.

1942. Glenn Miller receives a gold award for his track - *Chattanooga Choo Choo*

180•62

Lyceum Tavern, 354 Strand

Aldwych Theatre

179•62

150

Eye Spy Intelligence Magazine

Several key propaganda recordings were made here on behalf of the government's PWE and other likewise organisations, but workers also gave their opinion on the quality of German tapes. MI6 puzzled over how Hitler could one day deliver a speech from northern Germany, and just hours later be heard talking in the south. It soon became clear Berlin was producing pre-recorded lectures which made pin-pointing his real location problematic, as of course, London never gave up on the possibility of finding and eliminating him.

Little public information exists about the identity of the main British propaganda players who were attached to the studio, but great wartime stars like American forces band leader Glenn Miller recorded here.

Crowsley Park
176•99
© SHAUN FERGUSON

A BLOW TO MORALE

An Air Ministry building near the popular **ALDWYCH THEATRE [179•62]** hosted the vitally important headquarters of Her Majesty's Stationary Office (HMSO). Here a dedicated team of intelligence propaganda specialists supplied by Bush House, worked tirelessly on the posters which adorned thousands of buildings across the UK; from anti-Nazi works to other memorable posters warning citizens of German spies and that simple, but iconic message - *'Keep Calm and Carry On'*. That message became even more important when a V1 missile struck the area damaging various buildings, including the Aldwych Theatre which had its facade blown away. Poster production was affected - so too staff recreational visits to the theatre.

However, a popular pub frequented by the many intelligence staffers working in the area - the **LYCEUM TAVERN, 354 STRAND [180•62]** was not damaged. If only walls could talk!

Posters produced by HMSO - some warning of German spies

Eye Spy Intelligence Magazine

151

Aldwych Theatre
In 1944 a V1 cruise missile struck the area badly damaging the theatre's splendid facade

SPY SITES OF LONDON

VIII
A Very Dirty Business
The Irregulars - Throwing Away the Rule Book

As we have learned, the Special Operations Executive's first headquarters was on Caxton Street, within St. Ermin's Hotel. As the SOE grew, its operations became more frequent - and officials recognised its need for more central London office space. However, those charged with liaison between MI6 and the SOE sensed growing animosity, the latter having performed brilliantly and bravely against Nazi forces occupying Europe.

On 31 October 1941, the organisation moved to a permanent residence at **64 BAKER STREET** [181•55]. Agents and personnel were called 'Baker Street Irregulars' after the group of boys who helped the fictional detective Sherlock Holmes. He too 'resided' in the same street. And of course, visitors to London will find the **SHERLOCK HOLMES MUSEUM** on **BAKER STREET** [182•15]. The SOE was also known as 'The Old Firm', 'The Racket' and 'The Baker Street Boys'.

At **BAKER STREET STATION** [183•15] visitors can find artwork reflecting the site's ties to the legendary detective - here colourful tiles sporting a pipe-smoking silhouette of Holmes adorn the walls. More sombre, however, is the Baker Street Memorial to former train employees who fought and died in WWI.

The foyer inside St. Ermin's Hotel

THE RAPID GROWTH OF SOE

SOE was fronted by a cover agency known as the Inter-Services Research Bureau. Agent training, interviews, debriefing etc. were conducted at country houses referred to as Stations. Other sites were used for research and equipment production. Here all manner of devices were made, including instruments for sabotage, espionage and false documentation. Some stations were dedicated to wireless transmissions, all of which left MI6 annoyed. It didn't help either that SOE was attracting the very best agents and increasing its staffing levels that would dwarf its established cousin. At its height, SOE had a staggering 10,000 employees of which 3,000 were field agents and support staff. This, in comparison to MI6 whose numbers were still in the hundreds.

Interestingly, the term 'Station' was to become an accepted part of CIA and MI6 terminology (CIA Field Station, for example).

RELOCATION, DISTRIBUTION AND AGENT TRAINING

SOE's huge staff had outgrown number 64, and soon offices and flats at **82 BAKER STREET (ST MICHAEL'S HOUSE)** [184•55], and **83 BAKER STREET (NORGEBY HOUSE)** [185•55] were acquired. In

SPY SITES OF LONDON

64 Baker Street
SOE headquarters

Baker Street Station WWI memorial to employees who died in the service of their country

Sherlock Holmes Museum, Baker Street

Sherlock Holmes tiles in Baker Street Station

SPY SITES OF LONDON

183•15

Baker Street Station

later years, some parts of the buildings would be used by MI5 and MI6.

By 1943, SOE was so large it consumed another slice of a major building - this time the nearby **MONTAGU MANSIONS [186•55]**.

After the war, intelligence researchers discovered that SOE had occupied much of **BICKENHALL MANSIONS [187•55]**.

The SOE's Scandinavian sections were located at **CHILTERN COURT, BAKER STREET [188•55]**, and for SOE operatives enroute to Europe, many stayed briefly at Berkeley Court in Glentworth Street close to the Baker Street headquarters.

In the British countryside, SOE had several training houses and special sites used to manufacture a wide variety of equipment - much of it used for undercover operations. In London, one its technical sections was located at **221 BAKER STREET [189•15]**. Here special garments were made by the clothing branch, while other stations forged documents, created new identities, special weapons and tested gadgets and so on. Explosive specialists at **35 PORTLAND PLACE [190•55]** designed ingenious bombs while at **20 CRANLEY PLACE [191•47]** SOE ran a safe house for its agents - later used by MI6.

Besides British agents, the SOE realised that it was essential to use foreign nationals who had a far better

184•55
82 Baker Street
(St. Michael's House)

Eye Spy Intelligence Magazine

155

SPY SITES OF LONDON

83 Baker Street
(Norgeby House)

185•55

192•55

Orchard Court, Portman Square

understanding of their respective countries in relation to language, terrain, transport and customs. Henceforth the SOE established training centres across London. Many of these locations still exist today.

SOE was made up of several sections. For example, Section F, which occupied premises in **ORCHARD COURT, PORTMAN SQUARE [192•55]**, made contact with and subsequently trained new recruits for operations in France. One of its leading operatives was Vera Atkins - described as the "heart of F," by a British intelligence official. Many agents spoke French (though not all were natives) and had some connection to France. All were incredibly brave - save one who decided to disappear with three million French Francs intended to pay for operations by the SOE. After the war Atkins searched Europe in an effort to find out what had happened to many of her missing colleagues - some who were already dead. When training in London, Atkins used a former MI6 safe house at **NELL GWYNN HOUSE, SLOANE AVENUE [193•44]**.

A fascinating SOE branch was based at **56 QUEEN'S GATE [194•47]** and **TREVOR SQUARE [195•47]** which housed the Camouflage Department Workshop. It would later relocate to concealed rooms on the ground floor of the **NATURAL HISTORY MUSEUM, 26 CROMWELL ROAD [196•46]**. Two other sections were based here: the Demonstration Room and Station XVb (SOE exhibitions).

Just as interesting, we learned that the bus stop directly outside the museum was another pick-up point for MI5 operatives travelling to locations across the city. Special buses would take dozens of female staffers to its Wormwood Scrubs headquarters.

A NEST OF ALLIED SPIES

A proliferation of other WWII intelligence sites can be found in the Belgravia area. **18B EBURY STREET [197•42]** reportedly housed an MI6-OSS (USA - Office of Strategic Services) liaison unit known as X-2. Further down the street at **22A EBURY STREET [198•42]**, a young Ian Fleming resided, and before him, the previous occupant was Sir Oswald Mosley of the British Union of Fascists!

156   Eye Spy Intelligence Magazine

186•55
Montagu Mansions

194•47
56 Queen's Gate

188•55
Chiltern Court, Baker Street

SPY SITES OF LONDON

187•55
Bickenhall Mansions

(The BUF's headquarters at 1 Sanctuary Buildings were always under surveillance by MI5). 22A was also used as an overflow residence when the nearby Ebury Court Hotel at **26 EBURY STREET [199•42]** (now Tophams Hotel) was fully occupied. During WWII all manner of intelligence figures stayed in the hotel which was recommended (and probably staffed or monitored) by operatives from MI6 and the SOE.

At the impressive **140 PARK LANE [200•55]**, SOE ran another element

190•55
35 Portland Place

221 Baker Street

Trevor Square

dedicated to obtaining intelligence in Holland. However, there were a multitude of errors and many Dutch SOE agents were captured and executed. For the Germans it was an intelligence treasure trove and in later years several books outlined this intelligence debacle - including one titled *Error of Judgement: SOE's Disaster in the Netherlands, 1941-1944*. There were warnings from MI6 that the SOE's Dutch network had been compromised, but these were seemingly ignored.

That a further warning from a senior cypher clerk working for a certain Leopold Samuel Marks was also dismissed, was nothing short of appalling. Marks was one of the UK's most brilliant cryptographers who went on to write the best-selling book *Between Silk and Cyanide*. The son of an antiquarian bookseller in London, he was introduced to the world of intelligence inadvertently by his father, when he deciphered the bookshop's unusual (and most puzzling) price coding.

Marks joined the armed forces and went to Bedford to train as a cryptographer. Soon after he took an exam at Bletchley Park where he was judged to have failed. Unbeknown to examiners, while other students used code books

20 Cranley Place
SOE safe house. Later acquired and used for a number of years by MI6

View down Portman Square

Nell Gwynn House, Sloane Avenue

SOE agent Vera Atkins

to help - Marks simply used his brain. Thereafter he joined the SOE and went on to help organise agent training and operations. Installed as head of SOE's codes and ciphers, Marks commanded a staff of 400 and briefed many agents personally before they embarked on their mission. One such SOE agent was the legendary Indian-born Noor Inayat Khan - agent codename Madeleine. She was caught and paid with her life at the dreadful Dachau concentration camp in 1944. She wasn't the only female SOE agent to die as history records.

Marks is still affectionately referred to by former Bletchley Park codebreakers as 'the one that got away'. Sadly, his father's bookshop where he first learned of the significance of codes - **84 CHARING CROSS ROAD [201•62]**, has long since closed - replaced by a modern restaurant. However, his work for SOE and the wider intelligence community will never be forgotten. Today, Marks' book remains the best selling of all titles in Bletchley Park's museum shop. As for the SOE operation in Holland, one of Marks' men said that he believed all the radios used by SOE's Dutch agents were "under German control." MI5 investigated, and concluded nothing was amiss - but they were wrong and many lives were lost.

THE RECRUITING HOUSE

It's strange to imagine that a number of SOE and MI6 sites used in WWII remain unidentified. Some undoubtedly will be revealed in time, probably through Freedom of Information Act (FOIA) requests or Britain's 50 Year Secrecy Rule (which can be extended indefinitely depending on the nature of the information you are trying to obtain). One impressive building that we know was once occupied by British Intelligence sits on the corner of Northumberland Avenue, a stone's throw from Parliament and amidst other government buildings.

Once upon a time **ROOM 238** in the **VICTORIA HOTEL, NORTHUMBERLAND AVENUE [202•62]** housed senior SOE recruiters who definitely didn't conform to regular military recruiting methods. Here prospective candidates were interviewed in the

160

Eye Spy Intelligence Magazine

SPY SITES OF LONDON

196•46

Natural History Museum, 26 Cromwell Road

The MI5 'bus stop' outside the Natural History Museum

hope that they would be selected to perform dangerous missions in France and the wider European theatre. It was but one of a number of SOE safe houses. Some authors have suggested that until recently the building, now called Nigeria House and hosting the Nigerian Embassy and High Commission, was still used by the British intelligence community to conduct interviews!

199•42

197•42

18B Ebury Street

Ebury Court Hotel (Tophams), 26 Ebury Street

Eye Spy Intelligence Magazine 161

SPY SITES OF LONDON

201•62
84 Charing Cross Road
Site of the famous Marks and Company bookshop

NOT SUCH A GENTLE TOUCH

That SOE agents from different countries are still being remembered and celebrated is testimony to their astonishing bravery.

One female agent born in Paris in 1921, but raised in London, was Violette Bushell Szabo. She was brought up in her family home in **BURNLEY ROAD, STOCKWELL [203•49]**.

198•42
22A Ebury Street

Photograph taken by Steve Crook of the great Leo Marks at the opening of the Violette Szabo Museum in Wormelow, Hertfordshire in 2000

Szabo's father was killed in October 1942, at the Battle of El Alamein. At the time she was selling perfume behind a shop counter, but her father's death prompted her to apply for a post with the SOE, where she was probably interviewed in the Victoria Hotel. However, Szabo suffered an injury during training and

162

Eye Spy Intelligence Magazine

SPY SITES OF LONDON

200•55

140 Park Lane
SOE Dutch units were based here

had to wait until late 1944 for a chance to use her skills. Codenamed Louise, and on just her second mission, Szabo was quickly captured. During her subsequent captivity she was interrogated, tortured and then finally executed on or about 5 February 1945 at Ravensbruck concentration camp (female inmates numbered over 90,000). It had been a miserable experience for the young lady. Three other SOE female agents were shot at this camp: Denise Bloch, Cecily Lefort and Lilian Rolfe.

In 2001, a mural featuring various notable people was opened in Stockwell, now known as the Stockwell Memorial Gardens **(See Site 252•25)**. Szabo appears alongside the likes of Vincent Van Gogh and perhaps more poignantly, James Bond! In 2008, a splendid bronze bust honouring Szabo was also unveiled on the **ALBERT EMBANKMENT [204•23]**.

205•62

Princess Anne unveils Noor Khan's memorial sculpture in 2012 at Gordon Square Gardens

Noor Inayat Khan

163
Eye Spy Intelligence Magazine

202•62

203•49

Former Victoria Hotel, Northumberland Avenue
SOE recruiting centre

Burnley Road, Stockwell

Gordon Square Gardens, Bloomsbury

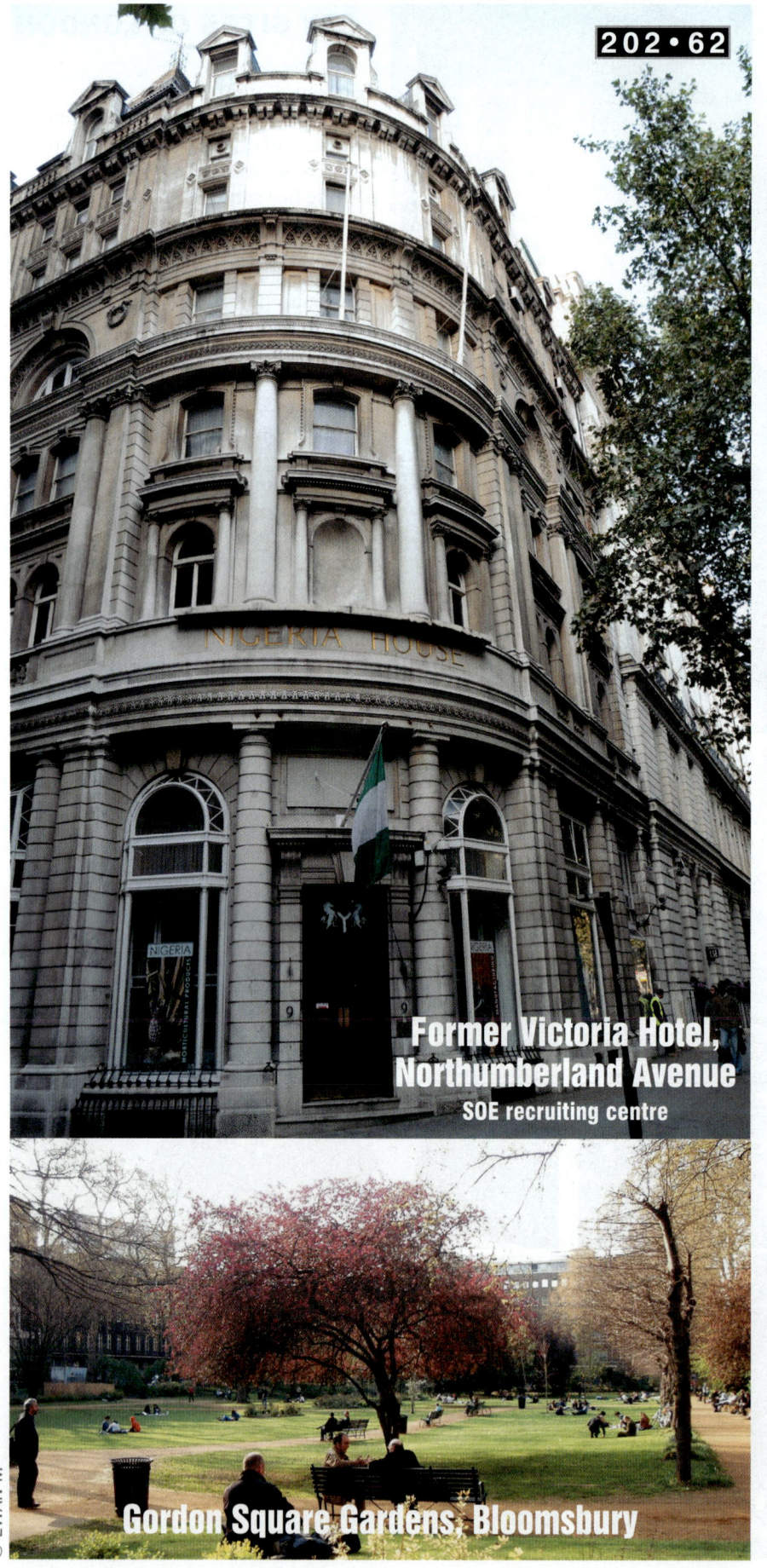

Four years later Noor Inayat Khan, was also honoured. A splendid sculpture was unveiled in **GORDON SQUARE GARDENS, BLOOMSBURY [205•62]** by Princess Anne - close to the Bloomsbury house where she lived as a child. The agent, who operated in the Phono spy network in Europe, was posthumously awarded the George Cross for revealing nothing to her Gestapo interrogators, this despite ten months of torture. For the record, Khan was the first female radio operator for the SOE in France.

Whilst non-operational in London, two popular destinations for the SOE (men and women) were the **CAFE DE PARIS, 25 COVENTRY STREET, PICCADILLY [206•55]** and the **TURF CLUB, BENNETT STREET, PICCADILLY [207•42]**. Here they could enjoy a cabaret and a good meal. The Cafe de Paris venue is still open today and has recently celebrated its 90th anniversary. However, the Turf Club relocated to 5 Carlton House Terrace in 1965.

SOE Memorial, Albert Embankment

Below: Actress Virginia McKenna (seated) at the opening of the Stockwell Mural

Left: This monument sits on Albert Embankment, River Thames (opposite MI5 HQ) and honours the brave men and women from various nations who served with the SOE during WWII. The statue features SOE agent Violette Szabo who was captured and executed by the Nazis. She revealed nothing during her ordeal

© STEVE CROOK of www.powell-pressburger.org

Some 55 senior female agents were employed and used by SOE - 13 in total lost their lives.

THE WHITE MOUSE

Nancy Wake is another legendary SOE female agent. After operating as a courier for the French Resistance, becoming the Nazis most wanted operative, she left France for the UK. She lived at the **STAFFORD HOTEL 16-18 ST JAMES'S PLACE [208•42]** which at the time was used by British and American military forces. Thereafter she returned to France and led a significant Maquisards force in multiple operations along with Vera Atkins.

After the war she continued to work with British Air Intelligence up until 1957. In the 1960s the Australian-born Wake departed the UK for her native country. However, in 2001 she returned to England and took up permanent residence at one of her old haunts... the Stafford Hotel!

Nancy died in 2011, aged 98, and her ashes were scattered in France where she performed so bravely during the war. In the intelligence world she will always be remembered by her codename - The White Mouse.

The contribution made by women of many nations to the Allied war effort was significant. From munitions girls, to supply pilots and land girls, their role was recognised in 2005, when **THE WOMEN OF WORLD WAR II MEMORIAL, WHITEHALL [209•42]** was dedicated. Seventeen individual sets of clothing and uniforms symbolise the hundreds of jobs women performed during the war. The actual type face used in the statue replicates that found in wartime ration books.

Eye Spy Intelligence Magazine

Violette Szabo   Denise Bloch   Lilian Rolfe   Cecily Lefort

Ravensbruck female concentration camp

206•55

Cafe de Paris, 25 Coventry Street

Eye Spy Intelligence Magazine

Nancy Wake

208•42
Stafford Hotel,
16-18 St James's Place

207•42
Turf Club, Bennett Street
(Former location)

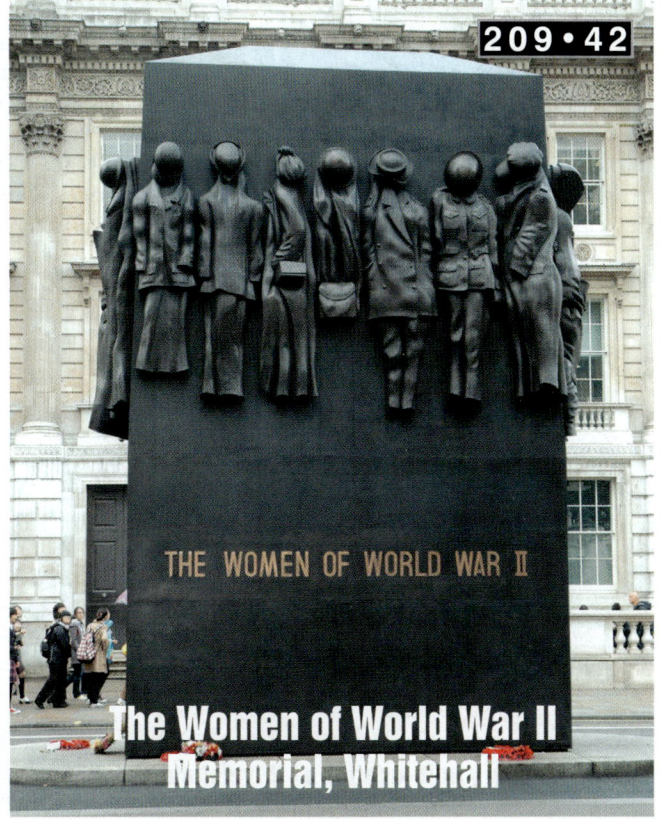

209•42
THE WOMEN OF WORLD WAR II
The Women of World War II
Memorial, Whitehall

Eye Spy Intelligence Magazine 167

Naval Intelligence Chief - John Henry Godfrey

36 Curzon Street

THE STAY BEHIND OPERATIONS

Winston Churchill may have displayed a fearless public face, but at the beginning of the war he recognised that there was a very real chance of invasion.

The SOE was born and evolved from a number of ideas, one of which was to create Auxiliary Units - a resistance-type organisation that would operate in the UK disrupting and striking at every opportunity in what could be described as guerrilla warfare.

One man involved with early planning was military intelligence man Peter Fleming, the elder brother of MI6 and Naval Intelligence Division officer and future author Ian. Some 3,500 operatives were trained for future local defence operations.

As the war progressed, the term 'stay behind' was also attached to overseas operations, in this case SOE and resistance fighters volunteering to remain in place in the most difficult of circumstances. One top secret operation that was a tri NID-SOE-MI6 affair concerned the strategically important location of the Rock of Gibraltar. The peninsula on the edge of neutral Spain was used as a vital base by British Intelligence to monitor shipping in the Mediterranean Sea. It was also an excellent location in helping to place agents in Europe and Africa. There was every reason to believe it would fall into the hands of the Germans, especially after British Intelligence learned of Berlin's Operation Felix - a plan to capture the Rock. Thus the Director of Naval Intelligence, Rear Admiral John Henry

© GAIUS CORNELIUS

An Auxiliary unit location at Wivelsfield showing the emergency exit

Bruce Cooper pictured with researcher Martin Nuza revisits the MI6-NID stay behind cave

Eye Spy Intelligence Magazine

Bruce Cooper pictured with researchers Martin Nuza and Jim Crone

Dr Bruce Cooper's family in the MI6-NID radio room

Rock of Gibraltar

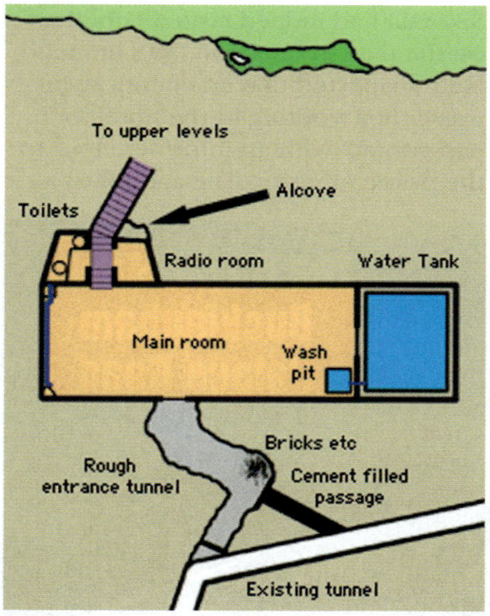

Dr Bruce Cooper pictured in 1942. This wartime hero died in 2010 aged 96

Godfrey, came up with a ruse that in the event of German capture, a team of communications specialists would remain on the Rock in a secret cave and radio intelligence back to London for as long as possible.

The planning for the mission took place at **36 CURZON STREET, MAYFAIR [210•55]**, the home of Godfrey. Senior MI6 officials arrived at the residence and a plan to build the stay behind cave, codenamed - Operation Tracer - was developed.

One brave officer who volunteered was Dr Bruce Cooper. He duly arrived at the British outpost with colleagues in 1942. The cave was chosen and equipment and supplies installed. But with pressure mounting against German forces on the Eastern Front, the threat of an attack diminished, and Tracer never went operational. However, similar stay behind operations did take place across Europe.

As for Godfrey, one of his best friends was Ian Fleming. There are many real intelligence people who Fleming is said to have based his Bond film characters on, including - 'M' (agent Bond's MI6 superior). Godfrey was Fleming's senior commander in the Naval Intelligence Division and commenting on media suggestions it was he who the 'M' character was fashioned on, Godfrey replied: "Fleming turned me into that unsavoury character 'M'."

Eye Spy Intelligence Magazine

169

SPY SITES OF LONDON

Photograph showing proximity of Rubens Hotel (right) to the Royal Mews opposite

Wladyslaw Sikorski

MYSTERY OF THE GIBRALTAR AIR CRASH AND LONDON PHONE CALL

Another visitor to Gibraltar in July 1943, was Wladyslaw Sikorski, Prime Minister (in exile) of Poland. He was on a stop-over enroute to England after visiting Polish troops in Cairo, Egypt. Seconds after taking off on the final leg of his journey, his Liberator II aircraft crashed into the harbour. Many intelligence experts believed the crash was not an accident, and few can explain why a number of bodies, including that of his daughter, had simply disappeared from the wreckage. But there was skulduggery afoot.

Sikorski, together with his Polish Government-in-exile was of course based at the Rubens Hotel in London **(See Site 019•42)**.

MI5 began its own probe and discovered that six weeks *prior* to the incident, a receptionist had received a telephone call from an unidentified caller saying Sikorski had been involved in an aeroplane crash in Gibraltar. Officials could not say if this was a prank, warning or simply a bizarre coincidence. Nevertheless, Sikorski had indeed visited Gibraltar on the date in question. MI5 immediately suspected that an enemy agent was either working in the hotel, or had contact with an informer close to the prime minister. The agent was

211•42

The Royal Mews, Buckingham Palace Road

170

Eye Spy Intelligence Magazine

Memorial to the Polish service personnel who were executed on Stalin's orders at Katyn and elsewhere

simply "over enthusiastic" according to our sources. The Service secretly sent a small unit under cover to the hotel to establish if anyone was connected to the crash.

MI5 had further reason to investigate Sikorski's death with the utmost urgency, for directly across the road from the Ruben's Hotel is the **ROYAL MEWS, BUCKINGHAM PALACE ROAD [211•42]**. This important location, which falls under the jurisdiction of the Lord Chamberlain's Office, provides transport for the Queen and the Royal Family. And we are not just referring to the horse-drawn carriage. The Palace's motor vehicle pool is also serviced here; and vehicles are despatched to collect foreign dignitaries from their residences and take them to their destinations. MI5, according to our sources, hurriedly established a team of Watchers at the location to monitor all comings and goings, and almost certainly embedded its own personnel. Above the Mews lived coachmen, drivers, service staff, grooms and essential workers. Together with officers engaged in the investigation at the hotel, MI5's presence seemed to indicate that it was seriously considering the politically sensitive event in Gibraltar was not an accident.

The suggestion is of course, that Sikorski's itinerary was deliberately leaked or secured in an underhand fashion by someone employed either at the hotel or Royal Mews; or that it was given to a third party. The information then found its way to a country opposed to his leadership. And immediately some intelligence men from both MI5 and MI6 suspected Russia.

If the aeroplane crash was sabotage, what had Sikorski or his exiled government done that provoked such a response? The answer probably lay buried thousands of miles away in the Katyn Forest. In 1943, German forces discovered the graves of an astonishing 22,000 Polish troops, many from an elite corp and intelligence officials

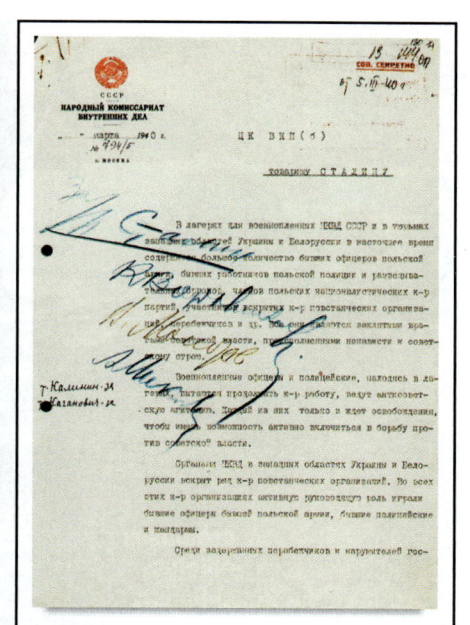

TOP SECRET: Letter to Stalin which resulted in the appalling execution of 22,000 Polish troops. German forces found the mass grave at Katyn and soon the Nazi propaganda machine went into overdrive - even producing posters such as this one announcing the *'Forest of the Dead at Katyn'*. Sikorski's own spy agency also informed him of Stalin's guilt

who had been captured by the Russians when Moscow invaded Poland on 17 September 1939, this as part of the German-Russia Molotov-Ribbentrop non-aggression Pact. By now of course, Germany was fighting Russia and when Berlin announced the discovery of the mass grave, and gave details of the manner in which

Eye Spy Intelligence Magazine

The Royal Mews organises and services vehicles used by the Royal Family and dignitaries

Portland Place
Wladyslaw Sikorski Statue

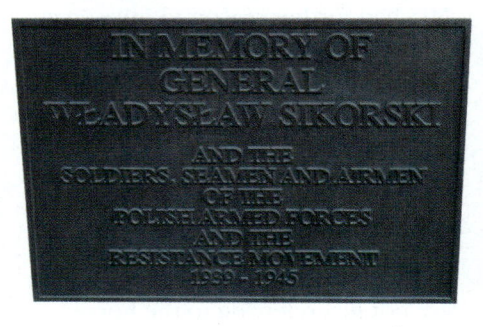

Embassy of Poland, 47 Portland Place

the Polish troops had been killed, there was a real furore.

Moscow blamed the Nazis, and its stance would continue for decades until the 1990s when Russia acknowledged its involvement. A top secret document written by Soviet police chief Lavrenty Beria was discovered dated 1940. Addressed to Stalin, he proposed the execution of Polish prisoners of war. Stalin agreed and the Katyn executions began.

Back in London - April 1943, Sikorski knew the truth and pointed an accusing finger at Stalin. This all happened at a delicate stage of the war, with Russia's Red Army at last managing to push the German Army back a little. Nevertheless, at the Rubens Hotel, a furious Sikorski and the Polish Government held audiences with a plethora of political officials and his own intelligence chiefs who retained good contacts with the Polish underground, some of whom were fighting with Station 43 - the Polish SOE element.

In the end the Poles demanded that the International Red Cross be allowed to investigate the crime. At this very moment Stalin severed all relations with the Polish Government. The political situation was spiralling out of British control, especially because Churchill had been obligated to declare war on Germany by the Polish-British Common Defence Pact.

Some historians admit that the best way the matter could be quickly resolved, was by removing the man at the centre of the mess - Sikorski, who quite rightly wanted to find out the truth. If MI5 did locate anything untoward - a security breach or similar, this still remains archived and under lock and key. MI5 has released but a paucity of material connected to the crash, leaving intelligence and military historians alike quite puzzled.

As for the cause of his death, this has never been ascertained. However, a memorial plaque on Gibraltar uses the phrase *'mysterious accident'* in relation to the aeroplane crash. This in itself is probably a good enough clue to what caused his demise - many intelligence people believe he was assassinated. Indeed, an official declassified letter released in 1969, to Cabinet official Sir Burke Trend from Sir Robin Cooper, another Cabinet man and former pilot, says: *'Security at Gibraltar was casual, and a number of opportunities for sabotage arose while the aircraft was there'*. Cooper didn't or would not say if he believed Sikorski was murdered, but whilst dismissing British involvement,

SPY SITES OF LONDON

A very revealing clue on this memorial to Sikorski in Gibraltar. Polish and UK intel ties remained remarkably strong, despite the incident on Gibraltar

Churchill and Sikorski (far left)

he did say, "the possibility of his murder by persons unknown cannot be excluded." And there is no reference whatsoever to intelligence supplied by MI6. The Service discovered that Sikorski's aeroplane was parked alongside a Russian aircraft on Gibraltar carrying the person of Soviet Ambassador Maisky and a few officials who were guarded by a small Russian Army delegation.

Perhaps more relevant, MI6 man and KGB agent Kim Philby was in overall charge of intelligence happenings in a region that included Gibraltar. He would have been fully informed of Sikorski's journey. The incident remains one of the greatest mysteries of World War Two.

A statue of Sikorski was erected in PORTLAND PLACE [212•55] close to the country's embassy. It was unveiled by the Duke of Kent in 2000. A memorial to the victims of the Katyn massacre can also be found at Cannock Chase in Staffordshire.

All of Poland's armed forces in exile were headquartered or represented in London. For example, from 1939-1945, **28 WIMPOLE STREET** [213•55] was the headquarters of the Polish Navy which had an important naval intelligence liaison section. Interestingly, its address today is shown as **51 NEW CAVENDISH STREET** [214•55], which is indicative of the post-war renumbering of addresses. This is just around the corner from what is today's 28 Wimpole Street.

Another clue to why so many researchers remain confused is because right next to the original naval headquarters is a hand-written sign declaring 30B Wimpole Street! Little wonder there was a sigh of relief when in 2013, a plaque was affixed by the Polish Heritage Society UK on the real building declaring it hosted the Polish Navy during the war.

Following Germany's conquest of mainland Europe, many governments like Poland, decided to establish their base of operations in London. Most had an intelligence element which would prove invaluable in future years. Some of these are examined next.

For MI5 and MI6, such venues provided an intelligence windfall, but they also proved problematic, as many organisations were very nationalistic.

Today's 28 Wimpole Street did not host the Polish Navy headquarters in London as some researchers believe - or did it?

28 Wimpole Street

Eye Spy Intelligence Magazine

173

214 • 55

51 New Cavendish Street

THIS BUILDING HOUSED THE HEADQUARTERS OF THE POLISH NAVY DURING 1939-1945

SOE

THE IMAGINATION AND GENIUS OF THE SOE LABORATORY

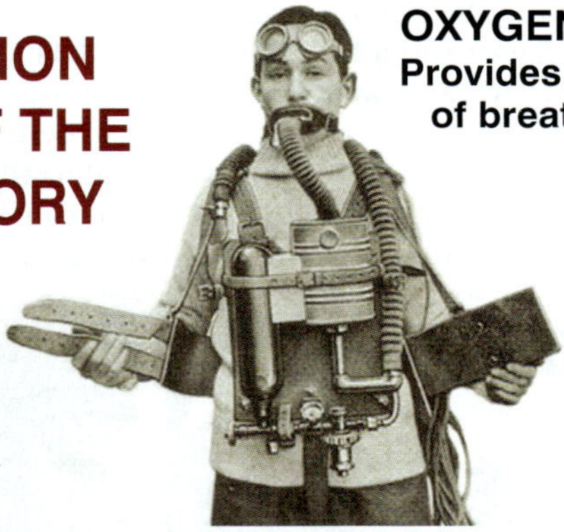

CROSSBOWS

'Little' and 'Big Joe'

OIL CAN BOMB

OXYGEN BOTTLE
Provides 90 minutes of breathing time

KEY WITH SECRET COMPARTMENT

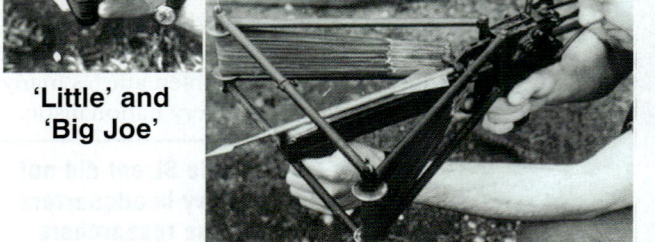

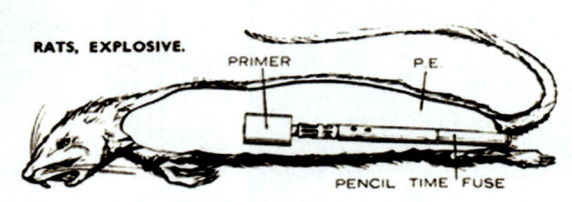

EXPLODING RAT

Eye Spy Intelligence Magazine

CHOCOLATE BOMB

The chocolate bomb was made of steel with a thin covering of real chocolate. When a piece was broken off, the canvas was revealed and pulled. After seven seconds delay the device detonated

FOOT PRINT DEVICE

Created specifically for a Far East SOE operation

WELROD 9MM FIREARM

Bolt-action suppressed firearm also used by the American OSS

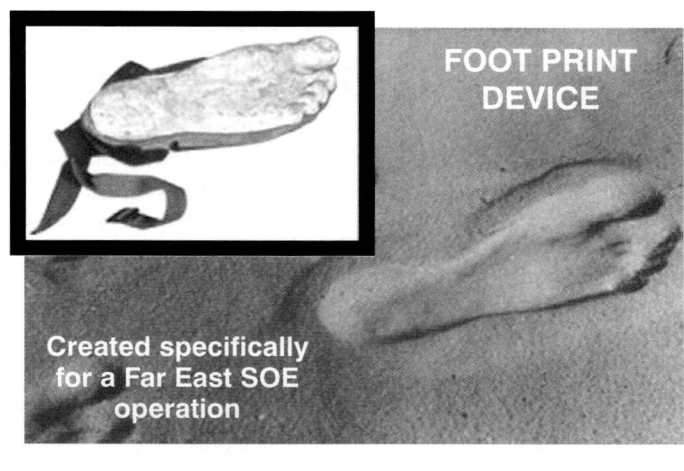

THE WELBIKE

Quickly assembled one-seater folding motorcycle - not a particular SOE favourite

BOOBY-TRAPPED CASE

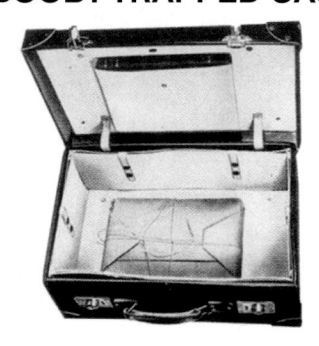

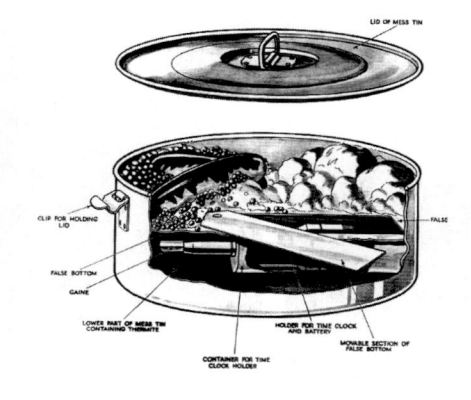

EXPLODING MESS TIN BOMB

PIPE PISTOL

Eye Spy Intelligence Magazine

SOE FORGERY SECTION

Agents operating in occupied Europe required proper documentation to travel and present if challenged. The SOE's Forgery Section had in its ranks some of the best counterfeiters in the world. This fake passport, perhaps created by a humorous staffer, shows Adolf Hitler. The red 'J' means the holder is Jewish, and note also the Government of Palestine stamp.

An agent shows a resistance fighter how to assemble a gun blindfolded

SOE AGENT TRAINING

SOE instructors show underground operatives how to fire a variety of weapons. This photo was taken in Warsaw, August 1944

German troops inspect a military train blown-up by an SOE-trained unit in Poland, April 1944

SOE agents attend a demolition class at Milton Hall, Peterborough, just one of many large estates used by the organisation

Eye Spy Intelligence Magazine

IX

SPY SITES OF LONDON

Exiles and Guests
London Homes for Friends in Need...

Poland was but one of a number of governments-in-exile from occupied nations which used residences in London to support their military and intelligence agencies during World War Two.

Belgium's Military Intelligence, for example, occupied **32 EATON SQUARE [215•42]**. This organisation had threads to both MI6 and the SOE and following the Allied invasion of Europe in 1944, its operatives were active behind enemy lines. So too the government of Holland which had managed to remove much of its main intelligence apparatus to London.

Following invasion, Queen Wilhelmina of Holland wanted to stay in the country to help bolster resistance. She was eventually forced to leave for Britain in May 1940. A few days later Holland surrendered and established its government at 77 **CHESTER SQUARE [216•42]**.

Naturally there were tensions between the monarchies, but after describing Hitler as the "arch enemy of mankind," and broadcasting to the Dutch people in a genuine effort to boost morale, Wilhelmina succeeded in gaining the respect of many people in

215•42

32 Eaton Square

Eye Spy Intelligence Magazine

SPY SITES OF LONDON

220•42

4 Carlton Gardens
The Free French headquarters of Charles de Gaulle occupied in 1940

GENERAL CHARLES DE GAULLE President of the French National Committee set up the Headquarters of the Free French Forces here in 1940

216•42

77 Chester Square

---

the UK and Holland. She herself eventually moved to a quiet residence in South Minns in bordering Hertfordshire - a decision which almost cost her life after a Luftwaffe bomber decided to target the small town.

Dutch citizens were particularly keen to help the war effort and many joined the SOE. But there were serious problems and the fear of infiltration evident in the minds of SOE controllers. Many agents were compromised and captured, leading to a degree of mistrust between Holland and Britain. For example, two agents, codenamed Sprout (Pieter Dourlein - Dutch Navy) and Chive (Johan Ubbink) were actually interrogated by MI5 following missions in Europe. MI5-SOE spycatcher Major Geoffrey Wethered believed Chive could have been a double agent and was arrested before Operation Overlord (the invasion of Europe). Dutch officials protested and a high-level meeting between intelligence officials took place at the

Queen Wilhelmina 1942

NEDERLANDERS

VOOR UW EER EN GEWETEN OP! - TEGEN HET BOLSJEWISME
DE WAFFEN SS ROEPT U!

SPY SITES OF LONDON

[218•43]

Brixton Prison

operations should fall within its remit. This proposal was rejected.

Agents Chive and Sprout on their return to England were immediately detained and taken under guard to **BRIXTON PRISON [218•43]**. Here they were locked up and interrogated by MI5. Both agents protested their innocence and advised MI5 that a security breach had occurred. They

Chester Street address. The actual government-in-exile address for the Netherlands was **STRATTON HOUSE, PICCADILLY [217•55]**.

The German Army recruited an estimated 25,000 Dutch citizens into several fighting forces, including the Waffen SS. This may have been the stimulus for some suspicion. It should again be noted, for a matter of record, the disastrous events surrounding SOE Dutch operations that led to the capture of more than 50 of its operatives. Many documents detailing this incredibly important moment have been lost, whilst others remain classified. The MI6 memo sent to the SOE warning that the Dutch SOE had been penetrated does still exist - so too SOE's negative response. MI6 thereafter were adamant that SOE

CITY OF WESTMINSTER — HEADQUARTERS OF THE NORWEGIAN GOVERNMENT-IN-EXILE LOCATED HERE 1940-1945 — ROYAL NORWEGIAN EMBASSY

[221•47]

Kingston House North, Prince's Gate

Eye Spy Intelligence Magazine

179

SPY SITES OF LONDON

Netherlands Government-in-exile headquarters

217•55

Stratton House, Piccadilly

GE ZIJT VRIJI
PIETER GERBRANDY PRIME MINISTER OF THE KINGDOM OF THE NETHERLANDS
5 MAY 1945

YOU ARE FREE!
FROM MAY 1940 UNTIL AUGUST 1945 THE NETHERLANDS GOVERNMENT FOUND REFUGE HERE IN STRATTON HOUSE

government-in-exile in Britain was France. Charles de Gaulle established the headquarters of the Free French at **3-4 CARLTON GARDENS [220•42]**, after his arrival in London in June 1940. The building nestled between UK government establishments and intelligence houses making it an ideal location.

More on the activities of the French exiles shortly.

THE SHETLAND BUS OPERATION

From 1941 until the end of the war, Norway's London-based SOE contingent ran the famous operation now known as the Shetland Bus, transporting agents to and from occupied Norway to Britain on fishing vessels. These dangerous missions were later supported by very fast submarine chasers.

The operation was headed by Leif Larsen and coordinated from the remote Lunna House on Shetland. Larsen himself participated in over 50 trips between Norway and Scotland. By the end of the war, the boat service had transported nearly 200 agents into the country and returned 73 to the safe shores of Scotland. Forty-four

pointed the finger of blame at a Major Bingham, head of the Dutch SOE element. This allegation was rejected by officials. Records show that of the 50 SOE agents sent to Holland, 43 were greeted by a waiting German guard. The history surrounding the Dutch SOE surely needs more research and openness.

Belgium too supplied its fair share of brave men and women to the SOE. Its main section operated from **6 BELGRAVE SQUARE [219•42]**. The best known and most powerful

Leif Larsen

© MARIT LARSEN

180

Eye Spy Intelligence Magazine

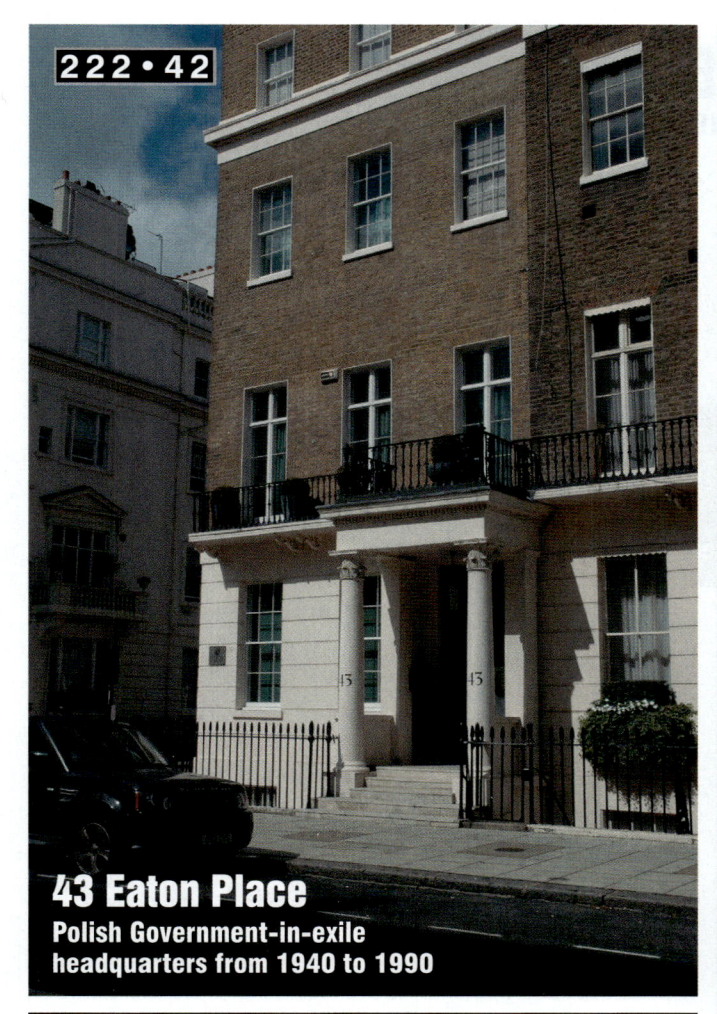

43 Eaton Place
Polish Government-in-exile headquarters from 1940 to 1990

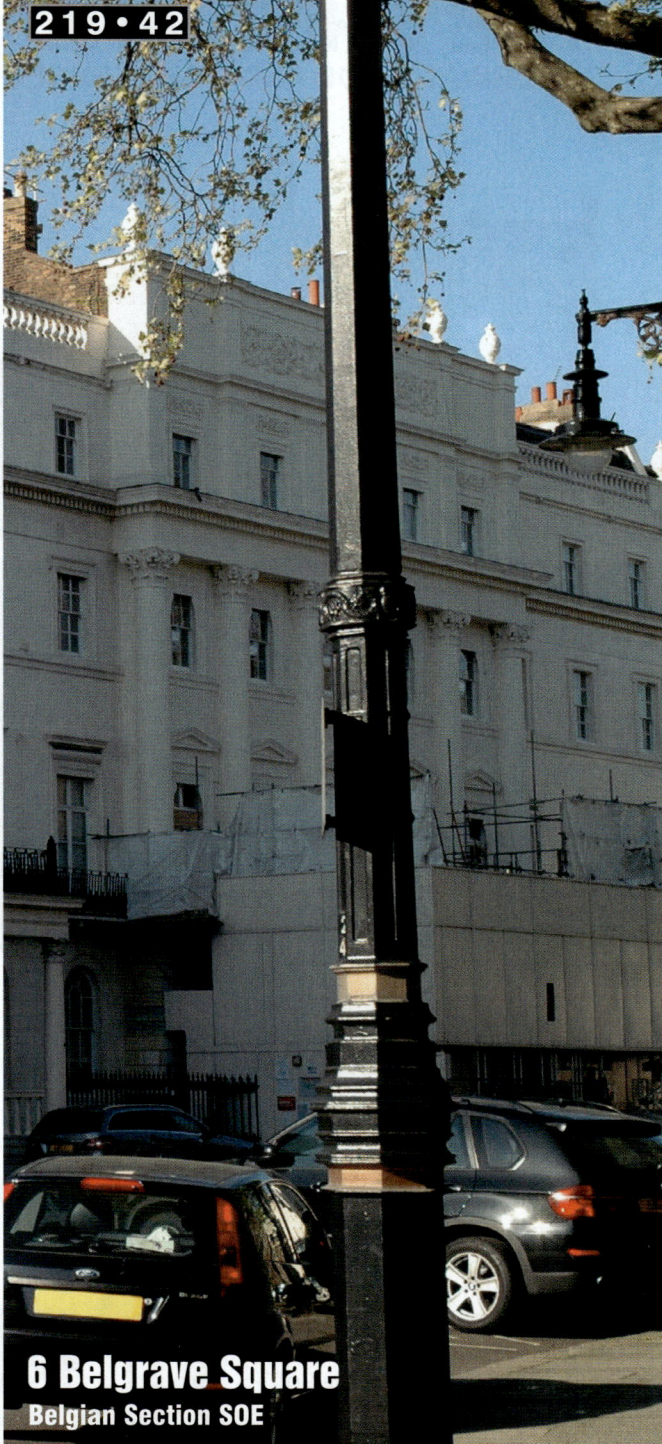

6 Belgrave Square
Belgian Section SOE

members of this valuable 'shuttle service' lost their lives, but the organisation had provided a vital link to the country which caused Berlin many problems.

Though most of the operations were planned at Lunna House, they were overseen and assisted by intelligence elements based at **KINGSTON HOUSE NORTH, PRINCE'S GATE [221•47]** - home to the Norwegian Government-in-exile. The building, now slightly modernised, contained an incredibly vital intelligence and military element that had a permanent liaison with the SOE and MI6. Indeed, its intelligence staff, in regular contact with resistance fighters back in Norway, played a pivotal role in providing information on Nazi ambitions in the country, including using Norway as a base to create an atomic bomb. The remarkable bravery of Norway's resistance operatives in WWII, should not be underestimated.

THE SHETLAND BUS
NORWAY'S SOE AND RESISTANCE HEROES

Shetland Bus Memorial, Shetland

Lunna House, Shetland. Operations were coordinated from here

Model of submarine chaser

Scalloway, Shetland - home port of the Shetland Bus vessels

STATION 43, BOMBS AND ASSASSINS

When World War Two finally ended, and the Soviets raised what Churchill called an "Iron Curtain," many countries were in limbo. The Polish Government-in-exile was the first to announce itself as a "Western and independent nation" - establishing a base at **43 EATON PLACE, KNIGHTSBRIDGE [222•42]**. Here it remained until 1990 and the fall of Communism.

Reference should also be made to the Poles who joined the SOE Polish element. The origins of this important unit can actually be traced back before the SOE was even formed. Krystyna Skarbek, the daughter of a Jewish family in Warsaw, was a founding member of the Polish unit. She had been introduced to MI6 in early 1940 through a contact and friend of German-born British journalist Frederick Voigt. Her daring exploits in Europe are well documented, but not so her alleged one-year long relationship with a well known MI6 man.

MI6 contact man Frederick Voigt

In 1941, she took on the operational name of Christine Granville, which after the war was officially recognised. Sadly her life was taken by an assassin on the streets of London outside what was the **SHELBOURNE HOTEL, 1-3 LEXHAM GARDENS, EARLS COURT [223•60]** in June 1952. Her killer was an obsessed employee of the respected gentlemen's **REFORM CLUB, PALL MALL [224•42]**. Granville had rejected the advances of porter Denis Muldowney so he took revenge.

He was executed by hanging in September 1952. It was an appalling incident, and a sad end to a women who had dared to venture into the darkest corners of Europe.

A book written in 1954 by Xan Fielding, a woman Granville had saved during the war, contains the opening dedication: *'To the memory of Christine Granville'*. She was buried

182

Eye Spy Intelligence Magazine

SPY SITES OF LONDON

The memorial to the Polish SOE agents of Station 43

Skarbek is buried at St Mary's Catholic Cemetery, Kensal Green

SOE agent Krystyna Skarbek

at **ST MARY'S CATHOLIC CEMETERY, KENSAL GREEN [225•16]**.

The Polish SOE unit, which had several hundred agents, was known as the Cichociemni or The Dark and Silent. The Poles were based at **AUDLEY END HOUSE [226•99]** (SOE Station 43, or Secret Training Station 43), just outside Saffron Walden in Essex, close to London. Over 500 agents passed through Station 43 - a memorial to the 108 Polish SOE agents who didn't return - now stands in its grounds.

Founded in 1836, the Reform Club makes the spy site listing for a number of reasons. Some of its members are famous intelligence figures, including former MI5 Director-General Dame

1-3 Lexham Gardens (Shelbourne Hotel)

Eye Spy Intelligence Magazine

1840s drawing of the central saloon at the club

Stella Rimington. The club was also used as a fictitious meeting location by MI6 officer and author Graham Green in his spy novel *The Human Factor*. However, in past years it was indeed a location used by the intelligence services to recruit personnel.

Originally it was a central hub for those aligned to the Liberal Party, but now it has no political allegiance whatsoever. Today's Reformers, a title taken from those who pledged support for the Great Reform Act of 1932, are drawn from many backgrounds, but are generally regarded as professionals. Unlike some gentlemen-only venues, the Reform Club changed its membership rule in 1981, allowing female members. Though no longer a political venue, its outlook is said to be progressive, and the building also hosts an impressive library of 75,000 volumes.

224 • 42

The Reform Club, Pall Mall

MENACE FROM ABOVE AND DISBELIEF

On 2 September 1940, three men left the Reform Club just as the Luftwaffe started to drop bombs in and around Pall Mall. The incident was described in the wartime diaries of one of the men - MI5 spycatcher Guy Liddell. The other two individuals were in fact Guy Burgess and Anthony Blunt - unbeknown to Liddell - both already in the pay of Soviet Intelligence.

And British Intelligence would have to start getting used to the Luftwaffe's falling bombs, the first cruise missiles and rockets as we shall discover...

226 • 99

Audley End House - SOE Station 43

184

Eye Spy Intelligence Magazine

AIR INTELLIGENCE IGNORED

In World War Two British Intelligence was inextricably linked to various military units and the country's defence and security forces worked as one. However, besides debate, discussion and concession, there was often downright rejection of some analysis being produced by each other's respective analytical wings. This was evident in the story of Germany's V1 and V2 projects.

Some Air Ministry intelligence officials believed the programme was real, others were convinced it was nothing more than propaganda. What is absolutely clear, is that some officials in London ignored valuable intelligence and photo reconnaissance imagery that should have provided a clue. That all changed on 13 June 1944, when a huge explosion rocked an area in **GROVE ROAD, MILE END [227•05]**. When the emergency services arrived, they recovered the bodies of eight civilians. Any doubt Germany had created a serious new weapon of menace was now a thing of the past - this despite earlier RAF bombing raids on the secret German research facility of Peenemunde in August 1943. It was here, of course, German military scientists had focused their attention on development of the

Adastral House
Air Ministry headquarters including air intelligence elements

Much re-worked since it was badly damaged by a V1 cruise missile in 1944

© REDVERS

228•62

227•05

THE FIRST FLYING BOMB ON LONDON FELL HERE 13 JUNE 1944

Air Council meeting

Air Council meeting of the Air Ministry in July 1940. During later stages of the war, it was heavily influenced by the powerful Air Intelligence Branch which also provided counter-measures for attacks by the V1 and V2. The Council considered and approved a variety of defensive and offensive weapons.

Eye Spy Intelligence Magazine 185

SPY SITES OF LONDON

A V1 on ramp at Imperial War Museum, Duxford

The V1 strikes Aldwych

COURTESY: NATIONAL ARCHIVES

V2 rocket, but Mile End had suffered a strike by another 'vengeance weapon' - the V1.

Despite the fact that London, by 1944, had a functioning spy network criss-crossing vast areas of Europe, the Nazis had managed to strike the city. Public fear and morale was viewed with equal concern in relation to the damage such weapons could cause. Much changed again just two weeks later when a V1 struck Aldwych, impacting between the important locations of the **AIR MINISTRY BUILDING (ADASTRAL HOUSE) [228•62]** and Bush House. The time was 2.07pm, and the area busy with workers. Also badly damaged was **AUSTRALIA HOUSE [229•62]**, where that country's intelligence

229•62

Australia House

© JAMIE BARRAS

186

Eye Spy Intelligence Magazine

SPY SITES OF LONDON

230•62

80 Strand
Former site of the Cecil Hotel - parts of which still exist and were occupied by the Air Ministry and its intelligence section

Poster advertising dance evenings at the Hotel Cecil

A fragment of the V1 that struck between the Air Ministry and Bush House

Air Chief Marshal Glen Torpy

Part of the original facade of the Hotel Cecil remains on the Strand.

The bombings caught Britain off guard. The war was going well; America had joined the fight and the invasion of Europe by Allied forces had just begun.

An official said that at the time of impact, some Air Ministry staffers were "sunbathing on the roof of the building." Ministers met to discuss a plan to down-play the event. An initial report was prepared for the media, claiming that some 48 people had been killed in the attack. But the truth was far more shocking, and for the intelligence services it was a dreadful blow.

Workers at Bush House, a building that supported many MI6 fronts and media projects, had been blown out of the building, such was the force with which this missile struck. Other government and RAF officials were lost amongst the twisted wreckage of the Air Ministry.

In a deliberate disinformation ruse, we have been told that Churchill authorised the release of a signal acknowledging death and destruction had occurred, but the role of many who died was not given. Indeed, the exact number of deaths is still a matter of contention, but it is higher than the official 48. About 400 others were seriously wounded and a further 200 suffered minor injuries.

division was housed. Another famous landmark was also damaged - Aldwych Theatre had its facade blown away. This disrupted the activities of the Air Ministry Committee which used to meet at **CECIL HOUSE**, later **HOTEL CECIL [230•62]** that was requisitioned during World War One. At the time it was the largest hotel in Europe. In 1930, much of the building was demolished. A formidable rebuild took place and two years later it was renamed Shell Mex House. However, since the departure of Shell Mex the building is simply known as 80 Strand. During the war it was occupied by the Ministry of Supplies and various intelligence elements. In 2008, a plaque was unveiled by Air Chief Marshal Glen Torpy which notes its one-time location as the first headquarters of the Royal Air Force.

Eye Spy Intelligence Magazine

187

SPY SITES OF LONDON
IMPERIAL WAR MUSEUM

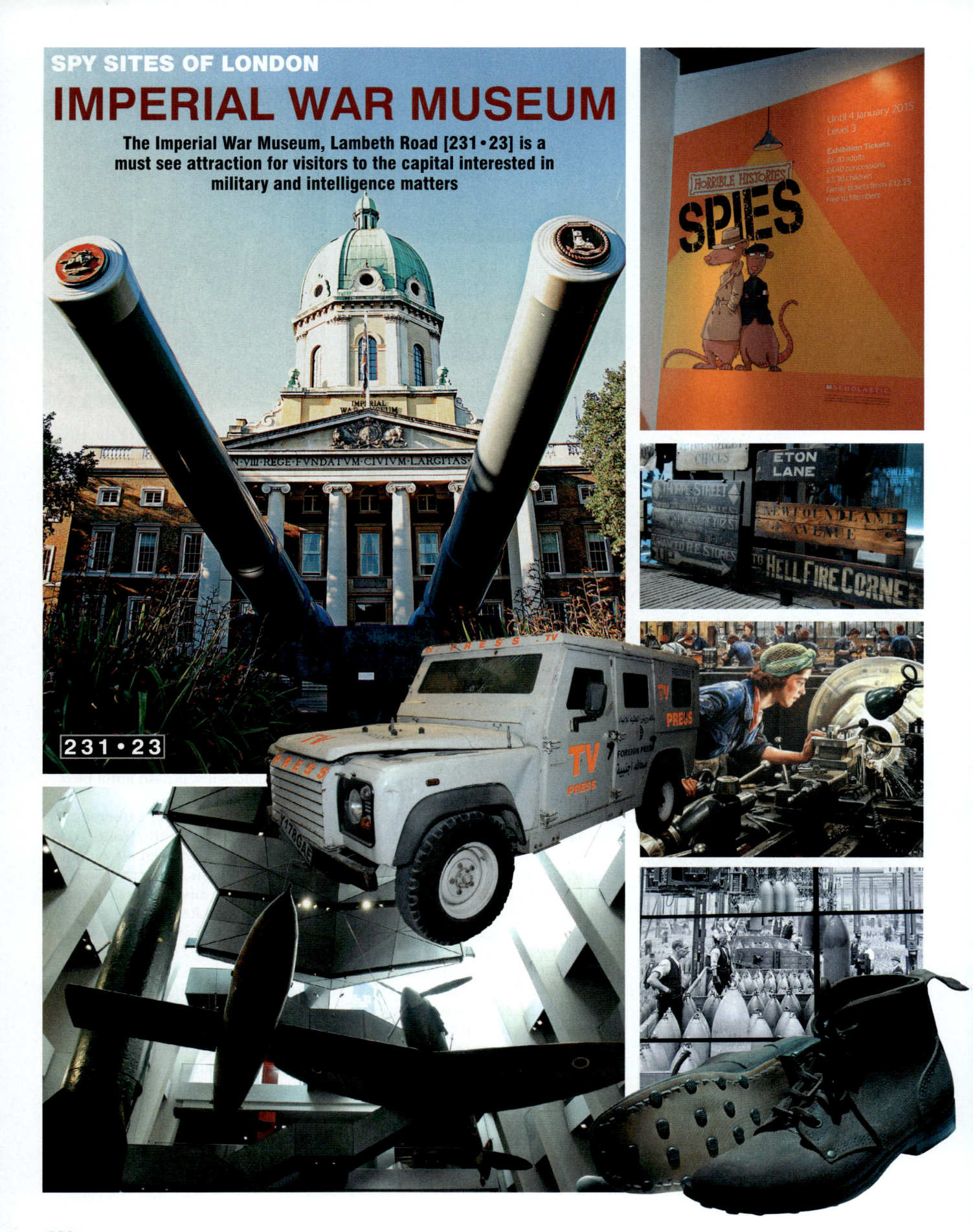

The Imperial War Museum, Lambeth Road [231•23] is a must see attraction for visitors to the capital interested in military and intelligence matters

Eye Spy Intelligence Magazine

SPY SITES OF LONDON

X

A Most Secret War
OSS, MI9 and Hidden Tunnels

Unbeknown to most visitors to London, and certainly not by the pilots of Germany's wartime Luftwaffe bombers, Churchill and many senior military and intelligence figures used a top secret labyrinth of tunnels under Whitehall and Downing Street. On occasions, Churchill also used the maze to reach a very special location - The Duck and Goose - his favourite city pub! Other notable figures who frequented the bar included Lord Kitchener, George Bernard Shaw and William Gladstone. The tunnel system was used primarily to access important buildings without having to venture outside onto the streets of London, which suffered dreadful damage from Goring's flying marauders and the incoming rockets and missiles towards the latter stages of the war.

Similarly, it was an effective method of concealing the identities of dignitaries

232•42

William Gladstone served as British Prime Minister on no fewer than four occasions. He was fully aware of a secret passage which was used to frequent a well protected pub

and senior political and military officials as they made their way from one meeting to another. Their presence in the capital was considered too important to risk exposure.

The sub-sub basement link to the pub was in fact part of a secret passage to the immense embankment building of 2 Whitehall Court **(See Site 034•42)**. It was first intended as a railway tunnel from nearby Scotland Yard to Waterloo to carry freight. The actual building was the location of MI6's early headquarters, when the Service (and MI5) used an entire upper floor. After World War Two broke out, Whitehall Court was again occupied by the War Office and MI5.

Royal Horseguards Hotel, Whitehall Court

Eye Spy Intelligence Magazine

189

234•42

1 Whitehall Court
In January 1992, the IRA detonated a car bomb here

233•42

Royal Tank Regiment Memorial, Whitehall

Today of course, much of this historic building is occupied by the 280 bedroom 5 star **ROYAL HORSEGUARDS HOTEL [232•42]** (Guoman Hotels). Its One Twenty One Two restaurant is actually named after the original telephone number of Scotland Yard. In 1989, it made a fleeting appearance in the James Bond movie - *Octopussy*. The hotel was in fact used by British Intelligence staffers during WWI.

Directly outside the hotel's entrance is the splendid British Army **ROYAL TANK REGIMENT MEMORIAL [233•42]** dedicated to the Royal Tank Regiment (RTR), depicting the crew of a WWII Comet tank. It was unveiled by HM Queen Elizabeth in 2000. The RTR participated in D-Day and it was this famous regiment that carried Winston Churchill over the River Rhine as Allied forces moved ever closer to Berlin.

190

Eye Spy Intelligence Magazine

Horse Guards Parade in the grounds of the Old Admiralty Building

© LUCIA WALLBANK

235•42
Horse Guards Building
View from Whitehall Avenue

236•42

War Memorial Horse Guards

© ANON

SPY SITES OF LONDON

Memorial plaque and statue to the Royal Tank Regiment outside the Royal Horseguards Hotel

In 2009, following a £16 million revamp, the hotel reopened its doors. Guests now have the opportunity of embarking on an internal spy tour of some of its secret passages and rooms. You can also enjoy a drink specially named after Britain's wartime leader - The Churchill - in his most favoured drinking place!

The Royal Horseguards Hotel is a great supporter of the charity - Help for Heroes.

The site also hosts the **NATIONAL LIBERAL CLUB** founded in 1882, at **1 WHITEHALL COURT [234•42]**. In World War One it was used by Canadian troops. When Churchill became prime minister in May 1940, the club quickly put back his 1915 portrait which had been hidden away for years. In less than a year members were taking it down again - this after the club was hit by a Luftwaffe bomb.

Close by is the **HORSE GUARDS BUILDING [235•42]**. Situated between Horse Guards Parade and Whitehall, the location was used by the army as the headquarters for the London District and Household Cavalry. Visitors will find an impressive war memorial at **HORSE GUARDS [236•42]** and is the location for an annual parade and dedication service.

Whitehall Court therefore, tucked amidst military buildings and other government offices, has a fascinating intelligence and military history. So

Eye Spy Intelligence Magazine

SPY SITES OF LONDON

Grosvenor Street
The OSS initially wanted to occupy various offices in this famous London Street

239•55
68 Brook Street
OSS agent training house

too another area of London which hosted agents, spy training and sabotage schools, and the offices of a certain American called William Casey, who would become the Central Intelligence Agency's first Director.

THE FEARLESS OFFICE OF STRATEGIC SERVICES (OSS)

The American Office of Strategic Services (OSS) was modelled on MI6 and the SOE. Via these important British organisations the OSS was delighted because it now had access to far more materials and resources to tackle the Germans in Europe.

The OSS conducted most of its agent training in the UK, indeed, its central European Operations Unit was also located in London at **72 GROSVENOR STREET, MAYFAIR [237•55]**. Another early OSS-related location was **40 BERKELEY SQUARE [238•55]**. This address was also occupied by liaisons from the Ministry of Economic Warfare which was the controlling political body of the SOE. Of course like SOE, OSS had safe houses and training schools dotted about the capital. A famous OSS location can be found at **68 BROOK STREET [239•55]**, where analysis, training and the equipping of OSS

OSS Director William Donovan

Eye Spy Intelligence Magazine

40 Berkeley Square
Site of an early OSS headquarters and offices of Ministry of Economic Warfare

18 Grosvenor Square

Brutons, 15 Bruton Lane

agents took place. At its height, OSS had over 10,000 operational personnel, many of them passing through the Brook Street and Grosvenor Street sites.

Like the SOE, the OSS also had female agents - every bit the equal of their male counterparts. They were billeted at **49 UPPER BROOK STREET, MAYFAIR [240•55]**. One famous agent was Virginia Hall who received the US Distinguished Service Cross from OSS head General William Donovan in 1945. Hall's dangerous work in Europe is now legendary.

An important OSS office was established at **18 GROSVENOR SQUARE [241•55]**. Staffers here coordinated with US Naval Intelligence.

A popular haunt for both OSS and SOE operatives was **BRUTONS PUBLIC HOUSE, 15 BRUTON LANE [242•55]** off Berkeley Square. Sadly

Eye Spy Intelligence Magazine   193

72 Grosvenor Street
WWII [Europe] headquarters of the OSS

Operating under the noses of MI5 and SOE in London - brilliant OSS spy recruiter - Joseph Gould

it closed but has since reopened as Mr Frogg's bar.

AN INDEPENDENT SERVICE

Despite being based in London and surrounded by British Intelligence agencies, Donovan was keen to ensure his operation kept its own identity. Nevertheless, this led to inevitable tri-service tensions. OSS refused to allow MI6 an insight into its codes, communications and more dangerous operations, but it relied on MI6 to organise transport and was utterly dependent on the British services for dropping agents into conflict zones. Analysts in MI6 believed internal OSS security was poor and feared intelligence breaches - this was probably why early mistrust ensued. There was also, at times, a cross-over with SOE and OSS personnel operating in some cases in the same areas.

But in 1943, a liaison and cooperation agreement between the UK and USA over signals intelligence was formalised, a situation which still exists today. This helped lessen tensions.

It should also be noted that Donovan was keen to foster good relations between all of the US intelligence elements, and for the record, as Co-ordinator of Information, invited a certain Allen Dulles to help in this endeavour. Relevant to British Intelligence, in 1941 Dulles occupied offices in the Rockefeller Center in New York which were rented and occupied by MI6's British Security Coordination

The OSS London Labour Desk - essentially an agent recruiting house for the organisation

OSS operatives in training near London for the dangerous Tool missions in Germany

194

Eye Spy Intelligence Magazine

49 Upper Brook Street
Female OSS agents were billeted here

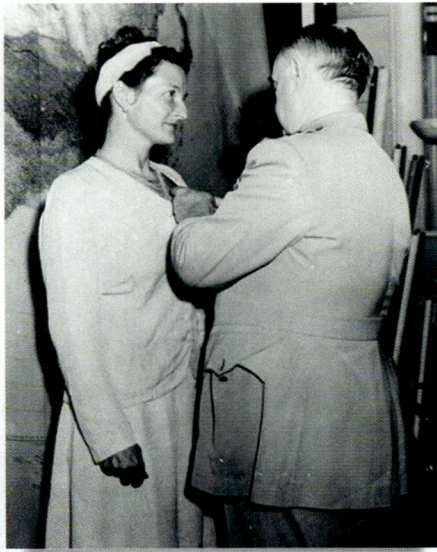

OSS head General William Donovan presents Virginia Hall with the US Distinguished Service Cross in 1945

which had schemed to get America involved in the war! More on the BSC story shortly.

When the Allies eventually circled Berlin two years later, there was much talk about how MI6 did not have one single agent inside Germany. Donovan's men could not believe Britain had relied so heavily on intelligence gleaned from products such as ULTRA, and from the RSS and GC&CS.

This was not to say the OSS fared much better. However, recognising serious intelligence gaps, the OSS sought to secure the services of German nationals willing to help the Allies.

The OSS launched its own intelligence gathering programme in London seeking out exiles it believed could help. The man behind this operation was Joseph Gould. He sought persons of German origin living in London to act as agents for a number of special operations, one of which was codenamed Tool. Most recruits were trained at an OSS base in Ruislip, though lived in the borough of Hampstead. The so-called 'Free Germans' would eventually provide invaluable intelligence to the OSS. Much more on this remarkable wartime story can be read on the CIA's web site (library/archive section).

In June 1944, the OSS despatched over 200 agents to Germany. From its own Secret Intelligence Branch (SIB) in London, OSS would launch over 100 operations between invasion and the end of the war. Chosen to lead the SIB was William J. Casey.

Eye Spy Intelligence Magazine

This splendid painting by the artist Jeffrey W. Bass shows OSS agent Virginia Hall in a barn in France in 1944. She is transmitting secret messages on a suitcase radio with the aid of a bicycle-powered generator. Hall lived in Europe and was first employed by British Intelligence training Resistance operatives

Old Metropole Hotel, Northumberland Avenue

Another critical judgement made by MI6 was one against its ally and former adversary - Russia. MI6's hierarchy warned that beyond the collapse of Germany, a new and immense foe would emerge. MI6 created Section IX, a directorate or branch dedicated to countering Soviet espionage and sabotage. And though proud of their foresight, MI6 and MI5 made errors that would have global implications - it had already started to appoint emerging talents such as Kim Philby. There were also the first real signs that MI6 might disappear forever, consumed by the far larger SOE.

With the war against Germany almost won, Churchill was faced with a dilemma - what to do with the SOE which had served the country so well. Some politicians and military officials were of the mind that the UK and the West would soon need the SOE to counter the 'Red Menace' that wasn't budging from the plains of Eastern Europe. MI6, which was under the auspices of the Foreign Office wanted SOE shut down, or at the very least put under its control. Lord Roundell Palmer, 3rd Earl of Selborne, who had oversight of the SOE and was effectively responsible for its operations, wanted to keep the organisation alive responded to the suggestion: "To have SOE run by the Foreign Office would

William Casey - first Director of the CIA and ex-SIB staffer

196

Eye Spy Intelligence Magazine

SPY SITES OF LONDON

The Great Central Hotel is now the Landmark

Great Central Hotel, Marylebone Road

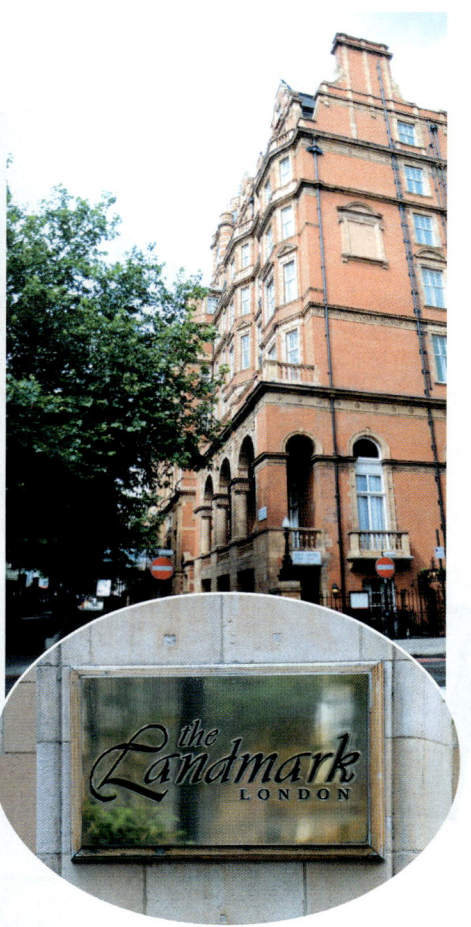

Much intelligence was gleaned here by debriefing POWs who managed to escape from occupied Europe

WWII British POW Red Cross Parcel

be like inviting an abbess* to supervise a brothel."

Churchill surprisingly dithered and failed to act one way or another, and the decision was effectively taken out of his hands when he lost the next general election. Labour Prime Minister Clement Attlee was also dismissive of SOE, despite this worldwide organisation having a network of agents and communications in place. SOE was officially dissolved on 15 January 1946, and some 300 operatives from the Special Operations Branch moved to MI6. SOE's training and research bodies were also handed over to MI6, whose senior officials celebrated and congratulated each other on a 'great victory'.

* Abbess - Superior of a convent

Eye Spy Intelligence Magazine

SPY SITES OF LONDON
246•42 Palace Street

247•08 Princess House, Princes Street
Postwar MI6 training school. Espionage tradecraft was taught here by senior staffers

Please note: Some maps and Internet mapping sites show the address as Prince's Street. However, the street sign is Princes Street

Clement Atlee

THE QUIET INTELLIGENCE GATHERERS

Helping to secure victory in Europe had propelled the British Secret Service to heights not before seen. MI6 and MI5 were at that time the most powerful intelligence agencies in the world, and with MI6's electronic intelligence arm - shortly to separate into a genuine third spy organisation, Britain was well set to tackle its old adversary - Russia. However, before engaging with the sites that will forever remain in Cold War legend, it's well worth remembering that British and then American Intelligence learned a great deal from the brave prisoners of war (POWs), who managed to escape from German POW

245•55

Harry Gordon Selfridge

Selfridges, Oxford Street

A SIGSALY unit

Part of the SIGSALY communications system at the NSA Museum in Fort Meade, Maryland. As a sidebar to the story of Selfridges, Russian Cold War spy Gordon Lonsdale used the store to meet his KGB contacts

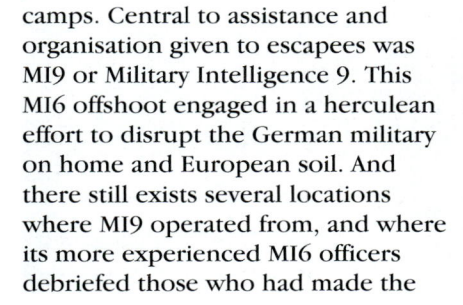

camps. Central to assistance and organisation given to escapees was MI9 or Military Intelligence 9. This MI6 offshoot engaged in a herculean effort to disrupt the German military on home and European soil. And there still exists several locations where MI9 operated from, and where its more experienced MI6 officers debriefed those who had made the 'glorious home run'. Utilised in the early part of the war, the **GREAT CENTRAL HOTEL, MARYLEBONE ROAD [243•15]** was a debriefing site run by the War Office.

By 1943, part of the site was occupied by MI9 specialists and military commanders who in time, would carefully glean intelligence from escapees.

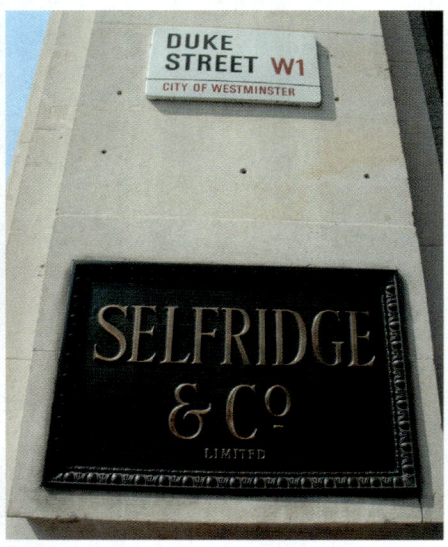

MI9 moved its headquarters outside the capital to Wilton Park in the Chilterns after the original Escape and Evasion section based at the **OLD METROPOLE HOTEL, NORTHUMBERLAND AVENUE [244•62]** was bombed (1940). However, it retained an operations' room in the War Office. More interesting was its agent briefing room at 5 St. James's Street **(See Site**

Eye Spy Intelligence Magazine

199

SPY SITES OF LONDON

276•42) - a flat purchased by Claude Dansey from BSC chief Sir William Stephenson. Here all kinds of ideas were discussed to conceal equipment into Red Cross parcels for prisoners to make good their escape. In later years, both MI5 and MI6 used this address as a safe and planning house.

SECURE COMMUNICATIONS

SIGSALY was the WWII codename given to a top secret secure communications line between Churchill and Roosevelt. The system was inaugurated on 15 July 1943, following a conference between US and British military officials. The original plan called for one of the terminals to be installed in the White House, but Roosevelt, aware of Churchill's penchant for calling at all hours of the night, decided to have the Washington unit moved to the Pentagon with extensions to the White House and the Navy Department building!

In London, the bulk of the SIGSALY equipment was actually stored in the basement of **SELFRIDGES DEPARTMENT STORE, OXFORD STREET [245•55]**. The communication system was fitted with an extension to Churchill's war room, approximately a mile away. The name SIGSALY was not an acronym but just a random codename.

SPY TRAINING SCHOOLS

Following MI6's feud with the SOE, which was described by MI6 officer Captain Henry Kerby, as "the biggest, bitterest internal battle of our intelligence services," the Service moved quickly to re-establish itself throughout the capital. Several training schools outside of its main headquarters were created. Even today, MI6 has several unspecified and top secret locations which are operational in respect of officer and staff training. These of course are classified and even journalists have difficulty in obtaining precise details. Some locations, or suspected locations, have been mentioned in one or two London publications. We have learned that because of today's instant communication channels and information access, especially via the Internet, MI6 and other likewise organisations retain some training locations for short periods, often of course, under second-party names. This was also the case following WWII.

In late 1945 or early 1946, MI6 occupied a building on **PALACE STREET [246•42]**. Here former SOE trainers taught new recruits a plethora of spy tradecraft gleaned from the

Kingsway Tunnels, 39 Furnival Street
Note the huge ventilation opening

249•62
Chancery Lane Tube

SPY SITES OF LONDON

Note the proximity to the entrance of 138-142 Holborn Bars, High Holborn

138-142 Holborn Bars, High Holborn

Built between 1879 and 1901, one underground passage is connected to Kingsway. Its relevance is not known

actions, operations and ruses performed during the war. This station replaced a training school created by MI6 in Sloane Square (**See Chapter 15**) that operated from 1940 through to the end of 1945. Another larger spy school emerged in rooms at the impressive **PRINCESS HOUSE, PRINCES STREET*** **[247•08]**. All of these would operate for a generation and then be shut down - primarily because of the fear of compromise. MI6 and MI5 sought to consolidate their strong postwar positions by adding various branches and seeking greater autonomy from Whitehall.

COLD WAR CALLING - ROOMS WITH NO VIEW - MI6's UNDERGROUND CENTRE

In 2008, a series of WWII-era bomb-proof tunnels were advertised for sale. Situated about 100ft under the streets of London, the **KINGSWAY TUNNELS, 39 FURNIVAL STREET [248•62]** were originally built in 1942 to protect civilians from the bombers of Hitler's Luftwaffe (capacity - 8,000-10,000 civilians with limited provisions). However, two years later, MI6 and a number of other agencies quietly established a secret facility here - primarily to protect sensitive equipment and store documentation. Rumours abound about its precise use, as no sooner had the war ended with Germany in May 1945, the one-mile long tunnel was allegedly stripped bare. Researchers are not convinced this happened!

At point of sale it was owned by the telecommunications company BT Group PLC. This might also give an indication as to its use since 1945!

When news of its sale was announced, a BT spokeswoman said: "We're looking for a purchaser with the imagination and stature to return the tunnels to productive use. The site has a fantastic history and, now that we have no requirement for it for telecommunications use, it is right that we should offer it to the market. Here's hoping it has a fantastic future as well."

Some 400 tons of highly sensitive documents belonging to the Public Record Office (now the National Archives) were stored here. When the site was taken over by the General Post Office (GPO), which also ran Britain's telecommunications network, the papers seemingly became the property of the GPO.

By 1953, as far as we can ascertain, the Kingsway Tunnel ran the UK's entire machinery to connect overseas telephone calls. These were controlled by a self-contained telephone exchange system also inside the complex. Among the calls routed in, out and via Kingsway was allegedly the 'hot line' which connected the Kremlin with the Communications team at the White House in the 1960s... just in case of a misunderstanding involving the armed forces, or the accidental launch of a nuclear missile.

During the latter part of the war, a number of MI6 personnel were based at the facility, though few clues regarding what these staffers actually

*** Two variants of spelling exist Princes Street and Prince's Street**

Eye Spy Intelligence Magazine

201

SPY SITES OF LONDON

251•19

Downside Crescent, Belsize Park

did exist. However, it's likely that after the war the telecommunications equipment installed became a good source of intelligence for MI6 and MI5. Similarly, we understand that Kingsway or Furnival as some intelligence watchers call it, was considered a vital location in respect of keeping Britain's major cities and military facilities connected [telecommunications]. During the 1962 Cuban missile crisis, the facility was a hive of activity, an indication that Britain was doing its utmost to intercept calls from the Soviets to Fidel Castro in Havana.

Of equal importance, the tunnel ran all the way to an underground complex at Ingersoll House and Bush House on Kingsway **(See Sites 169•62 and 128•62)**, where it joined with Melbourne Place Tunnel. Here a platform still exists. There is little doubt the Kingsway Tunnel complex was called as such because it began underground at Kingsway - one of the most important intelligence hubs during WWII and the Cold War.

Part of the MI6 facility carried on under **CHANCERY LANE TUBE STATION [249•62]** and the impressive building called **HOLBORN BARS, HIGH HOLBORN [250•08]**, a clue perhaps to where staffers all of half a century ago entered and exited. A sub-level corridor was reportedly built, and there is a very real possibility that this descends to 200ft below London. One report even suggests Kingsway

254•45

Clapham South

could have been developed after the war into an emergency nuclear command centre, capable of supporting several hundred government workers. How much truth there is in this report, is debatable. Another unconfirmed report states that the line and location may have once been proposed as an emergency escape route for the Royal Family.

At least three entrances (or exits) to Kingsway exist. Besides Furnival Street, a door at 32 High Holborn (Chancery Lane Station) is said to lead to a lift and stairwell to the facility.

Many such buildings were designed and built in WWII by the government with one thing in mind - security - for both the public and official organisations. Look hard enough in the capital, and you may just come across existing buildings which seem very much out of place, but have a fantastic history. **DOWNSIDE CRESCENT, BELSIZE PARK [251•19]** is a great example. Beneath this white-painted

SPY SITES OF LONDON

252•25 Stockwell Air Raid Shelter
After WWII the facility was used by the government and armed forces

structure is a huge facility that supports a variety of rooms and accommodation tunnels.

Another facility - **STOCKWELL AIR RAID SHELTER [252•25]** falls beneath Stockwell Tube Station. On the surface, part of the complex has been painted by local artists as a memorial. Completed in 1942 and opened at the height of the V1 and V2 attacks, the facility has been used by various government bodies ever since.

The **GOODGE STREET TOTTENHAM COURT ROAD [253•62]** deep level shelter (West entrance) is next to Whitfield Memorial Church and is called the Eisenhower Centre. This is because for over a year it was used as a secure communications and control facility for the US commander and his staff. After the war, the British Army used the shelter until the mid-1950s.

However, the authorities, armed forces and indeed the intelligence services, soon found such out-of-sight and protected locations ideal in respect of concealing operations and functions. Such buildings appeared across the country, in major towns and the countryside and within a decade, many were being utilised as Cold War command centres; others as communication hubs between the regions and London. In a number of cases, the overland architecture is identical.

253•62 The Eisenhower Centre, Goodge Street

Eye Spy Intelligence Magazine

London has numerous puzzling buildings and sites linked to a subterranean world. The doors seen here under Waterloo Bridge, and the track below in Southampton Road, both lead to the Kingsway subway

Eric Arthur Blair (George Orwell) broadcasting to listeners in Eastern Europe from Bush House in WWII

Take for example Goodge Street and **CLAPHAM SOUTH [254•45]**. Some complexes outside London even housed nuclear weapons.

Thus these strange and often bizarre-looking concrete structures represent a very important chapter in the history of Britain. A simple pillbox could be a clue to a significant location.

By the Spring of 1945, Nazi Germany was close to collapse and the world prepared to celebrate. But privately in the intelligence offices of Whitehall, MI6 and the SOE, officials who previously worked with the Soviets to topple Hitler realised trouble loomed. Moscow had an aggressive agenda and within a very short space of time, London and Washington accepted the notion that the Red Army had no intention of pulling back eastwards once victory was assured. Indeed, in March 1946, *The Observer* wrote: *'George Orwell... after the Moscow conference last December, noted Russia began to make a cold war on Britain and the British Empire'*.

It was reference to an essay Orwell published in October 1945, following the end of the war and the atomic bomb attack on Japan. The 'Cold War' term has been used ever since in the context of an East and West world armed with nuclear weapons - but one that could never envisage their use again - complete with a chilling caveat that it might one day happen.

THE RUSSIAN 'GHOSTS' LURKING WITHIN MI5 AND MI6

Ever since Orwell's perceptive comments, the West and East have traded blows in a plethora of secret wars... all perpetuated by espionage and intelligence gathering.

Unbeknown to MI5 and MI6, Britain had a group of traitors already established within its intelligence community - spies who had started to pass secrets to Moscow. Others walked London's streets in an attempt to glean secrets about Britain's atomic research and arsenal.

But before we examine the buildings and streets made famous by the likes of Burgess, Maclean, Blunt, Philby and the 'fifth man' - John Cairncross - collectively known as the Cambridge Spies, let us now investigate the many ultra secret organisations, spies and operations which ultimately brought about Victory in Europe.

OFFICE OF STRATEGIC SERVICES

OSS GALLERY, CIA HEADQUARTERS, LANGLEY

COMPASS

'CALTROP' TYRE SPIKE

WILLIAM DONOVAN STATUE

OSS CLOTH PATCH

OSS BOOK OF HONOUR

SILK ESCAPE AND EVASION MAP

COURTESY: CENTRAL INTELLIGENCE AGENCY

SPY SITES OF LONDON

This belonged to OSS staffer Stella Uzdawinis. Her family did not learn of her secret work until after her death when they discovered the pendent

WOODMAN'S PAL KNIFE

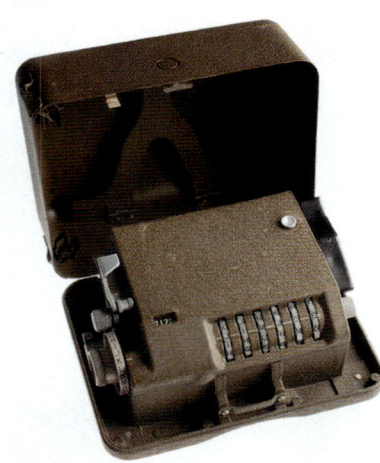

FAIRBAIRN-SYKES FIGHTING KNIFE

MATCHBOX CAMERA

M-209 MECHANICAL CIPHER MACHINE

IRRAWADDY AMBUSH
OSS Detachment 101 ambush Japanese troops

COURTESY: CENTRAL INTELLIGENCE AGENCY

206

Eye Spy Intelligence Magazine

SPY SITES OF LONDON

XI
The Illusionists
Ministries for Disinformation and Mischief

The brilliant author Graham Greene was a literary genius who found himself working within the propaganda section of British Intelligence. After moving to London from Hertfordshire, Greene lived at **14 CLAPHAM COMMON NORTH SIDE [255•45]** until 1940. He was forced to leave the residence after the Luftwaffe had dropped a bomb damaging the building.

Greene was a frequent visitor to **RULES RESTAURANT, 35 MAIDEN LANE [256•62]** believed to be London's oldest restaurant. Notable authors, playwrights and intelligence figures have all dined in this splendid restaurant, including MI6 and MI5 officer John Le Carre (David John Moore Cornwall). Le Carre's works, of course, including *The Spy Who Came In From The Cold,* are arguably the finest novels ever written on the subject of espionage.

Greene's books *Our Man in Havana, The Third Man, The Confidential Agent, The Quiet American* and *The Human Factor* reveal his deep interest in the intelligence game. And of course, MI6 contact man Alexander Korda later turned *The Third Man* into an atmospheric motion picture.

Greene joined MI6 in July 1941, following a short term serving with

14 Clapham Common, North Side
The famous author and long-time MI6 officer Graham Greene lived here

Eye Spy Intelligence Magazine 207

SPY SITES OF LONDON

257•62

Senate House, Ministry of Information
Now part of the University of London

256•62

Rules Restaurant, 35 Maiden Lane, Covent Garden

© TOM MORRIS

The Philosophy Library, Senate House

the incredibly important propaganda section of the **MINISTRY OF INFORMATION (MOI)** based at **SENATE HOUSE [257•62]**, now part of the University of London. The MOI worked under the auspices of the Committee for Imperial Defence, formed in 1902 by Prime Minister Arthur Balfour. It had operated briefly during World War One, but was resurrected in 1935 because of the probability of war with Germany. At the time of Greene's appointment, the controller of the MOI was BBC founder John Reith, who once lived at **6 BARTON STREET [258•42]**.

During the war Reith also took on a naval commission, and in 1943 was

SPY SITES OF LONDON

258•42
6 Barton Street

John Le Carre, former MI6 and MI5 officer and author of some of the best spy books ever written

appointed Director of the Combined Operations Material Department at the Admiralty. Though he was a media man, Reith did have many associates who worked in the intelligence community.

Prime Minister Arthur Balfour

John Reith (inset) Minister of Information lived at 6 Barton Street. Another MI6 man in the person of T. E. Lawrence lived at number 14 Barton Street. Indeed, the area seems to have been one favoured by Service staffers and intelligence community in general

The MOI had links with various desks operated by MI6, and threads to other military and political offices including the powerful Political Warfare Executive (PWE). The WWII organisation closed within 12 months of the war ending, but many of its key functions were kept - this resulting in a government organ known today as the Central Office of Information.

Greene's recruitment was surprising because whilst studying at Oxford in 1922, he joined Britain's Communist Party (CPGB). However, delve a little deeper and you will find he was recommended by his sister Elisabeth who was already in the employ of MI6, her husband was in fact the MI6 Station Chief in Paris. Greene's work with MI6 took him to places overseas including Sierra Leone. He was controlled by none other than double agent Kim Philby, who at the time Greene regarded as his friend. He wrote a letter describing his African assignment, part of which read: *'This is not a government house, and there is no larder: there is also a plague of house flies which come from the*

Eye Spy Intelligence Magazine

SPY SITES OF LONDON

Fidel Castro in East Berlin 1972. Graham Greene's interviews with such people were of immense use to British Intelligence

Charlie Chaplin's statue in Vevey, Switzerland. The comic genius was investigated in the 1950s by MI5. Graham Greene also moved to Vevey

African bush lavatories round the house'.

Officially, Greene returned to London in 1942, and in 1944 duly handed in his notice to his MI6 line manager - but he never relinquished his ties with the Service. As an author Greene was able to secure interviews with important world figures such as Fidel Castro and Ho Chi Minh, undoubtedly filing reports of these and many more encounters to MI6!

It should be noted that Greene's uncle, Sir William Graham Greene was prominent in Britain's powerful Naval Intelligence Division, always regarded by the government as the country's pre-eminent intelligence body. However, another family member, his older brother Herbert actually worked as a spy for the Imperial Japanese Navy in the 1930s. Cunningly Herbert failed to

39 Methley Street

Camera Club, 16 Bowden Street

SPY SITES OF LONDON

Photograph showing proximity of Charlie Chaplin's house to the famous Camera Club

MI6 contact man - Graham Greene

tell Tokyo that he was also submitting his reports to MI6! Another brother, Hugh, would later be appointed BBC Director-General in 1960.

In 1966, Greene departed Britain and eventually retired to Vevey on Lake Geneva, Switzerland.

As a footnote to Greene's most interesting career, the author, perhaps in an attempt to secure information, visited KGB double-agent Kim Philby in the late 1980s in Moscow - long after his former head had defected to Russia. We understand that Greene may have supplied intelligence to his main MI6 contact well into the 1980s. And beyond all of this, Greene's books are essential reading for spy enthusiasts, and one can be assured that some of the characters, situations and plots that he devised and wrote about, are probably based upon his own experiences and that of the intelligence contacts he undoubtedly retained long after leaving MI6.

THE SECRET LIVES OF CHARLIE CHAPLIN

Now, for those connoisseurs of intelligence, another man who had been investigated for his suspected links to Communism also lived in London - the great cinematic clown Charlie Chaplin (real name Charles Spencer). After the war, the FBI asked MI5 to investigate Chaplin's suspected Moscow ties, and though the Service failed to find any real evidence of this, an investigative team did find itself in the midst of a real mystery - this as they sought background on the iconic actor. Chaplin lived at various addresses in the city, including **39 METHLEY STREET [259•25]** and **287 KENNINGTON ROAD [260•25]**.

Chaplin's Security Service file reveals that MI5 mounted an investigation into the strange circumstances of his

Charles Spencer - Charlie Chaplin

Hard to believe this is the great cinematic clown - Charlie Chaplin pictured in 1916. In later years, at the request of the FBI, MI5 would launch an investigation into his alleged Communist links. The Service would find information about his identity that puzzled many in the intelligence world

Eye Spy Intelligence Magazine

211

SPY SITES OF LONDON

birth. Born in 1889, he was one of the silent era's biggest stars, featuring in such terrific movies as *The Tramp* (1915). However, he was viewed with suspicion in the United States because of his alleged links to and support of Communist groups. Whilst some intelligence figures in the US considered his downtrodden movie parts as "too leftist," MI5 believed he was more of a "progressive type or radical," rather than a Communist.

MI5 launched its official investigation in 1952 at the personal request of FBI Director J. Edgar Hoover, because he hated all things 'red'. He privately denounced Chaplin as, "one of Hollywood's parlour Bolsheviks."

It was always believed Chaplin was born in the Walworth district of London, but when MI5 started its enquiries, there was no official record of the performer's birth, despite much literature saying in 1891 he was living with his elder brother, Sydney in the south of the city: *'It would seem that Chaplin was either not born in this country or that his name at birth was other than those mentioned',* an MI5 note concludes.

Charlie Chaplin satirising Adolf Hitler in the 1940 film *The Great Dictator*

BACKGROUND

MI5 investigated Chaplin's political allegiances and personal background, including a long-standing rumour that Charlie Chaplin was an alias and the performer's true name was Israel Thornstein. There was no trace of him in the birth records at London's part-government occupied **SOMERSET HOUSE [261•62]** on the Strand.

Though respectful of its US counterparts' request, MI5 was content to let the mystery of Chaplin's birth remain. In reality, the Security Service could not properly ascertain where Chaplin was born. Other British agents were sceptical of American claims that the star was a Communist threat, and John Marriott, head of MI5's counter-subversion branch, said the Bureau's

260•25
287 Kennington Road
Another Charlie Chaplin residence

A young Chaplin without his familiar hat and moustache

Eye Spy Intelligence Magazine

SPY SITES OF LONDON

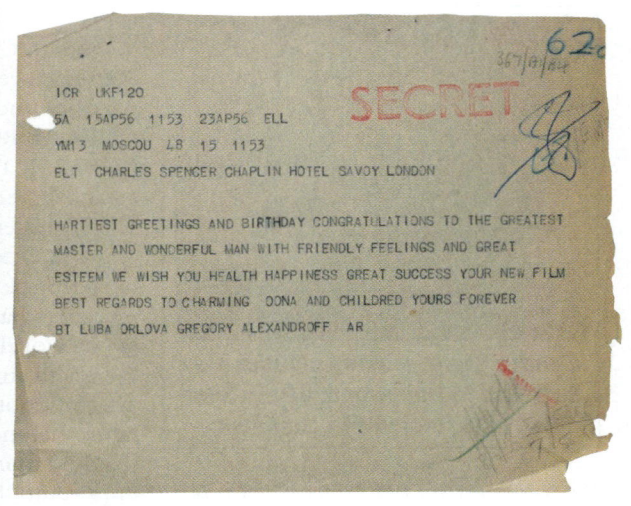

FBI Director J. Edgar Hoover requested MI5 examine Chaplin's possible Communist links. Above: MI5 interception: A letter to Chaplin from a Moscow admirer

"allegations were unreliable." In one released paper written by Marriott in 1952, he wrote: *'It is curious that we can find no record of Chaplin's birth, but I scarcely think that this is of any security significance'*.

However, the Service watched Chaplin for several years. The Chaplin Dossier as it is known, is full of newspaper reports about the actor, and other interesting correspondence, including letters from Russia addressed to *'Comrade Charly Chaplin'* sent to the extreme left-wing publication and Communist supportive title *Challenge*.

This held no sway with Hoover, and as Chaplin sought to enter the United States in 1952, Bureau counter-intelligence officers conspired with senior Washington officials and he was refused entry. Chaplin subsequently settled in Switzerland until his death in 1977.

MI5 enquiries continued throughout the 1950s but by 1958, the Service was adamant Chaplin posed no threat: *'We have no substantial information of our own against Chaplin, and we are not satisfied that there are reliable grounds for regarding him as a security risk. It may be that Chaplin is a Communist sympathiser but on*

MI5 searched for information here that could link Chaplin to Communism - what they found was quite bizarre

Somerset House, Strand

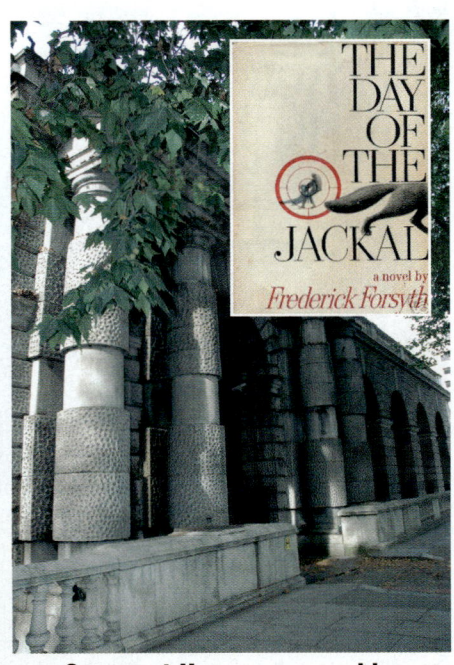

Somerset House was used by Frederick Forsyth in his book *The Day of the Jackal* - as an assassin sought a new birth certificate and identity

Eye Spy Intelligence Magazine

SPY SITES OF LONDON

Charlie Chaplin with socialist Max Eastman in Hollywood, 1919. Such liaisons fuelled FBI suspicion

the information before us he would appear to be no more than a progressive or radical'.

Chaplin married four times - and on two occasions to girls aged just 16. Nevertheless, the genius of the silver screen became Sir Charles Chaplin in March 1975, two years before his death aged 88. Visitors can find a splendid statue of this complex figure in **LEICESTER SQUARE [262•62]**.

Visitors to Chaplin's address at Methley Street need only walk a few paces to find the famous **CAMERA CLUB, 16 BOWDEN STREET [263•25]**. The club is the oldest such establishment in the world (formed 1885) and entry is free to the public. Many fine exhibitions have been hosted here and a number of previous members have threads to the intelligence world, including Frederick Sidney Cotton. He was an inventor, aviator, photographer and a leading figure behind the process which resulted in colour photography. Just as important - his work on aerial photographic reconnaissance before and after WWII. Cotton was a personal friend of Winston Churchill, George Eastman (Eastman-Kodak fame) and Ian Fleming.

Somewhat of a renegade, Cotton often clashed with his superiors. After losing his commission he still maintained links with the intelligence world and acted as a consultant to the Admiralty.

Cotton, who was later awarded an OBE, lived at the magnificent Astor House, now known as **TWO TEMPLE PLACE [264•62]** near Somerset House. In 2011, the building began displaying regional artwork and is opened to the public during exhibitions. Its name derives from the founder of the famous Waldorf Hotel in New York City - William Waldorf Astor.

Frederick Cotton

THE MINISTRY OF TRUTH

The stunning architecture of Senate House was also the inspiration for author George Orwell's description of his fictitious Ministry of Truth in his acclaimed, but controversial novel *Nineteen Eighty-Four*.

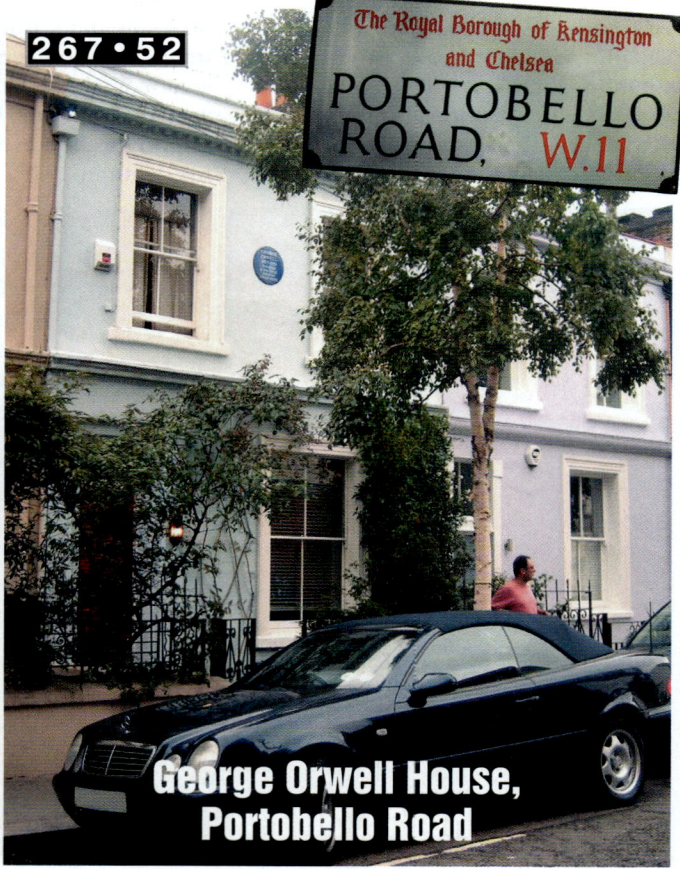

© YAIR HAKLAI

262•62

Leicester Square
Charlie Chaplin statue

267•52

George Orwell House, Portobello Road

214

Eye Spy Intelligence Magazine

SPY SITES OF LONDON

264•62

2 Temple Place
Formerly Astor House

© JAMIE BARRAS

Orwell, born Eric Arthur Blair, travelled to Spain in 1937 during that country's civil war, embarking on a mission he described as a "fight against fascism." After receiving a bullet wound, he returned to England and recuperated at the home of his brother-in-law (Laurence O'Shaughnessy) at **24 CROOMS HILL, GREENWICH [265•24]**. Some intelligence analysts believe it was at this moment he was then placed under surveillance by MI5, and interest in his left-wing beliefs were heightened following a review of his

George Orwell

265•24

24 Crooms Hill, Greenwich

Eye Spy Intelligence Magazine

215

University College Hospital
Gower Street Entrance

A plaque of George Orwell can be found close to the Royal Free Hospital on the corner of Pond Street and South End Road (The bookshop has long gone)

GEORGE ORWELL
WRITER 1903··1950
LIVED AND WORKED IN
A BOOKSHOP ON THIS SITE
1934··1935

book - *The Road to Wigan Pier* - which had been criticised even in the Communist paper the *Daily Worker*.

Orwell met his wife Eileen, the sister of O'Shaughnessy at a party in 1935, at **77 PARLIAMENT HILL, HAMPSTEAD [266•19]**. This was the former lodging address of Orwell and soon the couple made it their home. His earlier residence, on **PORTOBELLO ROAD** is now called **GEORGE ORWELL HOUSE [267•52]**.

When war did break out, Eileen interestingly, began work at the Censorship Department in London.

Orwell joined Britain's Home Guard, this after his trying to find a job within various military forces, including the Air Ministry. Eventually, however, he did find service with an intelligence element as a commentator for the BBC to counter propaganda broadcasts by the Nazis to India. He secured the services of various contributors including T. S. Elliot. Orwell left the BBC in late 1943, but not before it had been recorded that he met with a certain Peter Smollett, an official at the Ministry of Information who in later years was exposed as a Soviet spy. This meeting led to problems in publishing one of his most famous books -

Animal Farm: A Fairy Story. Some commentators considered the work an attack on the Communist regime - which had been - after all, a wartime ally. By this time, we understand from intelligence sources that MI5 Watchers were already surveilling Orwell - a man they could never quite understand...

In 1947, Orwell left London for good and set about writing his most famous work - *Nineteen-Eighty-Four*. At the same time he passed lists of people he thought unsuitable for publication to the anti-Communist Foreign Office element - the Information Research

77 Parliament Hill, Hampstead

Adam von Trott - on trial for conspiracy to kill Adolf Hitler

Eye Spy Intelligence Magazine

270•15
5 Cambridge Gate

Department. That list would remain top secret until 2003. He returned to the city after falling ill and died on 21 January 1950 at **UNIVERSITY COLLEGE HOSPITAL, EUSTON ROAD [268•15]**. A plaque honouring Orwell can also be found on the site of a bookshop where he worked on the corner of **POND STREET** and **SOUTH END ROAD [269•19]**.

Orwell had many friends in the intelligence game, including David Astor of *The Observer* newspaper who invited him to contribute articles. Astor had liaisons with at least one anti-fascist wartime German, Adam von Trott zu Solz, a diplomat and solicitor, who was involved in the daring 1944 plot to assassinate Adolf Hitler. Astor had befriended von Trott whilst studying at Mansfield College in Oxford. Trott, it should also be noted, was the great-great grandson of John Jay, one of the founding fathers of the United States of America.

Perhaps Orwell's closest friend in British Intelligence was author and MI6 man Malcolm Muggeridge who visited him frequently after he had fallen ill. He was drafted into the Ministry of Information in early 1940, but said it was an "appalling set up." (The agency - not his draft). In 1942, he was transferred into the effective

MI6 officer Malcolm Muggeridge

271•42
Cabinet War Rooms, King Charles Street (Churchill Museum)

Eye Spy Intelligence Magazine

SPY SITES OF LONDON

Sketch of Oliver Stanley commissioned by the Ministry of Information

Intelligence Corp, and towards the end of the year had found his vocation in MI6. Muggeridge was friends with many, many MI6 officers and contact men, including Arthur Ransome, the Leeds-born author best known for his iconic work - *Swallows and Amazons* - a series of books for children.

Muggeridge, who lived at **5 CAMBRIDGE GATE [270•15]** also spent time working for MI5 whilst a senior editor at the *Daily Telegraph*. He had threads to a substantial intelligence and propaganda organisation and monitoring endeavour known as the London Controlling Section (LCS). His title was Special Correspondent.

MI6 often recruited journalists during the war as liaisons. Alan Pryce-Jones, editor of *The Times Literary Supplement* was one such person. The *Daily Telegraph's* Foreign editor S. R. Pawley another. Pawley ran a network of journalists and reporting agents for the newspaper abroad.

THE LONDON CONTROLLING SECTION - DECEPTION KINGS

Overseeing many of Britain's wartime deceptions was the London Controlling Section. Formed in 1942 as an element of the Joint Planning Staff, the group which consisted of intelligence, military and political figures, was presided over by Winston Churchill. It met regularly in the basement of the Cabinet War Rooms which is now a major London tourist attraction

The actual Cabinet War Rooms or Churchill War Museum as it is known today, falls within part of the basement structure of The Treasury Building. Its construction began in 1938 and was operational for the duration of the war. On the table at LCS meetings the committee would place a so-called 'dancing faun' statue to represent the ruses de geurre (ruses of war) played by its representative organisations

known as the **CHURCHILL WAR ROOMS, KING CHARLES STREET [271•42]**. Opened in 2003, a visit to this museum and subterranean complex which was actually built under the **TREASURY BUILDING, GREAT GEORGE STREET [272•42]** is an absolute must.

The Treasury Building, Great George Street

272•42

SPY SITES OF LONDON
LONDON CONTROLLING SECTION - DECEPTION KINGS

Bedroom-office of Brendan Bracken - Minister of Information

CABINET WAR ROOMS
The nerve centre of Britain's war effort
SECRET
KEPT UNDER LOCK AND KEY

With cigar in hand - this figure must represent Churchill!

Eye Spy Intelligence Magazine 219

274 • 42

Admiralty Citadel, Horse Guards

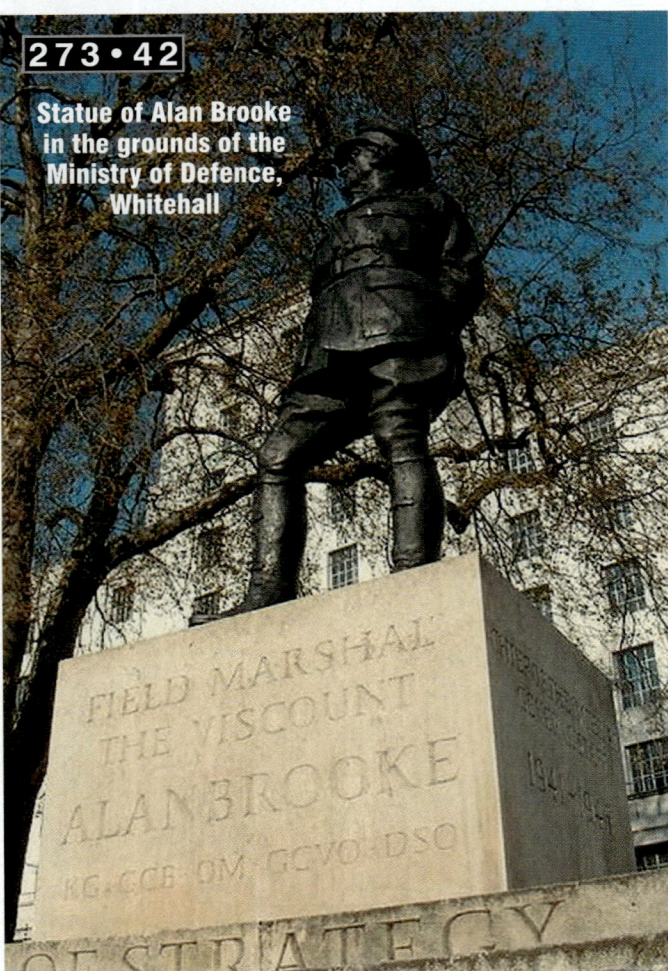

273 • 42

Statue of Alan Brooke in the grounds of the Ministry of Defence, Whitehall

The LCS kept a replica statue of this dancing faun on its conference table as a reminder of the ruses the organisation played

© SABRINA ROBERJOT

General Sir Allan Brooke Chief of the Imperial General Staff

SPY SITES OF LONDON

The primary function of the LCS, which was overseen by Secretary of War Oliver Stanley, was to coordinate and plan worldwide deception and cover operations. These would then be submitted to organisations such as MI6 and the SOE for action. The belief and support of such covert action was probably spurred on by the incredible success of the British Security Coordination (BSC) which used all manner of ruses and ploys. This powerful MI6 organisation undoubtedly helped bring America into the war, though many intelligence papers relevant to this secret agency remain closed. The work of the BSC is examined next.

Thus with Hitler still in control of most of Europe, the LCS was given powers to approve a wide variety of operations, some that today would be considered distasteful.

Those agencies involved with developing and performing deception operations had a permanent liaison at meetings of the LCS. Gatherings in London were held whereby the nature and purpose of proposed ventures could be discussed, analysed and if necessary, halted or enlarged. As the endeavour continued, an American intelligence official was drafted into the committee; like his colleagues he too had the authority to propose all manner of schemes.

CHURCHILL'S STORYTELLER

A key member of the LCS's deception team was one of Britain's most popular thriller writers - Dennis Wheatley. Known as 'Churchill's Storyteller', Wheatley would write many of his most creative works in Churchill's bunker. As head of a team of writers, artists, special effects personnel and producers, he provided disinformation to publishing houses, broadcasting stations and other media outlets with one single goal - make the material realistic enough to interest Germany's High Command. Wheatley would also play a part in one of the most incredible deception operations of all time codenamed Mincemeat - to

'Churchill's Storyteller' - Dennis Wheatley - a member of the London Controlling Section

Eye Spy Intelligence Magazine

221

SPY SITES OF LONDON
275•47

Victoria and Albert Museum, Cornwall Gardens

disguise invasion plans of Europe. This too is examined shortly.

Other key personnel on the committee included a variety of intelligence and military commanders, including General Sir Allan Brooke, Chief of the Imperial General Staff. He was close to Churchill and Montgomery and had good relations with several intelligence men involved with the running of decidedly shadowy branches. After the war, Brooke was privately dismayed that Churchill and others had taken the credit for many of the operations green-lighted by him, often under difficult circumstances. Nevertheless, this great thinker had remained by Churchill's side throughout the war, and many of the LCS's most daring and outrageous operations were the result of Brooke's 'sixth sense'. In 1994, a **STATUE** of **ALAN BROOKE [273•42]** was unveiled outside the Ministry of Defence headquarters, Whitehall.

The LCS, whose first Controlling Chief was John Bevan, was so secret that details of its existence and function were not released until 1969 by Sir Ronald Wingate. He served with the equally shadowy Ministry of Economic Warfare.

A VAST MONSTROSITY

Close to the War Rooms and other Whitehall buildings (probably connected by a labyrinth of underground tunnels), is the **ADMIRALTY CITADEL [274•42]**. Construction began in 1940 and the huge bunker-type building was intended to thwart German bombers. Located just behind the Admiralty building on Horse Guards Parade, its concrete roof is a staggering 20ft thick. The citadel was also to be used as a fortress in the event of invasion, and gun positions (openings) can still be seen, though the authorities have tried to tone-down the hideous appearance of the building with vines. Today the citadel is used as a military communications centre. Winston Churchill said the building was a "vast monstrosity."

OPEN SOURCE INTELLIGENCE

Many well known buildings in London were used to host government offices in wartime Britain. Indeed, it is evident that in future years historians and intelligence researchers will probably come across more hidden 'gems'. One such building put to good use was the **VICTORIA AND ALBERT MUSEUM, CORNWALL GARDENS, SOUTH KENSINGTON [275•47]**.

Open source intelligence (OSINT) was collected by numerous organisations such as the LCS, PWE and MOI from newspapers, magazines, broadcasts and archives. Such was the government's need for information, ASLIB (Association of Special Libraries), with the support of various information and propaganda offices, including MI6 and MI5, installed an array of microfilm cameras in a secret upper floor of the museum. Here staffers received dozens of boxes every day containing published material from all over the world. This also included publications from neutral countries, which still displayed and sold German newspapers and journals. After translation, hundreds of reels of microfilm were created every week and despatched post-haste to relevant government offices, including military and intelligence officials. The information was particularly useful in determining the mind-set of German government officials and its military planners.

© DAVID DILIFF

SPY SITES OF LONDON

XII
British Security Coordination
MI6 and a Man Called Intrepid

Few historians would reject the notion that the British Security Coordination (BSC) was a hugely influential and powerful covert intelligence organisation. Yet surprisingly it was headquartered in New York City's Rockefeller Center - Midtown Manhattan to be precise, following a brief period in Wall Street. Overseen by the UK Government in London, hundreds of MI6 officers and liaison staff were deployed here, including some under the guise of Passport Control officers. The BSC ran secret operations under the noses of Washington and in various South and Central American countries. Established in 1940 on the orders of Winston Churchill, its primary role was to secure American support against the Nazis - by any means.

Headed by Canadian businessman and entrepreneur William Stephenson (codename Intrepid - assigned by

MI6's Claude Dansey lived here - a former property owned by Sir William Stephenson - head of the powerful BSC

5 St James's Street

Eye Spy Intelligence Magazine

223

SPY SITES OF LONDON

Entrance to 5 St James's Street

23 Bruton Street
The SOE's Colin Gubbins worked from an office at this address

Churchill himself), historians also accept that the BSC evolved into one of the greatest autonomous spy organisations dutifully assisted by some very surprising people. Stephenson himself was a brilliant intelligence officer and had the necessary genius to understand evolving situations and what was required to achieve success. He was known as the 'Quiet Canadian', but in truth he was ruthlessly efficient and utterly focused.

The BSC integrated and utilised nine distinct organisations and subjects, including MI6, SOE, censorship, codes and ciphers, security, and communications. CIA historian Thomas Troy said: "In the Western hemisphere William Stephenson ran them all."

Stephenson was originally one of Claude Dansey's Z agents and owned a safe house at **5 ST JAMES'S STREET [276•42]**. This he duly sold to Dansey as it was near to his beloved White's Club. As a point of interest, following Dansey's death in 1947, MI6 officer and author Graham Greene moved into the flat.

The BSC operated front companies, spies and a subtle, but clever undercover programme using media personalities and writers. This assured good publicity for the UK. There were many prompts from the BSC to friendly US editors to run stories piling pressure on the public to help get America to physically join with Britain in the war against the Nazis. Besides infiltrating the media, unions and public service organisations were also targeted.

Officially registered as the British Passport Control Office in New York, the BSC was at the centre of British propaganda, psychological warfare and intelligence collection and manipulation. Not only did it engage in spy operations across North and South America, but the BSC utilised and liaised with organisations such as the SOE in an effort to secure information.

FBI chief J. Edgar Hoover and other US State Department officials were furious about the BSC and its infiltra-

Sir William Stephenson and badge of the BSC

tion of many US media outlets, however, because of the friendship between Winston Churchill and President Roosevelt, Hoover was somewhat powerless. This friendship is recognised by a splendid statue of the men sitting together on a bench in **NEW BOND STREET [277•62]**. The BSC also provided the FBI with intelligence on suspected Nazi spies, but 'grinding teeth' is a phrase most apt to describe Hoover's feelings about the situation.

Stephenson and Hoover agreed to tolerate each other, on the condition that MI6 did not try and recruit US agents. The BSC ignored this and by the time America declared war on Japan and Germany, the UK had hundreds of US operatives and friends who would today, be described as agents, assets and contacts. These people, from newspaper owners to regular journalists, were even provided with MI6 code numbers referencing their location by state. More teeth grinding by Hoover.

As well as securing US support for the war, the BSC ran a plethora of its own agents to infiltrate German businesses and even slipped beautiful female spies into the Vichy and Italian embassies to gather intelligence. Indeed, dozens of spies under the control of various British agencies were often active on behalf of the BSC.

Historian William Boyd wrote: *'What eventually occurred [in] 1940 and 1941 was that BSC became a huge secret agency of nationwide news manipulation and black propaganda. Pro-British and anti-German stories were planted in American newspapers and broadcast on American radio stations, and simultaneously a campaign of harassment and denigration was set in motion against those organisations perceived to be pro-Nazi or virulently isolationist (such as the notoriously anti-British America First Committee - it had more than a million paid-up members).*

'Stephenson called his methods 'political warfare', but the remarkable fact about BSC was that no one had ever tried to achieve such a level of 'spin', as we would call it today, on such a vast and pervasive scale in another country. The aim was to change the minds of an entire population: to make the people of America think that joining the war in Europe was a good thing'.

It's not really known just how many BSC agents and collaborators worked

Friends across the Pond. A splendid sculpture of wartime leaders - Franklin D. Roosevelt and Winston Churchill can be found at New Bond Street. Roosevelt was supportive of the BSC and provided covert assistance

Berkeley Square [278•55]

10 Adam Street

towards the UK government's ultimate objective, but estimates range from 2,000-3,000 - an astonishing figure and one that almost defies belief.

A journalist from the *Washington Post* who read the BSC history said: "Like many intelligence operations, this one involved exquisite moral ambiguity. The British used ruthless methods to achieve their goals; by today's peacetime standards, some of the activities may seem outrageous. Yet they were done in the cause of Britain's war against the Nazis - and by pushing America towards intervention, the British spies helped win the war."

FAMOUS AND SURPRISING INTELLIGENCE PEOPLE OF BSC

Stephenson, using his many media contacts, including people such as the Korda brothers, helped secure the services of many famous figures in the film, media, business, literary and music fields. Noel Coward, Roald Dahl, Dick Ellis, Ian Fleming, Gilbert Highet, Dorothy Maclean, Eric Maschwitz, H. Montgomery Hyde, David Ogilvy, Ivan Sanderson, Amy Elizabeth Thorp, Frank Foley to name but a few. The classic song *A Nightingale Sang in Berkeley Square,* written by Albert Eric Maschwitz, was adopted as the signature tune for the intelligence staffers of Baker Street - almost certainly because so many intelligence hubs surrounded **BERKELEY SQUARE [278•55]**. Interestingly, this became one of the songs which helped keep morale up throughout the war - and morale Stephenson recognised - was important.

Maschwitz, a writer, entertainer and broadcaster was targeted by Stephenson, for unbeknown to those outside the intelligence world, he was already a member of MI6's D (Destruction) Section. As a warfare specialist, and like so many intelligence officers, he was placed on active service with several of the so-called Baker Street Irregular organisations, including the SOE and Political Warfare Executive.

Dorothy Maclean pictured in 2008

Interestingly, Maschwitz, like the SOE's Colin Gubbins, worked from **23 BRUTON STREET [279•55]** poignantly situated next to Berkeley Square. The D-Day spy Popov - agent

SPY SITES OF LONDON

1 Dorset Square
Free French Forces headquarters

Plaque honouring British and Free French Forces who worked from 1 Dorset Square and those who fought and died in Europe

Tricycle - also operated from here. Much of the block appears to have been occupied by British Intelligence.

However, away from the hustle of SOE, PWE, MI6 and BSC, Maschwitz lived at **10 ADAM STREET [280•62]** off the Strand.

BSC - BAKER STREET CLUB

To understand just how all these organisations and individuals were linked, take for example Cyril Mills, an MI5 officer and the son of Bertram Mills, the famous circus owner. Just like film production companies, orchestras or any civilian entity that can travel abroad, even in times of growing menace, British Intelligence was keen to use their experiences and thoughts to build up a picture of events in Europe and the Americas. Mills, a trained pilot, was flying over Germany in 1936 and spoke of an "extraordinary build up of the military." When he returned to London, he mentioned this to friends and was quickly interviewed by officials. He was later recruited by MI5.

Bertram Mills Circus directors, and of course Cyril, once lived and worked from **1 DORSET SQUARE [281•15]**.

MI5's Cyril Mills

Following the establishment of SOE elements in the area including military and intelligence offices around nearby Baker Street, the building was duly handed to the SOE's RF Section.

This unit was the organisation's link with Charles de Gaulle's Free French codebreakers and a frequent visitor was perhaps the world's greatest codemaker - Leo Marks.

Eye Spy Intelligence Magazine

227

51 Cumberland Terrace

Stornoway House, 13 Cleveland Row

Stornoway House. Lord Beaverbrook hosted many BSC meetings here with Churchill and other leading intelligence figures from the organisation

William Stephenson

Mills became particularly close to Juan Pujol Garcia, a D-Day spy codenamed Garbo and often guided his work. He was then chosen to firm-up links with the security services in the United States. Thereafter, via his connections with BSC, he became MI5's representative in Canada. After the war he retired to a luxury apartment at **51 CUMBERLAND TERRACE [282•15]**. Of course, Wallis Simpson, Duchess of Windsor and the wife of King Edward VIII who abdicated his throne in order to marry her, also lived here.

THE BSC'S MEDIA KING

Another Canadian-born operative utilised by British Intelligence and the BSC was William Maxwell Aitken (Lord Beaverbrook), owner of the powerful *Daily Express*. He had played a pivotal role as Minister of Information in WWI. Twenty years later, Beaverbrook was called upon again as a minister for disinformation and to help draw America into WWII. Called the First Baron of Fleet Street, he lived and worked from the spectacular **STORNOWAY HOUSE, 13 CLEVELAND ROW [283•42]**. It was at this address Beaverbrook, Stephenson, Churchill and various other members of British Intelligence met to discuss and plan future operations.

Beaverbrook was one of Churchill's closest friends. Indeed, he was soon

Stephenson receives the US Medal of Merit from William Donovan

appointed Minister of Aircraft Production and later Minister of Supply. He was also one of the main figures behind the formation of the BBC.

The Deputy head of the BSC was MI6 officer Charles 'Dick' Howard Ellis who joined Stephenson in New York in 1940. He was responsible for making contact with and recruiting many of the people associated with BSC.

In 1918, Ellis joined the Intelligence Corp and was awarded an OBE. By

The Grand Buildings, 1-5 Strand

284•62

© JAMIE BARRAS

Eye Spy Intelligence Magazine

229

54 Wynnstay Gardens [285•60]

33 Tedworth Square [286•44]

John Burdon Haldane

1923 he was working for MI6 in Paris and various other European capital cities in the guise of a newspaper correspondent. In 1938, just prior to his role with BSC, Eye Spy learned Ellis worked from a secret MI6 office at **THE GRAND BUILDINGS 1-5 THE STRAND [284•62]**. Here he supervised the Service's monitoring of German Embassy telephone lines.

The intelligence officer lived at **54 WYNNSTAY GARDENS [285•60]** and also **33 TEDWORTH SQUARE [286•44]**. After the war, Ellis found himself at the centre of a major Cold War spy scandal as we shall discover.

Professor John Burdon Haldane was the nephew of WWI Secretary of State for War 1st Viscount Richard Haldane. He worked on a floating mine project on the River Thames which utilised the power of waves to detonate explosives. The device was intended to be a counter-measure to thwart invasion barges which Germany hoped would carry its army across the Channel. Like Dick Ellis, his name would emerge in later years as a possible double agent. Haldane, who was in fact the Chairman of the Communist newspaper - *The Daily Worker,* lived on **PARK VILLAGE EAST [287•15]**. It seems inconceivable that

287·15
Park Village East

his activities did not attract the attention of MI5 both during and after the war.

Another of Stephenson's BSC agents suspected of working for a foreign power was Cedric Belfrage. He was a journalist, translator and co-founder of the radical US newspaper the *National Guardian*. In 1937 Belfrage joined the Communist Party of the United States. However, after the war his activities attracted the attention of the FBI and in 1947 he was interviewed by Bureau agents. Eight years later he was deported back to Britain. Belfrage's treachery would not be revealed until decades later when it emerged he had been passing the content of Churchill's conversations with BSC to the Russians.

288·55

Louis de Wohl

Grosvenor House, Park Lane

The Royal Borough of Kensington and Chelsea
ABINGDON VILLAS, W.8

289•60

46 Abingdon Court Villas, Kensington

DIVERSITY OF BSC STAFFERS

The BSC was truly a diverse organisation with numerous directorates established to tackle every possible scenario. To achieve this, Stephenson required the expertise and experience of many people some may have considered strange or eccentric.

One such man was the famous Hungarian astrologer Louis de Wohl. Stephenson recognised that Hitler was often influenced by his own personal astrologer, thus through de Wohl, the BSC planted numerous stories in the world's media that would attract German attention. Many of these stories would of course turn out to be true because the BSC was manipulating the press and feeding it information which contained an element of truth. The objective was to confuse and mislead. BSC knew de Wohl's work was being taken seriously by Hitler because of the attention it attracted in Berlin. Similarly, some decisions made by Hitler were in direct response to de Wohl's predictions. Besides his work for the BSC, the astrologer assisted Britain's propaganda directorates and SOE.

When in London, de Wohl, who held an American passport, stayed at the Athenaeum Club **(See Site 031•42)** and at a safe house operated by MI5 at **GROSVENOR HOUSE, PARK LANE [288•55]** (now a Marriott hotel). Despite his fame, De Wohl died in 1961 leaving just £800 in his will.

Another unlikely character used as a spy by BSC was stage magician Jasper Maskelyne. He created large scale illusions involving camouflage. One such example involved the use of a huge mirror which reflected a model German battleship sailing up the River Thames. It was very convincing. He is

Dummy Sherman Tank

A young Julian Huxley pictured in his Intelligence Corp uniform

232

Eye Spy Intelligence Magazine

SPY SITES OF LONDON

also credited with building an inflatable 'dummy army' complete with aircraft and tanks. This was invaluable on the run-up to D-Day as the imaginary army was placed well away from the real launch points of the invasion force. Maskelyne lived at **ABINGDON COURT VILLAS, KENSINGTON [289•60]**.

BSC's attention to detail was incredible. The SOE manufactured improvised bombs which looked like dung. Professor Julian Huxley, head of London Zoo at Regent's Park and a former member of the Intelligence Corp, advised Stephenson's technical team on its appearance, colour, size and texture depending on which area SOE agents were operating. Huxley, who was born in 1887 and lived at **61 RUSSELL SQUARE [290•62]**, had many intelligence connections. In 1927 he resigned his chair at King's College to take up full-time work with H. G. Wells, a key member of Britain's WWI propaganda bureau Wellington House which evolved into Crewe House. Stephenson used Huxley's experience in various ways and drew upon his knowledge of biology and deception. Huxley met with his intelligence contacts at a safe house in nearby Cambridge Gate **(See Site 270•15)** which borders Regent's Park. He lived at **31 POND STREET, HAMSTEAD HEATH [291•19]** from

BSC man Jasper Maskelyne (far right) and his magic troupe in Nairobi. CIRCA. 1950

291•19
31 Pond Street

292•41
Dryden Road

Eye Spy Intelligence Magazine

233

290·62
61 Russell Square

Colonel Bailey (far right) pictured with his wife in Tibet. CIRCA. 1927

1943 to 1975 the year of his death. Huxley was knighted in 1958 for services to his country, and at this residence a plaque, said to be the "loveliest in London," can be found.

Age was of no concern to Stephenson, which is evidenced in the recruitment of a man who would be nicknamed 'The Mail Carrier'. Colonel Frederick 'Eric' Bailey, who operated for MI6 in WWI, was 60-years-old when he was appointed as King's Messenger to Central and South America aiding the BSC. He carried ULTRA intelligence and communications material deemed so sensitive it could not be transmitted even in code.

Bailey's reputation for bravery was sown in WWI as Britain and Russia wrestled for supremacy along the Himalayan borders. The agent used his passion for butterfly collecting, photography and big game hunting as cover to secure intelligence for MI6.

As a former political officer of Tibet, he became another invaluable and most trusted member of Stephenson's team. After the war, Bailey returned home to his residence on **DRYDEN ROAD, HARROW [292·41]**.

GENESIS OF THE CENTRAL INTELLIGENCE AGENCY (CIA)

Stephenson's main liaison in the United States was William J. Donovan, a powerful figure with the ear of President Roosevelt.

Donovan was invited to Britain to examine the war effort and the intelligence machinery. Stephenson explained the role of MI6 and the SOE, and convinced the American his country should embark upon the formation of such organisations. That didn't go down too well with FBI chief Hoover - who headed the country's only civilian-based intelligence gathering service. However, it was a significant moment in the world of intelligence, for that London meeting sowed the seed for the creation of the famous international US intelligence service - the Central Intelligence Agency (CIA).

Whilst on a research trip to London, Donovan met with British agent Joan Bright, a stenographer. Her recruitment is interesting. In 1939 she was told by a friend that a job vacancy might be available if she went to St James's Park Underground Station at 11.00am. Bright was instructed to wear a pink carnation. It was a strange suggestion but one she decided to go along with. She was met by a govern-

William Donovan

59 Queen's Gate
293•47

ment official who led her across the road to MI6 headquarters at the Broadway Buildings. Here she was asked to sign the Official Secrets Act.

Thereafter Bright's prowess for intelligence work grew and she became a key liaison figure in several organisations, including the BSC. Her most important role was running Churchill's Special Information Centre situated deep underground in Whitehall. The facility was known as the Rotundas and originally consisted of three buildings bounded by Great Peter Street, Marsham Street, Horseferry Road and Monk Street. Sadly this most important facility no longer exists.

Bright formed a personal relationship with the MI6 and NID intelligence officer Ian Fleming. He was of course attached to the BSC and attended the top secret special agent training facility which Stephenson helped to create known as Camp-X in Canada. Bright once said of Fleming: "He was awfully attractive and fun but very elusive. I think he was a ruthless man... he would drop somebody if he didn't want them any more. That would be it."

It is quite possible the couple met occasionally at Bright's apartment at **59 QUEEN'S GATE [293•47]**. It's also said that Fleming used some of her attributes to create his fictional character Miss Moneypenny in his James Bond spy novels.

Another of Bright's intelligence associates at Military Intelligence (Research) was the well known actor and romancer David Niven. Though not necessarily attached to the BSC, he did work with Stephenson on various film projects. Niven was part of an Army film unit which made two pictures *The First of the Few* and *The Way Ahead*. Both were produced to encourage the United States to join Britain against the Nazis. Most

David Niven

Eye Spy Intelligence Magazine   235

St James's Park Station - scene of a most unusual recruitment encounter

295•55

44 Park Street, Mayfair

interestingly, and probably no coincidence, in 1979 Niven played Stephenson in the television mini-series *A Man Called Intrepid*. Amusingly, Niven used 28 St James's as his wartime address - this of course just happens to be Boodle's Club - a venue often frequented by intelligence staffers! And just like another of Stephenson's team, Jasper Maskelyne, Niven lived at Abingdon Court Villas **(See Site 289•60)**.

One of Niven's associates was the actor Peter Ustinov. He tried to find employment with British Intelligence but failed an exam. His father, Jona Baron von Ustinov (better known as Klop Ustinov), fared a little better.

Prior to the war, Klop had worked for a German news agency but later joined MI5. He was also handler of agent Wolfgang zu Putlitz who furnished information about Hitler.

One of Klop's associates was Moura Budberg, who at the beginning of the war worked for the propaganda unit - Joint Broadcasting Committee. Budberg had befriended many senior intelligence officials but there was deep suspicion in London she was a double agent - a Communist spy. At her apartment - **68 ENNISMORE GARDENS, KNIGHTSBRIDGE [294•47]** she often hosted cocktail parties. Many intelligence and government figures would attend. And it was

Jona Baron von Ustinov - Klop

through one of her guests - H. G. Wells - she met and eventually worked with BSC official - Hungarian-born Alexander Korda (Sándor László Kellner). Budberg was known as the 'Mata Hari of Russia',* while Klop was undoubtedly one of Britain's most underestimated and important spies.

LONDON FILMS

Korda headed by far the most important commercial cover used by MI6 - London Films - a feature film company. His work, along with that of his brother Zoltan, would be of immense help to Stephenson. Korda was recommended by his close friend - Robert Vansittart, a senior British diplomat and brilliant analyst who had the ear of Churchill and British Intelligence. He recognised that a film company could legitimately operate abroad and carry equipment supplying overseas agents.

Vansittart, who lived at **44 PARK STREET, MAYFAIR [295•55]** had

* Mata Hari - suspected Dutch-born German spy executed by the French in 1917 - real name Margaretha Geertruida MacLeod nee Zelle

SPY SITES OF LONDON
294•47
68 Ennismore Gardens

MI6 contact man Robert Vansittart

opposed Hitler long before war broke out and suggested Britain take a tough stance against Berlin following a visit to Germany in 1936. There is little doubt his suspicions about appeasement and Nazi aggression were proven correct. Of interest, he was also second cousin to MI6's Thomas Edward Lawrence, better known of course as Lawrence of Arabia.

Korda worked from **21-22 GROSVENOR STREET [296•55]** from 1936 to 1939, assisting the government on various projects. One of the more unusual was helping to build Camp-X, the agent training facility in Canada where he created realistic locations replicating German sites for exercises. Korda recruited Hollywood make-up artists to help develop disguise techniques, and agents were given acting lessons. Some of his films, for example - *That Hamilton Woman* - were viewed as British propaganda by critics in a still neutral United States. Korda shared his time between the UK and USA, which led later intelligence writers to call him a "courier for Churchill." By 1943, Korda had returned to London and started to make films again, but the climate was tough and opportunities few. Nevertheless, by then he had been knighted by King George VI - and not just because of his work in the film industry. For the record, some film production actually took place behind the Grosvenor Street address inside a small mews house.

Alexander Korda resided in **AVENUE ROAD [297•22]** a short distance from his brother Zolton in **FROGNAL GARDENS [298•19]**. A third brother, Vincent, art director for Alexander, travelled the world in an effort to secure the services of actors and actresses, some of whom were used by the BSC and its propaganda arms. He operated from **32 WILTON PLACE [299•42]**. Also situated here - the

Suspected double agent Moura Budberg pictured in 1972

Eye Spy Intelligence Magazine

SPY SITES OF LONDON

296•55

Alexander Korda

21-22 Grosvenor Street

Sir ALEXANDER KORDA 1893-1956 Film Producer worked here 1932-1936

BERKELEY HOTEL [300•42], a fashionable and popular WWII venue frequented by British Intelligence and SOE officials and agents. Perhaps the most famous MI6 officer to dine here was Sidney Reilly - the so-called 'Ace of Spies'. Of interest, the Berkeley was later used by the KGB as a meeting point between agents and handlers. One such aspiring spy was William Marshall. He met with his controller at the hotel, but was arrested in 1952 before he could do any real damage.

Vincent Korda's son, Michael, also worked in intelligence as a language specialist in the RAF.

Another Korda connection to the BSC can be found in the person of Harford Montgomery Hyde, a barrister, biographer and MI6 officer (Section D) who worked for Claude Dansey on many overseas operations. Interestingly, whilst in London he shared an office with Guy Burgess - who was already in the employ of the Russians. Hyde's friendship with Stephenson continued after the war and once a year he would visit him in Bermuda at his home in the Princess Hotel. This location had been the headquarters of a BSC/MI6 front known as the British Imperial Censorship. Amongst its various tasks the organisation sought to identify German spies operating in the United States.

In 1962 Hyde published *The Quiet Canadian* a controversial book which covered the activities of the BSC. Hyde became assistant editor of the *Law Reports* until 1947 and was legal advisor to British Lion Film Corporation - run of course by Korda. Hyde operated from St. Ermin's Hotel **(See Site 140•42)** but worked at **4 BRICK COURT [301•08]** just off the Strand. Interestingly, whilst operational in London, Hyde also stayed at 32 Wilton Place - an address used by Vincent Korda.

The BSC operation in Bermuda also provided a plethora of intelligence on German communications in North and South America. An MI6 officer attached to the facility was Naval Intelligence Division man Ivan T. Sanderson. He used his knowledge of biology and his writing skills to secure contacts with many useful people in the US media and would eventually become a press agent in New York. And as evidence again that

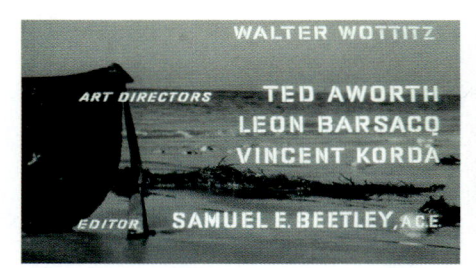

End credits for the picture *The Longest Day* - the Allied invasion of Europe - note Vincent Korda

Stephenson cared little about the background interests of some of his associates, he ignored the fact that Sanderson had a fascination with the paranormal and was a member of the Society for the Investigation of the Unexplained based at the British Museum! Undoubtedly many interesting meetings and discussions took place at his residence at **7 CHESTER MEWS** off **WILTON STREET** [302•42].

Unbeknown to many, but of no surprise to intelligence watchers, the famous Hollywood actor Laurence Olivier also assisted Alexander Korda and the BSC. Besides his acting career, Olivier worked for the SOE's early propaganda arm Electra House **(See Site 163•08)**.

Based in America, he quietly played a vital role in influencing leading figures (including diplomats) that the United States should join Britain against Germany. It was Winston Churchill who requested that Korda secure the services of Olivier. This brilliant actor met his future wife Vivien Leigh whilst acting together at the Old Vic Theatre **(See Site 503•23)**. They lived at **DURHAM COTTAGE, 4 CHRISTCHURCH STREET** [303•44] between 1937 and 1956.

THE PORT WATCHERS

Security and intelligence collection were crucial to organisations such as MI6. And in times of war, information is gleaned from numerous private companies and government bodies. Undoubtedly one of the most important entities was the **BRITISH PORTS ASSOCIATION** at **AFRICA HOUSE**,

300•42 Berkeley Hotel, Wilton Place

298•19 Frognal Gardens

297•22 Avenue Road

Eye Spy Intelligence Magazine

SPY SITES OF LONDON

In WWII, the Princess Hotel, Bermuda, hosted the British Imperial Censorship - a BSC-MI6 front. It also became home to BSC director Sir William Stephenson

Laurence Olivier worked for SOE and the BSC

© ALLAN WARREN

64-78 KINGSWAY [304•37]. This organisation was of use to Claude Dansey and the Passport Control Office, but even more so to the BSC. One of the BSC men who used this address was statistician Doctor Herbert Sichel. He was a shadowy figure but a master of recognising the importance of data attached to cargo.

The BSC established a network of agents and observers on merchant ships crossing the Atlantic. Many of the operatives were recruited from the crews who would write reports. Much focus was upon the manifests (cargo) and passenger lists. BSC agents would also be deployed in the ports of Britain and America in order to intercept and report upon unusual activities. Stephenson was concerned that Germany was still importing materials for the war effort through bogus companies and third parties.

After the war Sichel established the Operational Research Bureau. And it is here one can understand why he was of such immense help to Stephenson. The ORB discipline considers the application of advanced analytical methods - this 'application' helped the BSC make considered decisions.

The BSC operated numerous unusual directorates which collectively combined to make the organisation a most

301•08

4 Brick Court (off Strand)

299•42

302•42

32 Wilton Place

7 Chester Mews off Wilton Street

303•44

Durham Cottage, 4 Christchurch Street

Eye Spy Intelligence Magazine

241

SPY SITES OF LONDON

304•37
Africa House, 64-78 Kingsway

flexible and powerful entity. It could draw upon the experiences of earlier WWI British Intelligence efforts in the theatres of disinformation and psychological warfare. One such organisation associated with these fields was of course Wellington House **(See Site 066•42)** which helped shape and control public opinion. In 1921, three years after the war ended, it evolved into what became known as the **TAVISTOCK INSTITUTE, 120 BELSIZE AVENUE [305•19]**. And it was to this institute that Stephenson turned again to help manipulate American thinking.

PSYCHOLOGICAL WARFARE

One man who worked at Tavistock was Aldus Huxley (the brother of Julian who headed London Zoo and assisted the BSC and SOE), a writer who experimented with psychological drugs. He wrote two controversial novels - *Brave New World* set in a dystopian London and *The Doors of Perception*. He would later go on to work for the CIA in the Agency's controversial MKULTRA project.

Another Tavistock man was MI6 officer David Ogilvy, known affectionately as the 'father of advertising'. He worked for George Gallup's British Institute For Social Research and Public Opinion. Ogilvy was also a BSC officer who utilised his knowledge of human behaviour applying the Gallup Technique to intelligence decision making - this was of immense use to Stephenson in understanding how ordinary Americans felt about the war.

Aldus Huxley

David Ogilvy

© FALLING ANGEL

242

Eye Spy Intelligence Magazine

Sigmund Freud

Conveniently he worked at the British Embassy in Washington DC. Towards the end of the war, Ogilvy's research was also used by Eisenhower's Psychological Warfare Board. In 1962 a *Time* magazine writer called him "the most sought-after wizard in today's advertising industry." At the time of his recruitment by MI6, Ogilvy lived in **RAVENSCROFT AVENUE [306•17]**.

One of the three founding members of the Tavistock Centre was Edward Bernays - described as a "pioneer of public relations and propaganda." He was in fact the nephew of another famous man - Sigmund Freud - the founding father of psychoanalysis. Interestingly, visitors to this most unusual London site will find a statue of Freud in the grounds of the centre. Today Tavistock is a specialist mental health trust. Freud's last residence in London was turned into the **FREUD MUSEUM, 20 MARESFIELD GARDENS, HAMPSTEAD [307•19]**.

Best known for his children's books, author Roald Dahl served in the RAF as a fighter pilot and then as an intelligence officer. He was soon targeted by the BSC.

Dahl began supplying intelligence to Stephenson on US affairs and worked closely with David Ogilvy and Ian Fleming. Regarded as one of the greatest story-tellers for children of the 20th century, Stephenson recognised that his experience in this field would be useful as a "communicator for British interests in America." He had been recruited into MI6 in 1942

Sigmund Freud's statue at the Tavistock Centre

305•19

Tavistock Centre, 120 Belsize Avenue

Eye Spy Intelligence Magazine

243

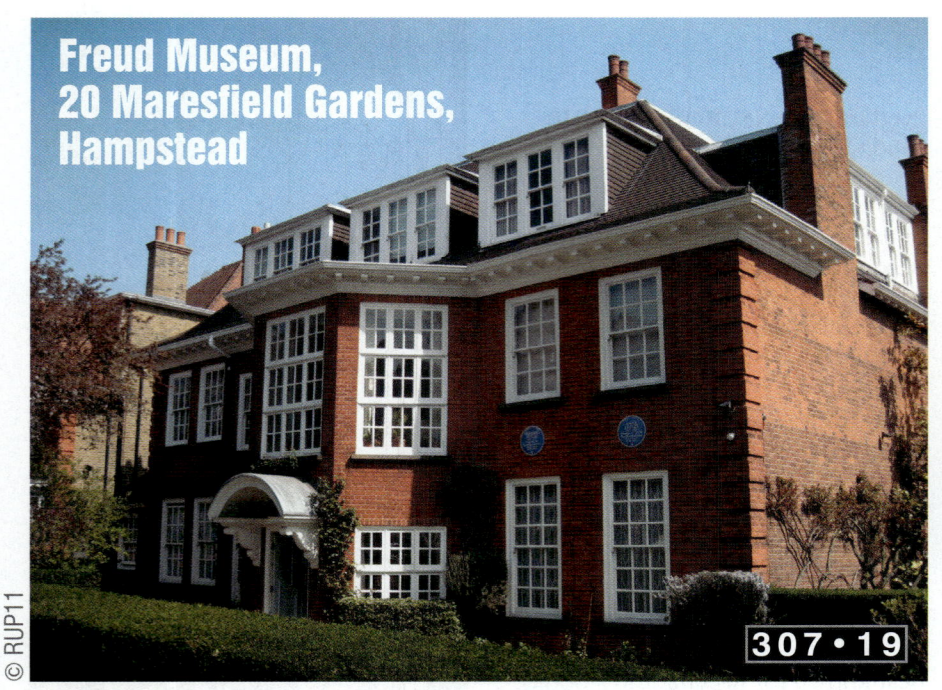

Freud Museum, 20 Maresfield Gardens, Hampstead

307•19

Roald Dahl

by Britain's Under Secretary of State for Air Harold Balfour (later Lord Balfour) at the **ROYAL AERO CLUB, 119 PICCADILLY [308•55]**. A founding member of the club was MI6 Chief Mansfield Cumming. A short time later he became the Assistant Air Attache at the British Embassy in Washington DC. His double life as a spy and writer now began. Dahl lived and worked for 36 years from **81-83 HIGH STREET, GREAT MISSENDEN, BUCKINGHAMSHIRE [309•99]** some 20 miles northwest of London. The building now hosts the Roald Dahl Museum and Story Centre.

As a point of reference, visitors to Piccadilly can find the **RAF CLUB, 128 PICCADILLY [310•55]** and the **CAVALRY & GUARDS CLUB, 127 PICCADILLY [311•55]**. One long-time member of the Cavalry & Guards Club was MI6 man Anthony Cavendish. He often had drinks here with KGB spy Kim Philby and was a personal friend of MI6 Chief Maurice Oldfield.

A MONUMENTAL SPY OPERATION

Of course Stephenson's efforts to sway American public opinion worked. And when the Japanese attacked the US Navy facility at Pearl Harbor on 7 December 1941, the United States joined the war. Even so, the BSC

306•17

Ravenscroft Avenue

244

Eye Spy Intelligence Magazine

SPY SITES OF LONDON

Cavalry & Guards Club, 127 Piccadilly

Harold Balfour of the Air Ministry recruited Roald Dahl at the Aero Club

RAF Club, 128 Piccadilly

continued to operate and assist spy operations in Europe and elsewhere. Several of the so-called D-Day Spies were attached to the BSC, and the intelligence these agents provided would prove invaluable. Stephenson built up good relations with many of the spies who were primarily operating in Europe - another indication of his wide intelligence remit. His attention to detail would again prove invaluable in the run-up to the Allied invasion of Europe in 1944.

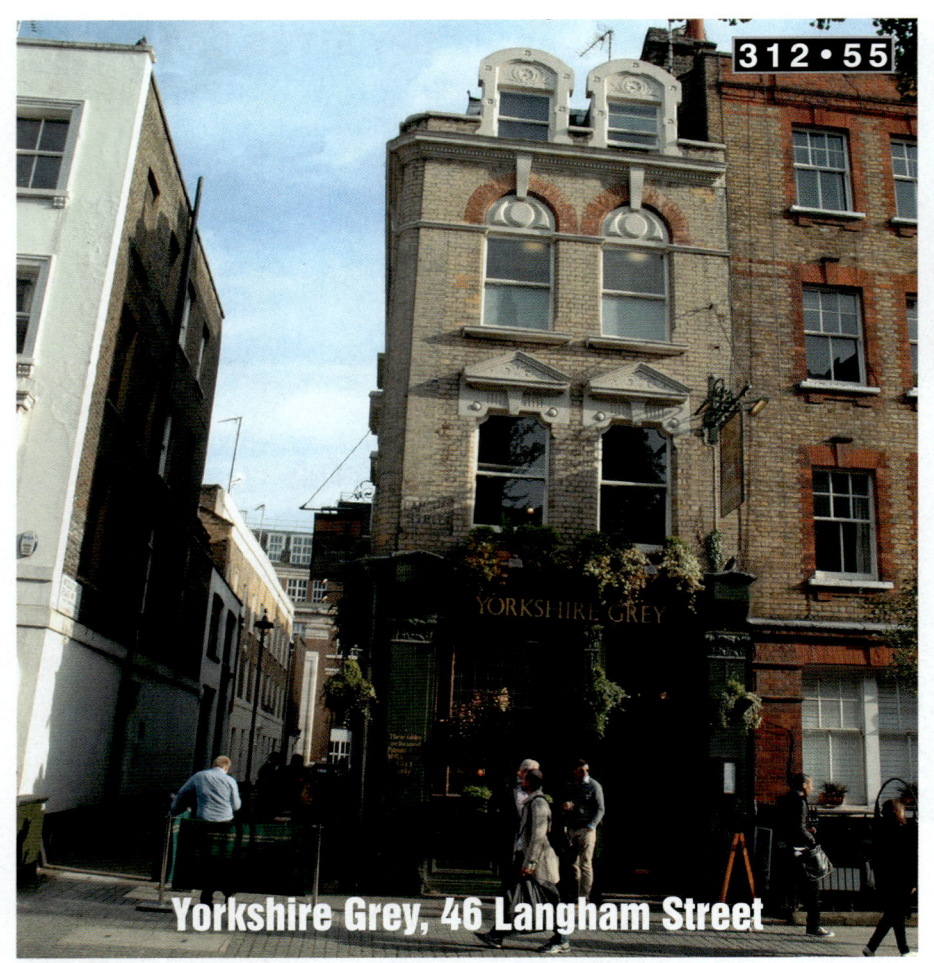

Yorkshire Grey, 46 Langham Street

81-83 High Street, Great Missenden

When D-Day finally arrived, Stephenson's work was almost concluded. However, until then the deception, subterfuge, psychological warfare, espionage and 'dirty tricks' continued.

One little known address where the BSC first began its underhand work to secure popular American public support was not in the United States, but a small public house known as the **YORKSHIRE GREY, 46 LANGHAM STREET [312•8]**. Even before the first Luftwaffe bombs had begun to fall on London, undercover BSC men met

Royal Aero Club, 119 Piccadilly

246

Eye Spy Intelligence Magazine

The Yorkshire Grey. A WWII meeting place where carefully trained BSC spies sought to influence American journalists sent to cover the war in Europe. Note the photo of the nearby BBC headquarters at Portland Place

and drank with many American journalists who had been despatched to Britain to cover the war. And when the bombs did start to decimate the city, these meetings became even more important. Influencing the US press through subterfuge had begun. But for the Allied agents sent to mainland Europe as Germany conquered nation after nation, their ultra dangerous work had only just begun.

BRITISH SECURITY COORDINATION CAMP-X AND A LICENCE TO KILL

Unofficially known as Camp-X, the paramilitary agent training installation of the British Security Coordination was established on 6 December 1941, at Whitby, Ontario, Canada, through the co-operative efforts of the governments of Canada and Britain. The facility was the brainchild of Sir William Stephenson after Winston Churchill instructed him to "create the clenched fist that would provide the knockout blow" to the Axis powers. Ironically, the camp opened just one day before the attack on Pearl Harbor by the Japanese.

Camp-X's location was chosen with a great deal of thought: a remote site on the shores of Lake Ontario, yet only 30 miles across the lake from the United States. It was ideal for bouncing radio signals from Europe, South America, and of course, between London and the BSC headquarters in New York.

The commanding officers of the Camp soon realised the impact of Camp-X. Requests for more agents and different training programmes were coming in daily from London and New York. Not only were they faced with training agents who were going to go behind enemy lines on specialised missions, but now they were receiving requests to train agent instructors as well. These would be recruited primarily from the United States for the OSS (Office of Strategic Services) and for the FBI. Soon there were trainers training trainers for new camps being established in America.

Camp-X Museum

The psychological aspect of training was most critical. As crucial as the agent's training in silent killing and unarmed combat was the development of their ability to quickly and accurately assess the suitability of a potential partisan. Agents had to recognise a would-be recruit by being alert at all times and in any situation. They were trained to listen for a comment about a government,

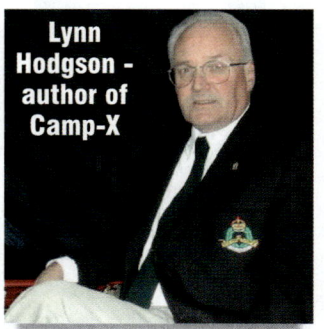

Lynn Hodgson - author of Camp-X

the Nazis or how the war was progressing, and to subsequently engage the individual in conversation. Allied agents were trained in all espionage activities - sabotage, subversion, deception, intelligence and other special tasks.

Eye Spy Intelligence Magazine

247

OPERATION ANTHROPOID
CAMP-X, FAIRBAIRN AND ASSASSINATION

Eye Spy Canadian editor Lynn Hodgson secured an intelligence file which proved Fairbairn trained the agents who killed leading Nazi Reinhard Heydrich in 1942

Agent trainers William Fairbairn and Rex Applegate

Reinhard Heydrich's car following the attack

Camp-X helped establish a major communications link between North and South America and European operations of SOE. Codenamed Hydra, the resulting short-wave radio and telecommunications centre was the most powerful of its type. Largely hand-made by a few gifted Canadian radio amateurs, Hydra played a central role in the tactical and strategic Allied radio networks.

Less well known is the fact that the first commandant of Camp-X was scheduled to be none other than Kim Philby - the KGB spy in British Intelligence.

Kim Philby had served briefly as an instructor at Beaulieu, the top-notch SOE finishing school in England. He was stationed there along with fellow KGB conspirators Guy Burgess and Donald Maclean. While at Beaulieu, Philby contributed to the writing of the SOE Syllabus, or training manual. Whether upon instructions from Moscow, or of his own accord, or both, Philby managed to convince his superiors in MI6 that he was of far greater value to the British in England than he ever could be in Canada.

Had MI6/SOE insisted upon Philby's transfer, how vastly different might the outcome of the secret spy wars of 1940 to 1963, and beyond, have been?

The only thing that remains of Camp-X is a small strip of grassland known as Intrepid Park, but visitors to its former location will find a splendid museum.

• Operation Anthropoid agents received their final briefing at the Czech Government-in-exile headquarters in London (See Site 379•56).

CAMP-X TRAINING:
Colonel William Fairbairn illustrates the art of 'silent killing'. Within moments of shaking hands with Fairbairn, an unsuspecting man can only muster up a silent gasp before what would have been certain death

Eye Spy Intelligence Magazine

SPY SITES OF LONDON

XIII Interrogation & Interpretation
Deceit, Danger and Aerial Spies

Throughout the war Britain ran a host of military organisations all connected to intelligence gathering, and though not actually under the direct control of MI5 and MI6, they were inextricably threaded together through a network of offices and administrators: their importance grew as D-Day loomed. Two areas vital to this endeavour was the interrogation of Axis prisoners and photographic analysis. Both relied heavily on the covert assistance of spies and deception.

Lt. Colonel Robin 'Tin Eye' Stephens was an MI5 officer and the Commandant of Camp 020, a facility within **LATCHMERE HOUSE** in the village of **HAM COMMON, SOUTH LONDON** [313•50] where German agents were interrogated and often turned. One well known inmate was Rudolf Hess, Hitler's deputy. Before then, the building was used in World War One to treat soldiers suffering from psychological problems - doctors here first referenced the phrase 'shell shock'.

Another building where MI5 undertook interrogations was the sinister-

WHATEVER'S IN HIS POCKETS, YOU MAY WANT IT, INTELLIGENCE NEED IT! HAND IT OVER

Colonel Robin 'Tin-Eye' Stephens

Camp 020, Latchmere House, Ham Common [313•50]

Eye Spy Intelligence Magazine 249

Royal Victoria Patriotic Asylum

Covert wartime MI5 interrogation centre

looking **OLD VICTORIA ASYLUM IN WANDSWORTH [314•40]**. Suspected spies, traitors and collaborators all eventually found their way to the centre. The man who conducted interviews here was the legendary Dutch-born MI5 interrogator Lt. Colonel Oreste Pinto.

Another interrogation centre at **TRENT PARK, ENFIELD [315•99]** was run by the Combined Services. This usually received high-ranking Nazis who had already spent time at an MI5 facility known as the **LONDON CAGE, 13 KENSINGTON PALACE GARDENS [316•60]** (now occupied by the Russian Embassy and the ambassador's residence).

The main building believed to house the majority of prisoners (1-3) was demolished in 1961 but two other buildings as well as the ambassador's residence still exist. These are **5 KENSINGTON PALACE GARDENS [317•60]** (consular section) and **6-7 KENSINGTON PALACE GARDENS [318•60]** (chancery housing Russian diplomatic mission and chancellor).

Colonel Alexander Scotland

Colonel Alexander Scotland commanded the Cage which became infamous for reports of torture, degradation and humiliation. It was a truly secret camp, kept even off the official Red Cross lists (until one guard developed a conscience and tipped-off the organisation about its existence). Conditions here were a world away from Scotland's luxury apartment at **21 CLARENCE GATE GARDENS, GLENTWORTH STREET [319•15]**.

Every morning when Scotland arrived at the Cage he would declare, "abandon all hope ye who enter here."

13 Kensington Palace Gardens

7 Kensington Palace Gardens

The London Cage, 5-6 Kensington Palace Gardens

German POWs

There has always been confusion over the exact location of the so-called London Cage. Eye Spy is quite satisfied its main centre is today 5-6 Kensington Palace Gardens, occupied by the Embassy of the Federation of Russia. Other nearby buildings were also used by MI9, MI5 and Special Branch to interrogate prisoners

13 Kensington Palace Gardens

Scotland and Stephens disliked each other and the former was officially banned from Camp 020 after he allegedly struck a prisoner he was interrogating. Scotland had been a guest at the camp and Stephens was so furious to have his own rules ignored by an officer that he later went on to resist all further requests for outside interrogators to visit 020.

Most of the cells at Trent Park had been bugged by MI5 which enabled the Service to glean information that helped provide an insight into the war situation and morale of the German Army in general. Similarly, deception agents posing as prisoners would generate rumours and false stories - this in an attempt to stimulate discussions.

SPY SITES OF LONDON

Latimer House, Buckinghamshire
320•99

The existence of the German rocket station at Peenemunde was first exposed by prisoners at Trent Park

THE FRENCH INTELLIGENCE KILLING ROOM OF DUKE STREET

Though the interrogation methods used by Britain may have seemed harsh to German POWs, they were nothing compared to a secret London facility operated by Free French Forces. Here officers from the Bureau Central de Renseignements et d'Action (BCRA), an intelligence section, received suspected Vichy French spies and Communists.

The BCRA had evolved from a 1941 service created by General Charles de Gaulle. He lived with his family at **99 FROGNAL [321•19]**. Besides opulent living quarters, the impressive residence, now a convent, was used to host meetings with government and military officials, including some from the BCRA.

BCRA personnel had embedded agents in occupied France and on the whole was a very useful partner to the SOE and MI6. But incidents of a more distasteful nature would sour relations and create a great deal of mistrust.

TORTURE OF MI6 AGENTS

The SOE did have a liaison officer who collected snippets of intelligence from the BCRA, but it was largely an autonomous operation, and its methods were brutal. Indeed, we understand secret files still exist which report upon the harsh interrogation of three men who were actually MI6 agents.

When the body of one of the agents, who had already been interviewed by British Intelligence on his return from

Besides the 10,000 troops who passed through Trent Park, 59 high-ranking German generals were also kept prisoner here. They were the main focus of the bugging operation which was operated from a site known as the M Room and overseen by MI6 officer Colonel Thomas Kendrick. This endeavour proved its value on more than one occasion. For example, information on German V-1 and V-2 rocket sites was secured; and admissions that some German officers had participated in the murder of thousands of Jewish citizens.

Other less harsh interrogation centres also existed throughout the country. Two fairly quite close to London include **LATIMER HOUSE, BUCKINGHAMSHIRE [320•99]** and a little further away Wiltern House in Wiltshire. However, just like the London Cage, some researchers believe Rudolf Hess spent time at Latimer House and like most prisoner centres, MI5 eavesdropped on conversations.

Another Combined Services Detailed Interrogation Centre operated at the Tower of London. Outside the capital was the notorious Camp 020R (R=Reserve Detention Centre) at Huntercombe in Nuffield in Oxon. There were nine such sites in the UK, some based at race courses and there was even one sited at Preston North End football club in Lancashire.

SPY SITES OF LONDON

315•99

Trent Park, near Cockfosters

319•15

21 Clarence Gate Gardens, Glentworth Street

France, was found dead in the cellar at the BCRA headquarters, close to Selfridges at **10 DUKE STREET [322•55]**, there was uproar. However, perhaps in a bid to temper Anglo-French relations, the official verdict was that the man had killed himself by hanging.

But Special Branch detectives noticed a variety of injuries inflicted on the prisoner during his interrogation. Some intelligence men in MI6 and MI5 suspected he had been hanged (after death) to mask these wounds and to create the illusion of suicide. It transpired the MI6 agents were simply following protocol in not revealing certain facts - a brave decision which resulted in more beatings.

As the war progressed, British Intelligence became increasingly uncomfortable with the goings on in Duke Street. This led to MI5's Guy Liddell writing a note on 14 January 1943 in his famous wartime diary: *'Personally, I think it is time that Duke Street was closed down'*. This of course is exactly what happened.

One US naval intelligence officer, sickened by what he had learned, then started to speak about the cellar - known as the 'torture chamber'. A report filed by the officer says: *'The*

© ROGER MARKS

Eye Spy Intelligence Magazine 253

PASSING THROUGH THE LONDON CAGE

Colonel Scotland interrogated many important and high ranking Nazis, including General Kurt Meyer who faced the death penalty for his role in the murder of Canadian soldiers in WWII. Scotland admitted Meyer received "milder treatment" following the public outcry after the atrocity had "grown cold."

Another Nazi who passed through the London Cage was SS General Sepp Dietrich. He was responsible for the murder of British POWs in 1940. Scotland also interrogated several SS and Gestapo officers who ordered the shooting dead of 50 Allied prisoners who escaped from Stalag Luft III in 1944. This shocking incident was made into the motion picture - *The Great Escape*.

Stalag Luft III's Kommandant Von Lindeiner-Wildau was arrested (by the SS) and court-martialled for allowing so many prisoners to escape. He was fortunate to survive. At the end of the war he surrendered to British forces and spent two years at the London Cage. The intelligence he provided to Special Branch was incredibly useful. Wildau was freed in 1947 after evidence showed he was respected by many of the inmates and had followed the Geneva Accords on the treatment of Prisoners of War. Several Gestapo officials were executed for their role in the massacre.

Rudolf Hess was moved from one location to another in an effort to conceal his whereabouts

The Tower of London

SS General Sepp Dietrich

Left: Frederich Wilhelm Von Lindeiner-Wildau

General Kurt Meyer - ordered killing of Canadian soldiers

Memorial to the 50 Allied soldiers who were shot dead after being recaptured following a mass escape from Stalag Luft III

men at Duke Street were hard, cruel and unscrupulous. They remind me of the Nazi Party officials and workers I knew in Berlin. Duke Street sounded very much like the notorious city concentration camp, Columbia-Haus, formerly run by the SS in Berlin'.

The US military operated a covert counter-intelligence section from **300 OXFORD STREET [323•55]** which is today the John Lewis store. The office - called Room 102 - supplied Washington with reports on the activities of the BCRA. These would not have sat comfortably with officials, nor would they have helped those charged with organising joint operations with the French. Events at Duke Street will also have been discussed at two important locations used to launch operations in France and elsewhere. **32 WEYMOUTH STREET [324•55]** was used to house French SOE agents before they were secreted onto the continent. A little further along the street at **59 WEYMOUTH STREET [325•55]** the US Army operated an important signals section.

So concerned were government ministers, that some people held at Duke Street were allegedly allocated monies from MI5's coffers - this to compensate for their suffering.

Details of what happened in this building eventually leaked to other officials and politicians. However, in

SPY SITES OF LONDON

Churchill and Charles de Gaulle

1943, de Gaulle decided to take flight and move to Algiers. The French stayed in London, but with the war nearing its end, this darkest of matters was quietly dropped.

Various addresses in London have been proposed for the centre. However, the original building was demolished, but the steps leading to the cellar where the alleged torture and killings took place remain.

There is another **10 DUKE STREET, ST JAMES'S [326•42]** in London which some people believe is the address of the French intelligence service. However, this is incorrect but the building does host a Masonic Lodge, described as one of the most "mysterious bodies in international Masonic circles" and it too has steps leading to a cellar.

Aliens arriving from Germany or Italy were housed at Internment Camp 001 at the **ORATORY SCHOOLS, BURY WALK [327•44]**. Here they were questioned by friendly officials and greeted with a handshake, cigarette, pot of tea and a proclamation - "welcome to the land of liberty." However, if deemed a 'person of interest' by MI5 they were quickly relocated to Latchmere House 020 for more rigorous interrogation.

General de Gaulle broadcasting from a BBC studio, probably Bush House

COURTESY: BBC

The Bury Walk location had been used in WWI as a school for exiled Belgian children. Its history is inextricably linked to the Cadogan family. Opposite the Oratory is St Luke's Church and the Cadogans owned all the land

321•19

99 Frognal
Charles de Gaulle resided here with his family during the German occupation of France

Eye Spy Intelligence Magazine

255

SPY SITES OF LONDON
300 Oxford Street

Room 102 - WWII US counter-intelligence section

Saint Luke's Church, Chelsea

foreign exiles. In 1952 he was appointed chairman of the board of governors at the BBC by Winston Churchill. Cadogan lived at **18 SLOANE GARDENS [328•42]**.

and had been patrons of the church since it was built in 1819. At the time Camp 001 was created, Sir Alexander Cadogan was Permanent Under Secretary for Foreign Affairs and a central figure in British policy-making. He also had a plethora of intelligence links and it seems likely he suggested the use of the Oratory for processing

Whilst some of the sites used for interrogation were tough, MI5 did use other more luxurious venues. One such location was a suite at the **WALDORF HOTEL, ALDWYCH**

A US intelligence officer compared the interrogation centre at 10 Duke Street to the notorious Columbia-Haus concentration camp in Berlin run by the SS. This photograph shows the memorial to the camp's victims

SPY SITES OF LONDON

322•55
10 Duke Street

French officers from the Bureau Central de Renseignements et d'Action (BCRA) ran a gruesome interrogation and torture centre from its cellar

The stairs leading to the interrogation cellar

[329•62]. However, this was used mainly for suspected Nazi spies. In the 1950s and 1960s, it was a known meeting point for Soviet agents.

THE ALLIED AERIAL SPIES AND PHOTOGRAPHIC ANALYSIS

To the planners of D-Day, photographic intelligence was just as important as that gleaned from German POWs and British agents operating in Europe. Central to the analysis was the specialist RAF Intelligence Branch which operated out of **DANESFIELD HOUSE, RAF MEDMENHAM** near **MARLOW, BUCKINGHAMSHIRE** [330•99].

US and British military intelligence spent months flying over the coastline of France securing millions of aerial images which made a mosaic of Hitler's Atlantic Wall and revealed its many defences. They also allowed commanders to identify weak points and places which would allow the invasion forces to deploy.

Without aerial photographic intelligence, it is certain the Allies would

Alexander Cadogan (left) and Lord Bevan at Gatow Airport, Berlin, 1945

COURTESY: US ARMY SIGNALS CORPS

Eye Spy Intelligence Magazine 257

SPY SITES OF LONDON

326•42
10 Duke Street, St James's

have suffered thousands of additional casualties and the operation could have ended in failure.

RAF Medmenham supported a dedicated photo reconnaissance unit (PRU) that was eventually designated the Central Interpretation Unit (CIU), and became part of MI4. By 1945, the unit, which consisted of 1,700 personnel, had a staggering daily intake of 25,000 negatives and 60,000 prints. By the end of the war, some 5,000,000 prints had been processed.

PEGASUS BRIDGE HOLES AND EXPLODING STAKES

One objective on D-Day (6 June 1944) was the early capture of several bridges behind the German defences. This was to be achieved by landing gliders and deploying troops. A series of reconnaissance photos taken of Pegasus Bridge (Benouville Bridge) in Normandy, France, showed a strange number of holes had been dug in fields surrounding this important crossing. Analysts at Medmenham concluded these were intended to support hundreds of wooden stakes that held an inter-connected network of explosive charges. Should a glider strike one on landing, they would all detonate.

Luckily, the counter-measure was to be made active on 7 June 1944 - just one day after invasion. For the record, the British 6th Airborne Division did manage to secure the bridge after all its gliders landed safely.

JAMMING SYSTEM DOMINO AND BATTLE OF THE BEAMS

Another immensely important RAF element was its scientific division (Technical Intelligence). This proved crucial in the defence of the skies as German bombers, using effective systems of radio navigation, began their raids against Britain.

The RAF hurriedly researched counter-measures. A system was developed which essentially involved jamming and distorting the bombers radio waves and targeted the Luftwaffe's Knickebein system (amongst others). Central to the early part of the operation was the powerful BBC transmitter at **ALEXANDRA PALACE [331•99]** for the frequencies used by the Luftwaffe were within those covered by this facility. The jamming system

324 • 55

32 Weymouth Street

327 • 44

Oratory Schools, Bury Walk

The Royal Borough of Kensington and Chelsea
BURY WALK, S.W.3

SPY SITES OF LONDON

325 • 55

59 Weymouth Street
A US Army Signals Section was based here in WWII

329 • 62 Waldorf Hotel

was codenamed Domino and first became active in February 1941. Initially the Germans simply assumed their equipment was faulty. However, as the counter-measure signal was increased it rendered the bombers' system useless. This secret aerial war was later called Battle of the Beams by war historians.

SEEKING OUT INADVERTENT TRAITORS AND FOOLS

Marie Christine Chilver, born in London in 1920, was recruited as an agent provocateur to make contact and befriend prospective MI5, MI6 and SOE agents and occasional serving personnel to discover if they

SPY SITES OF LONDON

Danesfield House, RAF Medmenham

330•99

Another view of Danesfield House - now a hotel

© HERTZSPRUNG

328•42

18 Sloane Gardens

would refrain from divulging information concerning their work and private lives. Codenamed Fifi, one of her primary tasks was to travel throughout the UK to meet agents in simulated enemy territory, often in hotels, bars and clubs. MI5 and SOE instructed her to use the potential agent's real name - a tactic employed by the Gestapo - and then judge their reaction. Fifi would deliver her verdict on candidates - described as 'prey' - and their suitability, especially to provocation. These operations were called 96 Hour Schemes and/or Four Day Field Tests. Chilver felt some guilt when her actions led to the disqualification of operatives and candidates.

The original Pegasus Bridge on display in the Pegasus Museum

New Pegasus Bridge

Glider counter-measures

A replica of the first Airspeed Horsa glider to land at Pegasus Bridge on display at the Pegasus Memorial

Her multi-lingual skills were of immense use to SOE in determining the suitability of foreign agents and candidates. She often found herself performing what were called Silent Schemes - because the recruit could not speak English. This was not a concern of course, because they would be deployed in France, Norway, etc. - their home countries.

Chilver's reputation was growing in British Intelligence, and her name was even kept secret from SOE trainers. However, it is almost certain senior SOE heads Maurice Buckmaster - leader of the French element and Colin Gubbins - who would assume command over the entire organisation, knew of her. Legendary MI5 officer Maxwell Knight insisted that she only be referred to as "our special agent." Knight had long been opposed to MI5's policy of only using male spies and was very supportive of Chilver.

By 1942, her identity was stripped again and she was given a new Legend.* She became Christine Collard.

* Historical background, biography, work record etc. supported by documentation

Photo Intelligence - Utah Beach - D-Day landing site

RAF/US ARMY AIR FORCE PHOTOGRAPH

Photo analysts decided these holes were intended to support glider counter-measures - wooden stakes connected to explosives

British troops secure Pegasus Bridge - note the close proximity of the landed glider in the field - upper right

COURTESY: WAR OFFICE ARCHIVE/IMPERIAL WAR MUSEUM

`331•99` **Alexandra Palace, Muswell Hill**

© NELJS FLICKR

`333•46` **9 Nevern Road**

The Royal Borough of Kensington and Chelsea
NEVERN ROAD, S.W.5

Eye Spy Intelligence Magazine

Inverness Terrace, 39 Porchester Gate

9 Nevern Road

Marie Christine Chilver

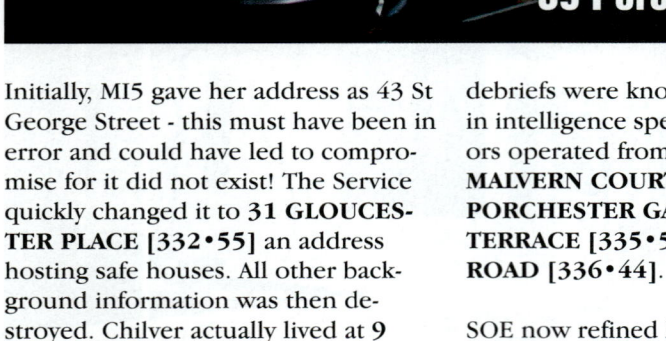

Initially, MI5 gave her address as 43 St George Street - this must have been in error and could have led to compromise for it did not exist! The Service quickly changed it to **31 GLOUCESTER PLACE [332•55]** an address hosting safe houses. All other background information was then destroyed. Chilver actually lived at **9 NEVERN ROAD [333•46]**.

After the Schemes concluded, Chilver would write a report and hand-deliver it to her MI5 handlers, of which there were three or four - each having jurisdiction over a particular area. The debriefs were known as Post Mortems in intelligence speak. Her MI5 superiors operated from offices at 14 **MALVERN COURT [334•47]**, 39 **PORCHESTER GATE, INVERNESS TERRACE [335•56]** and **16 HANS ROAD [336•44]**.

SOE now refined her role further and MI5 approached Edward Hulton (an MI5 and MI6 contact man involved with British media and propaganda organisations) who owned Hulton Press Ltd. They duly arranged a bogus press card and a fictitious position as a freelance French journalist writing articles for *Housewife* magazine. Interestingly, and perhaps laced with a little MI5 humour concerning her undercover work, one feature was titled: *'Continentals, Compliments, Corsages and Kisses on the Wrist'!*

As the war progressed and SOE operations in Europe intensified, Chilver was now travelling to cities and towns more frequently and performing numerous 96 Hour Schemes every week. Interestingly, one file concerning Chilver shows the legendary MI5 address - Box 500. Some staffers and intelligence watchers still use the term when speaking about the Service!

After the war she assisted MI6 in Germany and then retired. Chilver died in 2007 aged 86. She never spoke about her secret work throughout her fascinating life.

14 Malvern Court

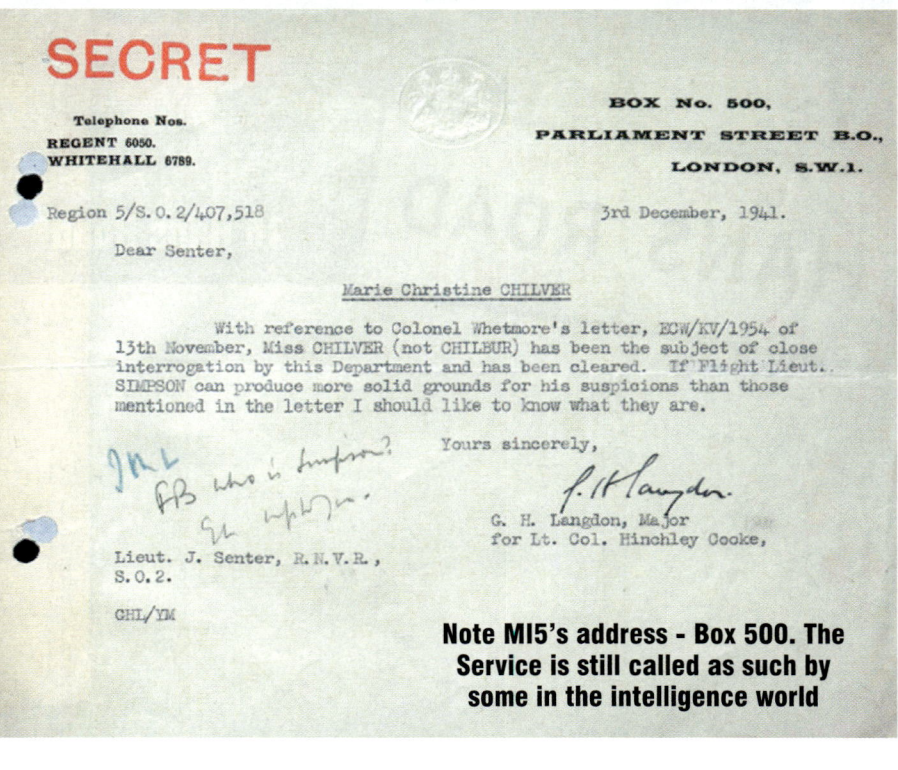

SECRET

Telephone Nos.
REGENT 6050.
WHITEHALL 6789.

BOX No. 500,
PARLIAMENT STREET B.O.,
LONDON, S.W.1.

Region 5/S.O.2/407,518

3rd December, 1941.

Dear Senter,

Marie Christine CHILVER

With reference to Colonel Whetmore's letter, ECW/KV/1954 of 13th November, Miss CHILVER (not CHILBUR) has been the subject of close interrogation by this Department and has been cleared. If Flight Lieut. SIMPSON can produce more solid grounds for his suspicions than those mentioned in the letter I should like to know what they are.

Yours sincerely,

G. H. Langdon, Major
for Lt. Col. Hinchley Cooke,

Lieut. J. Senter, R.N.V.R.,
S.O.2.

CHI/YM

Note MI5's address - Box 500. The Service is still called as such by some in the intelligence world

SPY SITES OF LONDON
336•44

332•55

16 Hans Road

31 Gloucester Place

SPY SITES OF LONDON

XIV
Games of Deception
Operation Mincemeat and Jermyn Street

On Field-Marshal Bernard Montgomery's advice, the War Office requisitioned the quiet buildings of St Paul's School, Hammersmith, which had been evacuated in 1939 to help finalise the immense plan for the Allied invasion of Europe. Though the school no longer exists, near the site a large map of Europe used by the wartime commander takes pride of place in the Montgomery Room at the new St Paul's built close to Hammersmith Bridge.

On 15 May 1944, Montgomery and US General Eisenhower, plus other military chiefs, presented the plans of invasion to Winston Churchill and King George VI in the school lecture theatre. A plaque commemorating this historic event can be found at the entrance to **ST PAUL'S GARDENS AND OPEN SPACE, HAMMERSMITH ROAD [337•59]** near Colet Gardens.

St Paul's School - CIRCA. 1900

St Paul's Gardens, Hammersmith 337•59

Through these gates Allied officials presented the D-Day plans for the invasion of Europe to Winston Churchill and King George VI

Field-Marshal Bernard Montgomery. Though he worked closely with Eisenhower, there were tensions

Eye Spy Intelligence Magazine

267

SPY SITES OF LONDON

A statue of the wartime commander can also be found in the grounds of the Ministry of Defence, Whitehall **(See Site 730•42)**. Montgomery was born in **OVAL HOUSE, 52-54 KENNINGTON OVAL [338•25]**, close to the famous cricket ground.

General of the Army, Dwight D. Eisenhower, Supreme Commander, Allied Forces, used **20 GROSVENOR SQUARE [339•55]** as his headquarters. US military intelligence officers and OSS agents occupied offices at 18 Grosvenor Square **(See Site 241•55)**.

From here Eisenhower commanded earlier operations such as Torch (North Africa) and Avalanche (Italy), but it was Overlord, the invasion of Europe which was discussed in the school in Hammersmith that proved fatal for Hitler. The American's

Statue of Bernard Montgomery in the grounds of the Ministry of Defence, Whitehall

268

Eye Spy Intelligence Magazine

SPY SITES OF LONDON

Norfolk House, 31 St James's Square

Left: SHAEF commanders at a conference in London. Left to right: Lieutenant General Omar N. Bradley, Admiral Sir Bertram Ramsay, Air Chief Marshal Sir Arthur Tedder, General of the Army Dwight D. Eisenhower, General Sir Bernard Montgomery, Air Chief Marshal Sir Trafford Leigh-Mallory and Lieutenant General Walter Bedell Smith

SHAEF: NORFOLK HOUSE

Former headquarters of SHAEF and early workplace of a certain KGB spy - Anthony Blunt. Moscow therefore was privy to a plethora of important intelligence. Blunt's brother, Christopher, also worked at Norfolk House and was honoured by the US military for his exceptional research.

UK and USA officials met here to plan the D-Day operation under the auspices of SHAEF. Overseen by Dwight Eisenhower, deception plans were agreed upon to confuse the Nazis. However, Anthony Blunt's skulduggery enabled the Russians to pass the Abwehr all manner of false reports and disinformation, helping the Soviets reach and ultimately capture Berlin first.

Dedication at Norfolk House to Dwight D. Eisenhower's planning and execution of Operation Overlord

Dwight D. Eisenhower

Eye Spy Intelligence Magazine

SPY SITES OF LONDON
General view of Grosvenor Square North

339•55

In This Building Were Located The Headquarters of General of the Army Dwight D. Eisenhower Commander in Chief Allied Force June - November 1942 Supreme Commander Allied Expeditionary Force January - March 1944

Eisenhower's headquarters were at number 20

commitment to a free Europe and his support of Britain is recognised on a plaque at **NORFOLK HOUSE, 31 ST JAMES'S SQUARE [340•42]**. It was presented by the US Department of Defense and the family of Eisenhower on 4 June 1990, the centennial year of the general's birth, and the 46th anniversary of the beginning of Operation Overlord - D-Day.

A splendid statue of Eisenhower can also be found outside the US Embassy in Grosvenor Square **(See Site 649•55)**.

But these legendary operations would not have been possible without intelligence, deception, skulduggery, planning and luck. One incident above all encapsulates all of these factors, and was codenamed Operation Mincemeat.

OPERATION MINCEMEAT - THE MAN WHO NEVER WAS

In 1942, as the Allies continued to make steady ground in North Africa and other parts of the Mediterranean theatre, Berlin and Rome recognised an attack on Italy would probably take place sooner rather than later. German forces were strong and so a plan was generated in London to deceive the opposition into thinking invasion would take place at a certain location, forcing a major troop reinforcement of the area. And then of course, Allied forces would attack elsewhere.

Charles Cholmondeley

Statue of Dwight D. Eisenhower outside the US Embassy

270

Eye Spy Intelligence Magazine

341•47

18 Queen's Gate Place Mews

342•60

5 Vicarage Gardens

Ewan Montagu

The intelligence ruse would involve allowing the body of a dead British officer, carrying plans of the invasion location, to be washed up on the shore of neutral Spain. Of course MI6 was fully aware any information recovered would probably end up with German diplomats and then be wired to Berlin. However, this wasn't really the problem. First a body had to be found, second the documentation had to be convincing, and third - Berlin had to be wholly satisfied this was not an intelligence deception.

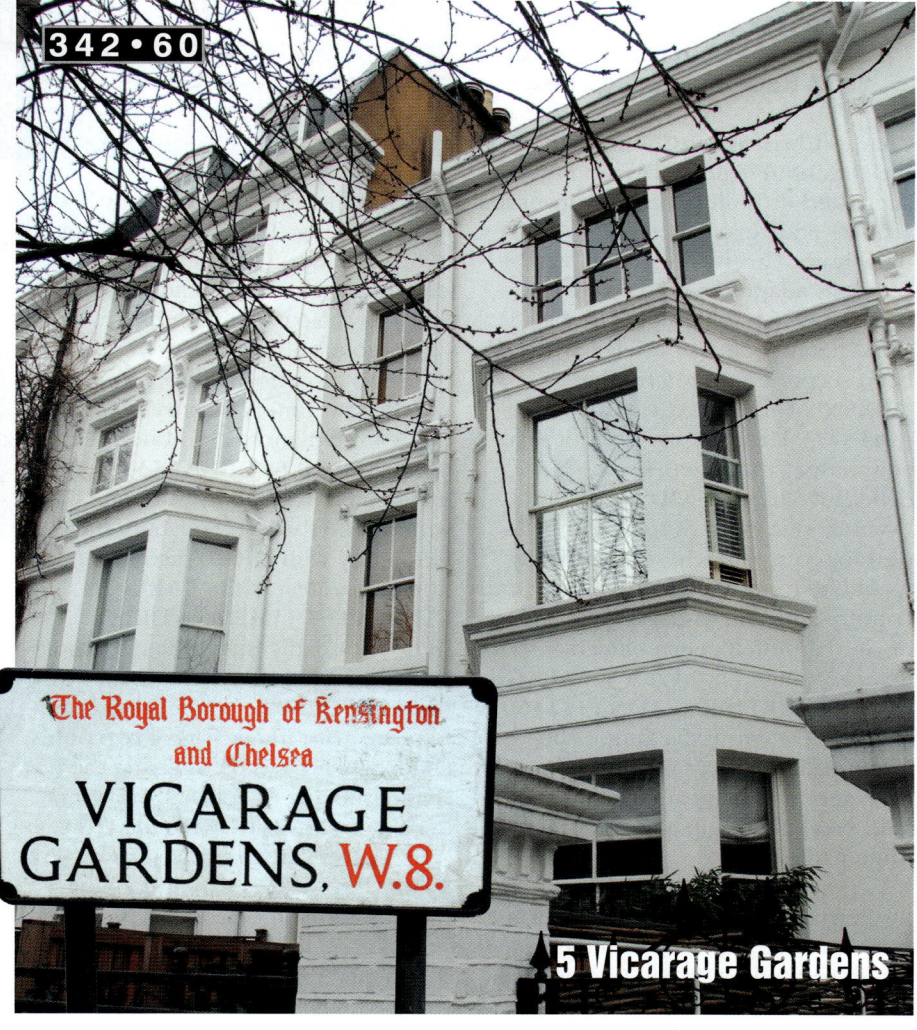

Combined Operations Headquarters (COHQ) which assisted Operation Mincemeat, was strategically positioned in Whitehall just a 100 yards from 10 Downing Street

Richmond Terrace, Westminster
Ukrainian demonstrators opposite Downing Street protest about Russian interference in their country in 2014. Behind them, Richmond Terrace, which hosted the Combined Operations Headquarters

Richmond Terrace (right) sits next to the Ministry of Defence HQ. In the distance - the London Eye

Charles Christopher Cholmondeley of the Naval Intelligence Division first suggested dropping the body from the air over France still attached to a parachute. This was rejected, but the plan was adapted by the Twenty Committee which ran the Double Cross agents. Cholmondeley, who had been seconded to MI5 lived at **18 QUEEN'S GATE PLACE MEWS [341•47]**. He was a member of that committee, and together with his colleague, another NID man Lt. Commander Ewen Montagu, they developed a plan whereby the body would be found in waters off a neutral country and one with a large presence of German intelligence officers - Spain. Montagu lived at **5 VICARAGE GARDENS, KENSINGTON [342•60]** and in 1953 wrote the famous book, *The Man Who Never Was,* based upon Operation Mincemeat. Three years later he appeared in a movie of the same name.

Sir Bernard Spilsbury, Britain's foremost forensic pathologist at the time was consulted by British Intelligence. He duly advised that in order for the operation to succeed, the body had to be convincing. The corpse and cause of death had to give the impression that the airman died in an air crash. Spilsbury also explained that in Spain - a Catholic country - they were often reluctant to perform autopsies. It was not the first time Spilsbury, who at the time of the planning of Mincemeat lived at **18-20 FROGNAL [343•19]**, had been consulted by MI6, nor would it be the last. Spilsbury met frequently with MI6 to discuss Operation Mincemeat at the **CARLTON CLUB, 69 ST JAMES'S STREET [344•42]**. Sadly this brilliant pathologist committed suicide in 1947. Insiders believe he never quite came to terms with the deaths of two of his children who had died during the war. Before moving to Frognal, Spilsbury lived at **31 MARLBOROUGH HILL, WESTMINSTER [345•22]** from 1912-1940. Here visitors can find a blue plaque commemorating his life.

In January 1943, the body of Michael Glyndwr, aged 34, was selected: he had died from phosphorus poisoning. Coroner Bentley Purchase secretly assisted the operation and arranged for the corpse to be removed from St Stephen's Hospital, Fulham. It was then stored at St Pancras Mortuary before being transported to a secret location in Hackney Mortuary and dressed in suitable military attire.

Meanwhile plans were also made to build a special canister that enabled the body to be packed in dry ice. In order that the crew of HMS Seraph

SPY SITES OF LONDON

343•19
18-20 Frognal

344•42
Carlton Club, 69 St James's Street

Sir Bernard Spilsbury met here with intelligence officials to discuss the type of corpse needed for Operation Mincemeat

Sir Bernard Spilsbury played a pivotal role in the planning of Operation Mincemeat

selected for the operation did not become suspicious, the canister containing the corpse was marked 'Optical Instruments'. After the 'cargo' was released in Spanish waters, the body of a Major William Martin was found by a Spanish fisherman. And within a short time, just like the NID had hoped, along came German spy Adolf Clauss and the rest is history.

As part of this brilliant operation, documentation found on the dead body included genuine accommodation receipts from the **NAVAL AND MILITARY CLUB, CAMBRIDGE HOUSE, 94 PICCADILLY [346•55]**. Affectionately called the In and Out Club, (see photo to understand why), British Intelligence were convinced this location would be known to the Germans as it was frequently used by MI6, MI5 and military officers - and had been for decades. One former member was MI5's Vernon Kell.

Over the years it had gained a reputation as a spy recruiting club used by various services. Interestingly, at **42 HALF MOON STREET [347•55]** another entrance to the original club was located. Less obvious, this door was very convenient for intelligence staffers based on the street and used by female guests who were covertly invited - often to stay the night!

Eye Spy Intelligence Magazine   273

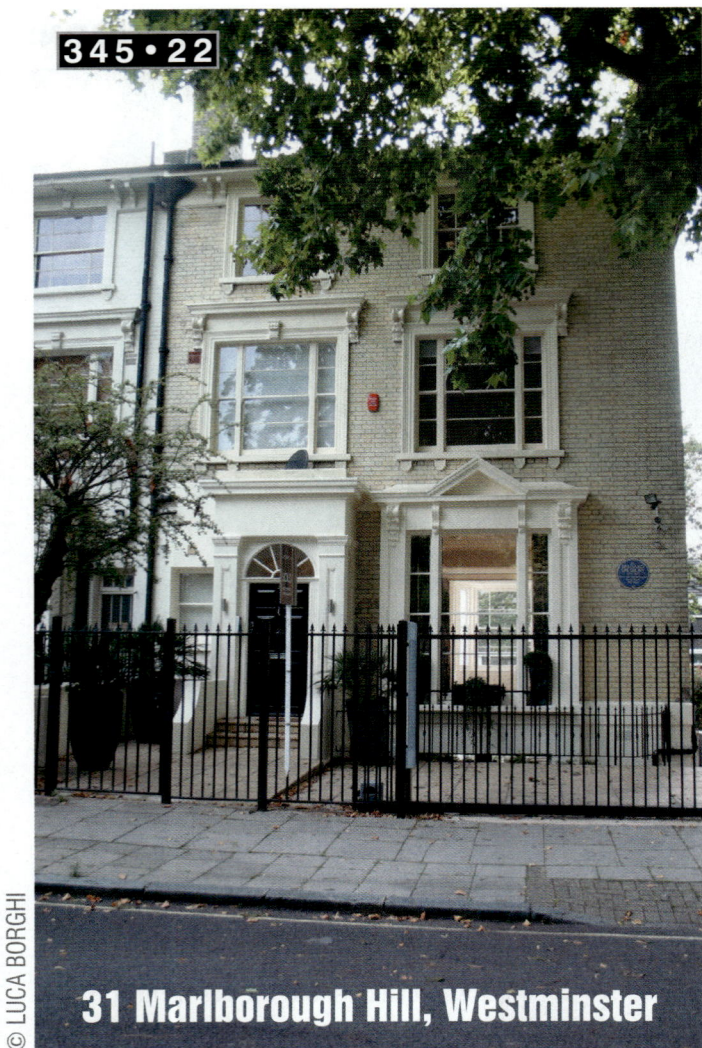

42 Half Moon Street
Side entrance to the Inn and Out Club, 94 Piccadilly

31 Marlborough Hill, Westminster

Navy and Military Club, 4 St James's Square

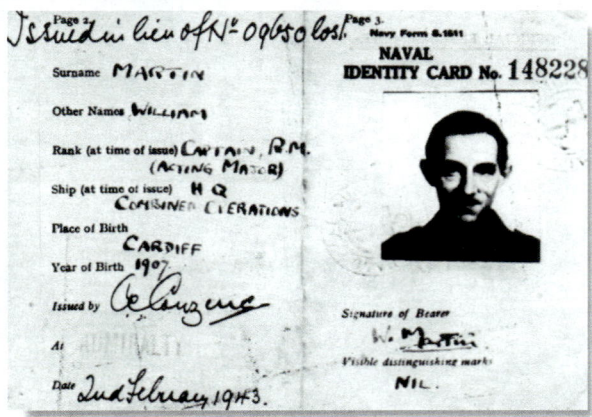

Major Martin's identity card

SPY SITES OF LONDON

346•55

The new Navy and Military club building has retained the famous In and Out signage

94 Piccadilly - In and Out Club
Former location of the Navy and Military Club - better known as the In and Out Club because of the vehicle signs at the entrance

Additional deception items found by the Germans included a photograph of a woman called Pam and two love letters. Pam was in fact Nancy Leslie, an MI5 operative. To further augment the scenario of a relationship, a receipt dated 19 April 1943 from the exclusive London jewellers - **S. J. PHILLIPS, 113 NEW BOND STREET [348•55]**. Phillips have relocated a few hundred feet away to **139 NEW BOND STREET [349•55]**, but the site of their former premises still exists.

Another receipt for a new shirt purchased from the world famous **GIEVES & HAWKES TAILORS, 1 SAVILE ROW [350•55]** had been slipped into Martin's wallet. Both these locations were known to German Intelligence - Gieves being a manufacturer of high-class tailor-made military uniforms, especially for senior officers in the British armed forces. Political and intelligence officials also shopped here. The smart shop can boast an envious client list: Winston Churchill, Lord Nelson, The Duke of Wellington, Mikhail Gorbachev and President Bush plus many celebrities all bought clothes here.*

There was also a certain Guy Burgess who paid the shop a visit just hours

* Gieves acquired Hawkes in 1974

Eye Spy Intelligence Magazine

SPY SITES OF LONDON

348•55
113 New Bond Street

When Operation Mincemeat was launched, S. J. Phillips Ltd occupied this building in New Bond Street. Inset: 'Pam' - MI5 operative Nancy Leslie

COURTESY: NATIONAL ARCHIVES

before he and another fellow Soviet spy made their escape to Russia. Their story features soon.

Meanwhile, other items found on Major Martin's body included letters from a Lloyd's Bank manager demanding an overdraft be paid off. That Martin should be carrying such convincing documents was further augmented by an introduction letter from Admiral Louis Mountbatten to Admiral Sir Andrew Cunningham, Commander-in-Chief of the Mediterranean Fleet. On the letter - the actual address of the vitally important

349•55
S. J. PHILLIPS LTD
139 New Bond Street

ROYAL NAVY

The Board of Admiralty regrets to announce the following casualties which have been sustained in meeting the general hazards of war. Next-of-kin have been notified:—

OFFICERS
KILLED

A/Capt. Sir T. L. Beevor, Bt., R.N.; T/Lt. D. A. Burgass, R.N.V.R.; Lt. J. L. Fraser, R.N.V.R.; Lt. P. F. S. Gould, D.S.C., R.N.; T/Sub-Lt. (A) J. H. Hodgson, R.N.V.R.; T/Sub-Lt. (A) K. R. Joll, R.N.V.R.; Rear-Admiral P. J. Mack, D.S.O.; T/Lt (A) G. Muttrie, R.N.V.R.; T/Lt. (A) G. Raynor, R.N.V.R.; T/Sub-Lt. J. N. Wishart, R.N.V.R. ROYAL MARINES.—T/Capt (A/Major) W. Martin.

DIED FROM WOUNDS OR INJURIES
T/Sub-Lt. (A) J. Hall, R.N.V.R.; T/Lt. A. G. D. Heybyrne, R.N.V.R.

The London Times announces Major Martin's death - 4 June 1943

Combined Operations Headquarters - **COHQ 1A RICHMOND TERRACE [351•42]**. This office had been purposely established to harass the German armed forces on the continent by conducting lightening raids. At the time, Mountbatten headed the operation. Thus everything surrounding Martin seemed very plausible. The SOE and MI6 soon reported German forces were on the move, thus alerting London the plan had worked. A statue of Cunningham, whose nickname was

SPY SITES OF LONDON

350·55

Gieves & Hawkes, 1 Savile Row

Admiral Sir Andrew Cunningham

Admiral Cunningham's statue in Trafalgar Square

'ABC', can be found in Trafalgar Square. He was trained at the **OLD ROYAL NAVY COLLEGE IN GREENWICH [352·24]**, a must-visit location.

Mention must also be given to well known writer Dennis Wheatley and his deception team who worked for the London Controlling Section (LCS). They helped the Naval Intelligence Division throughout, drawing information from past ruses and public thinking - advising what might work and what would probably be seen as

Admiral Louis Mountbatten

Inside Gieves and Hawkes. Note the drawings of Charlie Chaplin and 007 actor - Sean Connery - both clients of the famous tailors

Eye Spy Intelligence Magazine

277

SPY SITES OF LONDON

352•24

Old Royal Naval College, Greenwich

353•39

Prince of Wales Theatre, Coventry Street

1 Becmead Avenue

355•42

278

Eye Spy Intelligence Magazine

354•42

Waterloo Place

Crimean War Memorial

357•60
81 Victoria Road

nothing more than deception. Wheatley, who lived at **1 BECMEAD AVENUE [353•39]** was an important intelligence contact man and a close friend of NID officer Ian Fleming (amongst others). Indeed, it's probably because of Fleming that he was invited to help the operation.

The mind-boggling attention to detail on the items recovered by the Germans on Martin's corpse can also be found in a solicitor's letter discussing his personal affairs. This was written on letter-headed paper of the legal office of McKenna & Co. Indeed, Ian Wilson who controlled British D-Day spies Dusan 'Dusko' Popov and Johny Jebsen actually worked here. Further research revealed the company were based at **14 WATERLOO PLACE [354•8]** near the splendid Crimean War Memorial and a minute's walk from the recruiting and gentlemen's clubs of Pall Mall, including the Athenaeum, Carlton and RAC.

Accurate dating and stamping of all receipts, letters and tickets was

Eye Spy Intelligence Magazine

SPY SITES OF LONDON

Keynes Lodge, 32 Gloucester Road, Teddington

Margaretha MacLeod, better known as Mata Hari executed as a spy by the French in 1917

crucial. But had the Spaniards and Abwehr examined them a little more carefully, they may well have found discrepancies surrounding ticket stubs for a show at the **PRINCE OF WALES THEATRE, COVENTRY STREET** [355•42] on 22 April 1943. These conflicted with other documents. As it transpired, they did not.

The London Times of 4 June reported the deaths of several officers in a tiny column - *'The Board of the Admiralty regrets to announce the following casualties'.* A. W. Martin was noted as *'Killed'.* Such detail and planning is testimony to the brilliant organisation of the NID and XX Committee.

As for Major Martin, he was buried in the Cemetery of Solitude in Huevlva, where he was brought to shore. A plaque commemorating this homeless figure can be found on the war memorial in Aberbargoed, Wales. An

Nancy Astor

Geo. F. Trumper, Duke of York Street

280

Eye Spy Intelligence Magazine

inscription in Welsh says: *'Y Dyn Na Fu Erioed'* which translates to - *'The Man Who Never Was'*.

As for the private members In and Out Club at Piccadilly, it no longer occupies the original building also known as Cambridge House. However, its leadership have paid homage to it at their new residence which can be found at **4 ST JAMES'S SQUARE [356•42]** - the former residence of Nancy and Waldorf Astor - the latter himself being an intelligence contact man. The club have painted 'in' and 'out' on the two pillars aside its entrance.

IAN FLEMING, OPERATION MINCEMEAT & JERMYN STREET

Popular opinion credits Ian Fleming with the idea of Operation Mincemeat. However, the original idea of using a corpse carrying bogus identification papers was conceived by former WWI intelligence spycatcher Basil Thomson. Thomson, one of the original staffers of the Secret Service Bureau, also wrote detective novels, including *The Milliner's Hat Mystery* (1937). In this case a body was discovered in a barn. Thomson's research was discussed as early as 1940 by NID officials and is the true genesis for Operation Mincemeat.

Thomson worked closely with MI5's Vernon Kell and interviewed several high profile suspected spies, including Mata Hari and Carl Hans Lody **(See Chapter 2)**. In 1919, he was appointed Director of Intelligence at the Home Office, but left two years later following a disagreement with Chancellor Lord George.

It should also be noted that Thomson, whilst operating for British Intelligence, lived at **81 VICTORIA ROAD, KENSINGTON [357•60]**, and was Ian Fleming's idol. Sadly he would never learn of the success of the operation for he died in 1939, this after relocating to **KEYNES LODGE, 32 GLOUCESTER ROAD, TEDDINGTON [358•50]**.

Dukes Hotel, 35 St James's Place

G. F. Trumper, 9 Curzon Street
Heywood Hill bookstore is located next to Trumper's

Eye Spy Intelligence Magazine

Aleister Crowley

Another nearby location used by some Mincemeat operators is **DUKES HOTEL, 35 ST JAMES'S PLACE [359•42]**. This can be found in a courtyard a two minute walk from Pall Mall and Jermyn Street. This splendid hotel was said to be Ian Fleming's favourite drinking location, and it was here his love of the Martini was born. Undoubtedly many secret issues were discussed here, perhaps even the outcome of Operation Mincemeat!

This part of London is synonymous with the world of spies and espionage, and another man connected to Fleming had a very dark persona. His name was Aleister Crowley who lived above **93 JERMYN STREET [360•42]**.

Crowley had a deep interest in the occult and Fleming, through his

Another view of Hawes and Curtis

Hawes and Curtis, 34 Jermyn Street

Turnbull and Asser, 71-72 Jermyn Street

Marilyn Monroe

Eye Spy Intelligence Magazine

93 Jermyn Street

Floris, 89 Jermyn Street

interrogation of Rudolf Hess, Hitler's deputy, had learned of Hitler's fascination with the occult and astrology. Fleming suggested to the NID that Crowley be allowed to interview Hess to help understand the role of occult in Nazism. However, MI5's Maxwell Knight thought differently and he refused to allow Crowley access.

On a final note concerning Crowley, some intelligence watchers believe the man friends called 'The Beast', was in fact already in the service of MI6.

HAIRCUTS, SUITS, PERFUMES AND CIGARS

A favourite location used by Fleming and other intelligence officers was Geo. F. Trumper - a gentleman's barbers and perfumers. Trumper first opened in 1875 at **9 CURZON STREET, MAYFAIR [361•55]**. Its famous range of scents are named after some recognisable names in intelligence and military history - Astor, Wellington, Curzon, Marlborough. The establishment offered much discretion and privacy - the booths were actually separated by velvet curtains.

Of course, visitors to Trumper's would have noticed Heywood Hill bookshop right next door **(See Site 413•55)**! One of the workers at the shop was Nancy Mitford of the infamous Mitfords. Her sister, Diana was married to Oswald Mosley the Nazi sympathiser - both of whom were imprisoned in WWII. In 2010 Trumper opened a second outlet in the area, **1 DUKE OF YORK STREET [362•42]**.

One perfume and cologne shop frequented by the famous is **FLORIS, 89 JERMYN STREET [363•42]**. Established in 1730, its visitor list includes Winston Churchill, Florence Nightingale and Marilyn Monroe. Ian Fleming and his colleagues also purchased quality scents from this establishment, indeed, his favourite was simply called Floris No.89.

Daniel Craig at the Australian premiere of the 007 picture - *Skyfall*

Eye Spy Intelligence Magazine

283

A Cuban Davidoff cigar sits next to a bottle of Dom Perignon champagne. No doubt 007 would have approved!

Intelligence men have for decades made a bee-line for shirt-makers **TURNBULL AND ASSER, 71-72 JERMYN STREET [364•42]**. And interestingly, virtually all the actors to have played the fictitious MI6 officer 007 have sourced their shirts from the establishment - this to add an air of authenticity to the production.

Another of London's most famous and oldest shirt-makers is **HAWES AND CURTIS, 34 JERMYN STREET [365•42]**. Dating back to 1664, the shop has served many interesting folks down the years!

When speaking of Fleming and Jermyn Street it's perhaps amiss not to mention his love of cigars and cigarettes. He purchased his cigars at the world famous **DAVIDOFF CIGARS, 35 ST JAMES'S STREET (OFF JERMYN STREET) [366•42]**.

And for the intelligence staffers who worked in the street and could take a break, they often spent an hour or two taking in a show at the tiny, but famous **JERMYN STREET THEATRE, 16B JERMYN STREET [367•42]**.

Jermyn Theatre, 16B Jermyn Street

Davidoff Cigars, 35 St James's Street

284

Eye Spy Intelligence Magazine

XV

The D-Day Spies
Double Cross, XX Committee and Victory

SPY SITES OF LONDON

British Intelligence ran hundreds if not thousands of spies and agents during WWII, many were drawn from organisations such as the SOE, others having risen through the ranks or passed through training schools. However, as evidenced by events in New York and the BSC, ordinary civilians, professionals and celebrities were also prepared to help. They received invaluable assistance from foreign nationals who fled their country in the wake of German invasion. Many of these joined British spy agencies or fought with resistance groups. There were of course rivalries, none more so obvious than that between MI6 and SOE, however, ultimately they recognised that cooperation and their goal of liberating Europe was better fought with a sense of togetherness. There was another avenue for spy recruitment - turning enemy agents - codenamed the Double Cross System.

6 Chesterfield Gardens

Eye Spy Intelligence Magazine

SPY SITES OF LONDON

371 • 55
Lansdowne Club, 9 Fitzmaurice Place

Art historian and MI5 officer Tomas Harris resided at 6 Chesterfield Gardens with his wife. For many years this impressive building hosted a most interesting drinks circle, which included KGB spies Blunt, Burgess and Philby. Also within the group - Dick White, who would go on to head both MI5 and MI6, plus MI5 men Guy Liddell and Victor Rothschild.

The intelligence flowing in and out of Double Cross needed careful scrutiny and evaluation. It was overseen by the secret Twenty Committee or XX Committee (it was called thus because double cross - XX is twenty in Roman numerals). Most of the spies secured by the organisation were in fact working for the Nazis, though were not necessarily German nationals.

By late 1942, dozens of German spies were effectively under British control, many having passed through interrogation centres such as Camp 020 (Latchmere House). Having agreed to work for the British, their lives had been spared. At the head of Double Cross was MI5 man Lt. Colonel

Waterloo Station
Victory Arch, Waterloo Station

SPY SITES OF LONDON

Juan Garcia - agent Garbo

Thomas Argyle Robertson, better known as 'Tar', whilst John Masterman chaired the Committee which consisted of various intelligence officials from MI5, MI6 and the War Office. The operation, it should be noted, was also aided in part by German Abwehr officials who were willing to collaborate with Britain.

Robertson inherited a splendid apartment at **6 CHESTERFIELD GARDENS [368•55]** which was used for Double Cross meetings. After the war the address hosted an interesting drinks circle which included several famous spies and intelligence supremo Dick White. He would go on to head both MI5 and MI6. Other participants were Victor Rothschild and Guy Liddell from MI5 and interestingly, KGB spies Guy Burgess, Anthony Blunt and Kim Philby. Another MI5 officer attached to Double Cross also spent time here renting a room. He was art historian Tomas Harris who was the handler of a senior D-Day spy.

OPERATION FORTITUDE

The so-called D-Day Spies were a handful of agents utilised successfully in Europe to help prepare the ground for invasion. However, so many agencies were involved in deception

Dick White headed both MI5 and MI6

operations, essentially to convince the Germans an invasion force would land in one area, whilst the real force landed elsewhere, that readers are urged to research this monumental effort further. This ruse was codenamed Fortitude.

Eye Spy Intelligence Magazine

287

SPY SITES OF LONDON

Waterloo Station Clock. A well known meeting point on the concourse of the biggest station in Britain. Several spies also used the clock as a venue for covert meetings and signals

Actress Patricia Owens was the daughter of an MI6 double agent

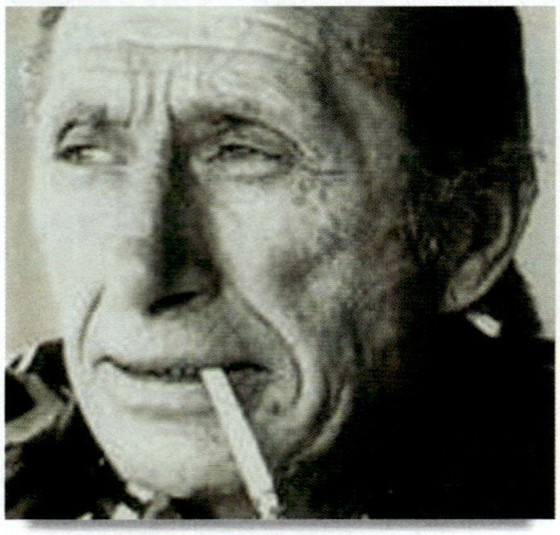

Popov - MI6 double agent codename Tricycle

It was just one part of an operation codenamed Bodyguard. That the spies MI5 had managed to turn were still supplying Berlin with carefully edited and controlled intelligence (all written by the Service and the XX Committee) was incredibly important. Whilst ever German defence troops were on standby in one region, it proved that Berlin still believed the double agents.

Much has been written about a handful of famous Abwehr spies associated with Double Cross, they include: Dusan 'Dusko' Popov - codename Tricycle; Lily Sergeyev - codename Treasure; Roman Czerniawski - codename Brutus; Elvira de la Fuente Chaudoir - codename Bronx; Wulf Schmidt - codename Tate; Eddie Chapman - codename Zig Zag; Arthur Owens - codename Snow and Juan Pujol Garcia - codename Garbo. It should be recognised that as many as 50 agents were involved in D-Day deception and many of them paid the ultimate price with their lives.

One person almost certainly on MI5's Registry was a 40-year-old Welsh electrical engineer and Royal Navy contract man by the name of Arthur George Owens. Owens was in fact an MI6 agent who had been paid a reasonable sum of money in the mid-late 1930s to bring back intelligence on German shipyards during his frequent overseas trips. MI5 suspected Owens was also working for the Abwehr. When confronted by counter-espionage officials, he said he was only passing on certain information thus enabling him even more access to areas of interest to MI6. This explanation did not sit well with MI5, but they continued to play along with him. As war ensued, MI5 started to round-up suspected spies, and Owens feared he would be next. He duly telephoned a Scotland Yard contact and arranged to meet him under the clock at **WATERLOO STATION [369•23]**. This location was, and still is, a favourite meeting place for Londoners and visitors to the city. Owens intention was to emphasise to government officials his ties with, and role play for MI6. However, the problem for Owens was compounded when his police

Johann Jebsen

Double agent George Owens was sent to Dartmoor Prison

Eye Spy Intelligence Magazine

SPIES, CRIMINALS & WANDSWORTH PRISON

Wandsworth Prison was used by the War Office during both World Wars. Many characters recognised in the intelligence world have been 'residents', including Nazi propagandist William Joyce, better known as 'Lord Haw Haw', seen here after his arrest by US forces in 1945. German spy Karl Richter was also imprisoned here. He managed to slip out of his handcuffs as he stood on the gallows.

In more recent times the former editor-in-chief of WikiLeaks - Julian Assange, was remanded here (See Chapter 24). His web site was responsible for uploading hundreds of thousands of leaked intelligence files.

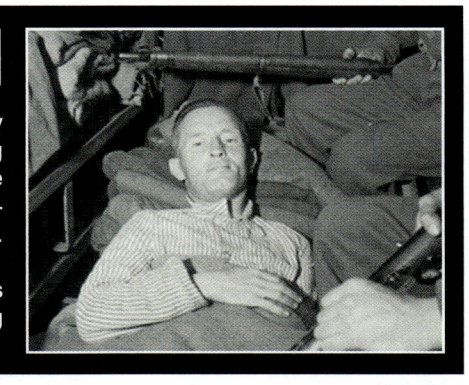

US warships ablaze at Pearl Harbor. Some historians believe Popov had intelligence on the Japanese attack - but this was not imparted

friend, along with MI5 officers pounced. He was arrested as a German spy and taken to **WANDSWORTH PRISON [370•40]**.

Owens was told that if he cooperated, he would avoid prosecution... and possibly execution. He agreed, and using his Abwehr codename Snow he once again made contact with his German handlers via a radio he had been given by Berlin. As far as the Nazis were concerned, Owens was still their agent-in-place and this was confirmed when he sent a message they had been patiently waiting for: *'Must meet you in Holland at once. Bring weather code. Radio town and hotel Wales ready'*. Unbeknown to Berlin - the signal had been relayed by Owens from his prison cell under the watchful eyes of senior MI5 men.

This one communication proved that operations such as Double Cross could work. As for Owens, MI5 were never comfortable with him, despite him identifying German agents. He ended his war days in the hospital wing of Camp 001 - Dartmoor Prison - also used to hold German POWs. And to his credit, Owens befriended prisoners in an effort to glean information which he immediately passed on to MI5. After the war, he secured an apartment at 501 Dolphin Square **(See Site 120•42)** before moving to Skipton in North Yorkshire. As a sidebar to the Owens story, his daughter was Hollywood actress Patricia Owens who featured in a number of pictures, but is best remembered for her role in the 1958 horror film, *The Fly* starring Vincent Price.

A MOST ENIGMATIC SPY

Whilst Owens was a low-grade spy, perhaps the most flamboyant agent run by Double Cross was Dusan 'Dusko' Popov codenamed Tricycle. Born in Yugoslavia, he had been recruited into German Intelligence by a friend, Johann 'Johny' Jebsen who invited Popov to join him at the Abwehr, which he duly did. Unbeknown to Popov at the time, Jebsen, who had Danish parents, was also working for MI6. Popov then offered his services up to British Intelligence after making contact with agents from MI6's Passport Control Office.

Popov moved to England - his direct handler was Tar Robertson. The men worked and socialised together and Popov fast gained a reputation for the high-life... and women. Indeed, his codename - Tricycle - is thought to have been issued because he liked to have three in a bed sex parties.

Popov and Robertson often discussed operations over a game of billiards at the private members club frequented by the aristocracy - **LANSDOWNE CLUB, 9 FITZMAURICE PLACE [371•55]**, former residence of Gordon Selfridge, founder of Selfridges department store.

Popov's case officer was MI5's Hugh Astor who lived at **18 CARLTON HOUSE TERRACE [372•42]**.

370•40 Wandsworth Prison

Eye Spy Intelligence Magazine

SPY SITES OF LONDON

373•55

Imperial House, 80-86 Regent Street
The building was used first by Russian spies, and then by MI5 and MI6 for concealing front companies and agent runners

Tar had of course played a role in Operation Mincemeat, but his attention was now focused upon the operation that would enable the end game of WWII.

In 1941, Popov received an order from the Abwehr in Berlin instructing him to create a spy ring in the still neutral United States - this was also sanctioned by MI5 and MI6. And despite MI6 advising Washington he was working for the British, FBI chief J. Edgar Hoover was having none of it. Some analysts believe that this was a major error, especially when Pearl Harbor was attacked.

Historians have since suggested MI5 man Guy Liddell should have been a little more forceful in advising Hoover that Popov was carrying vital intelligence on Pearl Harbor. Others suggest this was deliberately withheld by Britain, recognising any attack on a US base or protectorate would trigger America's entry into the war. Because of Popov's now tri-party role, parts of Double Cross were sometimes referred to as Triple Cross. Popov worked under cover of an MI5 front company situated within **IMPERIAL HOUSE, 80-86 REGENT STREET [373•55]**, humorously called Tarlair Ltd. In the 1930s, this location housed the American Refrigerator Company - and proved a perfect front for Russian London NKVD agent handler William Goldin (real name - Alexander Orlov).

There is also an interesting sidebar to the story of Popov. He met and worked with MI6 man Ian Fleming in various parts of Europe, but in particular the Mediterranean. Many intelligence writers believe Popov, more than any other secret agent, has the strongest claim to be the real-life model on which Fleming would base his spy character - James Bond - 007. For those who believe espionage is a glamorous occupation, one only has to read Popov's 1976 book - *Spy Counter Spy* - to understand the dangers of this occupation, especially in times of war.

SECRETS OF CLOCK HOUSE

Popov lived at various locations including one he references in his book as Clock House, a one-storey apartment. This has been sought after for years by historians.

Popov said he had to move out of Clock House because a V-1 missile had struck nearby in 1944 and shattered his windows. Investigating bomb site impact areas we were drawn to Rutland Gate.

Richard Meinertzhagen

SPY SITES OF LONDON

Eresby House, 44 Rutland Gate [374•47]

Hole in the Wall, Rutland Gate [375•47]

Rutland Gate contains dozens of splendid Victorian buildings which line both sides of the street, yet one seems very much out of place - **ERESBY HOUSE, RUTLAND GATE [374•47]**. This is a relatively modern structure and after a little research we discovered the original building had been destroyed in 1940 during another Luftwaffe bombing raid. A famous occupant was Sir William Gore Sutherland Mitchell. He was Air Chief Marshal and RAF Director of Operations and Intelligence.

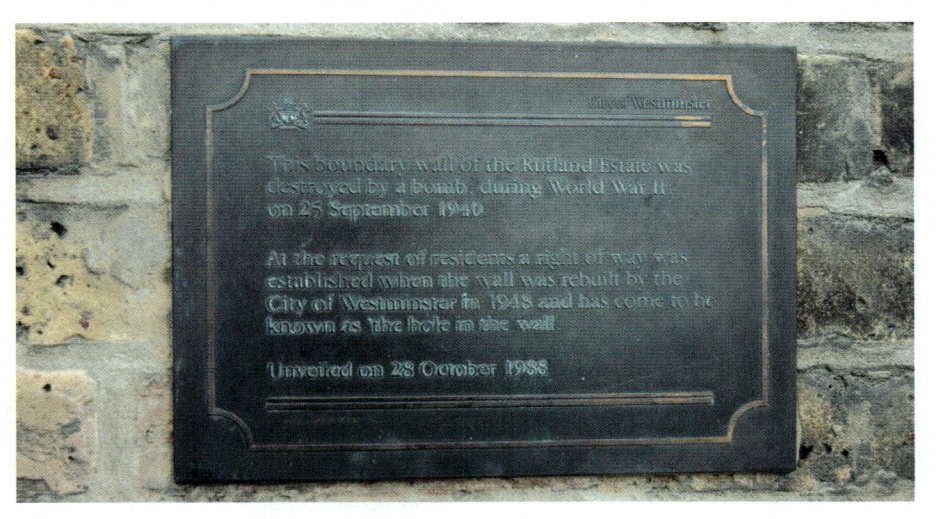

A plaque behind the building can also be found where the bomb ripped through a rear wall. This hole was made into a gateway and is called **THE HOLE IN THE WALL [375•47]**. We walked through and discovered a one-storey building nearby featuring a splendid clock. **CLOCK HOUSE, RUTLAND GATE [376•47]** one of the 'holy grails' of British spylore had been discovered. The clock appears to be identical to that which can be found on the **RUSSIAN ORTHODOX CHURCH 67 ENNISMORE GARDENS [377•47]** just off Rutland Gate.

Further research was of course required. The building's original address was 3 Rutland Mews West. It was once the home of the Lord Mayor of London, but far more importantly, it was the residence of Richard Meinertzhagen, a British intelligence officer who participated in many operations especially in Africa, Asia and parts of the Middle East. He claimed to have worked with MI6 man T. E. Lawrence - but not all is clear

Eye Spy Intelligence Magazine

SPY SITES OF LONDON

Clock House, Rutland Gate
One of the 'holy grails' of British spylore

about his past. Author Brian Garfield who wrote the *Meinertzhagen Mystery* said he "bamboozled everyone - he was a colossal fraud, liar and charlatan." Nevertheless, in 1939 he was assigned to Military Intelligence which might explain his connections to Clock House. More significant was another occupant, Lord Chancellor Frederic Maugham, the brother of MI6 officer Somerset Maugham. Popov, who moved into the residence in 1943, hosted many meetings with Tar Robertson and other Double Cross associates at Clock House. Popov's case officers were MI5's Billy Luke and Ian Wilson **(See Chapter 14)**.

Forced out of Clock House whilst repairs were undertaken, Popov's desire to continue his charismatic lifestyle can be evidenced from the fact that he insisted on being moved to the **SAVOY HOTEL, THE STRAND [378•62]**. Here he continued to be briefed on operations. The hotel was used throughout WWII by MI5 to interview suspects. Some suites were fitted with eavesdropping devices whilst other rooms were searched for bugs. This was because many notable guests, including Winston Churchill, Lord Mountbatten and Charles de Gaulle, to name but a few, all held regular meetings here. Other visitors included Ernest Benes, leader of the Czechoslovak Government-in-exile and his Foreign Minister - Jan Masaryk.

THE ALLEY AND TAP

The address of the Czechoslovak Government-in-exile, which housed a Military Intelligence section, was **3-8 PORCHESTER GATE, BAYSWATER ROAD [379•56]**. The Blitz later forced officials to move out of the capital but not before a crucial SOE-BSC operation had been planned.

Jan Masaryk memorial, Prague

Russian Orthodox Church, Ennismore Gardens 377•47

Czech-trained SOE operatives plotted to assassinate leading Nazi Reinhard Heydrich in 1942 in Prague **(See Chapter 12)**. The agents, some from an undercover resistance movement known as Out Distance, were actually trained by William Fairbairn of the British Security Coordination Camp-X facility. Once this was completed they were taken to London where planning began at Porchester Gate.

Unbeknown to most Londoners, Czech visitors familiar with Operation Anthropoid still make their way to Porchester Gate to an adjoining alley where the agents were photographed prior to European operations.

As for Masaryk, he was assassinated by the KGB in 1948 in Prague - probably because of his past ties to the West and his suspicion of Russia.

18 Carlton House Terrace 372•42

Eye Spy Intelligence Magazine

378•62

Savoy Hotel, The Strand

384•20

55 Elliot Road

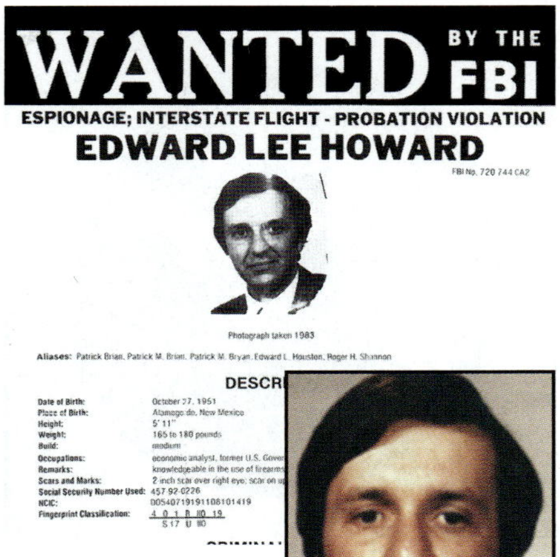

WANTED BY THE FBI
ESPIONAGE; INTERSTATE FLIGHT - PROBATION VIOLATION
EDWARD LEE HOWARD

The subsequent images were used to create bogus passports and new identities. The exact location, known in spylore as **THE WALL AND TAP [380-•56]** is marked by an external tap which was not there in the war.

On a slightly lighter note, in 1940, the Savoy's Italian waiters were removed and despatched to the Bertram Mills Circus in Berkshire which had been refurbished as an internment camp. Cyril Mills was of course an MI5 agent which might explain why he assisted the Service in this endeavour.

Perhaps to celebrate the successful invasion of Europe and his work for Double Cross, Robertson invited Popov to lunch with him on Christmas Day 1944, at **QUAGLINO'S RESTAURANT, 16 BURY STREET [381•42]**.

The establishment was and still is one of London's finest eating places; famous visitors include members of the Royal Family and of course, senior intelligence and diplomatic figures who once dined here. Popov no doubt agreed. Of further interest, Quaglino's was also used by FBI officers in 1984, who over a meal, interviewed CIA case officer Edward Lee Howard. He was suspected of passing intelligence to the KGB. Howard escaped to Russia through Helsinki and for the record, was found dead in 2002 with a broken neck in his apartment. Shortly before this, he said he was prepared to enter into a plea bargain to return to the

Eye Spy Intelligence Magazine

379•56

3-8 Porchester Gate, Bayswater Road

Wall and Tap
Operation Anthropoid agent Adolf Opalka - note the bricks on his photo. The tap was not there in WWII

380•56

City of Westminster plaque:
1940-1945
THIS BUILDING HOUSED THE CZECHOSLOVAK GOVERNMENT-IN-EXILE MILITARY INTELLIGENCE SERVICE

OPERATION ANTHROPOID WAS PLANNED HERE IN OCTOBER 1941, WHICH LED TO THE ASSASSINATION OF THE NAZI LEADER REINHARD HEYDRICH IN PRAGUE ON 27 MAY 1942

EMBASSIES OF THE CZECH AND THE SLOVAK REPUBLICS
FREE CZECHOSLOVAK AIR FORCE ASSOCIATION - JAN KAPLAN ARCHIVE

THE GARBO DECEPTION

MI6 double-agent, Juan Pujol Garcia MBE, born in Spain, codenamed Garbo (German codename Arabel), made an accurate warning of the invasion to his German handler - but purposely just a little too late to have any deadly impact. His reputation in Berlin, therefore, had been enhanced.

Garbo came to Britain in 1942 after he had been rebuffed three times by MI6's Spanish section. Following the Service's decision not to employ him he formulated a plan.

Garcia approached German Intelligence in Madrid and offered up his services to the Abwehr. This was of course a ruse - but he believed it would make him more useful to MI6 and more employable. And of course it worked. In the UK, Garcia's handler was Tomas Harris and like Popov, meetings were held at 6 Chesterfield Gardens. Together, Harris and Garcia developed an imaginary team of 27 agents to convince the Germans he was a reliable spy.

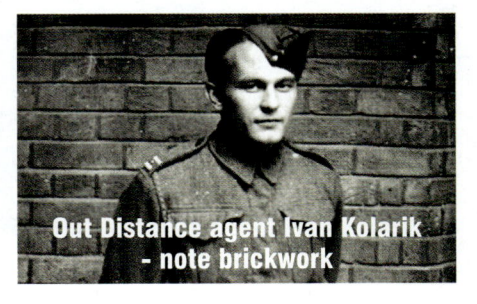

Garcia lived and worked at **35 CRESPIGNY ROAD, HENDON [383•20]**, an MI5 safe house. It was from here that MI6 established a radio transmitter which was used to send misleading communications to Berlin, including the progress of the bogus spy ring.

Another radio station used by Garcia operated from **55 ELLIOT ROAD, HENDON [384•20]**. Signals here were sent to the Germans in Madrid.

Out Distance agent Ivan Kolarik - note brickwork

United States. As for Popov, in 1947 he married Janine. They continued to live in London until around 1951 at **10A GROSVENOR SQUARE [382•55]**.

Ernest Benes  **Jan Masaryk**  **Reinhard Heydrich**

Eye Spy Intelligence Magazine

295

Quaglino's, 16 Bury Street [381•42]

10A Grosvenor Square [382•55]

One of the most important transmissions concerned Operation Fortitude. Garbo reported that Normandy was a diversion and the real attack would come at Calais. Hitler was provided with this intelligence and it may well have led him to hold back his reserves from Normandy. It was a resounding Double Cross success, and one founded on deception, disinformation and confusion. Living and working next door with his wife at either 33 or 37 Crespigny Road was MI5 radio specialist Ted Poulton.

THE SAFE CRACKER

One of the most controversial figures to have worked for MI6 is Eddie Chapman - agent Zig Zag - a flamboyant career criminal, expert safecracker and a man who loved society women and blackmail. His reputation as a London gangster was well known and he participated in several high profile break-ins. Chapman used a garage at **39 ST LUKES MEWS [385•52]** as a safe house and on one occasion blew up a safe at the site whilst trying to gain access.

Before the war and following several arrests and a prison term, he fled to Jersey. Whilst on the island he was jailed again for burglary and received a two-year prison sentence. Unfortunately for him, Jersey was then occupied by the Germans. Chapman's desire for freedom resulted in him offering to spy for the new authorities. And the Abwehr duly accepted him. Unbeknown to Chapman or Berlin, through ULTRA, MI5 had already learned of his new role.

Chapman or agent Fritz as he was codenamed, was sent back to Britain to use his explosives' knowledge to blow up the DeHavilland factory in Hertfordshire. Eventually he turned himself in to local police and was soon in the hands of MI5. A harmless explosion at the factory enhanced Chapman's reputation. Interestingly, this was performed by Jasper

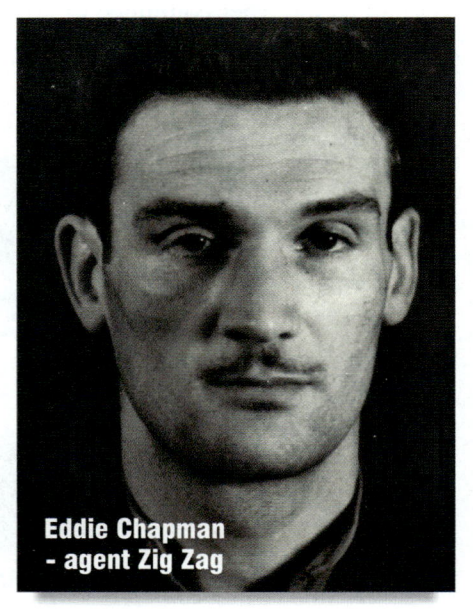

Eddie Chapman - agent Zig Zag

296

Eye Spy Intelligence Magazine

SECRETS OF THE RITZ HOTEL
A VENUE FOR ALL SEASONS AND REASONS

The splendid RITZ HOTEL, 150 PICCADILLY [386•55] has a plethora of surprising links to the intelligence world. In WWII, because of its sturdy construction, it was considered a safe venue for world leaders to meet and its air raid shelter was popular with the rich and famous. Unbeknown to those using the hotel, the steel used in the building was actually manufactured in Germany!

It was used regularly by Churchill, de Gaulle and Eisenhower for summit meetings and the planning of operations such as D-Day. The meetings were often held during dinner at the hotel's Palm Court Restaurant.

When MI5 was forced out of Wormwood Scrubs after it was hit by a bomb, they found alternative accommodation at 57-58 St James's Street (See Site 142•42). As a result, the Ritz became the staff canteen of the Security Service and its spies. One such intelligence person who breakfasted there everyday was Guy Burgess. He would of course soon be recruited by the KGB and become part of the infamous Cambridge Spy Ring.

The famous British D-Day spies Dusko Popov - Tricycle and Juan Pujol Garcia - Garbo, both met their MI5 handlers at the hotel. Popov even had a suite here where he entertained his female friends. After the war, Popov was made a British citizen and awarded an OBE. Fittingly, the presentation was made in the cocktail bar at the Ritz.

The Ritz Hotel, 150 Piccadilly

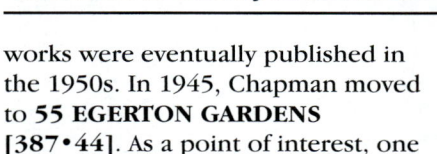

Maskelyne, the stage magician and BSC operative. As part of the ruse, newspapers even carried reports of the bogus explosion.

Chapman became bored with his new lifestyle and he was soon dropped by MI5 which considered him a security risk. Interestingly, the Service sent him to 35 Crespigny Road to be minded by officials. Not surprisingly he disappeared again and next turned up in Norway where he became engaged to a woman - not informing her he was already betrothed! Eventually he returned to the UK to report back to Berlin on the accuracy of V1 strikes. Under British Intelligence control again, he broadcast false coordinates thus convincing the Germans their missiles were striking important targets, whilst in truth, many were simply falling short or over-shooting.

By 1944, he was no longer in the employ of MI5. After the war he wrote two books about his activities which broke the Official Secrets Act. The works were eventually published in the 1950s. In 1945, Chapman moved to **55 EGERTON GARDENS** [387•44]. As a point of interest, one of Chapman's case officers was MI5's

Eddie Chapman became engaged to MI5 agent and Norwegian resistance fighter Dagmar Lahlum - this at a time when he already had a fiancee

Eye Spy Intelligence Magazine

297

SPY SITES OF LONDON
383·20

One of the two houses either side of agent Garbo's residence was occupied by an MI5 radio specialist

35 Crespigny Road, Hendon

385·52

39 St Lukes Mews

Ronnie Reed. It was Reed's photograph used on the identity card of Major Martin - the corpse used in the deception operation codenamed Mincemeat **(See Chapter 14)**.

D-DAY, BABS AND GANGSTERS

Russian-born Nathalie 'Lily' Sergeyev, who trained as a journalist in Paris, was recruited into the Abwehr in 1941 following the fall of France. Two years later she was sent to Madrid taking with her her beloved dog Babs. It was here she approached a UK intelligence officer and offered to work for Britain. Unfortunately for her, UK quarantine regulations meant her dog had to be left in Gibraltar. It was a decision which could have been fatal for Double Cross. Nevertheless, once in the UK - agent Treasure began transmitting false information about the approaching invasion of Europe.

Sergeyev operated from an MI5 safe house at **16-23 RUGBY MANSIONS, BISHOP KINGS ROAD [388·54]** but was later relocated to **39 HILL**

Eye Spy Intelligence Magazine

Chapman pictured with a Rolls Royce

STREET, MAYFAIR [389•55] after threatening to reveal Double Cross to the Germans - this after she learned of the death of Babs.

This building is divided into flats, and our research interestingly showed that at the time of Treasure's relocation, none other than MI6 Chief Lt. Colonel Stewart Graham Menzies used number 35 Hill Street as an office.

Sergeyev was given a secret Abwehr code that she should transmit if her cover was blown. She threatened to broadcast the code as D-Day approached in revenge for Babs. She eventually revealed this to Tar Robertson who just seven days after invasion, told her that she was no longer in the employ of Britain.

Sergeyev relocated to the United States where she died in 1950 - but

387•44

55 Egerton Gardens

COURTESY: NATIONAL ARCHIVES

Lily Sergeyev's identification card

390•37

61 Richmond Park Road

Eye Spy Intelligence Magazine

299

SPY SITES OF LONDON

388•54

16-23 Rugby Mansions, Bishop Kings Road

not before writing a memoir in which she described her former employers as gangsters.

AGENT BRUTUS

Roman Czerniawski, whilst in the Polish Air Force, offered to establish a spy network for the Allies in occupied France. However, he was captured by the Germans in 1941 who said they would grant him his freedom if he went to spy for the Abwehr in England.

He accepted, but once in London he made contact with the authorities and explained he wanted to work for the British. MI5 duly recruited him and assigned him the codename Brutus. Like other agents, Czerniawski started to broadcast bogus intelligence back to Germany. However, he was arrested for insubordination. To conceal his new role the affair was kept quiet and he was released after just two months. This MI5 believed would alert the Germans. Thereafter, he was no longer allowed to operate his radio alone from an innocuous address at **61 RICHMOND PARK ROAD [390•37]**. MI5 monitored his broadcasts and only permitted low-grade snippets of intelligence to be imparted. Initial German suspicion evaporated and by late 1943 he was once again transmitting important disinformation. He became an integral part of the D-Day deception plan. Czerniawski had a central London flat at **41 REDCLIFFE SQUARE, KENSINGTON [391•34]**.

391•34

Redcliffe Square, Kensington

© CHEMICAL ENGINEER

Eye Spy Intelligence Magazine

SPY SITES OF LONDON

39 Hill Street, Mayfair

ESPIONAGE AND THE HIGH LIFE

Elvira de la Fuente Chaudoir - codename Bronx - was the daughter of a Peruvian diplomat who grew up in Paris. She enjoyed an affluent life and frequented some of the city's more glamorous locations. After the fall of France, Chaudoir moved to London where she continued to enjoy the high life. She tried to enlist with the Free French Forces but was told she was unsuitable. During an evening out at the **CONNAUGHT HOTEL, CARLOS PLACE, MAYFAIR [392•55]** Chaudoir attracted the attention of MI6's Claude Dansey who overheard her complaining about the decision. He recognised this was an opportunity for recruitment. Her lifestyle conformed to the German pre-conception that spies belonged to the upper echelons of society. After all, much useful gossip could be overheard at the gaming tables and bars of leading establishments and this Dansey recognised.

An approach was made thereafter and she duly agreed to work for MI6. Dansey explained she would be assigned a mission that meant returning to France in 1942.

In Paris, and just like Dansey, the Abwehr thought her Peruvian status could be useful; she was thereafter recruited and returned to England as a German spy. She had regular contact with her German handler but continued to assist the secret British Normandy ruse. Eye Spy learned that she occupied a mews house in **PAVILION ROAD [393•42]** near Sloane Street. In the vicinity was 21 Sloane Street which was being used by MI6 to host a front company. This building was demolished and today visitors will find the Millennium Hotel. Next door was another MI6 safe house. Interestingly, MI6 also operated a spy training school at **SLOANE SQUARE [394•42]** from 1940-45. Just where this facility was actually based has been impossible to determine.

Chaudoir was paid a considerable salary by the Germans to maintain her flamboyant lifestyle. This included many nights of gambling at the tables of **CROCKFORDS CASINO, 30 CURZON STREET [395•55]** and the bar and bridge tables at the Ritz Hotel. She reported back to Berlin, under MI6 instruction, that she had overheard conversations from drunken guests about British troop movements and fabricated rumours of advanced weaponry, including electric-powered canoes. This was deemed accurate by the Abwehr and helped keep divisions of German troops away from the real landing points of Normandy.

THE LONGEST SERVING DOUBLE CROSS AGENT

Another Abwehr agent who was allowed to live the high life was

Eye Spy Intelligence Magazine

301

392•55

Connaught Hotel, Mayfair

395•55

Crockfords Casino, 30 Curzon Street

Sloane Square — 394•42

Tate Britain, Millbank — 396•42

Pavilion Road — 393•42

Danish-born Wulf Schmidt, later known as Harry Williamson. After being parachuted into England in September 1940, British Intelligence immediately secured his services. He was to become the longest serving agent in the Double Cross System.

Codenamed Leonhard by the Abwehr, he contacted Berlin insisting his finances were running short, thus in the Spring of 1941, the Germans despatched Carl Richter to deliver money to Schmidt. Richter was soon caught, tried and hanged at Wandsworth Prison **(See Site 370•40)**. Thereafter, the Abwehr made contact with the naval attache of the Japanese Embassy who duly passed the agent £200 in a newspaper. Schmidt's MI5 codename was Tate, not because he frequented the Tate Gallery, as some spy authors believe, but because he looked rather like Harry Tate, the famous music hall comedian!

Schmidt 'worked' as a photographer for the *Watford Observer*, it was excellent cover. He managed to convince the Germans that he was loyal right to the end. When hostilities ceased, he went to live with his superior officer Tar Robertson on his farm in Hertfordshire.

As for the gallery, now called **TATE BRITAIN, MILLBANK [396•42]** it is but a few minutes walk from MI6 and MI5 headquarters and a well known meeting place for the intelligencia!

SECRET MEETING LOCATION

One top secret meeting place where Robertson, Masterman and other officials from the XX Committee met with agents to discuss operations, was **THE GARDEN LODGE, 1 LOGAN PLACE [397•60]**. This walled location still exists and was once the residence of Tomas Harris. Besides hosting meetings for the D-Day spies, other intelligence officers from MI5 and MI6 including David Liddell, Victor Rothschild, Anthony Blunt, Dick White, Kim Philby and Tim Milne would meet and socialise here.

Eye Spy Intelligence Magazine   303

SPY SITES OF LONDON

Brazilian fans of the legendary rock star Freddie Mercury take photographs outside the Lodge. Hundreds of messages left by visitors from around the world can be seen attached to the wall. It is likely few really know the significance of this address to the intelligence world

At some point the residence was purchased by the musician Freddie Mercury of the famous rock band Queen. He actually died in the house in 1991. His fans from all around the world still make a bee-line for the address to pay homage to their hero and post messages on the outer wall. Little do they know of its secret intelligence past.

THE TOP SECRET TUNNEL OF RUTLAND GATE

Our researches in Rutland Gate did not stop with Clock House. We discovered that at the outbreak of war, residents of one entire side of **RUTLAND GATE [398•47]** were asked to leave their houses and the buildings 'seconded' by the government. They were informed that they could return once victory was assured. Officials from Whitehall soon moved in and various military offices sited their headquarters here. However, we also learned that building contractors started to appear. Indeed, we can now reveal that the cellars of these grand residences were knocked through to create a secret tunnel which ran all the way to the **HYDE PARK BARRACKS [399•47]**. A resident who returned to her house in 1945 explained to us why:

"The tunnel had a transit lane which used to carry shells to the barracks and the anti-aircraft guns in Hyde Park. Some of the cellars, which were very deep, were used to store weapons and ordnance. The tunnels then went elsewhere." Indeed, we soon learned that it wended its way to the famous Harrods department store, another to the Hyde Park Hotel and a further branch to the now disused **BROMPTON ROAD TUBE STATION [400•44]**. The station was closed to

397•60

The Garden Lodge, 1 Logan Place

304

Eye Spy Intelligence Magazine

Rutland Gate
The cellars of these houses - requisitioned by the War Office - were used to transport shells and supplies through a secret tunnel

the public in 1934 and purchased by the War Office. Additional floors were added during the war and it was used by the Royal Air Force and Royal Navy to help coordinate the city's air defences. The shaft to the Piccadilly Line still exists though it was bricked-up many years ago, but it is still accessible by foot. We also learned part of the building was occupied by Britain's wartime propaganda section - Ministry of Information. Undoubtedly it was also used by British Intelligence, indeed, it is rumoured Hitler's Deputy Rudolf Hess was interrogated

Brompton Road Station

The disused Brompton Road Station sits opposite the Oratory and Holy Trinity Church

WWII anti-aircraft guns in Hyde Park 1939. A secret tunnel was built under Rutland Gate to store and transport shells to the gun placements

Eye Spy Intelligence Magazine

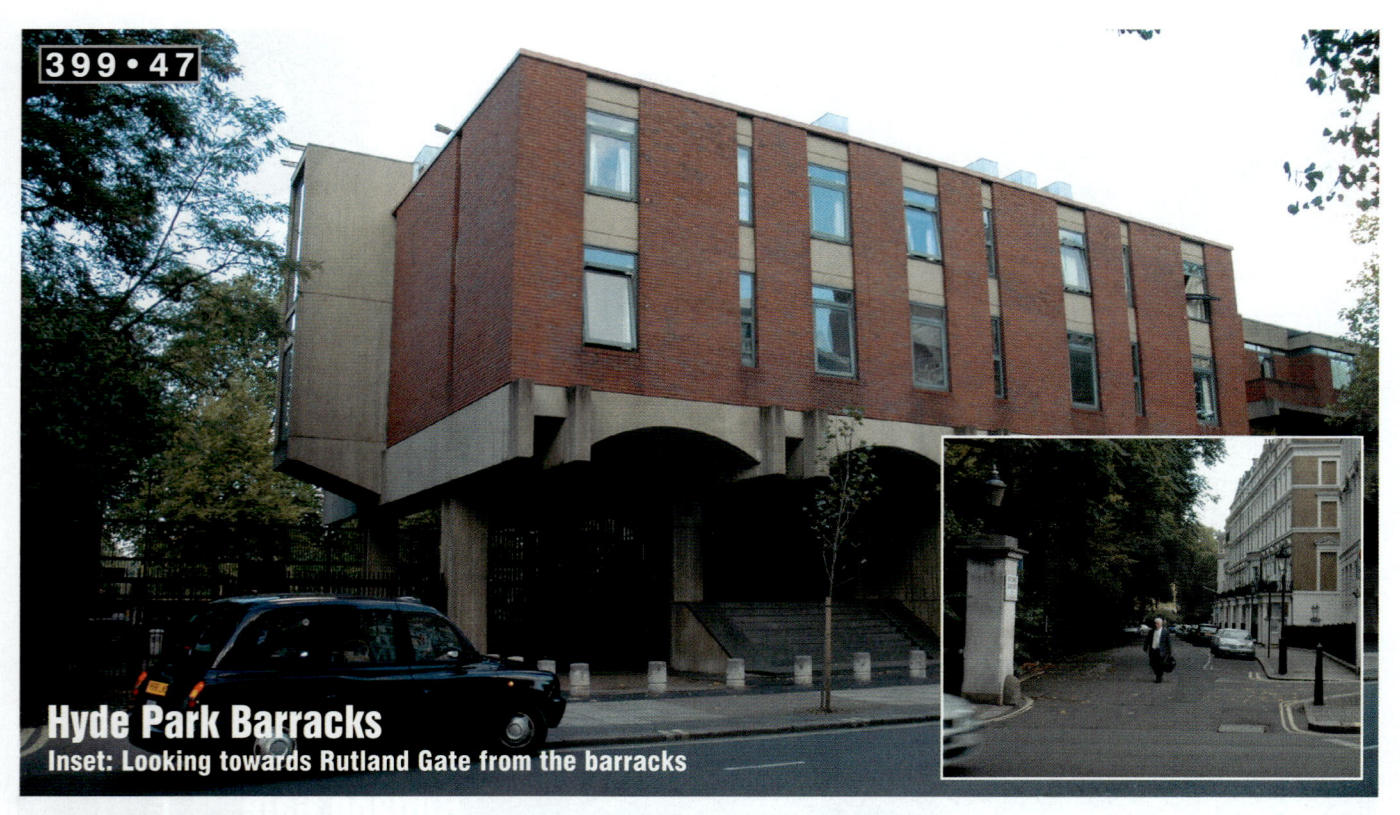

Hyde Park Barracks
Inset: Looking towards Rutland Gate from the barracks

Hyde Park Hotel
(Now the Mandarin Hotel)

here in 1941. In 2014 it was sold by the Ministry of Defence for £53 million for use as luxury apartments.

The tunnel which led to Harrods carried away bomber parts and parachutes which were manufactured in the building's basement.

A little further down Brompton Road was the **HYDE PARK HOTEL, 66 KNIGHTSBRIDGE [401•56]** (now the Mandarin) and Winston Churchill lived here during the war. The hotel boasts its own private tunnel entrance to Hyde Park which once connected to the underground tunnel. Churchill hosted many important meetings with his inner circle, and it is known both MI5 and MI6 officials often met with the wartime leader here. The hotel was described as "Westminster's alternate place of government," because Churchill's Cabinet would dine in the restaurant. In the 1950s, a fourth floor suite was commandeered by MI5 for use as an operations room.

Many fascinating characters linked to the world of spies lived on Rutland Gate and are examined shortly, suffice it to say this is one area of London which is certainly worth a visit!

SPY SITES OF LONDON

General Dwight D. Eisenhower

US troops storm Omaha Beach, Normandy, 6 June 1944

D-DAY

The Normandy landings on 6 June 1944 - codenamed Operation Neptune - were a success, though thousands of Allied troops died in the biggest seaborne operation of all time. The deception operation - Bodyguard - had indeed misled the Germans into thinking the invasion would take place elsewhere. It would be extremely unfair to credit any particular agency, office, authority or individual - so many people played a part and their collective contribution ultimately proved pivotal. However, there is no doubt without the cunning of British, American and Allied intelligence, and the bravery of agents such as the D-Day spies, the task of landing 250,000 troops in France would have been made even more difficult. This chapter has focused on a few of the agents who risked everything, but historians accept that the operation was multi-faceted and thousands of 'surprise spies' played a part - perhaps even inadvertently. One such person was US band leader Glenn Miller.

PROPAGANDA SUCCESSES

It is known that in 1944 Glenn Miller was approached by US Intelligence and its Psychological Warfare Division (PWD). He was asked to make a number of broadcasts as the D-Day invasion and related operations neared. This was tied in with a secret US organisation known as ABSIE (American Broadcasting Station in Europe) and operated by the Overseas Branch of the Office of War Information. This powerful intelligence-led agency consolidated various news outlets and coordinated broadcasts from 1942 until 1945. All very hush, hush and overseen by General Eisenhower's Supreme Allied Expeditionary Force (SHAEF). ABSIE first broadcast in late April 1944, a few weeks before invasion. It was a combined effort with the BBC, whose officials visited General Eisenhower's quiet residence

Glenn Miller

Whilst propaganda broadcasts affected German morale, Allied spirits were kept high by the songs of artists such as Vera Lynn. She became the 'sweetheart' of British forces and is pictured here singing at a munitions factory in 1941.

During WWII she joined ENSA (Entertainments National Service Association) and sang for troops in several countries. Many of her songs became armed forces favourites, including *We'll meet Again* and of course, *A Nightingale Sang in Berkeley Square* which was adopted by the SOE

SPY SITES OF LONDON

Dinah Shore

in **TELEGRAPH COTTAGE, WARREN ROAD [402•99]** several times - as did of course, a plethora of highly important people.

Following D-Day, Miller travelled to Abbey Road with his Army Air Force (AAF) musicians and recorded various songs. After each song ended, a

402•99
Telegraph Cottage, Warren Road

General Dwight D. Eisenhower resided at this location for much of the war. The original Telegraph Cottage no longer exists, but the new build on this private lane retains its famous name

General Dwight D. Eisenhower,
Supreme Commander, Allied Forces Europe

General Eisenhower lived in Telegraph Cottage, Warren Road, from 1942 to 1944. This property formerly stood about 750 yards along Warren Road.

This plaque was erected by the Royal Borough of Kingston Upon Thames to commemorate the 50th anniversary of VE Day and VJ Day 1995

General Jimmy Doolittle

SPY SITES OF LONDON

German-speaking girl called Isle started to chat with Miller. She was in fact a real German called Isle Weinberger who was, we are informed, a translator. There were also messages to German forces urging them to stop fighting. Miller also spoke in German about the war effort, and one message proclaimed: "America means freedom and there's no expression of freedom quite so sincere as music." Several broadcasts were recorded and featured a variety of singers, including music with German lyrics sung by artists Johny Desmond and Dinah Shore. The first programme was aired on 8 November 1944 titled - *Music For The Wermacht*.

British Intelligence reported that despite intense efforts by the Germans to jam the broadcasts, the project had been successful. Miller's songs and ABSIE's endeavours had succeeded.

Senior Allied commanders celebrate at Rheims shortly after General Eisenhower addressed the German mission which had just signed the unconditional surrender document. L-R: General Ivan Susloparov (Soviet Union), Lieutenant General Frederick E. Morgan (British Army), Lieutenant General Walter Bedell Smith (US Army), Captain Kay Summersby (US Army) (obscured), Harry C. Butcher (US Navy), General of the Army Dwight D. Eisenhower (US Army), Air Marshal Arthur Tedder (Royal Air Force)

Abbey Road Studio

ENSA concert party for British troops at a chateau in Normandy just six weeks after invasion

Eye Spy Intelligence Magazine

309

Celebrations in Piccadilly Circus

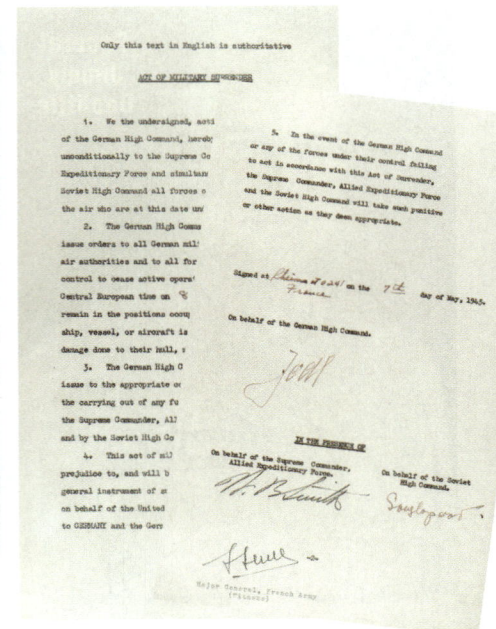

But just as they drained German enthusiasm for the war, they were equally effective in lifting Allied troop morale. General Jimmy Doolittle commented: "Next to a letter from home, that organisation (ABSIE) was the greatest morale builder in the European Theatre of Operations."

Ironically, these were the last recordings ever made by Miller with his band; the iconic music man disappeared on a flight from RAF Twinwood Farm in Bedfordshire to Paris on 15 December 1944. That the great Glenn Miller was actually a member of the Psychological Warfare Division has been discussed by some authors. This has never been proven, but it seems evident that the musician must have known via those who worked at Abbey Road, and others who used the broadcasts, that his endeavours had far more to do with psychology and 'hearts and minds' than the brilliance of his music - as good as it was!

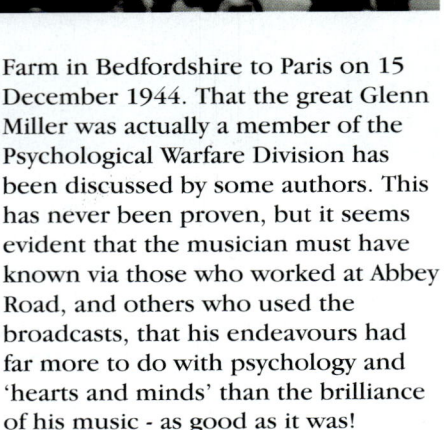

7 May 1945 - Surrender document signed by Germany at Reims

The BBC also used the studio to produce a variety of radio broadcasts, and intercepted Axis recordings were sometimes sent to analysts who helped ascertain their authenticity and date. Much of the wartime work carried out at Abbey Road Studios remains a closely guarded secret.

7 Bedford Square

310

Eye Spy Intelligence Magazine

404•19

1-3 Willow Road

SPY SITES OF LONDON
405•23

Alexander Fleming House

STRANGE BUT TRUE

Operating in the war years had proven difficult for British Intelligence, but one interesting affair did at least offer a little light relief.

At the outbreak of war, former MI6 man Ian Fleming lived in a splendid Victorian Terrace house at **WILLOW ROAD, HAMPSTEAD (number 2) [403•19]**. He would soon be joined by architect Erno Goldfinger. Goldfinger applied to build a very futuristic structure at **1-3 WILLOW ROAD [404•19]** right next door to where Fleming lived. It was very much out of keeping with the other houses in the street. Goldfinger's design was modernistic to say the least. Residents, including Fleming, opposed its construction, but it was approved by the council anyway. This so infuriated Fleming that in his third James Bond 007 book - *Goldfinger* (1964) - the villain was of course named Auric Goldfinger. Interestingly, in the subsequent movie, Goldfinger's factory resembled the house that everyone in Willow Road hated! Erno Goldfinger responded by naming a tower block complex in Southwark **ALEXANDER FLEMING HOUSE [405•23]** (now called Metro Central Heights).

Visitors to London are advised that since 1995, the modern building on Willow Road has been managed by the National Trust and is open to the public. You must however obtain a dated ticket. Goldfinger resided here with his wife until his death in 1987, but worked from offices at **7 BEDFORD SQUARE [406•62]**.

Though there is no information linking Goldfinger to the world of intelligence, it is puzzling that he once considered buying the fabled Clock House **(See Site 376•47)** occupied by several important MI6 officers and agents!

WILLOW R^{**D**} **N.W. 3.**

2 Willow Road
Ian Fleming's 1939 residence on the right - Goldfinger's modern creation is on the left

403•19

Eye Spy Intelligence Magazine   **311**

Carlyle Mansions, Cheyne Walk

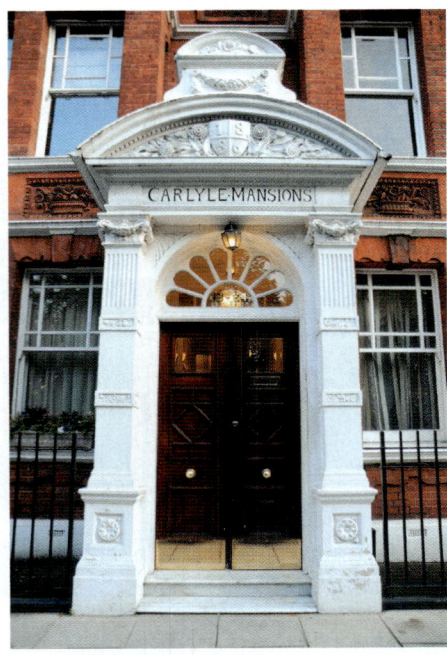

408•44

407•42

From 1953 through 1964, Fleming lived in an apartment with his wife Anne and their young son Casper, at **16 VICTORIA SQUARE [407•42]**. Indeed, Fleming celebrated the launch of his first book *Casino Royale* just four weeks after moving from his home in **CARLYLE MANSIONS, CHEYNE WALK [408•44]**. MI6 man Malcolm Muggeridge would spend a great deal of time with Fleming in an upper room, drinking and discussing the latest happenings.

16 Victoria Square

Ian Fleming's residence

SPY SITES OF LONDON

XVI
A Street of Strange Secrets
Rutland Gate and People of the Serpentine

A few hundred feet from Rutland Gate is Hyde Park's famous Serpentine Lake. Created in 1730, no doubt it has welcomed many of the interesting people who lived in the street, including those of the spying fraternity. The wartime government of Britain had shown much interest in using Rutland Gate to its fullest potential, thus we too chose to examine some of its most interesting residents.

Richard Meinertzhagen, the adventurer, military officer and controversial MI6 man who lived at Clock House was actually born at **18 RUTLAND GATE [409•47]** in 1878. His mistress lived next door at **17 RUTLAND GATE [410•47]**. Meinertzhagen built an underground passage between the houses which would allow them to meet secretly away from the watching eyes of other residents!

Another resident of number 17 was Churchill's favourite historian - Arthur Bryant who had connections to GCHQ and MI6 and moved in the upper echelons of government. In 1943 Bryant visited the codebreaking centre

View of the Serpentine looking towards Hyde Park Barracks and Rutland Gate

Eye Spy Intelligence Magazine

313

SPY SITES OF LONDON

Richard Meinertzhagen pictured in Kenya 1915

at Bletchley Park where he delivered a lecture. During the event he was introduced to Stella a codebreaker whom he subsequently married. Bryant's neighbour was one Oswald Mosley, and he would often write to Churchill informing of his dubious activities. However, one of his biggest detractors was historian John Plumb who said Bryant was himself a Nazi and fascist sympathiser!

Another Churchill - Lord Alfred Spencer-Churchill, a politician and army officer, once lived next door at **16 RUTLAND GATE [411•47]**. He was the son of the 6th Duke of Marlborough. Prior to these residents, Henry Northcote, 3rd Governor-General of Australia lived at 17 Rutland Gate. He was a politician and Foreign Office staffer who had military and intelligence links.

At **26 RUTLAND GATE [412•47]** lived the infamous Mitford sisters - Nancy, Pamela, Diana, Unity, Jessica and Deborah. Diana married Brian Guinness of the brewing dynasty. She left him in 1933 and in 1936 married Oswald Mosley. He had left his wife, Lady Curzon who was the daughter of intelligence man Lord Curzon. Mosley of course was the founder and head of the British Union of Fascists and was constantly under surveillance by MI5. Both would be arrested in the war and together with their new son, were interned at Holloway Prison.

Unity had a complete obsession for Adolf Hitler and was in his inner circle of friends. She spent five years in Germany and once appeared with him on a balcony in Vienna. After Britain declared war on Germany she shot herself in the head but the bullet did not kill her.

Nancy, like her sister Jessica was a devout Communist. Nancy was also a writer and in 1942 went to work for Heywood Hill Books at **10 CURZON STREET [413•55]** in the heart of Britain's intelligence community. This store of course supplied Communist material. Opened in 1936, the establishment still exists at the address selling old, new and antiquarian books.

Deborah Mitford married Lord Andrew Cavendish, the younger son of Lord Devonshire. Mitford then took the title Dame Deborah Cavendish,

Lord Northcote

409•47

Houses on Rutland Gate East

Oswald Mosley

314

Eye Spy Intelligence Magazine

SPY SITES OF LONDON

410•47 Rutland Gate West

412•47 26 Rutland Gate

413•55 G. Heywood Hill Books, 10 Curzon Street

411•47 Rutland Gate looking South

Eye Spy Intelligence Magazine

315

414•47

28 Rutland Gate
Used by SOE and OSS officials during WWII, the building now hosts the Austrian Consulate

Cecil Harcourt-Smith

operated in the Middle East in WWI. Very spiritual, he began writing and focused on the ordinary soldier and the afterlife. Pole instituted the 'Silent Minute' which is now used throughout the world to honour victims, deaths and to pray for peace. In 1919 King George, on Pole's suggestion, dedicated 11 November as Remembrance Day to honour British war dead. Similar ceremonies now take place across the world. In Britain, it is also known as Poppy Day and towns across the country lay poppy wreaths at specially built war memorials. A huge annual event takes place at the **CENOTAPH, WHITEHALL [415•42]**.

Cecil Harcourt-Smith was an archaeologist and director of the Victoria and

Cenotaph, Whitehall

Duchess of Devonshire. She became the public face of the splendid stately Chatsworth House in Derbyshire.

Around the same time of the Mitfords' occupancy, **28 RUTLAND GATE [414•47]** was being used by the French Government-in-exile. It was frequented by SOE and OSS agents who would receive guidance and materials to help with their secret missions in France. Violette Szabo the famous SOE agent was honoured here. In 1946 her family posthumously accepted the George Cross on her behalf. She was of course executed (gassed) in February 1945, along with three other agents following their capture by the Nazis. The address was later acquired by the Austrian Government (consulate) which remain here today. Other foreign consulates can also be found in the street: Sudan, number 32 and Germany number 4.

A famous British intelligence officer in the person of Major Tudor Pole lived at **27 RUTLAND GATE [410•47]**. Pole

© CHRIS NYBORG

Eye Spy Intelligence Magazine

415•42

The Cenotaph, Whitehall
Remembrance Day 11 November

416•47

Rutland Gate West

Western Australian Governor Malcolm McCusker lays a wreath in Kings Park

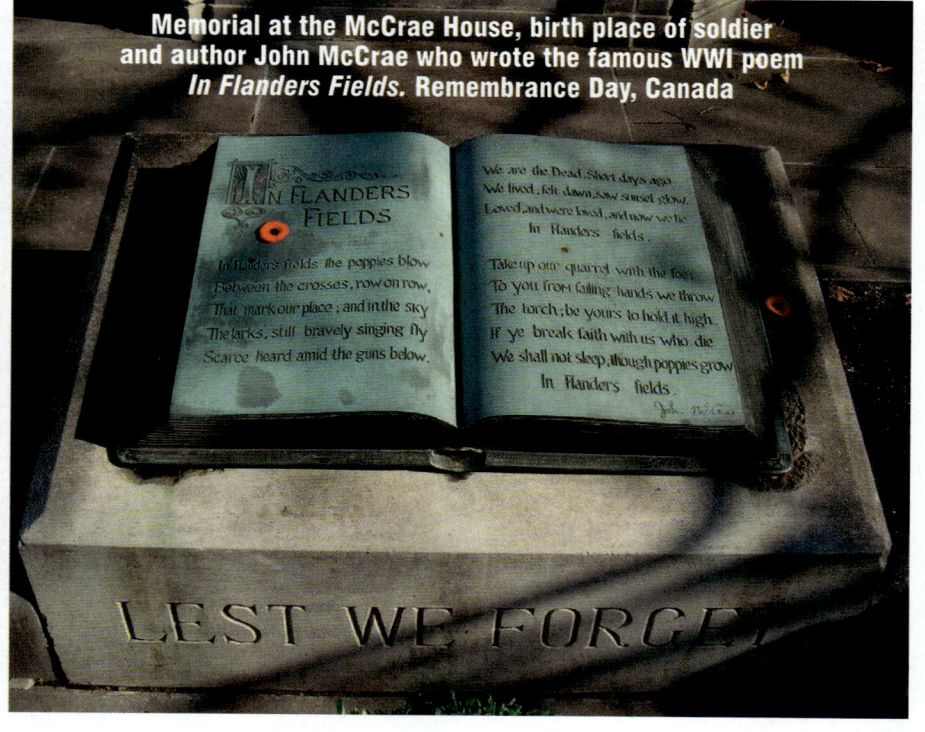

Memorial at the McCrae House, birth place of soldier and author John McCrae who wrote the famous WWI poem *In Flanders Fields*. Remembrance Day, Canada

Albert Museum. He was also a navy intelligence contact man in WWI. Well versed in Middle East diplomacy, unsurprisingly some of his friends also worked in intelligence, including Somerset Maugham (MI6). Harcourt-Smith lived and operated from **62 RUTLAND GATE [416•47]**.

Following the end of hostilities in WWII, Sir Robert Craigie chaired the United Nations War Crimes Commission. As former British Ambassador to Japan 1937-1941, he was charged with examining alleged atrocities. Craigie lived at **52 RUTLAND GATE (See also Site 416•47)**.

Sir Austen Chamberlain was half-brother of Neville, British Prime Minister. He held many significant government posts from the 1920s and became First Lord of the Admiralty in the Intelligence Division of Douglas Haig. Haig of course commanded the British Expeditionary forces in Europe

Eye Spy Intelligence Magazine   317

SPY SITES OF LONDON

Austin Chamberlain

from 1915 to the end of World War One. He was also commander at the infamous battles of Somme, Ypres and the 100 Day Offensive. In Whitehall, visitors will find a statue of **EARL HAIG [417•42]**. At the time he lived at 58 Rutland Gate.

Another well known WWI British Army officer with ties to Rutland Gate is Staff Captain Sir Herbert Lawrence. He maintained links to his intelligence friends after retiring in 1919 - this after entering the world of international banking. His job afforded him many opportunities to travel overseas! Lawrence lived at **32 RUTLAND GATE [418•47]**.

One person with deep connections to the slightly darker areas of British Intelligence and its propaganda, psychological and deception arms was Sir Francis Galton. He was the half cousin of Charles Darwin who himself had connections to the intelligence world through work being performed at the Tavistock Centre **(See Site 305•19)**. Galton was a psychologist, eugenicist, inventor and statistician.

He was first to apply statistician methods to study human behaviour. He introduced the use of questionnaires and surveys for collecting data on human communities. This was of immense importance of course to William Stephenson and the British Security Coordination. The BSC employed his methods in an effort to understand American public opinion to the war raging in Europe in 1940.

Galton, who lived at **42 RUTLAND GATE [419•47]** is most remembered for devising a method for classifying fingerprints. He visited the Tavistock Centre and collected the fingerprint markings of youngsters. A plaque honouring Galton's fingerprint work can be found at Rutland Gate.

Briefly, other past well known residents of this famous street include Ava Gardner, Prince Bertil of Sweden and interestingly, Annie Chapman, a Jack

417•42

Statue of Field Marshal Earl Haig, Commander of British forces in France 1915-18

Earl Haig Memorial

418•47

32 Rutland Gate

Eye Spy Intelligence Magazine

419•47

42 Rutland Gate

SIR FRANCIS GALTON
1822 - 1911
EXPLORER . STATISTICIAN
FOUNDER OF EUGENICS
LIVED HERE FOR FIFTY YEARS

Sir Francis Galton lived here. The house sits next to the new build at 43-44 which first attracted our attention to the street

Sir Francis Galton

SPY SITES OF LONDON

Ava Gardner

the Ripper victim who worked as a maid here. She was murdered in 1888.

THE ATOMIC SPY AND RUTLAND GATE

Perhaps one of the most famous houses on the street is **PARK HOUSE, 24 RUTLAND GATE [420•47]**. Based here was the secretive Department of Scientific and Industrial Research. Amongst its employees was Herbert Wakefield Banks Skinner who worked on atomic weaponry and radar.

During the latter part of WWII, Skinner went to America to work on the

GHASTLY MURDER IN THE EAST-END. DREADFUL MUTILATION OF A WOMAN.

Ripper victim Annie Chapman

Eye Spy Intelligence Magazine   319

SPY SITES OF LONDON
Park House, 24 Rutland Gate

Britain's once secret Department of Scientific and Industrial Research was based here

ultra-secret Manhattan Project - which of course resulted in the first atomic bomb. His research was performed at the Telecommunications Research Establishment, Berkeley University in California.

Skinner was a close friend of Klaus Fuchs - better known in spylore as the 'atomic spy'. More on him later, suffice it to say Skinner confronted Fuchs about his suspicions that he was a KGB spy seeking information on the project.

Fuchs, unable to lie to his good friend said nothing, thus MI5 was informed and an investigation launched.

Ironically, Skinner died in Geneva in 1960 whilst on a visit to the European Organisation for Nuclear Research headquartered there.

And finally, a scheme to build a block of flats at 3-4 Rutland Gate was proposed by architect Erno Goldfinger, but thankfully nothing came of his idea!

SPY SITES OF LONDON

XVII
KGB Spies, Treason & Venona
Communist Spies in London

When 'Captain Black' of the War Office entered a plush apartment in **5 BENTINCK STREET [421•55]**, little did he know he was about to make the biggest mistake of his life. Black was in fact Guy Liddell, head of MI5's counter-espionage branch and one of the Service's most experienced officers. He had been invited to the apartment by Victor Rothschild, a top Cambridge scientist and fellow MI5 man who was keen to introduce his former French teacher to Liddell. That man was Captain Anthony Blunt and his host was recommending him to the Security Service.

The date was June 1940, and is significant in that Liddell had inadvertently recruited a top Russian asset who would go on to spy for Moscow for years. Another room in the building was occupied by an equally interesting character - Guy Burgess - he too would join the KGB. And this wasn't the only address where Russian agents within British Intelligence fraternised with their colleagues - such gatherings also took place at the home of intelligence man and art collector Tomas Harris in 6 Chesterfield Gardens, former residence of MI5 man Tar Robertson (See Site 368•55).

It's also poignant that in July 2009, exactly forty years after he was unmasked publicly as a KGB spy, the

In 1940, Anthony Blunt was introduced to MI5's Guy Liddell by Lord Rothschild at this address

KGB agent Anthony Blunt

5 Bentinck Street

Eye Spy Intelligence Magazine

321

SPY SITES OF LONDON

Trinity College, Cambridge

British Library released Blunt's memoir. Blunt was the so-called 'fourth man' in an infamous grouping known as the Cambridge Spy Ring; other members were Kim Philby, Donald Maclean, Guy Burgess and John Cairncross. Four of them had previous connections to Trinity College in the 1930s and hailed from an intellectual elite. Most, if not all were members of a secret debating society called The Apostles.

MI5 had battled hard to stop the influence of Communism spreading throughout the UK in the 1920s and 1930s, but the men, despite dreadful tales of repression in Russia, were intent on helping Moscow. They were not really a spy ring as such, and some were decidedly unfriendly to each other, but they all had two things in common - they were traitors and all would ultimately work for the intelligence services of both Britain and Russia.

Much has been written about the men and their exploits have filled many books. In the East they remain legendary figures - a throwback to the days when the NKVD (People's Commissariat for Internal Affairs) and its successor, the KGB, were feared worldwide. In Britain, the Cambridge men remain a point of fascination. Lest we forget, their actions resulted in the deaths of many British and Western agents.

Other Communist sympathisers and spies existed of course, and one address in London was a 'hotbed' of activity. And it was here that the controller of the Cambridge spies resided. So too a number of other

430 • 55
Leconfield House, Curzon Street

In 1945, MI5 moved its headquarters from St James's Street to Leconfield House. The building has been modernised since the Security Service departed in 1976, though it still retains its original name. MI5's Registry was situated in the basement. Interestingly, it once sported port hole-type windows - machine gun posts - just in case the Germans decided to visit London. The building also housed an MI5 staff bar called the Pig and Eye

Eye Spy Intelligence Magazine

SPY SITES OF LONDON

Isokon Building, Lawn Road Flats, Belsize Park

UNDER SURVEILLANCE - LAWN ROAD FLATS

The **ISOKON BUILDING, LAWN ROAD FLATS, BELSIZE PARK** [422•19] will forever be linked to Soviet spies and Communist supporters plying their underworld trade in the 1930s and 1940s. This iconic building was the first in Britain to use reinforced concrete in its architecture, but its residents were probably more remarkable than its ultra modern design and construction.

Opened in 1934, the building contained 34 flats and though each had a small kitchen, many occupants opted to use a large communal area to cook. In 1937 this was converted into the Isobar. Residents enjoyed various services as part of their rental including a laundry and shoe shine. For those living in Lawn Road Flats, this was truly a different way of living.

characters, spies, artists, writers, poets, historians, sculptors, codebreakers, intelligence officers, broadcasters etc. An eclectic mix of personalities.

RESIDENTS AND VISITORS

Edith Tudor Hart was a photographer and Soviet NKVD spy. She played an important role in the recruitment and development of Soviet spies. Her codename was Edith and she met the important spy Arnold Deutsch, the Cambridge Spy Ring controller in Vienna in 1926.

In future years Hart acted as a courier for Russian agents, including Anthony Blunt and CPGB spymaster Robert Stewart.

Arnold Deutsch

Eva Collet Reckitt was an heiress and Soviet spy who ran Collet's bookstore on Charing Cross Road (**See Site 107•62**). This of course imported and sold radical Communist books, and it seems little wonder that like her Moscow-supportive friends, she too chose to live in the flats.

Kuczynski family: Barbara, Brigitte, Jurgen and Margueritte - were once described as the most successful family of spies in espionage history. Along with other members of the family, including Ursula - a Soviet GRU spy codenamed Sonja, they are credited with helping German-born Russian scientific spy Klaus Fuchs to secure intelligence on the atomic bomb project. Indeed, it was Jurgen who Fuchs approached in 1941 for help - thus drawing in the entire family who were all ardent Communists. Fuchs, who held British citizenship worked at the Los Alamos National Laboratory in the USA and was

Eye Spy Intelligence Magazine

323

SPY SITES OF LONDON

Mornington Crescent Tube Station
`423•15`

Klaus Fuchs was an agent of Russia who passed secrets to the Soviets about the United States Manhattan A-bomb programme. On one occasion in 1946, he was due to meet his KGB controller at MORNINGTON CRESCENT STATION [423•15]. Told to carry a copy of *Life* magazine, while his controller would be carrying a stack of books, Fuchs froze and never turned up - fearing MI5 men were watching. It was more likely he had been tipped-off by a KGB spy inside British Intelligence.

in a prime position to steal vital information. After he was exposed by his long-time friend Herbert Skinner in 1949, Fuchs was arrested. Following weeks of questioning by MI5, he finally admitted he was a spy in an office occupied by RAF Intelligence at Shell Mex House **(See Site 230•60)**.

Once news of his arrest came to the attention of the Kuczynskis, Ursula, who also went by the name Ruth Werner, fled to East Berlin. She was later awarded the Order of the Red Banner. Ursula was also said to have been an early controller of another Lawn Road Flats resident - Melita Norwood - the longest operational Russian spy in Britain.

AGENT HOLA

Norwood began working for the important British Non-Ferrous Metals Research Association (BNF) in 1937 as a clerk, a job she would hold down for 40 years. As secretary to the Research Superintendent, she had access to a

324

Eye Spy Intelligence Magazine

424•15
81-103 Euston Street

Klaus Fuchs

Melita Norwood

425•15

Regnart Buildings, behind Stephenson Street

plethora of research papers. It was also in 1937 that Norwood, a Communist Party member, was recruited by Soviet Intelligence and given the codename Hola. She would go on to pass information to Moscow on Britain's atomic bomb project codenamed Tube Alloys - of which much test documentation was stored at BNF. And as a

Eye Spy Intelligence Magazine

428 • 42

112 Eaton Square

426 • 62

Leicester Square
A bronze statue of the famous author Agatha Christie

© ALLAN WARREN

Famous sculptor Henry Moore was a resident of Lawn Road Flats

matter of record, the KGB trusted her far more than the likes of Blunt, Burgess, Philby and Maclean. Some officials even described her as the "most important female KGB agent of all time."

The BNF was located at **81-103 EUSTON STREET [424•15]** with its main laboratories tucked away in the **REGNART BUILDINGS** behind **STEPHENSON STREET [425•15]**.

Despite MI5 watching both the BNF building and Lawn Road - examining its residents with much curiosity - it was not until 1992 the Security Service learned the truth about Norwood. Amazingly, she was not charged.

Brigitte Kuczynski was married to suspected Soviet spy Anthony Lewis. He worked with the BBC's Research Department. Another broadcaster, Trevor Blewitt, was a suspected contact man with the CPGB.

Agatha Christie - investigated by MI5

A surprise occupant included the famous sculptor Henry Moore who unbeknown to many was a member of the famous Artists Rifles **(See Chapter 3)**. The poet and Bletchley Park codebreaking centre officer Charles Orwell Brasch also resided here for a time.

Agatha Christie, who lived here between 1941 and 1948, wrote her one and only spy book at this location - *N or M?* The book had attracted the

Eye Spy Intelligence Magazine

Lawn Road Flats resident - CIA man Charles Fenn recruited Ho Chi Minh. In 1946 Minh became godfather to the daughter of French Resistance fighter Lucie Aubrac

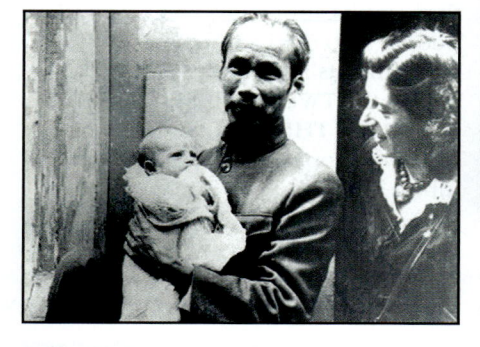

58 Sheffield Terrace

attention of MI5 because of her apparent knowledge of British Intelligence; the supposed antics of German spies and Fifth Columnists in London and that one of the book's characters was called Bletchley. This may well have been sourced from her husband - RAF intelligence officer Max Mallowan.

Visitors to London can also find a wonderful bronze statue of the author at the end of **CRANBOURNE STREET, LEICESTER SQUARE [426•62]** and a blue plaque at her previous residence - **58 SHEFFIELD TERRACE, KENSINGTON [427•60]**.

The CIA had evolved from the OSS in 1947 and one of its earliest operators was British-born Charles Fenn. He served with the OSS and in 1945, is credited with recruiting Ho Chi Minh, the Vietnamese leader. Fenn was also a propaganda specialist.

OSS chief William Donovan was full of praise for Fenn and awarded him the Bronze Star for valour. Ironically, when he returned to London he moved into the flats in 1949 where he would remain until 1954.

In 1946, Minh, who fought against the Japanese, became godfather of Elizabeth Aubrac, daughter of Lucie. She had been a member of the French Resistance during WWII and helped produce the underground publication *Liberation*. In 1944, she relocated to London after her identity was revealed. The genesis of Minh's connections to France were probably created through the French Resistance units fighting in Indo China.

In 1937, a regular dining event started in Lawn Road. Hosted by the Half-Hundred Club, a food and wine society, the club had 25 members who could bring one guest - hence its name. Amongst its membership Soviet agent and journalist William Ewer and interestingly Julian Huxley, ex-British Security Coordination and Director of the Zoological Gardens, London Zoo. Occasionally the club dined at the zoo. Suspected Soviet agent and journalist Francis Meynell was also a resident and club member.

Regular visitors to the flats included British Communist and Soviet agents Len Beurton and Alexander Foote.

THE SPY RECRUITER - CODENAME OTTO

A most influential and important KGB spy, Arnold Deutsch - Cambridge spy ring controller - lived at Lawn Road Flats together with his wife Josefine, an experienced radio operator and

Eye Spy Intelligence Magazine

SPY SITES OF LONDON

Kim Philby

Soviet spy. Deutsch is credited with recruiting Kim Philby in 1934 and thereafter Donald Maclean, Guy Burgess, Anthony Blunt and John Cairncross. As for his demise, there is much debate in the intelligence community. Some historians believe he was captured and killed by the Nazis, whilst others insist he escaped to South America under a false identity. However, it is possible he drowned when the SS Donbass carrying him on a mission to the United States in 1942, was attacked and sunk, probably by a U-boat.

As a point of interest, Hermann Deutsch was uncle to the Kuczynskis who lived just a few feet away in Lawn Road Flats.

STRANGE DAYS AND RIPPLES FROM THE WAR

There were many accusing fingers pointed at those suspected of working against Britain's interests after the war. One was at John Amery, the brother of Julian and son of Leo Amery, a noted

Leo Amery

John Amery's arrest in Italy 1944

British statesman and First Lord of the Admiralty. Whilst Julian was an MI6 officer and later CIA contact man who fought bravely against the Nazis in Europe, John was a fascist who wanted to establish a British volunteer force to fight with Germany.

John Amery also produced propaganda for Berlin much to the angst of British Intelligence. Arrested in Italy, the man who was actually despatched to bring him back was Alan Whicker who moved in significant intelligence circles. Whicker would become a hugely successful television presenter on *Whicker's World*.

John Amery was executed on 19 December 1945 at Wandsworth Prison. Julian lived at **112 EATON SQUARE [428•42]**.

One significant memorial to many people who died at the hands of the Communists after they were repatriated is the **TWELVE RESPONSES TO TRAGEDY, THURLOE SQUARE [429•47]**, opposite the Victoria and Albert Museum (**See Site 275•47**).

Commissioned by Prime Minister Thatcher, the original statue was damaged by vandals.

429•47

Twelve Responses to Tragedy

Thurloe Square

THIS MEMORIAL WAS PLACED HERE BY MEMBERS OF ALL PARTIES IN BOTH HOUSES OF PARLIAMENT AND BY MANY OTHER SYMPATHISERS IN MEMORY OF THE COUNTLESS INNOCENT MEN WOMEN AND CHILDREN FROM THE SOVIET UNION AND OTHER EAST EUROPEAN STATES WHO WERE IMPRISONED AND DIED AT THE HANDS OF COMMUNIST GOVERNMENTS AFTER BEING REPATRIATED AT THE CONCLUSION OF THE SECOND WORLD WAR.

MAY THEY REST IN PEACE

431•44
18 Carlyle Square

MI6 officer and KGB agent Kim Philby - codenamed Stanley - lived in this end-of-terrace house

MOSCOW'S BIG-TIME PLAYERS - FLAMBOYANT AND HARD DRINKING SPIES

In 1945, MI5 as a post-war institution found itself on the move - this time to the larger premises that would remain its home for many years - **LECONFIELD HOUSE, CURZON STREET [430•55]**.

Against the backdrop of deep suspicion between the West and East following the end of the war, British Intelligence moved swiftly to reorganise itself. However, by now the Soviets had established spies in Britain and most held important posts allowing them to secure secret information.

PHILBY: Harold Adrian Russell, born 1912, was probably lured to Moscow after witnessing Nazi supporters crush the Socialist Party in Austria in 1933. He was nicknamed 'Kim' - after the Indian boy-spy in Rudyard Kipling's stories. In 1940, his Communist cohort Guy Burgess proposed him for employment in MI5. Eventually he would serve with Section IV (MI6) and then head Britain's counter-intelligence efforts against Russia (Section IX anti-Soviet counter-intelligence) - an intelligence disaster for MI5 and MI6. In 1949, MI6 sent him to Washington DC to work at the British Embassy and liaise with CIA officials.

Philby organised an impromptu press conference at the home of his mother in November 1955 after being cleared of working for the Soviets. "I have never been a Communist," he said

Eye Spy Intelligence Magazine 329

Clifford Chambers, 10 New Bond Street

26 Medway Street

MI5 had been oblivious to Philby's background and even a Registry note on him read: *'Philby - NRO - Nothing Recorded Against'*. Historians agree that this proves MI5 was still recruiting via the 'old boys network' and recommendations from elitists and the Establishment. As for Philby, MI6 man and author Graham Greene, who worked with him said: "Few officers in the history of MI6 have been as well liked within the Service." Indeed, he was very well liked by MI6 Chief Sir Stewart Menzies and even touted as a future 'C'. Problematic too was the fact that he had access to MI6's own [Central] Registry of 'persons of interest', contacts, agents and worldwide officers. He reportedly spent hours digesting its content, and undoubtedly passed Moscow the names of many important people opposed to the policies of the USSR. It's unlikely we will ever know just how many British agents perished after being outed by Philby. Kim Philby lived at **18 CARLYLE SQUARE [431•44]**.

BURGESS: Guy Frances de Moncy, born 1911. In 1935 Burgess found work in the banking industry, after his Cambridge friend, Victor Rothschild, persuaded his mother to employ him as an investment advisor for £25.00 a week. He became assistant to a right-wing politician who was central to a

Burgess lived here in 1945

Guy Burgess

Eye Spy Intelligence Magazine

38 Chester Square

In 1935, Burgess resided in a top floor flat in this Belgravia building. By this time he was already in the pay of his Soviet spymasters

136 Ebury Street
Morgan Goronwy Rees lived here

pro-Anglo-Nazi outfit, before ending up with the BBC. The earlier ruse would confuse intelligence watchers after he joined MI6 (Section D) in 1940, but it was perfect cover. However, he was left out in the cold when the Special Operations Executive took over Section D. He would eventually serve in the diplomatic corp of the Foreign Office and worked as a secretary in Washington DC, under Kim Philby. In 1950 he was summoned back to the UK for serious misconduct. His intelligence career was short lived but he remained a useful KGB asset after returning to the BBC. Burgess occupied a number of addresses in the city, including **38 CHESTER SQUARE [432•42]** and a three bedroom flat at **CLIFFORD CHAMBERS, 10 NEW BOND STREET [433•55]**.

He also lived at **26 MEDWAY STREET [434•42]** (apartment) for a while from 1945. One guest who visited him here was fellow spy Donald Maclean.

As a side issue to Burgess's espionage, the name Goronwy Rees has often surfaced in spylore. A military intelligence officer with links to MI6, he was charged with keeping the D-Day invasion plans secret. Rees resided at **136 EBURY STREET [435•42]**, and often wrote of his friendship with Burgess. Rees lived at other locations in the city, but **26 CAVENDISH AVENUE [436•22]** was described as the family home.

Some authors believe Rees, who was acquainted with several intelligence officers and his Cambridge friends, was himself suspected of being a KGB asset, though this has never been proven. Similarly, there is a feeling within the intelligence world that Rees may have had something to do with exposing Burgess and Maclean.

This rumour began after a drinking session at the **GARGOYLE CLUB, 69 DEAN STREET [437•55]**. A drunken Maclean accused Rees of "ratting on him" to MI5 that he was a Russian spy. "You used to be one of us," Maclean exploded. This club, along with the nearby **MANDRAKE CLUB, MEARD STREET [438•55]** (off Dean Street) was popular with intelligence and government figures as well as artists and tourists. It was also frequented by Communists, including Philip Toynbee, the son of Arnold an MI6 officer.

As Maclean increasingly feared he was becoming more exposed, his drinking worsened and on one occasion threw Toynbee into the bandstand at the Gargoyle Club. Thereafter he was given the nickname - 'The Lurcher'.

Another popular drinking venue for Britain's spies at the time could be

HeyJo Members Club, 91 Jermyn Street
Maclean, like many UK intelligence officers was a frequent visitor to the HeyJo Club situated in the basement of what today is the Abracadabra Restaurant. Interestingly, the HeyJo Members Club still exists

found in the basement of the Abracadabra Restaurant - the **HEYJO MEMBERS CLUB, 91 JERMYN STREET [439•42]**. Maclean was a frequent visitor. In 2005, owned by a Russian, it was in the news again after MI6 agent and former FSB man Alexander Litvinenko was poisoned with the deadly radioactive isotope Polonium-210. Traces of polonium were found in the HeyJo after Litvinenko drank at the venue.

Another club of note that is included in the popular 1950s spylore of London and associated with the Cambridge Spy Ring is **PRATT'S, 14 PARK PLACE, ST JAMES'S [440•42]**. Maclean, Burgess, Philby and Cairncross were all members. Interestingly, Duncan Sandys, Churchill's son-in-law, was also a member and the first person ever to be convicted under the Official Secrets Act in 1939!

One of the favoured restaurants used by Maclean and Burgess was the fashionable **L'ETOILE, 30 CHARLOTTE STREET [441•55]**. It was popular with many MI5 and MI6 officers, including Ian Fleming. The restaurant can still be found here today.

BLUNT: Anthony Frederick, born 1907, was the son of a clergyman. In 1937 he joined the **WARBURG INSTITUTE, WOBURN SQUARE [442•62]** famous for its cultural and art history. Three years later he transferred from the Intelligence Corp (military) to MI5. He became a liaison between the Service and SHAEF (Supreme HQ Allied Expeditionary Force) based at Norfolk House in St James's Square **(See Site 340•42)**. Blunt handled intercepted diplomatic bags from a number of embassies in London. This enabled his secondary employer - Russia - access to a wealth of intelligence. Blunt's intelligence career was enhanced when he secured a place on the Joint Intelligence

Duncan Sandys

Eye Spy Intelligence Magazine

CAVENDISH AVENUE NW8 — CITY OF WESTMINSTER

436•22

26 Cavendish Avenue
Goronwy Rees former family home

Service (JIC) and occasionally acted as MI5's representative. Blunt would be knighted and find impressive jobs as the King's Surveyor of Pictures and Director of the **COURTAULD INSTITUTE OF ART [443•62]**.

In his parallel occupation, he was regarded as a top recruiter for the KGB. After he confessed in 1964 to being a Soviet spy (he managed to obtain immunity from prosecution in return for his cooperation), he was stripped of his knighthood. In later years he admitted he felt remorse at not being able to continue his career in art, but said nothing about his treachery against the State.

As a most puzzling finale to the spying career of Blunt, intelligence watchers note that Blunt's departure from MI5 was unusual in that Moscow never attempted to keep their agent in place. They simply left him to his own fate. This decision still causes much debate today, as some commentators believe he was actually deflecting

438•55

Mandrake Club, Meard Street off Dean Street

Burgess and Maclean were often visitors to the Mandrake Club

Eye Spy Intelligence Magazine

333

SPY SITES OF LONDON

440•42

Pratt's, 14 Park Place, St James's

437•55

69 Dean Street
The building hosted the famous Gargoyle Club

Maclean accused Goronwy Rees of exposing him to British Intelligence at this address

441•55

L'Etoile, 30 Charlotte Street

© ADAM SINGER

attention away from an even more powerful spy within British Intelligence. For the record, he is the only known spy who was allowed to use his real name as his codename - Tony.

Others note Blunt and his associates were fearful that MI6 and MI5 had gained access to the spy ring via Soviet defectors. The truth lies probably somewhere in the middle. As for his home, after the war Blunt spent 30 years living in a plush apartment at **20 PORTMAN SQUARE [444•55]**. Before this, he and his inner circle of friends and cohorts partied at his pre-war residence at **30 PALACE COURT, NOTTING HILL [445•56]**.

The deflection theory surrounding Blunt is enhanced by statements from

334

Eye Spy Intelligence Magazine

SPY SITES OF LONDON

a Soviet [agent] 'walk-in'.* In August 1945, Konstantin Volkov entered the British Consulate in Istanbul, Turkey. He told officials who he was and that he had knowledge of two Russian spies inside British Intelligence. Unfortunately, Volkov's intelligence reached London and found its way to Philby. Weeks later a heavily bandaged man was seen boarding a Russian military flight at Ankara enroute to Moscow. It was probably Volkov who had been exposed and, before MI6 could get him out of the country, the KGB pounced. The likes of Blunt and Philby now realised that their well-being was threatened by Soviet intelligence officers who knew exactly what their true role was in London. As for Philby, this was a warning shot that would soon turn into rapid fire when news reached him of another Soviet defection in Canada.

Ironically, Blunt's great uncle, Wilfred Scarwen Blunt, diplomat, poet and traveller was once a friend of Winston Churchill. He resided at **15 BUCKINGHAM GATE [446•42]**. His work for the government's various intelligence sections in their embryonic stages is not well known, but he carried secret messages to British agents in the Middle East.

Another strange quirk of fate not widely known, is that Anthony Blunt's brother, Christopher, also worked at SHAEF; and furthermore, he resided at **15 GERALD ROAD [447•42]**. His neighbour was none other than MI6 man Noel Coward living at number 17! **(See Site 054•42)**.

MACLEAN: Donald Duart, born 1913, was the son of a Liberal politician and grew up in **6 SOUTHWICK PLACE [448•56]**. After entering the British Foreign Diplomatic Service he was hailed as a potential ambassador.

But Maclean concealed secrets - he was a committed Communist who had agreed to spy for Russia: he was also an alcoholic, had a penchant for orgies and was gay, which at that time was considered problematic as it

A statue of King William III in St James's Square. To the right and the tallest of the buildings is Norfolk House where Anthony Blunt worked as a liaison with SHAEF - Supreme HQ Allied Expeditionary Force. Blunt's brother, Christopher, also worked here and was honoured by the US military for his exceptional work

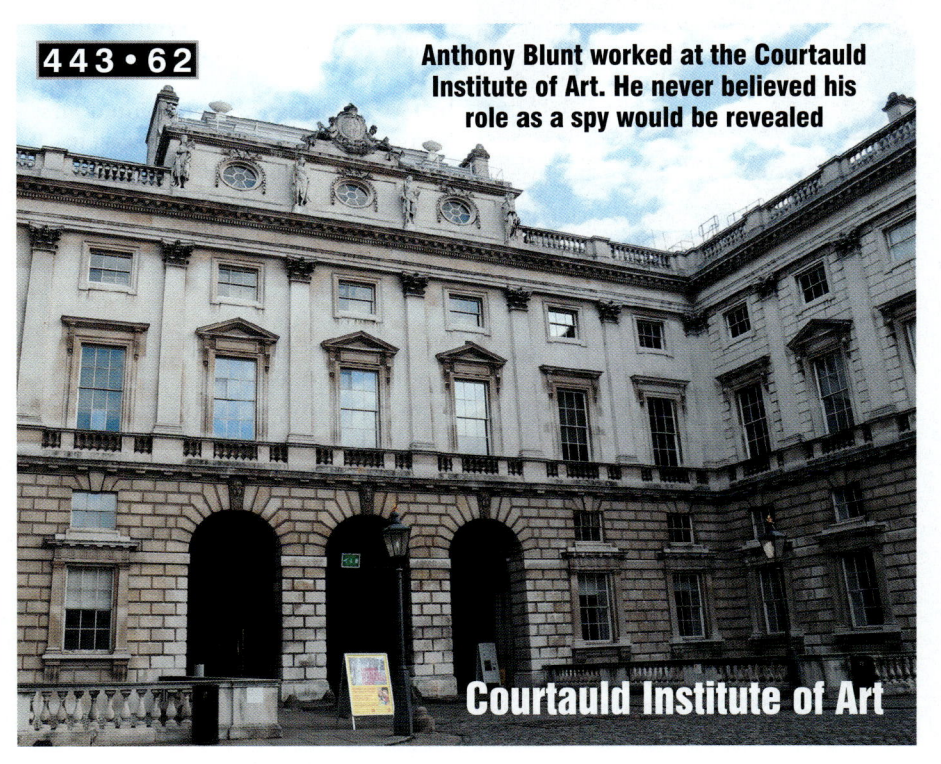

443•62

Anthony Blunt worked at the Courtauld Institute of Art. He never believed his role as a spy would be revealed

Courtauld Institute of Art

Walk-in - typically a person who voluntarily offers to spy for a foreign agency

444•55
20 Portman Square

For thirty years Blunt lived in a luxurious apartment here

Alan Nunn-May and Igor Gouzenko

left him exposed to blackmail. These perceived weaknesses were exploited by the Russians and soon Moscow's spies had photographed him in a variety of compromising situations.

In 1944, Maclean was appointed First Secretary to the British Embassy in Washington, which was ideal in that he could acquire intelligence on America's nuclear ambitions, and the fast-developing Anglo-American relationship.

Thousands of miles away, Canadian Intelligence had been handed a real 'gem' of its own with the defection of Soviet cipher clerk Igor Gouzenko who worked at the Russian Embassy in Ottawa. Philby had learned of the incident but unlike the Volkov affair, could do little about it. Gouzenko revealed details of some 20 Russian agents operating in North America, and also a person by the name of Alan Nunn-May - a Cambridge man and nuclear scientist. He was a friend of Donald Maclean and worked on Canada's atomic bomb project (1942 to 1945) and had duly imparted information to the Soviets. In February 1946, MI5 swooped when he returned to occupy a post at King's College. Nunn-May was jailed for 10 years.

MI5 failed to link Maclean, who lived at **SEYMOUR PLACE [449•55]** with Nunn-May.

VENONA AND SPY GAMES IN LONDON

For much of the time the Cambridge spies were looked after by one of the

SPY SITES OF LONDON

445 • 56 — **30 Palace Court**

Blunt once lived in this residence and often partied with his Communist friends - including KGB spy Guy Burgess

457 • 44 — **138 King's Road, Chelsea**

Former Markham Arms pub - Kim Philby's favourite. Contact with Anthony Blunt was re-established here several years after Burgess and Maclean escaped

446 • 42 — **15 Buckingham Gate**

Eye Spy Intelligence Magazine

337

Warburg Institute, Woburn Square

442•62

Seymour Place

449•55

KGB's top spy handlers in London. MI5 had absolutely no idea about the activities of a certain Yuri Modin.

Modin used all the tricks of spy tradecraft to meet with his agents **(See Chapter 20)** and liked to converse in busy tube stations such as Mornington Crescent **(See Site 423•15)**, though Burgess and some of his colleagues preferred the pubs of Soho.

Another well known KGB-agent meeting location was the **PIGALLE CLUB, PICCADILLY [450•55]**. Besides business, the venue was undoubtedly used by the likes of Maclean and his associates to socialise. Ironically, it had been a firm favourite with Britain's wartime SOE agents.

In the USA, an intelligence effort spearheaded by the NSA known as VENONA, sought to identify a suspected spy linked to Britain's Foreign Office. Analysts discovered that every two weeks a person codenamed Homer visited New York. An intercepted message in 1944 discussed a pregnancy. The evidence was actually pointing to Donald Maclean. MI5 Watchers decided to surveil him across London and tapped his telephone, but that one piece of evidence which could trap the spy was never forthcoming.

Nevertheless, MI5 was now convinced Maclean was KGB. In later years, Philby wrote that Moscow agreed to get him out of London before he could talk - just in case he revealed the identity of other associates.

In Moscow, a plan was hatched that would enable Maclean to flee the UK in the summer of 1951. Fellow Russian agent Guy Burgess was tasked with travelling to London to help

452 • 55

Flemings Hotel, Half Moon Street

450 • 55

The Pigalle Club, Piccadilly

448 • 56

6 Southwick Place

Donald Maclean's boyhood home

Eye Spy Intelligence Magazine

15 Gerald Road

447•42

Anthony Blunt's brother, Christopher, lived here. His neighbour was MI6 man Noel Coward

organise his departure, however, he was in the United States. The KGB arranged that Burgess should receive three speeding tickets in one day infuriating his superiors back in Whitehall. The plan worked a treat and he was recalled to the UK for breaching his diplomatic privileges.

Back in England, MI5 were working with the FBI to set up the interrogation of Maclean. It was too late. On 25 May, Burgess and Maclean decided to escape. Burgess had already booked two ferry tickets to France - one for himself and one for an American called Bernard Miller who he had befriended on his return to England.

This ticket would of course be used by Maclean. Knowing they were under surveillance, and to thwart their MI5 Watchers, it was necessary to act as if everything was normal.

Half Moon Street, Mayfair

Just hours before he departed, Burgess purchased a new coat and suitcase at Gieves & Hawkes, 1 Savile Row. Ironically, during his entire time in Moscow, he continued to purchase his suits from Savile Row

340

Eye Spy Intelligence Magazine

454•55

Former location of Wheeler's Oyster Bar

19-21 Old Compton Street

451•55

Green Park Hotel, Half Moon Street

That morning Maclean received a coded telegram from Western Union sent by Philby in Washington. Philby had learned both Maclean and Burgess were to be interviewed and told the agents to act immediately. Maclean went to work as usual at the Foreign Office, this after enjoying an early drink at the RAC Club. Burgess, meanwhile visited the **GREEN PARK HOTEL, HALF MOON STREET [451•55]** with Miller where they enjoyed a drink. The hotel sits just yards away from the Navy and Military Club (In and Out Club) and was popular with intelligence staffers. Also on Half Moon Street - **FLEMINGS HOTEL [452•55]**. This too was frequented by the intelligence community, and one visitor was of course Ian Fleming himself. It should be noted Flemings Hotel, built in the 1700s is not connected in any way to

Garages and former workshop behind Welbeck Motors

Eye Spy Intelligence Magazine

SPY SITES OF LONDON

455•55
Wigmore Street

Escape to Moscow - Maclean and Burgess collected their hire car here

Wheeler's of St James's. A restaurant bearing the same famous name at 72-73 St James's Street

the iconic writer and MI6/NID officer Ian Fleming.

After departing the hotel, the two men strolled in Green Park before Burgess left to go to the Reform Club alone.

Burgess the superyacht specialists on Pall Mall. Ironically the reflection in the window is actually that of the Reform Club. On the day Burgess and Maclean fled, the former went to the club for a glass of whisky. Both men escaped by boat to France

While at the club, Burgess asked a porter to call **WELBECK MOTORS, 7-9 CRAWFORD STREET [453•16]** to hire a car for 10 days. With MI5 continuing surveillance on the men, Maclean visited the famous **WHEELER'S OYSTER BAR, 19-21 OLD COMPTON STREET [454•55]**. This has long since gone and visitors will now find a bar. However, you can find Wheeler's of St James's fish restaurant at 72-73 St James's Street.

By now, the spies recognised they were being followed. The hire car was driven to **WIGMORE STREET [455•55]** and readied for their getaway. Burgess then drove to Savile Row to the famous Gieves and Hawkes **(See Site 350•55)** tailor, picked up a new suitcase and coat and contacted Maclean notifying him everything was ready for their journey to the south coast. After dinner they drove to Southampton and boarded the cross channel ferry Falaise to St Malo. Thereafter they caught a train to Paris and changed again for Moscow.

Neither man would ever return to the UK, but in later weeks it emerged Burgess had accidentally left a number of papers in his London flat that if discovered, would have compromised Blunt, Philby and himself.

It transpired that after the men disappeared, Guy Liddell asked Blunt to help search Burgess's apartment. There's little doubt Blunt found and subsequently destroyed the papers.

Philby had shared the flat with Burgess and one might assume MI5 thought it impossible he didn't know what his friend was up to. Not so, and with MI6 being ultra protective of their man, plus the fact that there was no real evidence against Philby - he was off the hook - this despite two MI5 interrogations at Leconfield House. The CIA were not so forgiving - the agency told MI6 their officer would no longer be welcome in Washington DC. Thereafter MI6 caved in and Philby was forced to resign.

Nevertheless, Philby avoided MI5's every trick to get him to admit his guilt and confess to being a KGB spy.

The public of course, had been made aware of the escape of Burgess and Maclean, but were oblivious to the shadowy goings-on surrounding Philby. That was until 1955. The

SPY SITES OF LONDON
7-9 Crawford Street
Former site of Welbeck Motors

Grove Court, Holly Mews

76 Warwick Square
When Cairncross joined the Foreign Office in 1936 - he lived here. He would later betray his country

Eye Spy Intelligence Magazine

343

458•47

3 Rosary Gardens

RECRUITING HOUSE

This Kensington terrace residence once housed the Soviet Union's consulate; was a work station for the Novosti Press Agency and from time to time, used as a safe/meeting house for KGB agents and diplomats.

The building holds a much darker and controversial secret. It was here that author Andrew Boyle, in his book *The Climate of Treason,* suggests Kim Philby was recruited as a spy by Moscow.

Another author, Robin Bruce Lockhart, the son of MI6 man Bruce Lockhart, in *Reilly: The First Man,* says a Russian national by the name of Rostovsky operated a number of agents within the British Government from this location, adding credence to Boyle's writings. However, Eye Spy sources say that such activities could hardly have gone unnoticed by MI5, who had for years placed a Watchers team in an address nearby. The surveillance operatives might just have asked a question or two if Philby had turned up...

government was forced to make a statement about Philby's possible involvement with the defection of the two former intelligence officers. Amazingly, on 7 November, Foreign Secretary Harold Macmillan proclaimed Philby's innocence and the KGB asset duly held a party with the press at his mother's basement flat in **GROVE COURT, HOLLY MEWS** [456•34]. MI6, whose Chief was now Sir John Sinclair after Menzies had retired in 1953, sent Philby to Beirut working under the guise of a journalist. The move did not please MI5 or

Though several top KGB spies had been uncovered, MI5 would soon be interrogating an even higher ranked official - its own Director-General

344

Eye Spy Intelligence Magazine

the watching CIA who were still convinced Philby was a traitor. Nevertheless, there he remained until 1960.

After Maclean and Burgess fled to Moscow, Philby chose to avoid contact with Anthony Blunt for three years. However, in 1954 both men re-established contact in Philby's favourite pub - **MARKHAM ARMS, 138 KING'S ROAD, CHELSEA [457•44]** today a coffee shop and bank.

Philby's demise came in 1962 after a chance meeting between MI5 officer Victor Rothschild, and Flora Solomon, a former Jewish friend of Philby. Solomon was annoyed that Philby had penned a few articles in his reporting capacity that she considered anti-Israeli. So she told Rothschild that Philby had once tried to recruit her as a KGB agent. Experienced MI6 officer and Beirut Station Chief Nicholas Elliott, a close friend of Philby and Trinity College graduate, confronted him with the story. Strangely he admitted he was a Russian spy but after being offered a deal guaranteeing immunity from prosecution if he rumbled his other friends, he disappeared from Lebanon on 23 January 1963. MI5 officers monitoring the situation in London believed the KGB had secretly smuggled him onto a Russian merchant ship in the dead of night. In the summer of 1963, Philby surfaced in Moscow.

Some intelligence writers have speculated that Philby was first recruited as a KGB agent in the Soviet consulate at **3 ROSARY GARDENS [458•47]**. This has never been confirmed.

THE FIFTH MAN

CAIRNCROSS: John. In later years it emerged there was a fifth Cambridge man under the KGB's wing - John Cairncross, born 1913. By 1937 Cairncross had joined the Communist Party and was acquainted with Burgess and Blunt. Whilst living at **76 WARWICK SQUARE [459•42]**, he found work in the Foreign Office, conveniently alongside Donald Maclean.

460•47

SPY SITES OF LONDON

27 South Terrace

John Cairncross

Cairncross was a true sleeper agent and in 1940 joined GC&CS at Bletchley Park allowing him access to ULTRA material - much of which he passed to the Russians. Towards the end of the war, he also held a position with MI6. Cairncross was connected to some degree in the Russian plot that saw intelligence on Britain's atomic weapons programme end up in Moscow. He was definitely not a 'bit player' as some intelligence watchers once believed.

One man unconnected to the Cambridge spies, but nevertheless of interest to Russia was Foreign Office radio operator William Marshall. He was an operative in the Diplomatic Wireless Service and lived at **27 SOUTH TERRACE [460•47]**. In July 1952 he was sentenced to a very lenient five years in prison for

SPY SITES OF LONDON

461•41 Dog and Fox, Wimbledon Village

© JESSICA MULLEY

espionage - the judge saying he had been "led astray." British Intelligence insisted Marshall had information to impart to the KGB though this was never fully understood or properly presented in the resultant court case.

Marshall, who had previously worked in Moscow, was arrested on 13 June 1952 along with Soviet Second Secretary Pavel Kuznetsov at Canbury Park Gardens. It was the second occasion they had met here. Earlier, the two men had performed a lengthy anti-surveillance operation to thwart possible MI5 Watchers. One of their meeting points was the public house - **DOG AND FOX, WIMBLEDON VILLAGE [461•41]**. However, MI5, which had been alerted by a suspicious Foreign Office staffer, had the two men 'under control'. Shortly after Kuznetsov claimed diplomatic immunity and was released.

462•55 Brown's Hotel, 33 Albemarle Street

END GAME FOR BLUNT

In 1964, just months after Philby's reappearance in Moscow, an American by the name of Michael Straight, editor of the *New Republic* magazine, wrote that he had been *'talent-spotted by none other than Anthony Blunt in the 1930s'*. It was enough to re-ignite MI5's interest in Blunt. MI5 spycatcher Arthur Martin confronted him with the allegation, and told him Britain would not seek his prosecution if he cooperated in full.

Leo Long

Fellow counter-espionage officer Peter Wright held six interviews with Blunt at **BROWN'S HOTEL, 33 ALBEMARLE STREET [462•55]**. Faced with public humiliation, Blunt named Cairncross and fellow Apostles Society member Leo Long as Russian spies. Long had been Deputy Head of Military Intelligence (MI14) in the British sector of Germany after the war, though by 1952, had retired. In later years it was alleged Long's codename was Elli.

Though Cairncross and Long admitted their guilt, MI5 could have nabbed Cairncross much sooner had they investigated further a number of handwritten notes left by Cairncross that were found in Burgess's flat after he fled the country - these were the ones missed by Liddell but secretly removed by Blunt.

The affair was a bitter blow to MI5, which had previously pointed an accusing finger at MI6 and its seemingly endless conveyor belt of Soviet spies. Blunt was a friend of Dick White - the only person to head both MI6 and MI5, and Guy Liddell's right-hand man. If proof were ever needed that British Intelligence had been penetrated to its core, this was it. There were also officers and commentators who suggested the Soviets had infil-

Margaret Thatcher

trated the Service even higher - perhaps to its very summit. In time this would lead to the interrogation of MI5's Director-General and his deputy. The stories surrounding Blunt and the antics of Cairncross had yet to be fully reported upon in the press.

In 1979, Prime Minister Margaret Thatcher acknowledged Blunt's treachery - thanks in part to warnings issued by Goronwy Rees. Blunt was stripped of his knighthood, disgraced publicly and died four years later, but not before leaving a few notes about his regrets to the British Library. He lost his house in Portman Square and

After leaving the Courtauld Institute of Art, Blunt lived here until his death in 1983

Portsea Hall, Portsea Place [463•56]

Yuri Andropov

moved into a flat in **PORTSEA HALL, PORTSEA PLACE [463•56]**. His final residence.

In Moscow 1963, Burgess had fallen victim to the bottle and died. Maclean, and especially Philby, fared much better. Maclean finally died from drink and depression in 1983, by which time his wife and children had left him, but Philby, after years of similar hard drinking, became a trusted advisor to Yuri Andropov - head of the KGB. Andropov went on to become leader of the Soviet Union. Philby died in Russia in May 1988. He was buried with full KGB honours. As for the 'fifth man' Cairncross, in 1990 MI6 interviewed Soviet defector KGB Colonel Oleg Gordievsky at a safe house in London. He said, "far from being a small fish, Cairncross was as good as anyone, except Philby in the 'Cambridge Five'." Cairncross died in 1995.

Yuri Modin, the spies KGB handler, said the five men were not a team as such, but were given much priority in 1943. Most of the men had worked alone feeding information via contacts to Moscow.

As for this chapter in the history of Britain's secret services, the spy ring had inflicted immeasurable damage to MI5 and MI6 in respect of their standing. Yet the spying games had just begun. And there was also deep suspicion that British Intelligence had been penetrated much higher up the ladder by the KGB.

Nicholas Elliott, Kim Philby's friend and MI6 controller was one of the Service's most experienced Station Chiefs. Whilst in London he lived at **88 ST JAMES'S STREET [464•61]**. Philby's betrayal had deeply affected Elliott - and it came at a time when he

SPY SITES OF LONDON

88 St James's Street

464•61

Russian stamp commemorating the life and work of Kim Philby 1990

was still being criticised after another perceived MI6 debacle involving the surveillance of a Russian warship. Friends and colleagues alike warned Elliott was so depressed they believed he was close to ending his life.

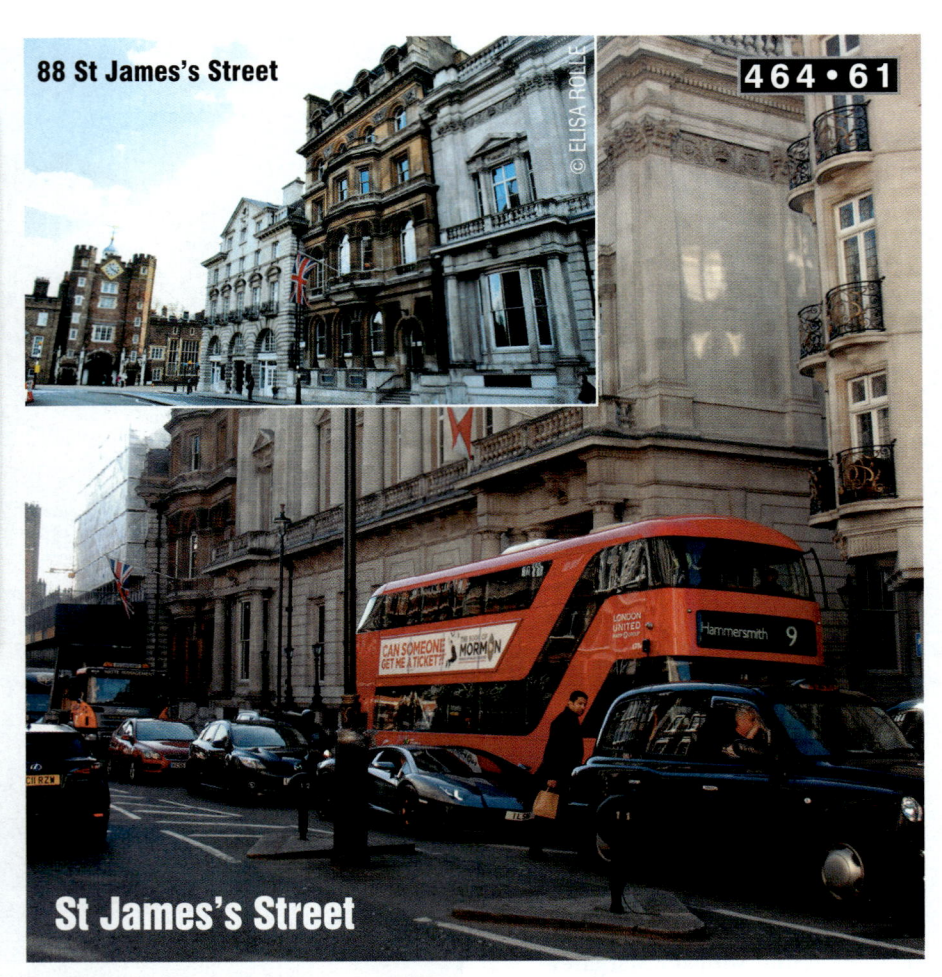

St James's Street

465•44

2A Hans Road

348

Eye Spy Intelligence Magazine

SPY SITES OF LONDON

Lionel 'Buster' Crabb

THE CRABB AFFAIR 1956

In 1956 Commander Lionel 'Buster' Crabb's controller was Nicholas Elliott. Crabb, an experienced diver, lived in a safe house at **2A HANS ROAD, KNIGHTSBRIDGE [465•44]**. Elliott invited him to head an unauthorised Naval Intelligence Division mission to examine the advanced hull of the Ordzhonikidze, a visiting Soviet warship in April 1956. The vessel was part of a goodwill flotilla carrying none other than First Secretary Nikita Khrushchev and other Soviet ministers to the UK for meetings with Prime Minister Sir Anthony Eden.

During the dive Crabb disappeared and it sparked one of the most enduring spy mysteries of all time. There were rumours he had been captured, shot, drowned and even killed by his own side - all of which were unproven. A few months later and just down the coast, the headless body of a frogman was found by local fishermen. Was it Crabb? This question has never satisfactorily been answered for the man who formally identified Crabb has since retracted much of his testimony. In between, the British secret services did everything to conceal what had happened on that fateful day - even from the prime minister. Hotel registers where Crabb stayed were removed and police officers told to keep quiet.

When Downing Street eventually learned of the operation, ministers were furious - but simply had no option but to keep quiet. Eden told Parliament:

"It would not be in the public interest to disclose the circumstances in which Commander Crabb is presumed to have met his death. While it is the practice for ministers to accept responsibility, I think it is necessary in the special circumstances of this case to make it clear that what was done was done without the authority or knowledge of Her Majesty's ministers. Appropriate disciplinary steps are being taken."

Anthony Eden forced MI6 chief Major-General John Sinclair to resign. He was then replaced by Sir Dick White, the experienced head of MI5.

Nikita Khrushchev

Despite the fact that some official British papers on the case have been released, intelligence watchers note that other Crabb documentation is

1950s. A Russian sailor prepares to dive. Inset: Lionel Crabb - he was probably killed by Russian divers

Prime Minister Sir Anthony Eden

Eye Spy Intelligence Magazine

349

SPY SITES OF LONDON
466•39

4 Greyswood Street, Tooting

deemed so sensitive it can't be viewed until 2057.

In 1994, Nicholas Elliott, the MI6 man generally thought responsible for planning the operation, wrote his memoirs and mentioned the operation. He believed Crabb died from respiratory trouble - noting the diver was a heavy smoker and that his equipment probably failed. He said: "Crabb did not die as a result of any incompetence. Nor did he lose his life as a result of any action by the Russians."

The devices used to examine the Ordzhonikidze's hull had been built by a top secret General Post Office electronics unit headed by John Taylor. The unit worked closely with British Intelligence on all manner of covert projects including one regarded as the most daring ever performed in the Cold War. That operation is examined next.

As for poor Lionel Crabb, a Royal Navy request to honour its missing diver was rebuffed by English Heritage (EH). Officials wanted to place a blue plaque on **4 GREYSWOOD STREET, TOOTING [466•39]** - Crabb's birthplace. However, this was rejected because EH said his story lacked "historical significance." This of course is nonsense and according to our

14-16 Regent Street

467•42

SPY SITES OF LONDON

intelligence sources, Crabb's murky work for MI6 was almost certainly responsible for this bizarre decision.

VENONA: TO SPY OR NOT TO SPY

In 1943, the fledgling US Intelligence Community began its search for enemy spies in a programme which would develop into the VENONA Project. This ran until 1980. In 1995, the VENONA papers were made public and surprisingly, several members of the UK's famous British Security Coordination and other well known characters were named in the files.

One person previously unconnected to the escape of Burgess and Maclean is also mentioned - Kitty Harris. Codenamed Ada in VENONA, she had an apartment at **14-16 REGENT STREET [467•42]**. Harris joined the Communist Party in 1923 and in 1931 was recruited into the OGPU (Joint State Political Directorate) an early forerunner of the KGB. She served in various European capitals and was eventually sent to London to manage a safe house and act as a courier.

468•20
40 Crespigny Road

Before the outbreak of WWII, Harris made contact with Donald Maclean and a relationship developed. Acting as a cut-out* between Maclean and his Soviet controller Yuri Modin, she assisted in the removal of 45 boxes of British intelligence papers. Her liaison with Maclean ended when he married Melinda Marling who would later join him in Moscow. Of further interest, Marling later became romantically involved with Kim Philby.

Our research into Harris uncovered a most unusual and conflicting piece of evidence about her death.

Harris is said to have died in Russia and laid to rest in Gorky in 1966. And yet, UK archive records show she died in a London hospital. On her death certificate - her place of residence at the time - **40 CRESPIGNY ROAD, HENDON [468•20]**. This is just a few doors away from the safe house used by MI5 and D-Day spies Juan Pujol Garcia (agent Garbo) and Eddie Chapman (agent Zig Zag).

Other VENONA papers connected to Soviet spies reveal the names of three important British Intelligence officers. The Deputy head of Stephenson's wartime British Security Coordination - MI6 officer Charles 'Dick' Howard Ellis; Cedric Belfrage and John B. S. Haldane. Belfrage, an alleged GRU agent, was described as a spy recruiter codenamed Intelligentsia.

469•57
29 Ranelagh Gardens

A thoroughly trusted intermediary to pass or transport communications/material etc.

Eye Spy Intelligence Magazine

351

470•46

52 Coleherne Court

Incredibly, a fourth Briton, film-maker Ivor Montagu, the younger brother of Ewen Montagu and one of the masterminds behind Operation Mincemeat **(See Chapter 14)**, is also identified as an alleged Soviet spy for the GRU codenamed Nobility. During the war he lived at **29 RANELAGH GARDENS, CHISWICK [469•57]**.

Montagu, a Communist sympathiser, had been identified by Simon Davidovitch Kramer, Secretary to the Soviet Military Attache in London who described him as "head of the X-Group spy ring." Interestingly, MI5 intercepted a telegram from Montagu to Charlie Chaplin in 1952 saying: *'How sorry I was to have missed you in London'*.

The US intelligence was backed by a file hidden deep in the MI6 vaults. In 1945, Walter Schellenberg, a captured Nazi spy controller identified Charles Ellis as a German agent **(See Chapter 5)**. It is alleged after being blackmailed he agreed to work for the Soviets. There is evidence that Moscow had threatened to expose his brother-in-law who was working for Russia if Ellis did not switch sides. He would end his career in MI6 in 1953 after a tenure in the Far East.

Ellis was never arrested or charged but a lengthy covert investigation codenamed Emerton ensued. His former superior at BSC William Stephenson did not believe Ellis had betrayed his organisation, despite him being an ardent supporter of Communism. These were serious allegations and several intelligence authors focused on the information. In later years MI6 Chief Sir Maurice Oldfield was said to have forgiven Ellis after he

471•55

20 Half Moon Street

352

Eye Spy Intelligence Magazine

CAMBRIDGE SPIES - REFLECTIONS

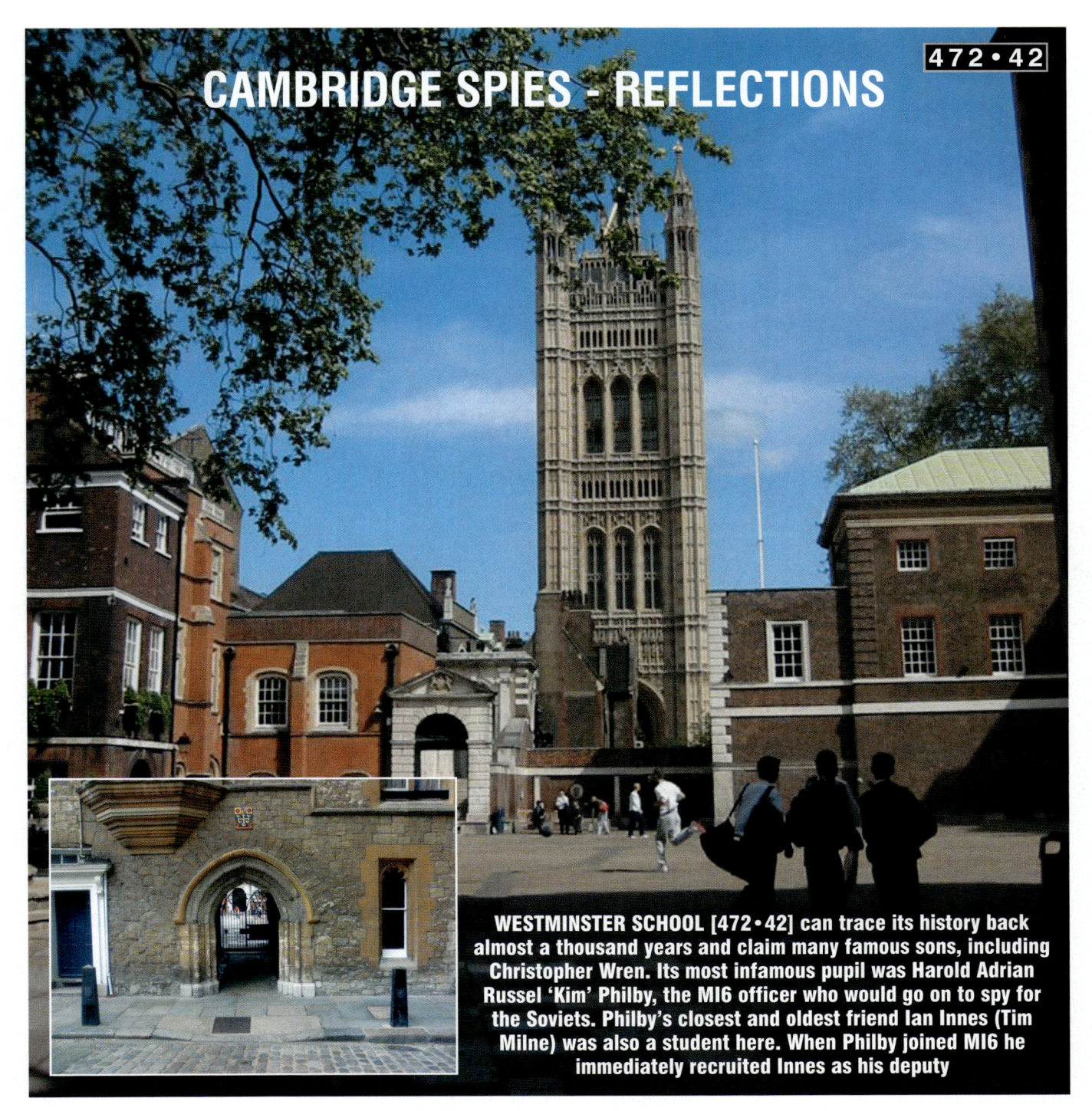

WESTMINSTER SCHOOL [472•42] can trace its history back almost a thousand years and claim many famous sons, including Christopher Wren. Its most infamous pupil was Harold Adrian Russel 'Kim' Philby, the MI6 officer who would go on to spy for the Soviets. Philby's closest and oldest friend Ian Innes (Tim Milne) was also a student here. When Philby joined MI6 he immediately recruited Innes as his deputy

supposedly confessed in 1965 having spied for the Germans and then the Soviets for almost 40 years. It was alleged he "sold vast quantities of information about MI6 to the Germans." In 1953 he began preparations to relocate to Australia - the country of his birth. At the time Ellis lived at **52 COLEHERNE COURT [470•46]**. A full 30 years later the spy writer Chapman Pincher again accused Ellis of being a spy. Prime Minister Margaret Thatcher refused to confirm or deny the allegation.

John Haldane retired in the 1950s and moved to India and like Ellis he was never charged. There was a similar outcome for Ivor Montagu - he too simply walked.

As for Cedric Belfrage, his name appeared on nine pages identified only as UNC/9. These revealed that the content of Churchill's telephone calls to Belfrage's bureau chief were being directed back to Moscow. The CIA believed UNC/9 was in fact Belfrage. He retained an apartment in London at **20 HALF MOON STREET [471•55]**. Here of course existed a plethora of buildings and locations, including clubs and hotels frequented by British intelligence staffers, and the address may well have been used by other operatives.

Irving Street, Covent Garden

William Colby (right) - a member of Le Cercle

Many people find it astonishing that despite some fairly convincing evidence, none of the men were brought to book. It is quite feasible that after discussions with the Americans, MI5 thought it best not to proceed - for the CIA and NSA did not want the Russians to know about VENONA which had enabled the US to decipher Soviet wires.

A COLD WAR SECRET SOCIETY

Established in the 1950s, Le Cercle is a most secretive group founded by French intelligence man Jean Violet. With alleged threads to Opus Dei, it's rumoured Violet was promoted to head Vatican Intelligence. Le Cercle's membership includes senior politicians, diplomats, business people, military and intelligence officials. The organisation has no headquarters and has been likened to another secret society - the Bilderbergers. Le Cercle was opposed to Communism thus attracted both UK and US intelligence people during the height of the Cold War. Former MI6 man Anthony Cavendish and politician Julian Amery were members.

Following the death of Cavendish in 2013, The *Daily Telegraph's* obituary made reference to his and Amery's involvement in Le Cercle:

'He was also a leading figure, with Julian Amery, MP, in running Le Cercle, a very private discussion group composed of leading figures from the international business and intelligence communities, which meets twice a year, usually invited by a head of state in some hospitable host country. He much enjoyed the conspiracy theorists' misinterpretation of Le Cercle's activities'.

Though shrouded in mystery, Le Cercle once reportedly met at a private club in **IRVING STREET, COVENT GARDEN [473•62]** and White's Club **(See Site 131•42)**.

Eye Spy understands that senior CIA men Bill Casey and William Colby were long-time members. Other attendees to Le Cercle meetings include President Richard Nixon and Henry Kissinger.

In 1993, British politician Alan Clark wrote in his diaries that Le Cercle was funded by the CIA. A scandal in the late 1990s involving another UK politician and Le Cercle member featured in the press and a few more details of the organisation emerged.

As of 2014, it is believed Le Cercle has around 200 members. A list of those supposed members has been circulated on the Internet.

SPY SITES OF LONDON

XVIII
Room at the Top
MI5, Internal Suspicion and KGB Spy Games

One London spy story which never fails to generate debate - is that of MI5 Director-General Roger Hollis and his supposed links to the KGB. Hollis lived at **6 CAMPDEN HILL SQUARE [474•60]**. Before that, **18 ELSHAM ROAD [475•54]**.

According to former MI5 man Peter Wright, Hollis was "undoubtedly a Russian spy" and insinuated he often walked home via **HYDE PARK [476•56]** enabling him to make contact with his KGB handler. These claims are still rejected by the Security Service. On its web site MI5 says: *'In 1981 allegations were published that Sir Roger had been a Soviet secret agent. These were investigated and found to be groundless'*. This is followed by: *'Reference is made to the Trend Inquiry of 1974 that cleared Hollis of that suggestion'*.

Indeed, in 1979, when Margaret Thatcher spoke of Anthony Blunt's treachery, she exonerated Sir Roger Hollis, head of MI5 from 1956-65.

However, Igor Gouzenko, the GRU (Soviet Military Intelligence) intelligence officer who defected in 1945, thought differently. After Gouzenko walked into the hands of Canadian Intelligence - leaving his cover as a cipher clerk in the Ottawa Embassy, he

Sir Roger Hollis
COURTESY: THAMES HOUSE/MI5

provided invaluable intelligence on a major spy ring in Britain. After a debrief in Britain by MI5 and MI6, Gouzenko returned to Canada.

In 1972, he was asked back to the UK by MI5, but for reasons of personal safety, was wary about another liaison. Gouzenko actually feared an assassination attempt by British Intelligence and he wanted to make sure that if it happened, he would have a friendly witness. He said he didn't want to end up dead - the victim of a 'manufactured suicide', referring to an incident involving Czechoslovakian diplomat Jan Masaryk in 1948 **(See Chapter 15)**.

The evidence here suggests Soviet agents threw Masaryk out a window in Prague. If Gouzenko was to pass away - it must be seen as murder - at least that was what the defector believed. Nevertheless, he decided to meet with MI5 officers in Toronto.

CODENAME ELLI

According to a friend, Gouzenko was "indignant" after meeting UK officials. He said that they had shown him his original 1945 briefing. "It was fabricated," he said. "It was such nonsense that the person who interviewed me had to be a Soviet agent. The interview had me talking of British spies in the Kremlin. There were no British spies in the Kremlin." Gouzenko, had in fact, explained that a high-ranking British intelligence officer codename Elli was working for the Russians. The suggestion being Elli was indeed Hollis, though Gouzenko at that time failed to say whether the spy was a man or woman.

His friend asked: "Why didn't you say something at the time, in 1945?" Gouzenko replied: "I wanted to check the transcript for corrections, but since I didn't have security clearance, I wasn't allowed to see what they had written." He was then invited to reveal who had interviewed him. "I don't know... they wouldn't tell me... but he was a Soviet agent," he proclaimed. The interviewer was Roger Hollis...

Eye Spy Intelligence Magazine

SPY SITES OF LONDON

6 Campden Hill Square
474·60

From 1943 to the day he retired as Director-General in 1965, Roger Hollis lived in this townhouse in Holland Park. According to the likes of Peter Wright and Chapman Pincher, Hollis always walked home from work, despite having use of a chauffeur driven car courtesy of MI5. Pincher's hugely controversial books - *Their Trade is Treachery* and *Too Secret Too Long,* list a plethora of incidents and case files which he believes proves Hollis was a KGB mole. There's even a theory that he chose to walk home via Hyde Park - enabling him to meet his Russian contact

Hyde Park
476·56

It has been said Hollis walked home through Hyde Park to meet his KGB handler - an unproven allegation

SPY SITES OF LONDON

475 • 54

In 1938, Roger Hollis lived in this house before moving to Oxford in 1940 - the wartime home of MI5's Registry (Blenheim Palace)

18 Elsham Road

477 • 55
33 South Audley Street

Hollis and his deputy Mitchell were interviewed at this former MI5 safe house

After Gouzenko defected, Kim Philby, head of Section IX of MI6 (Soviet Affairs), contacted him and said he should tell his story to Roger Hollis. During the debriefing, Gouzenko maintained Hollis seemed indifferent to his intelligence showing Soviet infiltration of MI5: "The mistake in my opinion in dealing with this matter was that the task of finding the agent was given to MI5 itself. The results even beforehand could be expected to be nil," Gouzenko said. Indeed, it's widely known that Hollis initially cast doubt on Gouzenko - thus managing to deflect attention away from Elli.

Another man who was suspected of being a Russian spy was Graham Russell Mitchell, Deputy-Director of MI5 appointed second-in-command under Hollis in 1956.

Mitchell commanded a staff of around 30-40 to investigate Soviet spies, many of whom were plying their trade under diplomatic immunity via the Russian Embassy. He resided just outside London in a remote house near Chobham, Surrey.

The evidence relating to Mitchell and the KGB, was definitely more persuasive in nature than that on Hollis, according to some intelligence historians. MI5's own officers soon started to search for clues. Mitchell's house was bugged and even his office at the Service's own headquarters in Leconfield House was monitored. In this case, cameras were carefully pushed through holes in the floorboards of the office directly above Mitchell's. Another closed-circuit camera was installed behind a two-way mirror over his office door.

Eye Spy Intelligence Magazine

L'Ecu de France 108-110 Jermyn Street

18-21 Jermyn Street

Similarly, his telephone was bugged according to Peter Wright. However, far from being covert, Mitchell once looked at the mirror and shouted "why are you doing this to me?" The DDG was fully aware he was being surveilled. And MI5 soon realised this when he began to watch the Watchers on his way to and from work.

At an MI5 safe/meeting house, in nearby **33 SOUTH AUDLEY STREET [477•55]**, Hollis and Mitchell were interviewed by internal security on several occasions - under the auspices of Operation Peters. So concerned were intelligence advisors to Downing Street [that the Service was being run by officers loyal to Moscow] that in Audley Street, MI5 fitted numerous listening devices and cameras recording every comment and filming every response. Indeed, bugs were everywhere, including in the bathroom, under the staircase and in the entrance hall. More Watchers surveilled the scene from opposite the building. It was all to no avail and no evidence was ever uncovered, at least none that was revealed publicly. This didn't stop a plethora of books being published on the affair.

For the record Mitchell, who was always regarded as somewhat of a mystery man, quietly stepped down after the internal interrogations.

Chapman Pincher

Mitchell's fifth floor office in Leconfield House was bugged by MI5

MONTPELIER PLACE SW7
CITY OF WESTMINSTER

478•47

Dear chessfriend Mitchell,
Frankfurt/Main, 30.11.50
J beg your pardon, Sir, but J was very badly ill. J had a-Lungenentzundung, schwereKiefervereite rung and last not least-schwere Nierenblutungen. J hope J am recovered now and J am enabled to continue our game in the same quickly way as before.
What news meanwhile? Have you already won some games? Or have you finished some others?
In our game J play:
19. ...... c7-c5/37 35
20. Lb3 - a4/23 14.
With best wishes
very sincerely
Yours

6 Montpelier Place

He joined MI5 in 1939 via a contact man in the Conservative Party. At the time he lived at **6 MONTPELIER PLACE [478•47]** - this after graduating from Oxford University.

MI5 spycatchers were aware that the Soviets used games of chess to communicate - and Mitchell was a brilliant chess player often engaging in games with players outside the UK. In this case moves were written on postcards.

Central to the case were the ripples still issuing from the Cambridge Spy Ring affair which would continue to expand.

One man in particular who was convinced of Hollis's double life was the outspoken *Daily Express* defence journalist Chapman Pincher. At the time the newspaper was Britain's biggest selling daily. He was a close friend of Peter Wright and in 1981 wrote the controversial book *Their Trade is Treachery,* which outlined the reasons why he believed Hollis was KGB. The book was an instant bestseller and the evidence, which was fairly convincing, seemed to indicate

The Soviets often communicated with their agents using chess moves. MI5's Deputy-Director Graham Mitchell was an avid player and this only increased speculation he was a double agent

Eye Spy Intelligence Magazine

359

481•18
Dollis Hill
The main GPO research station has been turned into apartments

there was substance to his suspicions. Pincher would also connect Hollis to a spy scandal involving a senior British politician and a Russian intelligence officer which shook the British Government in the 1960s.

Chapman had a plethora of contacts in the intelligence world and would write further spy books. Perhaps fortuitously he lived in a flat at **18-21 JERMYN STREET [479•42]** - one area of the city frequented by intelligence officials. He secured so many leaks that one critic likened him to a urinal! In 2013, Pincher turned 100, and in a rare interview with the BBC, again reiterated his views on Hollis.

DINNER WITH SPIES AND A SECRET DESERT

L'Ecu de France was a very popular French restaurant at **108-110 JERMYN STREET [480•42]** (now occupied by Church's Shoes). It was also Chapman Pincher's favourite restaurant. The journalist, whose flat was just a short distance away often took his secret sources to dine here. Pincher believes many of his encounters and even innocent social occasions here were bugged.

For decades frequented by government and foreign officials, L'Ecu de France was of much interest to MI5 and MI6 monitoring all the comings and goings. When the restaurant finally closed its doors in the 1970s, there was a surprise for MI5. The Service had installed microphones to listen and record the conversations of dignitaries and 'persons of interest' who dined here - some undoubtedly attached to the Soviet Union and its satellites. As officers removed the bugs, they discovered a second set of recording devices secreted under tables favoured by notable figures working for the government or the intelligence community. These were the property of the KGB!

SECRETS OF DOLLIS HILL

Some of the bugs used in Audley Street, Leconfield House and at Mitchell's house were developed by a rather clever, but clandestine bunch based at the General Post Office's (GPO), special research facility at **DOLLIS HILL [481•18]** in North London. At the time, this huge centre was responsible for distribution of mail and communications in the UK and beyond. Naturally, certain rooms were manned by men and women from all three British secret services - MI5, MI6 and GCHQ. Other operatives, known as Seals and Flaps [teams] would steam-open thousands of letters and packages received from, and sent to, all parts of the world. Indeed, MI5 man Peter Wright once said: "One room was like a sauna... cluttered with boiling kettles used to peel open envelopes." Much of the mail and packages searched originated from Russia and Eastern Europe.

Peter Wright

SPY SITES OF LONDON

Opening mail at Dollis Hill was just a tiny part of the station's intelligence work. At one point, MI5 and MI6, through the GPO's 170 regional post centres employed a staggering 5,000 people as postal censors - one can only image how many letters were opened. Though scaled down in size - the MI5 operation continued unabated at Dollis Hill until the 1980s - but it didn't stop the mail intercepts. Units were simply moved out of the capital

One intercept product developed at Dollis Hill was tested to the fore at a particular location monitored and used by MI5 - **CLARIDGE'S HOTEL, BROOK STREET [482•55]**. The hotel, which dates from 1812, is one of the world's most famous places to stay when in London. Situated on the corner of Brook Street and Davies Street, it is close to the popular tourist sites of Hyde Park, Park Lane, Bond Street and Oxford Street. During WWII it was home to a number of prominent guests, including the exiled King Peter of Yugoslavia. Churchill, wanting to make the family feel at home, declared his room Yugoslav territory. He also placed some Yugoslavian soil under the bed where King Peter's son, the Crown Prince Alexander was born in suite 212 in July 1945. This, so the King could honestly say his son was born in his own country.

After WWII, state delegations from all over the world stayed at Claridge's and many of these would be invited to attend a banquet in their honour at Buckingham Palace. Eventually it became traditional for visiting statesmen to return the hospitality by hosting a banquet for the Queen at Claridge's. This was far too good an opportunity for MI5 to pass up. The Security Service decided to use what was known in the trade as SF or Special Facilities to monitor targeted guests. SF was actually created and initially run by Dollis Hill in 1942.

The telephone division of the General Post Office (GPO) would only provide SF to its 'special customers' - notably Special Branch, MI5, MI6 and a few shadowy outfits. Basically SF converted a telephone into a bugging device. When SF was used, the effect stopped the disconnection and the mouthpiece was still enabled allowing the eavesdropper to hear conversations in the room. Back at the Moorgate Exchange **(See Site 164•11)**, monitors simply recorded the spoken word or sound. A more advanced system was eventually created codenamed Cabman by its MI5 users. Sadly, this marvellous little trick was leaked to the Russians very

Eye Spy Intelligence Magazine

King Peter II

Claridge's Hotel, Brook Street

early on by KGB spy Anthony Blunt. But, Moscow never let on for obvious reasons.

MI5 used SF on Roger Hollis and his deputy Graham Mitchell. As for Claridge's, the Service started using the feature on rooms delegated for 'persons of interest'. The problem was, people suspected they might be bugged and often asked for an alternative room. In the end, according to Peter Wright, MI5 simply bugged all the rooms and the exchange.

Dollis Hill housed a most important element of British Intelligence as daring as it was technically clever - the Post Office Special Investigations Research Unit headed by John Taylor. He was described as an "electronic whiz kid" by colleagues. His team liaised closely with MI5 and MI6 producing various pieces of specialist equipment and often going into the field to conduct operations. Indeed, the GPO had long enjoyed a productive relationship with the intelligence services. This began in 1914, when the Post Office established a Research Branch as part of its engineering division at Dollis Hill.

During WWI, censors at Dollis Hill worked feverishly to monitor letters, telegrams and every conceivable communication - save there be spies

MI5 was uncertain if targets would use the 'special rooms' at Claridge's that were primed with listening devices... so they bugged all of them!

SPY SITES OF LONDON

112 Central Park Road
The legendary Tommy Flowers - inventor of Colossus lived here. Flowers work enabled British Intelligence to decrypt signals from German FISH cypher machines

483•06

passing secrets or servicemen and members of the public inadvertently revealing important information. At its height, the censors, operating under the auspices of MI5, employed a staggering 5,000 people to sneakily open and read mail.

By the 1930s, Dollis Hill had grown into an important intelligence station. And when WWII broke out, it was engineers from Dollis Hill who supplied vital equipment and expertise to the codebreaking centre at Bletchley Park.

One of Dollis Hill's most famous engineers was Thomas 'Tommy' Harold Flowers. In WWII he designed the Heath Robinson - a machine capable of decrypting signals from Germany's FISH cypher machine. Without his research team's input and its engineering prowess, ULTRA intelligence would not have been so forthcoming from Bletchley's Colossus machine. This provided the Allies with Germany's complete order of battle around D-Day. However, it should be stated that Colossus, the brainchild of Flowers, had its early doubters; Bletchley Park was initially unconvinced about the machine. Nevertheless they encouraged him to proceed which he did - controversially funding the project himself.

A Colossus machine was rebuilt by the late Tony Sale and is on display at Bletchley Park

Dollis Hill and Tommy Flowers in particular, certainly helped save thousands of lives and shortened the war considerably. For his efforts, he was awarded an MBE in 1943. Ironically after the war, the government gave him a paltry £1,000 which hardly dented the amount of money he had personally invested in Colossus. Yet typical of this great wartime hero, Flowers shared the award with the staff who helped build and test the machine.

Born at 160 Abbot Road, Poplar in the East End, his house is no longer there. However, after the war he moved to **112 CENTRAL PARK ROAD, EAST HAM [483•06]**.

Flowers was honoured in 2013 by British Telecommunications which commissioned sculptor James Butler to produce a life-sized bronze bust. An unveiling ceremony - *A Portrait of Tommy Flowers* - took place at BT's Adastral Park Centre in Suffolk.

But one event alone would elevate Dollis Hill to its highest standing ever

Eye Spy Intelligence Magazine

SPY SITES OF LONDON

THE GREAT TOMMY FLOWERS

BT unveiling ceremony of *A Portrait of Tommy Flowers*
1. A Portrait of Tommy Flowers. 2. Sculptor James Butler examines his work. 3. Attending the unveiling ceremony (L-R): Trevor Baylis (inventor), James Butler, Kenneth and Sue Flowers (son and daughter-in-law of Tommy Flowers). 4. Kenneth and James Butler with clay model

within British (and American) intelligence... Operation Stopwatch.

SATYR AND ENGULF

Other bugs almost certainly made by experts attached to MI5 and Dollis Hill were codenamed Satyr and Engulf. Satyr targeted encryption devices, typewriters and comptometers, while Engulf recorded the key thumps from typewriters. Later variants also identified variations in the mains current made by electric motors. These could be analysed and the letters used determined.

Though MI5 bugged embassies throughout the city, including the **EGYPTIAN EMBASSY, SOUTH STREET [484•55]** and a diplomatic building attached to the **EGYPTIAN EMBASSY, 2 LOWNDES STREET [485•42]** during the Suez Crisis in the 1950s, it mainly targeted Soviet-bloc countries. One such operation, again in the 1950s, ended disastrously for an MI5 eavesdropping team who were sent to bug the **EMBASSY OF POLAND, 47 PORTLAND PLACE [486•55]**. The intention was to place listening devices inside the wall of an adjoining building which was unoccupied. Poland was of course part of the Warsaw Pact and an ally of Russia. It was hoped that the bugs would be able to detect conversations made in rooms and on the telephone. However, at 3.00am, one of the MI5 men placed his foot on a rotting floorboard and the entire ceiling collapsed making a sound that mimicked a small bomb explosion. The team beat a hasty retreat but undoubtedly those inside the Polish Embassy would by now have been alerted!

486•55
Embassy of Poland, 47 Portland Place

Eye Spy Intelligence Magazine

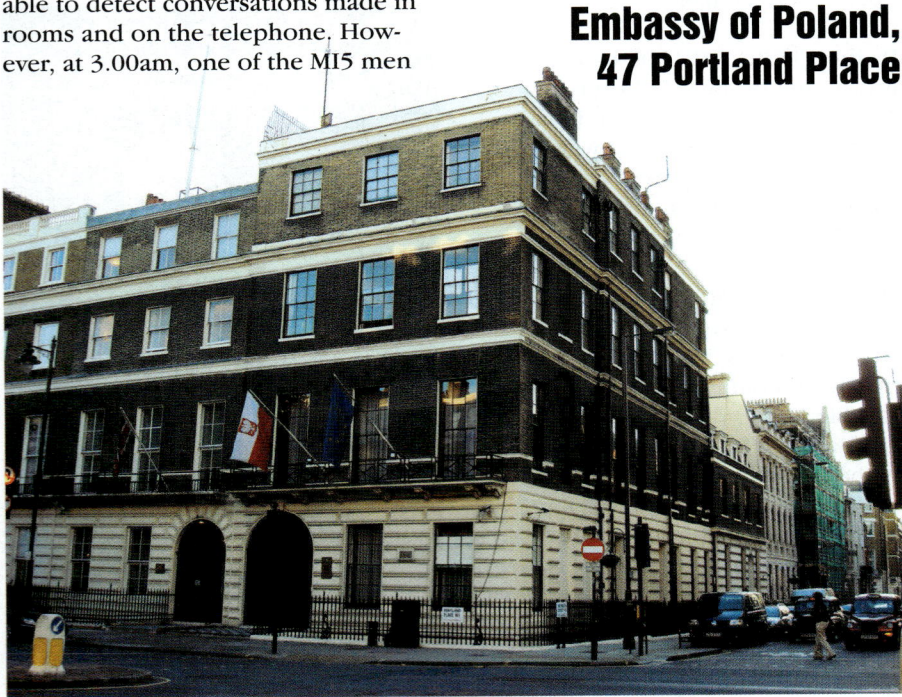

SPY SITES OF LONDON

484•55 Egyptian Embassy, South Street

485•42 Egyptian Consulate, 2 Lowndes Street

MI6, OPERATION STOPWATCH AND A KGB SPY

In 1954, John Taylor was invited by MI6 (Section Y) and the CIA to a meeting at 2 Carlton Gardens **(See Site 037•42)** in the affluent Pall Mall area of London. It was also the former home of a certain Lord Kitchener famous for his image on a poster proclaiming: *'Your Country Needs You'*. Well, the secret service certainly needed Taylor and his Dollis Hill outfit, for what they had in mind was a little more complex than the bugging of a simple hotel phone. The plan was to dig a tunnel under East Berlin and tap into Soviet telephone cables. This would enable monitors to record thousands of Warsaw Pact conversations from the heart of this Cold War city. The underground lines had been located by a German MI6 agent who provided a plethora of information, including the whereabouts of the phone cables which also carried KGB traffic. Taylor called on experienced MI6 engineer and technician John Wyke for assistance, and a plan was hatched. A 6ft wide tunnel was dug from a decoy American building and ran for 1500ft buried 14ft underground. On 21 April, after a complex dig and engineering feat, the first communication was received.

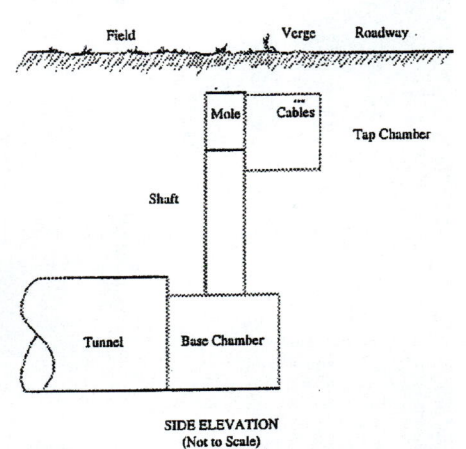

MI6 diagram of the shaft and tunnel

During his many secret meetings with MI6 on Stopwatch, Taylor, Wyke and their liaisons stayed at the famous **BERNERS HOTEL, BERNERS STREET, FITZROVIA [487•55]**. We also discovered that when Taylor journeyed to America for further meetings, he was booked on a ship using an MI6 front company called Express Travel and Trans Co.

Wyke, who was later awarded an OBE, lived at **12 PASSFIELDS, BROMLEY ROAD, LEWISHAM [488•32]**.

SPY IN THE CAMP

The Stopwatch intercepts were managed by a US voice-processing centre employing 317 people. Over 360,000 calls were transcribed from 50,000 reels of tape. In total, analysts for Stopwatch or Gold as the Americans called it, typed an astonishing six million hours of teletype traffic - manually.

Eye Spy Intelligence Magazine 365

Berners Hotel, Berners Street

The CIA's Bill Harvey had control of Stopwatch or Gold as it was called in the United States

The problem was, in attendance at the meetings of Stopwatch* at Carlton Gardens was MI6 man George Blake. Unbeknown to anyone in the room - he was a Soviet agent. Blake had been assigned to take minutes of the top secret liaisons - which he duly did. After he left the premises he immediately met with his KGB handler and handed him the precious notes, thus even before work had started on the £25 million tunnel, the Russians knew exactly what was going to be dug under their feet. When Moscow decided to reveal the tunnel in April 1956, the KGB made no reference to the fact they had been fully aware of its existence from day one.

Dollis Hill was eventually run down in the 1960s, and its various intelligence elements distributed elsewhere; for example, the cryptographic unit was absorbed by GCHQ. A name change saw the GPO (the mail and telephone service was divided) become British Telecommunications and Royal Mail. Its technical section was moved out of

Soviet officials invite journalists to take photographs of the tunnel after it was publicly revealed by Moscow

12 Passfields, Bromley Road

* Blake first started to document Stopwatch on 22 October 1953. A full report of the operation was submitted to Moscow in February 1954

Eye Spy Intelligence Magazine

SPY SITES OF LONDON

This extraordinary photograph published courtesy of David Stafford from his splendid book - *Spies Beneath Berlin*, shows Royal Engineers taking a break during the digging of the Berlin Spy Tunnel

2 Carlton Gardens. Dollis Hill men met here at the headquarters of MI6's Y Section to discuss building the Berlin Spy Tunnel and tapping into Soviet telephone cables

MI6 officer and Dollis Hill liaison man John Wyke is pictured on the right. It has been suggested the man on the far left is the legendary John Taylor

London to a new site in Suffolk (BT Laboratories Martlesham). The main building at Dollis Hill now hosts about 50 plush apartments, though a part of the facility, created to support diplomatic meetings and known as The Churchill Paddock opens twice a year for tourists (check for opening times). This underground room was first used by the Cabinet on 3 October 1940, but Churchill thought it was too far to journey, despite it being much safer than his second choice at the North Rotunda in Marsham Street near Downing Street.

As for Mr Blake - he still had plenty of fruitful days ahead of him - spying for the Russians and exposing one of Britain's top MI6 agents in Moscow - GRU Colonel Oleg Penkovsky.

THE DAMAGING LEGACY OF GEORGE BLAKE

Blake had joined MI6 in 1944 and later admitted that he presented "every single important intelligence snippet that came across his desk to the Soviets." Posted by MI6 to Korea in the early 1950s, he was taken prisoner in the North. Ultimately released in 1953, MI6 put the story out that he had been brainwashed by the Soviets while in captivity. Others believe MI6 had intended to use him as a double agent against the KGB. The problem was, he was acting only as an agent of Russia. Blake's treachery led to the deaths of 40 Western agents, and the dismantling of at least one MI6 and CIA spy network operating in the East. Indeed, his biggest crime was probably exposing Penkovsky who was eventually executed.

Penkovsky had been assigned by the KGB to acquire technological secrets as part of a trade delegation to London in 1961. However, for several days he met with MI6 men at the **MOUNT ROYAL HOTEL [489•55]** in a special room to impart information - this behind the backs of other

MI6 officer and KGB spy George Blake compromised Operation Stopwatch before it had even started

Continued on page 369

Eye Spy Intelligence Magazine

367

A BAG OF SECRETS
LISTENING AGENCY EXPOSED IN A PUB

After the war, Britain's top secret codebreaking organisation which had been based at Bletchley Park was quietly moved to Eastcote in Middlesex. In 1951, GCHQ's existence was still a guarded secret, so too its first director Sir Edward Travis. Travis was incredibly security conscious and had this to say about the subject in a secret memo written in 1945: *'While we were fighting Germany it was vital that the enemy should never know of our activities here. At some future time we may be called upon to use the same methods'.* The work of those at Bletchley Park is now acclaimed, but at the time and for years thereafter, they too were sworn to silence. "Absolute security must be maintained," Travis told his staff.

Sir Edward Travis

Travis was one of Britain's most senior and important intelligence figures. For several years he had been deputy to Alastair Denniston at the Government Code and Cypher School (GC&CS), the forerunner of GCHQ.

Henceforth, Travis would not have been amused at the strange goings-on six years later in THE OLD BELL TAVERN, 95 FLEET STREET [490•08] - a pub frequented by dozens of reporters and newspaper people working in Fleet Street - home to most of the country's best-selling daily and weekend nationals.

The head of personnel security at the Foreign Office, a man called Arthur Askew, gave a number of interviews in the pub to *Sunday Express* journalist Eric Tullett. Askew spoke about Eastcote and a chap called Travis. A grateful Tullett took notes and was now in possession of an astonishing secret. Askew told the reporter he should clear the interview with the Foreign Office before publication. But a security breach had already occurred.

Fleet Street

The two men parted but astonishingly Tullett left without his briefcase containing his interview notes. However, barmaid Marie Cockburn found the briefcase and handed it to the police - they in turn contacted MI5. A Security Service officer posing as policeman 'A Pelling' made contact with Tullett, gave him back the case, and told him to be more careful in future. The affair did not sit well with MI5 or British

The Old Bell, 95 Fleet Street

Intelligence as a whole. Senior MI5 officer, Sir Dick White, who shortly thereafter was appointed Director-General, contacted the Foreign Office and issued a stern warning saying any reference to Eastcote would cause "Sir Edward Travis much pain."

All of this happened at a particularly sensitive time for MI5, for In May 1951, of course, Guy Burgess and Donald Maclean escaped to Russia.

As for Tullett, he went on to write a number of features based on his Askew interviews about spies and intelligence. Major parts, however, were re-written and some internal censorship occurred because of government pressure. There was no mention of Eastcote or the wartime work of Bletchley Park. The true operational secrets of GCHQ would not be made public for another 23 years, but it could have been so very different. A few months after the fiasco, in April 1952, Travis stepped down as the organisation's director.

As for The Old Bell, built by famous English architect Christopher Wren, it is one of the city's oldest pubs and its connections to the media and Fleet Street date back to 1500 - when the building once supported an early printing press!

Definitely worth a visit.

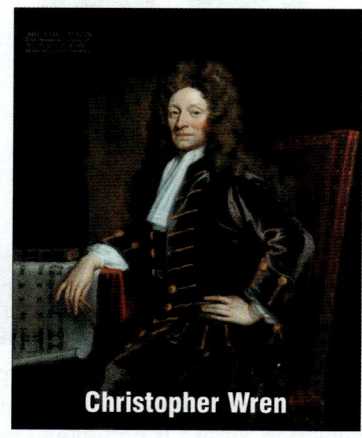

Christopher Wren

Eye Spy Intelligence Magazine

SPY SITES OF LONDON

5 All Soul's Place

During part of his career working as a double agent George Blake lived here in a small apartment at the end of the alley

Russians in his team. It was an intelligence treasure trove as the spy spoke about Russia's nuclear programme; revealed the identities of KGB and GRU men in the West, how they performed spy tradecraft and Russia's military strength. Some 5,000 crucial documents were secured by MI6 and the CIA. Eventually the Russians were tipped-off about his dealings with MI6 and he was arrested, tried and executed - supposedly in a grim fashion.

The list of possible candidates who exposed Penkovsky is long. Some intelligence watchers say it was Blake, others believe it was Roger Hollis. There is even a theory his role was compromised by people in America.

Main passage which runs into the Paddock Bunker - Dollis Hill

Mount Royal Hotel (Thistle Hotel)

Eye Spy Intelligence Magazine

369

SPY SITES OF LONDON

The Ivy, 1-5 West Street, Covent Garden

493•62

Despite this, the West had learned a great deal about Russia's military strength, its intentions, and who was spying in London and Washington.

The legacy of Penkovsky's work for the West still had a little way to run. The Russian had been recruited via a British diplomat and an MI6 front company run by businessman Greville Wynne out of **19 UPPER CHEYNE ROW [491•44]**. Wynne had transferred from MI5 to MI6 in 1959, at which time he lived at **14 THE LITTLE BOLTONS [492•34]**. He had made contact with Penkovsky at a trade exhibition in Moscow.

It was at **THE IVY, 1-5 WEST STREET, COVENT GARDEN [493•62]** where future Chief Dickie Franks, secured the services of Wynne. The restaurant was a location frequently used by MI6 to wine and dine business people and industrialists in an effort to secure information and make associations.

Interestingly, both Wynne and Blake would find themselves entering **ARTILLERY MANSIONS, VICTORIA STREET [494•42]**. This was a special MI6 research station which housed a debriefing centre for the Service's many business agents. When Penkovsky was finally outed, the Russians held on to Wynne after he was detained by friendly KGB forces outside a hotel in Budapest, Hungary. Sentenced to eight years in prison, he walked free in 1964 in exchange for a key KGB spy captured in London.

Blake, who had a small flat at **5 ALL SOUL'S PLACE [495•55]**, was eventually

Oleg Penkovsky - MI6 agent

Michael Randle helped George Blake escape

370

Eye Spy Intelligence Magazine

491•44
Penkovsky contact-man Greville Wynne (MI6) lived here and operated his 'export business' from this address

19 Upper Cheyne Row

496•51

28 Highlever Road
Blake was hidden in this safe house following his escape

14 The Little Boltons

492•34

SPY SITES OF LONDON

500 • 55

Classic Cinema, 96-98 Baker Street

497 • 42

Royal Over-Seas League, Park Place, St James's Street

501 • 55

117 Great Portland Street

SPY SITES OF LONDON

Lonsdale's used the lift shaft control as a dead letter drop

498•15

The White House, Albany Street

502•99

45 Cranley Drive
The Krogers bungalow in Ruislip, Middlesex
© PAUL BEAUMONT WWW.ENIGMA2000.ORG.UK

outed by senior Polish military intelligence officer and defector, Michael Goleniewski. He had been liaising with the CIA since 1959. However, like all those involved in the Berlin Tunnel, Blake had been cleared of any suspicion. Ironically, he was re-interviewed at Carlton Gardens, confessed and subsequently sentenced to 42-years in prison. In October 1966, two sympathisers - Michael Randle and Pat Pottle helped Blake clamber over Wormwood Scrubs Prison **(See Site 141•53)** wall and into a waiting car. Blake was ushered away to a nearby safe house at **28 HIGHLEVER ROAD [496•51]** before starting his long journey to his beloved Russia via East Germany.

THE PORTLAND SPY RING

Goleniewski was pivotal in exposing what would become known as the Portland Spy Ring. The Pole said, "Russia had recruited an Englishman whose name began with H," and who had connections to the Royal Navy. MI5 soon identified Harry Houghton - an employee at the Underwater Weapons Establishment, Portland. Houghton was surveilled with his mistress, Ethel Gee by MI5 Watchers and in July 1960, was seen exchanging packages with another man - later identified as a Canadian businessman using the name of Gordon Arnold Lonsdale. He was in fact an experienced KGB officer.

Soviet stamp issued to commemorate the life of Molody, a.k.a. Gordon Lonsdale

In 1955 Lonsdale came to Britain and used his connections as a member of the **ROYAL OVER-SEAS LEAGUE, PARK PLACE, ST JAMES'S STREET [497•42]** to secure a residence in the **WHITE HOUSE, ALBANY STREET [498•15]** near Regent's Park. Houghton would make contact at **THE BUNCH OF GRAPES PUB, 207 BROMPTON ROAD [499•44]**. He signalled an exchange was ready by carrying a newspaper in his left hand. Lonsdale used the toilet cistern in the **CLASSIC CINEMA, 96-98 BAKER STREET [500•55]** to hide covert radio parts and materials used in the espionage. In this case they were secreted in water-tight condoms.

After learning of Lonsdale's address in the White House, MI5 occupied the flat next door and started installing listening devices in the party wall. He was often seen at the **MIDLAND BANK, 117 GREAT PORTLAND STREET [501•55]** (now HSBC), and in September, when he left for a lengthy journey abroad, MI5 paid the bank a visit and found that he owned a deposit box. Inside they discovered a tiny KGB camera, writing instruments, and a lighter which concealed

Harry Houghton

Eye Spy Intelligence Magazine

373

499•44

Rudolf Abel (second from left) and Konon Molody (second from right) with KGB Chairman Vladimir Semichastny

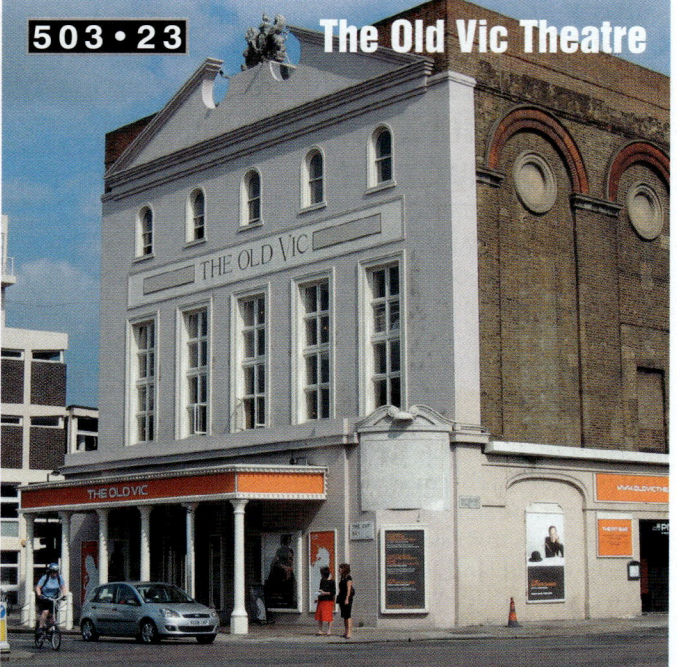

503•23 The Old Vic Theatre

MI5 triggered an operation here enabling Special Branch to arrest Lonsdale and his cohorts outside the theatre

The Bunch of Grapes, 207 Brompton Road

One Time Pads **(See Page 99)**. MI5 carefully opened the pads, transcribed the code and re-sealed them - thus Lonsdale had no idea his future radio communications to Moscow were being listened to by GCHQ. MI5 then placed a Watchers team opposite the bank to surveil his future visits.

When Lonsdale returned to the UK, instead of going straight to his flat he travelled to a small bungalow at **45 CRANLEY DRIVE, RUISLIP, MIDDLESEX [502•99]**. His hosts were Peter and Helen Kroger. MI5 started to monitor the Krogers from the house of a cooperative neighbour directly opposite.

The operation was headed by senior MI5 D-Branch man Arthur Martin, who though convinced the spy ring was larger than just four persons, decided that it should be broken - save the Russians act after learning of Goleniewski's defection. On 7 January 1961, Special Branch officers swooped on Lonsdale, Houghton and Gee outside the **OLD VIC THEATRE [503•23]** after a signal from MI5 that documents had just been exchanged at nearby Waterloo Train Station.

The Krogers house was also raided, and MI5 found all manner of spy paraphernalia, including false passports, microdot equipment and invisible ink. A few days later a high-speed radio transmitter was found under the kitchen floor. The FBI helped British Intelligence identify the couple as Morris and Lona Cohen - US citizens who had been part of a Russian spy network in the 1940s. Lonsdale, it transpired, was in fact Konon Trofimovich Molody, an experienced KGB officer who had previously worked with the Krogers spymaster in America - Rudolf Abel.

SPY SITES OF LONDON

494•42
Artillery Mansions, Victoria Street

Former location of a top secret MI6 research centre. Besides regular visitors such as KGB agent George Blake, MI6 front company operatives would be debriefed here - including businessman Greville Wynne

Molody was eventually exchanged for Greville Wynne in 1964 - the spy swap taking place in Berlin. Intelligence insiders say the deal was very advantageous to the Soviets who had one of their top spies in England returned... this in exchange for a somewhat amateur Wynne.

As a footnote to this spy case, the building used by the Royal Over-Seas League held sad memories for one past spymaster - Maxwell Knight and one that almost cost him his job in MI5. The Royal Over-Seas League is a private members club with addresses throughout the world. In 1935, and after an unhappy marriage, the wife of Knight, Gwladys, (both members) booked into the London address. She took a massive dose of barbiturates and aspirin and died. Her family blamed Knight and a criminal inquest followed. Knight survived the scandal and continued to work for MI5. The location was used by many in the intelligence world at the time.

AGENT TOP HAT

One of the CIA's best agents inside Russian Intelligence in the 1960s was GRU Major General Dmitri Polyakov - codename Top Hat. Via the FBI, MI5 learned that the Russians had acquired guided missile documents from an English source. The trail soon led to MI6 man Frank Bossard, an employee in the Air Ministry. He had document-copying paraphernalia tucked away in a suitcase at the **LEFT LUGGAGE OFFICE, WATERLOO STATION [504•23]**. During his lunch break he would remove papers from his office and duplicate them at the **IVANHOE HOTEL, GREAT RUSSELL STREET [505•62]** (now Bloomsbury Street Hotel) - this after checking in as

Eye Spy Intelligence Magazine

SPY SITES OF LONDON

505•62

97 Great Russell Street
Former Ivanhoe Hotel

© JAMIE BARRAS

504•23

The old Left Luggage Office is now occupied by Bonapartes cafe bar

Left Luggage Office, Waterloo Station

Towards the end of WWII, Waterloo rail staff opened a suitcase which had been unclaimed for many weeks in an effort to trace its owner. They were shocked to find it was stuffed with thousands of pounds worth of banknotes. Special Branch and MI5 officers soon arrived at the scene. It was always rumoured the money was actually a pay-off for a spy - though just who he or she was has never been determined.

John Hathaway. He would then return the papers to their relevant drawers at work. Bossard used several dead letter drops (DLD) to leave the material for his spy handler - who in return would deposit a small wad of cash. Operational instructions were played on Radio Moscow - a particular song representing a meeting point or an aborted operation, for example.

Bossard had been recruited by the KGB in the mid-1950s, whilst stationed in Bonn, West Germany. After Polyakov's tip-off, MI5 Watchers started to surveil his movements. It didn't take long to find his meeting points, one of which was the public house - **RED LION, DUKE OF YORK STREET [506•42]**. Indeed, he had actually been recruited here by a Russian spy who said he shared Bossard's hobby - coin collecting. Special Branch eventually arrested Bossard after MI5 monitored him leaving documents in a drain pipe - another DLD. In 1965, Bossard admitted his guilt and was duly sentenced to 21-years in prison. He died in jail in 1978.

A 1960s traitor was War Office worker Staff Sergeant Percy Allen. After finding himself in financial difficulties,

Train Arches of Charing Cross
War Office worker Staff Sergeant Percy Allen was arrested here as he tried to sell British secrets

507•62

376

Eye Spy Intelligence Magazine

SPY SITES OF LONDON

506•42

Red Lion, 2 Duke of York Street
Frank Bossard met his KGB handler here - a location the two men would use in future liaisons

509•99
Pinner Station

510•99
Pinner Church

Science Museum, Exhibition Road

508•47

SPY SITES OF LONDON

511•42
14 Ryder Street

Former MI6 premises used to support various branches. KGB spy Kim Philby worked here (Section V). During the early part of the Cold War it was used to debrief Soviet defectors. The building also contained elements of RAF Intelligence and other War Office desks

Allen sought out Middle East officials who he hoped would buy documents on UK estimates for troop numbers in the region. He chose to meet his potential buyers under the arches at **CHARING CROSS STATION [507•62]**. His luck eventually ran out when MI5 Watchers observed him time and time again wandering about the place. He was arrested at his favourite underground spot by Special Branch officers. In court, he received a ten-year prison sentence for his spying - though it later transpired he had received less than £110 in payment for the intelligence papers.

Another member of HM armed forces who decided to cash in on the Cold War climate was Douglas Britten. In 1963, shortly before his posting to Cyprus - Britten was approached by a KGB spy outside the **SCIENCE MUSEUM, EXHIBITION ROAD, KENSINGTON [508•47]**. The man called himself Yuri and like Britten, said he was a radio enthusiast. Britten had been recruited. On Cyprus he performed various acts of espionage. Amongst the material discovered by MI5 following his arrest, instructions for agent contact. The document described the route he should take from **PINNER STATION [509•99]** to **PINNER PARISH CHURCH [510•99]**. He would be approached by a man outside the church's lychgate who would ask: "Could you tell me the way to the local library?" To which Britten should reply: "Unfortunately not. I don't live here."

He was eventually tried and sentenced to 21-years in jail.

SPY FREE TIMES?

By the end of 1965, MI5 Director-General Sir Roger Hollis retired, and after more soul-searching (and investigations), the Service was satisfied British Intelligence was free of all moles and KGB spies. But suspicion of espionage was never too far away, and

Prime Minister Harold Wilson

with a Labour Government taking office in Downing Street, some senior MI5 and MI6 men feared Communism might spread its wings via Prime Minister Harold Wilson. Some even believed Wilson was a KGB spy. This is examined shortly.

Many Soviet defectors were questioned about KGB infiltration at **14 RYDER STREET [511•42]** - an important building which supported several MI6 branches - but Wilson's name was never mentioned. It was during the latter part of WWII that MI6's counter-espionage Section V moved to Ryder Street, though the Service has long since relocated from this address.

512•55

14-17 Great Marlborough Street

Martin Furnival Jones

MI5 spycatcher Arthur Martin, who once interviewed the notorious spies Blunt, Maclean and Burgess was disappointed when Director-General Roger Hollis opted not to force a legal case against KGB spy Anthony Blunt.

Despite being warned off, and then ultimately suspended by Hollis (because he was insistent Soviet spies remained in MI5), Arthur Martin, along with colleagues Martin Furnival Jones, a former Director-General of the Service and Peter Wright, went to see Dick White - then head of MI6.

Martin had a good relationship with White, who had recruited him into MI5 from the RSS. He explained that it was their belief Hollis or Mitchell were

Eye Spy Intelligence Magazine   379

Itar-Tass headquarters in Moscow. The organisation has 70 offices in Russia and 68 overseas bureaus

the Director-General's main office was relocated here. Christopher Andrew, who wrote the official history of MI5 - *The Defence of the Realm: The Authorized History of MI5,* described the building as "MI5's new headquarters," though it did use at least six other premises throughout the capital. Today the building is numbered 14-17 and has been thoroughly modernised.

REACH OF THE KGB

An internal government report prepared by intelligence officials revealed the global reach and power of the KGB. It was a deeply disturbing document. In early 1970, Russian Intelligence had an espionage budget of £1,500 million - 50 times more than MI5 and MI6 put together. A lot of the money was being used, according to analysts, to fund the KGB's huge spy network in Britain. It concluded KGB spies were operating in their hundreds in 'legitimate concerns' and businesses such as the state-owned airline Aeroflot, Tass News Agency and Russia's Trade Mission.

KGB agents. White supposedly convinced Hollis that Mitchell should be monitored, henceforth all the bugging that ensued in his office at Leconfield House. Nevertheless, in 1963, Mitchell took early retirement. He died in 1984.

When asked about the alleged double agents, former KGB colonel and MI6 agent Oleg Gordievsky, said that any suggestion Graham Mitchell or Roger Hollis were Soviet spies was "simply ludicrous."

In 1965, MI5 moved a host of its branches to a single building leased from Great Universal Stores at **15-17 GREAT MARLBOROUGH STREET [512•55]** near Oxford Circus. Even

The Lubyanka building, Moscow - home to Russia's KGB

380

Eye Spy Intelligence Magazine

SPY SITES OF LONDON

IXX

Too Hot to Handle
Spy Case that Shook the Establishment

As to underline the strange world of espionage in the Cold War climate, Eye Spy learned via a former intelligence contact that British and Russian intelligence officials would often socialise at a club known as **EVE'S, 189 REGENT STREET [513•42]**. The manager, aware of their role and nationality would reserve special tables for MI5 and MI6 officers making sure they were next to known KGB officers and Soviet diplomats. Indeed, they became so familiar with each other that in the end all talk of intelligence matters ceased. "The evenings were full of joviality and for a few hours every weekend the adversaries could have passed as friends," we were told. Nevertheless, that the venue was not bugged or surveilled seems unlikely.

Eve's opened in 1953, and was one of those locations that celebrities made a bee-line for. Famous visitors included Frank Sinatra and Judy Garland is said to have made her last performance here.

3 Chester Terrace, Regent's Park   515•15

John Profumo, Minister of War lived here at Nash House

John Profumo

A GRIPPING SPY DRAMA

In the early 1960s, the club had two interesting new guests - British Minister of War John Profumo and London socialite Christine Keeler. The couple would become entangled in one of the great spy drama's and sex scandals of the era. Like many of the famous clubs of the period, Eve's no longer exists, closing its door in 2003. However, a new Eve club has since opened at nearby **3 NEW BURLINGTON STREET [514•55]**.

As Britain recovered from the embarrassment created by the actions of

Eye Spy Intelligence Magazine

Valerie Hobson

Chester Terrace
Another view of Profumo's residence where he lived with his wife - actress Valerie Hobson. Former Prime Minister Margaret Thatcher also resided here until her death in 2013. Of interest, the terrace has the longest unbroken facade (nearly 300 yards) in Regent's Park

Philby, Burgess, Blunt and other members of the Cambridge Spy Ring, another great spy story was developing. The case involved the country's Secretary of State for War, John Profumo, a glamorous socialite in the person of Christine Keeler, and Soviet naval attache Yevgeny Ivanov.

Profumo, who lived at **CHESTER TERRACE, REGENT'S PARK [515•15]** would eventually resign, an action which ultimately rocked Harold Macmillan's government resulting in its fall at the next election. And despite details of the affair being published at the time, numerous intelligence files and diplomatic papers have remained unseen for over half a century.

Historians had hoped that classified material on the case, called the Profumo Affair, would be released in 2014. However, it has now emerged that the information contained therein is so sensitive that its release won't even be considered for another quarter-of-a-century, much to the dismay of intelligence watchers.

A BLATANT COVER-UP?

On 21 June 1963, Prime Minister Harold Macmillan summoned Lord Denning and asked him to conduct an inquiry to investigate if British national security had been threatened. His findings, published in a 1963 paper entitled *'The Denning Report'*, supported the government's view that whilst the events were unfortunate and embarrassing, security had not been breached.

This wasn't how many intelligence writers viewed the situation, noting the sensitivity of the case and the players involved. Journalists too, thought Denning was being aloof, dismissive and highly protective, perhaps fearful the commentary of other leading figures might exacerbate the scandal.

Denning interviewed over 150 people linked to or who had knowledge of the affair. Some of the resultant information did appear in his 70,000 word report but a great deal did not. Nor did the identities of everyone concerned become public knowledge. And the reason for this is simple: Denning had promised "absolute confidentiality," and that is the key phrase being used today to defend the current government's position.

Central to the affair, and an admission perhaps of the sensitivity of the secret papers, many historians believe other senior and well-known figures, some probably holding a position in the

Prime Minister Harold Macmillan

Prime Minister Harold Macmillan invited Lord Denning to investigate the case - behind closed doors - and "guaranteed confidentiality" to over 150 people who provided information. This guarantee is still being used today as an excuse not to release material to the public

government of the day, may feature. It is believed at the time even MI5 Director-General Roger Hollis was not made privy to all the facts.

RELEASE DATE POSTPONED

In the summer of 2013, questions were raised about if and when the material would be released. Remarkably, Cabinet Spokesman for the

Soviet spy - Yevgeny Ivanov

Eve's Club, 189 Regent Street
Location of a popular venue for intelligence officers from both the East and West

New Burlington Street

Eye Spy Intelligence Magazine

383

SPY SITES OF LONDON

17 Wimpole Mews
MI5 and KGB contact man Stephen Ward lived here

Another view of Wimpole Mews

Lords, Lord Wallace of Saltaire, responded by announcing that the government was still unsure if the papers should be destroyed or released. However, though the decision not to release them in 2014 was made, an official said the documents will be "permanently preserved." Essentially this means that anyone previously linked to the spy scandal will be dead by the time they reach the archives.

Historian and expert on the machinery of government, Professor Peter Hennessy, said the papers are simply "too hot to handle," and that they may not be released for another 50 years - 2064 being the earliest date.

It was details supplied by MI6 agent Oleg Penkovsky that had first alerted MI5 to Ivanov, who was in fact a senior GRU man. In the early 1960s he became the focus of the A4 Watchers.

STEPHEN WARD

A central character involved in the case was London osteopath Stephen Ward who lived at **17 WIMPOLE MEWS [516•55]**. In 1947, he established his practice at **19 CAVENDISH SQUARE (HARCOURT HOUSE) [517•55]**. By 1960 he had a plethora of society, political and aristocratic clients whom he regularly treated including members of the Royal Family. He also secured new consulting premises at **38 DEVONSHIRE STREET [518•55]**. One only has to take a quick scroll down his client list to understand just how popular he was. Winston Churchill, Princess Margaret, Prince Philip, Elizabeth Taylor, Ava Gardner and Frank Sinatra to name but a few. Ward was almost certainly a KGB contact man, but he also liaised with the likes of MI5 Director-General Roger Hollis. Indeed, Hollis visited Wimpole Mews on more than one occasion.

Ward loved the social scene in London and creating contacts; he also had a passion for glamorous women, including Christine Keeler. As a reasonable artist, he would often paint nude models at the **PAINTBOX CLUB,**

517•55

SPY SITES OF LONDON
Harcourt House, 19 Cavendish Square

Stephen Ward clients - Princess Margaret, Winston Churchill and Prince Philip

84A GREAT TITCHFIELD STREET [519•55]. His entry into the world of socialites began at the home of Fleet Street artist and cartoonist Arthur Ferrier and his wife Freda. They lived in **WILTON ROW, KNIGHTSBRIDGE [520•42]** - their house having established itself for some of the best parties in London. Only a social circle of around 300 people, including West End personalities and the city's elite were invited to attend.

Ward's relationship with Christine Keeler was at the very least strange, and readers are urged to study many fascinating books published on his involvement with Keeler and the Establishment. At the height of her affair with Profumo and Ivanov, the showgirl lived at **63 GREAT CUMBERLAND PLACE [521•55]**. Just prior to this she rented an apartment at **2-3 PARK WEST PLACE (Flat 164) [522•56]** and her night-time adventures are generally associated with Soho and in particular **MURRAY'S CABARET CLUB, 16-18 BEAK STREET [523•55]**. Opened in 1933, it was another member-only venue frequented by celebrities and of course, Ward.

One of Keeler's closest friends at the time was Mandy Rice-Davies - a fellow club hostess. The pair would attend parties and clubs across the city - and

Eye Spy Intelligence Magazine

385

Christine Keeler

Frank Sinatra
© WILLIAM P GOTTLIEB COLLECTION

Elizabeth Taylor
CIRCA. 1960s

Devonshire Street W1
City of Westminster

518•55

38 Devonshire Street

naturally at times associate with various characters - some from the underworld. The women moved in together at **1 BRYANSTON MEWS WEST [524•55]** owned by notorious slum landlord Peter Rachman - well known for his exploitation of tenants. Eventually allegations emerged that both women had at one stage been Rachman's mistresses. "It was all very dark and seedy," according to Keeler. The address was also used by Stephen Ward as a safe house. He moved in temporarily following a shooting incident in the city - forcing Rice-

Stephen Ward's consulting rooms

Davies out of the property. It later transpired that Rachman had installed a two-way mirror to watch couples on the bed. The mirror had in fact been purchased from Diana Doors, a well known actress at the time.

It was Ward who actually introduced Keeler to John Profumo at a function at **CLIVEDEN, BUCKINGHAMSHIRE [525•99]**, a sprawling estate to the West of London and residence of prominent businessman, politician and horse breeder 3rd Viscount Astor in 1961 **(See chapter end note)**. Just before WWII began, Astor worked as the Parliamentary Secretary to the First

386

Eye Spy Intelligence Magazine

SPY SITES OF LONDON

Wilton Row [520•42]

Arthur Ferrier's illustration of Agatha Christie characters - the amateur detectives Tommy and Tuppence from a 1923 issue of *The Grand Magazine*

Lord of the Admiralty Sir Samuel Hoare. Hoare himself was later despatched to Spain in 1940 as British Ambassador.

One of his primary tasks was to keep Spain out of the war, and he almost certainly played a role in British intelligence collection and subterfuge.

Many famous people had been entertained by the Astors at Cliveden, including Winston Churchill, Rudyard Kipling, Joseph Kennedy, Mahatma Gandhi, F. D. Roosevelt, George Bernard Shaw, Charlie Chaplin and T. E. Lawrence. Interestingly, the family also owned a number of small cottages in the grounds. In 1957, one of these buildings called **SPRING COTTAGE [526•99]** was leased by Stephen Ward and in future years, he and Keeler would spend weekends at Cliveden.

Unbeknown to Profumo, but not MI5, Keeler had also started to date Yevgeny Ivanov. Ivanov may well have been a Russian naval attache, but he was also in the service of the GRU. Whether or not Ivanov sought to use Keeler to get close to British Intelligence figures is a matter of conjecture.

In the midst of this most complex affair was Stephen Ward - a supplier of intelligence to both MI5 and the KGB. It was at the popular **KENYA COFFEE HOUSE, 20 MARYLEBONE HIGH STREET [527•55]** where Ward met with MI5 contact man William

First Lord of the Admiralty, MI6 contact man and later British Home Secretary - Sir Samuel Hoare

© GEORGE GRANTHAN BAIN COLLECTION

84A Great Titchfield Street [519•55]

Former location of the Paintbox Club

Eye Spy Intelligence Magazine

16-18 Beak Street, Soho

Former location of Murray's Club

33 Devonshire Street

Shepherd in 1961. A plan was later discussed to trap and turn Ivanov by making him vulnerable to blackmail.

When news of Profumo's involvement with Keeler broke, the minister initially denied the affair. He was married to actress Valerie Hobson, who herself had a rather interesting encounter with one of Britain's most secretive intelligence contacts - this in the person of Alexander Korda. She played a leading role as a German spy in the 1939 film *The Spy in Black*. One central figure pushing for a parliamentary investigation was George Wigg (later Lord Wigg). He soon started passing snippets of information to Labour Party leader Harold Wilson who in 1964, would be installed as prime minister following Macmillan's demise. Wigg ensured the case was pursued to the full. It later transpired Wigg was in fact Wilson's primary liaison with MI5 and MI6. He lived at **26A WARWICK SQUARE, ST GEORGE'S DRIVE [528•42]** a location used to meet his intelligence friends.

Nevertheless, national security was at risk. Indeed, Keeler later claimed that Ward asked her to try and secure details from Profumo of when America was going to install nuclear warheads in West Germany. She also inadvertently acted as a courier for him, delivering envelopes to the Russian Embassy. Just what they contained remains a mystery - Keeler herself admitted she "had no idea."

By now Keeler was living with her friend Paula Hamilton-Marshall at **33 DEVONSHIRE STREET [529•55]**. And it was during these tumultuous years that Keeler, who had ambitions of becoming a top model, had her most famous photographic shoot. Photographer Lewis Morley had a studio above **THE ESTABLISHMENT CLUB, 18 GREEK STREET [530•55]** - premises once occupied by the satirical magazine *Private Eye* - a publication still monitored today by the intelligence world. It was here he took the photograph of the model and show girl sitting near-naked astride an Arne Jacobson chair.

522 • 56

2-3 Park West Place
Christine Keeler rented an apartment here at the time of her liaisons with Profumo, Ivanov and other Establishment figures

63 Great Cumberland Place

521 • 55

Eye Spy Intelligence Magazine

389

SPY SITES OF LONDON

ELABORATE STING OR SUICIDE?

Ward was arrested and charged not with espionage, but securing and supporting his affluent lifestyle from the "immoral earnings of call girls" - an accusation he vigorously denied - and one many intelligence watchers still find amusing today. However, on 30 July 1963, whilst staying with his friend Noel Howard-Jones at **20 VALE COURT, MALLARD STREET [531•44]**, he reportedly overdosed on sleeping tablets. As he was being taken to **ST STEPHEN'S HOSPITAL [532•34]** a jury at the Old Bailey Court found him guilty. On 3 August Stephen Ward died.

As for Christine Keeler, she was sentenced to nine months in prison at **MARYLEBONE MAGISTRATES COURT, 181 MARYLEBONE ROAD [533•15]**. This was also the location where Ward had first appeared on 28 June 1963, for the committal proceedings of his trial. Ironic also, that Keeler then moved into a flat at **31 CHESTER CLOSE NORTH [534•15]** - just 100 yards away from Profumo in Chester Terrace.

There has always been much suspicion about Ward's death, even in the intelligence community. Rumours and speculation abound that he was killed to protect members of both the government and Establishment, though this has never been proven. However, it was hoped that with the release of further papers in 2014 connected to the affair, some additional clues may have surfaced.

1 Bryanston Mews West

524•55

Stephen Ward - an MI5 agent who almost certainly worked for the KGB as well. Some historians believe Ward was killed to protect Establishment and Society figures

Cliveden House

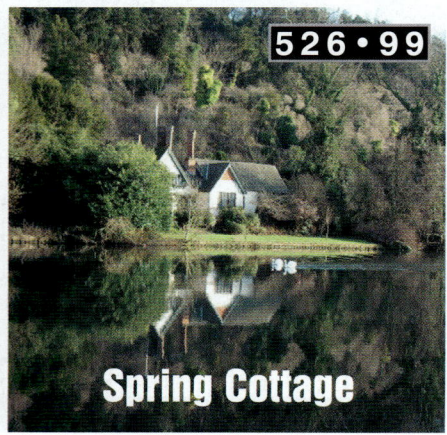

525•99

Spring Cottage

526•99

Eye Spy Intelligence Magazine

SPY SITES OF LONDON

527 • 55
Former Kenya Coffee House. Stephen Ward met his MI5 contacts here and a plan was devised to trap Ivanov. Keeler and her associates were also regular visitors

20 Marylebone High Street

528 • 42

26A Warwick Square

530 • 55

18 Greek Street

Eye Spy Intelligence Magazine

391

SPY SITES OF LONDON

531 • 44

20 Vale Court, Mallard Street
Stephen Ward overdosed in a flat at this address. Three days later he died

A book by barrister Geoffrey Robertson QC - *Stephen Ward Was Innocent, OK,* seems to support the case for a great miscarriage of justice. He argues that two senior judges, Chief Justice Lord Parker and Lord Widgery, who would assume that position, had allegedly concealed evidence from the Ward jury.

The information contained therein has now been presented to the Criminal Cases Review Commission (CCRC) in an effort to have the original conviction overturned. Amongst those attending the launch of the book, was Mandy Rice-Davies, who at the time of the Profumo Affair was Christine Keeler's closest friend. Also in attendance, Andrew Lloyd Webber who wrote a play - *Stephen Ward the Musical* which ran at London's Aldwych Theatre in 2013.

Commenting on the Ward affair, Mr Robertson said: "The conviction of Stephen Ward stands as the worst unrequited miscarriage of justice in modern British history and it is now time for it to be overturned." He is not without support.

Another book, *The Secret Worlds of Stephen Ward* by investigative authors Anthony Summers, a Pulitzer Prize Finalist and Stephen Dorril, the latter being the acclaimed author of *MI6: Fifty Years of Special Operations,* goes further. They claim to have uncovered evidence that MI5 was behind the overdose - this in the form of information supplied by an MI6 contact man. In 1987, the authors wrote *Honeytrap: The Secret World of Stephen Ward,* which focused on the more controversial aspects of the case and linked former US President Kennedy to the affair.

MURDERED BY MI6 ASSET?

In the new book, Lee Tracey, described as an SIS asset, says he was told by another MI5-MI6 contact man in the person of a Polish emigre Stanley Rytter, that he was actually paid to kill Ward. Tracey said: "He

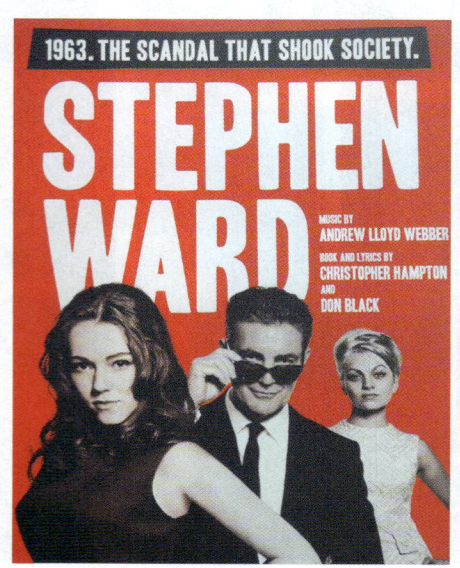

Andrew Lloyd Webber

SPY SITES OF LONDON

St Stephen's Hospital 532•34

Ward was taken to St Stephen's Hospital - renamed St Stephen's Centre (right). The main building was demolished in 1989 - replaced by Chelsea and Westminster Hospital

Mandy Rice-Davies

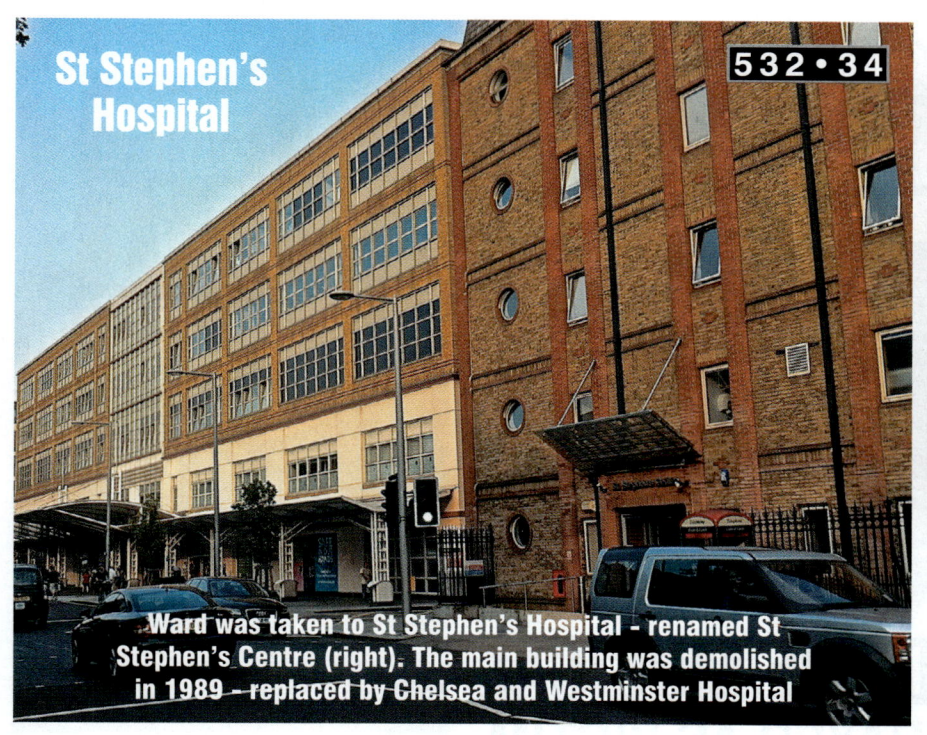

[Rytter] convinced Ward that he ought to have a good night's sleep and take some sleeping pills. He let Ward doze off and then woke him again and told him to take his tablets. Half an hour or so later, he woke Ward again and told him he'd forgotten to take his sleeping pills. And so it went on... until Ward overdosed. It might sound far-fetched, but it's the easiest thing in the world to do. Once the victim is drowsy, he will agree to almost anything."

It is an extraordinary allegation, though the actual overdosing theory is not new and has been proposed on a number of occasions. However, it is the statement by Tracey, a man now in his eighties, that sent ripples through the intelligence community, and may be another reason why the Profumo documents are deemed so sensitive that they can't be released. As for Tracey, he also said MI6 engaged him in an operation to watch several people closely associated with Stephen Ward.

Stephen Dorril said Ward was initially identified by a freelance MI6 operative in the 1950s, as a person who may be of use to the Service. "This came in 1961, when he was introduced to Yevgeny Ivanov," said Dorril. The authors note that events turned complex when MI5 appeared on the scene, but the Security Service did not believe Ward was a security risk.

The two men met at the **GARRICK CLUB, 15 GARRICK STREET [535•62]** a private members club in the heart of London's theatreland. It was a popular haunt for many in the intelligence community and its membership list boasted several well known MI6 and MI5 officers, including the likes of Somerset Maugham and Malcolm Muggeridge. Thereafter Ward and Ivanov became friends.

Ivanov and Ward also met frequently at the **CONNAUGHT CLUB, SEYMOUR STREET, EDGWARE ROAD [536•56]** to play Bridge.

PARTING NOTES

Christine Keeler still believes Ward was KGB, and notes in her book, *Christine Keeler: The Truth At Last*, revealed at the time of his death, concerns were raised over how Ward secured the sleeping tablets.

For a point of record, Eye Spy was told in 2002 by an MI5 contact man who knew Ward and many of his intelligence associates, that he was "definitely involved in intelligence collection for the Soviets." That he may have

533•15

Marylebone Magistrates Court, Marylebone Road

Eye Spy Intelligence Magazine 393

STEPHEN WARD THE MUSICAL
MI5 AGENT PORTRAYED AS VICTIM

Sir Andrew Lloyd Webber's play, *Stephen Ward The Musical,* portrayed Ward as the victim of an Establishment plot, effectively a 'fall guy' who found himself in the middle of a sex and spy scandal. Speaking about the new investigations, Webber admits they are of interest.

Ward's remaining relatives believe the stature of Sir Andrew and the musical may yet help to clear his name and restore his reputation. Michael Ward, 69, a solicitor and Ward's nephew, said that his uncle was "stitched-up" and that the charges were designed to deflect attention away from the Profumo business. Michael's brother, Jonothan, 68, supports this viewpoint calling the affair "one of the worst cases of character assassination of the 20th century."

been a double or even a triple agent remains a possibility. Sceptics of the assassination theory point to the suicide note left by Ward, and his resignation to the fact that everyone was against him - including trial judge Mr Justice Marshall. Some observers believe he had been overly intent on influencing the jury.

One sentence in Ward's suicide note revealed his state of mind at the time: *'After Marshall's summing up, I've given up all hope'.*

Fifty years after the death of Ward and the Profumo Affair, there remains a great deal of interest in one of Britain's most infamous 'sexpionage' cases. As for Sir Andrew Lloyd Webber's play, it received mixed reviews.

DEATH OF WINSTON CHURCHILL

What the great wartime leader Winston Churchill made of the scandal is anyone's guess. Sadly he died on 28 January 1965 at his home - **28 HYDE PARK GATE [537•47]**.

Visitors to Parliament Square can find a splendid statue of Churchill though his famous cigar is somewhat conspicuous by its absence. Churchill was honoured across the world and even

31 Chester Close North

Garrick Club, 15 Garrick Street

535•62

Mandy Rice-Davies pictured in 2013. She passed away a year later

hotel developer Eric Miller named his new building **THE CHURCHILL, 30 PORTMAN SQUARE [538•55]**. Of interest to the intelligence community, Miller ran Prime Minister Harold Wilson's office. Miller had links to the left and was treasurer of the Socialist International - a worldwide association seeking global socialism. He committed suicide in 1977, just seven years after the hotel opened. At the time he was being investigated for money irregularities.

* The Astor family gave the estate to the National Trust in 1942, on the premise that they could continue to live in the mansion. The family departed Cliveden in 1968, following the death of Lord Astor.

537•47

28 Hyde Park Gate

Churchill statue in Parliament Square

Eye Spy Intelligence Magazine395

Churchill Hyatt Hotel, 30 Portman Square

Winston Churchill lived and sadly died here on 28 January 1965

Connaught Club, Seymour Street

Ivanov and Ward met here frequently to play cards. The famous Victory Services Club is also located here

SPY SITES OF LONDON

Spy Tradecraft
Dead Letter Drops and Brush Passes

London is a huge city with a population of around eight million. This increases dramatically when workers commute into its heart from the sprawling suburbs. It is rich in history and tradition; has wonderful architecture and a diverse population. It also has a train network called the Tube or Underground that moves hundreds of thousands of people every day. A KGB handbook described the Tube as: *'Ideal for espionage and the running of agents'*. London was considered far more suitable for spy operations than Washington DC. The writer no doubt having tested the streets for himself.

Besides its own facilities at the Russian Embassy and out-buildings in Kensington, Soviet agents also had support offices located within legitimate businesses and state-funded operations. One such concern was situated at **THE LODGE, 13 OAKLEIGH PARK NORTH, WHETSTONE, BARNET [539•13]**. Residents recall aerials and antennas and records reveal it had a huge basement. Russians would be seen coming and going and there is little doubt it was a major spy centre used by agents. In the early 1940s, Churchill had allowed Moscow to establish a radio facility to broadcast to its nationals. It was considered a propaganda site. After the war it was developed further and run by Tass - the Soviet News Agency. MI5 was fully aware of its importance to the KGB and it seems far too much of a coincidence that at **TOWER HOUSE, 17-19 OAKLEIGH PARK NORTH, WHETSTONE, BARNET [540•13]**, the Admiralty and GCHQ developed a huge site. Part of its remit was to monitor and intercept Soviet transmissions, but it seems evident that visitors to Tass were also surveilled.

Much speculation abounds over when the Russians departed and Tass moved out. Some residents and papers suggest it was in 1951, though we were informed it was operational until 1961. Either way, both buildings have since been demolished - replaced by houses at number 13 and flats at 17 (Greenleaf Court). There remains two more mysteries associated with this street. First it has been suggested British Intelligence built a tunnel running underneath **15 OAKLEIGH PARK NORTH, WHETSTONE, BARNET [541•13]** towards the Soviet station. Sandwiched between the sites, this building remains intact. And then there are stories linking Rudolf Hess - the Nazi deputy leader to Whetstone. According to some, Winston Churchill met with Hess at the British site. Though the Hess story may sound like fiction, it is worth pointing out that but a few miles away is Trent Park **(See Site 315•99)** where German POWs were housed and bugged by MI5. As for the underground tunnel, it

13 Oakleigh Park North
Once the location of the Tass News Agency and a major KGB spy centre

Eye Spy Intelligence Magazine

**Greenleaf Court,
17 Oakleigh Park North**
Former site of Tower House a
GCHQ and Admiralty centre

15 Oakleigh Park North

Holy Trinity Church

is known the government were concerned about the demolition of number 17 in the 1990s - reference to a cellar being made.

Unlike those KGB agents exposed in the quiet street in Whetstone, in the hustle and bustle of central London KGB officers met with their agents and operatives with relative ease. The environment was most suitable and clandestine meetings took place in parks, cafes, rail stations, public houses and museums. It might be a little more difficult today with a sprawling CCTV network that can capture a visitor 500 times on a single day in the city. Not so during the height of the Cold War.

DEAD LETTER DROPS

Several locations where KGB spies used to hide packages and messages have been identified in recent times. These are known of course as dead letter drops (DLD), though some agents call them dead letter boxes (DLB). The Russians call them Duboks. Retrieving and inserting materials from such locations is a spy trait that continues today. A DLD can be anything from a tin can, to a hole in a tree or wall. Perhaps London's most famous KGB DLD can be found inside the magnificent **BROMPTON ORATORY, BROMPTON ROAD** [542•47]. Here packages and instructions were tucked away behind a marble pillar situated on the right just inside the front door.

Another DLD is but a two minute walk behind the building - in the grounds of **HOLY TRINITY CHURCH** [543•47]. To the right of the statue of St Francis of Assisi is a tree in front of a wall - the DLD was sandwiched here. The KGB handbook described this as *'fairly inconspicuous'*.

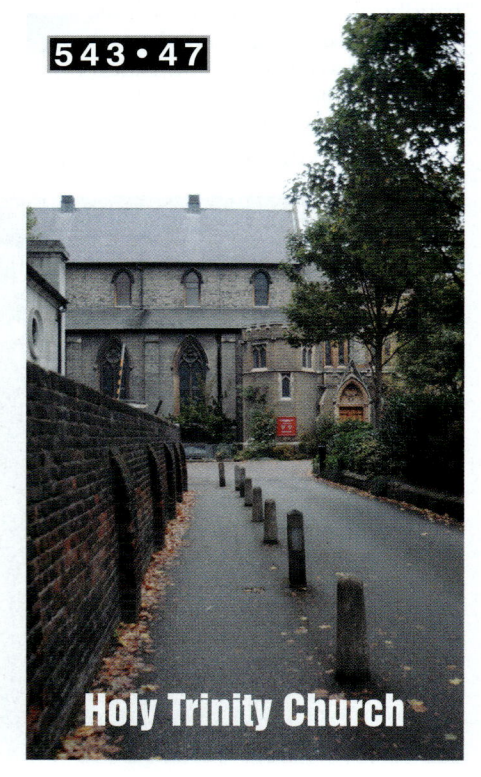

SPY SITES OF LONDON

542 • 47

The location of a famous KGB dead letter drop

Brompton Oratory, Brompton Road

The author examines the DLD inside the grounds of Holy Trinity Church

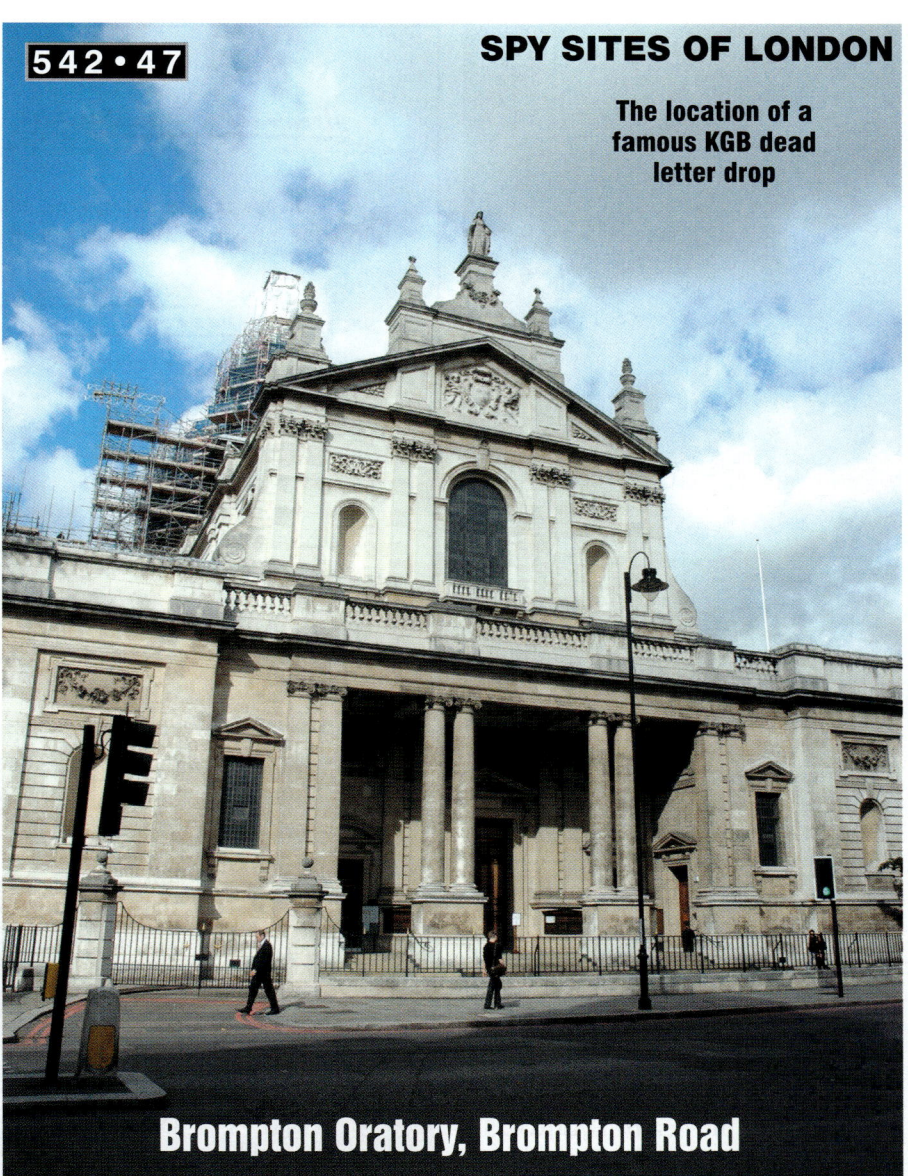

Another view of Holy Trinity Church

Statue of St Francis of Assisi. Circled is the DLD

Eye Spy Intelligence Magazine

SPY SITES OF LONDON

The splendour of Brompton Oratory

A KGB document identifying the DLDs in Brompton Road

It's almost certain that defector Oleg Gordievsky revealed a whole host of KGB DLDs when he defected. MI6 have never commented on just what they found - or the identity of the visitors to these sites. Hopefully the gardener was cleared of any suspicion!

There were several other reasons why this location was popular with the KGB. If operatives suspected MI5 Watchers were monitoring them, they would walk to the nearby **HARRODS, 87-135 BROMPTON ROAD [544•42]** department store. With so many entrances, exits, staircases and floors, it was relatively easy to lose anyone who was following. However, there is always the possibility that the **CAFE DAQUISE [545•47]** near South Kensington Station, might have had something to do with the positioning of the Brompton Road DLDs. Famous for its East European cuisine and the number of high-profile spies who were once frequent visitors, including Anthony Blunt and society girl Christine Keeler. Her Soviet lover, Yevgeny Ivanov would often meet her for lunch here - the Russian Embassy being in walking distance. Though modernised inside, it's certainly worth a trip to the Cafe Daquise (reservations preferable) for lunch.

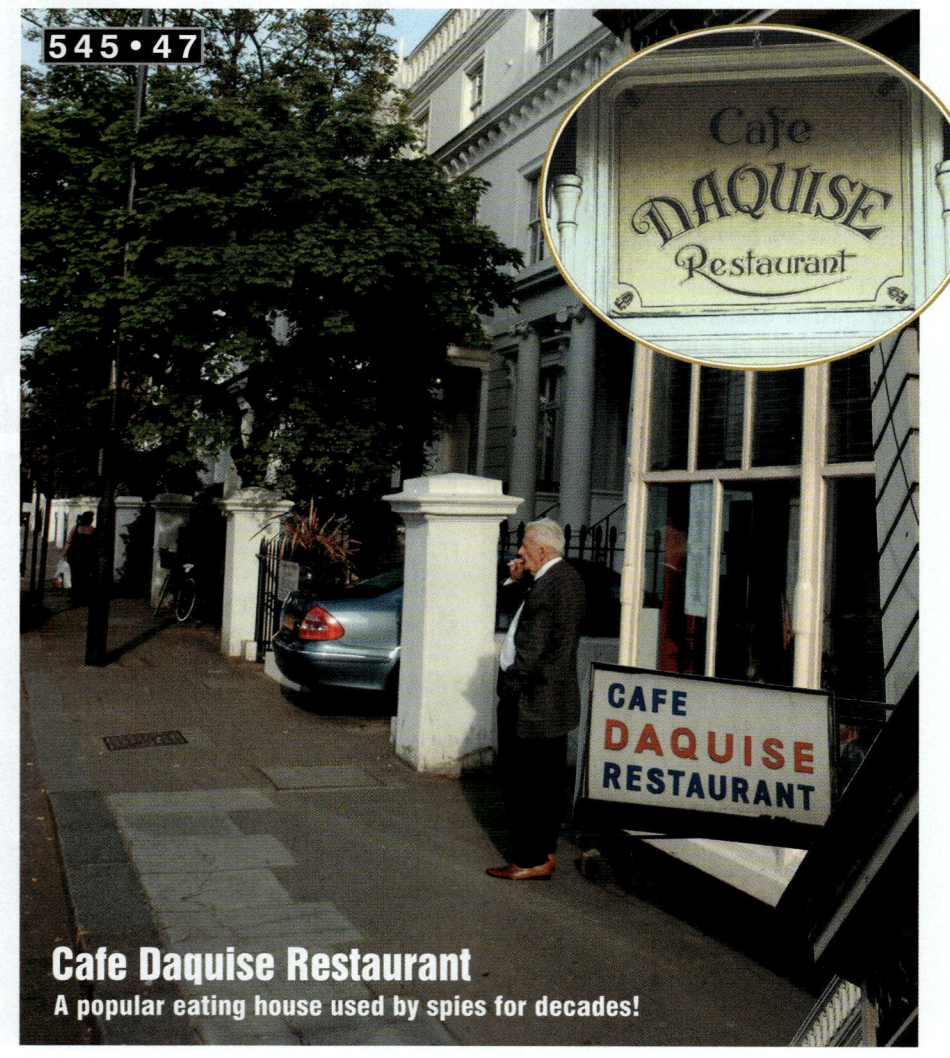

545•47

Cafe Daquise Restaurant
A popular eating house used by spies for decades!

400

Eye Spy Intelligence Magazine

SPY SITES OF LONDON

Harrods, Brompton Road

The James Bond movie *Skyfall* featured in an exhibition of all things 007 at Harrods in 2011

The Cafe Daquise has retained its famous sign

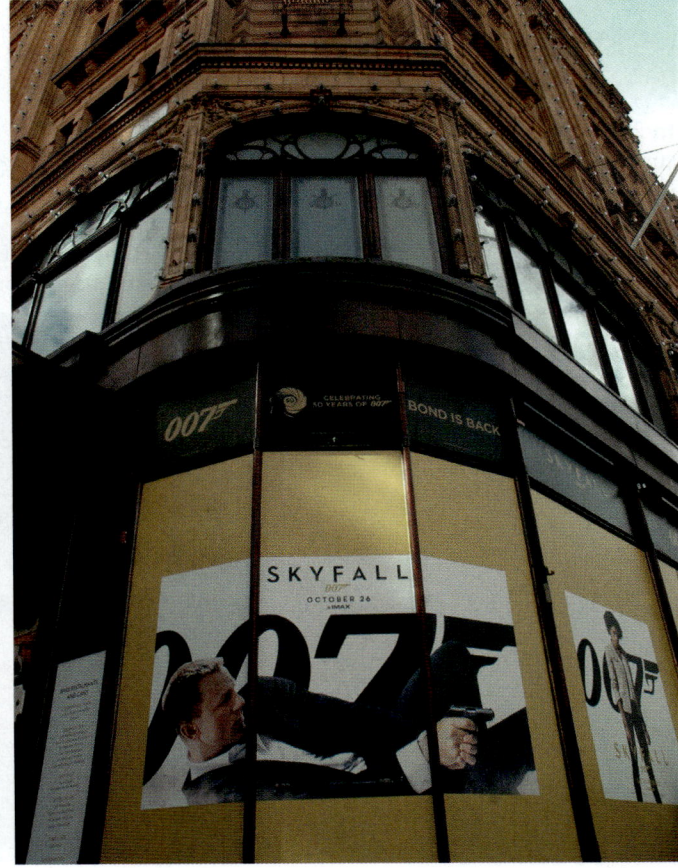

Audley Square
The lamp post may well have been number 8 when used by Russian spies – but today it has been renumbered 2

Marylebone Passage

St George's Gardens

In 2005, the restaurant suffered a serious fire, but its owners used the insurance money to redecorate the interior and exterior in an identical fashion to that before the fire... including the bric-a-brac which adorns its walls! However, since then new owners have changed the interior decor again.

The Brompton DLDs seem inextricably linked to two other sites in the city.

According to intelligence gleaned by MI6, a KGB agent would chalk a blue mark on a particular **LAMP POST** in **AUDLEY SQUARE [546•55]**, recorded as being number 8 in the street. Once this was done, he would

Eye Spy Intelligence Magazine

check to see if his handler had seen the message by visiting a bench in nearby **ST GEORGE'S GARDEN [547•01]**, a small park area. It's not certain what was written or left at the bench, perhaps another chalked mark, but once he was satisfied contact had been made, he duly departed for Brompton Oratory to either leave or pick up messages or packages. For the record, the lamp post is now numbered 2! The famous British spy author Chapman Pincher, who sadly passed away in 2014 at the grand age of 100, once wrote that MI6 had a string of safe houses (watch locations) on Brompton Road. One must consider the possibility they were strategically placed to monitor the comings and goings of suspected Soviet agents.

Cutting the corner off Margaret Street and Wells Street is the historic **MARYLEBONE PASSAGE**, and the now closed **PRING AND ROSE PRINTERS [548•55]**. It's a little known fact that at the height of the Cold War, some British agents would use the alley to meet with their spy handlers and converse or pass on materials. It was also a useful location to draw any possible opponent (surveillance operative) into the open, for once entered, there is only one exit. Known as a choke point, MI5 could mount counter operations to identify foreign watchers. Pring and Rose closed in the 1960s, but it is understood the factory was occasionally used by British Intelligence. Around the corner at **12-13 WELLS STREET - THE CHAMPION PUB [549•55]**. Its stained glassed

The Champion, 12-13 Wells Street

Mark Birdsall and BBC security editor Gordon Corera discuss espionage on the Tin and Stone Bridge

Tin and Stone Bridge, St James's Park

Eye Spy Intelligence Magazine

403

553•60

Planetree House, Duchess of Bedford's Walk

Planetree House complex today - the contact point is probably buried beneath the building

John Vassall (left) exposed by KGB officer and CIA spy Yuri Nosenko

and officers belonging to Britain's own intelligence services favoured one particular site - undoubtedly chosen for its quiet central location. This is known in spylore as the **TIN AND STONE BRIDGE, ST JAMES'S PARK [550•42]** opposite Buckingham Palace. One famous spy who regularly met here with his associates was MI5 man Peter Wright. Other officers from MI6 also started their journey here - interviewing contacts

552•08

Farringdon Station

windows pay homage to explorers, pioneers and sportsmen. Like a number of drinking houses in London, it too became popular with those who worked in the intelligence community around Oxford Street.

It's not just foreign spies who use specific locations to engage in mischief in London - for decades agents

404

Eye Spy Intelligence Magazine

551•55

Gerrard Street, Chinatown

SPY SITES OF LONDON

whilst strolling peacefully around the park. Of course they were being watched all the while by friendly forces - trying to identify inquisitive KGB operatives! However, it has been rumoured that the bridge is still occasionally used as a meeting point by today's 'spooks'.

Perhaps the least known agent-meeting site is in and around **GERRARD STREET, CHINATOWN [551•55]**. It's hard to believe that some of the restaurants and bars, knowingly and unknowingly host spies from across the world - especially those of a Chinese persuasion!

Perhaps allied to the DLD is an espionage technique known as the brush pass. In this case materials are passed by hand to an associate using slight of hand. Two people walk towards each other and at a given moment are close enough to hand over a package, for example. Lots of variants exist - two identical briefcases could be used. One operative may sit

A bus stairwell is called dead ground as it provides cover and can also be used to perform a brush pass if both participants' timing is immaculate

Eye Spy Intelligence Magazine

405

Bag exchange

down on a bench and place their briefcase on the floor. Thereafter he or she is joined by another person who places their briefcase close to that of their accomplice. Moments later they depart with each other's case.

Exchanges can take place in restaurants and at sporting events. Other popular locations used to perform this act in London include buses and the Tube. Both busy environments and difficult to monitor. **FARRINGDON STATION, ISLINGTON [552•08]** was but one of a number of known locations used by the KGB in the 1950s and 1960s to conduct brush passes, though they undoubtedly occurred elsewhere in the city.

Admiralty man John Vassall had worked as a clerk at Britain's embassy in Moscow in 1954. His lifestyle had made him a target for entrapment by the KGB and from 1956 to 1962 he was forced to pass a plethora of intelligence and military files to his spy handler - this after he had been posted back to London. Intelligence from Soviet defectors Anatoli Golitsyn and then Yuri Nosenko led MI5 to Dolphin Square **(See Site 120•42)** and special teams soon bugged his flat. It wasn't until a year later when officers burgled his flat that they found spy cameras and other materials. Besides meeting his Russian contact at various locations in the city, Vassall used to draw a pink circle on a tree or fence in the garden of **PLANETREE HOUSE, DUCHESS OF BEDFORD'S WALK [553•60]** - if he needed to make contact.

Brush passes are very difficult to monitor

Prince Albert

406

Eye Spy Intelligence Magazine

SPY SITES OF LONDON

The Albert, 52 Victoria Street

In its 2014 annual report, SAPO, the Swedish Security Service, published this cartoon-like drawing depicting a brush pass in a park!

One of the most popular pubs frequented and used as a meeting point throughout WWII and the Cold War by all manner of spies and intelligence people, was **THE ALBERT, 52 VICTORIA STREET [554•42]**. During the war it became a popular haunt for MI6 and SOE personnel who were headquartered at the nearby St. Ermin's Hotel.

Built between 1845 and 1852, it was originally known as The Blue Coat Boy, but changed its name to The Albert in honour of Queen Victoria's late husband. Situated in the heart of London between Parliament and New Scotland Yard it survived the Blitz.

Its carvery is well known in the city and past visitors to the public house include Royalty, prime ministers, politicians of note and leading businessmen.

Eye Spy Intelligence Magazine

SPY SITES OF LONDON

556•55
Statue of Eros, Piccadilly Circus

555•55
Telephone Box, Grosvenor Square

Other known locations used to trigger or signal meetings between friendly agencies are the old blue-coloured **PUBLIC TELEPHONE BOX, GROSVENOR SQUARE [555•55]** near the US Embassy and the steps below the **STATUE OF EROS, PICCADILLY CIRCUS [556•55]**.

In today's electronic age where espionage is often performed daily via the Internet, a visit to these historic locations where all manner of espionage and intelligence was practised and discussed, is akin to a journey back in time.

PROPERTY AND SAFE HOUSES

In the UK, many agent meeting points and places used to support spy operations are actually funded by the public. Unbeknown to most people, British Intelligence, because of its secret role, once used The Treasury as a front organisation to secure buildings (for various purposes, including operations and safe houses). However, The Treasury's accounts were examined and approved by the government's Chief Auditor who was not party to the need of such premises. Thus every year he or she was surprised to find the state now owned a plethora of seemingly unoccupied houses in the upmarket London districts of Mayfair, Belgravia, Chelsea and Kensington. This arrangement dates back before the war, and we are uncertain if it continues today.

Nevertheless, because of its historical links to the intelligence community, it's another reason why The Treasury is included in this book **(See Site 272•42)**.

Spy author Chapman Pincher accused MI5 Director-General Roger Hollis of using tradecraft in Hyde Park

408

Eye Spy Intelligence Magazine

SPY SITES OF LONDON

XXI
Menaces and Moves
More Spies and Relocation of Service Sites

One still unresolved chapter in British Intelligence history concerns the allegations that Prime Minister Harold Wilson was actually a KGB asset. He served two terms as premier - 1964-70 and 1974-76. Wilson himself was convinced that some officers in MI5 had plotted to overthrow him and he became obsessed with security - advising his closest associates that he believed the Service had bugged his office at Downing Street. He even feared troops based in the city would be reluctant to come to his assistance if the plot was engaged.

The allegation that he was to be overthrown came from MI5 officer Peter Wright. He said that up to 30 people were involved in the plot - a figure he would later revise to just a handful. No-one really knows if the story is true, but Wilson, a trade unionist supporter did have friends in Moscow. His name also appears in an MI5 Registry file - under Norman John Worthington codename - Olding. In Moscow Wilson was given various KGB codenames including Dream. In the USA, the FBI called him Top Cat! There is also evidence to suggest that Moscow tried to recruit him when he visited the city. Senior CIA man James Angleton was convinced of this and launched an investigation codenamed Oakleaf.

Harold Wilson was convinced of an MI5 plot to topple him

Downing Street and Whitehall from the air

© FLIGHT IMAGES OF LONDON

Eye Spy Intelligence Magazine

409

SPY SITES OF LONDON

Transport House, Bradley Street, Smith Square [557•42]

John Stonehouse

Several of Wilson's closest friends in government were also surveilled by MI5, including John Stonehouse - described by an MI5 officer as a "KGB contact man."

The revelations by Wright again caused uproar, but were dismissed by MI5. Nevertheless, MI5 continued to monitor many of Wilson associates, especially those in Britain's powerful trade unions who backed Labour. One such man was Jack Jones, a Communist Party of Great Britain (CPGB) member who in the 1970s was General Secretary of the Transport and General Workers Union (TGWU) and head of the Trade Union Congress (TUC). The TGWU headquarters were at **TRANSPORT HOUSE, SMITH STREET [557•42]**, close to Parliament. This location was monitored by MI5 and its telephone lines rumoured to have been intercepted.

Jones was definitely a 'person of interest' to MI5, especially because he was said to have held more sway over Wilson than his own ministers. It would later be alleged by Soviet defector Oleg Gordievsky, that Jones and his wife Evelyn, were Soviet agents. Some intelligence watchers believe the couple were active between 1964 and 1968, whilst other reports state he may have been a mole for 45 years. Jones was in MI5's Registry and it is claimed the Service bugged the headquarters of the CPGB in King Street in 1969 **(See Site 109•62)** to listen to his conversations. Reports also suggest that in 1970, MI5

74 Ruskin Park House, Champion Hill [558•31]

Jack Jones

410

Eye Spy Intelligence Magazine

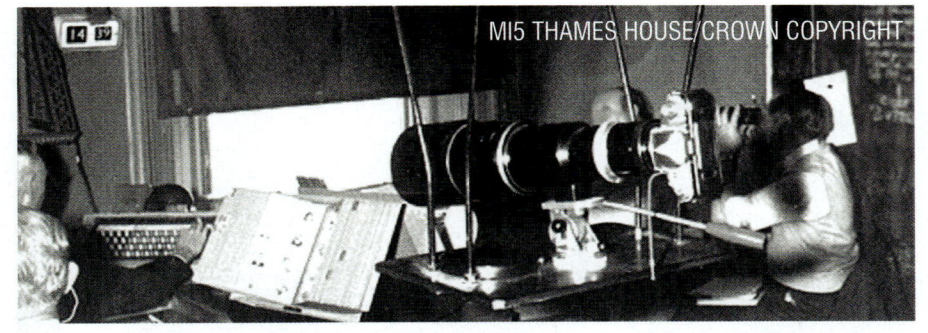

SPY SITES OF LONDON

MI5 monitor the movements of KGB personnel in London. In 1971, Britain ordered 105 suspected Russian spies out of the country following an operation codenamed Foot

on the orders of a new prime minister in the person of Conservative Edward Heath, ordered the telephone at Jones's council flat at **74 RUSKIN PARK HOUSE, CHAMPION HILL [558•31]** to be monitored. So worried was Heath that he instructed all calls made by Downing Street to Jones be recorded.

Jack Jones died in 2009. And for the record, Gordievsky claimed to be his KGB case officer. Quite remarkable.

OPERATION FOOT

Of the Wilson-KGB theory, sceptics point to a pivotal day in September 1971 for Anglo-Soviet relations. Wilson, after receiving intelligence secured by MI5 and MI6 concerning Soviet spy activities in Britain, began to prepare for the removal of 105 diplomats and intelligence officers in an operation codenamed Foot. This followed a stark warning by MI5 that the Soviet espionage arm threatened to 'swamp' its meagre resources.

TOWERING INTERCEPTION

One of Harold Wilson's first duties after he was elected prime minister in 1964, was to open the most iconic modern building in central London. Yet few people know of its connection to the world of espionage. **LONDON'S BT TOWER (BRITISH TELECOMMUNICATIONS), 60 CLEVELAND STREET [559•55]** was officially opened on 8 October 1965. Standing at over 550ft tall, the concrete and glass building dwarfed its neighbours, but not everyone supported its construction, which had been conceived and commissioned by the GPO (General Post Office) in 1961. Despite this, it was hailed as being a positive symbol for a modern 20th century Britain, and in terms of its architecture, the country had not seen anything like it.

Atop the building, which was originally known as the Post Office Tower, a revolutionary revolving restaurant afforded superb views of London, but

MI5 Director-General Sir Martin Furnival Jones warned his counterpart in MI6 about Soviet interceptions from the Post Office Tower. Initially, his concerns were ignored

Eye Spy Intelligence Magazine

411

SPY SITES OF LONDON

Temple Fortune Hill, Hampstead

560•17

Sir Martin Furnival Jones

it's what was contained below that so interested all three arms of British Intelligence - MI5, MI6 and GCHQ. The structure was a hub of advanced communication instruments and microwave channels beaming conversations to every corner of the country and beyond. And lest it be forgotten, the GPO's long tradition in assisting British Intelligence operations, from the Berlin Tunnel to the bugging of Soviet dignitaries and suspected agents in the city.

The public's fascination with the tower meant that it soon became a prime site tourist attraction, and its doors were opened on 19 May 1966. In the first year it attracted almost one million visitors, including over 100,000 who dined in the lofty restaurant aptly named Top of the Tower. However, because of its significance, it also attracted the attention of the Irish Provisional Army (IRA). And on 31 October 1971, a small terrorist bomb detonated in the toilet of the restaurant. This resulted in its temporary closure. A decision was then taken that once the lease on this part of the structure to Butlins expired in 1980, it would not be renewed. A year later, access to the building was also stopped and the public could only admire the tower from street level. In 1992, the building was renamed the BT Tower.

Intelligence officials asked that the tower not be identified on Ordnance Survey Maps, despite the fact that it could be seen from vast distances and was one of the tallest structures in the country. This bizarre situation continued until 1993, when the building was officially recognised in Parliament. However ironic that decision seemed, the Cold War was at its height and the tower played a central and pivotal role in Britain's air early warning system. Dozens of smaller towers were built across the country in key regions to keep communications open in the event of a nuclear attack. All lines were threaded to the BT Tower and beyond.

MI5 WARNING

Eye Spy has learned that at least two years before the Post Office Tower's completion, MI5 submitted a top secret review to its counterparts in MI6. Security Service officials said that any intelligence traffic sent or received by the building's microwave instrumentation would be vulnerable to Soviet interception, primarily via its embassy in Kensington Gardens. The report was signed off by MI5 Director-General Sir Martin Furnival Jones.

Jones, who stepped down in 1971 and retired a year later lived at **TEMPLE FORTUNE HILL, HAMPSTEAD [560•17]**. He was superseded by Sir Michael Hanley.

SPY SITES OF LONDON

Kelvedon Hatch, Brentwood, Essex

Sir Michael Hanley

Nevertheless, Jones' action concerned MI6 engineers who often worked alongside security personnel attached to the GPO, and who were planning to install a link and office staffed specifically by the Service. MI5 had considered that the line-of-sight between the Russian Embassy and the tower was unhindered and not restricted by other buildings.

The MI5 situation report was passed to the Foreign Office which asked for a second opinion. This was provided by FO technicians and analysts who argued that because of the amount of calls, channels and signals passing through the tower (150,000 an hour) "Soviet Intelligence would be unable to pick and select."

With much haste, MI6 installed its own communication system which was ready and operational by the time the tower was opened. The Service was now in a position to liaise with its overseas outposts and friendly agencies, and at the same time, glean additional intelligence via foreign telephone calls routed through the building's intricate machinery.

The situation infuriated MI5 counter-espionage men who, through various means, learned that Moscow was intercepting all manner of calls. But the Security Service had yet to prove beyond any doubt, MI6 signals traffic was being captured at will. A report was sent by MI5 to the Foreign Office about intercept concerns. A codeword - *'Cabbages and Kings'* was used to describe *'inconsequential rubbish'* or ordinary public calls being listened to by the KGB. This in itself meant MI5's warning was still being ignored, thus a secret plan was formulated to finally convince the FO's boffins they were wrong and in danger of exposing British Intelligence secrets.

Kelvedon Hatch emergency broadcasting tower was linked to the BT Tower

At some point in the 1970s, a decision was taken by MI6 to close down its tower operation and secure sites were explored elsewhere. But there is an ironic twist to this most fascinating story. Within months of MI6's departure, MI5 decided to occupy the same office in an effort to bolster its counter-espionage potential in the city. It too would depart for less obvious locations in future years, leaving the tower to function properly and as intended by those who had conceived it in the first place!

LINKS TO THE WORLD

Many of the tower's dishes were strategically positioned and connected to numerous important intelligence and security sites, including the secret Cold War underground nuclear bunker at **KELVEDON HATCH, BRENTWOOD, ESSEX [561•99]** and air traffic control at West Drayton. Radar signals and an array of domestic communications also passed through the tower, including military and intelligence traffic.

Eye Spy Intelligence Magazine   413

SPY SITES OF LONDON

Kelvedon Hatch, which could support over one hundred personnel is now a museum and a must-visit location. Building started on the facility in 1952 and it operated until 1992 when it was decommissioned.

MOSSAD AND VENGEANCE

Whilst the KGB was obviously British Intelligence's main protagonist, the agents of many foreign services were operating on London's streets, and some were engaged in activity a world away from espionage... including Israel's Mossad.

Steven Spielberg's absorbing and controversial 2005 film - *Munich* candidly replayed the supposed actions of a Mossad assassination squad as they hunted down senior planners of the infamous 1972 Munich Olympics massacre. Eleven Israeli athletes were brutally murdered on the Games campus by members of the Black September terrorist group. Within weeks of the outrage, the Mossad was directed to create a small ultra-secret active service unit that was given free reign to hunt down those responsible. This meant using unorthodox killing methods, new identities, bogus documentation, a plethora of safe houses, international bank accounts, and more importantly, operating in friendly countries right under the noses of organisations such as MI5 and MI6. It is widely believed the group also used diplomatic contacts and some underworld characters to source intelligence. The overall codename for this outrageously conceived plan was Operation Wrath of God.

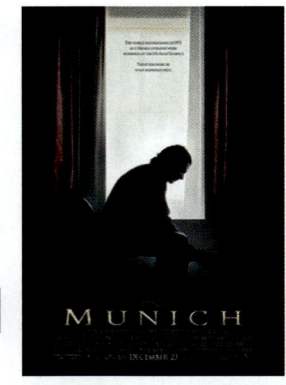

A most strange occurrence connected to Mossad's search team occurred at the **HOTEL EUROPA, DUKE STREET/ 10-13 GROSVENOR SQUARE [562•55]** in 1974 (now known as the London Marriott Hotel). As the Mossad attempted to make contact with an informer, an agent called Carl was himself assassinated. Yet no body was ever recovered by the UK authorities, no press reports appeared, nothing exists in the archives, hotel staff seemed oblivious and today's contacts are devoid of any knowledge.

The event still causes much discussion amongst senior MI5 and MI6 staffers - perhaps reluctant to believe such things could happen without their knowledge and on their 'manor'.

Apartments used by the Israeli athletes at the 1972 Olympic Games in Munich

Ali Hassan Salameh - top of Mossad's Operation Wrath of God hit list

BACKGROUND

In early May 1974, the Mossad team led by a man called Avner were given an opportunity to meet with a contact man in London who reportedly knew the whereabouts of primary target - Ali Hassan Salameh. The intelligence was itself sourced in the city as Salameh had an eye condition and had reportedly booked into a London clinic to see an eye specialist. The informant apparently knew which one.

Avner and two associates - Carl and Hans - travelled to London on 9 May and checked into the Europa Hotel. Their brief was to simply wait in the lobby of the **GROSVENOR HOUSE HOTEL, PARK LANE [563•55]**, here the informant would make contact. However, there was no pre-set date, just a time - between 10.00am and 4.00pm so the men took shifts - waiting and watching. Another surveillance point was set up on the corner of the square at **9 DUKE STREET [564•55]** which afforded a good view of the street and hotel entrance.

Avner decided that if contact was made between any member of the team and the informant, for security reasons they should make their way

SPY SITES OF LONDON
Former Europa Hotel used by Mossad personnel throughout the 1970s

London Marriott Hotel, 10-13 Grosvenor Square

individually to the nearby **BROOK GATE** entrance of **HYDE PARK** [565•55]. The remaining two operatives would perform counter surveillance to ascertain if the meeting was being surveilled. Of interest, visitors to this location will now find the Animals in War Memorial. No contact was forthcoming so Avner explained that in the morning it might be best if Carl and Hans left for Europe to rejoin their colleagues - he would take responsibility and meet the informant alone. That evening, after dinner, Avner left to hunt down a few souvenirs for his wife. Arriving back at about 10.00pm, he looked inside the hotel's Etruscan Bar - as Carl would often enjoy a drink before retiring.

Grosvenor House Hotel, 86-90 Park Lane

9 Duke Street

Eye Spy Intelligence Magazine

565 · 55
Brook Gate, Hyde Park

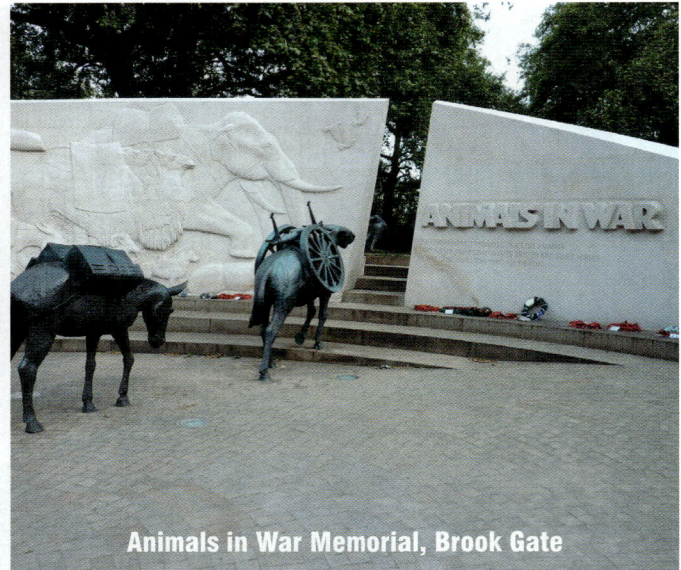

Animals in War Memorial, Brook Gate

Had the Mossad informant presented himself at the Grosvenor House Hotel, the plan was to walk to the nearby Brook Gate entrance of Hyde Park near Speaker's Corner. Intelligence on Ali Hassan Salameh would be imparted here

The bar was empty save a young, slim and attractive blond woman who spoke English but had a foreign accent. Avner ordered a beer and the two struck up a conversation. The Mossad man noticed her distinct musky perfume. Though an intimate few hours might have been in the offing, he declined her tempting suggestion of another drink upstairs.

Avner, perhaps reluctantly, decided to head to his room which was situated a short distance away from Carl's. As the lift doors opened, Carl stepped out and said he was going to the bar for a drink. Avner declined his offer of a beer and said he had a postcard or two to write. Early next morning Avner ate breakfast but was puzzled by Carl's non-appearance. He knew his colleague would never risk being late for an aeroplane flight. He knocked on the door of his room; no response forced him to use an old trick to gain access. He slid a credit card behind the lock and the door opened (this would not have been possible had the lock been engaged from the inside). Carl was laying on his back under the covers. A small hole was visible in his chest and blood and gunpowder surrounded the wound. His friend had fallen victim to an assassin's single bullet... a professional's signature. The musky perfume was again evident.

At 9.00am he placed a *'Do Not Disturb'* notice on Carl's door and telephoned Hans who was waiting at the safe house. He calmly said "the movie's off tonight... I'll talk to you later." It was the codeword which signalled a situation of extreme peril. Hans fled and made haste to a pre-arranged meeting place in Frankfurt, Germany. Carl's body was quietly removed via the Europa's rear service door by another Mossad team - MI5 oblivious of the situation.

THE SUSPECTS

There is also a certain character known to have had many contacts in London opposed to the existence of Israel - Illich Ramirez Sanchez, better known in the intelligence world as 'Carlos the Jackal'.

Service entrance behind the former Europa Hotel. It was here Carl's body was removed by an underworld team on behalf of the Mossad

Eye Spy Intelligence Magazine

In 1970, Nydia Romero de Tobon, an attractive female moved to London after splitting up with her Colombian husband. A revolutionary at heart, she soon fell for the charms of Sanchez - who had been appointed as a representative of Palestine's Popular Front. He had also been given a list of high profile figures that he was required to kidnap or assassinate - and that list now took him to London. De Tobon became a key operative for the Jackal and she sought out a safe house for him - a first floor flat in **PHILLIMORE COURT, KENSINGTON HIGH STREET [566•60]**.

He had previously attempted to assassinate the President of the Zionist Federation of Great Britain and had

THE LILLEHAMMER AFFAIR
MOSSAD'S GRAVEST ERROR?

Known as The Lillehammer Affair, this was undoubtedly one of the Mossad's lowest points in its turbulent history. On 21 July 1973, as the hunt for those responsible for the Munich outrage continued, a Mossad team mistook Moroccan waiter, Ahmed Bouchiki for Ali Hassan Salameh. As the innocent Bouchiki walked home with his pregnant Norwegian wife after an evening at the cinema in Lillehammer, Norway, Mossad agents pounced. He was shot dead at close range. Bouchiki had lived in the country since 1966. Six of the nine-strong team who participated in this part of the Wrath of God operation were arrested by Norwegian security services. Five operatives were found guilty and sentenced to several years in prison, all were released within 22 months and deported back to Israel.

Though Tel Aviv eventually paid compensation to Bouchiki's family, Israel has never acknowledged it was behind the error.

Ahmed Bouchiki

The Jackal used this address (first floor flat above bank) as a safe house

566•60
Phillimore Court, Kensington High Street

Eye Spy Intelligence Magazine
417

Earl's Court Square
In 1971, MI5 triggered a raid at the address but failed to understand the significance of a bogus Italian passport that was on the mantelpiece

liaisons with many underworld characters and groups throughout Europe. He was also a friend of the PLO-spawned Black September and vehemently supported the Palestinian cause. Sanchez lived at **12 WALPOLE STREET, CHELSEA [567•44]** but used a number of safe houses in the city. On 22 December 1971, MI5 launched a huge operation which saw armed Special Branch officers raid one of his addresses in **EARL'S COURT SQUARE [568•46]** - this in connection with the hunt for an acquaintance. Illich had stored a plethora of materials at one of his safe houses - enough to have warranted his arrest had they been discovered. However, MI5 did find a bogus Italian passport but amazingly believed Illich when he said it belonged to a friend. Another interesting find was a copy of Frederick Forsyth's book - *Day of the Jackal*. Despite this bungle, the Jackal was now on MI5's radar.

However, Illich was part of an international terrorist world that was determined to remain firmly out of reach of its biggest enemy - the Mossad. Using the cunning of a master spy, Illich travelled the world liaising and performing acts of terrorism which astonishingly were not linked to him. As for his connections to the events in Munich in September 1972, Illich told David Yallap, author of the critically acclaimed book - *To the Ends of the Earth*: "That is fantasy... in September 1972 I was teaching Spanish at the Langham Secretarial College in Park Lane, attending the LSE (London School of Economics), helping my mother and having a lot of fun."

12 Walpole Street, Chelsea

Eye Spy Intelligence Magazine

SPY SITES OF LONDON

Queen's Grove, St John's Wood [569•22]

Carlos the Jackal - one of the world's most notorious terrorists is serving life in a French prison

Though at an early stage of his career, Illich was personally behind the December 1973 London attack on Sir Edward Sieff, president of Marks and Spencer and a leading British-Jewish businessman. The Jackal surveilled Sieff to his house in **QUEEN'S GROVE, ST JOHN'S WOOD [569•22]** and shot him, but Sieff survived. A few weeks later in January 1974, a bomb explosion at the Israeli **BANK HAPOALIM, 81 GRACECHURCH STREET [570•08]** was also connected to the assassin. The bank closed in 2013.

The Jackal was a regular visitor to the public house - **DUCKS AND DRAKES, PRINCESS SQUARE, BAYSWATER [571•56]** (now called the Prince Edward). Here he met his new girlfriend Angela Baranca. Reluctant to take Baranca home because of his family, the couple rented the top floor flat at nearby **24 HEREFORD ROAD, BAYSWATER [572•04]** above a launderette. The lovers also met frequently at the **QUEENS HOTEL, INVERNESS TERRACE [573•56]**.

MI5 believed the bank attack was the work of Illich, but the evidence was spurious. It's little surprise, therefore, that many intelligence watchers believe that Carlos the Jackal may well have had a hand in the incident at the Europa Hotel.

And a final twist that may connect the killing of Carl, the Europa Hotel and the Jackal, came in August 1978. The hotel was also used by employees from Israel's security conscious national air carrier - El Al. The airline has never lost an aircraft in decades of operations, despite being targeted on numerous occasions. However, an underworld contact learned about the hotel's contract with El Al and passed this intelligence to an operational PFLP cell. Operatives had managed to outflank MI5 and establish a safe house in the city. As the El Al crew started to board a coach which had been booked to take them to Heathrow Airport, PFLP terrorists pounced and threw several grenades towards the vehicle. Other gunmen joined the attack. One air hostess died, as did a terrorist. Soon after the Europa Hotel closed.

81 Gracechurch Street [570•08]

Eye Spy Intelligence Magazine

572•04 **24 Hereford Road**

573•56

Queen's Hotel, Inverness Terrace

571•56

Ducks and Drakes, Princess Square
(Now the Prince Edward)

SPY SITES OF LONDON

574·60

Embassy of Israel, South Kensington
© DANIEL TAUB

A STRANGE TWIST OF FATE

The **EMBASSY OF ISRAEL, SOUTH KENSINGTON [574·60]** was targeted by mail bombs in 1972. Around 50 letters had been posted from Amsterdam to Israeli diplomatic missions around the world. One in particular was devastating. In London, Dr Ami Shachori, Israel's agriculture attache opened a letter which duly exploded - he was killed instantly. However, within minutes a signal was sent out to all Israeli embassies, consulates and missions about the attack. Dozens of letter bombs were successfully intercepted and disabled. A resulting investigation blamed the terror group Black September.

What's ironic in this case is that eight letter bombs had been sent to Israel's London embassy addressed to different staffers. Several had been intercepted by MI5. Four did make it to the embassy - three of which were identified and made safe. As for the unfortunate Shachori, a week or so earlier he had purchased a packet of Dutch flower seeds - and the Amsterdam postal mark made him believe it was his order arriving from Holland. On 12 September 2012, a special ceremony took place at Israel's embassy to mark the 40th anniversary of his death.

The attacks on Israeli diplomatic targets would continue. In June 1982, a gunman from the FTC (Fatah Revolutionary Council), headed by the notorious terrorist Abu Nidal, shot and severely injured Shlomo Argov, Israel's 53-year-old Ambassador to London, on the steps of the **DORCHESTER HOTEL, PARK LANE [575·55]**.

A SURPRISE TARGET

One surprising entry in MI5's 1970s Registry was John Lennon of the pop group The Beatles. The FBI were intent on removing him from the United States because of his campaigning against the Vietnam War. They called upon MI5 for any material that could be of use in building a case for his deportation. One Security Service file alleges that he funded the Workers Revolutionary Party in Britain, which was a Trotskyist group; gave money to *Red Mole*, a Marxist publication and backed other controversial groups. Just before he moved to America, Lennon lived at **34 MONTAGU SQUARE [576·55]** with his partner Yoko Ono. He was undoubtedly surveilled by the Security Service.

575·55

Dorchester Hotel, Park Lane

Ambassador Shlomo Argov

Eye Spy Intelligence Magazine

576•55

34 Montagu Square
John Lennon's former residence

John Lennon with television host Tom Snyder in 1975

BRITISH INTELLIGENCE - A SHIFT IN THE OPERATIONAL DYNAMICS

MI5 was involved in a chilling war with the Provisional IRA. However, it was barely represented in Northern Ireland with MI6 and other undercover services the main players. This would change in later years, but for now the Security Service was extended and its officers and agents engaged in shadowy wars with both spies and terrorists. Naturally, its Registry was burgeoning with the names added of those suspected of supporting the IRA.

With such a shift in the operational dynamics of MI5, the Service started to investigate a move to an enlarged location. Quite simply, with more employees, more directorates and more enemies and targets, it was running out of room. New technology was also coming on line, and the rooms and internal building structure at MI5's Leconfield House were simply too old and complex.

MI6 had been much quicker off the mark, though they were to make two disastrous choices for new headquarters. The splendid Broadway buildings had all but been emptied by early 1965 and many of its branches had been relocated to a new skyscraper. Built in 1961, and originally intended as a hotel - the **EMPRESS STATE BUILDING, EARLS COURT [577•46]**

SPY SITES OF LONDON

Empress State Building, Earl's Court

was a truly modern structure - chosen to reflect a modernising MI6. Three or four floors were occupied by a disgruntled staff and soon moves were afoot to seek out pastures new. Astonishingly, civil servants in the Foreign Office chose **CENTURY HOUSE, WESTMINSTER BRIDGE ROAD [578•23]** - a dismal 22-storey tower block that sat a few hundred feet from Lambeth North Underground Station. It was an appalling decision and MI6 staffers were soon complaining Soviet agents were identifying them even before they had turned up for work. Similarly, the open-plan offices were clearly visible through the large glass windows. Nevertheless, MI6 would remain here for the best part of thirty years.

Near to MI5 headquarters at Leconfield House, is **CURZON STREET HOUSE [579•55]**. This building was chosen in 1976 as an MI5 site for several reasons, not least for its security and maze of underground walkways and subterranean rooms. Rumours exist that it was here the Royal Family stayed on several occasions during the height of the Nazi bombing blitz in WWII. And it was in this building (or under it), that the precious Registry was housed. In 1955, it contained a little over two million names, but this had increased by the mid-1970s, though to what extent is unknown. Today, the building has been thoroughly modernised and sports a new facade.

While MI5 had found a suitable location for its Registry, it still had to find a new headquarters. And just like MI6's land planners - they got it wrong. In 1976, MI5 moved to **140 GOWER STREET [580•62]** and a

Gower Street Former location of MI5 headquarters

Eye Spy Intelligence Magazine

423

SPY SITES OF LONDON
Century House, Westminster Bridge Road

578•23

MI6 moved into this tower block in the 1960s, and though they would remain here for 30 years, staff were never comfortable. Inset: Century House before redevelopment. CIRCA. 1970s

581•23
Waterloo Bridge

Georgi Ivanov Markov

building described like those built in postwar Dresden or an Eastern Bloc country. The only thing in its favour was its total anonymity!

THE UMBRELLA MURDER

There's an old saying in the spying game that's often used to explain the subject's more darker side - 'it's a dirty business'. And one aspect that provides ample evidence of this 'cloak and dagger' world is murder... or as the CIA dictionary describes it - *'A Wet Job'*. London, too, has had its fair share of murder mysteries associated with the intelligence world.

In 1978, MI5 were involved in a most puzzling investigation involving its old adversary - the KGB. Georgi Ivanov Markov, a Bulgarian dissident felt a sharp stab in his leg as he waited for a bus on **WATERLOO BRIDGE [581•23]**. Nearby a man holding a umbrella apologised, hailed down a London cab, and disappeared. Sadly for Markov, it was no ordinary umbrella - the device shot a deadly ricin-filled pellet into his leg.

Markov had left Bulgaria in 1969 to work as a journalist in London. Within a short space of time he found employment as a broadcaster for the BBC's World Service, based at Bush House **(See Site 128•62)**. He also wrote scripts for Radio Free Europe and other organisations opposed to

424

Eye Spy Intelligence Magazine

579·55

Curzon Street House

ONE CURZON STREET

The building once housed MI5's important Registry

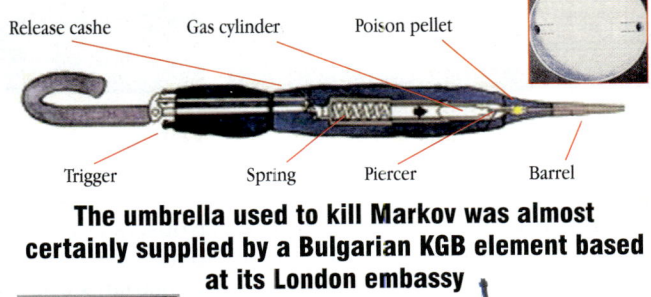

Release cashe — Gas cylinder — Poison pellet
Trigger — Spring — Piercer — Barrel

The umbrella used to kill Markov was almost certainly supplied by a Bulgarian KGB element based at its London embassy

583·47

Another view of Gower Street

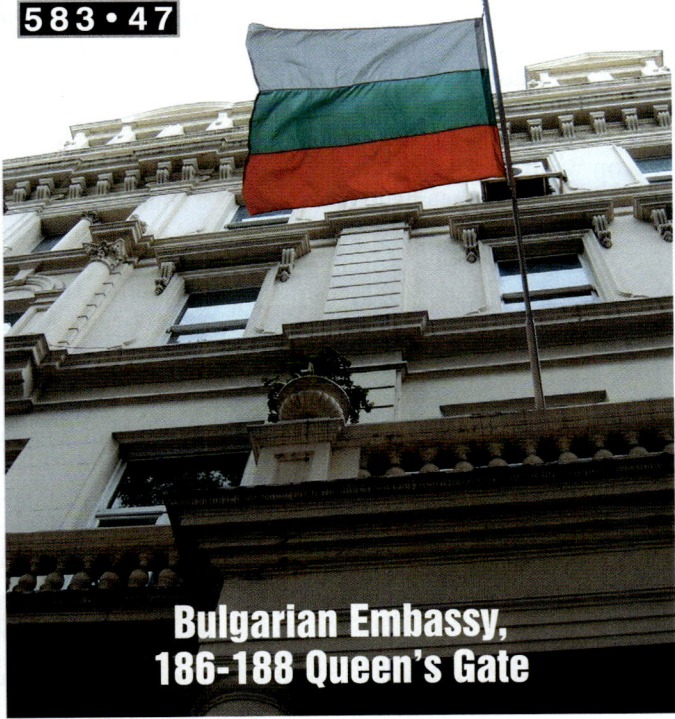

Bulgarian Embassy, 186-188 Queen's Gate

Eye Spy Intelligence Magazine 425

Waterloo Bridge has changed little since Markov's death, but he would not recognise today's modern London skyline

582•35

Within hours of Markov's death he was taken here. MI5 men were already waiting and soon government scientists found traces of ricin in his blood

Sheepcote Lane Morgue (Now a nursery)

The former BBC station at Bush House

the rule of Communism. His views were seen as disloyal back in Bulgaria, a country which had a very powerful intelligence service. As the broadcasts continued, a decision was taken by the KGB in Moscow to silence Markov. An agent arrived in London with a carefully constructed umbrella that concealed a deadly secret. On 7 September, Markov, who was celebrating his 49th birthday, was waiting for a bus on Waterloo Bridge. As a stranger passed he felt a sharp pain. A hired KGB assassin codenamed Piccadilly had delivered a fatal blow by firing the ricin-laced pellet through Markov's trousers and into his leg. The minute pellet was coated with wax and as the Bulgarian's body temperature rose, the wax melted allowing the ricin to enter his bloodstream - he died four days later. His body was taken to **SHEEPCOTE LANE MORGUE [582•35]** where MI5 men were waiting. This was the starting point of a chilling investigation that would run for almost 30 years. In 2006, intelligence researchers named the alleged assassin as Francesco Gullion - he has never been tried for Markov's murder. There is little doubt the operation had been supported by the KGB section at the **BULGARIAN EMBASSY, 186-188 QUEEN'S GATE [583•47]**.

For the record, Markov's grave can be found in a small churchyard at Whitchurch Canonicorum in Dorset.

MI6-CIA LIAISONS

The death of Markov shocked both British and American Intelligence. This was not the first time a dissident who was an MI6 contact man had been assassinated, but the fact that it took place in London was unnerving. MI6 and the CIA have cooperated closely for decades, and Langley has a dedicated team based in London at the US Embassy. The CIA and FBI helped MI5 in its worldwide hunt for Markov's KGB assassin.

In London, the Agency managed a number of Cold War outposts. These have long since closed. One such facility that operated into the early 1990s, was sited between **19-23 UPPER BROOK STREET [584•55]**. This was the former office and temporary residence of Lt Colonel Stewart Menzies, Chief of MI6 from 1939-1952. At some point in WWII, the building was occupied by US military intelligence officials and according to Eye Spy intelligence sources, was retained for use by Washington throughout the Cold War. We understand that the CIA's Covert Operations Office, codenamed LCPIPPIT, was relocated from 72 Grosvenor Street **(See Site 237•55)** formerly used by

Eye Spy Intelligence Magazine

SPY SITES OF LONDON

584•55

19-23 Upper Brook Street

Upper Brook Street

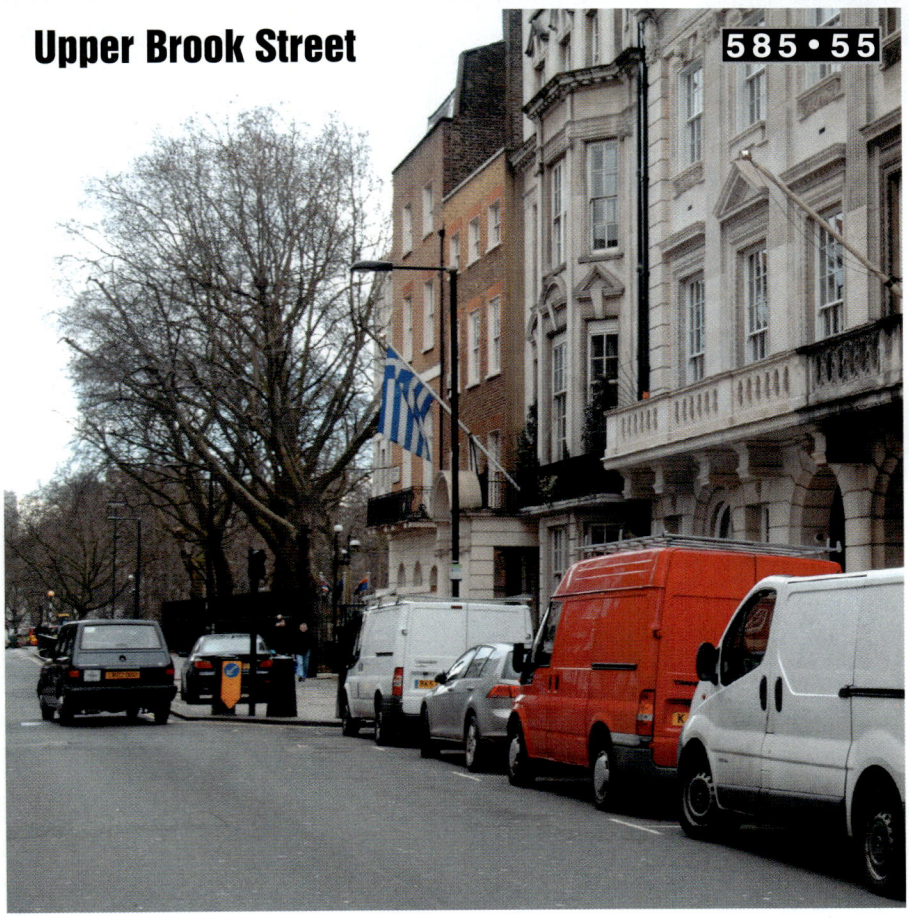

585•55

the OSS, to 23 Upper Brook Street. Another **UPPER BROOK STREET [585•55]** building close to the US Embassy was used to assist OSS and later Agency operatives. Documentation and transport was organised here. And for the record, in WWII, Admiral of the Fleet Louis Mountbatten (Lord Mountbatten) used number 27 Upper Brook Street as an office and residence, sadly this has been replaced by a new build.

SAFE CRACKERS, SILENCERS AND ASSASSINS

Iraq dictator Saddam Hussein always kept his friends close - but his enemies even closer. He was insistent that his spies keep a close eye on political opponents - especially in foreign lands.

This was no more apparent than on the streets of London. MI5 had a permanent team monitoring the coming and goings at the Iraq Embassy ever since General Abdul Razak al-Naief, a former Iraqi Prime Minister living in exile, was assassinated by a

Eye Spy Intelligence Magazine

427

586·55

Bryanston Square, Marylebone

21 Queen's Gate, Kensington

587·47

hitman on the streets of Mayfair on 9 July 1978. It turned out the assassin was operating from the embassy. Interestingly, some official records associated with the case file are so sensitive that they will not be considered for release until 2038. Also in London in 1978, Ayad Allawi, who in 2005 became interim Prime Minister of Iraq, survived an assassination attempt at his home in Kingston-Upon-Thames by an agent sent by Saddam Hussein. Allawi and his family were living in exile at the time and he was a vocal opponent of the Iraqi leader. The assassin attacked Allawi with an axe as he slept in his bedroom, almost severing his leg. He was hospitalised for nearly a year. Some intelligence watchers note his close relationship with MI6.

Six years earlier an attempt to assassinate Al-Naief had been foiled by his wife outside their sixth floor flat at **BRYANSTON SQUARE,** **MARYLEBONE [586·55]**. In this case Mrs Al-Naief bravely threw herself in front of her husband as a gunman opened fire. The would-be assassin had posed as a journalist and arranged an interview at the flat.

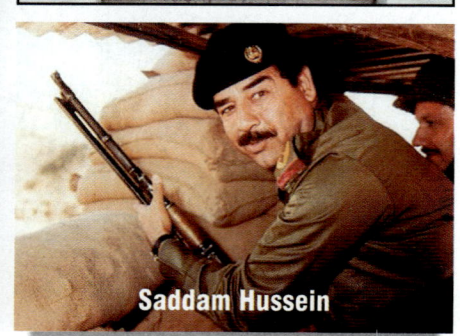

Prime Minister Allawi and President Bush

Saddam Hussein

428

Eye Spy Intelligence Magazine

Following Iraq's invasion of Kuwait in 1990, Saddam's diplomats left **21 QUEEN'S GATE [587•47]**. Thereafter the building was boarded up - this after a search by Special Branch and MI5 officers. When a new government replaced Saddam in 2003, Iraqi diplomats returned to the building and discovered a total of 12 unopened safes. A team of safe crackers were called in to open the boxes - eleven were empty, but watching officials were shocked when a twelfth revealed four machine guns, ten hand guns complete with silencers, an Uzi machine gun, ammunition and countless items associated with the spying game, including false documentation and identity papers. MI5 immediately called in weapons specialists to remove the firearms.

The Security Service had finally discovered the weapons used by the rogue Saddam spy ring which regularly hired assassins to eliminate the country's opponents - as happened to General al-Naief. Also in the safe were miniature spy cameras, recorders and several bugs - an indication Saddam's spies were most active - even against staff working inside the embassy. But, perhaps the strangest find of all was an electronic cattle-prodding device - the favoured tool used by Saddam's secret police to torture victims.

ASSASSINATION AND BOMBS

In 1979, Sir Maurice Oldfield, former 'C' of MI6 (1973-1978), was selected by Downing Street to head Britain's intelligence and security effort against the IRA. After WWII Oldfield spent much time abroad, including postings to Washington DC and Singapore. However, he retained an apartment at **17 MANSON PLACE [588•47]** behind Queen's Gate.

The IRA's terror cells were now operating on the mainland and never afraid to take on British Intelligence. In the 1970s, an IRA bomb detonated outside the restaurant at 33 South Audley Street **(See Site 477•55)** - this the former MI5 safe house used to

17 Manson Place

Crescent Mansions, 113 Fulham Road

Eye Spy Intelligence Magazine

429

Brooks's Club, 60 St James's Street

Assassinated - Lord Louis Mountbatten

interrogate Hollis. More audacious was the attempted bombing at **MARSHAM COURT, MARSHAM STREET [591•42]** - the new London home of Oldfield - the man selected by premier Margaret Thatcher to tackle the terror group. A little over twelve months later, Oldfield stepped down.

Even more daring was the assassination of Shadow Northern Ireland Secretary Airey Neave. The former Colditz Camp escapee and MI9 intelligence agent was killed on 30 March 1979, after his car was blown up as he left the underground **HOUSE OF COMMONS CAR PARK [592•42]**.

Neave's superior at MI9 was Michael Bentine, the founding member of the *Goons,* a popular comedy series on television. Bentine also mooted the idea of establishing a counter-terrorist section within 22 SAS.

Initially, New Scotland Yard believed the assassination was carried out by the IRA, however, another Republican terrorist group - the Irish National Liberation Army (INLA) later claimed responsibility for Neave's death. At the time, Neave lived at **CRESCENT MANSIONS, 113 FULHAM ROAD [593•44]**.

The IRA struck again on 27 August 1979. Lord Louis Mountbatten, 1st Earl Mountbatten of Burma and former WWII Supreme Allied Commander, had been holidaying at his cottage in Mullaghmore, Ireland. Whilst sailing in Donegal Bay, a bomb exploded on his yacht killing him, two grandsons and a local boat boy. Dowager Lady Braybourne died the next day as a result of her injuries. The incident rocked the country and caused much upset in the Royal Family. Mountbatten, who lived at **2 WILTON CRESCENT, BELGRAVIA [594•42]** was Prince Charles' Great Uncle and a wartime favourite commander of Winston Churchill. Lady Braybourne was actually the Godmother of Charles.

On the same day, the British Army suffered one of its biggest post-war losses. An attack at Warrenpoint on the Northern Ireland border with the Republic, resulted in the deaths of 18

Brooks's Club formed in 1764

Eye Spy Intelligence Magazine

soldiers. The troops had fallen victim to two booby-trapped bombs. Another particularly appalling incident occurred in July 1982, when a bomb devastated a troop of the Household Cavalry in Hyde Park. Eleven military personnel died in the attack - four from the Blues and Royals and seven bandsmen of the Royal Green Jackets. Memorials to the dead soldiers can be found in **REGENT'S PARK [595•15]** and **HYDE PARK [596•42]**. Seven horses were also killed in the attack claimed by the IRA.

RECRUITING CLUB CLOSES

In 1978, one of the most famous gentlemen's clubs closed its doors.

Opened in 1857, **ST JAMES'S CLUB, 106 PICCADILLY [589•55]** was extremely popular with foreign diplomatic and intelligence officials. Notable members included Winston Churchill and for a time Ian Fleming lived here. It was also used by visiting intelligence staff from friendly nations.

After it closed, the club's membership merged with **BROOKS'S, 60 ST JAMES'S STREET [590•42]**.

SPY SITES OF LONDON

589•55

St James's Club, 106 Piccadilly

591•42
Marsham Court, Marsham Street

Eye Spy Intelligence Magazine

431

House of Commons Car Park

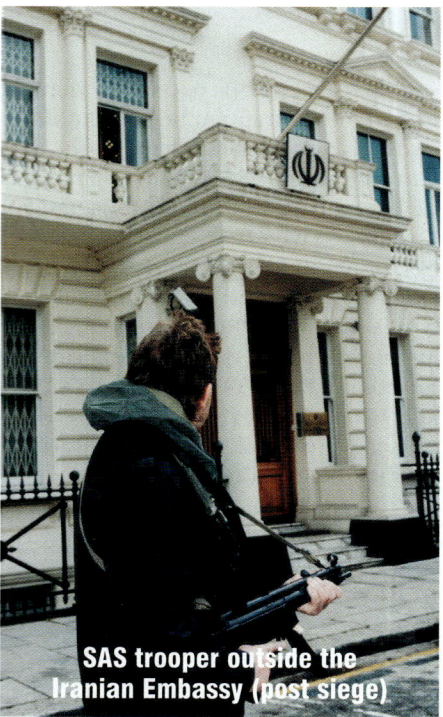

SAS trooper outside the Iranian Embassy (post siege)

THE IRANIAN EMBASSY SIEGE OPERATION NIMROD

On 30 April 1980, six Middle East terrorists opposed to the Iranian revolution of 1979, and demanding the liberation of the Arabistan region in Khuzestan, Western Iran, stormed the **EMBASSY OF IRAN, 16 PRINCES GATE [597•47]**. Led by Salim Towfigh, the group rented two flats at **20 NEVERN PLACE [598•46]**. After being thrown out because of their late night drinking and bringing prostitutes onto the premises, they secured a three bedroom flat at **105 LEXHAM GARDENS [599•60]**. Interestingly, one of the men with Towfigh was an Iraqi Army officer described in his passport as an Iraqi Ministry of Industry official. 'Ali' was actually an intelligence contact man who arranged the property rental and asked a letting agent to ensure the group's baggage and belongings be returned to Baghdad on a certain day. He held two covert meetings at **24 QUEEN'S GATE [600•47]** and **55 QUEEN'S GATE, SOUTH KENSINGTON [601•47]** which intelligence officials believe were attended by 12 terrorists. Not by chance, the Embassy of Iraq was a few feet away at 21 Queen's Gate **(See Site 587•44)**.

The men belonged to a terrorist outfit calling themselves the Group of the Martyr. They assembled at the **ALBERT MEMORIAL, KENSINGTON GARDENS [602•47]** before walking to the embassy. The sole police officer on patrol that day, Trevor Lock, was enjoying a cup of coffee with an embassy official. Seconds later the gunmen forced their way in. Embassy officials and other people, including two BBC news men were in upstairs rooms. At that moment, an embassy official pressed a security button which alerted New Scotland Yard that something was occurring. This marked the beginning of an extraordinary six days, ending only when several SAS units stormed the building in an operation codenamed Nimrod.

Specialist MI6 and MI5 technicians dropped listening devices down the building's chimney pots, whilst other bugs were fixed on adjoining embassy walls. At the rear of the building, various command centres were

Members of the UK's secret Force Research Unit (FRU) in Northern Ireland fought a secret war with dissidents. The FRU is now defunct

Eye Spy Intelligence Magazine

SPY SITES OF LONDON

594•42
2 Wilton Crescent, Belgravia

595•15
Regent's Park Memorial

596•42
Hyde Park Memorial

597•47
Embassy of Iran, 16 Princes Gate

COURTESY: RUSTY FIRMIN

Eye Spy Intelligence Magazine

SPY SITES OF LONDON

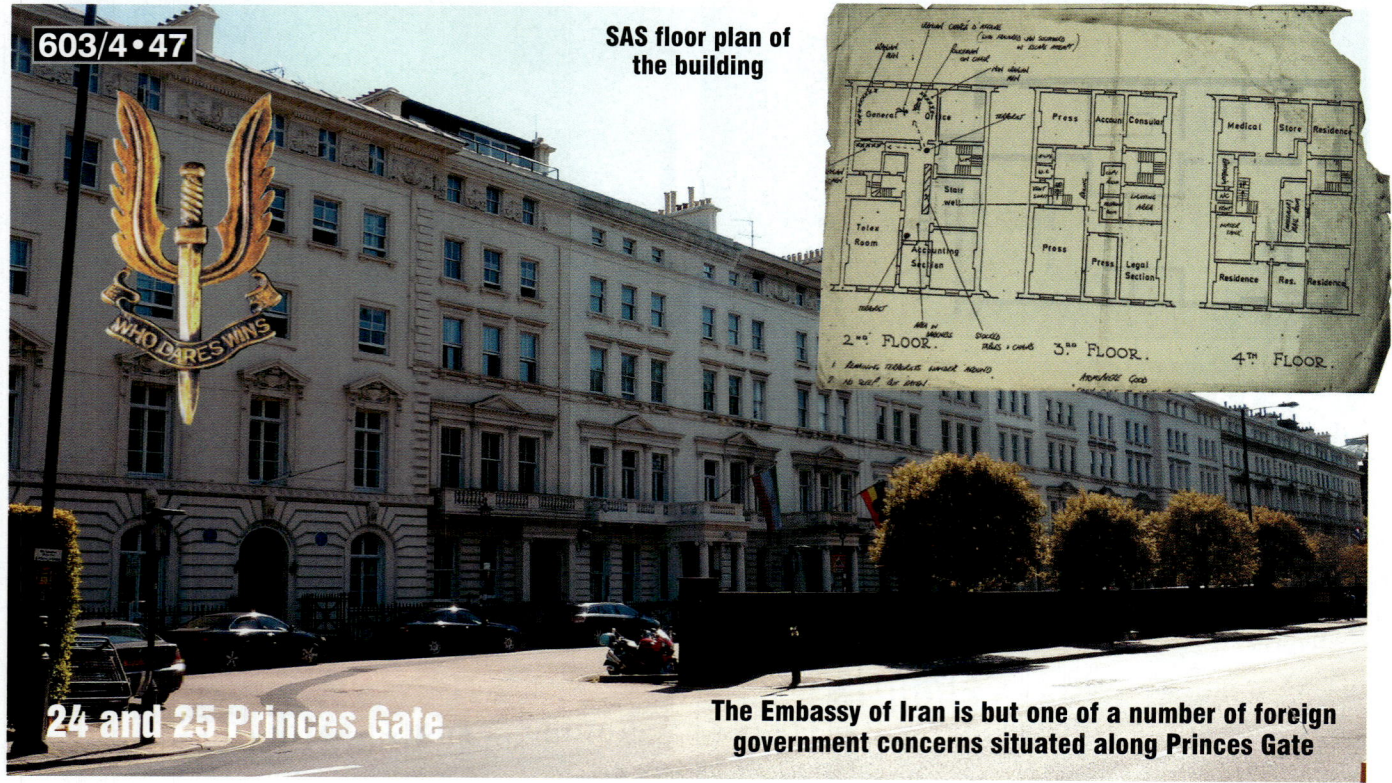

599 • 60

598 • 46

The Royal Borough of Kensington and Chelsea
NEVERN PLACE, S.W.5

105 Lexham Gardens

20 Nevern Place

603/4 • 47

SAS floor plan of the building

24 and 25 Princes Gate

The Embassy of Iran is but one of a number of foreign government concerns situated along Princes Gate

SAS troops, including Rusty Firmin (centre - no gloves) enter the Iranian Embassy

COURTESY: RUSTY FIRMIN

MI6 and MI5 specialists dropped listening devices down these chimneys at the Iranian Embassy

Sami Muhammad Ali -a.k.a. Salim

606•47

Embassy of Ethiopia, 17 Princes Gate

601•47

55 Queen's Gate

Eye Spy Intelligence Magazine

435

SPY SITES OF LONDON

Rendezvous site for the six terrorists - a short walk from the Iranian Embassy

602•47

Albert Memorial, Kensington Gardens

600•47

24 Queen's Gate

A reflective Rusty Firmin outside the Iranian Embassy. Rusty was part of the SAS team which freed the hostages and killed all but one of the terrorists. In 2011, Firmin wrote about the siege in his best-selling book - *Go! Go! Go!*

established by New Scotland Yard, MI5 and MI6, and of course, the SAS. New Scotland Yard counter-terrorist specialists used the headquarters of the **ROYAL SCHOOL OF NEEDLEWORK, 25 PRINCES GATE [603•47]** and a day later occupied **24 PRINCES GATE [604•47]** which was being used as a nursery at the time. The troopers had been waiting at a holding area in **REGENT'S PARK BARRACKS, ALBANY STREET [605•15]**.

Britain's policy has been never to negotiate with terrorists, and after a hostage was shot dead, police negotiators faded into the background. The SAS men, most of whom had travelled to the city from the Regiment's Hereford barracks, were called in to execute Nimrod assembling at 14

SPY SITES OF LONDON

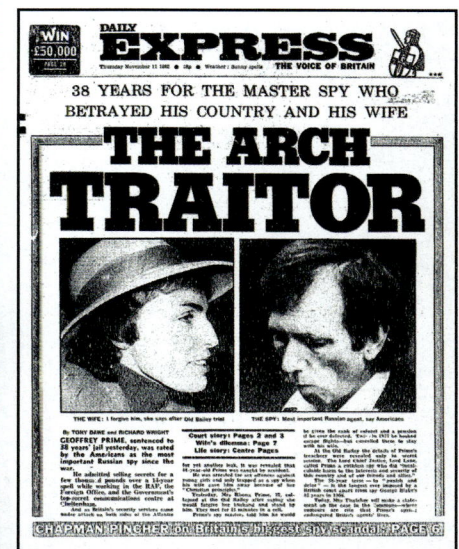

A New Scotland Yard marksman provides protection to fellow officers and SAS soldiers who assembled at the rear of the Iranian Embassy

COURTESY: RUSTY FIRMIN

THE ARCH TRAITOR — *Daily Express:* 38 YEARS FOR THE MASTER SPY WHO BETRAYED HIS COUNTRY AND HIS WIFE

Princes Gate, the former residence of US Ambassadors to Britain **(See Site 152•47)**. Salim, and his cohorts, were doomed.

At the **ETHIOPIAN EMBASSY, 17 PRINCES GATE [606•47]**, a security element consisting of counter-terrorist troops, police, medical personnel and other officials gathered. Indeed, the adjoining balcony was used by some of the hostages to make good their escape when the assault began on 5 May 1980. When the shooting finally stopped, five terrorists, including their leader, Salim Towfigh, lay dead in various rooms and halls of the burning embassy. Twenty hostages were rescued. It was one of the SAS's finest moments.

PRIME-TIME SPYING

If MI5 Watchers had their hands full surveilling IRA and other terrorist groups, the Service still had to find time to catch KGB spies. In 1981, acting on a tip-off from the police investigating a sex case, MI5 discovered the KGB had an agent in place for the best part of 13 years - a former RAF man by the name of Geoffrey Arthur Prime. After being called up for national service, Prime sought to further his career by training as a Russian linguist. Posted to RAF Gatow in Berlin in the 1960s, he was inspired by Communism. It was here Prime was recruited by the Soviets.

Returning to the UK, he landed a job at GCHQ - the KGB now had an agent

605•15 — Regent's Park Barracks, Albany Street

Daily Mail: Army storm siege embassy — **SAS GETS THEM OUT ALIVE**

Eye Spy Intelligence Magazine

SPY SITES OF LONDON

Camelford House, 89 Albert Embankment
Note proximity to MI6 headquarters

well-placed in British Intelligence. However, posing as a decorator called Williams, Prime made an indecent approach towards a young girl. His car was traced and soon his spying games came to the attention of MI5. At his trial in November 1982, various espionage products were shown, including one time pads, radios, invisible inks etc. He was jailed for 38 years, though was released after serving exactly half his sentence.

The fall out between the US and UK was immense. GCHQ was the sister agency of America's NSA and there was real concern in Washington about such infiltration. It was rumoured the White House threatened to withdraw intelligence cooperation unless tighter security was brought into play. However, through MI6's persistence and daring, Britain was about to receive a phenomenal boost to its counter-espionage operations.

TINKERBELL EXPOSED

In 1980, details of a top secret telephone tapping operation codenamed Tinkerbell were revealed in the media.

The programme was hosted at the **CENTRAL OFFICE, 93 EBURY BRIDGE ROAD [607•42]** opposite Chelsea Barracks. Little remains of the original building which has been demolished. However, the revelations

93 Ebury Bridge Road

GCHQ, Cheltenham
Geoffrey Prime worked here. Photo shows original buildings

438 Eye Spy Intelligence Magazine

Chantry House, Ecclestone Street

608•42

MI6 agent and senior KGB officer - Colonel Oleg Gordievsky

610•52 42 Holland Park

caused uproar and questions were raised about the MI5-police operation in Parliament.

Despite the furore, the programme relocated to **CHANTRY HOUSE, ECCLESTONE STREET [608•42]** and then **CAMELFORD HOUSE, 89 ALBERT EMBANKMENT [609•23]**. This building sits right next to today's MI6 headquarters which when Tinkerbell was operational of course, did not exist!

THE DEFECTION OF A MASTER KGB SPY

In September 1985, KGB Colonel Oleg Gordievsky defected leaving behind a trembling KGB. The agent had already tipped-off MI6 that an MI5 operative - Michael Bettany was passing secrets to the Soviets.

In April 1983, Bettany discovered the address of London's top KGB man in the city. He duly popped an envelope offering his services in the letter-box of **42 HOLLAND PARK [610•52]**.

He explained if the Russians were interested, they should place a drawing pin on the sign above the underground entrance to **PICCADILLY CIRCUS STATION [611•55]**. Also in the letter were details about dead letter drops where information could be secreted and picked up.

Soviet Rezident, Arady Guk, was suspicious of the letter offering British Intelligence secrets so he discussed the matter with his second-in-command - Oleg Gordievsky. The MI6

© GREG BOKOLSKY VIA DAVID HAMER

Eye Spy Intelligence Magazine

439

Piccadilly Circus Station - South Entrance

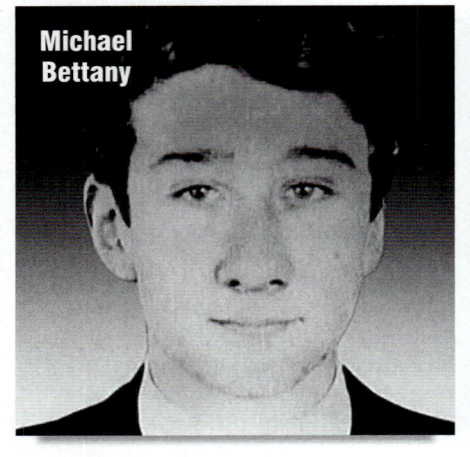

Michael Bettany

Soviet Rezident, Arady Guk

Roberto Calvi

agent duly informed his contacts in London and before Bettany could give Moscow London's entire counter-espionage and intelligence plans, he was arrested. Nevertheless Bettany had indeed passed on a number of highly sensitive files.

One location Gordievsky used in a KGB surveillance operation in 1983, was the **DUKE OF KENDAL PUBLIC HOUSE, 38 CONNAUGHT STREET [612•56]**.

Guk claimed he had secured the registration numbers of five MI5 surveillance vehicles which he said had been following him. Gordievsky monitored who was tracking his superior officer and duly tipped-off MI6 that their colleagues in MI5 had been uncovered.

There's more on Gordievsky shortly, suffice it to say the KGB never forgave him for defecting and in 2008, he became the victim of an attempted assassination.

GOD'S BANKER: DEATH UNDER BLACKFRIARS BRIDGE

"When you play with fire - expect to get burnt." These words were used by a New Scotland Yard detective in the investigation into the death of financial 'king pin' Roberto Calvi in 1982. Nicknamed 'God's Banker' because of his ties to the Vatican, Calvi's death remains unsolved.

The Exocet missile and French-built Argentinian Navy Super Etendard warplane posed the biggest risk to UK forces. Calvi's death seems linked to a shadowy affair to secure the missiles

Eye Spy Intelligence Magazine

Chelsea Cloisters

SPY SITES OF LONDON

In the early 1980s, Calvi was chairman of Banco Ambrosiano - in which the Vatican held a significant stake. He also had connections to a number of murkier outfits, including a masonic lodge known as P2 or Propaganda Due. Here, his liaisons with Italy's elite - including the hierarchy of the country's intelligence services - SISMi (military) and SISDE (civilian), were sown. Unfortunately for Calvi, the Mafia also had large sums of money tied up with his bank, and they were none too happy (like other customers), when it started to get into trouble. Also around this time, Britain had locked horns with Argentina in the battle for the Falkland Islands. MI5 and MI6 both were watching carefully various arms and front companies attached to Buenos Aires, as well as staffers of the **ARGENTINE EMBASSY, 65 BROOK STREET [613•55]**. One of the companies had recently moved from an office (coincidentally next to MI6's London Station - VBR) on Vauxhall Bridge Road to the port of Hamburg in Germany. The Argentine Purchasing Commission were monitoring the near completion of ten warships destined for the Argentine Navy.

It's a rather complex and lengthy story to link the intelligence aspects, but Calvi's bank was involved in part with financing the deal, and with an arrangement to purchase Exocet missiles from neighbouring France via third parties. The Exocet, MI6 was told, represented the biggest threat to UK forces in and around the Falklands, especially warships.

Duke of Kendal, 38 Connaught Street

Argentine Embassy, 65 Brook Street

Eye Spy Intelligence Magazine

441

SPY SITES OF LONDON

Blackfriars Bridge

Calvi was found swinging from this beam - his pockets stuffed with bank notes

Whatever Calvi's exact role in the demise of Banco Ambrosiano, in 1981 he was given a four-year prison term in Italy for illegal foreign currency deals. However, with an appeal pending, Calvi fled Italy on 10 June 1982. Using a disguise and a bogus passport, he flew into Gatwick Airport, London, on a private aeroplane.

He stayed in a shabby service apartment at **881 CHELSEA CLOISTERS**

[614•44]. On 17 June he was last seen alive at the Queen's Arms pub in Draycott Avenue (now closed). Friends say he seemed depressed. Early next morning a postman found him hanging from scaffolding under **BLACKFRIARS BRIDGE [615•08]**. MI5 and New Scotland Yard officers believed his death was unusual. Indeed, it later transpired that he had almost certainly been killed on the banks of the River Thames 300 yards away, and then carefully hoisted under the bridge to make it look like suicide.

Spy author Nigel West said: "Calvi was the key player in Argentina's efforts to acquire Exocet reloads and represented the Junta's last chance to change the course of the Falklands conflict." For more background, do read West's revealing book - *The Secret War for the Falklands*. Though some believe more shadowy forces in MI6 or their 'cousins' in the CIA acted to remove Calvi, West says this is simply untrue. However, he does not rule out the possibility that other dark forces were at work.

The Queen's Arms has long disappeared - but the nearby Queen's Head public house is open.

The Queens Head on Tryone Street

As for the conflict with Argentina, normal diplomatic relations were not resumed until 1990, this following the resignation of Prime Minister Margaret Thatcher.

THE RADIO SIGNAL

On 2 April 1982, Argentina media announced that the country's armed

442   Eye Spy Intelligence Magazine

Langham Hotel, Portland Place

616•55

SPY SITES OF LONDON

HOTEL [616•55]. So ironic that with all its communications prowess, that British Intelligence had to learn of the status of the islands via a radio ham!

THE LONDON SANCTION

Exiled Seychelles leader, activist and dissident Gérard Hoarau was assassinated on the doorstep of his home in Greencourt Road, Edgware in November 1985, by an unknown assailant. New Scotland Yard later identified the weapon used in the attack as a Sterling machinegun - the type issued to the Seychelles Police. Interestingly, the same model was used in the murder of police constable Yvonne Fletcher outside the Libyan Embassy a year earlier (more on this case shortly).

Two people responsible for the electronic surveillance deployed against Hoarau did appear in court where it was ruled they played no part in his death.

Technical details surrounding the bugging operation on London's streets was staggering. A Seychelles dissidents' meeting hosted at the **SWALLOW INTERNATIONAL HOTEL, CROMWELL ROAD, KENSINGTON [617•46]** was targeted. Here an attractive woman arranged flowers which impressed and distracted a hotel porter as bugs were planted in the hotel's rooms.

Even Mr Hoarau's meetings over a meal were not immune from such practice. "No one's going to notice an extra waiter who changes an ashtray or a pepper pot," said one of the surveillance operatives. The murder of Hoarau has never been solved.

forces had taken the Falkland Islands. Neither British Intelligence nor the Ministry of Defence could confirm this. As frantic efforts were made to make contact with the islanders, inside a building occupied by the BBC, reporter Laurie Margolis discovered the truth.

Situated on the top floor was an amateur radio station. And it is here Margolis listened to a broadcast made by a radio enthusiast from the Falklands: "We have now been taken over... the government denies this but we are under their control."

The message was routed to Whitehall and suddenly the government realised the truth. The building where Margolis received the communication is now the splendid **LANGHAM**

Swallow International Hotel, Cromwell Road
(Now Marriott Hotel Kensington)

617•46

STASI AGENT

In the 1980s, unbeknown to MI5, a spy working for the East German Stasi was operating on the streets of London. His name and nationality are not known, only his codename - Eckart. The man worked at the **ROYAL INSTITUTE OF INTERNATIONAL AFFAIRS (RUSI), WHITEHALL**

Eye Spy Intelligence Magazine

443

RUSI, Whitehall

34 Belgrave Square

France 1939. General Gort and Lt. General Henry Powell

The Viscount Gort

[618•42], a British defence and security think tank. Here he came into direct contact with people like Prime Minister Thatcher and leading officials. For six years he passed information to his controller at the **EMBASSY OF THE FEDERAL REPUBLIC OF GERMANY, 34 BELGRAVE SQUARE [619•42]**. His espionage was only revealed in 2000 following the release of decoded files from the former spy agency. Of interest, the Belgrave building was once home to General the Viscount Gort (John Vereker) who was commander-in-chief at Dunkirk 1939.

Eye Spy Intelligence Magazine

SPY SITES OF LONDON

XXII
The New Professionals
Cold War Ends as New Millennium Beckons

During the 1980s, British Intelligence was attracting media and public attention like never before. MI6 had been criticised in the press for not understanding the signs that Argentina would invade the Falkland Islands in the South Atlantic in April 1982. However, though MI5 was acknowledged and discussed regularly, it was still a big 'no, no' to whisper the words 'Secret Intelligence Service' in Parliament.

There were also a spate of revealing books about the spy services, none more controversial than former MI5 man Peter Wright's *Spycatcher*. Indeed, more than one spy location, or ruse can be sourced from Wright's work. MI5 operations, especially those involving the Service's clever surveillance and bugging teams, were discussed, so too the furious rows over KGB infiltration. And despite government attempts to stop its publication, the book came off the presses in Australia and became a worldwide best-seller notching up sales of over two million. Experts now believe no damage was done to British Intelligence.

POLICE DEATHS AND CONTROVERSY

The shadowy war between Britain's security services and the IRA was continuing, and the terror group was receiving arms and explosives aplenty from a predictable source - Libya.

On 17 December 1983, an IRA bomb exploded on Hans Crescent near Harrods killing three police officers - Sergeant Noel Lane, Constable Jane Arbuthnot and Inspector Stephen Dodd. Three civilians also died and a further 90 people were injured. A splendid memorial can be found outside **HARRODS, BROMPTON ROAD [620•42]**. Indeed, each year a special service takes place outside the store. MI5 and MI6 were satisfied the explosives had been sourced in Libya.

In 1984, MI5 found itself embroiled in a massive controversy which rumbles

Harrods Memorial, Brompton Road

COURTESY: NEW SCOTLAND YARD

Chief Superintendent Adrian Roberts honours those who died on the 30th anniversary of the IRA bomb

Eye Spy Intelligence Magazine

445

SPY SITES OF LONDON

Hilda Murrell (COURTESY: WEST MERCIA POLICE)

Memorial in St James's Square to WPC Yvonne Fletcher — 624•42

CND marchers protest in London

on today. It began following the brutal abduction and murder of Hilda Murrell, 78, an outspoken campaigner against nuclear weapons and a former staffer at the Bletchley Park codebreaking centre. As a member of CND (Campaign for Nuclear Disarmament), she attended numerous rallies and had vigorously opposed Britain's nuclear weapons policy.

Ms. Murrell was also the aunt of a former naval intelligence officer involved in the sinking of the Argentine warship the General Belgrano in the Falklands War. Some intelligence watchers believe her house was broken into by agents searching for sensitive papers linked to the controversial incident.

When she was found dead in March 1984, there were accusations aplenty that she had been eliminated by British Intelligence. None of this was true of course, but the conspiracy theories grew and were not helped by ill-timed comments linking the affair to the Falklands War.

It took almost thirty years to bring Murrell's murderer to book. In 2003, new DNA forensics pointed to Andrew George, who was just 16 at the time.

However, George's family have long maintained he is innocent, and in 2013, legal campaigner Michael Mansfield QC, asked that a commission of inquiry be established to look into the case. He described the security services as "major suspects."

ST JAMES'S SQUARE SHOOTING

In 1984, members of Libya's diplomatic corp at the **LIBYAN PEOPLE'S BUREAU, 5 ST JAMES'S SQUARE** [621•42], reacted with deadly violence to a protest by dissident Libyans. Someone within the building fired a gun killing WPC Yvonne Fletcher. Britain froze fearing a reaction could make vulnerable some 7,500 Britons working in the North African country. MI6 was tipped-off by the KGB that the shooter was a Libyan diplomat. After an eleven day siege the Bureau emptied under police guard, and the killer of Fletcher escaped scot-free - much to the annoyance of New Scotland Yard and its security detail which had surrounded the building.

GCHQ had intercepted a signal sent from Tripoli by Libyan leader Colonel Muammar Gaddafi asking for *'demon-*

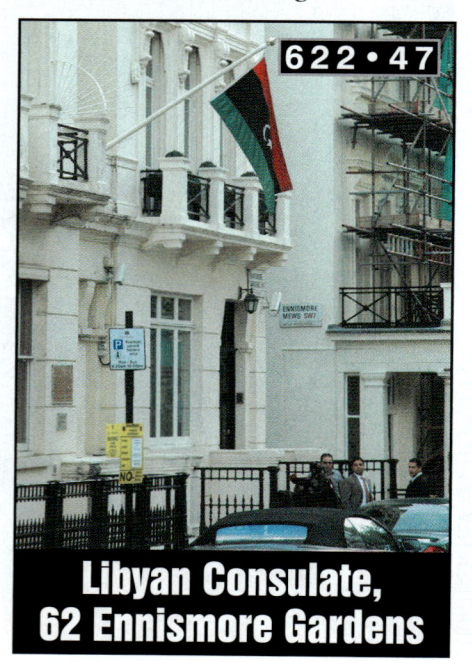

Libyan Consulate, 62 Ennismore Gardens — 622•47

446

Eye Spy Intelligence Magazine

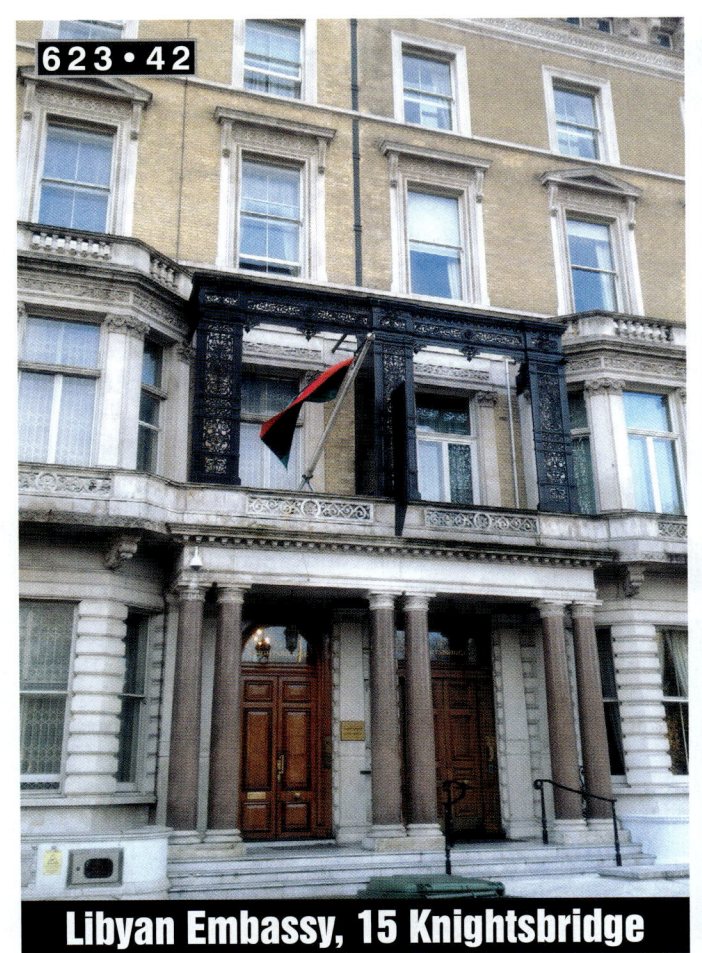

Libyan Embassy, 15 Knightsbridge

Former Libyan People's Bureau

strators blood' the previous evening. However, few could have expected that his London staffers would kill a British police officer.

One of the prime suspects was Omar Ahmed Sodani. After the shooting he fled to the **LIBYAN CONSULATE, 62 ENNISMORE GARDENS, KNIGHTSBRIDGE [622•47]**.

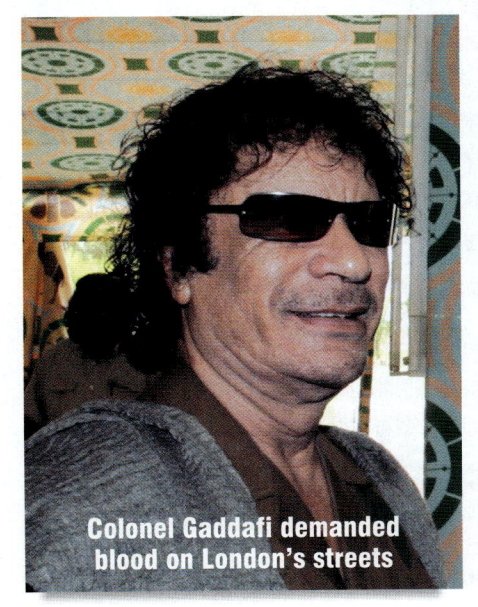

The diplomats were eventually allowed to depart and the gunman escaped. However, Sodani was detained in Libya in 2011 following the collapse of Gaddafi's regime. He has since dismissed claims he was involved in the shooting. Libya has a new embassy at **15 KNIGHTSBRIDGE [623•42]** which is run by representatives of the National Transitional Council (NTC). They have vowed to help New Scotland Yard bring to justice the killer[s] of Yvonne Fletcher.

A memorial to the police officer can be found in **ST JAMES'S SQUARE [624•42]**.

But this outrage would pale in significance compared to events that shattered the night sky over the Scottish border town of Lockerbie in December 1988. Libyan JSO agents had placed a bomb onboard Pan Am Flight 103 which duly exploded killing 270 people. Libyan leader Colonel Gaddafi eventually accepted responsibility for the air outrage. JSO officer Abdelbaset al-Megrahi was the only person ever jailed for the attack but released on compassionate grounds in 2009 after being diagnosed with cancer. He died in May 2012.

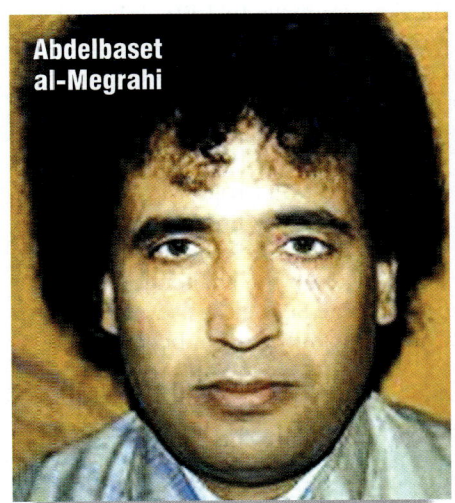

Colonel Gaddafi demanded blood on London's streets

Abdelbaset al-Megrahi

Eye Spy Intelligence Magazine

447

626•55 MI5 occupied offices here

Bolton Street

Dame Stella Rimington

Service was also spreading its wings to various locations across the city and occupied additional offices in **BOLTON STREET [626•55]**. However, its general staff were overjoyed when news came that its dreadful Gower Street headquarters was destined for the builders' bulldozer. News leaked out that the Service would be returning to a refurbished **THAMES HOUSE, MILLBANK [627•D]** on the River Thames after decades of travelling across the city. On 30 November 1994, Prime Minister John Major officially opened the building. But there was another controversy that would spark a security alert. A journalist had

BERLIN WALL AND COLD WAR THAW

Nearing the end of the decade, colleagues in MI6 and the CIA were reporting on a genuine warming of relations between the West and the Soviet Union. And when Reagan and Gorbachev started to talk, there was a real chance the Cold War, which had started to thaw, would melt away altogether. By 1990, the Berlin Wall had been tumbled and a new sense of freedom swept across Eastern European countries. This didn't mean espionage would stop, but for a time it slowed down!

THE FIRST FEMALE MI5 DIRECTOR-GENERAL

The IRA was not going away - unlike the Communists. In 1991, it launched an audacious mortar bomb attack on Downing Street. The projectile missed its target, but it was evidence enough MI5 had to stay alert.

A year later, MI5 broke with tradition and appointed its first-ever female Director-General. Stella Rimington would take up the challenge of modernising the Service as the countdown to the new millennium began.

For a time, MI5's special A4 Watchers had a building all of their own - occupying part of **EUSTON TOWER, 286 EUSTON ROAD [625•15]**. The

625•15

Euston Tower, 286 Euston Road

Brief home of MI5's A-Branch and the Service's famous A4 Watchers

Eye Spy Intelligence Magazine

SPY SITES OF LONDON

US President Ronald Reagan and Soviet Secretary General Mikhail Gorbachev at the 1985 Geneva Summit

Supergun designer Gerald Bull

somehow managed to get into the building during its overhaul and take several photographs of a new top secret mini railway line that ushered reports and Registry files across the huge complex.

SECRECY OF MI6 LIFTED

In 1992, a flurry of press reports suggested MI6 was about to be officially recognised by Prime Minister John Major - this as intelligence sources said a move away from Century House was imminent. MI6's existence was never a secret - it's just one of those bizarre situations that was allowed to continue - much to the puzzlement of the country. When premier Major made his statement in Parliament, he also said he would "sweep away some of the cobwebs surrounding its secrecy."

As lorries started to transport equipment out of Century House, driving to the impressive £250 million **VAUXHALL CROSS [628•25]** building, it didn't take long for the media to realise where MI6 was moving. Designed by architect Terry Farrell, the waterside building sits prominently amidst the apartments and offices in the area. It had actually been purchased for government use in 1988.

Terry Farrell designed Vauxhall Cross

629•55

Inn On The Park Hotel, Hamilton Place
(Now Four Seasons Hotel)

Eye Spy Intelligence Magazine

449

SPY SITES OF LONDON
628•25
85 Vauxhall Cross

Semper Occultus

MI6-SIS SECRET INTELLIGENCE SERVICE
VAUXHALL CROSS HEADQUARTERS

Terry Farrell's building under construction - 1991
© STEPHEN WILLIAMS

The electronic centre of MI6's worldwide operation

Visitors can take a cruise on the River Thames that passes in front of MI5 headquarters and exits right next door to the MI6 building!

Eye Spy Intelligence Magazine

These overhead views reveal the building's complex design dubbed 'Legoland' by some of the Service's employees

© FLIGHT IMAGES

Eye Spy Intelligence Magazine

451

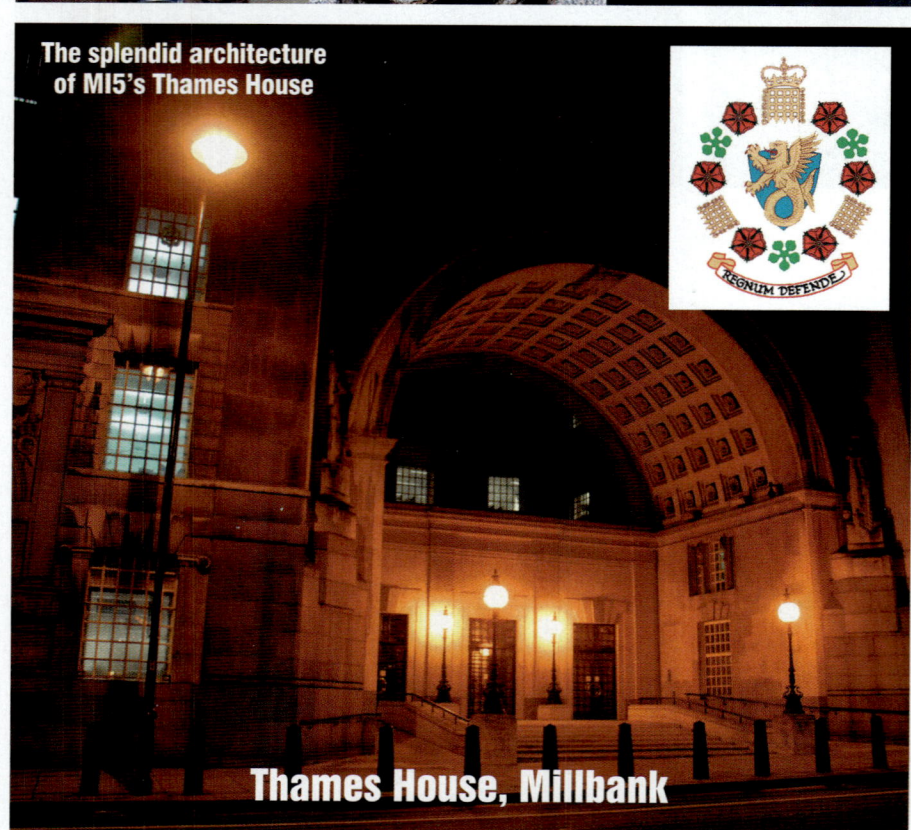

MI5 THE SECURITY SERVICE
THAMES HOUSE HEADQUARTERS

MI5 headquarters at Thames House was officially opened in November 1994. Since then, the number of employees has almost doubled

Stella Rimington

The splendid architecture of MI5's Thames House

Thames House, Millbank

452

Eye Spy Intelligence Magazine

The relocation was overseen by outgoing MI6 Chief Sir Colin McColl who was replaced by Sir David Spedding.

By 1994, the move was nearly complete, and now both MI5 and MI6 sat virtually opposite each other on the River Thames. This was also the year MI6 was officially recognised in the Intelligence Services Act.

PROJECT BABYLON AND MATRIX CHURCHILL

Sir Colin was at the helm of MI6 when a British company became entangled in a controversial business deal with Saddam Hussein's Iraq involving a long range rocket project.

Matrix Churchill, an engineering firm based in Coventry sold machines and components which were allegedly used in Saddam's secret weapons programme. Four company directors were put on trial, but the case collapsed mysteriously when it was revealed the government had advised the company on export licences. There was an alleged intelligence link which elevated the case - called the Matrix Churchill Affair - by the world's media.

It transpired that the company's Managing Director, Paul Henderson, met with an intelligence man at the renowned **INN ON THE PARK HOTEL, MAYFAIR [629•55]** (now Four Seasons Hotel) in 1988 and again in 1989. Part of the conversation centred around Canadian supergun designer Gerald Bull and the Space Research Corporation; Bull was linked to Iraq's enormous gun project codenamed Babylon. On 22 March 1990, the designer was assassinated in Brussels by an alleged Mossad hitman.

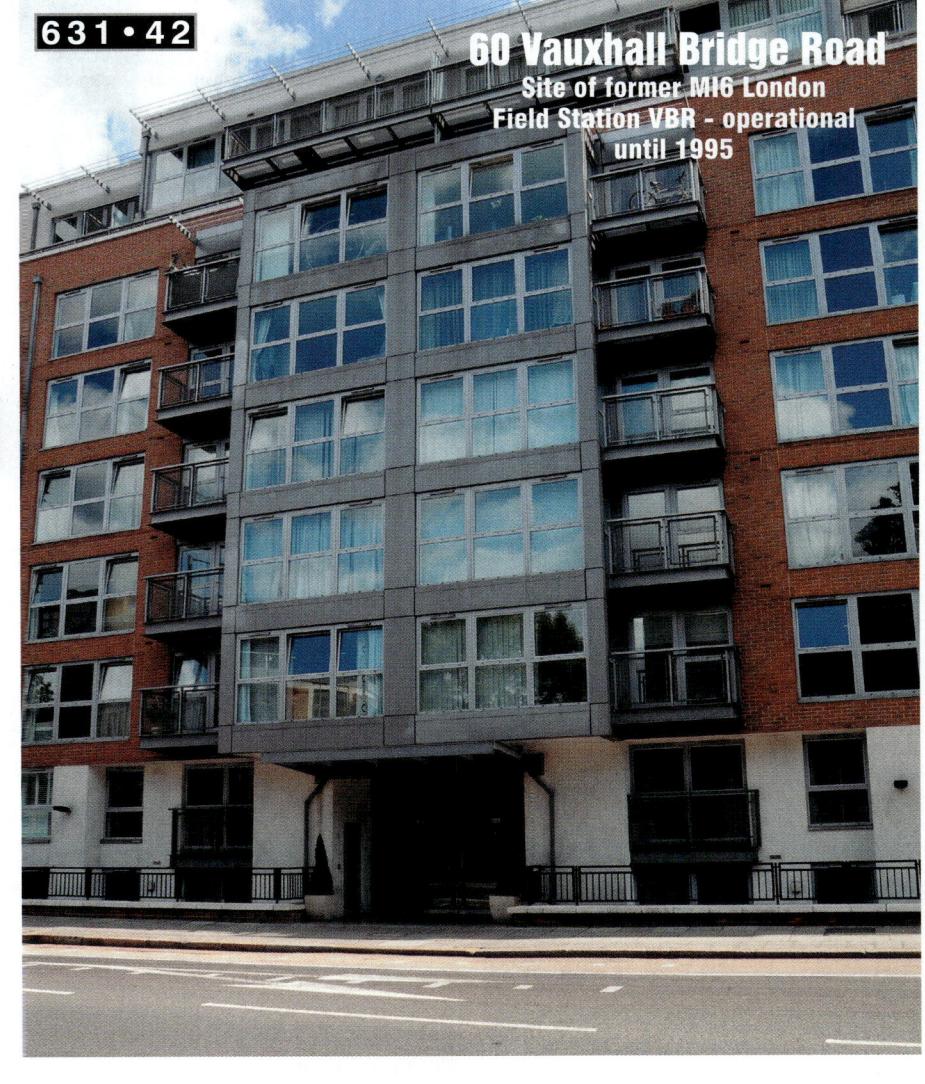

Interestingly, in St James's Park, visitors can find the **INN THE PARK [630•42]**, a popular cafe often mistaken for the hotel where Henderson held his secret meetings!

FATAL FLIGHT OF ZD576

The intelligence community of Britain was shaken to its foundation again on 2 June 1994, following an air disaster on the Mull of Kintyre in Scotland. For reasons unbeknown to many, 25 intelligence officers from various

631•42

60 Vauxhall Bridge Road
Site of former MI6 London Field Station VBR - operational until 1995

630•42

Inn The Park, St James's Park

Eye Spy Intelligence Magazine

453

SPY SITES OF LONDON

632•46

29 Gowan Avenue

services, including senior counter-terrorist men, were allowed to fly together on a short flight from Belfast to Inverness. The Chinook helicopter crashed and the resultant inquest blamed pilots Jonathan Tapper and Rick Cook. It later transpired they were the victims of a shadowy affair and were used as scapegoats.

A WELCOME CHANGE

For the staff of MI6, their new headquarters was simply sensational; incorporating several recreational areas and even a gymnasium. Of more importance was its functionality - and its electronic capability linking it to MI6 field stations across the world.

With the opening of Vauxhall Cross came the closure of one of the Service's worst kept secrets - MI6 actually had a field station in the capital separate from its headquarters. In 1995, MI6 moved out of **LONDON STATION VBR** or **60 VAUXHALL BRIDGE ROAD [631•42]**. It had occupied the site since 1955, and though much speculation exists concerning its whereabouts today - intelligence watchers believe it simply moved into the new building.

Today it's possible to take a boat ride (see www.londonducktours.co.uk) along the River Thames and exit right next to the new headquarters of MI6. The journey also takes you past MI5's Millbank headquarters.

Similarly, you can stroll down a walkway directly in front of the Vauxhall building and spend time enjoying the scenery from a well-maintained benched area. Looking at the building - nicknamed 'Legoland' by the personnel who work there, it's hard not to be impressed. One last note on Century House - the Service's former headquarters. When developers moved in they discovered MI6 had not quite secured an underground complex. This was rumoured to house a nuclear bomb shelter and other Cold War memorabilia.

A SHOCKING ASSASSINATION

On 23 April 1999, NATO bombers struck a building in the Yugoslavian

633•62 University College London

637•58

Ealing Broadway

634•55

David Copeland

Admiral Duncan, Old Compton Street

capital of Belgrade, this as the country splintered into various states following a bloody civil war. The CIA had identified the building as a Serbian intelligence centre, but it was in fact just a civilian television station. Seventeen people died, including many journalists. An intercepted signal revealed that in response, Zeljko Raznatovic, a Serb paramilitary commander, ordered that BBC Director-General John Birt be killed. The police increased his security, thus an assassin was told to kill the most popular and well-known broadcaster of the day - Jill Dando, 37. Her address was secured from a CD containing Britain's electoral roll manufactured in Belgrade itself.

On 26 April, a lone gunman confronted her on the steps of her home at **29 GOWAN AVENUE, FULHAM [632•46]**. Despite the fact that she was killed in a very professional manner - a single bullet to the head, Barry George, a 41-year-old fantasist who lived nearby was arrested, charged and later jailed for life. Police had uncovered a photo of him in SAS guise.

In 2001, and in honour of her life, the Jill Dando Institute of Security and Crime Science (JDI) opened within the **UNIVERSITY COLLEGE LONDON (UCL), BLOOMSBURY [633•62]**. It became the first university institute in the world devoted specifically to criminal science. As for George, his conviction was quashed in 2007 and a year later he was acquitted of the crime.

ADMIRAL DUNCAN BOMBING

Just four days after the shooting dead of Jill Dando, MI5 and New Scotland Yard investigated another shocking incident. A bomb had been detonated inside **THE ADMIRAL DUNCAN, OLD COMPTON STREET [634•55]** - a public house in the heart of the city's Soho district. It was the third such incident in recent weeks - bombs having exploded in Brixton and Hanbury Street. Three people were killed in the pub attack and over 50 injured.

Neo-Nazi David Copeland was arrested and a year later sentenced to a minimum of 50-years in prison. His actions were an attempt to stir ethnic and homophobic tensions in London.

1999 was a busy year for the authorities. MI5 faced embarrassment when it was revealed that no charges were to be brought against Melita Norwood, the KGB spy who had operated for decades. She had passed secrets to Moscow whilst in the employment of British Non-Ferrous Metals Research Association **(See Site 424•15)**. Her role as a spy had actually been revealed some years earlier in 1992 by Soviet defector Vasili Mitrokhin.

Eye Spy Intelligence Magazine

SPY SITES OF LONDON

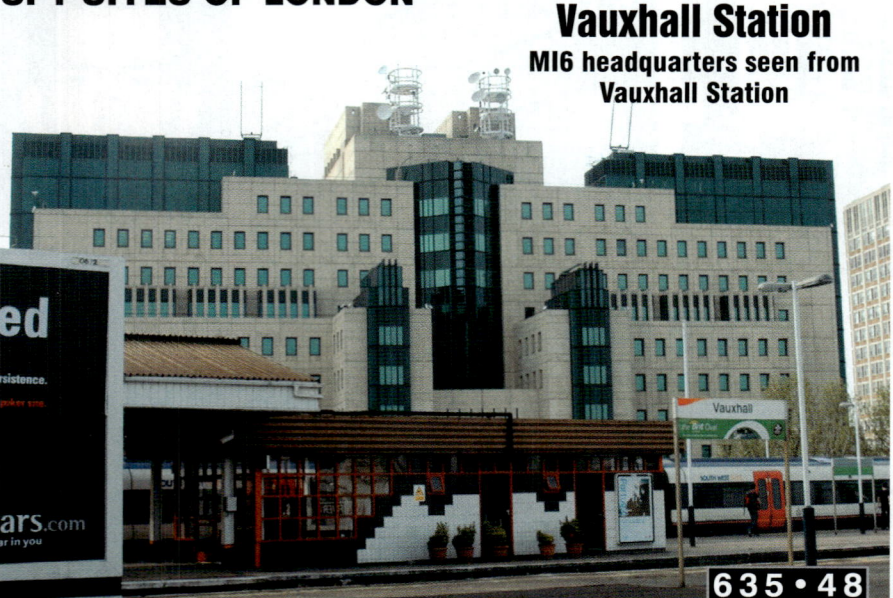

Vauxhall Station
MI6 headquarters seen from Vauxhall Station

635•48

MI6 HEADQUARTERS: ATTACK ON VAUXHALL CROSS

Some of MI6's old guard had disapproved of the new openness of the Service, and they considered such a prominent headquarters as a security risk. Their fears were part-realised on 20 September 2000, when an offshoot of the IRA - the Real IRA - fired a rocket-propelled-grenade (RPG) at the building from the nearby train embankment at **VAUXHALL STATION, VAUXHALL CROSS [635•48]**. Though it struck, the damage was only superficial and there were no casualties. After this incident, MI6 introduced additional security measures.

MI5 believed the terror cell responsible for this audacious attack were also involved in other operations in London and based in Oxford.

In June 2000, a bomb containing Semtex exploded directly under **HAMMERSMITH BRIDGE [636•59]**. The device had been attached to a girder. It wasn't the first time terrorists had targeted this iconic bridge. In 1996, the IRA had planted the biggest Semtex device ever on mainland Britain. Despite two of four detonators engaging, the device did not explode.

On 3 August 2000, a massive car bomb did explode on **UXBRIDGE ROAD, EALING BROADWAY [637•58]** causing extensive damage.

THE NEW MILLENNIUM FEARS

By 2000, MI5 was devoting more time and resources to capturing terrorists and thwarting attacks than countering espionage. MI6 and GCHQ were also engaged in this deadly game of 'cat and mouse'.

Unbeknown to many, ten addresses in London were raided in connection with Osama bin-Laden in the summer of 2001 - prior to 9/11. MI5 contacts told Eye Spy in May of that year al-Qaida was planning a major attack - "though not necessarily on British soil."

However, the spying game never ends and there remained the constant threat UK secrets could be stolen or sold by those seeking to secure cash. Indeed, unlike previous years when a plethora of spies operated in the belief they were actually aiding their own country, a new generation had emerged - intent only on financial reward. One such person was Ian Parr, 46, who wanted to sell secret technology owned by his employer - defence contract company British Aerospace.

In March 2001, MI5 learned of his mischief, and posing as a Russian agent called Aleksei (the buyer), an undercover MI5 officer induced him to part with his materials over a pint of beer at the **CROWN THISTLE HOTEL, TOWER BRIDGE [638•01]**. Parr said he wanted a total of £130,000 for information on the top secret BAE cruise missile project codenamed Storm Shadow. The sting, codenamed Operation Dragonfly, worked perfectly and Parr was arrested by Special Branch officers in Southend following another meeting with Aleksei.

636•59

Hammersmith Bridge

© ALEX MULLER

Thistle Hotel, Tower Bridge

MI5 discovered a British Aerospace worker was attempting to sell UK secrets to a foreign country

Also in 2001, another British Aerospace employee - Rafael Bravo was arrested after MI5 learned he was wandering about London touting sensitive military information. This included details about radar and aviation systems, circuits for the Apache helicopter and Harrier GR7 jump jet and a file containing an electronic warfare programme belonging to the US Army. Bravo worked as a security guard at the firm's Stanmore plant in London and over a period of time quietly secreted the files out. As he tried to find potential buyers, an MI5 undercover agent posing as a Russian official made contact with him and a meeting was arranged at the **WHITE HOUSE HOTEL, EUSTON [639•15]**. MI5 and Special Branch officers waited patiently in the bar - pretending to be guests and business people eating lunch and enjoying a drink. As soon as Bravo handed over the documents, he was arrested. In due course, the bungling spy received a seven-year prison sentence.

Such instances of espionage belong in the opportunist section, but even amateurs can be dangerous. There was much more concern in the mid-2000s, following a huge event in Moscow involving former and serving

Former KGB officer President Putin increased number of Russian spies in London

members of Russia's intelligence services. President Vladimir Putin, himself a former KGB officer, called for a "massive resurgence" in the country's spying operations - much of it aimed directly against the UK. And within weeks, a top secret MI5 assessment warned that at least 100 fully-fledged SVR and FSB spies had sought out new pastures in London - intent on stealing secrets and finding Britons or anyone willing to help their cause.

ASSASSINATION OR ACCIDENT?

MI5 found itself investigating an unusual death in the person of revered Egyptian actress Soad Hosni, star of many excellent movies. She had intelligence links and moved to London after suffering a back injury which forced her to leave Egypt. At 9.10pm on 21 June 2001, a friend saw Hosni standing on the balcony of

The hotel (left) sits opposite the magnificent Tower Bridge

Eye Spy Intelligence Magazine

457

White House Hotel, Euston

Soad Hosni

an apartment at **8 COLLINGHAM ROAD, MAIDA VALE [640•46]**, West London. He was puzzled when he failed to find Hosni inside, but then saw a lifeless blooded body on the pavement below. The fall had killed the actress instantly.

Some people close to Hosni believe she had been clinically depressed and this may have contributed to her state of mind - hence suicide. Her death occurred on the anniversary of Abdel Halim Hafez's birthday - a close friend who was a major influence on her career. However, others believe she was an agent for MI6 collecting information on high-profile figures. It's even been suggested she was used to frame prominent personalities. Friends and close associates say she was writing her memoirs at the time of

111 Old Church Street

8 Collingham Road, Maida Vale

458

Eye Spy Intelligence Magazine

SPY SITES OF LONDON
296-302 Borough High Street
Former MI6 training school

the incident - allegedly to raise money to pay for mounting debts. A number of journalists contend that she was killed because of what was contained in the manuscript.

At the inquest, which closed on 11 July 2003, the verdict was given as suicide. New Scotland Yard did not think Hosni's death was suspicious and the case was closed. It's a finding the Hosni family are still challenging.

Bizarrely, in 1974, Egyptian General al-Leithy Nassif, former head of the presidential guard under the late Egyptian President Sadat, also 'threw himself off' a balcony in the very same tower block in Maida Vale.

TRAINING NEW FRIENDS

Though officials in the West believed they had won the Cold War, the KGB was still far from finished - and despite a name change to FSB - the old guard continued to play the great game on the streets of London. However, MI6 sensed a real opportunity to gather intelligence in a more open Russia. With this in mind, the Service started to cooperate, liaise and then train operatives from former Soviet-bloc countries. Indeed, it's said many agents were trained at MI6's Fort Monckton spy school on the outskirts of Portsmouth. Known as The Fort within the intelligence community, this facility teaches operatives all manner of spy tradecraft. However, there were a number of top secret London-based centres used by MI6 to train spies to infiltrate the former Soviet Union from East European nations. Many of the operatives who attended such a spy school at one Chelsea address - **111 OLD CHURCH STREET [641•44]** - were refugees. The idea being to resettle them back in their native countries where they would act as sleeper agents.

And in the not-too distance past, hundreds of British intelligence officers were trained in a non-descript building at **296-302 BOROUGH HIGH STREET [642•23]**.

Though the Service still operates satellite sites in London, most training today is performed at its headquarters, Fort Monckton and other complexes - including military bases.

A training site which operated for years was based in **MATTHEW PARKER STREET [643•42]**. This MI6 office was also relocated to Vauxhall Cross.

WHISTLEBLOWERS

One particular problem that causes no end of concern for any intelligence service is disgruntled staff - especially when disputes can't be solved amicably. The fear for organisations such as MI5, MI6 and GCHQ, is that operational details and secrets may be revealed. Despite the fact that personnel sign the Official Secrets Act, some ex-employees have written books, or contributed to titles describing what they consider operational failures.

The Big Breach by former MI6 officer Richard Tomlinson appeared in early 2000. His most controversial claims relate to an alleged MI6 operation to assassinate Slobodan Milosevic, the

Matthew Parker Street
Site of former MI6 training and research centre

Former MI5 officers David Shayler and Annie Machon have been critical of their former employer

3 Carlton Gardens

645•54

Charles House, Kensington High Street

GCHQ, Cheltenham
© FLIGHT IMAGES

The courtyard and gardens inside GCHQ
© JAMES DENNISON

SPY SITES OF LONDON
CONTRASTING FORTUNES

Charles House on Kensington High Street once played host to various branches and elements of MI5 and MI6. The activities of those who served here remain top secret though it is believed several key international operations were either planned here, or supported by Charles House staff. In 2009, the local council gave the go-ahead for the total redevelopment of the site.

Contrast this to the fortunes of GCHQ, which for years operated from old H-type buildings in Cheltenham. In 2004, the Service moved to a stunning new futuristic headquarters in the town

Richard Tomlinson

former Yugoslavia leader, and also concerns Princess Diana who was killed in a car accident in Paris. Tomlinson, who hints at an intelligence plot, was interviewed for his job at **3 CARLTON GARDENS [644•42]**. And at around the same time, former MI5 man David Shayler helped write *Defending the Realm*. In 2004, Katherine Gunn of GCHQ was cleared of leaking intelligence material on the Iraq war to the press. Gunn, who was sacked, said she did it as a "matter of conscience." She too went on to produce a book. Coincidentally, in 2004, GCHQ moved into its new futuristic circular-shaped headquarters in Cheltenham nicknamed the 'doughnut'. At the same time, MI5 and MI6 departed satellite

Eye Spy Intelligence Magazine 461

SPY SITES OF LONDON

646•08
Union House, St Martin's Le Grande

Slobodan Milosevic

offices in **CHARLES HOUSE, KENSINGTON HIGH STREET** [645•54].

Some commentators said the publications were pointless, but undoubtedly they revealed - in part - the intricate workings of British Intelligence. As for relevance to our journey across the capital, while Tomlinson was interviewed for his job in Carlton Gardens, Shayler referred to his meeting point as "an unmarked building in the busy Tottenham Court Road."

Perhaps more interestingly, he also claimed MI5 once ran a mail tampering unit at **UNION HOUSE, 18-40, ST MARTIN'S-LE-GRAND** [646•08] near St. Paul's Cathedral. The building sat alongside Armour House. Echoes here of Peter Wright's 'kettle and sauna room' at Dollis Hill! No doubt after a hard day's work staffers enjoyed a drink at the Lord Raglan public house which sits just a few yards away.

Since 2005, MI5 has relocated many of its support facilities to a single host site that is naturally secret. One of those is the vehicle test and engineering centre that maintains the Service's A4 Watchers cars. However, just a few short years ago that centre could be found on **STREATHAM HIGH ROAD** [647•39]. Before that, vehicles were serviced and sometimes modified in

Lord Raglan Public House

© DUNCAN RIMMER

462

Eye Spy Intelligence Magazine

Streatham High Road
647•39

garages on Barnard Road near Clapham Junction. MI5 decided to leave after its own surveillance teams spotted KGB agents snooping all over it. And so the Service opted to use some non-descript car showrooms and a depot on Streatham High Road. This too didn't really stay secret for long, and was mentioned in a documentary film by journalist Duncan Campbell. It was inevitable, therefore, that MI5 decided not to try and keep it secret from the KGB any more. The garages were knocked down in 2008. As for MI6, some of its officers in the 1940s used a small top-secret garage at **CLARGES MEWS [648•55]**.

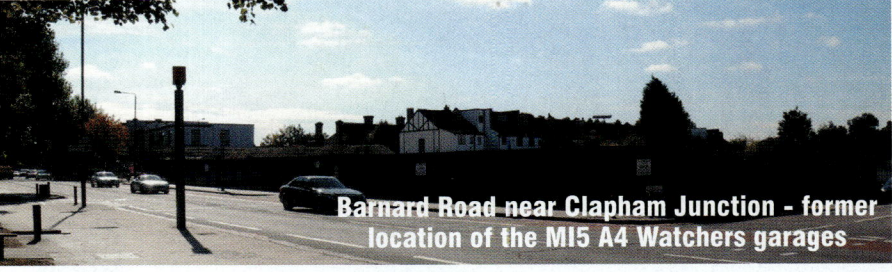

Barnard Road near Clapham Junction - former location of the MI5 A4 Watchers garages

Clarges Mews off Curzon Street
648•55

Vehicle locations used by MI5 and MI6 officers today are top secret

MI6 agents used this quiet street to garage a number of its London vehicles

Eye Spy Intelligence Magazine

463

SPY SITES OF LONDON

11 SEPTEMBER 2001
THE DARKEST DAY

The world of intelligence failed to undercover the plot which would change the way in which services such as MI6 and the CIA operated in future years. The attack on America resulted in 3,000 deaths. Four years later London suffered simultaneous attacks by the same group - al-Qaida

11 SEPTEMBER 2001 - DYNAMICS OF INTELLIGENCE COLLECTION CHANGES FOREVER

When terrorists struck several targets in the United States on 11 September 2001, the world changed forever. There was a real chance Britain would become embroiled in a global fight against al-Qaida. The dynamics of MI5 and MI6 operations also altered, though at least by then a peace accord

Damage to the Pentagon after terrorists crashed a hijacked airliner into the building

US Embassy, 24 Grosvenor Square

had been signed in Northern Ireland and the war against the IRA had effectively ended. There would still be dissident attacks by breakaway elements, but now the real enemy was one which had little sympathy for civilians - al-Qaida.

That London could not avoid the new threats posed by al-Qaida, was evidenced in 2002. An alleged plot had been foiled concerning the hijacking of a European airliner enroute to London. The media reported the aircraft was to be flown into the **US EMBASSY, 24 GROSVENOR SQUARE [649•55]** in an operation similar to that which had devastated New York and Washington a few months earlier.

Other plots to attack the embassy and its staffers are numerous and despite added security, US officials said the building was "not safe from attacks." In 2013, the US announced a new embassy was being built at **NINE ELMS, BATTERSEA [650•48]**. This modern building has numerous security features - many of which are top secret.

Though the building is protected by various counter-measures, the Department of State recognised that its position in London made it an inviting target

A statue of the great Cold War warrior President Ronald Reagan outside the embassy

Eye Spy Intelligence Magazine

465

SPY SITES OF LONDON

ICONIC SYMBOL OF AMERICA

The current US Embassy in Grosvenor Square was granted Grade II Listed status which means the building cannot be demolished. Construction started in the 1950s and the embassy opened officially in 1960. Atop the building sits the iconic golden eagle monument. Eye Spy has learned that officials are considering relocating this famous structure to the new embassy.

US Embassy, Nine Elms, Battersea

In 2003 Britain went to war in Iraq on the premise of an intelligence report written and compiled by MI6. Essentially the Service said Saddam Hussein had stockpiles of weapons of mass destruction (WMD) which could be readied for use in a short time period. Too short in the opinion of Prime Minister Tony Blair, who along with his counterpart in America - George Bush, decided to invade.

BBC Defence correspondent Andrew Gilligan claimed the government had effectively taken MI6's fairly low-key report on Iraq's WMD and "sexed it up." There was outrage and Downing Street targeted the Corporation like never before.

Gilligan's intelligence had to have come from a very senior source, and following an incident in Oxfordshire on 17 July 2003, it was evident from whence it came.

The new US Embassy under construction. Like most US embassies and diplomatic missions, security is provided for by the US Marine Corp and the Diplomatic Security Service

SPY SITES OF LONDON

651 • 62
Charing Cross Hotel

652 • 42
Ministry of Justice, 102 Petty France

Dr David Kelly

A government scientist in the person of Dr David Kelly walked out of his home in Abingdon and sat in a field next to a tree. He duly took a number of painkillers and slit his wrist. He bled to death.

Kelly was a Ministry of Defence scientific advisor and a former member of a specialist UN team which had previously investigated Iraq's WMD. He was not convinced at all regarding the government's report.

Kelly had come under immense pressure and was questioned in

Andrew Gilligan

COURTESY: DIPLOMATIC SECURITY SERVICE/DIPLOMATIC BUREAU

Eye Spy Intelligence Magazine

467

SPY SITES OF LONDON
653•42

Pakistan Embassy, 34-36 Lowndes Square

Parliament about his stance. He remained defiant, but after his secret meeting with Gilligan, it was obvious the journalist would want to air his story.

Kelly met with the investigator at the **CHARING CROSS HOTEL [651•62]** where the MOD man outlined his reasons for opposing war.

Days after his death it was discovered he had sent an e-mail to a journalist in New York saying: *'There are dark players at work'*.

Indeed, several leading medical professionals joined together and said the wounds on his body were not consistent with suicide. Many people still believe Kelly was murdered.

Seven years later the **MINISTRY OF JUSTICE, 102 PETTY FRANCE [652•42]** published its classified findings into Kelly's death in order to maintain public confidence. The MOJ also released details of the post mortem which concluded the scientist had killed himself. This still did not satisfy everyone, and Dr Kelly's death remains a dark talking point in Britain's intelligence history.

As a point of reference, the building occupied by the MOJ was occupied by the Home Office for years. As the regulator of MI5, it hosted many important intelligence meetings.

AGENT NOTATION AND MI5 BUGGING OPERATION

There was more controversy for British Intelligence in November 2003, when details emerged of an alleged MI5 operation to place listening devices, remove documents, acquire codes for sending secret messages and generally infiltrate a London-based foreign embassy. Legal restrictions prevented the media from publishing the identity of the embassy, though details appeared on the Internet just hours later. It was the **PAKISTAN EMBASSY, 34-36 LOWNDES SQUARE [653•42]**. Within a week, a Pakistan official declared: "We know it was our embassy, we want Britain to tell us what happened."

According to *The Sunday Times*, an agent codenamed Notation allegedly received a five-figure sum from MI5 for facilitating the operation. He was told not to bank the money in the event that it would "arouse the suspicion of the Inland Revenue." The agent, controlled by a handler called Claire, moved about the embassy with virtual impunity as he carried out building repair work. MI5 took photos, then examined the telephone system and a closed-circuit television monitor as possible locations for bugs.

Notation said the operation was badly managed and wrote to Ann Taylor, chairman of the UK's Parliamentary Intelligence and Security Committee. He referred to MI5's "bad tradecraft" and was fearful the espionage might put him in jeopardy. In the end, he resigned because he found the job "too stressful."

Just what MI5 was allegedly searching for remains a mystery!

Things were a little more clear a few months later when eavesdropping devices were discovered at the Connolly House headquarters of Sinn Fein in Belfast. MI5 Director-General Eliza Manningham-Buller acknowledged the Security Service had installed the bugs.

News also emerged that another plot to attack London had been thwarted, probably with the assistance of US Intelligence. In this case al-Qaida planned to hijack an airliner from mainland Europe and crash it into **CANARY WHARF [654•02]** - the expensive business heartland of the city and location of many skyscrapers.

SPY SITES OF LONDON

The Ministry of Justice (building in centre) now occupies the long-time headquarters of the Home Office. The building on the right is the former headquarters of MI6 at Broadway

Sir John Scarlett

INFILTRATION AND MI5 SUB STATIONS

Responding to the new terror threats, MI5 placed agents inside various UK universities in an effort to identify possible terrorist suspects. There was also talk of opening regional headquarters - this to counter illegal activities more quickly outside London. Indeed, a year later the Home Office confirmed new outposts in Manchester, Leeds, Birmingham and Glasgow were to be built and supported by local counter-terrorism police forces.

On 1 August 2004, the government announced John Scarlett had been selected as new Chief of MI6.

One of his first tasks was to answer questions and allegations concerning the Service and the death of Princess Diana in Paris 1997. Former New Scotland Yard Commissioner Sir John Stevens had been asked to head Operation Paget, after several conspiracy theories linked MI6 to events in France.

Sir John also faced problems, when under a Freedom of Information Act request, files were released that linked the Service to a French Intelligence operation that resulted in the deliberate sinking of the Greenpeace vessel - the Rainbow Warrior in 1985.

And then more trouble as a Greek magazine named the MI6 Station Chief in Athens, and accused his team of abducting Pakistani immigrants.

It was a candid reference to the CIA's controversial Extraordinary Rendition programme. In this case Langley was abducting suspected al-Qaida

Britain introduced a new threat-level system in an effort to advise and make the public more aware of emerging threats to security

Eye Spy Intelligence Magazine

469

SPY SITES OF LONDON
Canary Wharf

654•02

terrorists around the world and interrogating them at secret locations.

However, whilst these accusations could be dismissed as speculation, Sir John had little defence as an MI6 spying operation in Moscow was compromised and broadcast on Russian and world television.

MI6 officers were recorded in a Moscow park uploading and removing electronic data from an advanced communication device disguised as a rock. Several officers had their photos and identities revealed. This effectively ended their role as covert field officers. As for the 'spy rock', it now sits proudly in the KGB Museum in Moscow, alongside other espionage artefacts...

NEW THREAT LEVEL SYSTEM

On 1 August 2006, the UK introduced a new national threat level system.

The British Government unveiled details as part of an effort to make the nation's security system clearer and more useful to the public. The new guide streamlined the old seven-point threat-level method down to five levels:

- low (an attack is unlikely)
- moderate (an attack is possible but not likely)
- substantial (an attack is a strong possibility)
- severe (an attack is likely)
- critical (an attack is expected imminently)

Downing Street was forced to act after a huge number of people complained about the lack of information imparted by officials. Government buildings and facilities have used threat level models for years, but most members of the public were oblivious to the system.

FSB covert film footage showing an MI6 officer with the 'spy rock' in a Moscow Park

Eye Spy Intelligence Magazine

SPY SITES OF LONDON

XXIII
British Intelligence Shaken
Terrorists Strike in London - 7 July 2005

On the morning of 7 July 2005, four Britons recruited by al-Qaida travelled from the north of England to London intent on murder. They carried rucksacks containing improvised explosive devices. Just before 9.00am, explosions ripped through carriages on trains just outside **EDGWARE ROAD STATION [655•15]** and **ALDGATE STATION [656•01]**. A bomb then exploded on a train travelling between **KING'S CROSS STATION [657•8]** and **RUSSELL SQUARE STATION [658•62]**.

A fourth bomber blew himself up around an hour later on a bus. By chance, the explosion occurred outside the **BRITISH MEDICAL ASSOCIATION HEADQUARTERS (BMA), TAVISTOCK SQUARE [659•62]** which at the time was hosting a conference. Delegates ran to the scene and helped the injured and dying.

In total, 52 people lost their lives. Special Branch and Counter-Terrorist Command (CTC) officers based at **NEW SCOTLAND YARD, 8-10 BROADWAY [660•42]** working with MI5 soon identified the culprits. The bomb factory and a number of safe houses were discovered 200 miles away in Leeds, but there were no arrests, despite MI5 having a list of

Eye Spy Intelligence Magazine

THE LONDON STATIONS AT THE CENTRE OF 7/7

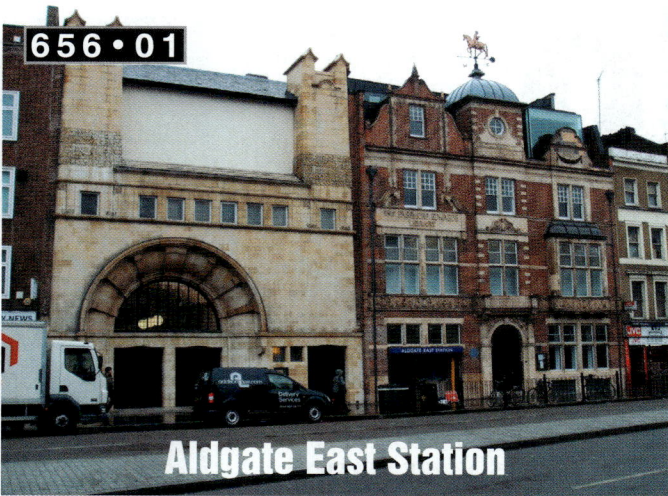

Russell Square Station

Edgware Road Station

King's Cross Station

Aldgate East Station

7/7 Memorial, Hyde Park

SPY SITES OF LONDON

MI5 Director-General Eliza Manningham-Buller and Home Secretary David Blunkett. Buller told Eye Spy "7/7 was the darkest moment in her intelligence career"

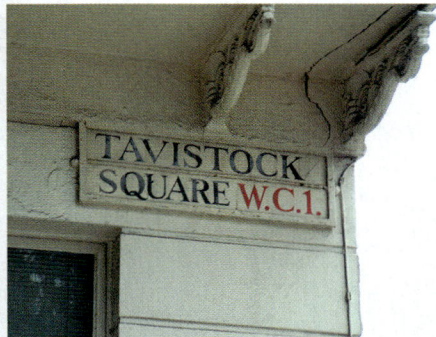

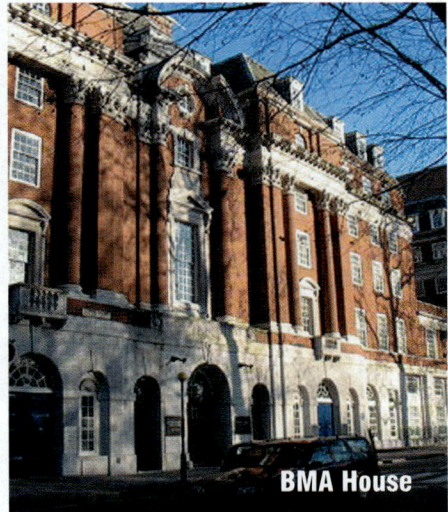

COURTESY: THAMES HOUSE/MI5

BMA House

659•62

Tavistock Square

nearly 30 suspects. A memorial to those who died in the attack can be found in **HYDE PARK [661•55]**.

Just hours after the 7/7 bombings, Prime Minister Tony Blair called an emergency meeting of **COBR[A] (CABINET OFFICE BRIEFING ROOMS), 70 WHITEHALL [663•42]**. This body consists of senior security and emergency officials as well as other officers dependent on the type of crisis situation encountered. In this case, New Scotland Yard, MI5 and MI6 officials were in attendance as well as transport and emergency services personnel.

Two weeks later on 21 July, another group of five terrorists attacked London transport again. The gang attempted to detonate home-made bombs on trains entering several stations, including **WARREN STREET STATION [662•15]** and on a Number 26 bus in Shoreditch. However, and very fortuitously, in every case the bombs failed to work properly and the devices did not explode. All the men fled.

Amongst the clues left by the men was a gym card belonging to Hussein Osman - and an address - 21 Scotia Road. Armed with this clue the police and MI5 launched an operation codenamed Kratos which sadly, would go badly wrong, resulting in the shooting dead of an innocent civilian.

Eye Spy Intelligence Magazine

473

Special Branch, Counter-Terrorist Command and other police elements, including Royal protection officers - all belong to New Scotland Yard - though are not necessarily based here

New Scotland Yard, 8-10 Broadway

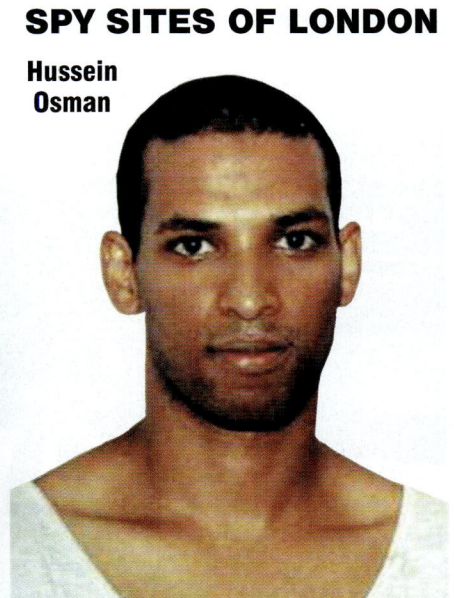

SPY SITES OF LONDON

662·15

Warren Street Station

Hussein Osman

663·42

Cabinet Office, 70 Whitehall
The gates of Downing Street are visible

SPY SITES OF LONDON

Heathrow Express

A SURVEILLANCE OPERATION GOES BADLY WRONG

Less than 24 hours after the failed attack, armed surveillance officers watched a man they believed was Osman exit a building on Scotia Road and walk towards **STOCKWELL TUBE STATION [664•49]**. They were ordered not to let him board a train, but this he managed to do. He was challenged and shot dead.

Sadly it transpired this was a case of mistaken identity - the victim was actually Charles de Menezes - a Brazilian-born electrician. In 2008 an inquest returned an open verdict on his death.

ARREST OF THE 21/7 BOMBERS

The would-be bombers were soon identified from CCTV and arrests followed. The actual bomb factory was on the ninth floor of **CURTIS HOUSE, LADDERSWOOD WAY [665•10]**. Here CTC made two arrests. The gang had purchased over 600 pints of peroxide which was mixed with liquid hydrogen and other substances.

These two cases signalled the real beginning of a secret war between the security services and al-Qaida. However, not that MI5 had been oblivious to the threat. In 2003 Kamel Bourgass stabbed and killed Manchester policeman Stephen Oake who was part of a team of officers sent to arrest him. Bourgass had fled London and was wanted in connection with a deadly ricin plot and (proposed) attack on the Heathrow Express train to Paris. Earlier MI5 and CTC officers raided his small flat above a chemist at **352 HIGH ROAD, WOOD GREEN [666•16]** and what they found prompted a nationwide hunt for Bourgass.

In March 2004, MI5 and New Scotland Yard under the auspices of Operation Crevis raided an Access storage facility near Heathrow Airport. A huge amount of ammonium nitrate had been stored here by al-Qaida opera-

664•49 Stockwell Station

Police officers at the station following the shooting of Charles de Menezes

Charles de Menezes

Ticket gate at Stockwell Station

Eye Spy Intelligence Magazine

Outside Stockwell Station is this mosaic memorial to the unfortunate Charles de Menezes

tives intent on bombing nightclubs, railways and the country's power and transport infrastructure.

Those arrested in connection with al-Qaida and terrorism are regarded as most dangerous. And in such cases in London, prisoners are always proc-essed at the high security **PADDINGTON GREEN POLICE STATION [667•56]**. The 21/7 bombers and a number of suspects who ended up at the US Guantanamo Bay prison, were all held here. It has been described as the most important counter-terrorist station in the country.

In another successful operation, a plot by al-Qaida terrorists to secure red mercury was also stopped. In this case a journalist assisted New Scotland Yard and MI5. A terror gang met with an undercover reporter who said he could supply a kilo of red mercury. A deal was brokered at Liverpool Street Station **(See Site 125•08)** under the eyes of MI5 and watching police. The group were willing to pay £500,000 for the mercury.

On 9 September, the gang were arrested as they left another meeting at the **HOLIDAY INN HOTEL, BRENT CROSS [668•18]**.

665•10

668•18
Holiday Inn Hotel, Brent Cross

Curtis House, Ladderswood Way
Inset: Two of the 21/7 bombers surrender to police at the flats

Location of an important MI5 sting operation

Eye Spy Intelligence Magazine

SPY SITES OF LONDON

666 • 16

Kamel Bourgass lived in the flat above the chemist

667 • 56

352 High Road, Wood Green

Paddington Green Police Station, 2-4 Harrow Road

Eye Spy Intelligence Magazine

SPY SITES OF LONDON

XXIV
Intelligence Services Evolve
Spies, Assassins, Honeytraps and Bomb Plots

If ever an intelligence operation needed a stroke of luck it was one codenamed Overt. MI5 had surveilled around 20 suspects in London who were in the final stages of an airline terrorist plot that could have easily resulted in over 2,000 casualties. The terrorists planned to adapt plastic fizzy drink bottles to hold a special explosives' mix (base mixture primarily hydrogen peroxide). The soft drink containers would avoid airport detectors and their contents could be reconstituted (mixed) in the aircraft's toilets.

These were nervous times for MI5 the FBI and US Homeland Security. So too for a few political and security chiefs who were privy to the facts. All the while the CIA were watching intently, fearful that any attack could prove disastrous again for America.

MI5 and New Scotland Yard eventually identified the senior bomb plotters, secured valuable intelligence after bugging at least one terrorist safe house, and in the end thwarted the

669 • 03

Former New Scotland Yard anti-terrorist chief Andy Hayman

386A Forest Road, Walthamstow
The terrorist bomb factory in London bugged by MI5. Much evidence was gleaned here, including the identities of some of the bomb plotters

Eye Spy Intelligence Magazine

479

Forest Gate Police Station, 350-360 Romford Road

Operation Overt saved the lives of thousands of airline passengers

plot. But this hardly begins to touch upon the drama that was played out in the capital cities of Britain, America and Pakistan.

Known as the Liquid Bomb Plot, intelligence men like New Scotland Yard's counter-terrorist officials Peter Clarke and Andy Hayman, the amicable Homeland Security Secretary Michael Chertoff, and the former head of the NSA and D/CIA Michael Hayden were all involved. While US Intelligence wanted the plot stopped sooner, John Reid, Britain's tough-talking Home Secretary gave MI5 time to gather enough evidence to convict the entire terror cell and put them behind bars.

After assembling a massive 200-strong investigative team, MI5's objective was of course to determine the primary players, their target[s] and the bomb delivery mechanism. MI5's A4 Watchers directorate working with New Scotland Yard teams soon had the suspects under surveillance, but there was real concern that the security teams could stumble across each other because so many targets were being monitored. In the end the operation sorted itself out, and the suspects were identified. So too the primary bomb factory, the type of explosives and delivery method.

BREAKTHROUGH

While MI5 bugged the bomb factory at **386A FOREST ROAD, WALTHAMSTOW [669•03]**, purchased by the gang for nearly £140,000, a female surveillance officer observed one of the gang at an Internet cafe. She was instructed to reload his computer screen after the suspect departed. Disturbingly, up popped the flight times of seven US-bound aircraft. British Intelligence now knew the sheer enormity of the proposed terror operation.

All the while communications between the London gang and a terrorist controller in Pakistan were increasing. The man heading up the plot was well known to MI5 and his name sat high in its Registry.

In August 2006, Counter Terrorism Command launched numerous raids in the city and several suspects were arrested, charged and some jailed for life. Police were surprised the terrorists had purchased the property on Forest Road, for just a few hundred

The Bridge To China Town

feet away at **350-360 ROMFORD ROAD, FOREST GATE [670•07]**, is a major police station. 'Hiding in plain sight' is an intelligence term which comes to mind here.

Less than a month later, on 1 September, MI5 decided to end yet another plot that was moving beyond the drawing board. Al-Qaida operatives were detained at **THE BRIDGE TO CHINA TOWN RESTAURANT, 30 BOROUGH ROAD [671•23]** following a lengthy surveillance and eavesdropping operation. The gang had discussed various high profile targets including **THE LONDON EYE [672•23]**. Besides the restaurant address, various other locations on Borough Road were raided by 50 armed officers. The suspects were charged with terrorism offences.

ASSASSINS STRIKE IN LONDON AS MI6 AGENT KILLED

The KGB had a reputation for eliminating targets in bizarre ways, therefore when one of President Vladimir Putin's most vociferous opponents was poisoned in London, suspicion immediately fell upon its successor - the Federal Security Service (FSB).

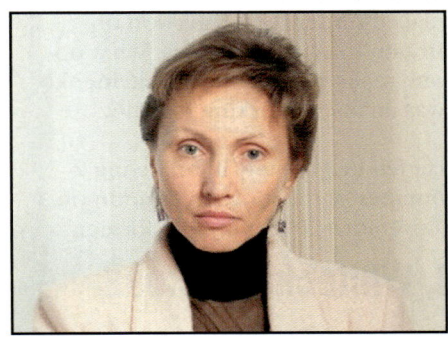

The London Eye

Marina Litvinenko

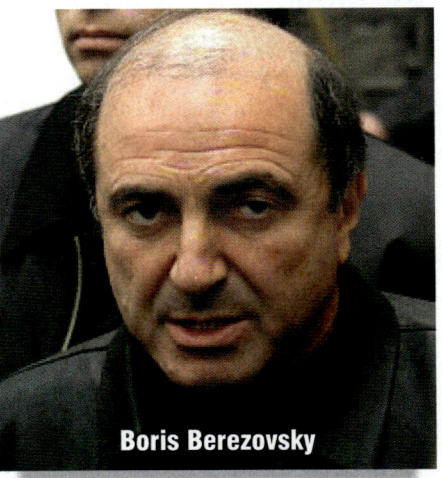

Boris Berezovsky

Alexander Litvinenko

Few people in the intelligence world have not heard of the strange death of Alexander Litvinenko, 43. He defected to Britain in 2000 with his wife Marina and their young son. The ex-spy worked for London-based Boris Berezovsky, a billionaire friend of former President Boris Yeltsin and a sworn enemy of President Putin.

Litvinenko provided Berezovsky with information on two bombings in Moscow and Volgodonsk in 1999 in which three hundred civilians died. Litvinenko said the incidents were a deception to generate support for a war against Chechnya. The files he passed on implicated Russian agents. Based on this information, Berezovsky produced a documentary called *Attack on Russia* which angered the Kremlin. Litvinenko then wrote a book with historian Yuri Felshtinsky - *Blowing Up Russia* - which further inflamed the situation.

Felshtinsky, a Russian living in the United States, had worked tirelessly to help the Litvinenkos in their quest to flee Russia. Berezovsky even provided

SPY SITES OF LONDON

Yuri Felshtinsky

Abracadabra Restaurant, 91 Jermyn Street

a private jet in this case to assist the exfiltration operation.

The former FSB officer was a constant thorn in the side of Moscow after he defected to the UK and launched a number of media campaigns against Putin's government accusing it of corruption and criminality. His writings and speeches were brushed aside by Moscow. Nevertheless, he was placed under the protection of Britain's security services. What no-one realised at the time - Litvinenko was an agent working for MI6.

He fell desperately ill following a number of meetings in London on 1 November 2006 with two former

University College Hospital, 235 Euston Road

Yuri Felshtinsky asleep on Berezovsky's private jet

Royal London Hospital, Whitechapel Road

intelligence associates, Andrei Lugovoi and Dmitri Kovtun and a third man Vyacheslav Sokolenko. Marina requested medical assistance for her husband - exactly six years to the day he had been granted asylum by the British authorities.

New Scotland Yard began an investigation after doctors discovered he had been poisoned. Specialists in London confirmed they had found significant quantities of thallium, a particularly nasty metal toxin once used in rat poison that is both tasteless and odourless. It transpired this was incorrect and new tests revealed Litvinenko had ingested the deadly radioactive isotope Polonium-210 - which was of military grade. As his condition deteriorated, he was secretly moved to **UNIVERSITY**

Eye Spy Intelligence Magazine

SPY SITES OF LONDON

Andrei Lugovoi

Dmitri Kovtun

A police officer stands guard outside the Litvinenkos residence

Mario Scaramella

New Scotland Yard police and forensic specialists search the Litvinenkos house for clues into his murder. MI5 officers are also on the scene

COLLEGE HOSPITAL, 235 EUSTON ROAD [673•15]. Sadly, he would die here, but not before revealing clues about his killers. His post mortem examination was conducted by a specialist team at the **ROYAL LONDON HOSPITAL [674•01]** which had been carefully selected by government nuclear specialists.

INVESTIGATION

Senior officials at New Scotland Yard and MI5 began retracing the days and weeks leading up to the poisoning. Officials also analysed several threatening e-mails sent to Litvinenko before the incident. Besides meeting the Russians he also met a mysterious Italian intelligence contact man called Mario Scaramella. Scaramella told Litvinenko he had some interesting information relating to the death of his friend Anna Politkovskaya who had been assassinated a month earlier in Moscow. The two men met at a pre-determined location in **PICCADILLY CIRCUS [675•55].** For decades this area has been a popular meeting point for intelligence people, agents and handlers. Litvinenko took Scaramella to the Japanese sushi restaurant - **ITSU, 67 PICCADILLY [676•55].** He ate while Marco showed him an e-mail print out containing a list of people, including FSB agents who were allegedly responsible for the death of Politkovskaya.

Litvinenko then met with the Russians at the **MILLENNIUM HOTEL, GROSVENOR SQUARE [677•55].** Here he drank a cup of green tea.

MI5 specialists and forensic experts searched the sushi restaurant, the

SPY SITES OF LONDON

Millennium Hotel, Grosvenor Square
Police arrive at the hotel - the location where Litvinenko was poisoned

Itsu Sushi Restaurant, 167 Piccadilly

Pescatori Restaurant, Dover Street

Millennium Hotel and Litvinenko's home. At all three locations they discovered traces of Polonium-210, a substance used in the chain reaction to detonate a nuclear bomb. The radioactive isotope is deadly if ingested or enters the body via a cut or other orifice. A single grain is sufficient to kill. Inside a teapot at the

New Scotland Yard and MI5 search the Litvinenkos family house

Millennium Hotel, significant traces of Polonium-210 were found. MI5 believe this is how Litvinenko was contaminated and assassinated.

MI5 and forensic specialists then retraced Litvinenko and the men's movements on 1 November. Traces of Polonium-210 were discovered at numerous addresses, including the **SHERATON PARK LANE HOTEL [678•55]** where the group met other associates. The men then enjoyed a drink at the popular **ABRACADABRA RESTAURANT, 91 JERMYN STREET [679•42]**, shortly after visiting **PARKES HOTEL, 41 BEAUFORT GARDENS [680•44]**. Contamination was found at both sites. However, of much significance were traces found at the **PESCATORI RESTAURANT,**

Police inside the offices of Boris Berezovsky's companies

Piccadilly Circus
Litvinenko met Italian intelligence contact man Mario Scaramella here

675•55

Eye Spy Intelligence Magazine

Parkes Hotel, 41 Beaufort Gardens

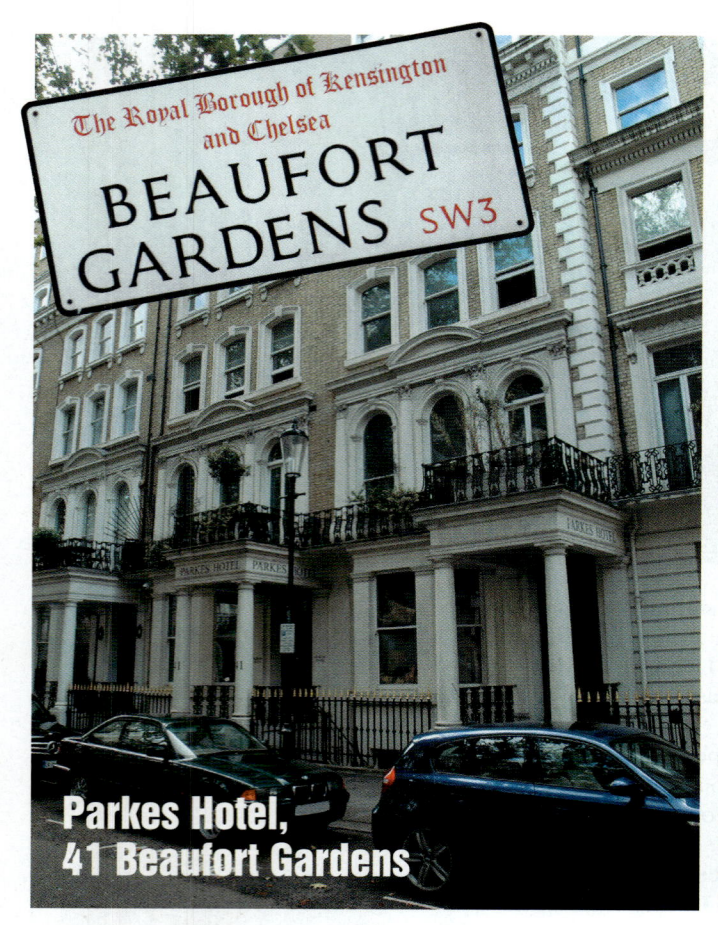

DOVER STREET [681•55]. Andrei Lugovoi had eaten here *before* he met Litvinenko and visited the other addresses. Additional sites were also investigated including offices occupied by Berezovsky's companies, at **25** and **58 GROSVENOR STREET [682•55] [683•55].** More traces of the radioactive isotope were found here.

Litvinenko passed away on 23 November. His grave can be found in **HIGHGATE CEMETERY [684•14].**

The agent's supporters were in little doubt as to who ordered the assassination. At the same time, and in a move described as "propaganda" by a Kremlin official, Britain announced former KGB officer and MI6 agent Oleg Gordievsky had been appointed

Sheraton Park Lane Hotel, Piccadilly

Oleg Gordievsky with Margaret Thatcher wearing his CMG medal

Highgate Cemetery

684•14

Companion of the Most Distinguished Order of the Saint Michael and Saint George (CMG) for services rendered. Interestingly, 007 author and MI6 man Ian Fleming made his fictitious agent James Bond a CMG in his book - *From Russia With Love*.

682•55

25 Grosvenor Street

683•55

58 Grosvenor Street

Eye Spy Intelligence Magazine

487

Prime suspect Andrei Lugovoi maintains he is innocent

MI5 DIRECTOR-GENERAL STEPS DOWN

In April 2007, Eliza Manningham-Buller, only the second woman to head the Security Service, stepped down. She served in MI5 for 33 years. At that time the Service was monitoring some 30 terror plots and had 1,600 people under various forms of surveillance. One of her last comments raised fears about the possibility of a biological attack, when she warned that more should be done to protect laboratories and research wings within universities. MI5 then embarked on a nationwide tour of the country advising organisations controlling security at such sites.

Buller's replacement was Jonathan Evans, 49, a counter-terrorism specialist. His experience in this field would be invaluable to Britain as the nation faced increasing threats and attacks.

Eliza Manningham-Buller

Alexander Litvinenko pictured in 1999

COURTESY: YURI FELSHTINSKY

HITMAN AT THE HILTON

One of Mr Evans first tasks was to thwart a plot to assassinate Russian billionaire Boris Berezovsky.

The operation, supposedly hatched in Moscow, was simple. Berezovsky would be lured to the **LONDON HILTON HOTEL, 22 PARK LANE [685•55]** (close to his offices) for a meeting where he would be shot.

Sources close to MI5 say the would-be assassin - a Russian, was followed to a number of locations in the capital where he tried to buy a hand gun. With the suspect was a young boy "who seemed to be acting as a lookout," an official said. To complicate matters further, it's understood MI5 officers had hired a room next to where Berezovsky was to meet with his intended killer. This suggests the would-be assassin was in fact lured to

Leicester Square

Eye Spy Intelligence Magazine

685 • 55

London Hilton Hotel, 22 Park Lane

THE LONDON SANCTION

Ashraf Marwan had lived quietly in the affluent Mayfair district of London for a number of years. The 65-year-old Egyptian billionaire was known in the intelligence world, but his connections with the Israeli spy organisation - the Mossad - were not. However, when he was publicly named as a double agent in 2003, for the part he played in the Egypt-Israel conflict in 1973, all that changed and Marwan told friends he felt vulnerable.

Vladimir Terluk

his destination believing Berezovsky had agreed to meet him.

A New Scotland Yard officer issued a brief statement: "We can confirm that a man was arrested on 21 June, and released into the custody of the immigration services on 23 June." The suspect was actually arrested on suspicion of conspiracy to murder in connection with an alleged attempt to assassinate the tycoon. The man was refused entry back into the UK for ten years.

Eye Spy later learned Berezovsky had been secretly flown out of the country prior to the arranged meeting. Sadly for him, it would not be the last attempt on his life.

In 2003, Berezovsky's personal security detail tricked an FSB contact man into a meeting at a venue used by Moscow's spies. The location was next to two **PHONE BOXES, LEICESTER SQUARE [686•62]** behind a gentlemen's underground toilet. The agent, Vladimir Terluk, admitted he was part of an operation to test just how easy it would be to get to Berezovsky. The plan was for an assassin to get close enough to the businessman to jab him with a poisoned pen.

Eye Spy Intelligence Magazine

489

Jonathan Evans

His fears were proven correct when on 27 June 2007, he was found dead on the pavement after he had seemingly fallen from the fifth floor of his luxury flat in **24 CARLTON HOUSE TERRACE [687•42]**. Marwan died instantly and MI5 and Special Branch were soon at the scene.

Later that day, Marwan should have attended a business meeting at the nearby **INSTITUTE OF DIRECTORS BUILDING, 116 PALL MALL [688•42]**. Bizarrely, one of the people in the building who was due to meet Marwan, actually saw two men of Mediterranean appearance standing on the balcony of Marwan's flat just seconds after he had fallen. Though his death was treated as suspicious, it was difficult to prove. Nevertheless, it transpired Marwan was close to completing a book on his role in the 1973 war, and some feared his expose would cause much embarrassment to certain agencies.

The two mysterious characters were never traced, but an indication that this case was far from a simple acci-

Ashraf Marwan

dent came after two vital pieces of evidence simply went missing. Firstly the manuscript was never found, but more importantly, the shoes that he was wearing when he fell disappeared after the body was removed. There

24 Carlton House Terrace

Eye Spy Intelligence Magazine

SPY SITES OF LONDON

688•42

Institute of Directors, 116 Pall Mall

were several plant pots on Marwan's balcony: because of an illness he would have been unable to climb over the rail, so detectives conjectured that if his shoes had dirt from the flower pots on the soles, he must have used them to help him climb over. If this was so, the verdict would have been suicide. With no shoes his death remains unexplained. However, Marwan's family are convinced he was killed by rogue elements of an intelligence agency to keep him quiet - evidenced by his stolen memoir and shoes. The case remains unexplained.

MOSSAD OPERATIONAL IN LONDON - AGAIN

Israel has always been concerned about its neighbours securing nuclear weapons, despite the fact that Tel Aviv has some 200 warheads of its own.

The Mossad was aware of a secret Syrian nuclear facility being built in the desert, but required more intelligence. Thus when it learned a Syrian diplomat was travelling to London carrying a batch of secret files on the site contained on a computer, it decided to launch a most audacious operation.

The Mossad team surveilled the diplomat leave the **SYRIAN EMBASSY, BELGRAVE SQUARE [689•42]**. They traced him to a hotel and watched him visit a restaurant for dinner. Operatives then surreptitiously entered his room and found his laptop computer which was not encrypted. Here they found all the technical blueprints for the nuclear site and a plethora of associated information, including leading scientists and others associated with the programme. In the Autumn of 2007, a commando raid was launched on the Syrian site and it was destroyed.

A FORTUNATE ESCAPE

Like every Thursday evening at the popular **TIGER TIGER NIGHTCLUB, 29 HAYMARKET [690•42]** in London's West End, partygoers had

Covert photographs of the secret Syrian nuclear reactor before it was destroyed

Eye Spy Intelligence Magazine

491

Syrian Embassy, 8 Belgrave Square

turned up in numbers to enjoy ladies night - a weekly event that attracts about 1,450 people. Hundreds of clubs and social establishments, including Tiger Tiger, had recently received a 50-page document from the security services advising staff to remain vigilant and security conscious. The file provided guidance and advice for management and staff alike. It was a timely reminder. At 1.25am on 28 June 2007, a unit from the London Ambulance Service was called to the club to tend to a person who had been injured in a fall. On their arrival, a medic noticed grey smoke issuing from the inside of a Mercedes parked in front of the nightclub. He quickly alerted police. At 1.40am several police officers arrived at the scene and examined the vehicle. Peering through the windows they noticed a number of propane gas canisters. It was a serious situation. On the back seat a mobile phone caught the attention of one of the officers. He instantly realised the vehicle was in effect, a giant IED (improvised explosive device). The officer disabled the phone from another device and walked quickly away. Officers later recovered about a dozen petrol cans (14 gallons) and an undisclosed number of bags containing industrial and household nails and tacks. The quick-thinking ambulance staff and policeman had averted a major attack and saved lives.

Unbeknown to the security services, outside the club, another Mercedes parked illegally in nearby Cockspur

Tiger Tiger Nightclub, 29 Haymarket

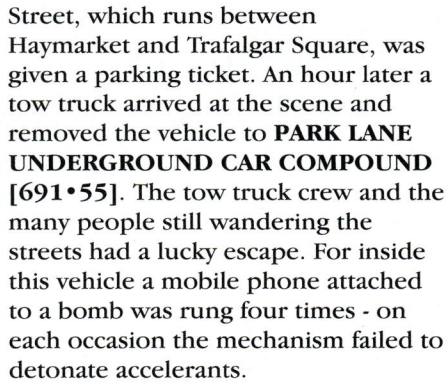

Street, which runs between Haymarket and Trafalgar Square, was given a parking ticket. An hour later a tow truck arrived at the scene and removed the vehicle to **PARK LANE UNDERGROUND CAR COMPOUND [691•55]**. The tow truck crew and the many people still wandering the streets had a lucky escape. For inside this vehicle a mobile phone attached to a bomb was rung four times - on each occasion the mechanism failed to detonate accelerants.

The al-Qaida terrorists fled the city that night and made their way to Scotland where they would attack Glasgow Airport. A major CTC-MI5 operation followed and the culprits were soon apprehended.

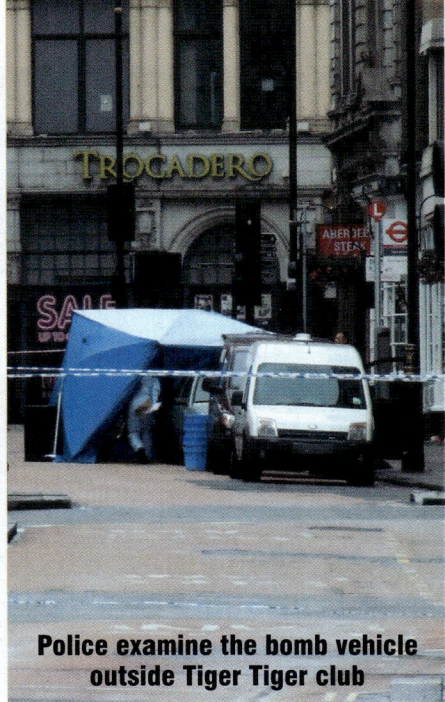

Newham Hotel, 349-353 Romford Road

Police examine the bomb vehicle outside Tiger Tiger club

Eye Spy Intelligence Magazine

The bombers fled Haymarket after hiring a London rickshaw

MI5 learned the bombers had visited London six weeks before the attack to select their target. The men stayed at the **NEWHAM HOTEL, 349-353 ROMFORD ROAD [692•07]**.

According to MI5, the area around Covent Garden was "meticulously researched."

INQUEST INTO DIANA DEATH

Ten years after the death of Princess Diana, 36, her lover Dodi Fayed, 42, and chauffeur and suspected MI6 agent Henri Paul, the final inquest opened at London's High Court on 2 October 2008. The jury of six women and five men selected by ballot, would decide if she was killed unlawfully, or if it was a simple tragic accident. In the end they ruled out foul play. One man who gave evidence was former MI6 Chief Sir Richard Dearlove. He too rejected any suggestion of a conspiracy to kill Diana. However, the ruling has not stopped the conspiracy theorists.

691•55

Park Lane Underground Car Compound

On Her Majesty's Postage Stamps

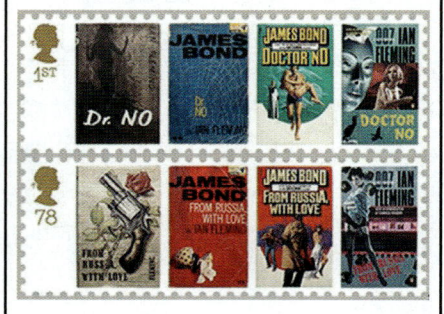

In January 2008, Britain's Royal Mail unveiled a set of postage stamps depicting the covers of Ian Fleming's James Bond 007 novels. The stamps marked the 100th anniversary of the author's birth in 1908.

Casino Royale, Dr No, Goldfinger, Diamonds Are Forever, For Your Eyes Only and *From Russia With Love* are some of the titles that appeared on the stamps.

Julietta Edgar, Head of Royal Mail Special Stamps said: "Fictional heroes don't come much more famous than James Bond, so it's entirely appropriate that we start our 2008 special stamp programme by honouring his creator, Ian Fleming."

Sir Richard Dearlove

COURTESY: PEMBROKE COLLEGE, CAMBRIDGE ANNUAL GAZETTE

494

Eye Spy Intelligence Magazine

AFTERNOON TEA AND POISON

In April 2008, MI6 agent and former KGB colonel Oleg Gordievsky claimed he had been the target of a Russian assassin in November 2007. Attending a function in the south of England, Gordievsky said someone had poisoned his food or drink with Thallium. Two days later he fell ill at his home in Guildford and was rushed to hospital. At the time nothing was reported in the press and details only began to surface six months later.

A furious Gordievsky said British Intelligence had not listened to his concerns, nor were they convinced about the poisoning. The former spy said: "I've known for some time that I am on a list drawn up by rogue elements in Moscow." Further information was not released and the affair was quietly closed.

Ex-KGB officer and MI6 agent Oleg Gordievsky

A forlorn Mr Fayed arrives at court for the opening of the inquest into the death of Princess Diana, his son Dodi and MI6 contact man Henri Paul

DATA DISASTERS

In June 2008, a senior intelligence official was suspended after two sets of important intelligence documents, prepared by the Joint Intelligence Committee (JIC), the UK's main advisory body on intelligence matters, were found by members of the public. They were left on trains in-coming and out-going from Waterloo Station in London. Three weeks later, in what appears to be an unrelated incident, the chairman on the JIC, Alex Allan, was found unconscious in a pool of blood in his home.

The first batch of secret files concerned the al-Qaida threat and a memorandum on the Iraqi security forces. They were handed in to the BBC by a bemused passenger. The papers were inside an orange-coloured folder and headed: *'Al-Qaida: Constraints and Vulnerabilities'* and describe al-Qaida's threat in Pakistan and Afghanistan. The report, commissioned by the Foreign Office and Home Office, the government departments which oversee MI6 and MI5, were marked classified *'UK Top Secret'* and each page was stamped *'For UK, US, Canadian and Australian Eyes Only'*. Also in the folder was a classified document about Britain's views on the capabilities of the Iraqi security forces, titled: *'Iraqi Security Forces: More or Less Challenged?'*.

The person responsible for the debacle turned out to be a senior civil servant who worked in the Cabinet Office's intelligence and security unit.

Within days of the security breach, it transpired a second batch of secret official files were found left on a train on the same day (11 June) and also on a Waterloo-bound train! These secret papers covered the UK's policies on tackling global terrorist funding, drugs trafficking and money laundering and emanated from an international conference attended by officers from the Financial Action Task Force (FATF).

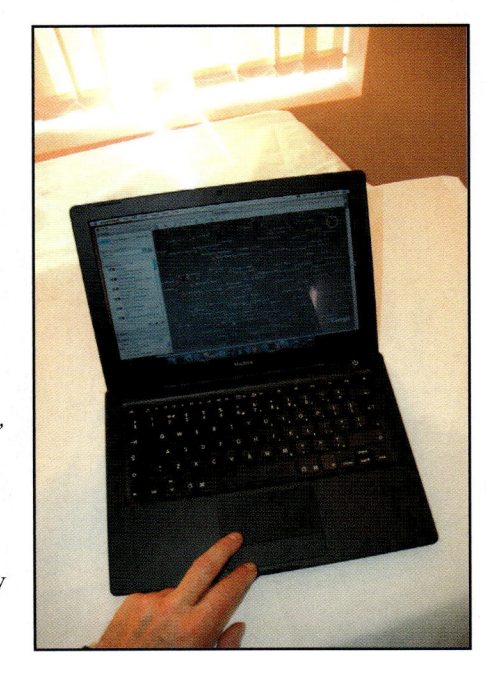

Eye Spy Intelligence Magazine

693•42

St James's Palace

Alexander Lebedev and Vladimir Putin

the Royal addresses would be reconnoitred in future months.

The investigation remains open - and other intelligence continues to be added to the Praline file today.

OPEN SOURCE

In March 2009, former KGB officer Alexander Lebedev, 49, purchased one of the UK's most important and long-running newspapers. Lebedev, a billionaire businessman, bought around 75% of the *London Evening Standard* newspaper for just £1.

The paper, based at **NORTHCLIFFE HOUSE, DERRY STREET [695•60]** has a circulation of just under 300,000, and passed into the hands of the *Evening Press*. This company was formed by Mr Lebedev and his London-based son Evgeny Lebedev, 28, and is owned by Lebedev Holdings.

Intelligence watchers greeted the purchase with much suspicion, but Lebedev said he is a strong believer in a free press and "would not interfere with the paper editorially." Sir Peregrine Worsthorne, former editor of *The Sunday Telegraph*, said the takeover was a sign of "national decline."

Lebedev, coincidentally, used the *Evening Standard* to gather intelligence (open source) when he was operating as a KGB spy in London!

CONTEST AND AWARENESS

In March 2009, senior intelligence and military officials publicly admitted that the possibility of al-Qaida detonating a radiological dispersal device (RDD - 'dirty bomb') or chemical bomb on

© JOHAN BILIEN

An investigation by the intelligence services and Ministry of Defence soon revealed the scale of the problem in respect of computer losses. Nearly 1,000 electronic devices had gone missing or were reported stolen from 2000-2008!

OPERATION PRALINE

In 2006, CTC officers from Leeds detained three men in connection with a terrorist plot that targeted the Royal Family. The men were stopped at Manchester Airport and after a search of a computer, numerous addresses associated with the Royal Household were discovered, including **ST JAMES'S PALACE [693•42]** and **KENSINGTON PALACE [694•56]**. Masses of terrorist literature was also found. MI5 and officers involved in the counter-terrorist operation codenamed Praline, were convinced the material signalled the beginning of a major terrorist endeavour and that

694•56

Kensington Palace

695·60

London Evening Standard, Northcliffe House, Derry Street

New Scotland Yard Police Assistant Commissioner Bob Quick

It was unusual for a government minister in the UK to impart (in such great detail) - assessments made by British Intelligence, but this is exactly what happened. The UK's international counter-terrorist measures are contained within a 174-page pseudo public-official awareness programme called CONTEST. Four primary areas are covered - Pursue, Prevent, Protect and Prepare... collectively they are known as 'The Four P's'.

OPERATION PATHWAY - AN ERROR AT DOWNING STREET

On 8 April 2009, reports of several police raids started to appear via the newswires at tea-time. Intelligence watchers were puzzled why so many intense and high-profile operations had taken place in daylight hours. Part of the answer to that question lay two hundred miles away in the heart of London with a forlorn senior police officer and a decidedly frustrated MI5.

Two hours into this huge precise and spectacularly well-coordinated operation, which began in Liverpool at around 5.00pm, police vehicles were already dispersing 12 suspected terrorists to holding cells in Birmingham, Manchester and Leeds. The very scale of this operation, involving hundreds of officers from a variety of forces and intelligence services, was

the streets of Britain was no longer an impossibility. Home Secretary Jacqui Smith, believed that terrorists on Britain's streets not only have the capability to build IED's (improvised explosive devices), but said "it's quite probable and realistic to think they will use them."

Police and journalists outside a suspected terrorist's house in Manchester

Eye Spy Intelligence Magazine

497

SPY SITES OF LONDON

Prime Minister Gordon Brown

evidence enough that this was not an immediate response event. The hidden hand of MI5's A4 surveillance section was all over this important operation. In Downing Street, Prime Minister Gordon Brown lost no time in announcing the police were dealing with a "very big terrorist plot."

Information of significance had been presented to him just days earlier at a COBRA meeting. The most powerful counter-terrorist figure in the country - Metropolitan Police Assistant Commissioner Bob Quick, had briefed senior ministers over a top secret ongoing operation that, according to government sources, was soon to reach its climax. However, that's not what some intelligence watchers close to MI5 believe.

Security officials and ministers then gathered for another morning briefing at Downing Street on 8 April. Mr Quick advised that North West Counter-Terrorist Command, aided by specialist police from Liverpool and Lancashire forces, were ready to "take down an al-Qaida sleeper cell."

That action was needed immediately, and the nature of the threat immense, seems to have overtaken this experienced officer. For unbeknown to him, as he exited the vehicle to walk the few paces into Downing Street, he was photographed carrying a bundle of documents outside of a translucent plastic folder. Mr Quick had been reading the papers in his car, but forgot to make good their security. Ninety-percent of the text of a document marked *'Secret'* was readable - if one zoomed-in on the paper... something which journalists and editors with a keen eye did. Had the media published or aired the content of this file, it would undoubtedly have alerted the targets in the north, and probably a number of individuals who were yet to be identified.

Operation Pathway had been exposed, so too the number of alleged terror suspects, their locations, the police forces involved, and the suspects dispersal locations. Pathway's end game was hurriedly brought forward and the raids began. The next day, Bob Quick resigned.

MI5 had wanted more time to gather information and this is evidenced by what happened over the next few weeks. Of the 11 men who were arrested - only one was ever brought to book - and he was jailed in America.

In September 2009, news leaked that experienced Foreign Office official and MI6 officer Sir John Sawers was to become the new Chief of MI6

NEW 'C' OF MI6 ANNOUNCED

On 16 June 2009, it was revealed Sir John Sawers would be taking over as the new Chief of MI6. There was also a leaked report that the Service was to hold a tuxedo and gown ball to celebrate its 100th birthday. The venue for the event was kept top secret!

100 Years of SIS DINNER DANCE

October 2009

Cocktails and Hors d'oeuvres at 7.30pm

Dinner at 8.00pm

Dancing 10.00pm - 1.00pm

Dress accordingly

Sir John Sawers steps out as MI6 Chief

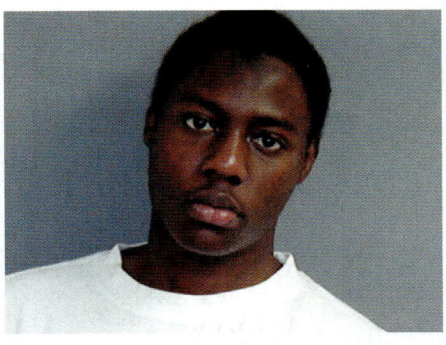

Umar Farouk Abdulmutallab

FBI explosives' experts replicated the device and discovered it would have blown a huge hole in the fuselage of the airliner causing a catastrophic event. A judge sentenced Abdulmutallab to five life terms plus 50 years - he will spend the rest of his life behind bars.

CYBER AND BANK SPECIALISTS

By 2010 it was no longer a surprise to find all three British Intelligence services placing adverts in the mainstream or specialist press. MI6 was even advertising for staffers on the London Underground! Such was the interest in joining the intelligence community, that in 2009, MI6 had nearly 300,000 applicants - but just 500 were successful.

THE UNDERWEAR BOMBER

On Christmas Day 2009, Umar Farouk Abdulmutallab, a Nigerian-born student living in London, attempted to bring down a Detroit-bound airliner using a specially designed bomb contained within his underwear.

Abdulmutallab, 23, studied at the engineering wing of University College London, and rented an apartment at **2 MANSFIELD STREET [696•55]**.

The terrorist boarded Northwest Airline Flight 243 in Amsterdam, and as the aircraft approached the USA, he tried to detonate the bomb, but even though it ignited, the device failed to explode. He was overpowered by passengers and arrested on arrival in Detroit.

Film crews and journalists gather outside 2 Mansfield Street

Eye Spy Intelligence Magazine

696·55

2 Mansfield Street

FORMER MI6 EMPLOYEE ARRESTED FOR ESPIONAGE

An MI5 counter-espionage team created a classic ruse to trap an ex-MI6 employee in a London hotel - this as he allegedly attempted to trade an external computer hard-drive containing a wealth of MI5 and MI6 operational secrets for a staggering £2 million. The Security Service discovered Daniel Houghton, 25, who resided at **ALLERTON HOUSE, ISLINGTON [697·10]**, had in his possession a large number of electronic secret and top secret files which would have provided any foreign service with a deep and revealing insight into how British Intelligence, in particular MI5, gathers its intelligence.

Britain's foreign intelligence arm also used the banking crisis as an opportunity to recruit out-of-work city financiers and analysts from the City or Square Mile. They were required for a special directorate involved in analysis of money laundering, terrorism financing, front companies, bogus government deals etc.

697·10
Allerton House, Islington

500

Eye Spy Intelligence Magazine

SPY SITES OF LONDON

Houghton, who was born in Holland but has dual British-Dutch nationality and is fluent in English, is said to have obtained the material whilst on active service for MI6 between September 2007 and May 2009.

Intelligence sources say that around August 2009, Houghton made a number of telephone calls to a potential foreign buyer (intelligence service). How MI5 obtained details of this action remain secret, but Eye Spy understands the Service was tipped-off by Dutch Intelligence. MI5's counter-espionage branch then made contact with Houghton and asked to see the 'goods'. An initial meeting took place in February 2010, the location was bugged by MI5. Houghton explained that he had down-loaded the information onto CDs and DVDs and secreted a copy at his mother's home in Devon.

A second meeting was then arranged in a central London hotel with two undercover MI5 operatives. Special Branch men and women watched developments as they mixed with guests. The location's exterior was also monitored and a specially chosen room fitted with recording devices.

On 1 March, Houghton arrived at the hotel and made his way to the lift and towards the primed room. Inside he allegedly handed over at least one memory stick, and the internal hard-drive of a laptop computer. After the contents were examined, the undercover MI5 team handed over a suitcase packed with a reported £900,000 in cash ($1.5m).

It is not known if the money was real, or a figure quoted to Houghton.

As soon as the exchange was made, Houghton bid farewell, left the room and pressed the button to summon a lift to the hotel lobby. At this precise moment a plain-clothed police team swooped and the suspect was handcuffed. As he was bundled into a police car, he allegedly shouted, "you've got the wrong man." He was subsequently charged with theft and a breach of the Official Secrets Act.

THE VYDIZHENET (THE PROTEGE)

In late June 2010, FBI chief Robert Mueller green-lighted one of the most extensive FBI counter-espionage operations ever undertaken. Over 100 FBI officers supported by various police forces, acted in unison and arrested ten suspected agents of Russia's overseas intelligence gathering agency - the SVR. This signalled the closure of an audacious Moscow Center programme to embed sleeper agents deep into American society. But unbeknown to anyone, officials in the Bureau, the CIA, MI6 and MI5, had already met to prepare an agent swap list for Moscow: operatives and people Washington wanted freed.

The document was prepared and signed off by Leon Panetta - Director Central Intelligence Agency (D/CIA), and addressed to Mikhail Fradkov, Russia's Foreign Intelligence Service chief. But before anything could happen, the FBI needed to act quickly, hence without warning and simultaneously, the Russian spy network was rounded-up.

The proper term used in the intelligence world for the type of agent the

Former MI6 staffer Daniel Houghton attempted to sell secrets to a foreign entity for £2 million

4 Thurloe Street [698•47]

NetFly, 5 Young Street, Kensington [699•60]

Anna Chapman

SVR had deployed in the United States is an 'illegal' - so called because they operate outside the relative safety shield of Russia's diplomatic corp. In the UK, they might be described as sub-agents. And despite the press branding most of the spies incompetent, at least two of the agents were experienced in espionage.

For the United States Intelligence Community (USIC) it was a major coup, and within hours of pleading guilty on 8 July, American and Russian diplomats were in deep discussion over the spy exchange which had, of course, been discussed by US intelligence officials two weeks earlier.

One of those arrested by the Bureau was Anya Kuschenko who used the name Anna Chapman. In 2002, she married Alex, an Englishman and lived at **4 THURLOE STREET [698•47]**. By now she was already known in the FSB as a Vydizhenet (protege). Building her Legend (historical cover story) she found employment at **NETJETS EUROPE, 5 YOUNG STREET, KENSINGTON [699•60]**. However, she was soon asked to elevate herself into loftier circles and joined Prince Harry's favourite nightclub **BOUJIS, 43 THURLOE STREET, SOUTH KENSINGTON [700•47]**. Here she was instructed to "get close to the Royal."

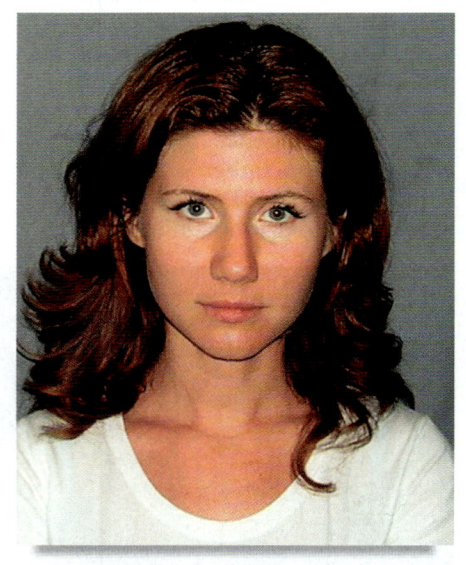

The SVR spy Chapman following her arrest by FBI counter-espionage officers in America

After Anna and Alex separated she was asked to leave for America in 2006. Her task, like that in London, was to climb the social, celebrity and political ladder. She received support from

502

Eye Spy Intelligence Magazine

Boujis, 43 Thurloe Street

Gareth Williams - GCHQ officer found dead in MI6 safe house

around a dozen SVR agents who had already embedded themselves into American society and were operating on the eastern seaboard.

However, the FBI rumbled the spies and a major surveillance operation secured all the evidence the Bureau needed to confirm they were committing espionage. By 2010, negotiations to release the spies in return for four Western agents and contact men held by Russia had concluded. As for Chapman, she has become somewhat of a celebrity in her own country, despite her failure as a spy.

Prince Harry

INCIDENT IN PIMLICO - BIZARRE DEATH OF GCHQ-MI6 MAN

On 23 August 2010, Gareth Williams naked and decomposing body was removed from **36 ALDERNEY STREET, PIMLICO [701•42]**.

There followed one of the biggest and most controversial investigations seen in London for years; for Williams was employed by GCHQ and on secondment to MI6 when he was discovered dead inside a padlocked sports bag.

Senior MI5 men visited the building with officers from New Scotland Yard and an MI6 liaison. The situation was viewed with concern - had he been the victim of an assassin or was his death the result of a sex game which went badly wrong? Either way, New Scotland Yard launched Operation Finlayson to find out what had really happened.

Holland Park Station
The last known movements of Gareth Williams were recorded by CCTV outside the station

Eye Spy Intelligence Magazine

701•42

36 Alderney Street

Williams living room as found by detectives investigating his strange death. Note the ginger wig - an item described as a "prop to confuse" and create doubt about his private life

COURTESY: NEW SCOTLAND YARD

By 25 August, the media rumour mill was in full swing with untrue stories concerning what detectives had actually discovered. A wardrobe containing dresses which would have fit the officer were discovered. Another report claimed he was gay with a propensity for visiting seedy bars, escort agencies and bondage. A journalist was told of "SIM cards from cell phones laid out in a ritualistic and macabre manner." The truth is more absorbing, but these case details were leaked to darken his image. Some suggest the dresses were intended to

A former MI5 agent and Eye Spy associate explains to a BBC Wales reporter why he believes Williams was murdered by a professional

703•23

Bar Code, Arch 69, Embankment

504

Eye Spy Intelligence Magazine

705·52

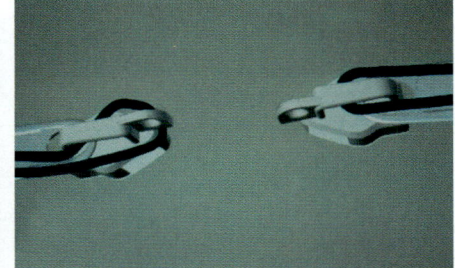

Patisserie Valerie, 94 Holland Park Avenue

British security expert Peter Faulding attempted to get into the bag and lock the padlock one hundred times.

Climbing into the bag and closing the zipper was possible, but he could not find a way to assemble and engage the locking mechanism from within.

Former soldier Jim Fetherstonhaugh (pictured) said his daughter had managed the feat

704·25

Royal Vauxhall Tavern, 372 Kennington Lane

Eye Spy Intelligence Magazine

505

community and in very close proximity to MI6 headquarters. The identity of the person for whom the second set of tickets had been purchased was never discovered.

As the investigation developed, it was learned he was seen in the company of people at the **PATISSERIE VALERIE, HOLLAND PARK [705•52]**. It later transpired these were his associates from MI6, perhaps his immediate superior. He was last seen alive on 14 August passing **HOLLAND PARK TUBE STATION [706•52]**.

Information then surfaced on two unidentified visitors to his flat, but they were later traced and eliminated from police enquiries.

Forensically, the scene was bizarre. There were few clues, but evidence did eventually emerge that another person was probably in the room when Williams died. However, the biggest mystery concerned how he got into the bag - was he ordered in and the second party closed the lock? Or did he somehow manage to climb in himself and manoeuvre the bag so the lock closed fast?

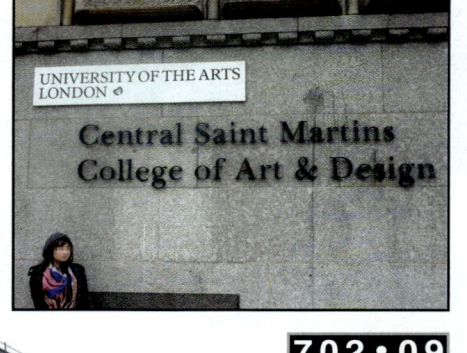

Security expert Peter Faulding said that whilst he duplicated Williams feat of getting into the bag, he failed on 100 occasions to engage the lock. However, former soldier Jim Fetherstonhaugh said his daughter, approximately the same size as Gareth, had managed to climb inside an identical bag and close it herself.

The room itself seemed to be 'stage managed'; little bits of evidence placed carefully here and there to arouse attention. A ginger wig on a chair caught the attention of detectives. Intelligence watcher Crispin Black said, "the death of Williams had the feel of a professional."

A former MI5 agent told Eye Spy the heating was nearly full on despite it being warm - this to help speed up decomposition of the body. Indeed, he also believes Williams was the victim of a professional assassin and the bag intended to carry his body away.

Investigators asked MI6 about his work, but cooperation was limited. Coroner Dr Fiona Wilcox ruled that Williams death was indeed suspicious.

Coroner Dr Fiona Wilcox

Crispin Black

be a present for a female friend and may have been part of his research into fashion. Williams studied clothing design at a night school in **CENTRAL SAINT MARTINS COLLEGE [702•09]**.

Williams occasionally drank at the **BAR CODE CLUB, ARCH 69, EMBANKMENT [703•23]**. Four tickets for two people were also found in his flat to events at the nearby **ROYAL VAUXHALL TAVERN [704•25]**. Both these venues are popular with London's gay community

702•09

Central Saint Martins College

506

Eye Spy Intelligence Magazine

707•08

708•42
Westminster Abbey

Stock Exchange, 10 Paternoster Square

THE RECONNAISSANCE MEN

MI5 infiltrated an al-Qaida terror cell that sought to bring more mayhem on the streets of London just days before Christmas 2010. Nine suspects were arrested on 20 December in a series of nationwide raids by officers from New Scotland Yard's Counter Terrorism Command and regional police forces. The arrests, which involved over 200 officers, were the result of months of careful investigation and an intricate surveillance operation in the capital that monitored several terrorist reconnaissance missions.

For much of 2010, MI5 had assisted several European intelligence services disrupt terror plots in Germany, Holland, Denmark, Belgium and France. With intelligence now suggesting a UK plot was reaching fruition, MI5 decided it was best to act, and in a coordinated police action, dawn raids took place in Birmingham, London, Cardiff and Stoke. Large amounts of information and materials were removed from a dozen or so properties. There was no official comment on what was recovered, other than a statement saying the "public were not in any danger."

Senior officers said the gang were deadly serious - this was the UK end of a plot that MI5 knew was part of a wider campaign initiated by those who support al-Qaida's Northern Project (planting operatives in European countries). A similar effort to strike American cities was enabled early in 2010, but disruptive efforts throughout the year by the FBI and

London Mayor Boris Johnson

CIA, meant that actions were limited and assigned to individuals.

PRIMARY TARGETS

When MI5 started to analyse information from computers and materials recovered at the raided addresses, other clues to the men's intentions became apparent. The group had various targets in mind including the **LONDON STOCK EXCHANGE, 10 PATERNOSTER SQUARE [707•08], WESTMINSTER ABBEY [708•42], CHURCH OF SCIENTOLOGY, BLACKFRIARS [709•08]** and the offices of Boris Johnson - the city's flamboyant mayor. These locations, complete with full addresses and post codes were found on a hand-written note next to a computer, and correlate with surveillance footage taken by MI5 of the men's journey around central London.

TO SPY OR NOT TO SPY?

In December 2010, Katia Zatuliveter, a 25-year-old Russian working as a parliamentary researcher for Liberal Democrat MP Mike Hancock, was arrested at Gatwick Airport and interviewed by MI5 at various hotels, including the **STRAND PALACE**

709•08

Mike Hancock

HOTEL [710•62]. This followed an MI5 briefing to the Home Secretary Theresa May on her alleged connections to the Russian foreign intelligence service, the SVR. Ms. Zatuliveter appealed against a deportation order, insisting that she was not a Russian spy. She began work for the MP in November 2006, soon after she arrived in the UK to study for a master's degree in peace studies at Bradford University.

She was quickly given a Commons pass and initially paid £250 a month before becoming Hancock's full-time researcher and parliamentary assistant. At the time, Hancock was MP for Portsmouth South, and sat on parliamentary groups for Azerbaijan and

Church of Scientology, Blackfriars

Eye Spy Intelligence Magazine

Portcullis House, Westminster [711•42]

Arundel House, 13-15 Arundel Street [713•62]

Ukraine as well as Russia. He was also a member of the Defence Select Committee, with whom he travelled to several former Eastern bloc countries.

Zatuliveter, who was born in Dagestan in the Caucasus, was first questioned by security officials when returning to the UK during the summer. She was arrested at the beginning of December after a briefing which apparently suggested the Security Service thought she was a sleeper agent. The case has faint echoes of the US spy scandal uncovered in 2010, when 10 Russian sleeper agents were deported from the United States. MI5 insisted she had liaised with a known Russian agent in **PORTCULLIS HOUSE, WESTMINSTER [711•42]**. This important building is opposite Parliament and houses Members of Parliament (MPs) offices, committee rooms and restaurants. MI5 Watchers also followed her to the **TRICYCLE THEATRE [712•21]** where a play called *The Great Game* was running. This only raised further suspicion amongst officials. Another alleged spy encounter took place at **ARUNDEL HOUSE, 13-15 ARUNDEL STREET [713•62]** during a meeting of the important Institute of Strategic Studies where she met a man called Boris. MI5 said he was a known SVR officer. By coincidence, she encountered Boris again outside **TEMPLE STATION [714•62]** - the inference being Boris was actually targeting or liaising with Zatuliveter.

Note proximity of Portcullis House to Parliament

Eye Spy Intelligence Magazine

SPY SITES OF LONDON

Katia Zatuliveter

Mr Hancock dismissed the spying allegations against Zatuliveter, telling one TV channel: "I think it is absolutely ludicrous. I have never had any inclination at all that Katia was anything other than a very conscientious worker. She had access to papers but none of them were in any way not public documents, in the sense that they were available at sometime, somewhere. I do not see what anyone would have benefited from that."

In November 2011, the Special Immigration Appeals Commission said it was satisfied Zatuliveter was not an SVR agent, despite MI5's information.

Tricycle Theatre, 269 Kilburn High Road

Temple Station

Strand Palace Hotel, 372 Strand

SPY SITES OF LONDON

A YEAR WITH MI6

In an unprecedented move, and as part of a number of events celebrating 100-years of MI6, British artist James Hart Dyke was invited to record the work of the Service for a full year. This resulted in a brilliant series of atmospheric oil paintings and sketches.

Dyke was also given permission to follow the organisation abroad, including Afghanistan, thus it was no surprise to see the odd canvas supporting spectacular views of this faraway land. But for balance, the artist compensated with views of London, including Battersea Power Station. This view was actually painted from the Service's Vauxhall Cross headquarters. James says that he had to duck so passersby on Vauxhall Bridge didn't see him. There are a number of London-based works, but it's important to remember that although a foreign intelligence collection agency, MI6 clearly performs much important work in the city.

Dyke's pre-project instruction to "show the world what it's like working for MI6," resulted in a series of dramatic works that caused much conversation and debate in the world of intelligence and art. The truth is, it could never have happened just a short time ago, and was indicative of Sir John Sawers (Chief of MI6) efforts to bring the Service out of the shadows. However, the idea was probably the result of the celebratory planning team created by Sir John's predecessor, Sir John Scarlett, who stepped down in 2009. The team worked on several projects which included organising a top secret dinner and ball for employees, and the release of a book - *MI6: The History of the Secret Intelligence Service, 1909-1949.* Sir John Scarlett was actually the main driver of the work and commissioned Professor Keith Jeffrey to research and write it.

Sir John Sawers

Sir Mansfield Cumming may not have approved of these happenings, but he would have been at the front of the queue to collect his powerful portrait by Dyke.

Like most people who venture through the front and back doors of Vauxhall Cross, James was carefully vetted by the Service's watchful monitoring unit.

The resultant public exhibition was hosted by **MOUNT STREET GALLERIES, 94 MOUNT STREET, MAYFAIR [715•55]** but not before some of the country's top spies had viewed the collection privately!

OPERATION ELLAMY

In 2011, the CIA finally caught up with Osama bin-Laden in Abbottabad, Pakistan. When the terror leader was killed two simple words were transmitted back to Washington - 'Geronimo EKIA' (target killed in action).

RESEARCH AND THINKING

It was in 1920 that a very important independent policy institution was formed in London - the Royal Institute of International Affairs based at CHATHAM HOUSE, 10 ST JAMES'S SQUARE [716•42]. Its mission is to help build a sustainably secure, prosperous and just world.

For the best part of a century the 'think tank' has hosted lectures, conferences and meetings by a plethora of world leaders, policymakers and leading figures, many attached or serving in the world of intelligence. Indeed, in 2011 former MI6 Chief Sir John Scarlett delivered a key-note speech.

Eye Spy Intelligence Magazine

'Waiting in the Hotel Room'

"There's a lot of hanging around. You're in a completely ordinary place, waiting for something quite extraordinary to happen... and often waiting for it for a long time" - James Hart Dyke

'Meeting an Agent'

Agent Giving Information to SIS Officer

FROM THE COLLECTION

'A YEAR WITH MI6'

© BY JAMES HART DYKE

Eye Spy Intelligence Magazine is grateful to James Hart Dyke for allowing reproduction of these works

© JAMES HART DYKE

SPY SITES OF LONDON

Police outside Buckingham Palace during President Obama's State visit

Thousands of miles away in Libya, MI6 became embroiled in another controversial incident. Two officers attached to a Special Forces element were despatched to the east of the country in an attempt to meet opponents of Colonel Gaddafi. The operation, codenamed Ellamy, had been compromised by local farmers who watched the team's helicopters descend in the desert.

Detained by a local militia, their equipment, including that used to communicate with London, was seized. Officials in the UK scrambled for an explanation - in the end the best they could come up with was that the men were looking for a hotel to check into!

The covert war to remove Gaddafi had begun, but events did not turn out as both London and Washington hoped, as the removal of the Libyan leader simply created a vacuum filled by fighting militias and more terrorists.

The Mall

Undercover US Secret Service officers stand on the Mall during President Obama's State visit to Britain in 2011

717•42

Eye Spy Intelligence Magazine

513

LONDON'S BIGGEST SECURITY OPERATION

In London the wedding of Prince William and Catherine Middleton initiated a massive MI5, military and police security operation as terrorists threatened to strike. Buckingham Palace was at the heart of the plot and special elements of the Army's Strategic Reconnaissance Regiment (surveillance) were called in to monitor the building and surrounding areas. Over 6,000 police were drafted in and some 100 SAS and SBS troops were also deployed. London was on lock down as never before.

Thankfully all went well and the couple married on 29 April 2011.

The city was also tense for the State visit of President Obama in 2011. Secret Service units manned special concealed points on **THE MALL [717•42]**. Other approaches to Buckingham Palace, which hosted a grand banquet, were also monitored.

Another headache for MI5 was just over the horizon - the 2012 London Olympic Games. The Security Service learned there would be a concerted effort by terrorists to disrupt the Games and plans were activated that ultimately led to surface-to-air missile batteries in **BLACKHEATH [718•30]** being assembled in the city.

BLETCHLEY PARK CODEBREAKERS HONOURED

In July 2011, HM Queen Elizabeth II, unveiled a new memorial in honour of the WWII codebreakers at Bletchley Park and its outposts known as Y Stations. One sentence at the back of the eight foot tall structure reads - *'My Most Secret Source'*.

THE ASSASSINATION LIST

In 2011, MI5 learned of a list containing the names of around 100 prominent business, political, military, intelligence and government figures that were the suspected targets of assassins. Some of the people lived in London, thus when a former Russian banker in the person of German Gorbuntsov was gunned down outside his apartment on **BYNG STREET, CANARY WHARF [719•02]**, a massive investigation began.

Rogue elements in Russia and Chechnya were believed to have been behind the attack and with the assistance of CCTV, MI5 soon had a

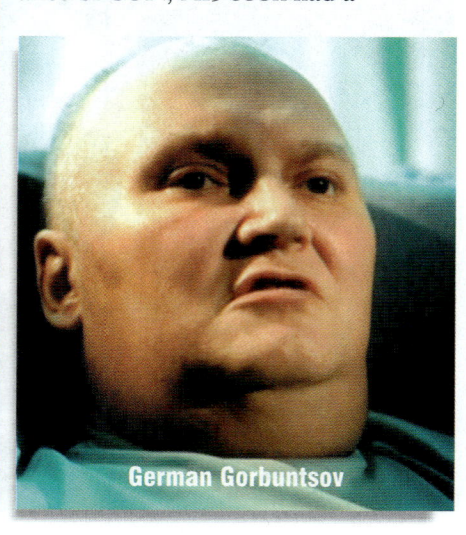

The new monument which HM Queen Elizabeth dedicated at a ceremony in 2011 in honour of the codebreakers of Bletchley Park and the Y Stations

German Gorbuntsov

Eye Spy Intelligence Magazine

A Rapier missile system is deployed on Blackheath Common. MI5 feared an airborne attack by terrorists during the 2012 Olympic Games

718•30

719•02

Byng Street
German Gorbuntsov was shot as he entered his apartment block

Army, police and intelligence officials discuss security prior to the 2012 London Olympic Games

BYNG STREET E.14
LONDON BOROUGH OF TOWER HAMLETS

Eye Spy Intelligence Magazine

SPY SITES OF LONDON

description of the gunman. Interestingly, the murder attempt was also linked to other assassination events in Europe, the Middle East and Russian satellite countries.

Gorbuntsov, who had been surveilled from his work place in Bishopsgate survived the attack, but others would not be so lucky.

Police discovered the weapon behind the **NORTH POLE PUBLIC HOUSE, 74 MANILLA STREET [720•02]** - it was a Soviet-era Makarov 9mm.

THE JULIAN ASSANGE AFFAIR

An international arrest warrant was issued for Australian-born Julian Assange, 40, the founder of a controversial Internet website WikiLeaks. The website was famous for uploading thousands of leaked classified intelligence documents and had caused no end of difficulties for US and British Intelligence.

Assange had been on bail in Sweden but fled to the UK. Swedish Police wanted to question him in connection with sexual incidents involving two women in Stockholm in August 2010. Following the allegations Assange's UK solicitor, Mark Stephens, said, "The honeytrap has been sprung... after what we've seen so far you can reasonably conclude this is part of a greater plan."

On 30 May 2012, Assange took the strange decision to breach the conditions of his bail and walked into the **ECUADOR EMBASSY, HANS CRESCENT [721•42]**. Within a few hours it was announced he had claimed political asylum. Many intelligence watchers, some of his supporters and even a few high-profile backers, believe he had made a grave error of judgement. New Scotland Yard said he was now subject to arrest. And for those high profile supporters who put up over £200,000 ($370,000) for bail, they could end up losing all their money.

North Pole Public House, 74 Manilla Street

Assange supporters outside the Ecuador Embassy also protested about the jailing of US trooper Bradley Manning who leaked thousands of documents to WikiLeaks

Eye Spy Intelligence Magazine

Ecuador Embassy, Hans Crescent

End of an era - the BBC World Service departs Bush House

MI5 and New Scotland Yard were forced to maintain a security presence outside the embassy in the event he tried to flee.

A year later a listening device was discovered in the ambassador's office. It was found around the same time he and the country's Foreign Minister were about to discuss what to do with Assange. An Ecuador official said a contract company had installed the bug on behalf of MI5 - a claim dismissed by the government.

Julian Assange

LONDON CALLING

Sadly, in 2012, the BBC World Service broadcast its last message from the iconic Bush House, Aldwych, home to this part of the global broadcaster for over 70 years. At its height of operations in WWII, over 1,400 people were employed by the BBC at the site. During the Cold War, Bush House transmissions were regularly jammed by the KGB.

Twenty-seven overseas stations and various foreign language units have now been relocated to the Corporation's Broadcasting House.

BRITISH INTELLIGENCE RECRUITMENT DRIVE

For the best part of a century opportunities to join organisations such as MI6 were limited to a select few. How technology and an ever changing world has altered the way in which people are now recruited. For years only a privileged number of men were given the task of finding prospective employees in the private clubs and elite establishments of London.

However, Foreign Secretary William Hague announced that the government, in conjunction with GCHQ, MI6 and MI5 was now supporting a new apprenticeship scheme which he hoped, would attract the country's most talented youngsters.

During a visit to the former WWII codebreaking centre, Bletchley Park, Hague also warned of the growing

Eye Spy Intelligence Magazine

SPY SITES OF LONDON

Former Chief of MI6 Sir John Scarlett and Foreign Secretary William Hague at Bletchley Park - supporting a new intelligence recruitment drive

Sub-Lieutenant Edward Devenney

SILENT SERVICE SPIES

threat posed by cyber attacks. Accompanied by GCHQ Director Iain Lobban, Hague said the apprenticeship scheme should be able to identify the best "experts from the 'X-Box' generation."

Hague noted all the intelligence services recognise the present generation of youngsters have already developed in the world of social media, gaming and interactive connectivity and this could be a huge asset.

The Royal Navy's submarine arm is known as the Silent Service. Maintaining security aboard the boats is of paramount importance to any navy. In 2013 it became embroiled in a spy scandal when one of its servicemen tried to sell secrets to the Russians.

© MINISTRY OF DEFENCE/CROWN COPYRIGHT

518

Eye Spy Intelligence Magazine

SPY SITES OF LONDON

British Museum, Great Russell Street

It wasn't the first occasion that a submariner had been involved in espionage.

On 3 September 1971, a Ministry of Defence (MOD) signal form marked *'Secret'* was generated by the Vice Chief Naval Staff. It was an advisory notifying a number of parties that a naval officer of Sub-Lieutenant rank had been acting on behalf of the Soviets and had already passed on documents to Moscow. It later transpired that a number were of the highest security gradings.

In the late 1990s, Chief Petty Officer Steven Hayden sold Gulf War data to *The Sun* newspaper. This information concerned a supposed plot by Saddam Hussein to launch anthrax attacks in Britain and was duly printed by the paper under a banner headline - *'Saddam's Anthrax in our Duty Frees'* on 24 March 1998.

Hayden received £10,000 for the story, doubtless gleaned from his work within Naval Intelligence. For that act, which perhaps falls more into the domain of Britain's Leveson Inquiry (press freedom investigation) than MI5, the officer was sentenced to one year in jail.

Another Royal Navy spy - Sub-Lieutenant David James Bingham made a few hundred pounds here and there for selling top quality information. In March 1972, he received a 21-year prison sentence for his betrayal, the motivation being the same as that of the later Official Secrets Act breach by the hapless Hayden - "horrendous financial problems." Intelligence files also make note of his wife's extravagance and how she had volunteered him as a spy to Moscow - this after she visited the Russian Embassy in London. Due to the intelligence classification of the information no details could ever be made public. For the

Royal Artillery Barracks, Woolwich

© MINISTRY OF DEFENCE/CROWN COPYRIGHT

Eye Spy Intelligence Magazine

New MI5 Director-General Andrew Parker - a counter-terrorism specialist. His appointment reflected the changing nature of much of the Security Service's work

record, Bingham died in a car crash in February 1997 - his Volvo car caught fire after he lost control and he was consumed by fire and smoke.

A NEW NAVY SPY AND MI5 STING

Sub-Lieutenant Edward Devenney offered a gold mine of information to agents he believed were from Russia's SVR. On 17 November 2011, he called the Russian Embassy on no fewer than 11 occasions. Not receiving a response he proceeded to take photographs of cryptographic data aboard HMS Vigilant. The data could have exposed NATO communications. MI5 became aware of his actions and decided to trap Devenney.

Knowing of his telephone calls to the Russian Embassy, two agents returned his call. A face-to-face meeting was organised at **THE BRITISH MUSEUM [722•62]** where contact was established. Devenney, believing he was meeting his Russian contact, was duly arrested by officers from New Scotland Yard's CTC on 6 March 2012. He received an eight year prison term.

Fusilier Lee Rigby

John Wilson Street

THE SHOCKING DEATH OF LEE RIGBY

One of the most appalling terrorist attacks in London occurred during the day in **JOHN WILSON STREET [723•28]** near the **ROYAL ARTILLERY BARRACKS, WOOLWICH [724•28]**. It was a crime so hideous that it left the country in shock.

On 22 May 2013, Lee Rigby of the Royal Regiment of Fusiliers was knocked down by a car driven by two al-Qaida terrorists. They then stabbed the young trooper to death. Both

The residents of Wootton Bassett show respect as fallen British armed forces personnel are repatriated

attackers received life sentences - one a whole life term.

Tributes to the young man were paid throughout the UK and a campaign launched for a permanent memorial to be erected at the site of the attack.

MI5 was facing a new kind of terrorist threat and its newly appointed Director-General Andrew Parker, 50, recognised that such actions were difficult to predict or stop.

That armed forces personnel and police in the UK were now being targeted was also evidenced in a terror plot that was thwarted in the town of Wootton Bassett (now Royal Wootton Bassett) whose residents regularly lined the streets to honour British troopers killed in overseas action. Another attack on a Territorial Army base in Luton was also derailed. In this case al-Qaida sought to use a remote controlled toy car packed with explosives. These incidents would not be the last.

THE BIGGEST LEAK OF INTELLIGENCE FILES

In June 2013, Edward Snowden an NSA and CIA contractor, began leaking an estimated 500,000 documents pertaining to intercept operations performed by NSA and GCHQ, the majority of them under the auspices of a programme codenamed PRISM. The damage done to the intelligence collection capabilities of America and Britain was considerable.

Snowden, who fled to Moscow via Hong Kong and sought sanctuary, selected just three media outlets to release his material. In the UK it was the *Guardian* newspaper that was given access to some extraordinary files. Journalist Glenn Greenwald was Snowden's primary point of contact.

Alan Rusbridger

The revelations were coming thick and fast and the intelligence services were powerless.

However, two managers from GCHQ visited the newspaper at its headquarters at **KING'S PLACE, 90 YORK WAY [725•09]**. The officers took photographs and notes. On 20 July 2013, after legal action was threatened, the media house agreed to destroy two hard drives using angle grinders in the presence of IT experts from GCHQ. The remnants were not removed. *Guardian* editor Alan Rusbridger said he would "rather destroy the copied files than hand them back to the NSA or GCHQ."

SPY SITES OF LONDON

Similarly, it emerged that cabinet secretary Sir Jeremy Heywood initially contacted the newspaper advising the files be destroyed as they would pose a "serious threat to national security should they fall into the wrong hands."

Rusbridger disclosed that the order came directly from 10 Downing Street. A request was made to return or destroy all the NSA files given to the newspaper.

It was perhaps a futile act as several intact copies and the original file still exist. These are held in Russia, Hong Kong, Brazil and Germany. Nevertheless, Snowden's espionage did immense damage and several terrorist groups altered the way in which they communicated and used the Internet.

THE CONTROVERSIAL DEATH OF A FALLEN RUSSIAN OLIGARCH

On 23 March 2013, the Russian billionaire, businessman and outspoken critic of President Putin, Boris Berezovsky, was found dead at his home in Berkshire.

New Scotland Yard were immediately called and his mansion tested for traces of radiation and other poisons. Obviously with the number of threats to his person and thwarted assassination attempts in previous years, the police were concerned he had been murdered.

There were similar fears in 2008, when Berezovsky's business associate Badri Patarkatsishvilli had been found dead in his mansion in Surrey. And just like Berezovsky, a specialist radiation team had been called in to check the premises.

The coroner said Berezovsky had taken his own life by hanging. Depression was mentioned, for he had lost over £100 million in a legal dispute with another London-based Russian billionaire Roman Abramovich, the owner of Chelsea football club.

However, other people believe he was assassinated and his death made to look like suicide. Berezovsky's former head of security, Sergie Sokolov is one such person. He believes darker forces linked to MI6 and the CIA were involved.

Russian Yuri Felshtinsky who helped the Litvinenko family get out of Russia was himself suspicious of the death of Berezovsky.

Eye Spy believes both Berezovsky and Patarkatsishvilli were on a Russian assassination list.

ALL CHANGE AT MI6 AND GCHQ

In the summer of 2014, Sir John Sawers, Chief of MI6, announced he was stepping down. Known as the man who lifted the Service out of the shadows, he was succeeded by counter-terrorism specialist - Alex Younger. This is indicative of how British

Guardian HQ, King's Place, 90 York Way

Boris Berezovsky

A carefully planned deception operation resulted in the escape of former FSB officer Litvinenko

Happier times. (L-R) Alexander Litvinenko, Boris Berezovsky, Akhmed Zakayev and Yuri Felshtinsky

© YURI FELSHTINSKY

Badri Patarkatsishvili

Intelligence views the current world climate.

In 2014, Britain's GCHQ intelligence service celebrated what was effectively its 100th year; and outgoing Director Sir Iain Lobban delivered his valedictory speech at the Churchill War Rooms **(See Site 271•42)**.

Speaking to an invited audience Sir Iain reflected on his three-decade long association with the world of intelligence and how the challenges have evolved. "From the Cold War to the present, the world continues to be a dangerous and unpredictable place," he said.

The Internet was also described as "challenging, enlightening but at times menacing." Sir Iain noted the amount of useful information which had been moved to the electronic platform which offered "unprecedented opportunities," but at the same time it had become a place where "less appealing aspects of human nature can be found."

That GCHQ was facing mounting challenges was aired too. However,

Alex Younger

despite the furore of the Edward Snowden NSA leaks, he emphasised that the "public interest is served by some things remaining secret." As for accusations of illegal searching made by Snowden, Sir Iain said: "The people who work at GCHQ would sooner walk out of the door than be involved in anything remotely resembling mass surveillance."

Eye Spy Intelligence Magazine 523

Sir Iain Lobban delivers his valedictory speech at the Churchill War Rooms

New Scotland Yard Police Commissioner Mark Rowley

As Sir John departed, MI5 revealed it had thwarted more dreadful plots involving a new terror group calling itself the Islamic State of Iraq and Syria (ISIS). Police arrested several people who had reconnoitred **SHEPHERD'S BUSH POLICE STATION [726•59]** and the **WHITE CITY TERRITORIAL BARRACKS [727•53]**. A number of photographs of police officers and armed forces personnel were discovered on the suspects electronic devices. At the same time a plot to attack the Remembrance Sunday event at the Cenotaph in Whitehall was also stopped.

New Scotland Yard Police Commissioner Mark Rowley also warned that the country faces mounting challenges.

Events in the Middle East, northern Africa and Ukraine have consumed much time in respect of MI6 analysts. The threat to Britain from terrorists and cyber hackers has never been greater, thus recruiting goes on and the intelligence community grows. It is difficult to predict the evolution of British Intelligence in the next 100 years, but it will undoubtedly be interesting.

And so that's it! We have journeyed across London and through time seeking out the intelligence secrets housed in an eclectic mix of buildings and streets that hardly begin to tell the story of the world's greatest espionage city. As the millennium progresses and new and historical case files emerge, this guide will undoubtedly grow. No doubt in future years another spy sites guide will appear identifying these locations, frequented and made famous by events of spy versus spy.

However, it would be unforgivable if we failed to end on a case file not involving espionage - the world's second oldest profession.

727•53

White City Territorial Barracks

SPY SITES OF LONDON

Russian Samovar

Shepherd's Bush Police Station

SPY VERSUS SPY

Thus we end our journey with a most amusing case file that typifies the ingenuity, resourcefulness, cunning and opportunism of those who operate in this shadowy world.

In 2009, Special Branch officers called MI5 concerning the discovery of a most unusual teapot presented to the Royal Family in 1991, by members of a newly formed Russian acrobatic team who were performing in Scotland. The object - an ornate Samovar - is a popular gift item, and the Queen Mother placed this one in the main living room at Balmoral Castle. Here the Queen hosted many world leaders and leading diplomatic figures. But there was something not quite right with this particular pot.

MI5 officers drove to Scotland, took one look at the Samovar and quickly ordered its removal from the room. There was every reason to believe it contained an elaborate listening device. And for those who point to the fact that bugs need batteries, this is not true... the Russians were producing listening devices so clever - some worked only on vibration. Of course, to pick-up the conversations, someone would need a receiver, or perhaps the gardener in the Royal grounds may just have been listening!

Either way, after decades of playing out the game of espionage in some of the most famous streets of London, this event proves MI5 still has a deep suspicion of everything KGB, but also a healthy respect for its cheek!

Queen Elizabeth II and Balmoral Castle

Eye Spy Intelligence Magazine

525

SPY SITES OF LONDON

SUPPORTING BRITAIN'S INTELLIGENCE SERVICES

Foreign Office
This department is responsible for overseeing and supporting global MI6 operations

10 Downing Street
728•42
The Prime Minister has close relations with all the UK's intelligence services

Home Office
729•42
Ministry diplomatically responsible for supporting MI5 operations

Ministry of Defence
730•42
Headquarters of the British Armed Forces. Within the MOD is a plethora of defence intelligence elements which work closely with MI5, MI6 and GCHQ

Eye Spy Intelligence Magazine

SPY AGENCY GCHQ REMEMBERS...

SPY SITES OF LONDON

The new openness of British Intelligence can be summed up in these remarkable photographs released by GCHQ. In 2014, some 1,400 staffers and defence personnel created a spectacular sight at the communications agency headquarters to help launch the Royal British Legion's poppy appeal. Within the grounds of the building, known affectionately as the 'doughnut', employees donned red ponchos in a display which measured 125ft.

The poppy, first used in 1921 by the American Legion to commemorate its WWI dead, was adopted by veterans across the then British Empire. It represents remembrance of the past (fallen troopers and staffers) and hope for the future.

© GCHQ CROWN COPYRIGHT

Eye Spy Intelligence Magazine

527

SPY SITES OF LONDON

Inside Down Street Station

Postscript

Eye Spy has sourced the vast majority of spy sites from open source literature, published works, archives, official documentation and from informed intelligence sources. Preparing the visual data alongside a candid commentary of events surrounding MI5, MI6, GCHQ (and other agencies) has been an enjoyable, but difficult task. Nevertheless, we believe this work reflects most of the significant (public) chapters in the story of British Intelligence and London buildings. No doubt the clandestine services could add significantly to this.

In time of course, other spy sites will emerge from past events and current happenings. An example of this is the abandoned **DOWN STREET TUBE STATION [731•55]**. In 2015, part of its secret history was spoken of after developers announced its sale. Opened in 1907, the Mayfair station was used by Winston Churchill and other senior military and political figures as a World War Two shelter and command room. Indeed, it also hosted Cabinet Meetings during the height of the Blitz because Downing Street was considered vulnerable. This was before the nearby fortified Cabinet War Rooms were readied **(See Site 271•42)**.

Churchill was never comfortable at Down Street and would describe it as the "barn" - this because the wind howled through its tunnels. Nevertheless, there were some comforts. Amongst items delivered by courier to the station during Churchill's stay, included bottles of 1928 Perrier-Jouet champagne and of course, his familiar Cuban cigars.

Sleeping quarters, typing and conference rooms and even a fully maintained kitchen were secretly built and maintained by a staff of 22 people and a dozen officials. There remain a number of tiles which carry the letter 'G'. These signify the location of a secure door where staff could shelter in the event of a poison gas attack.

Churchill later wrote of his experiences at Down Street: *'I used to go there once the firing started to transact my business and to sleep undisturbed. One felt a natural compunction at having more safety than most other people; but so many pressed me that I let them have their own way'.*

The station, which closed in 1932 due to low footfall, still retains its original facade.

DRINKS, REST AND REALITY

Readers may well have noticed our penchant for including several public houses, cafes and restaurants within this work! No doubt these will come in very handy after a few hours pounding the streets of London visiting spy sites. However, they are a deliberate inclusion intended to reflect the lives of those who work in intelligence and spies as ordinary and extraordinary people.

Winston Churchill complete with tin hat during the Battle of Britain

One public house not found in the manuscript is the **OLD RISING SUN, 79 MARYLEBONE HIGH STREET [732•55]**. Now a coffee shop, a regular visitor was Guy Burgess, he of the infamous Cambridge Spy Ring **(See Chapter 17)**. Sitting in the former pub one can only imagine his thoughts as he contemplated his great escape to his beloved Moscow with Donald Maclean... or his exposure, capture and possible execution. Espionage has its risks.

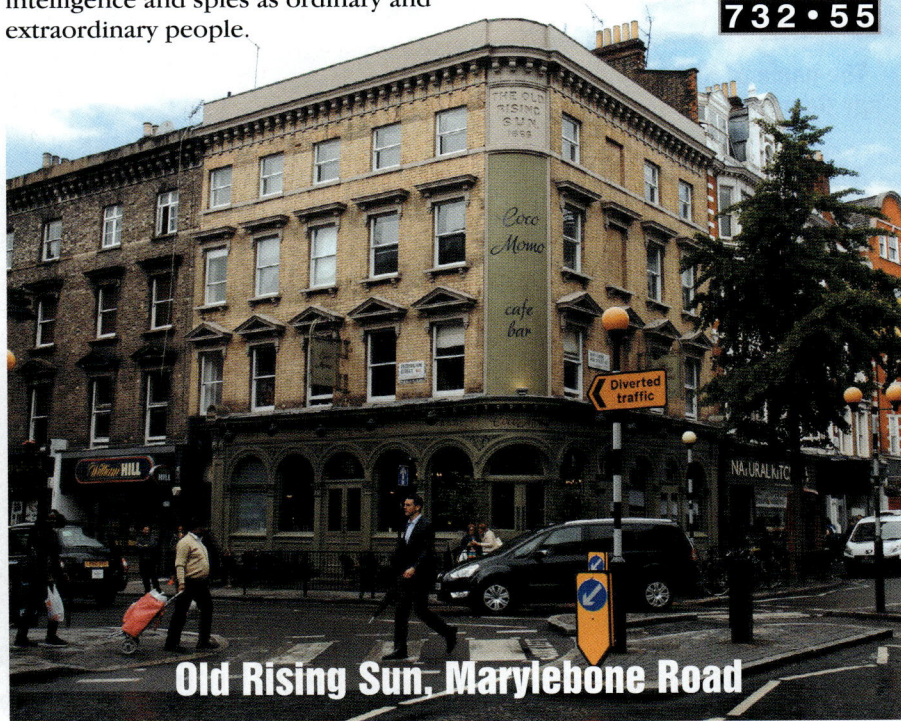

Another view of Down Street Station

Old Rising Sun, Marylebone Road

Eye Spy Intelligence Magazine

529

SPY SITES OF LONDON

BETRAYAL AND HOME IN TIME FOR SUPPER

Another site we sought to leave as a reminder of the great Cold War espionage battles between MI6 and the KGB is **CHARLEVILLE MANSIONS, BARONS COURT [733•54]**. In October 1953, MI6 officer and KGB spy George Blake made a bee-line for this address just hours after a most important event had taken place at 2 Carlton Gardens.

The home of KGB spy George Blake's mother

Charleville Mansions, Charleville Road

Powis Square, Bayswater

Another view of Powis Square

Blake had just participated in a meeting whereby MI6 and CIA officers discussed an incredible plan to dig a tunnel under East Berlin and tap into East German and Soviet telephone lines (See Chapter 18). After meeting with his KGB handler to impart the 'news', Blake slowly made his way to the Baron's Court address. And though historical literature identifies one of his places of occupation in London as 5 All Soul's Place **(See Site 495•55)**, at the time of his treachery, he was living in Charleville Mansions, the home of his mother.

ALWAYS A DANGEROUS GAME

Digesting the pages of this book one can see the world of intelligence and spies has changed dramatically in a little over a century. Cyber security, global border conflicts, organised crime, people trafficking, warped ideology and the on-going fight against international terrorism means that counter-espionage officers are being consumed with work outside their original remit. It is a modern and dangerous playground for today's intelligence services which face evolving and different challenges and threats. Yet one can find parallels to some of the topics mentioned above to those faced by the 'spy ghosts' of yesteryear. One MI6 officer who bravely operated in a climate of uncertainty and ultimate danger was of course Sidney Reilly.

Known as the 'Ace of Spies', Reilly charged across Russia sending his observations back to London as the embers of World War One were still glowing, and the Bolsheviks were seizing power. Much continues to be written about his exploits, and there is little doubt this member of Britain's first intelligence service, the Secret Service Bureau **(See Chapter 2)**, can take a seat alongside the country's most famous agents. A great deal of secrecy still surrounds his life and death, and also his *birth:* some papers and books state 24 March 1873. However, a 1904 note sourced from the Royal School of Mines in London (where Reilly applied for a post) states quite clearly 24 April 1877. And of further interest to ourselves, at this time the legendary spy was living at **9 POWIS SQUARE, BAYSWATER [734•52]**. Yet another spy site to visit!

Ten years of research and compilation has thus concluded in the publishing of *Classified: The Insider's Guide to 500 Spy Sites in London*. As with any project of this scale and size, information and leads on new spy sites surfaces every day. No doubt too that connoisseurs of the world of intelligence and espionage will bring to our attention locations that for reasons aplenty, we may have missed. We would love to hear from you!

SPY SITE LOCATOR AND INDEX
HOW TO USE THIS GUIDE

Each London spy site in the text has been issued with a unique number and a zone reference number. For example, former MI5 premises 73-75 QUEEN'S GATE is [017•55]. Please refer to post code map. You can identify how many spy sites are in each zone by using the map and index. For example, in Westminster (SW1 which is identified in the photo and the book's narrative as •42) 179 sites can be found!

Go to **http://www.eyespymag.com/spytours.html** to download a sample walk of Westminster for you to follow, or you can create one of your own by utilising one of the many web sites and apps available to tailor a customised walk. For mobile users, the Locacious App is free and extremely useful. For PC and Mac users, Community Walk allows you to programme the addresses into your computer which will identify the location and generate a walking map (distance, turn by turn, duration etc.).

Due to the size of the city and complex street layouts within some districts, we would recommend you use a London A-Z map to assist you. You can also download the A-Z App of London for your mobile device. All of the above platforms display the nearest tube station.

017 • 55
Spy Site Number • Zone Reference

There are Eye Spy recommended espionage guides in the city who regularly run walking tours. These fascinating walks are inexpensive and last a few hours. More details are available from Eye Spy - call 01756 770199

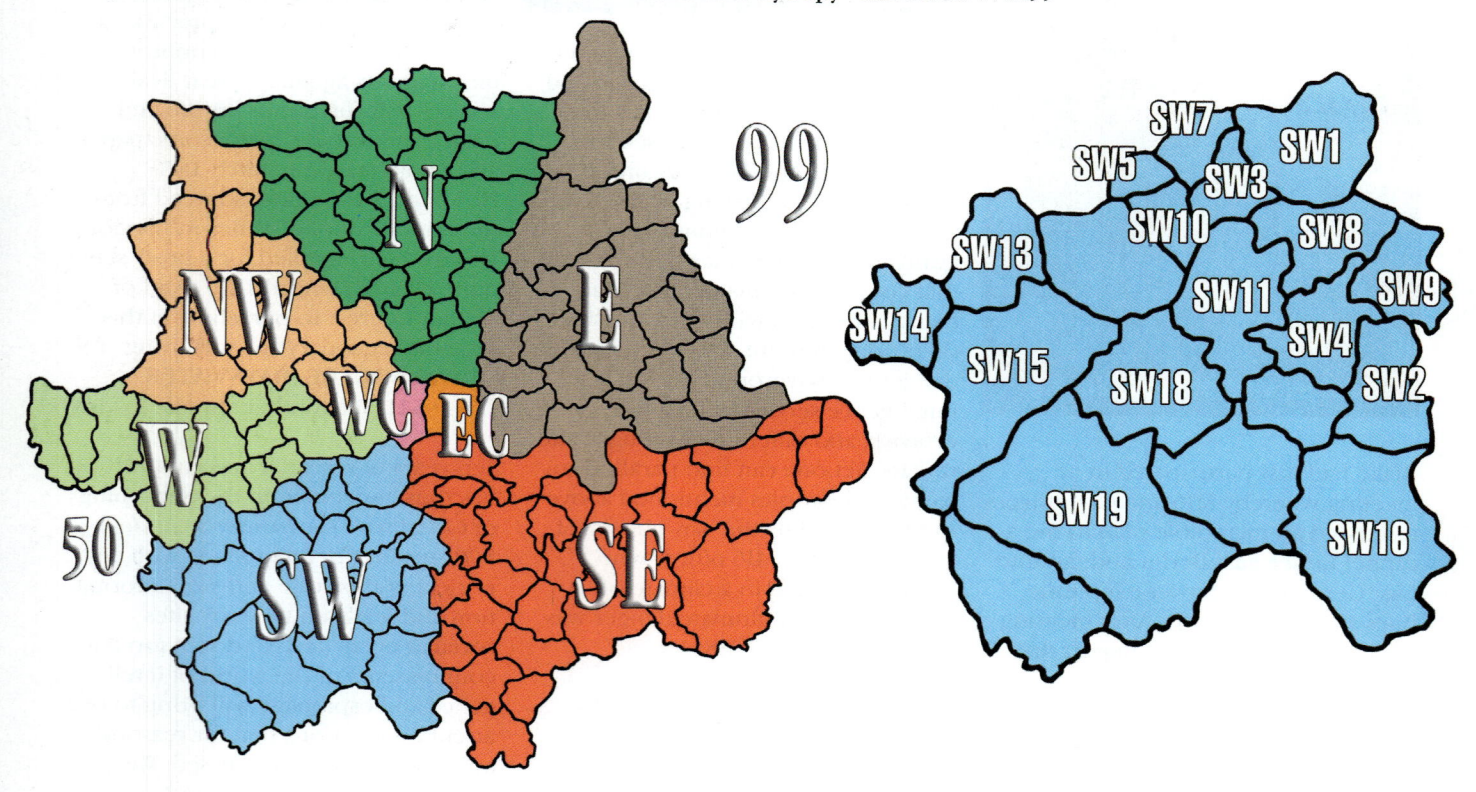

Eye Spy Intelligence Magazine

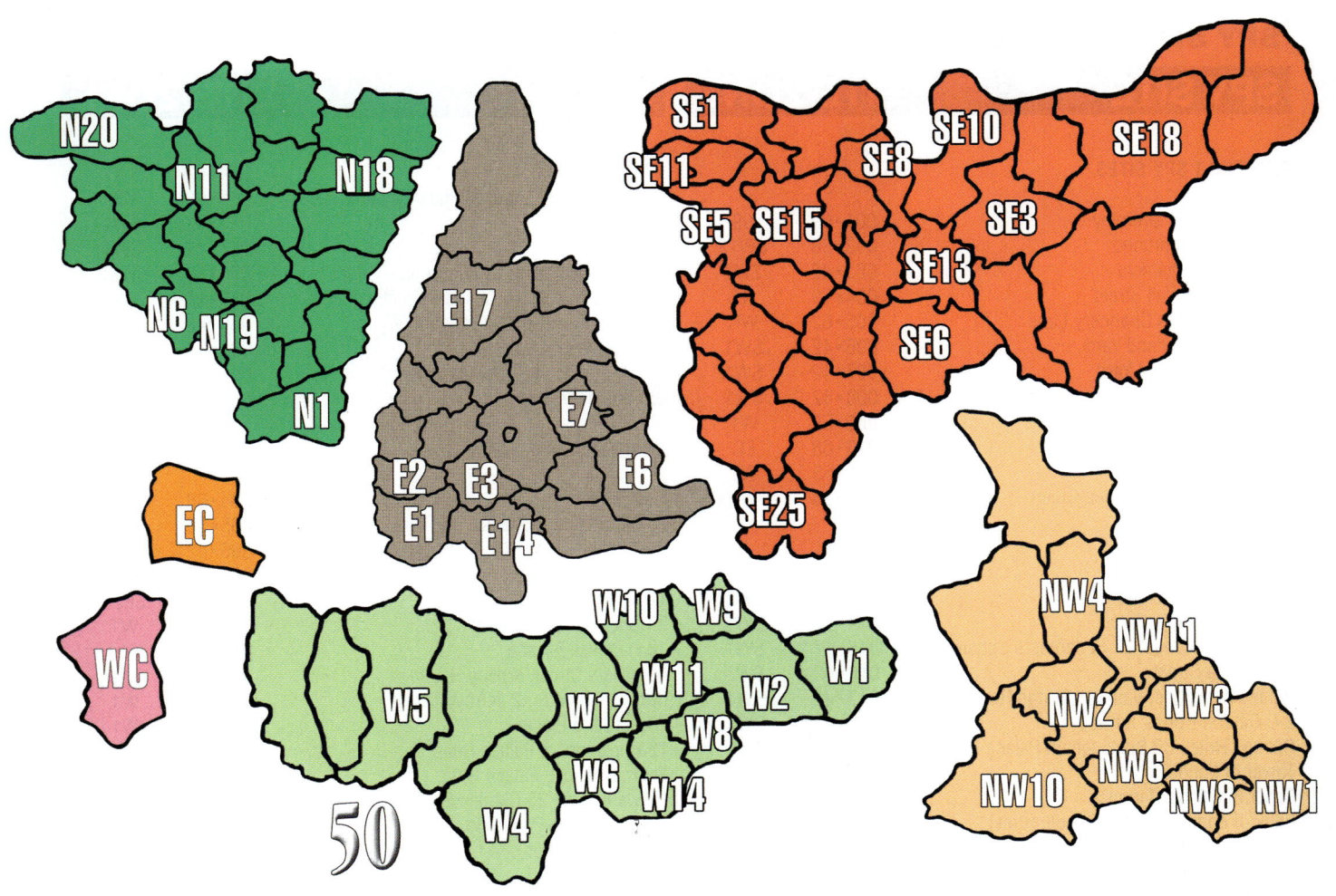

Zone/Number of Sites			Zone/Number of Sites			Zone/Number of Sites			Zone/Number of Sites		
•01	E1	5	•17	NW11	3	•33	SE8	1	•49	SW9	2
•02	E14	3	•18	NW2	2	•34	SW10	4	•50	TW11	3
•03	E17	1	•19	NW3	12	•35	SW11	1	•51	W10	1
•04	E2	1	•20	NW4	3	•36	SW13	2	•52	W11	7
•05	E3	1	•21	NW6	2	•37	SW14	2	•53	W12	2
•06	E6	1	•22	NW8	5	•38	SW15	1	•54	W14	12
•07	E7	1	•23	SE1	13	•39	SW16	3	•55	W1	158
•08	EC	23	•24	SE10	2	•40	SW18	2	•56	W2	13
•09	N1	3	•25	SE11	7	•41	SW19	3	•57	W4	1
•10	N11	2	•26	SE13	1	•42	SW1	179	•58	W5	1
•11	N18	-	•27	SE15	-	•43	SW2	1	•59	W6	4
•12	N19	-	•28	SE18	3	•44	SW3	23	•60	W8	21
•13	N20	3	•29	SE25	1	•45	SW4	4	•61	W9	2
•14	N6	1	•30	SE3	1	•46	SW5	8	•62	WC	56
•15	NW1	28	•31	SE5	1	•47	SW7	56	•99	London Outskirts	19
•16	NW10	2	•32	SE6	1	•48	SW8	2			

Eye Spy Intelligence Magazine

533

SPY SITES OF LONDON

SPY SITE	SITE/ZONE
CHAPTER 1 SPY SITES	
Scadbury Park, Bromley	001•99 99
Barn Elms, Richmond	002•36 SW13
Houses of Parliament	003•42 SW1
244-278 Crondall Street	004•09 N1
24 Old Buildings Chancery Lane	005•62 WC
7-11 Great Scotland Yard	006•42 SW1
3-5 Great Scotland Yard	007•42 SW1
New Scotland Yard, Victoria Embankment	008•42 SW1
16 Upper Grosvenor Street	009•55 W1
Coldbath Square, Clerkenwell	010•08 EC
1A Cato Street	011•55 W1
Milbourne House, Barnes Green	012•36 SW13
CHAPTER 2 SPY SITES	
Old War Office, Whitehall	013•42 SW1
16 Queen Anne's Gate	014•42 SW1
Winchester House, 21 St James's Square	015•42 SW1
64 Victoria Street	016•42 SW1
Ashley Mansions, Vauxhall Bridge Road	017•42 SW1
8-9 Carlton House Terrace	018•42 SW1
Rubens Hotel, 39 Buckingham Palace Road	019•42 SW1
Tower of London	020•08 EC
Paper Buildings, Temple	021•08 EC
Bank of England, Threadneedle Street	022•08 EC
84 Bedford Court Mansions	023•62 WC
16 Lydon Road	024•45 SW4
24 Orlando Road	025•45 SW4
Pentland House, Old Road	026•26 SE13
22 Fitzjames Avenue	027•54 W14
9 Holland Park Terrace	028•52 W11
27 Westminster Mansions	029•42 SW1
Royal Automotive Club, 89-91 Pall Mall	030•42 SW1
Athenaeum Club, 107 Pall Mall	031•42 SW1
Travellers Club, 106 Pall Mall	032•42 SW1
Rag Army & Navy Club, 36-39 Pall Mall	033•42 SW1
2 Whitehall Court	034•42 SW1
The Admiralty	035•42 SW1
201 High Street Deptford	036•33 SE8
2 Carlton Gardens	037•42 SW1
5 Cork Street	038•55 W1
Admiralty Arch	039•42 SW1
6 Chesterfield Street	040•55 W1
63 Earl's Court Square	041•46 SW5
16 Percy Circus	042•62 WC
Crown Tavern, Clerkenwell	043•08 EC
Marxist Library, Clerkenwell	044•08 EC
Fulbourne Street, Tower Hamlets	045•01 E1
Red Lion, Great Windmill Street	046•55 W1
Highgate Cemetery	047•14 N6
Mount Pleasant Sorting Office	048•08 EC
48 Walton Street	049•44 SW3
Watergate House, 13-15 York Buildings	050•62 WC
11 Fordham Court, De Vere Gardens	051•60 W8
14 Barton Street	052•42 W11
131 Waldegrave Road	053•50 TW11

SPY SITE	SITE/ZONE
17 Gerald Road	054•42 SW1
Noel Coward Theatre, St Martin's Lane	055•62 WC
5 Wilton Place	056•42 SW1
21 Pont Street	057•42 SW1
Adelphi Building, 1-11 John Adam Street	058•62 WC
Waterloo House, 16 Charles Street	059•55 W1
Greener House, 66-68 Haymarket	060•42 SW1
73-75 Queen's Gate	061•47 SW7
17-19 Buckingham Palace Road	062•42 SW1
35 Albemarle Street	063•55 W1
CHAPTER 3 SPY SITES	
Fleet Street	064•08 EC
Ye Old Cheshire Cheese, 145 Fleet Street	065•08 EC
Wellington House, 70 Buckingham Gate	066•42 SW1
46 Gillingham Street	067•42 SW1
12 Tennison Road	068•29 SE25
2 Upper Wimpole Street	069•55 W1
13 Hanover Terrace	070•15 NW1
43 Villiers Street, Kipling House	071•12 N19
Criterion Theatre, 2 Jermyn Street	072•55 W1
76 Portland Place	073•55 W1
13 Buckingham Palace Road	074•42 SW1
Thorney Court, Palace Gate	075•60 W8
Crewe House, 28 Charles Street	076•55 W1
49 Wimbledon Park Side	077•41 SW19
13 Mallord Street	078•44 SW3
31 Pandora Road	079•21 NW6
18 Eaton Place	080•42 SW1
59 Onslow Gardens	081•47 SW7
Burlington House, Piccadilly	082•55 W1
6-9 Carlton House Terrace	083•42 SW1
2A Melbury Road	084•54 W14
The Tower House, 29 Melbury Road	085•54 W14
1 Melbury Road	086•54 W14
8 Melbury Road	087•54 W14
Old Drill Hall, Duke's Road	088•62 WC
Little Holland House, 6 Melbury Road	089•54 W14
48 Langham Street	090•55 W1
10 Kensington Church Walk	091•60 W8
22 Melbury Road	092•54 W14
54 Broadway	093•42 SW1
St James's Park Station	094•42 SW1
21 Queen Anne's Gate	095•42 SW1
The Old Star, 66 Broadway	096•42 SW1
28 Queen Anne's Gate	097•42 SW1
3 Queen Anne's Gate	098•42 SW1
4 Queen Anne's Gate	099•42 SW1
34 Queen Anne's Gate	100•42 SW1
Admiralty Research Laboratory, Teddington	101•50 W10
CHAPTER 4 SPY SITES	
128 New Bond Street	102•55 W1
Chesham House, Chesham Place	103•42 SW1
49 Moorgate	104•08 EC
1-8 New Bond Street	105•55 W1

SPY SITES OF LONDON

SPY SITE	SITE/ZONE		SPY SITE	SITE/ZONE	
50 Outer Temple, 222 Strand	106•62	WC	**CHAPTER 7 SPY SITES**		
66 Charing Cross Road	107•62	WC	Bletchley Park, Milton Keynes, Buckinghamshire	156•99	99
Sanctuary Buildings, Great Smith Street	108•42	SW1	8 Beaumont Street	157•55	W1
16 King Street	109•62	WC	Faber Building, Russell Square	158•62	WC
25 Noel Street	110•55	W1	2 Warrington Crescent	159•62	WC
37 Old Compton Street	111•55	W1	7-9 Berkeley Street	160•55	W1
Foreign Office, King Charles Street	112•42	SW1	Berkeley Square House	161•55	W1
31 Pembroke Gardens	113•60	W8	17 Bruton Street	162•55	W1
Tedworth Square	114•44	SW3	Electra House, 84 Moorgate	163•11	N18
124 Cromwell Road	115•47	SW7	72 Fore Street	164•08	EC
38 Sloane Street	116•42	SW1	71 Chester Square	165•42	SW1
Beresford Gate, Woolwich	117•28	SE18	Blue Posts, 6 Bennett Street	166•42	SW1
82 Holland Road	118•54	W14	160 Cranmer Court	167•42	SW1
Charing Cross Station	119•62	WC	9 Vincent Square	168•42	SW1
Dolphin Square, Pimlico	120•42	SW1	Ingersoll House, 7-9 Kingsway	169•62	WC
Hammersmith Palais de Danse	121•59	W6	2 Fitzmaurice Place	170•55	W1
			Woburn Abbey, Bedfordshire	171•99	99
CHAPTER 5 SPY SITES			78 Margaret Street	172•55	W1
14 Cromwell Place	122•47	SW7	Bankruptcy Court, Carey Street	173•62	WC
Buckingham Palace	123•42	SW1	Seven Stars, 53 Carey Street	174•62	WC
36 Eaton Place	124•42	SW1	BBC Crowsley Park, Oxfordshire	175•99	99
Liverpool Street Station	125•08	EC	Caversham Park, Berkshire	176•99	99
22 Hans Place	126•42	SW1	BBC Broadcasting House, Portland Place	177•55	W1
Clive House, 70 Petty France	127•42	SW1	Abbey Road Studios, 3 Abbey Road	178•22	NW8
Bush House, Aldwych	128•62	WC	Aldwych Theatre, 49 Aldwych	179•62	WC
3 Albemarle Street	129•55	W1	Lyceum Theatre, 354 Strand	180•52	W11
Boodle's, 28 St James's Street	130•42	SW1			
Whites Club, 37-38 St James's Street	131•42	SW1	**CHAPTER 8 SPY SITES**		
46 Upper Grosvenor Street	132•55	W1	64 Baker Street	181•55	W1
4 Davies Street	133•55	W1	221 Baker Street	182•15	NW1
Devonshire Club, 50 St James's Street	134•42	SW1	Baker Street Station	183•15	NW1
East India Club, 16 St James's Square	135•42	SW1	82 Baker Street	184•55	W1
16 Cumberland Terrace	136•15	NW1	83 Baker Street	185•55	W1
15 Sunnymead Road	137•38	SW15	Montague Mansions, Marylebone	186•55	W1
Hoop Lane Cemetery, Golders Green	138•17	NW11	Bickenhall Mansions, Bickenhall Street	187•55	W1
Horseferry Road, Westminster	139•42	SW1	Chiltern Court, Baker Street	188•55	W1
St. Ermin's Hotel, 2 Caxton Street	140•42	SW1	221 Baker Street	189•15	NW1
Wormwood Scrubs	141•53	W12	35 Portland Place	190•55	W1
57-58 St James's Street	142•42	SW1	20 Cranley Place	191•47	SW7
24 Maple Street	143•55	W1	Orchard Court, Portman Square	192•55	W1
Victoria Street, Abbey House	144•42	SW1	Nell Gwynn House, Sloane Avenue	193•44	SW3
Ashley Gardens, Ambrosden Avenue	145•42	SW1	59 Queen's Gate	194•47	SW7
46 Campden Hill Road	146•60	W8	Trevor Square, Knightsbridge	195•47	SW7
4 Chesterfield Street	147•55	W1	Natural History Museum, Cromwell Road	196•46	SW5
			18B Ebury Street	197•42	SW1
CHAPTER 6 SPY SITES			22a Ebury Street	198•42	SW1
24 Onslow Square	148•47	SW7	26 Ebury Street Topham's	199•42	SW1
1 Grosvenor Square	149•55	W1	140 Park Lane	200•55	W1
18 Roland Gardens	150•47	SW7	84 Charing Cross Road	201•62	WC
47 Gloucester Place	151•42	SW1	Former Victoria Hotel (Nigeria House)	202•62	WC
14 Princes Gate	152•47	SW7	Burnley Road, Stockwell	203•49	SW9
50 Harrington Road	153•47	SW7	SOE Memorial, Albert Embankment	204•23	SE1
Evelyn Gardens	154•47	SW7	Gordon Square Gardens, Bloomsbury	205•62	WC
South Kensington Station	155•47	SW7	Cafe de Paris, 25 Coventry Street	206•55	W1
			Turf Club, Bennett Street	207•42	SW1
			Stafford Hotel, 16-18 St James's	208•42	SW1

Eye Spy Intelligence Magazine

SPY SITES OF LONDON

SPY SITE	SITE/ZONE	
Women of WWII Memorial, Whitehall	209•42	SW1
36 Curzon Street	210•55	W1
The Royal Mews, Buckingham Palace	211•42	SW1
Wladyslaw Sikorski Statue, Portland Place	212•55	W1
28 Wimpole Street	213•55	W1
51 New Cavendish Street	214•55	W1

CHAPTER 9 SPY SITES

32 Eaton Square	215•42	SW1
77 Chester Square	216•42	SW1
Stratton House, Piccadilly	217•55	W1
H. M. Prison Brixton	218•43	SW2
6 Belgrave Square	219•42	SW1
4 Carlton Gardens	220•42	SW1
Kingston House North, Prince's Gate	221•47	SW7
43 Eaton Place	222•42	SW1
1-3 Lexham Gardens	223•60	W8
Reform Club, 104 Pall Mall	224•42	SW1
Saint Mary's Catholic Cemetery, Kensal Green	225•99	99
Audley End House, Saffron Waldon, Essex	226•99	99
Grove Road, Mile End	227•05	E3
Adastral House, Kingsway	228•62	WC
Australia House, Aldwych	229•62	WC
80 Strand	230•62	WC
Imperial War Museum, Lambeth Road	231•23	SE1

CHAPTER 10 SPY SITES

Royal Horseguards Hotel, Whitehall Court	232•42	SW1
Royal Tank Regiment Memorial	233•42	SW1
1 Whitehall Court	234•42	SW1
Horse Guards Building, Whitehall	235•42	SW1
Horse Guards Memorial, Whitehall	236•42	SW1
72 Grosvenor Street	237•55	W1
40 Berkeley Square	238•55	W1
68 Brook Street	239•55	W1
49 Upper Brook Street	240•55	W1
18 Grosvenor Square	241•55	W1
15 Bruton Lane	242•55	W1
Great Central Hotel, Marylebone Road	243•15	NW1
Old Metropole Hotel, Northumberland Avenue	244•62	WC
Selfridges, Oxford Street	245•55	W1
Palace Street, Westminster	246•42	SW1
Princess House, Princes Street	247•08	EC
Kingsway Tunnels, 39 Furnival Street	248•62	WC
Chancery Lane Station	249•62	WC
138-142 Holborn Bars	250•08	EC
Downside Crescent, Belsize Park	251•19	NW3
Stockwell Shelter, Stockwell	252•25	SE11
Eisenhower Centre, Goodge Street	253•62	WC
Clapham South Shelter	254•45	SW4

CHAPTER 11 SPY SITES

14 Clapham Common, North Side	255•45	SW4
Rules Restaurant, 35 Maiden Lane	256•62	WC
Senate House, Bloomsbury	257•62	WC

SPY SITE	SITE/ZONE	
6 Barton Street	258•42	SW1
39 Methley Street	259•25	SE11
287 Kennington Road	260•25	SE11
Somerset House, Strand	261•62	WC
Leicester Square	262•62	WC
16 Bowden Street	263•25	SE11
2 Temple Place	264•62	WC
24 Crooms Hill	265•24	SE10
77 Parliament Hill	266•19	NW3
Orwell House, 22 Portobello Road	267•52	W11
University College Hospital, 235 Euston Road	268•15	NW1
George Orwell Plaque, Pond Street	269•19	NW3
5 Cambridge Gate	270•15	NW1
Churchill War Rooms, King Charles Street	271•42	SW1
Treasury Building, Westminster	272•42	SW1
Brooke Statue, Whitehall	273•42	SW1
Admiralty Citadel, Horse Guards	274•42	SW1
Victoria and Albert Museum, Cornwall Gardens	275•47	SW7

CHAPTER 12 SPY SITES

5 St James's Street	276•42	SW1
Roosevelt & Churchill Statue, New Bond Street	277•62	WC
21-22 Grosvenor Street	278•55	W1
23 Bruton Street	279•55	W1
10 Adam Street	280•62	WC
1 Dorset Square	281•15	NW1
51 Cumberland Terrace	282•15	NW1
Stornoway House, 13 Cleveland Row	283•42	SW2
Grand Buildings, 1 Strand	284•62	WC
54 Wynnstay Gardens	285•60	W8
33 Tedworth Square	286•44	SW3
Park Village East, Camden	287•15	NW1
Grosvenor House Hotel	288•55	W1
46 Abingdon Court	289•60	W8
61 Russell Square	290•62	WC
31 Pond Street	291•19	NW3
43 Dryden Road	292•41	SW19
59 Queen's Gate	293•47	SW7
68 Ennismore Gardens	294•47	SW7
44 Park Street	295•55	W1
21-22 Grosvenor Street	296•55	W1
Avenue Road, St John's Wood	297•22	NW6
Frognal Gardens, Hampstead	298•19	NW3
32 Wilton Place	299•42	SW1
Berkeley Hotel, Wilton Place	300•42	SW1
4 Brick Court	301•08	EC
7 Chester Mews	302•42	SW1
4 Christchurch Street	303•44	SW3
Africa House, 64-78 Kingsway	304•37	SW14
Tavistock Centre, 9 Fitzjames's Avenue	305•19	NW3
44 Ravenscroft Avenue	306•17	NW11
20 Maresfield Gardens	307•19	NW3
Royal Aero Club, 119 Piccadilly	308•55	W1
81-83 High Street, Missenden	309•99	99
RAF Club, 128 Piccadilly	310•55	W1
Cavalry and Guards Club, 127 Piccadilly	311•55	W1
Yorkshire Grey, 46 Langham Street	312•55	W1

SPY SITES OF LONDON

SPY SITE	SITE/ZONE	
CHAPTER 13 SPY SITES		
Latchmere House, Ham Common	313•50	TW11
Royal Victoria Patriotic Asylum, Wandsworth	314•40	SW18
Trent Park, Enfield	315•99	99
13 Kensington Palace Gardens	316•60	W8
5 Kensington Palace Gardens	317•60	W8
7 Kensington Palace Gardens	318•60	W8
Clarence Gate Gardens, Glentworth Street	319•15	NW1
Latimer House, Buckinghamshire	320•99	99
99 Frognal, Hampstead	321•19	NW3
10 Duke Street	322•55	W1
300 Oxford Street	323•55	W1
32 Weymouth Street	324•55	W1
59 Weymouth Street	325•55	W1
10 Duke Street, St James's	326•42	SW1
Oratory Schools, Bury Walk	327•44	SW3
18 Sloane Gardens	328•42	SW1
Waldorf Hotel, Aldwych	329•62	WC
Danesfield House, Medmenham, Bucks	330•99	99
Alexandra Palace, Muswell Hill	331•99	99
31 Gloucester Place	332•55	W1
9 Nevern Road	333•46	SW5
14 Malvern Court	334•47	SW7
39 Porchester Gate	335•56	W2
16 Hans Road	336•44	SW3
CHAPTER 14 SPY SITES		
St Paul's Gardens, Hammersmith	337•59	W6
52-54 Kennington Oval	338•25	SE11
Grosvenor Square	339•55	W1
Norfolk House, 31 St James's Square	340•42	SW1
18 Queen's Gate Place Mews	341•47	SW7
5 Vicarage Gardens	342•60	W8
18 Frognal, Hampstead	343•19	NW3
Carlton Club, 69 St James's Street	344•42	SW1
31 Marlborough Hill	345•22	NW8
In and Out Club, 94 Piccadilly	346•55	W1
42 Half Moon Street	347•55	W1
113 New Bond Street	348•55	W1
139 New Bond Street	349•55	W1
1 Savile Row	350•57	W4
Richmond Terrace, Westminster	351•42	SW1
Old Royal Naval College	352•24	SE10
1 Becmead Avenue	353•39	SW16
Waterloo Place, St James's	354•42	SW1
Prince of Wales Theatre, Coventry Street	355•42	SW1
Navy and Military Club, 4 St James's Square	356•42	SW1
81 Victoria Road	357•60	W8
Keynes Lodge, 32 Gloucester Road	358•50	TW11
Dukes Hotel, 35 St James's Place	359•42	SW1
93 Jermyn Street	360•42	SW1
G. F. Trumper, 9 Curzon Street	361•55	W1
Geo. F. Trumper, Duke of York Street	362•42	SW1
Floris, 89 Jermyn Street	363•42	SW1
Turnbull & Asser Ltd, 71-72 Jermyn Street	364•42	SW1
Hawes and Curtis, 34 Jermyn Street	365•42	SW1

SPY SITE	SITE/ZONE	
Davidoff, 35 St James's Street	366•42	SW1
Jermyn Theatre, 16b Jermyn Street	367•42	SW1
CHAPTER 15 SPY SITES		
6 Chesterfield Gardens	368•55	W1
Waterloo Station	369•23	SE1
Wandsworth Prison	370•40	SW18
Lansdowne Club, 9 Fitzmaurice Place	371•55	W1
18 Carlton House Terrace	372•42	SW1
80-86 Regent Street	373•55	W1
Eresby House, 44 Rutland Gate	374•47	SW7
Hole In The Wall, Rutland Gate	375•47	SW7
Clock House, Rutland Gate	376•47	SW7
Russian Orthodox Church, Ennismore Gardens	377•47	SW7
Savoy Hotel, Strand	378•62	WC
3-8 Porchester Gate, Bayswater Road	379•56	W2
Wall and Tap, Bayswater Road	380•56	W2
Quaglinos Restaurant, 16 Bury Street	381•42	SW1
10A Grosvenor Square	382•55	W1
35 Crespigny Road	383•20	NW4
55 Elliot Road	384•20	NW4
39 St Lukes Mews	385•52	W11
The Ritz Hotel, 150 Piccadilly	386•55	W1
55 Egerton Gardens	387•44	SW3
16-23 Rugby Mansions	388•54	W14
39 Hill Street	389•55	W1
61 Richmond Park Road	390•37	SW14
Redcliffe Square, Kensington	391•34	SW10
Connaught Hotel, Mayfair	392•55	W1
Pavilion Road, Kensington and Chelsea	393•42	SW1
Sloane Square	394•42	SW1
Crockford's Casino, 30 Curzon Street	395•55	W1
Tate Britain, Millbank	396•42	SW1
Garden Lodge, 1 Logan Place	397•60	W8
Rutland Gate	398•47	SW7
Hyde Park Barracks	399•47	SW7
Brompton Road Station	400•44	SW3
Hyde Park Hotel	401•56	W2
Telegraph Cottage, Warren Road	402•99	99
Willow Road	403•19	NW3
1-3 Willow Road	404•19	NW3
Alexander Fleming House, Southwark	405•23	SE1
7 Bedford Square	406•62	WC
16 Victoria Square	407•42	SW1
Carlyle Mansions, Cheyne Walk	408•44	SW3
CHAPTER 16 SPY SITES		
Rutland Gate East	409•47	SW7
Rutland Gate West	410•47	SW7
Rutland Gate South	411•47	SW7
26 Rutland Gate	412•47	SW7
10 Curzon Street	413•55	W1
28 Rutland Gate	414•47	SW7
Cenotaph, Whitehall	415•42	SW1
Rutland Gate West	416•47	SW7
Earl Haig Memorial, Whitehall	417•42	SW1

Eye Spy Intelligence Magazine

SPY SITES OF LONDON

SPY SITE	SITE/ZONE	
32 Rutland Gate	418•47	SW7
42 Rutland Gate	419•47	SW7
Park House, 24 Rutland Gate	420•47	SW7

CHAPTER 17 SPY SITES

SPY SITE	SITE/ZONE	
5 Bentinck Street	421•55	W1
Isokon Building, Lawn Road Flats, Belsize Park	422•19	NW3
Mornington Crescent Station	423•15	NW1
81-103 Euston Street	424•15	NW1
Regnart Buildings, Stephenson Street	425•15	NW1
Leicester Square	426•62	WC
58 Sheffield Terrace	427•60	W8
112 Eaton Square	428•42	SW1
Twelve Responses to Tragedy, Thurloe Square	429•47	SW7
Leconfield House, Curzon Street	430•55	W1
18 Carlyle Square	431•44	SW3
38 Chester Square	432•42	SW1
10 New Bond Street	433•55	W1
26 Medway Street	434•42	SW1
136 Ebury Street	435•42	SW1
26 Cavendish Avenue	436•22	NW8
69 Dean Street	437•55	W1
Meard Street	438•55	W1
HeyJo Club, 51 Jermyn Street	439•42	SW1
Pratt's, 14 Park Place	440•42	SW1
30 Charlotte Street	441•55	W1
Warburg Institute, Woburn Square	442•62	WC
Courtauld Institute of Art	443•62	WC
20 Portman Square	444•55	W1
30 Palace Court	445•56	W2
15 Buckingham Gate	446•42	SW1
15 Gerald Road	447•42	SW1
6 Southwick Place	448•56	W2
Seymour Place, Westminster	449•55	W1
The Pigalle Club, 215 Piccadilly	450•55	W1
Green Park Hotel, Half Moon Street	451•55	W1
Flemings Hotel, Half Moon Street	452•55	W1
7-9 Crawford Street	453•15	NW1
19-21 Old Compton Street	454•55	W1
Wigmore Street, Westminster	455•55	W1
Grove Court, Holly Mews	456•34	SW10
138 King's Road	457•44	SW3
3 Rosary Gardens	458•47	SW7
76 Warwick Square	459•42	SW1
27 South Terrace	460•47	SW7
Dog and Fox, Wimbledon Village	461•41	SW19
Browns Hotel, 33 Albemarle Street	462•55	W1
Portsea Hall, Portsea Place	463•56	W2
88 St James's Street	464•61	W9
2A Hans Road	465•44	SW3
4 Greyswood Street	466•39	SW16
14-16 Regent Street	467•42	SW1
40 Crespigny Road	468•20	NW6
29 Ranelagh Gardens	469•57	W4
52 Coleherne Court	470•46	SW5
20 Half Moon Street	471•55	W1
Westminster School	472•42	SW1
Irving Street, Covent Garden	473•62	WC

CHAPTER 18 SPY SITES

6 Campden Hill Square	474•60	W8
18 Elsham Road	475•54	W14
Hyde Park	476•56	W2
33 South Audley Street	477•55	W1
6 Montpelier Place	478•47	SW7
18-21 Jermyn Street	479•42	SW1
108-110 Jermyn Street	480•42	SW1
Dollis Hill, Brent	481•18	NW2
Claridge's Hotel, Brook Street	482•55	W1
112 Central Park Road	483•06	E6
26 South Street	484•55	W1
2 Lowndes Street	485•42	SW1
47 Portland Place	486•55	W1
Berners Hotel, 10 Berners Street	487•55	W1
Passfields, Bromley Road	488•32	SE6
Mount Royal Hotel, Bryanston Street	489•55	W1
The Old Bell, 95 Fleet Street	490•08	EC
19 Upper Cheyne Row	491•44	SW3
14 The Little Boltons	492•34	SW10
1-5 West Street	493•62	WC
Artillery Mansions, Victoria Street	494•42	SW1
5 All Souls' Place, Westminster	495•55	W1
28 Highlever Road	496•51	W10
Royal Over-Seas League, St James's Street	497•42	SW1
White House Hotel, Albany Street	498•15	NW1
Bunch of Grapes, 207 Brompton Road	499•44	SW3
Classic Cinema, 96-98 Baker Street	500•55	W1
117 Great Portland Street	501•55	W1
45 Cranley Drive, Ruislip	502•99	99
The Old Vic Theatre, The Cut, Lambeth	503•23	SE1
Waterloo Train Station	504•23	SE1
97 Great Russell Street	505•62	WC
Red Lion, 2 Duke of York Street	506•42	SW1
Arches, Charing Cross Station	507•62	WC
Science Museum, Exhibition Road	508•47	SW7
Pinner Train Station	509•99	99
Pinner Church	510•99	99
14 Ryder Street	511•42	SW1
17 Great Marlborough Street	512•55	W1

CHAPTER 19 SPY SITES

189 Regent Street	513•42	SW1
3 New Burlington Street	514•55	W1
3 Chester Terrace	515•15	NW1
17 Wimpole Mews	516•55	W1
Harcourt House, 19 Cavendish Square	517•55	W1
38 Devonshire Street	518•55	W1
84A Great Titchfield Street	519•55	W1
24 Wilton Row	520•42	SW1
63 Great Cumberland Place	521•55	W1
Park West Place	522•56	W2
16-18 Beak Street	523•55	W1
1 Bryanston Mews	524•55	W1

SPY SITES OF LONDON

SPY SITE	SITE/ZONE		SPY SITE	SITE/ZONE	
Cliveden House, Buckinghamshire	525•99	99	Empress State Building, Earl's Court	577•46	SW5
Spring Cottage, Buckinghamshire	526•99	99	Century House, Westminster Bridge Road	578•23	SE1
20 Marylebone High Street	527•55	W1	Curzon Street House	579•55	W1
26A Warwick Square	528•42	SW1	Gower Street	580•62	WC
33 Devonshire Street	529•55	W1	Waterloo Bridge	581•23	SE1
18 Greek Street	530•55	W1	Sheepcote Lane	582•35	SW11
20 Vale Court	531•44	SW3	186 Queen's Gate	583•47	SW7
St. Stephen's Hospital, Chelsea	532•34	SW10	19 Upper Brook Street, Mayfair	584•55	W1
Marylebone Magistrates Court	533•15	NW1	Upper Brook Street, Mayfair	585•55	W1
Chester Close North	534•15	NW1	Bryanston Square, Marylebone	586•55	W1
15 Garrick Street	535•62	WC	21 Queen's Gate	587•47	SW7
Victory Services Club, 63-79 Seymour Street	536•56	W2	17 Manson Place	588•47	SW7
28 Hyde Park Gate	537•47	SW7	106 Piccadilly	589•55	W1
30 Portman Square	538•55	W1	60 St James's Street	590•42	SW1
			Marsham Court, Marsham Street	591•42	SW1
CHAPTER 20 SPY SITES			House of Commons Car Park	592•42	SW1
			Crescent Mansions, 113 Fulham Road	593•44	SW3
13 Oakleigh Park North	539•13	N20	2 Wilton Crescent	594•42	SW1
17 Oakleigh Park North	540•13	N20	Regent's Park Memorial	595•15	NW1
15 Oakleigh Park North	541•13	N20	Hyde Park Memorial	596•42	SW1
Brompton Oratory, Brompton Road	542•47	SW7	16 Princes Gate	597•47	SW7
Holy Trinity Church, Brompton Road	543•47	SW7	20 Nevern Place	598•46	SW5
Harrods, Brompton Road	544•42	SW1	105 Lexham Court	599•60	W8
Cafe Daquise, 20 Thurloe Street	545•47	SW7	24 Queen's Gate	600•47	SW7
Audley Square	546•55	W1	55 Queen's Gate	601•47	SW7
St. George's Gardens	547•01	E1	Albert Memorial, Kensington Gardens	602•47	SW7
Marylebone Passage, Westminster	548•55	W1	24 Princes Gate	603•47	SW7
The Champion, 12-13 Wells Street	549•55	W1	25 Princes Gate	604•47	SW7
Tin and Stone Bridge, St James's Park	550•42	SW1	Regent's Park Barracks	605•15	NW1
Gerrard Street, Westminster	551•55	W1	17 Princes Gate	606•47	SW7
Farringdon Tube Station	552•08	EC	93 Ebury Bridge Road	607•42	SW1
Planetree House, Duchess of Bedford Walk	553•60	W8	Chantry House, Eccleston Street	608•42	SW1
The Albert, 52 Victoria Street	554•42	SW1	89 Albert Embankment	609•23	SE1
Grosvenor Square	555•55	W1	42 Holland Park	610•52	W11
Piccadilly Circus	556•55	W1	Piccadilly Station, South Entrance	611•55	W1
			38 Connaught Street	612•56	W2
CHAPTER 21 SPY SITES			65 Brook Street	613•55	W1
			Chelsea Cloisters	614•44	SW3
Transport House, Smith Square	557•42	SW1	Blackfriars Bridge	615•08	EC
Ruskin Park House, Champion Hill	558•31	SE5	Langham Hotel, Portland Place	616•55	W1
BT Tower, Cleveland Street	559•55	W1	Swallow International Hotel, Cromwell Road	617•46	SW5
53 Temple Fortune Hill	560•17	NW11	RUSI, Whitehall	618•42	SW1
Kelvedon Hatch, Brentwood, Essex	561•99	99	34 Belgrave Square	619•42	SW1
10-13 Grosvenor Square	562•55	W1			
Grosvenor House Hotel	563•55	W1	**CHAPTER 22 SPY SITES**		
9 Duke Street	564•55	W1			
Brook Gate, Hyde Park	565•55	W1	Harrods Memorial, Brompton Road	620•42	SW1
Phillimore Court, Kensington High Street	566•60	W8	5 St James's Square	621•42	SW1
12 Walpole Street, Chelsea	567•44	SW3	62 Ennismore Gardens	622•47	SW7
Earls Court Square	568•46	SW5	15 Knightsbridge	623•42	SW1
Queen's Grove, St John's Wood	569•22	NW8	Yvonne Fletcher Memorial, St James's Square	624•42	SW1
81 Gracechurch Street	570•08	EC	286 Euston Road	625•15	NW1
Prince Edward (Old Ducks And Drakes)	571•56	W2	Bolton Street	626•55	W1
24 Hereford Street	572•04	E2	MI5 Headquarters, Thames House, Millbank	627•42	SW1
Queens Hotel, Inverness Terrace	573•56	W2	MI6 Headquarters, 85 Vauxhall Cross	628•25	SE11
Israel Embassy, South Kensington	574•60	W8	Inn on the Park Hotel, Hamilton Place	629•55	W1
Dorchester Hotel, Park Lane	575•55	W1	Inn The Park, St James's Park	630•42	SW1
34 Montague Square	576•27	SE15	60 Vauxhall Bridge Road	631•42	SW1

Eye Spy Intelligence Magazine

SPY SITES OF LONDON

SPY SITE	SITE/ZONE	
29 Gowan Avenue, Fulham	632•46	SW5
University College London, Gower Street	633•62	WC
Admiral Duncan, Old Compton Street	634•55	W1
Vauxhall Station	635•48	SW8
Hammersmith Bridge	636•59	W6
Ealing Broadway Station	637•58	W5
Tower Hotel, Tower Bridge	638•01	E1
White House Hotel, Euston	639•15	N6
8 Collingham Road	640•46	SW5
111 Old Church Street	641•44	SW3
296 Borough High Street	642•23	SE1
Matthew Parker Street, Westminster	643•42	SW1
3 Carlton Gardens	644•42	SW1
Charles House, Kensington High Street	645•54	W14
St Martin's Le-Grand	646•08	EC
Streatham High Road	647•39	SW16
Clarges Mews, Mayfair	648•55	W1
24 Grosvenor Square	649•55	W1
Nine Elms, Battersea	650•48	SW8
Charing Cross Hotel, Strand	651•62	WC
Ministry of Justice, 102 Petty France	652•42	SW1
34 Lowndes Square	653•42	SW1
Canary Wharf, Tower Hamlets	654•02	E14

CHAPTER 23 SPY SITES

Edgware Road Station	655•15	NW1
Aldgate East Station	656•01	E1
King's Cross Station	657•15	NW1
Russell Square Station	658•62	WC
Tavistock Square	659•62	WC
8-10 Broadway, New Scotland Yard	660•42	SW1
7/7 Memorial, Hyde Park	661•55	W1
Warren Street Station	662•15	NW1
Cabinet Office, 70 Whitehall	663•42	SW1
Stockwell Station	664•49	SW9
Ladderswood Way	665•10	N11
352 High Road Wood Green	666•16	NW10
Paddington Green Police Station	667•56	W2
Holiday Inn, Brent Cross	668•18	NW2

CHAPTER 24 SPY SITES

386A Forest Road	669•03	E17
Forest Gate Police Station	670•07	E7
Bridge To China Town	671•23	SE1
London Eye	672•23	SE1
University College Hospital, 235 Euston Road	673•15	NW1
Royal London Hospital	674•01	E1
Piccadilly Circus	675•55	W1
Itsu, 167 Piccadilly	676•55	W1
Millennium Hotel, Mayfair	677•55	W1
Sheraton Park Lane	678•55	W1
Abracadabra, 91 Jermyn Street	679•42	SW1
Parkes Hotel, 41 Beaufort Gardens	680•44	SW3
Pescatori Restaurant, 11 Dover Street	681•55	W1
25 Grosvenor Square	682•55	W1
58 Grosvenor Street	683•55	W1

SPY SITE	SITE/ZONE	
Highgate Cemetery, Highgate	684•14	N6
London Hilton Hotel, Park Lane	685•55	W1
Leicester Square	686•62	WC
24 Carlton House Terrace	687•42	SW1
116 Pall Mall	688•42	SW1
8 Belgrave Square	689•42	SW1
Tiger Tiger Club, 29 Haymarket	690•42	SW1
Park Lane Underground Car Park	691•55	W1
Newham Hotel, 349-353 Romford Road	692•07	E7
St James's Palace, Westminster	693•42	SW1
Kensington Palace	694•56	W2
Evening Standard, Northcliffe House	695•60	W8
2 Mansfield Street	696•55	W1
Allerton House, Islington	697•10	N11
4 Thurloe Street, Kensington	698•47	SW7
5 Young Street, Kensington	699•60	W8
Boujis, 43 Thurloe Street, Kensington	700•47	SW7
36 Alderney Street, Pimlico	701•42	SW1
Central Saint Martins, King's Cross	702•09	N1
Barcode, Arch 69, Albert Embankment	703•23	SE1
Royal Vauxhall Tavern, 372 Kennington Lane	704•25	SE11
Patisserie Valerie, 94 Holland Park Avenue	705•52	W11
Holland Park Station	706•52	W11
Stock Exchange, 10 Paternoster Square	707•08	EC
Westminster Abbey	708•42	SW1
Church of Scientology, Blackfriars	709•08	EC
Strand Palace Hotel	710•62	WC
Portcullis House, Westminster	711•42	SW1
Tricycle Theatre, 269 Kilburn High Road	712•21	NW6
Arundel House, 13-15 Arundel Street	713•62	WC
Temple Station	714•62	WC
94 Mount Street, Mayfair	715•55	W1
Chatham House, 10 St James's Square	716•42	SW1
The Mall	717•42	SW1
Blackheath, Shooters Hill Road	718•30	SE3
Byng Street, Canary Wharf	719•02	E14
North Pole, 74 Manilla Street	720•02	E14
Ecuador Embassy, 3 Hans Crescent	721•42	SW1
British Museum, Great Russell Street	722•62	WC
John Wilson Street, Woolwich	723•28	SE18
The Royal Artillery Barracks, Woolwich	724•28	SE18
Guardian, King's Place, 90 York Way	725•09	N1
Shepherds Bush Police Station	726•59	W6
White City Territorial Army Barracks	727•53	W12
10 Downing Street	728•42	SW1
Home Office, 2 Marsham Street	729•42	SW1
Ministry of Defence, Whitehall	730•42	SW1

POSTSCRIPT SPY SITES

Down Street Station, Mayfair	731•55	W1
Old Rising Sun, 79 Marylebone High Street	732•55	W1
Charleville Mansions, Charleville Road	733•54	W14
9 Powis Square, Bayswater	734•52	W12